The Letters of
Virginia Woolf

Volume IV: 1929-1931

The Letters of Virginia Woolf

Volume IV: 1929-1931

Edited by Nigel Nicolson
and Joanne Trautmann

Harcourt Brace Jovanovich

New York and London

Originally published in England as A *Reflection of the Other Person*

Printed in the United States of America

First American edition 1979
B C D E

Library of Congress Cataloging in Publication Data

Woolf, Virginia Stephen, 1882–1941.
The Letters of Virginia Woolf.

Vol. 1 first published under title: The flight of the mind.
Vol. 2 first published under title: The question of things happening.
Vol. 3 first published under title: A change of perspective.
Vol. 4 first published under title:
A reflection of the other person.
Includes bibliographical references and indexes.
CONTENTS: v. 1. 1888–1912 (Virginia Stephen).—
v. 2. 1912–1922.—v. 3. 1923–1928.—v. 4. 1929–1931.—
1. Woolf, Virginia Stephen, 1882–1941—Correspondence.
2. Authors, English—20th century—Correspondence.
PR6045.072Z525   1975   823'.9'12   [B]   75-25538
ISBN 0-15-150927-1

'It is an interesting question—what one tries to do, in writing a letter—partly of course to give back a reflection of the other person.'

Virginia Woolf to Gerald Brenan
4 *October* 1929

Contents

Illustrations

3a was loaned by Professor and Mrs Quentin Bell; 7a by
George Rylands (phot. Cecil Beaton); 2a, 3c, 4a, 6b and 8
are the copyright of the Editor, and 7b of Lettice Ramsay;
2b is reproduced by permission of Quentin Bell and the
Berg Collection; 6a by permission of Mrs T. Parsons;
5 was photographed by Basil Fielding; 4b by Elizabeth
Williamson; and 8 by Susan Forbes.

Editorial Note

THE methods we have employed in editing the Letters of Virginia Woolf have been explained in the Notes attached to the first three volumes in this series, and need not be repeated here. As before, we wish to acknowledge primarily the great assistance which we have received from Quentin and Olivier Bell. Professor Bell, and his sister Angelica Garnett, are the owners of the copyright in the letters, and it is at their invitation that we have undertaken the editing of them. Olivier Bell is simultaneously editing Virginia Woolf's diaries (of which the originals are in the Berg Collection, New York Public Library), and she has allowed us to see transcripts of them in advance of her own publication, in order to avoid any inconsistency between the dating and annotation of the two documents, but we have quoted nothing from the diary that has not been previously published.

The letters have been printed verbatim, apart from the very occasional omission of words or sentences which might cause pain to people still alive. We have made it clear where such omissions have been made and at what length.

About thirty short letters or postcards have not been published because they concern nothing but social or business arrangements, most of which are mentioned again in another context.

The note 'Squiggly design' may puzzle some readers. It is a fanciful elaboration of Virginia Woolf's signature, which she sometimes used in ending her letters to Vita Sackville-West. An example was reproduced in Volume III, Letter 1862.

Some letters have reached us too late for inclusion in the relevant volume. Most will be published as an Appendix to Vol. VI in 1980, and we appeal to the owners and collectors of other Virginia Woolf letters unknown to us to send us facsimile copies before it is too late.

We acknowledge with gratitude four books on which we have specially relied: *A Bibliography of Virginia Woolf* (revised edition, 1967, now in course of further revision) by B. J. Kirkpatrick; *A Checklist of the Hogarth Press* by J. Howard Woolmer, 1976; *Virginia Woolf: The Critical Heritage*, edited by Robin Majumdar and Allen McLaurin, 1975; and (for this volume) *Virginia Woolf: 'The Waves': The Two Holograph Drafts*, transcribed and edited by J. W. Graham, 1976.

Jane Lancellotti has been an indefatigable researcher for this volume, and we thank her for the care she has taken to trace to their sources many obscure references in the letters, and to discover the identity of many people who briefly entered Virginia Woolf's life, and the books and articles which she read.

Once again we are indebted to Dr Lola S. Szladits, curator of the Berg Collection, New York Public Library, and the staff of the Library of Sussex University (particularly John Burt), which own the majority of Virginia Woolf's surviving letters, and to the owners of many others whose permission to publish them is acknowledged by printing their names at the foot of each.

For allowing Dr Joanne Trautmann to spend part of her academic year working on this volume, we are grateful to the Department of Humanities and its Chairman E. A. Vastyan, the Pennsylvania State University College of Medicine, Hershey, Pennsylvania. We also acknowledge with thanks the grant of travel funds to Dr Trautmann by the Institute for the Arts and Humanistic Studies, Pennsylvania State University, directed by Professor Stanley Weintraub.

Mrs Norah Smallwood of the Hogarth Press has been the most understanding of publishers, and T. & A. Constable the most painstaking of printers.

The following have willingly responded to our requests for help or information: Barbara Bagenal; Dr Wendy Baron; Professor Richard Braithwaite; Rohan Butler; Lady David Cecil; Lady Darwin; Angus Davidson; F. E. Drown; Angelica Garnett; Jeremy Hutchinson; Virginia Isham; Milo Keynes; James Lees-Milne; the staff of the London Library; Jean O. Love; Norman Mackenzie; Raymond Mortimer; Charles Murphy; Benedict and Adam Nicolson; George Rylands; Daphne Sanger; Richard Shone; Frances Spalding; George Spater; Charles Thomas; Mrs H. Thomas; and Julian Vinogradoff.

The typing of the letters has been shared between Valerie Henderson (assisted by Ann Erikson), Gretchen Hess Gage, June Watson, Diane Ruhl and Kimberly Kiscadden in the United States; and Pamela Kilbane and Jane Carr in England. In preparing the book for press we owed much to the secretarial help of Jane Carr, Lyn Dunbar and Marcia Rhodes.

NIGEL NICOLSON
JOANNE TRAUTMANN

Introduction

THIS volume covers only three years of Virginia Woolf's life, 1929 to 1931. They were years dominated by one woman and one book. The woman was Ethel Smyth; the book was Virginia's masterpiece, *The Waves*. There was almost no link between them. Virginia completed her book in spite of Ethel Smyth; and Ethel, like many other readers, found it difficult to understand, and its characters unsympathetic.

How different it had been in 1928! Then Virginia had written *Orlando* for and about Vita Sackville-West, and Vita was enchanted by it. They continued to see much of each other, but for Vita their love-affair was over; defused, as I suggested in the last volume, by the publication of the book. She made no breach with Virginia, but gently widened an existing gap. For Virginia it was not so easy. She still loved Vita. When they were together in Berlin in January 1929, she seems to have made some sort of declaration to her as they dined in the radio-tower which overlooks the city. The evidence in their subsequent letters (see particularly pp. 20n and 29) is obscure. If it was a renewed declaration of love, as it seems to have been, Vita was successful in dealing with it without causing her pain, and Virginia, who was humble in these matters, accepted Vita's implicit withdrawal. What cannot be in doubt is Virginia's continued need for her. When she was ill after her return from Germany, Vita was the only friend she wished to see, almost the only one to whom she wrote. She felt no regret or remorse about what had happened between them. She told her sister Vanessa Bell about it, casually, in a chemist's shop (p. 36).

However, she was not quite so resigned as she pretended. When Vita went walking in France with Hilda Matheson in July 1929, Virginia was tormented, saying that what pained her most was that Vita had concealed the plan from her until the last moment, an accusation which Vita, desperately anxious to keep her friendship and not to hurt her, flatly denied. But more than Virginia's momentary jealousy lay behind their slight tiff. She was distressed that Vita should choose as her new friends (how could she avoid the comparison with herself?) women who had weak intellectual gifts, whose lives were mainly social, and who trapped Vita into promiscuous behaviour and wasted her time. The charge was not quite fair. Hilda Matheson, for example, the first Talks Director of the BBC, was affectionate, competent, and widely admired for her steadfastness and good judgement. Nor was Vita distracted from her writing by these friendships. In these three years she wrote two of her most successful novels, *The Edwardians* and *All Passion*

Spent, both published by the Hogarth Press, as well as countless book-reviews and broadcast talks. She had reached her life's plateau. In these same years she bought Sissinghurst Castle, and began to create between its battered buildings one of the loveliest gardens in England, with the help of her husband, Harold Nicolson, who resigned from diplomacy to devote himself to literature and politics. They shared an idyllic life. Virginia had always recognised in Vita these competing interests, and made no more than token protests against them, but Vita was never quite sure how high she stood in Virginia's regard:

> "Now you write to me, and how do I know that the next minute you wont snatch up your pen again and write something completely different to Vanessa? and even you yourself dont know what you really mean" (Vita to Virginia. 22 August 1929. *Berg*).

It was a shrewd comment. Virginia often appeared unsure of her tastes. Take, for instance, the conflict in her mind between her wish to live in the world and out of it. One would have imagined (she often imagined it herself) that the place best suited to her was Monk's House, where she could write in peace, walk on the Downs, be spared travelling, and avoid the constant intrusion of self-invited guests. "I assure you", she wrote (2418), "that one walk here fills my poor old head with a sense of such natural happiness as I never get a whole summer in London." Whenever she escaped to Sussex, she invariably wrote like this about the purgatory of the city, but it was to London that she invariably returned. Often saying that she hated parties, in prospect or recollection, she could seldom refuse an invitation, because parties stimulated her. Disliking society people, and uttering wails of complaint when forced to associate with them, she could not bring herself to cut them out of her life. Indeed, they came to take precedence, but in terms of time only, of her old Bloomsbury friends ("wild, odd, innocent, artless, eccentric and industrious beyond words") who saw less of her because they were busier than these smart people, and had made new friends, as Virginia did herself. Few letters in this volume are addressed to Forster, Fry, Keynes, MacCarthy, Strachey, Sydney-Turner or Eliot, the companions of her youth and early middle age, and it was only at the very end of this period that John Lehmann brought into her life the new writers, Spender, Auden and Day Lewis. But when one of her older friends, Lytton Strachey, fell seriously ill in December 1931, there was no doubt where Virginia's deepest affections lay. At that moment her emotion was too strong for her to express it more than superficially. But earlier she had burst out in reply to Ethel Smyth:

> "Take away my affections and I should be like sea weed out of water; like the shell of a crab, like a husk. All my entrails, light, marrow, juice, pulp would be gone. I should be blown into the first puddle and drown.

Take away my love for my friends and my burning and pressing sense of the importance and lovability and curiosity of human life and I should be nothing but a membrane, a fibre, uncoloured, lifeless to be thrown away like any other excreta." (2222)

One of these friends was Ethel Smyth herself. It is surprising that they had not met before. They knew many people in common, including Vita, and each had long been interested in the other's work and personality. Virginia had attended at least two performances of Ethel's music, and had once seen her, in 1919, "striding up the gangway in coat and skirt and spats and talking at the top of her voice". She had also read with admiration the successive volumes of Ethel's autobiography, which were published step by step with her developing career. Ethel had read some of Virginia's books, but it was *A Room of One's Own* which finally compelled her to seek a meeting, since in it Virginia had expressed precisely, if less exclamatorily, what had become Ethel's *leit-motif*, the unequal struggle of women-artists to win recognition in a man's world.

In fact, Ethel had allowed this grievance to develop into an obsession. She retold her story many times in books and conversation, with a rising note of petulance and hurt pride, but she told it with such gusto, humour and eloquence that everyone forgave her, being willing to endure it for the sake of her friendship. Vita wrote charitably after her death that she was often a nuisance but never a bore, but her reiterated accusations of rejection and foul play were apt to strain credulity. Undeniably, Ethel had been obliged to fight to win attention, but so had many men-composers like Vaughan Williams and Arnold Bax, because the British taste for serious music was thinly spread. Fighting for a performance of her work gave her almost as much pleasure as composing it. Her combativeness, allied to her demonstrable talent, had produced results that made very little sense of her complaint that her music was ignored because she was a woman. Perhaps, indeed, it was the other way round. A woman composer was so rare a creature that her very existence excited wonder, and a woman who had added to her reputation in so many other ways—by her books, her public exuberance, her friends in high places, her two-months imprisonment as a suffragette—was regarded as a national phenomenon, a heroine with the right to blow her own trumpet, and her music was performed not only because it was fierce and novel, but because it was by Ethel Smyth. But never often enough to satisfy Ethel. In canvassing her work she was indomitable. To her the good and great were those who praised it and performed it, like Bruno Walter, Thomas Beecham and Donald Tovey. She did nothing to conciliate those who hesitated. When her opera *The Wreckers* was acclaimed in Leipzig, and the conductor refused to make the small changes she demanded for the second performance, she grabbed every sheet of the score from the orchestra-pit, and caught the next train to Prague. It was this sort of behaviour that made Ethel the terror of conductors, producers and music-publishers throughout the western world. After the first shock, they admired her for it, and so did the public. "One would have loved her less", wrote Edward Sackville West, "had she been more cautious. . . . She was, by any standard, among the greatest women this country has produced."

Ethel was quite unashamed of her egotism. In one of her books, *As Time Went On*—and time was always going on—she exclaimed, "I am the most interesting person I know, and I don't care if no one else thinks so." It was not conceit. It was pugnacious ambition, a confidence in her own worth. She despised women who hugged the shore: they should put out to sea. "The most boring thing in the world", she once wrote, "is doing things by halves." In another autobiographic book, *A Final Burning of Boats*—and she was always burning her boats—she cited as the three reasons why she remained undefeated, "An iron constitution, a fair share of fighting spirit, and, most important of all, a small but independent income."

She had often been in love with other women, and once deeply with a man, Henry Brewster, who figures largely in this volume, although he died in 1908. Brewster was born Anglo-American, but lived for most of his life in Italy, where he met Ethel as a girl. He was rich enough not to need a profession, and devoted his life to philosophy and poetry. He was married when Ethel first knew him, and remained faithful to his wife, but when she died, he and Ethel carried on their affair openly. "Why don't you get married, and have done with it?", asked a friend. "Because we don't want to have done with it", was Brewster's reply. He and Ethel maintained a vast correspondence, and he wrote the librettos for two of her operas. His death shattered her. She retained for him a veneration which many of her friends thought morbid and excessive. When Virginia first met her, she was about to reissue Brewster's philosophic dialogue, *The Prison*, with a Memoir by herself, and simultaneously based upon it an oratorio, her last major composition before extreme deafness destroyed her art. Virginia showed extraordinary patience for Brewster's memory, but he was one of several reasons why Ethel's pursuit of her seemed unlikely to succeed.

The pursuit began at a moment which could not have been more awkward for Virginia, when she was struggling with her most original book, *The Waves*. Ethel was nearly 72. Her deafness made conversation very difficult. She was a Dame of the British Empire. She was vehement, impetuous, and enjoyed rows, and was astounded when anyone regarded one of them as terminal. Once she stormed out of her beloved sister's house, paused at the village post-office and sent her a telegram: "Damn you, Mary Hunter, damn you, damn you". She talked, as she wrote, unceasingly about herself. She was cosmopolitan, as Virginia never was, although Mrs Pankhurst called her "a being whom only these islands could have produced". She was a snob, boasting royalty among her friends. She was in no real sense an intellectual. She was a golf-addict. She was arrogant, quick to take offence and full of grievance. She never apologised for interrupting. She insisted (as her biographer, Christopher St John, remarked) "on being liked by the people she admired". All this amounted to a character which in any other woman Virginia would have found intolerable. Yet she adored Ethel. Why?

Because Ethel had a directness, an uncompromising downrightness, a style, which set her apart from other people. "She shows up triumphantly through sheer force of honesty", Virginia had written to Lytton Strachey when she knew her only through her books. She came late into Virginia's life with such an accumulation of energy, love, ambition, fulfilment and despair that Virginia found her fascinating, not just for her past, but because she continued to burst through the weeks like paper-hoops, composing more music, more books, taking for granted that her love was reciprocated (and Virginia was always vulnerable to love), indifferent to snubs because a snub was nothing but another challenge, a writer whose pace was never less than top-speed and who expected the reader to ride pillion behind her, a composer whose music was as torrential as her talk, who once claimed that she made twelve new intimate friends a year, who gave adoration un-grudgingly, and whose pertinacity was irresistible. Had Ethel given up, Virginia would have given up. But Ethel never gave up. She cultivated their friendship like a prize marrow. "I don't think I have ever cared for anyone more profoundly", she wrote in her diary. "For 18 months I really thought of little else."

She was in love with Virginia, but her love could hardly be called physical, and certainly not uncritical. Virginia at first responded with alarm and embarrassment. She began by holding her up to Quentin and Vanessa as a figure of fun: "An old woman of 71 has fallen in love with me. . . . It is like being caught by a giant crab." In fact, Vanessa liked Ethel. They corresponded, discussing Virginia, who felt "rather like a mouse pinned out on a board for dissection". Virginia was half-amused, half-defensive, referring to "this curious unnatural friendship", fearing ridicule, fearing too deep an involvement. She was wary of her. They had both voyaged too far before berthing in the same dock. Ethel took the initiative with a volley of questions to which she seldom awaited the replies, even if she could hear them, but the replies could be repeated in Virginia's letters. Reading them, one hears their talk, the gradual unloading of all that cargo, more reticent on Virginia's side than on Ethel's, but gradually, under pressure, she yielded, and wrote to Ethel about matters that hitherto she had scarcely mentioned to anyone, her madness (2194), her feeling about sex (2218), the inspiration for her books (2254), and even her thoughts of suicide (2341). For Ethel she was reliving her entire life, because Ethel's curiosity was compulsive, and because Virginia became eager to explain herself to a woman who seemed suddenly the most sympathetic person she had ever known. For there was another side to Ethel. She could be maternal. "What you give me is protection. . . . Its the child crying for the nurses hand in the dark. You do it by being so uninhibited: so magnificently unself-conscious" (2342).

A mother Ethel might be, but not beyond reproach. Early in their relationship they quarrelled, twice. Once it was about Ethel's tedious complaints that her music was ignored. "For 3 hours she nailed me to my chair while she rehearsed the story of her iniquitous treatment by Adrian Boult. . . . One is perfectly powerless. She raves and rants. . . . Undoubtedly sex and egotism have brewed some bitter insanity" (2375). The other quarrel was more profound. Virginia wrote her almost the angriest letter she ever penned, when Ethel forced her to attend a smart party at Lady Rosebery's:

> "I dont know when I have suffered more. . . . I had been dragged to that awful Exhibition of insincerity and inanity against my will. . . . You liked the party—you who are uncompromising, truthful, vehement. 'Ethel likes this sort of thing' I said, disillusion filled me: all belief fell off me. 'And she has planned this, and worse still, subjected me to it. Gulfs separate us.' And I felt betrayed—I who have spoken to you so freely of all my weaknesses—I to whom this chatter and clatter on top of any art, music, pictures, which I dont understand,—is an abomination. Oh then, the elderly butlers, peers, champagne and sugared cakes! It seemed to me that you wantonly inflicted this indignity upon me for no reason, and that I was pinioned there and betrayed and made to smile at our damnation. . . There I was mocking and mowing, and you forced me to it and you didn't mind it." (2335)

Quentin Bell has summed it up astutely: "Virginia had, in fact, discovered that she was the stronger of the two. She could up to a point dictate the terms of their friendship" (Vol. II, p. 159). It had begun with passionate self-assertion on Ethel's part, with tolerance on Virginia's; it continued in mutual scolding; but after eighteen months, Virginia began to teach Ethel the elements of patience and humility, qualities which Ethel had never previously thought worth considering. Under Virginia's influence she became a little calmer, a little less prone to beat the cymbals. Vernon Lee had once compared her own relationship with Ethel to that between the Unicorn and the Lion. It was much the same with Virginia, whose defter strokes parried Ethel's mauling grasp. Her torrent of words seldom gave Virginia new ideas of permanent value, but she enjoyed the combat, admired Ethel, respected her. She was a horsefly, and paradoxically a solace.

Virginia's letters to Ethel Smyth were the most intimate she wrote at this period, because they were the most self-revealing. But her innermost thoughts, her literary plans, her melancholy and disillusion, were confined to her diary. With its publication by Olivier Bell (not level with these volumes of her letters, but separated from them by a knight's move), we shall soon be able to know Virginia Woolf better than we can know almost any other person of this century. The purposes of the diary and the letters differed. In her diary there was no need to answer anyone, no change of tone, no loss of continuity, no need for reticence about herself or her friends. Nobody would be hurt by it; there was no call on her to explain, conciliate or disguise. She could reprove herself, goad herself, as Boswell did in his journal, and Byron in his. If she conceived a plan, her diary would not hold her to it. The events of the week were used in the diary as illustrations of her state of mind; in the letters they took first place. Reflection and self-analysis and toying with ideas and phrases were the characteristics of the diary; the purpose of the letters was to communicate and entertain. If only Virginia's letters and critical essays had survived from her writings, she would be accounted a delightful and very clever woman; the diary and the novels proclaim her genius.

The diary and letters are complementary. Almost nothing is repeated from one into the other. Virginia tossed away an idea or a phrase as soon as she had minted it. Each fills the gaps left by the other, gaps created because many of her letters do not survive, and by what she deliberately withheld from her friends or did not bother to mention in her diary. They must be read side by side. Together they form the portrait of an artist in travail, but one who did not allow her creative anguish to suppress her gaiety. If the diaries seem more contemplative, and the letters more exuberant, it was because these moods alternated in her, and for each she adopted the appropriate vehicle, a hammock and a trampoline.

Nowhere are her two voices heard more distinctly than in the account she gives in the diary of the writing of *The Waves*, and by her references to it in her letters. The letters, to Ethel Smyth particularly, utter a periodic groan of protest about the impossibility of concentrating on the book when she was constantly interrupted, a hint that Ethel herself was a main culprit. But sometimes she revealed a little more:

> "I think that my difficulty is that I am writing to a rhythm and not to a plot. Does this convey anything? And thus though the rhythmical is more natural to me than the narrative, it is completely opposed to the tradition of fiction and I am casting about all the time for some rope to throw to the reader." (2224)

When she had finished the book, she exclaimed to Clive Bell, "It is a failure. Too difficult: too jerky: too inchoate altogether"; and, less seriously, to Quentin, she called it "the worst novel in the language"; and to Ethel, "fundamentally unreadable". After publication, as was normal with her, her retrospective ideas about the book swarmed uninhibited. She was prepared to discuss it with almost anyone who wrote to her about it.

But the agonising labour of writing *The Waves* was traced in detail only in her diary, some of which has already been published by Leonard in *A Writer's Diary* (1953). It was the most difficult literary task she ever undertook, and we know most about it, for not only did she record her progress privately in these two ways, but we have both her manuscripts, transcribed and edited with meticulous skill, with every erasure, every interpolation, by J. W. Graham.[1] This is not the place to analyse *The Waves*, nor to discuss its importance in Virginia's work and English literature. But a summary of how she wrote it is a necessary preliminary to this volume, because the pounding of the waves throbs, usually unheard, throughout it.

Virginia wrote the book in manuscript twice over, and it took her two years, July to July, 1929-31. The seed of the idea was sown by a chance letter from Vanessa two years earlier, but Virginia approached the task of writing it with misgivings, like a cross-country expedition, with "no great impulse; no fever; only a great pressure of difficulty" (AWD, p. 142). She wrote nearly sixty pages of the first draft, and then began it again. By Christmas 1929 it had begun to torment her: "I write variations of every sentence; compromises; bad shots; possibilities. . . . I wish I enjoyed it more" (AWD, p. 151). She fell ill, but as she lay in bed, it continued to ferment like wine in the cask. She returned to it, and it was finished by the end of April 1930. But only the first draft. With extraordinary pertinacity, she wrote it all over again, and a comparison between the two drafts suggests that she barely glanced at the first when writing the second. The theme remained unchanged, but she altered the structure and the title (she had originally called it *The Moths*, but moths play almost no part in the book), and in rewriting, it became a chain of soliloquies by six people from childhood to the approach of death, connected by 'interludes' describing the rising of the sun to its setting, and the rhythmic beat of the sea. Each afternoon Virginia typed out what she had written in the morning, and when the second draft was finished, she retyped it a third time, altering as she went, then had it retyped by a professional, and further revised it, and again slightly in proof. It was an astonishing feat of concentration. "Never", she wrote (AWD, p. 167), " have I screwed my brain so tight over a book." But her brain was not damaged by the two-year effort. She simply felt relief that it was over, and began, almost immediately, to write her next book, *Flush*, as a relaxation.

In spite of all the evidence, we will never know why Virginia Woolf recast *The Waves* so many times, nor why she made her detailed changes. Take, for example, this passage, describing Bernard's intended visit to Hampton Court. In her first draft it does not appear at all. In the second (Graham: p. 577):

> "I will go to Hampton Court and look at the red walls and the court-yards, and the seemliness of the trees, herded in black pyramids, symmetrically among flowers".

1. *Virginia Woolf: 'The Waves'. The two holograph drafts* (University of Toronto and The Hogarth Press, 1976).

In the printed book it became (pp. 174-5):

"Or shall I go to Hampton Court and look at the red walls and court-yards and the seemliness of herded yew trees making black pyramids symmetrically on the grass among flowers?"

There was something that displeased her in the first version; some tonal imbalance, some lack of precision not obvious to the reader. Such small changes give us a glimpse into her workshop, the garden-hut at Monk's House or the basement of 52 Tavistock Square. Virginia's letters tell us next to nothing about her methods of composition, except that the book owes much of its careful observation of nature and street-scenes to her daily walks on the Sussex Downs or through London. It was a private labour, the printed book the only public declaration of her intent. The life of her mind lay behind her life in the world, and her letters give us a faint conception of the relationship between them.

NIGEL NICOLSON
Sissinghurst Castle, Kent

Abbreviations at foot of letters

Berg: The Henry W. and Albert A. Berg Collection of English and American Literature in the New York Public Library (Astor, Lenox and Tilden Foundations).

Sussex: University of Sussex Library, Brighton.

Hatfield: The Marquess of Salisbury (Cecil Papers), Hatfield House, Hertfordshire.

Texas: The Humanities Research Center, The University of Texas, at Austin, Texas.

King's: King's College Library, Cambridge.

Letters 1978-2006 (January–February 1929)

On 16 January Virginia and Leonard went for a week's holiday to Berlin, where they were joined by Duncan Grant, Vanessa Bell and her younger son Quentin (now aged 18). Virginia's main purpose was to visit Vita Sackville-West, who was staying in Berlin for two months with her husband Harold Nicolson, then Counsellor at the British Embassy. The visit was not wholly a success. The Woolfs disliked the Germans, the city and its social obligations. During the journey back to England on 25 January Virginia was taken ill. The cause was partly the 'rackety' life they had led in Berlin, and partly a seasick sedative which she took on board the ship from Holland to Harwich, where she fell into a temporary coma. For a month she was more or less permanently bed-ridden, while London endured one of the worst frosts on record. Although she was able to write some journalism, she found it impossible to start her new novel The Waves. *She saw few visitors, and her main correspondent was Vita, who did not return from Berlin until the end of February.*

1978: To V. SACKVILLE-WEST   37 *Gordon Square, W.C.*1

6th Jan. [1929]

Owing to a mistake by me or you or Vanessa or all we do not want the rooms [in Berlin] as we are taking others. Could you possibly cancel them. We are extremely sorry for any inconvenience we may have caused you and must bear any expense incurred.

[*in Leonard's handwriting:*]
This has been written under dictation by Virginia who now refuses to sign. We are very sorry for the trouble but do you think you can cancel the rooms?

> Leonard
> Virginia Woolf
> Duncan Grant
> Roger Fry who does not
> know what it is all about
> but signs obediently.
> Quentin Bell
> Vanessa Bell

Berg

I

January 1929]

Telegram

Letter cancelled reserve two rooms from 17th three more from 18th. Woolf

Berg

1980: To V. Sackville-West   52 *Tavistock Sqre, WC*1.

Tuesday 8th January 1928 [1929]

I hope you have got the wire, and taken the rooms. You will think Im a little crazed. The truth is when I said to Vanessa Vita is taking us rooms, it rose in my mind that you meant in a pension, and the picture which then presented itself of us all sitting round a plant eating cold beef was so dismal that we instantly signed a round robin and sent it off. Next day, on reconsideration, I conceived of rooms in a hotel, and it seemed likely that they would be chosen with tact and insight, so, meeting Nessa over a very late breakfast,—I think Clive was pouring out his history to her—I re-settled the affair and wired.

Leonard and I shall arrive on the 17th, travelling by sea, by the Hook, your way. The others are going by Brunswick to look at a ceiling, and will arrive on the 18th.

We shall have one whole week, leaving on the 24th—but I dont think of that. What I think of is arriving and seeing Vita black and scarlet under a lamp with a dog on a string. As the train draws up the dog will run the wrong way round a pillar: Vita will thus be in difficulties; will bite her under lip, and so stride through a crowd of dumpling shaped greasy grey women to meet us.

What station it will be I will tell you later. Vita will say Hullo Virginia! Leonard will stoop and pat the dog. He will compare her with Pinker, and if you are tactful you will say "But Pinker's a much better colour, Leonard" and then we shall all feel happy.

I am as usual writing quicker than the clock ticks. I have been talking about V. Sackville West to a man called Wells—who is succeeding Crosby Gaige as publisher of pale green priceless editions.[1] The desire of his heart

1. Crosby Gaige, who lived in New York City, produced limited editions of English and American books, among them *Orlando*, for his Fountain Press. Early in 1929 James R. Wells, in partnership with Elbridge C. Adams, took over the Press from Gaige, and ran it in conjunction with his three other Presses (Bowling Green, June House, and Slide Mountain Press).

2

is to publish a book by V. Sackville West. He read a copy of Seducers[1] on the liner, and the title page was torn off. Being enchanted he went to the Librarian, who said "I'll look up the author's name in my catalogue" and then said "By Virginia Woolf." I had to disengage myself from his compliments. I said I would try to coax another Seducers, another Land[2] out of you.

But why am I writing so fast? I am in a mixed mood, flying before the fury of my own devils. They have started a pumping machine in the hotel basement which shakes my studio: 25 minutes pumping like the tread of a rhythmical Elephant; then 25 minutes silence. I try ear stoppers; I try patience; finally I am trying psychology. If, I say to myself, you can imagine that the pumping is the sound of Times clock made audible, which for all your life will measure the day into spaces of 25 minutes, you will take the sound into your bloodstream, where it will become noiseless as the beat of the heart. All is habit. So far I have not triumphed. There! it begins again.

And I am once more, though so ill-fitted for the part, a go-between Clive and Mary.[3] His disillusion, like that of a dinner table after a party, so depressed me that I volunteered help. So Mary dines with me tomorrow. So I shall be clawed between the two. And so nothing will come of it. Whats more, when I ran into Nessa's this morning there he was in spats and fur coat sitting over the fire. He had been seeing a lady off at Victoria, and staying with Dick Wyndham[4] and seeing Dottie:[5] and "Lifes whizzing so fast" he said, "I dont know if I'm awake or asleep". This is the one day I got into a fury with it all; and said "I will stand this no longer," and made off—to Greenwich by myself. What an adventure! How your bandits and skeletons pale beside it![6] Think—I had lunch in a shop. Think—I sat on the pier and saw the ships bowling up. Women were walking on deck. Dogs looking out of portholes. The Captain on The Bridge. Never was anything so romantic and lovely. And then I wandered about the hospital, and saw Nelsons coat that he wore at Trafalgar, and his white stockings, and almost wept. What a day it was! How I shall remember it to the end of my life. Lets go there together.

1. *Seducers in Ecuador*, Vita's short novel which was published by the Hogarth Press in 1924.
2. *The Land*, Vita's long pastoral poem, published by Heinemann in 1926. It was awarded the Hawthornden Prize in 1927.
3. Clive Bell and Mary Hutchinson had had a prolonged love affair which drew to a painful close in 1927-8, but they continued to see each other.
4. Richard Wyndham, the painter, who lived at Tickerage Mill, near Uckfield, Sussex.
5. Lady Gerald Wellesley, later Duchess of Wellington (1889-1956). She was a poet and edited the series of Hogarth Living Poets.
6. In *Twelve Days* (published by the Hogarth Press in October 1928), Vita described her journey through the wild country of Southern Persia.

I have written myself out of breath—30,000 words in 8 weeks;[1] and now want to dive and steep myself in other peoples books. I want to wash off all my own ideas. So I have been reading and reading, and making up a new little book for the Hogarth Press (if it survives) on six novels.[2] A good idea, d'you think? Picking six novels from the mass, and saying everything there is to be said about the whole of literature in perhaps 150 pages. I've been reading Balzac, and Tolstoy. Practically every scene in Anna Karenina is branded on me, though I've not read it for 15 years. *That* is the origin of all our discontent. After that of course we had to break away. It wasn't Wells, or Galsworthy or any of our mediocre wishy washy realists: it was Tolstoy. How could we go on with sex and realism after that? How could they go on with poetic plays after Shakespeare? It is one brain, after all, literature; and it wants change and relief. The text book writers cut it up all wrong (the telephone: Leonards mother: is sending us a cake—) and where was I? Literature is all one brain.

It suddenly strikes me, this will be my last letter to you. Wont it? That is rather exciting. But not your last to me. All our plans are run through by the Editor of The Nation.[3] We only get 5 days now, and go to some obscure Inn as far away as we can find in Dorsetshire perhaps, and perhaps end up on Thomas Hardy's doorstep. France is put off till June perhaps.

Will you be walking in soon? Won't that be exciting? Nothing compared with my brigands and so on, Vita will say. Never mind—she shall say what she likes, and be as condescending as she chooses provided she is kind to that poor Weevil, Virginia, and dog Grizzle who sends her love.

Orlando has now sold 13000 copies in America: thats the last time I mention him.

The [Berlin] station will be *Friederichstrasse*.

Berg

1981: To V. Sackville-West   [52 *Tavistock Square, W.C.*1]

[9? January 1929]

[*first page missing*]

. . . formula, which I'm a little sick of, for another love affair: but still, he [Clive] said, taking my arm and walking me round the Square—I in my blue pinafore—still I want you to speak to Mary [Hutchinson].

1. Of *Phases of Fiction* (*Bookman*, New York, April, May and June 1929).
2. She never carried out this plan.
3. Leonard had become Literary Editor of the *Nation & Athenaeum* (hereafter referred to as the *Nation*) in March 1923 and held the post until early in 1930. The Editor was Hubert Henderson.

I do nothing but try, vainly, to finish off a year's journalism in a week. If I can earn £400, by flights into the lives of Miss Burney and Miss Jewsbury,[1] then I can pitch every book away, and sink back in my chair and give myself to the wings of the Moths [*The Waves*]. But I doubt it. There are dates to look up. One can't simply invent the whole of Chelsea and King George the 3rd and Johnson, and Mrs Thrale I suppose. Yet after all, thats the way to write; and if I had time to prove it, the truth of one's sensations is not in the fact, but in the reverberation. When I have read three lines, I re-make them entirely, if they're prose, and not poetry; and it is this which is the truth. (Has Harold [Nicolson] read Lytton?)[2]

So my dearest, we shall soon meet again—pray the Lord not round an aspidistra in a Boarding House. We are coming in our shabbiest clothes; my mother in law has given me a coat like the pelt a sheep wears when its been on a high mountain alone for weeks—an old sheep.

With tact, we shall spend a good deal of time alone together. And you'll be loving and kind to Potto[3] wont you? And kind to Virginia? And you'll say that you love her in so many words, won't you, not leaving her to infer that she's on a par with the . . . oh damn you, you never told me Harold's word.[4]

A certain gloom lies over London. I am glad to be flying.

Virginia

Berg

1982: To V. Sackville-West   [52 *Tavistock Square, W.C.*1]

Friday [11 January 1929]

I wrote in such a hurry the other night that I expect I failed to explain that Leonard and I arrive at the Friederichstrasse station on Thursday at 5.21. and shall go to the Prinz Albrecht [Hotel] if we dont see you. Could you possibly let us have a line to say what street it is on, as its not marked in the Baedeker.

I see that one out of every 15 people has influenza in Berlin, so I'm arranging to catch it on the last day and stay on.

---

1. Review of *Zoe* and *The Half Sisters*, by Geraldine Jewsbury (*TLS*, 28 February 1929); and *Dr Burney's Evening Party* (*New York Herald Tribune*, 21 and 28 July 1929).
2. Lytton Strachey's *Elizabeth and Essex*, published in autumn 1928.
3. One of Virginia's pet names for herself when writing to Vita. A potto is an African lemur.
4. 'Stoker', Harold's and Vita's pet name for Hilda Matheson, one of Vita's most intimate friends. She was Talks Director of the BBC.

Lord! What unhappy letters you do write from Berlin![1]

V.

Let me know if you want anything brought.

Berg

1983: TO PHILIP GOSSE   52 *Tavistock Square, W.C.*1

11th Jan. 1929

Dear Sir,

I should be delighted to send you any letters from Sir Edmund Gosse to my father, if I could find them.[2] Unfortunately my father destroyed almost all his letters and it is only by chance, in most cases, that a few remain. I should be so sorry that there were none to him in your life of your father that I will look carefully through any papers I have. As I am just going abroad for a fortnight, I am afraid I must wait till I come back to do this.

I will let you know as soon as I can.

Believe me

yours sincerely
Virginia Woolf

Cambridge University Library

1984: TO WILLIAM ROTHENSTEIN 52 *Tavistock Square, W.C.*1

Typewritten
14th Jan 1929

Dear Mr Rothenstein,

Please forgive me for being so long in answering your letter. It was extremely good of you to send me the drawings,[3] which I have looked at with great interest. I had seen them years ago. I am not capable of any opinion about drawing—I never venture to give one—but I have the ordinary persons love of a likeness and desire to be reminded by portraits of real people and I have been greatly interested and pleased to find in your

1. For instance, Vita wrote on 6 January 1929: "You have no idea how miserable I am here. I almost cease to exist" (*Berg*).
2. Sir Edmund Gosse (1849-1928), the man of letters. Evan Charteris, not Gosse's son Philip, wrote *The Life and Letters of Edmund Gosse* (1931). The book contains no letters to Virginia's father, Leslie Stephen.
3. Of Virginia's parents. William Rothenstein drew a portrait of Julia Stephen in 1890 and one of Leslie Stephen in 1903. (See Volume I of this Edition, Letter 90.) Both drawings are reproduced in Rothenstein's *Portrait Drawings* (1926).

pictures a trace of my father and mother. They are more worn and sad than I remembered them; but no doubt this is accounted for by the fact of my father's illness. I admit that I think, perhaps with the partiality of a daughter, that my mother was more beautiful than you show her; but I am very glad to have these records of them, and must thank you very sincerely for sending them.

Yours sincerely
Virginia Woolf

[*in Virginia's handwriting:*]
Please excuse the typewriter but it is better than my handwriting.

Houghton Library, Harvard University

1985: To Helen McAfee   52 *Tavistock Square, W.C.*1

Typewritten
14th Jan. 1929

Dear Miss McAfee,[1]
 I am afraid that there is no chance of my being able to send you the article on Dr Burney by the tenth of February. I am only now beginning to work at it, and as I have other work to do at the same time I shall certainly not have finished it by then. Also I think it will be a good deal longer than I supposed. Would it not be as well to give up the idea, and I will find a home for it elsewhere?[2]
 Thank you so much for sending me the press cutting about Orlando. It was very good of you to write so kindly, and I am delighted to think that you enjoyed the book.
 With kind regards from myself and my husband.

Yours very sincerely
Virginia Woolf

Yale University

1986: To V. Sackville-West   [52 *Tavistock Square, W.C.*1]

Sunday [27 January 1929]

 Well, here I am in bed. I had to be hauled out of my berth at Harwich— a mixture of the somnifeine [Somnifène], flu, and headache—apparently. Quite drugged. But I'm better. Only of course the dr. makes me stay in

1. Managing Editor of the *Yale Review*.
2. See p. 5, note 1.

bed and do nothing. I wish it had happened in Berlin. I wish I could see you. Do write. I'm much better today. Berlin was quite worth it anyhow.

Love,
Virginia

The doctor just been—says its the flue and I shall be able to get up on Tuesday.

VW

Berg

1987: To V. Sackville-West   [52 *Tavistock Square, W.C.1*]

Monday [28 January 1929]

How nice to get your letter this morning—a great treat. I'm afraid I wrote you rather a dazed one yesterday. That blessed sea sick drug of Nessa's somehow went wrong and I had to be hauled along like a sack, but thats all right now, and so's the flue, and I've only got the usual headache which is better today.[1]

I daresay I shall get up tomorrow. I'm being rather strictly looked after though by Leonard and Ellie Rendel (the dr.)[2] and so can only write these scraps. I keep thinking of you and long—oh Lord how I long—that you would open the door and come in. I've seen no one, so you need have no fears. I do nothing but sleep. Pinker [spaniel] lies on the chair by the fire. Leonard comes in with a proof or the paper, Nelly brings me lemonade. I read the Times and drop it. I see you with extreme distinction—Well anyhow it was worth the week with you. I think of the tower and the lights and the waves and the shell room at Sans Souci and you, and you[3]—

1. Leonard wrote to Vanessa on this same date: "When I woke her in the morning [at Harwich] she was in a very curious state, so giddy that it was with the greatest difficulty I got her off the boat and into the train, as she could hardly walk and was in a kind of drugged state. She says she had only taken 20 drops. She has been in bed ever since. The giddiness lasted off and on for another 24 hours and she has now one of the oldfashioned headaches and a rather bad one. . . . My own theory is that she did too much in Berlin and that the late nights reduced her to the last gasp; she was on the point of a breakdown when she took the Somnifène which for some reason or other affected her wrongly" (*Berg*).

2. Dr Elinor Rendel, the daughter of Lytton Strachey's eldest sister, also called Elinor.

3. The 'tower' was the *Funkturm* in Berlin, where Virginia and Vita had dined; the 'waves' was the *Wellenbad*, a huge indoor swimming pool fitted with a wave-making machine; Sans Souci was Frederick the Great's palace at Potsdam, which the whole party had visited one afternoon.

Next week is Feb. 1st. so there's really not long to wait. But Lord! what a horror Berlin and diplomacy are! I'd no idea till I'd seen it. And I shiver at the thought of our behaviour about that lunch.[1] You and Harold were such angels. My love to him. *Write.*

V.

(Here's Leonard so I must stop)

Berg

1988: To V. Sackville-West   [52 *Tavistock Square, W.C.*1]
Tuesday [29 January 1929]

Dearest Creature,

Here is another selfish invalids bulletin, but I like to write to you, and you won't mind it all being about myself.

I am really better today, only still kept in bed. It is merely the usual headache which is now making me rather achy and shivery but passing off. And the dr has just been and says I shall get on the sofa tomorrow and may see someone on Thursday. Who would you like to see she says, and I think at once of ——— well, it aint Mary [Hutchinson] or Christa:[2] though I daresay to tease you I shall have Mary. and as I shall be in my nightgown— But no. I am very faithful. Its odd how I want you when I'm ill. I think everything would be warm and happy if Vita came in. And Vita's having tea with the American Ambassadors wife, I suppose: very smart and haughty. How you frightened me that night on the pavement! Potto still talks of it.

Its so odd to have gone straight from all that movement, and big houses, and street signs and wine and Vita to lying alone in bed up here without any interest. I've looked out of the window and see that Tavistock Sqre is very small and distinguished. L. is at the office. Nelly[3] out. So I'm alone. Pinker was sent up. She has worms and is very fat. I've got some rather nice photographs of Virginia;[4] but can't send them at the moment. I will tomorrow if I can. Please write, long long letters, all about yourself and if you like me. That is what I want. I dont really read anything with interest except your letters.

1. The Woolfs had refused to attend a lunch-party which Harold Nicolson had arranged for them. See Vanessa's account of the Berlin holiday in her letter to Roger Fry, quoted by Quentin Bell, *Virginia Woolf*, II, pp. 141-3.
2. Christabel McLaren, whose husband succeeded as the 2nd Lord Aberconway in 1934. She was a patron of the arts and had a salon in Mayfair.
3. Nelly Boxall, who had been the Woolfs' cook since 1916.
4. By Lenare. See plate 1. Vita thought Virginia looked 'mischievous' and 'tidy' in them (Vita to Virginia, 8 February 1929, *Berg*).

I've no ink up here, and this is becoming illegible. Lord! how I should like to see you!

Virginia

Berg

1989: TO V. SACKVILLE-WEST   52 *Tavistock Square, W.C.*1

Wednesday [30 January 1929]

Another 5 minutes conversation, all about myself as usual. Do you mind? Are you bored? You're the only person I write to.

I'm down on the sofa in the drawing room this evening. The Knole sofa[1]—very comfortable. I cant be bothered to find a pen so you must put up with pencil. These headaches are very odd. This time last week we were at Sans Souci—now I cant imagine walking across the Square. What d'you think happens? Leonard and the dr. says its my rackety life in Berlin. But why this change in 10 seconds? I'm really better, only rather cross that it takes so long. And that I cant see you. If you were to sit by me now I should be so happy. Brilliant ideas come into my head—scenes—solutions—but are extinguished. How does one write? I read half a page about Austin Dobson[2] and then drowse for an hour. Leonard brings in huge beef steaks. I say I'm afraid I shall be very strictly kept under for a time. No parties— no romances. But that suits you very well, you wretch. You want Potto and Virginia kept in their kennel—write dearest please anything that comes into your head—the more the better. I have no pain today but am only like a damp duster.

Love
V.

Berg

1990: TO V. SACKVILLE-WEST   [52 *Tavistock Square, W.C.*1]

Thursday [31 January 1929]

I shall now have my little treat of writing to Vita, I say to myself.

I wish I'd heard from you, but perhaps I shall. No I am not to see anybody—not Mary [Hutchinson] even. Dr Rendel can't imagine why I want to see Mary, (her cousin). There is such a thing as womanly charm I reply. Anyhow it aint allowed. I console myself by thinking that they wouldnt allow you either. I have been rather giddy, and have to keep lying down. It is something to do with the spirit level in my ears. There is a kind

---

1. A type of sofa with collapsible ends, of which the prototype is at Knole.
2. Henry Austin Dobson (1840-1921), the poet, critic, and biographer of several eighteenth-century figures, including Fanny Burney.

of mouse which turns for ever, because its ears have no spirit level. Would you like to see Potto turning for ever? Everything is put down to Berlin. I am never to walk round a gallery or sit up drinking again. All my adventures are to be lying down—which will suit, in some ways. Really I am rather better, and make up a book to be called The Moths [*The Waves*] hour after hour.

And what about Vita? poor poor Vita lying like a beautiful cat in a cage—and not a plain cage either, but a cage like the Albert Memorial. Lord! how the ugliness of Berlin remains with me!

We travelled back with the Rev. Herbert Dunnico[1] a labour MP, who had lunched with Kuhlman and with Schubert[2] and told L. all about it and abused the Duchess of Atholl:[3] theres the dear old Labour party atmosphere all over again I thought; and rejoiced that I was not labour and not anything: this is what makes one serene—these secret thoughts. Thats all my news—rather faded: and Kessler[4] is a bastard of the Kaiser's they say. Nelly [Boxall] is my only link with real life. I could tell you all about the party at the Harlands when George got drunk. They insisted that he should sleep in my bed and Nelly refused. George is Lotties young man, but Lottie doesnt mean anything serious; she's 38 after all.[5] And Nelly has taken away the latch key she gave her and wont see her till she gives George up. After all she cant have it both ways. I tells her. But thats enough.

I am now going to sleep, with Pinker in L's chair, looking very stately Love from us both.

And write dearest, if you have time, any scrap—

Virginia

Berg

1991: TO V. SACKVILLE-WEST   [52 *Tavistock Square, W.C.*1]

Friday [1 February 1929]

It was very refreshing to get your letter this morning—among such

1. M.P. for Durham (Consett), 1922-31, and Deputy Speaker of the House of Commons.
2. Richard von Kühlmann, formerly German Foreign Secretary, and Carl von Schubert, currently Permanent Under-Secretary of State at the German Foreign Office.
3. Katharine, Duchess of Atholl (1874-1960), was the first woman M.P. to be elected in Scotland, and in 1924-9 was parliamentary secretary to the Board of Education in the Conservative Government.
4. Count Harry Kessler, a prominent figure in the social and cultural world of Berlin. He supervised the printing of Vita's translations of Rilke.
5. Lottie Hope, who had come as parlourmaid to the Woolfs in 1916 and stayed until 1924, when she went to Virginia's brother, Adrian Stephen. Harland was manservant to John Maynard Keynes.

dreary ones. I have read it several times. Of course we would go to Long Barn[1] like a shot—you know. The dr. says though that I must be in bed another week anyhow and then be very quiet—oh this being very quiet!—so that I dont suppose we could get away till the middle of Feb, and then you'd soon be back.

But if London becomes intolerable I shall take you at your word. At the moment I'm so lethargic I dont think of anything but walking down to the sofa or up to bed. They give me stiff doses of bromide. Its rather nice. Ones head feels grown to the pillow. One floats like a log. I wake to write to you. The sight of you on [the] street at Berlin is my last record of humanity. There were two Germans in the carriage—fat, greasy, the woman with broken nails. The man peeled an orange for her. She squeezed his hand. It was repulsive. Perhaps in time one might come to think this complete unadornment beautiful—morally—after many many years. You deserve Rapallo[2] and I envy you. Heat—sun—anyhow clear air. Its lead and yellow here day after day. Oh how I liked your letter! There's nothing to be anxious about in me. The dr says its simply exhaustion and must take time, but theres nothing wrong. She has a silver stethescope and tells me every day that there is nothing wrong with my heart. What I can't understand is why, if theyre right about Berlin, I felt quite well there, only shivery that day at Sans Souci. However—I'm much better. Its a great refuge to think I could fly to Long Barn—How you cured me when I was ill before [June 1927]! Potto would be happy. I shall be in robust health by the time you're back—27 days now.

Write as often as you can—I do like your letters.

V.

Berg

1992: To Julian Bell   52 *T.S.* [*W.C.*1]

[3? February 1929]

My dear Julian,[3]

Many happy returns! To think that you are 21! And I carried you round the room in my arms once.

We send you a small cheque to buy a book or a bird or a chocolate cake—whatever you like—with our blessing.

1. The Nicolsons' house near Sevenoaks, Kent. Vita had offered it to Virginia for her convalescence.
2. Vita and Harold went to Rapallo on the north coast of Italy for a week's holiday.
3. Julian Bell, Vanessa's elder son, was an undergraduate at Cambridge. He was born on 4 February 1908.

The trapesing in Berlin was terrific. Nessa poisoned me with a seasick-draught. I sank into coma and am still in bed.

Are you writing poems? I should like to see them some day.

Write me a long long letter.

Yr loving Virginia

Quentin Bell

1993: TO V. SACKVILLE-WEST   [52 *Tavistock Square, W.C.*1]

Monday [4 February 1929]

Dearest—What a time your letters take to come! One posted Thursday comes this morning—to my great delight. You can't think what a difference it makes when they bring in a blue envelope. I'm still in bed—thats to say I stay in bed till after tea and then come down in my nightgown and lie on the sofa till after dinner, (as I'm doing now). I'm better, however—not so limp. And no pain for two days and no sleeping draughts, only Bromide. I've had this sort of thing before, especially after flue, slight though that was and it always takes some time to go off—Also the sea sick draught, which was veronal, made me more susceptible. But of course the dr and Leonard say its all the Berlin racketing (I daresay it was) on the top of the others. So I'm still prevented from seeing anyone—which may please you. You are still the only face I have in my minds eye. Therefore my letters are of an unthinkable dullness. Viola Tree[1] and Roger [Fry] and Lytton [Strachey] and Tom Eliot ring up and I think of their sailing about somewhere miles overhead, as if I were a fish at the bottom of the seas. Other people's lives become so decorative when one takes no part in them. I admit I rather like this solitude. Ones mind fills up like a sponge. I think of you. To own up, I rather like thinking of you shining at Embassies. I like to think of you all lit up among Nuncios and footmen. Its a weakness of mine. Part of your glamour, I suppose. On the other hand, Berlin glamour seems only that of Woolworths and Lyons Corner House—its immeasurable mediocrity still affects me. And you to be held under that arc lamp! Arent you a creature of the dusk? Very well. We will watch the moon rise together very soon at Long Barn. Bosquet[2] rang up this morning to ask if we were coming—as I think I said I dont see any immediate prospect, but it refreshes me to think we could go at any moment. I imagine I'm to go on like this till the end of the week and then sit up a bit and take little drives.

When shall I begin The Moths [*The Waves*]? Thats what I want to know. Theres that damned book on fiction [*Phases of Fiction*]—it still wants 10,000 more words—and such nonsense! and I darent leave it in the

1. The eldest daughter of Beerbohm Tree. The Hogarth Press had published her book, *Castles in the Air*, in 1926.
2. Audrey le Bosquet, Vita's secretary.

13

lurch again and write another Orlando—A woman writes that she has to stop and kiss the page when she reads O:—Your race I imagine. The percentage of Lesbians is rising in the States, all because of you. And did you yield to the red haired woman?[1] Please be explicit and honest. I shall be so lively when I get over this that I shall run amok at the least provocation. L's mother is worse, and has the nurse that nursed Lord Carnock.[2] They talk of you and the boys. Lawrences poems have been seized in ms by the police in the post.[3] Jack Hutch.[4] and L are going to work some protest—nothing will be safe—not this letter.

Let me have your address at Rapallo. I'm glad youre going tho' I dont like you to be further away. And send any scrap—a picture postcard even—

This is the longest letter I have written, and I'm not a bit tired. If I liked I could fill my pen and write in ink, but I'm abandoned to luxury. Thats all my news. Nothing is the matter, says the dr (to end medically as usual) except exhaustion—and she has made me breathe and stop breathing and say 99 till I am sick of it.

Yr.

Berg

Virginia

1994: To Vanessa Bell   52 *T.[avistock] S.[quare, W.C.*1]

Thursday [7 February 1929]

Dearest

I have been enjoying your letter extremely. This is only to say that there's no reason whatever to think it was your drug that did me harm—Elly says I may have had slight flue—but anyhow all the blame is put on Berlin and this would have happened anyhow, though possibly not in such a sudden way.

It was very odd, waking at Harwich in a state of apparent intoxication. Also, I took less than the proper dose, and it was from the same bottle you had taken.

I'm much better and am spending the day on the sofa today. and not in bed. I intend to begin work on Monday.

1. A photographer in Berlin who had shown Vita photographs "of an indecency which I won't describe" (Vita to Virginia, 31 January 1929, *Berg*).
2. Harold Nicolson's father, who died in November 1928.
3. The typescripts of D. H. Lawrence's poems *Pansies* were sent from abroad by post, opened by the Customs, and referred by them to the Home Secretary, William Joynson-Hicks, who described them in Parliament as "grossly obscene".
4. St John Hutchinson, the barrister, and husband of Mary.

Elly is rather severe, and I've only seen Helen,[1] who is thought less exciting than Mary.

The only gossip therefore is rather remote: I daresay you've heard that Angus has not got the Nat. Gall.[2] It has gone to an unknown man. Miss Ritchie[3] has been to ask L. to help—Angus she says, is now sunk into complete apathy, wont try for any job, and says he means to write plays with her—[*six words omitted*].

Then Partridge is said to be going back to Carrington[4] (Helen). Lady Carnarvon[5] is dead, after a lifetime of work among the Albanians. Nelly has had a complete break with Lottie and seized her latch key so that Lottie cant come here. The police have seized Lawrences poems in manuscript in the post—so this letter even may be taken and Jack Hutch. and Leonard are getting up a protest.

This is all the news.

It has been rather desperate being in bed a fortnight with this cursed disease, but Berlin was great fun in many ways—humans and pictures. Never again though. Even what I see of London from the window has an incredible distinction. Lord! how nice to see you again! So do ring up, when your back. I haven't seen Angelica,[6] but hear from Nelly that she's in great health and spirits. She was taking complete control of everyone.

B.[7]

Berg

1995: To V. Sackville-West   [52 *Tavistock Square, W.C.*1]

Thursday, Feb. 7th [1929]

There! does this ink convince you that I'm better!
A lovely letter from you just came. But I *am* telling you the truth. I'm

1. Helen Anrep, estranged wife of Boris Anrep, the Russian mosaicist. She was now living with Roger Fry.
2. Angus Davidson did not in fact apply for a position in the National Gallery. He had worked for the Hogarth Press, 1924-27.
3. Alice Ritchie published two books with the Hogarth Press, *The Peacemakers* (1928) and *Occupied Territory* (1930). Her family had come to England from South Africa in the First War, and Leonard called her 'a good and serious novelist' (*Downhill*, pp. 169-70). She also travelled books for the Press.
4. Ralph Partridge had married Dora Carrington in 1921, and both of them lived with Lytton Strachey. Partridge and Carrington drifted apart when she fell in love with Gerald Brenan, and he with Frances Marshall.
5. The step-mother of Lady Margaret Herbert, who had married George Duckworth, Virginia's half-brother.
6. Vanessa's daughter was then aged ten.
7. 'B.' stands for 'Billy', which in turn derived from Virginia's childhood nickname, 'Goat'.

not keeping anything back—only its rather difficult to explain. You see it was very odd—I went to bed at Harwich[1] rather cold and tired but apparently all right, took less than the usual dose of a seasick draught that Nessa had taken the week before—and woke up next morning completely drugged. Leonard had to drag me across to [from] the boat. My legs staggered and my head reeled. I slept in the train all the way to London; again he had to drag me into a cab. I went to bed. Shivered, ached, slept, had a little temperature; the doctor came next day and said I was certainly under the influence of some drug, and possibly influenza; but there was nothing in the dose to account for it: and therefore she thought I must be otherwise exhausted, but it would pass off. However, though the drug did pass off, and the temperature, I remained in what they call a state of nervous exhaustion—thats to say all the usual symptoms—pain, and heart jumpy, and my back achy, and so on. What I call a first rate headache. This, as you know, doesn't go at once; and what happens is one day one's better and one day worse. But on the whole I get more hours every day without any headache or heart or anything and today I've been on the sofa almost all day.

I cant yet talk much without this blessed old pulse beginning to rear like a kicking horse, but on the other hand my head is much less bothering —I read almost a whole manuscript carefully yesterday. These are the dull and sordid details—not much to send to Rapallo. But don't, for goodness sake, think I'm trying to spare you. I should tell you instantly if I felt bad.

No, I didnt feel tired in Berlin—I'd had three weeks rest before and felt very well. Thats the odd thing—but anyhow, if it was Berlin, you and your motor car made it infinitely less tiring than it would have been. I believe its partly that awful airlessness. But now lets talk of something else.

Lord, I'm glad to address this to Rapallo. The thought of you in Berlin makes me irritable. Now you'll have sea, and hills, and old women with hooked noses and maccaroni and olives—which is what I like to think of you against—wild, tossing, like a young mare; not that intolerable South Kensington and diplomacy—which is only South Kensington in extremis. Yes, I dare say it. Didn't I know Austen and Esme[2] when I was young? I gave your message to Leonard. But he doesn't correct proofs if its that that you hate him for—hate Harold and Hubert, not Leonard.[3]

1. Written in error for the Hook of Holland. The ship sailed to Harwich.
2. Esmé Howard, whose career was chiefly in diplomacy; George Duckworth was Secretary to Austen Chamberlain, 1902-5.
3. Vita had complained (4 February 1929, *Berg*) that in her latest *Nation* review the phrase 'sombre muse' had been printed as 'sombre nurse'. Virginia blames the error on Harold Wright, the Assistant Editor of the *Nation*, and Hubert Henderson, the Editor.

A slumber doth my spirit seal.[1] I have no earthly fears. Various people ring up and I dont see them. I hear that Valery [Valerie Taylor] is desperate because she was such a success in The Seagull—this proves that she can only act one character, her own. This came to me from my only visitor—not Mary—Helen Anrep—I like her because she's a true blood Bohemian: seduced, deserted, unfaithful, completely unusual and devoted to Roger.

Otherwise no news. Leonards mother is very bad and he has to go there. He is a perfect angel—only more to the point than most angels—He sits on the edge of the bed and considers my symptoms like a judge. He brings home huge pineapples: he moves the gramophone into my room and plays until he thinks I'm excited. In short, I should have shot myself long ago in one of these illnesses if it hadn't been for him. As it is, I hope to go into the Square next week: but as I say this sort of thing takes time; it must be let to wander about one's body like a policeman trying bolts; and theres no doubt I get many more times of complete comfort now. Ask Harold with my love in what book I should find Lady Bessboroughs letters? Life of Lord Somebody [Granville]—I cant remember who.

And give my humble duty to Max B. if you see him. And my love to Edith.[2] And write cards to me. And be happy. And come back soon. And love Potto and Virginia. How I dreamt of your mother last night! How I love you.

Berg

Virginia

1996: To Dorothy Bussy   52 *Tavistock Sqre., W.C.*1

Feb. 10th 1929

Dear Dorothy,

I was very pleased to get your letter—it was charming of you to write. I have been in bed for over a fortnight with some sort of flu that has a disastrous effect upon the nervous system. Elly has been giving me stiff tumblers of bromide. And your letter gleamed through my drowsiness like the fin of a silver fish. In fact I pulled it out and read it several times. But I wish I could have got more into my sketch of your mother.[3] When I came

---

1.   A slumber did my spirit seal;
                             I had no human fears:
                    She seemed a thing that could not feel
                         The touch of earthly years.
                                    (Wordsworth)

2. Max Beerbohm lived at Rapallo, where Vita had expected to find Edith Sitwell on holiday.

3. Lady Strachey, who died on 15 December 1928. Virginia had written her obituary in the *Nation*. Her daughter Dorothy, author of *Olivia* (1949), lived in France with her painter husband Simon Bussy and their daughter Janie.

to write (and it had to be scribbled in a great rush) I found the image of her somehow so important, so predominating in my mind—I was surprised, considering how little I had seen of her.

Yes, you are an arch-flatterer. Its done with an air of intense conviction on top of immense erudition and insight which is irresistible. I do hope our annual teas aren't doomed: you must come to London, if for them only. I would throw in 2 ices and a cocktail. Tell Janie I'm so glad she has begun to take liberties with me and the Sphinx [Leonard?]—high time she did. And excuse this handwriting. I am up, but write lying down.

Love, yrs aff
Virginia

Texas

1997: TO HUGH WALPOLE   52 *Tavistock Sqre., W.C.*1

10th Feb. 1929

My dear Hugh,[1]

You see how literally I obey your license not to answer letters. It is only selfishness that now drives me to the pen—I am in bed recovering from a week in Berlin, a little flue, what they call nervous exhaustion, vast draughts of bromide and other sleeping mixtures: have been in bed two weeks; shall only be allowed to creep round the Square this week; see visitors one by one and for a single hour only—you know the kind of thing —nervous people dropping their bags and saying its time they caught a train: all of which, slovenly though it is, leads up to the climax that I should like a letter from you.

What is diabetes like? I could write reams upon the effects on the nervous system of influenza. Another person's disease would be great fun. And another person's mind. And a flat in Piccadilly looking bang at the white bust of Queen Victoria—that pleased me so much. The raying paths of the park; and the Queen plump in the centre—or have I made this up? When you have had breakfast, do you look to see if the Royal Standard is broken at the palace? You see I am imagining your life, as I have at the moment none of my own—only imaginations drawn from books: (I am reading Beau Brummell's life,[2] Constable's life, a life of Trollope, and seven manuscript novels). I am trying to think where you are lunching; and dining; and then how you will be about 2 am saying something frightfully exciting to a young man in a corner. Up to that moment your life has been

---

1. Hugh Walpole (1884-1941), the novelist, who had presented Virginia with the *Femina Vie Heureuse* Prize in 1928 for *To the Lighthouse.*
2. Virginia's article on Brummell was first published in the *Nation* on 28 September 1929.

(to me) quite extraordinarily active; kindly, prosperous, and successful. I mean you've had 15 letters from admirers; 70 small cheques; one big one; requests for help; you have pushed aside the letters, and dipped your pen— you have then ridden white horses at a smart trot up to houses in the midst of trees where ladies are on the lawn—this is part of your 18th Century novel; And so on.

By the way, I'm going to read Hugh Walpole's novels; Shall I begin with the one I've just been writing—about the white horse trotting up to the lawn? I didn't tell you that I rang you up for 10 minutes one night— through the agency of Fielding, Sibyl's[1] maid who had your number, asking you to dine, asking you to come in to a party; and all the answer I got was a gigantic pop, like the cork being drawn from a champagne bottle in an empty room. Thats what happens at 99 [90] Piccadilly when you're not there.

Berlin was very exhausting; very large; very cold; lots of music: Count Kessler; Count Kühlmann, and Vita in black trying to be a diplomats wife with Harold to pull the strings. A pathetic sight, I thought.

No, I didn't much care for [Lytton Strachey's] Elizabeth and Essex— thats not the sort of imagination he has—he becomes all purple and gold, like the cheaper effects at the Pantomime: style to match; dum-dum-dum. Its odd how bad it is compared with the others (but no doubt I'm up a tree of my own and see this wrong.)

Yr
Virginia

Texas

1998: To V. Sackville-West   52 *T.[avistock] S.[quare, W.C.1]*
Tuesday, 12th Feb. [1929]

You have been an angel—letters every day and today a letter from Le Boski with your new address. Is it deep snow? Is it freezing? Is it fine? And are you tramping the hills? Questions I ask by the gas fire.

I am being kept very quiet today and so am rather grumpy. All my own fault. I insisted upon writing a little yesterday and so brought on the headache—or rather—for thats what it feels like,—tempted the rat to gnaw the nerves in my spine—fourth knob from the top. You must expect grumpy gloomy letters. Getting well is infinitely worse than being ill.

I have been out. I have twice walked round the square leaning on L's arm—very cold and ugly it was, and a cat had chosen to die on the path. Then I undress and lie on the sofa.

1. Lady Colefax, wife of Sir Arthur, who lived at Argyll House, Chelsea, and made it a centre of London's social and cultural life.

Today I have lain on the sofa—not dressed, and feel now much brighter clearer and less inclined to curse God for having made such a crazy apparatus as my nervous system. Is it worth it? I was asking this morning. In addition, the bath had frozen; no hot bath; the pipes downstairs had burst. Plumbers were knocking about in the walls. Then I ate a beefsteak and a pancake; L. wrapped me up warm; and I am very cheerful again. Its awfully difficult to say how long its going to take though. I agree it was the flu; but I think I was foolish also in Berlin—you dont realise what a valetudinarian life mine is, usually, so that what's nothing to anybody else is rackety to poor Potto. Never mind. I shall be in robust health by the 4th. But cant you look in for a bite on the 2nd? And I'm awfully tempted by the notion of a few days at Long Barn—as Le Boski insists.

But enough of these egotistical and invalidish woes. Dotty [Wellesley] came yesterday and L. said she was in an admirable temper, serene and kind. I didn't see her. I've seen Mary once—a little strained I thought; but then I think she may feel "I am 40, or this light is unbecoming"—I was too lazy to get up and arrange it. She was very 'nice,' as they say; I do like her;— in the way that I like her for making me think of pirates, sinister and swart, spearing fish remorselessly from the prow of a little boat. She is so intent on her game; and I see her watching the water and then casting her spear— Also she is decorative, and hunts, like a beast of prey, whatever it may be— a jewel, a toy: she had been to [the] Caledonian market and speared a hunting horn made of glass. She was dining with a young man, alone; incautiously, she told me his name, and I knew him, and she didn't, which discomposed her—huntress that she is. But how fascinating sincerity between women is —how terrifically exciting! She has been victimised by your red haired photographer[1] by the way. She sat to her and was sent in a bill for £5— but she is a crafty devil, Mary.

Thats all my news. Vanessa is back[2] and comes round and sits here, so I dont bother to see the enchantresses of London. We talk nursery talk. She wants me to buy a villa near her [at Cassis]—Shall I? London, society, talk, shops seem at this moment a waste of life. But then Vita? These illnesses are such a bore—4 weeks clean out of my life: when shall I write The Moths? I'm telling the doctor that its, as you say, due to suppressed randiness.[3]

1. See p. 14, note 1.
2. After leaving Berlin, Vanessa and Duncan Grant travelled to Vienna, Prague and Munich.
3. Vita had written soon after Virginia left Berlin: "You wont get this till after you have been to Long Barn, which I hope will have reminded you of me a little, and perhaps revived in you something of those feelings to which you gave such startling and disturbing expression in the Funkturm." In a later letter from Berlin, Vita accused Virginia of "suppressed randiness. . . . You remember your admissions as the searchlight [of the *Funkturm*] went round and round" (Both *Berg.*). See also p. 29.

Thats true. But also, its suppressed imagination. To write criticism is now like keeping my hand clenched, so much do I want to stretch and write fiction. And to see Vita. That would make me well. Seriously it would.

[*squiggly design*]¹ Potto and Virginia

I do hope you are happy, and want to know every detail—and send me a picture postcard please. Love to Harold.

Berg

1999: To Clive Bell   [52 *Tavistock Square, W.C.*1]
Postcard
[12 February 1929]

How nice it would be to get a letter from Clive. I am in bed, have been, and perhaps shall be: the effect of Berlin.
And no Clive to come to tea.

V.

Quentin Bell

2000: To Katherine Arnold-Forster
52 *Tavistock Square, W.C.*1
Feb. 13th '29

Dearest Ka,

I was stung with remorse seeing your handwriting today—to think I have never answered you! Being so vain too, your letter gave me exquisite pleasure. I never thought you would much like Orlando—and it is a great pleasure that Bruin whom I love and admire so much (for all sorts of qualities) should have turned over the work of such a scatterbrained and unsatisfactory character as I am (compared with Bruin) and smelt it and pawed it and growled quite melodiously over it. I was going to thank you for the bag of scent—thyme, lavender? What is it? all the little flowers that grow on the rocks² perhaps. I was going to write a long letter from Monks House, where we were, but then we went on a German tour with Nessa and Duncan and Quentin and I suppose Berlin, which is the ugliest of cities, did me in somehow, for I arrived at Harwich at 6am on 25th January in a state of intoxication—legs going one way—head another—and was put to bed here where I still am. Its said to be a touch of the flu, and Nessas seasick drug, and the usual amazingly ineffective state of what is called my nervous

1. See Editorial Note, p. xi.
2. At Zennor, Cornwall, where Virginia's old friend Ka Cox ('Bruin') lived with her husband, the painter Will Arnold-Forster, and their son Mark.

21

system. Elly is very strict, and I am lying in my drawing room, thinking over my past, but not allowed to write books or even see the human race—except for a moment. Nessa comes round and we gossip. But this is passing off, and I hope to be able to take part in life next week perhaps. If Bruin was round the corner, she should come in and have a spoonful of honey.

I liked your account of Mark. Why must he go to school in Geneva? Why must he learn French? Oh dear—why is life arranged with such crass stupidity? I mean I should like Mark to learn to read and then grow up with badgers and ravens—or remain the elf he was: you see I dont like the finished article. What a bore for you, too; not to have him. Angelica insists upon going to school. Julian and Quentin are exactly at the stage I was when I first knew you and Rupert and the Oliviers[1]— exacting, charming, combative. Does that describe me and you and the others 20 years ago?

I saw about the badger in the Manchester Guardian. It suggested Ka very powerfully—scuttling along, on its sturdy paws with its small round behind. A young Kennedy is now working for us in the Press and I hear a great deal about Cornwall.[2]

Yes, Ka, I am very pleased you liked Orlando. And write again.

V.

Mark Arnold-Forster

2001: To Nan Hudson   52 *Tavistock Sq.* [*W.C.*1]

[mid-February 1929]

My dear Nan,[3]

I am so sorry not to have seen you—is there still a chance? I've been in bed since we got back from Berlin; and still only drowse over the fire. Nevertheless I am constantly thanking you and Ethel—for ear stoppers, the joy of my life; for the desk; for your cookery book. We are going to have one of your dishes tonight: orange loaf. Last night it was Chocolate Cream. Bless Miss Hudson!

Nessa thinks you're just going [to Paris]—if so, love and farewell.

And I hope we shall meet soon.

Yr

Wendy Baron   Virginia

1. Ka Cox, Rupert Brooke (who was later her lover), and the four daughters of Sir Sidney Olivier were all members of the Cambridge group, called by Virginia the 'Neo-Pagans'.
2. Richard Kennedy had joined the Hogarth Press in May 1928 at the age of 16. He was the nephew of George Kennedy, the architect who had lived in Cornwall, where Virginia had spent her childhood holidays.
3. Nan Hudson was the life-long companion of Ethel Sands. Both were Americans by birth and both were painters. They lived in London and at Auppegard in Normandy, where Virginia had visited them.

Friday Feb. 15th [1929]

This must be sent to Berlin I suppose—alas! alas! Poor Vita fast in her cage again after her sniff of olive trees. She may be frozen, though, crossing the Alps.

Was it really true—about the mimosa and being warm after dinner [at Rapallo]?

Talk of icicles! You can see icicles 50 feet long—from the top story to the ground—in Tavistock Square.

As London has no provision for cold, we are in desperate states, all of us: most have no baths, no water closets, and some no gas fires, as the pipes are frozen. Our watercloset is our glory—the plug still pulls. No bath, though. Whats happened is that nature, having read a certain description of a frost (see O—o)[1] was so taken by it that she determined to do it better. Needless to say she does it infinitely worse: Not a flounder or an old woman to be seen at London Bridge. I wish I knew that you had crossed the Alps safely.

My letters have been awful—I know dreary invalidish egotism. Please forgive it. Its no good trying to get out in this cold, so I'm back on the sofa again, but dont much mind. I shall be in robust health by March 4th. Meanwhile I read vast masses of MSS. They plague my life out, these unhappy women and men, to read their mss myself and tell them how they cd. be improved.

I saw Lytton yesterday and he told me about Lady Bessborgh—it is Lord Granville[2]—the first one. How I adore Lytton!—except for his supercilious ways, which are on top: but rather baffling if one's rather used up in the head. Also the spectre of Queen Eth[3] stands between us. With the sensibility of an author he knows what I dont deny; and wont ask me; so we keep to trifles. Otherwise I see nobody but Nessa except that I'm to see Christa [McLaren]. I dont want to see anyone much—(there was a woman I once saw in a fish shop, by some glass bowls—what was her name? Nicols, I think—well I'd rather like to see her again.)[4]

Raymond[5] is said to return today with Lady Diana.[6] Clive is marooned in Paris with the prettiest girl in the movie world [Joan Firminger]; and has been completely happy for 3 weeks—but it wont last. A man called Dick Wyndham has come into our lives—he has the girls sister [Enid] in tow.

1. See Virginia's account of the Great Frost in *Orlando* (Hogarth, 1928, p. 33 ff.).
2. See p. 17.
3. Lytton's *Elizabeth and Essex*, which Virginia disliked.
4. Virginia repeatedly returned to the memory of Vita in a fishmonger's shop in Sevenoaks in December 1925, when their love affair began.
5. Raymond Mortimer, the literary critic, then aged 33, who had been in America.
6. Lady Diana Cooper (Manners), who had married Duff Cooper in 1919.

I see now why old women read novels—why Mudie [lending-library] flourishes—The meaning of British fiction has been revealed to me. Its a sort of pap-slop—something made digestible and sweet for invalids. (I live on codliver oil, now, and the taste clings to the crevices of my throat for hours). Novels glide me over the afternoon. In the evening I read Beau Brummell. I must now go back to "A woman of 40". And write the poor wretch a letter to say nothing can make this saleable though its wrung from her entrails and gives away every bitterness and sorrow of her life. She is half educated, deserted and lives on 15/- a week with a child.

Dottie [Wellesley] writes that her loneliness is a disease—she is hated of God and men.

I say how nice to see you

V.

Berg

2003: To Quentin Bell   52 *Tavistock Square, W.C.*1

17th Feb. 1929

My dear Claudian,[1]

(I am going to call you this, in order to give you another start in life.) I was very glad of your letter. Here I am still half in bed—I mean by that not that my legs are on a chair and my head on a bed but that I am on a sofa undressed (and by that I mean . . . but there will be no end to it if I have to explain all I mean.) Also I must write the hand of a MYOPIC ELEPHANT if you are to understand. Now it is a curious fact that to write a feigned hand falsifies the character. I feel simpler and saner and more like Helen [Anrep] and Lorna and Dorothy[2] when I write like this. When I write like this I feel vicious and dishonest and untrustworthy and full of delightful qualities. So you will never know me at my best. But eno', eno'—(as they say in Shakespeare).

The news is all a little erratic, as I am only allowed carefully chosen visitors, warranted not to excite, bite, kick, kiss, or anything else that makes life hectic and splendid—old Helen; (but I like her) and so on. Raymond [Mortimer] has just rung up to say he's back: and America's a ghastly country, of stunted development. Neither man nor woman has reached the age of puberty. They talk very slowly all day long and never listen. Also he made no money because he could never get a word in edgewise. Duncan's show[3] is on, but all I've heard of it is an idiotic, a senile, an incredibly vapid

1. Quentin Bell was named at birth 'Claudian Stephen', and for the first few months of his life he was known as Claudian. 'Quentin' was added later.
2. Lorna Acton and Dorothy Honey, Clive Bell's sisters.
3. An exhibition of Duncan Grant's work, 1910-29, at Paul Guillaume, Brandon Davis, Ltd. in London.

review in the Nation by Sickert.[1] That was Maynards choice.[2] (Maynard has the flu;) The great Tavistock news is that we have bought a Sun Singer (coffee and chocolate coloured) and sold the old umbrella.[3] This is a rash and daring experiment. The Sun Singer rolls off its lid and becomes open; rolls it on and becomes shut. We think we shall have it both ways; but we may be had.

Last night at 8.30 Nelly [Boxall] came in frantic to say that the basement was flooded and all our books under water. What is more she was within an inch of the truth. Imagine the idiocy of turning a tap full on with a frozen pipe! This is what the char did. Then she sobbed. Leonard baled with chamber pots and buckets. Our loss is well over—I forget what—call it £100. Coming upstairs, all the lights went out, and to consummate what was consummate already the drawing room door handle came off leaving me imprisoned inside and unable to gratify any desire of nature or affection until they could force the lock.

The scene from my window is a feeble copy of the frost scene in Orlando —icicles, dead cats, frozen bread and butter on the leads, a bird or two— but it is hoped that nature, seeing I can do it better—where's the old bumboat woman?[4]—will desist, and the use of the W.C. will be restored to us. Ours is almost unique of its kind—people ring up and say may they pay half a crown to any charity for the right to sit.

God! I had not meant to run on at this rate; but this big hand and the pleasure of writing to so CONGENIAL a CORRESPONDENT has—or have—seduced me. Please write again, and let us go at some length into the question of your new character. Quentin was an adorable creature and I'm sorry he's been sloughed (sluffed) like the gold and orange skin of the rare Mexican tsee-tsee snake. Why not be him and Claudian on alternate days? Claudian is a secretive marble-faced steady eyed deliberate villain. That is what his name indicates.

Not a word from Julian. It is thought that the frost took him one night and he is being used as a scratching post for cattle—but you know how these stories get about.

Your loving
Aunt
V.

Quentin Bell

1. Walter Sickert's review appeared in the *Nation* for 16 February 1929. He wrote in part: "Duncan Grant has become with the passage of years, in his line, the monarch of the longest standing in England."
2. Since 1923 John Maynard Keynes had been the Chairman of the Board of the *Nation.*
3. Their first car, also a Singer, bought in 1927.
4. *Orlando* (Hogarth, 1928), p. 35.

17th Feb. [1929]

Dear Miss Robins,[1]

I think that Mrs W. Arnold-Forster, who lives at Eagles Nest, Zennor, St Ives would know all about possible rooms or inns. She found us very good rooms a year or so ago. I have told her that you will write to her. I am sure she would be happy to do anything she could for you.

I am so sorry that I cant at the moment make any engagements. I have been ill and am still in bed. But might I write and suggest a time— I hope soon—when I could see you? I am so much interested in your suggestion.[2]

Yours sincerely
Virginia Woolf

Texas

Tuesday, Feb. 19th [1929]

Well, where are you? No letter since Saturday; and you may be in the snow among the wolves. Perhaps I shall hear tomorrow from Berlin, from your cage, the ornamental cage. But this time fortnight you'll be poking for the snowdrops at Long Barn.

And I have been for a little walk in Marchmont Street and bought a kettle (2/3) and some cars. (so they call carnations) and am now not dressed but sitting up like a woman of the world, over a little gas fire, for our pipes are choked. So you may infer that I am looking up; and shall be in rude health by the time rude health is needed. I wrote two pages yesterday; dull ones, but pages, with sentences and paragraphs; only about the Burneys,[3] who attract me less than The Moths, though.

Dotty is coming in I believe this evening. Raymond has been chattering on the telephone. Not a man or woman in the States has reached the age of puberty he says; and what is worse, he has made no money. Then Christabel has been and given me a brooch with a wolfs head on it—and you know how I hate presents. However she gave me what I adore—a long and detailed

---

1. The American-born novelist and actress (d. 1952) had been a friend of Virginia's mother. Miss Robins lived in Brighton with Octavia Wilberforce, who became Virginia's doctor at the end of her life. The Hogarth Press had published, in 1928, Miss Robins' *Ibsen and the Actress*.
2. That Elizabeth Robins should write her memoirs. See Letter 2037.
3. *New York Herald Tribune* (21 and 28 July 1929).

account of Zita Yungman's father, mother, and marriage; which led to a vast panorama of the Sitwells, in Italy, Zita saying "And I'll have a tray in my room", the bath not locking, Lady Ida [the Sitwells' mother], Stephen Tennant with his old nurse—what I call, perhaps foolishly 'real life.'[1]

You think reading Sterne is real life. I am sometimes pleased to think that I read English literature when I was young; I like to think of myself tapping at my father's study door, saying very loud and clear "Can I have another volume, father? I've finished this one". Then he would be very pleased and say "Gracious child, how you gobble!" (There's Miss [Hilda] Matheson ringing up to say they want to broadcast the frost and thaw in Orl—do tomorrow—Do I mind? No. Thats all right—) and get up and take down, it may have been the 6th or 7th volume of Gibbons complete works, or Speddings Bacon,[2] or Cowper's Letters." "But my dear, if its worth reading, its worth reading twice" he would say. I have a great devotion for him— what a disinterested man, how high minded, how tender to me, and fierce and intolerable—But I am maundering. And I cannot remember how many syllables disinterested has got. (here's a young man called Darwin[3]— almost broke in on me in my nightgown—an undergraduate. Never mind, he's been told to go.)

Blanche has written a long, very sugary, very acid, article on O——o; with so many hits [hints?] and double meanings one cant see the wood for the trees: something very arch about two birds flying together to France and alighting at Dieppe last autumn.[4]

We've just been sent the American edition of Twelve Days[5]—very dazzling and improper looking.

This time fortnight, I shall only have to ring up Weald 14 to hear a

1. Stephen Tennant was born in 1906, the fourth son of Lord Glenconner. He was a painter, good-looking, and intensely feminine. Zita Jungman was an exceptionally pretty girl who was a member of the young fashionable set in the 1920s. She was one of three daughters of Nico Jungman, the artist and picture-restorer, and of Mrs Richard Guinness.
2. James Spedding (1808-81) edited *The Life and Letters* of Francis Bacon in seven volumes (1861-74).
3. Robin (later Sir Robin) Darwin was then aged 19 and a Slade School student. He was the son of Virginia's old friend Elinor Monsell and her husband Bernard Darwin, the writer on golf. He became a painter and an art teacher, and in later life Rector of the Royal College of Art.
4. Jacques-Emile Blanche, the French portrait painter whom Virginia had met through Ethel Sands, wrote about *Orlando:* "Virginia Woolf seems to hide herself in rather arty and overpretty veils which her *afficionados*, hoping for a smile, offer her before she dances" (*Les Nouvelles Littéraires*, 19 January 1929).
5. Vita's second book of Persian travels, originally published by the Hogarth Press in 1928, and in America by Doubleday, Doran.

snuffle snuffling like a spaniel nosing about, with a wet muzzle and feathered paws.

But Lord! you may be among the cataracts frozen; write, anyhow, one line.

Virginia

Berg

2006: To V. Sackville-West   52 *Tavistock Square, W.C.*

Saturday Feb 23rd [1929]

I am glad that you have escaped the wolves, though it would have been a romantic death for you and might have suggested a second volume to O—o. Is your new novel[1] to be all about Potto? He thinks so. He is willing to help you in anyway he can. His past is full of adventure, he says; moreover the Bosman's[2] were great people in their way, Sackvilles after a kind.

This time next week—but I wont harp on it, for then you'll think of Harold on the platform.[3]

About Monday—anytime you name will suit me, but I shan't be alone for dinner, and I should like to see you alone, anyhow for a little. So let me know.

I have just seen the dr. I hope for the last time, and have had the usual lecture about resting and never being tired and never sitting up and never seeing too many people and never catching any single illness so long as I live.

I've been down to the Studio and done a mild morning's work on Miss Jewsbury.[4] So this illness is over, and next week I shall be risen like the morning star. Lord! how glad I am to use my wits again!

In order to steal a march on you, I had Elena Richmond[5] to tea yesterday; but no. I can make no impression on that woman. She is frozen, like a chicken left in the snow. With a pick axe one might hack out something. There is charm; she still holds her head like an Empress; but she nods and proses, and Raymond [Mortimer] came in and we were only conversational, not amorous. She livened, though, when you were mentioned. Not for years had she met anyone she liked so much. I bequeath her to you. She's dead to me; a casket of which I've lost the key.

1. Vita's 'new novel' was *The Edwardians*. She wrote of it to Virginia: "Such a joke it will be, and I hope everybody will be seriously annoyed" (21 February 1929, *Berg*).
2. In full, Virginia's joke name for herself (when writing to Vita) was 'Bosman's Potto'.
3. Vita returned to England on 28 February, leaving Harold Nicolson in Berlin.
4. See p. 5, note 1.
5. Wife of Bruce Richmond, Editor of the *Times Literary Supplement*. In previous years Virginia had been vaguely attracted by her.

But this is not altogether the case with Mary, Dotty, or Christabel—all of whom I find myself in touch with, though Dotty is set about with thorns, hard and pointed, 6 inches long. How you are not torn to pieces by her, God knows. She wrote to me and said—ah hah! Would you really mind if I replied in the same style, or perhaps a trifle warmer? Have you any of those feelings left that the nightingales and the splash of frogs on water sometimes call out in me, on hot May nights, at Long Barn, as I told you when we ate duck on the Funkel tower [*Funkturm*] (you know what I mean?) Have you any love for me? or only the appreciation which one member of the PEN has for another?

A novel that I refused to publish has been seized by the police: a vulgar book, but nothing in it to raise a hair.[1] Whats to be done with morality in England? If Harold would do a man's work there, instead of a flunkey's in Berlin—but hush, hush. "My Harold!" Isnt that what you'd say? Miss Storm Jameson says that Virginia Woolf is either a fallen angel or a changeling: she has no roots in common soil.[2] They had to broadcast the thaw too, the other night; for it is thawing; and on the whole we are rather less comfortable than before, as the drip is everywhere, and gas has failed. No baths again.

Clive comes back tomorrow, but is again off, and doesn't mind who knows that he has been bowled over by a movie star. Its like an old dandy fixing false whiskers—this mania to be the master of some chit. Mary is very much upset, and thinks I ought to control him. Will you? Say, I mean, that he's being ridiculous? For even Julian and Quentin think he goes too far. Its a bore, ones father's being laughed at.

Never mind anything though but come back to me and Potto. I dont see why I shouldnt have a day or two of convalescence at Long Barn—will you ask me?—although I shall be quite robust by then.

Virginia   [*squiggly design*]

Berg

1. *Sleeveless Errand*, by Norah C. James, was published in America and Paris. It was printed in England by Eric Partridge, but was confiscated by the police and never published.
2. The novelist and critic Storm Jameson (b. 1897) wrote about Virginia, in connection with *Orlando*: "Doubtless she suffers, weeps, laughs, herself—but not as a man does. As a fallen angel might. Or a changeling. Her genius, carefully tended, pruned, enriched, has no roots in our common earth" (*The Georgian Novel and Mr Robinson* 1929).

Letters 2007-2035 (March–May 1929)

As Virginia slowly recovered from her illness, her letters regained their vitality. Vita returned to England from Berlin at almost the same time as Vanessa left it for Cassis, and Virginia exchanged one of her two main correspondents for the other. She was finishing her long article Phases of Fiction *('My most hated book'), and revising as* A Room of One's Own *the two lectures which she had given at Cambridge at the end of 1928. At a deeper level she was pondering* The Waves, *which she had not yet begun to write. Her London social life was renewed, and she took short breaks at Rodmell, where she was planning an extension to Monk's House, a bedroom for herself opening on the garden and a writing-room above. Although she was temporarily irritated by Clive Bell's philandering, she developed a merry correspondence with his two sons, Julian and Quentin. Figures from the past like Sydney Waterlow drifted back into her life, and new friends like William Plomer entered it.*

2007: To J. D. Hayward   52 *Tavistock Square* [*W.C.*1]

[4 March 1929]

Dear Mr Hayward,[1]

It was very good of you to write to me about my article[2]—I never know whether these things are supposed to be secret or not—Anyhow, as you have guessed I am delighted to claim your praise, which is very welcome. I daresay one could have found out more about Miss Jewsbury; I had only one volume of her letters to go upon. I could not read more than one of the novels, and I expect that some old gentleman who has read all mid-Victorian memoirs will blast my theories completely. Her relation with Mrs Carlyle was interesting, and I had to be discreet.

Yours sincerely,
Virginia Woolf

King's

1. John Davy Hayward, the bibliographer and anthologist (1905-65).
2. Review of *Zoe* and *The Half Sisters*, by Geraldine Jewsbury (*TLS*, 28 February 1929). All *TLS* articles were then anonymous.

March 8th 1929

My dear Brett,[1]

I remember perfectly—Richmond [Hogarth House], Katharine, Garsington, Ottoline, tin trumpet with the ribbons—everything. Things seem to have changed prodigiously since you left—I dont quite know how.

Well, Murry's married again,[2] thats one thing, I know not whom, and Sydney is, or was—for he's come back ill—an Ambassador.[3] Kot[4] I saw on Christmas day washing up dinner in Acacia Road.—He's the same—precisely. We went and sat in his very small bare room—it was Katherine's—at the top of the house, and he gave me some Russian cigarettes, made by himself. He almost crushed my hand; he abused Murry; he spoke with enormous sincerity, staring at one out of his rather bloodshot eyes—just the same—It is a great pleasure to think of him there, but I never see him. Garsington is sold and Ottoline lives in Gower Street: as for Fredegond,[5] she has become a Roman Catholic; and I never see her, either; she lives near Cambridge, and is said to be very happy, cleaning furniture most of the time. The house is very very clean; and she never comes to London.

I don't see how I am to convey to you any facts of interest about myself. The address conveys nothing to you. We have a publishing business and a press in the basement and keep three clerks. Also we have a cottage in Sussex. You will have to come back—you cant imagine anything about us at that distance. Life is too complicated to be cut up in little dice and sent across the Atlantic for you to piece together. Yes I should like to see your pictures and to hear your Indian songs.

Do you live quite alone? I imagine porcupines opening the door with their quills. I wish you didn't make me imagine the mountains so furiously. I want to see them before I die. How long does it take to get there? Write again some day. I liked getting your letter; I was ill in bed and read it over

1. The painter Dorothy Brett, daughter of Lord Esher, had been an intimate friend of Katherine Mansfield and a frequent guest of Lady Ottoline Morrell at Garsington Manor, near Oxford. The 'tin trumpet' was an aid to Brett's deafness. After Mansfield's death in 1923 Brett followed D. H. Lawrence to Taos, New Mexico, where she died in August 1977, aged 93.
2. John Middleton Murry married Violet Le Maistre in April 1924. His first wife, Katherine Mansfield, died in January 1923.
3. Sydney Waterlow was British Ambassador in Addis Ababa, 1928-9. He had been in love with Virginia before her marriage, but she turned down his proposal, which he made even before he was divorced from his first wife.
4. S. S. Koteliansky, the Russian émigré who collaborated with Virginia on translations from Tolstoy.
5. Fredegond Shove was a poet and the daughter of Virginia's cousin Florence Fisher. She was married to the Cambridge economist Gerald Shove.

and over; but I have put off writing so long that you will have left New York, and will never get this. Tell me how you spend your day, accurately, minutely. But I'm very glad you like the Lighthouse. Would Katharine? I wonder.

Yours Ever
Virginia

University of Cincinnati

2009: TO DAVID GARNETT   52 *Tavistock Square* [*W.C.*1]

March 11th [1929]

Dear Bunny,[1]

How angelic of you to write—one doesn't expect to be thanked for an anonymous article in The Lit Supt.[2] This one was written in sheer idleness—you know my passion for pulling down all the memories in the house and lying on the floor surrounded by them. I was rather worried by the 72 volumes (or so) of Carlyle letters, and rather pleased to be so accurate in getting the bits together. I can't help thinking that 'transitions' arrange themselves almost automatically with facts to deal with: fiction leads one a much worse dance. Your old George Moore[3] conveyed his appreciation, much to my surprise. I've met him once or twice lately and been amused to watch him switching off the head of every possible daisy in the neighbour-hood—I think you alone survived last time. Otherwise it was "poor dear Henry James—deplorable, deplorable—" and so on. I find him, on these occasions quite fascinating. But I dont go with you all the way down the long smooth white undulating road of the novels.

As for Orlando (my egotism leads me back to the second page of your letter) God knows—I wrote it in such a tearing hurry that anything, horror or sublimity, may be there for all I know. You see, I can't correct, and I can't re-read; and I hate everything directly it is in cold print, and avoid it as I would last Sundays roast beef and Yorkshire pudding. So I shall never be a complete writer, as you are. These things should be said by word of mouth. It is years, (accurately, like my article on Jane [Carlyle]) since we met; and I never know how to lay salt on your tail. But I proved my affection to my own satisfaction the other night by getting really very worried by hearing

1. As a conscientious objector, David Garnett had spent the latter part of the war living with Vanessa Bell and Duncan Grant and working as a farm labourer. By 1929 he had published several books, of which the best known were *Lady into Fox* and *A Man in the Zoo*. He was married to Rachel ('Ray') Marshall, who died in 1940. In 1942 he married Virginia's niece, Angelica Bell.
2. On Geraldine Jewsbury and Jane Carlyle. *TLS*, 28 February 1929.
3. The Irish novelist was then 77.

of Rays illness. What an infliction it is to be fond of ones friends! How I hate being anxious! But I shall hear about her from Nessa.

Love to you both and do come and see us.

Yours ever
Virginia

Berg

2010: To Katherine Arnold-Forster
52 Tavistock Sqre., W.C.1

March 11th [1929]

Dearest Ka,

Well, I am recovered entirely owing to your Cornish cream, (but dont tell Mrs Manning Sanders[1] so—I am in the country getting well, I have just told her).

It was an amazing proof of the steadymindedness and goodheartedness of Bruin that she could think of cream when the poor beast must be run off her feet with voters and bishops.

I hope to leave the country while the Election[2] is on but shan't we see you before that?

Yr
Virginia

Mark Arnold-Forster

2011: To Vanessa Bell   [52 *Tavistock Square, W.C.*1]

[March? 1929]

1) Would you tell Grace [Germany, maid] not to bother her friend about the dress as I see I shan't have time to get stuff or anything, so I shall risk going to the party undressed.

2) I only sent one earring. I will send round the other.

to Bell. Decorator.

3) Have you got one of those tile tables? If so what price? or could you make one?

4) Could you make me 2 bouquets of artificial flowers for my green glass vases against the winter: and please quote best terms.

5. Could you estimate for painted dinner table.

6. Could you tell me what I owe for crockery?

Obedly
V. Woolf

Berg

1. Ruth Manning-Sanders, a friend and neighbour of Ka in Cornwall, had published two books with the Hogarth Press.
2. There was a General Election on 30 May.

Typewritten
20th March 1929

Dearest Quentin-Claudian

Look, I sit down the very minute I have yours to hand, not knowing even if I write to two of you or one. But then I am so pleased to get your letter— I like so much any scrap of offal that comes your way. So I must implore you to write at length. You know my appetite for facts. Nothing is too small, remote, large, or obscene. I am so bothered by writing about the obscene. At this moment I ought to correct an article[1] in a symposium of pundits upon that subject. If modern books are made pure, we shall read the classics I said; and then what happens? But all this is trivial worthless waste of time. It is fine. The buds are not visible but all the air is like a thin elastic veil, gently pressing on ones face. A blue veil it should be. Through this I see everything a little distorted. Beauty shines on two dogs doing what two women must not do. Thats a fact—Pinker got enmeshed with a fox terrier this very afternoon. Can you blame them? Beuty (spelt right) is everywhere. As for Clive, the canary with the shade off sings not more lustily. I hear his voice a mile off. What happened to him in Paris? What is his Poppet like? That I should ask you this! But anyhow she seems to have oiled his creaking feathers, and it is all to the good so long as it lasts. Julian is already caught in the Apostles web.[2] Ever since I have known them, they have spent their spare time spinning and intriguing, Lytton loves it. They think they can turn Maynard out; but they have thought this for twenty five years; whats more, talked of it. But Julian still thinks "This is the most tremendous thing that has ever happened!" Nessa is settling her life with a decision and ruthless rapidity that take the breath away. One day she has let [no. 37] Gordon Square; another sent Angelica to school; another hired a vast studio that smells like a stable in Fitzroy Street. We went and smelt it. Horses are better than cows says Leonard. I say Oh its the wax model of Queen Victoria (a sculptor has it) that smells so. But she is not going to take it. They will all be off to Cassis soon. Could I not spend a week with you in Paris?—a week of dreams on the banks of the Seine. A little furniture buying. A few pictures. Sitting smoking in cafés. Conversations with my dear Quentin. What delight! However whats delightful is always wrong. I want to write a serious book. I am all awash with too many words. I write nothing but criticism. Now if one writes imaginative works one has to stop talking. How is your painting? And what

1. The 'Censorship of Books', (*Nineteenth Century and After*, April 1929).
2. The Cambridge Conversazione Society, better known as the 'Apostles', a semi-secretive intellectual society to which Lytton Strachey, Maynard Keynes, Leonard Woolf and other Bloomsbury figures also belonged.

about life? I am going wandering through the elastic veil now to the London Library. That is an excuse for thinking about a book which I shall call the Moths [*The Waves*] I think—an entirely new kind of book. But it will never be so good as it is now in my mind unwritten.

We have got a new car. Please write now this instant wherever you may be whatever comes into your head.

Yr loving Virginia

Quentin Bell

2013: TO HUGH WALPOLE   52 *Tavistock Square, W.C.1*

31st March [1929]

Dear Hugh,

I got your message all right, and I was very sorry not to see you and for that reason. We are going away [to Monks] for a few days, but if you could come to tea on Tuesday 9th, I should be alone, and it would be a great pleasure to see you, about 4.30.

Yours
Virginia Woolf

Texas

2014: TO HUGH WALPOLE   *Monks House, Rodmell*
                                          [*Sussex*]

Friday [5 April 1929]

Dear Hugh,

Would it be possible for you to dine on Tuesday, (7.45) or to come to tea on Monday? Owing to what is said to be my mistake, I find I had arranged to go to Kew with Vita on Tuesday and shouldn't be back till six. I'm very sorry; but please arrange, somehow, something. Would you ring up or send a line anytime. I shall be in London on Sunday night after 7.

Your affate
Virginia Woolf

Forgive me my confusions.

Texas

2015: TO V. SACKVILLE-WEST   *Monks House, Rodmell*
                                          [*Sussex*]

5th April [1929]

"Not many women possess such great versatility as the Hon. V. Sackville-West . . . she has also the rare gift of enjoying solitude . . ." There you are—staring at me; not very congenial; rather frightening Potto; but awfully superb and tidy.[1] I must show it to Nelly when she comes to clear away the tea.

All this kind of thing is done at the command of Nelly—did you know that?

In God's name: yes: I have several sentences addressed to you with that beginning:

I.G.N. Come on Tuesday; to the basement, not a wink later than 3:

I.G.N: Do NOT bring Francis[2]—a dear old rattle headed bore.

IGN. Do NOT bring Dottie: This I feel strongly about. Twice lately she has utterly ruined my serenity with you; and I wont have it. Choose between us. Dottie if your taste inclines that way by all means; but not the two of us in one cocktail.

But listen. Hugh Walpole was coming; and I've put him off, and said I'm going to Kew with you. I mayn't be able to go to Kew, though, because I have had a dose or two of Chloral; and L. thinks it is walking that makes me sleep badly; I dont; never mind: we can sit and talk.

I cant be sure about dinner; I had to ask Hugh. Will you come? Only he mayn't come. Settle what you like when you come. Only don't be late this time.

Leonard's been having the rheumatism too. Its bitter, bitter. We missed the fine days—still the garden, the terrace, the view, even black and white in shower and wind make me wish—I'm not sure what—to write poetry; perhaps, and not an essay upon fiction.

Do you want a flat in Gordon Sqre [Vanessa's] very cheap?

Do you love me?

If you give me so much as a tuppenny mug from Woolworths, I never speak to you again. I told Nessa the story of our passion in a chemists shop the other day. But do you really like going to bed with women she said—taking her change. "And how d'you do it?" and so she bought her pills to take abroad, talking as loud as a parrot.

A mongoose has just run into the bathroom. Nelly is terrified.

Virginia

We come up on Sunday night

Berg

1. Virginia had seen an article in the *Morning Post* illustrated with a photograph of Vita by E. O. Hoppé.
2. Francis Birrell, son of Augustine Birrell, and a friend of Vita and Raymond Mortimer.

Tuesday 7th April 1929

Dearest Dolph.

This is a business letter. Vita turned up today at Monks, and is very excited about 37 [Gordon Square], which I told her about. Could you send her all details to Long Barn? Harold has written to say he is sending an ultimatum to the Foreign Office—if they wont let him live in London he's going to—I dont know what—I don't suppose he'll do anything. But probably they will want rooms in London.

She has a passion for your drawing room; wants to live there;

We are just back from Rodmell; doing the journey, you'll be glad to hear in record time, not *over* two hours; (not *under*—how exact I am!) It was perishing cold and divinely lovely; but life in my lodge even in a blanket, is impossible. Philcox came out and drew a sketch of two rooms in a jiffy: so I wait result; and tremble with excitement.[1]

Business again:

Could you let me have your account, if convenient: including 6 plates, one large green bowl; one bunch of decorative flowers; one small lampshade: do: lamp for diningroom. I am trying to clear off my affairs.

Could you tell me how I could make lavender blue? That inconceivable donkey, Daggett, has re-painted the mantelpiece;[2] and dotted it with sea-green. But if I go to a colour shop, should I ask for oil paint?—and is lavender blue a mixture? of what? Perhaps you remember the colour of the blue dots; a tender blue, like the blue of a chalk hill blue, or the sea at a distance, with chalk cliffs in the foreground.

Thanks to you I have now to plunge into society. You have thrown me on the streets. Sibyl is on me. I must dine with her and buy silk stockings They cost at least 14/6. Unless I can wear two old pairs: all your doing: and then there's Hugh Walpole tomorrow. I am aging rapidly and require a contemplative life with young things in the distance. I am going to write to Quentin—Claudian, I should say; whose letters are the best I know. How he can run that gift off into the eternal monotony of paint I know not. I daresay you are all as happy as grigs.

Leonard can't get off his jury; and there was a great excitement at Rodmell when a mongoose was seen running up the stairs as we sat at

1. Philcox was a local builder. The Woolfs planned the addition of two rooms, one above the other, as a bedroom and a workroom for Virginia. They were not completed until December. The 'lodge' was Virginia's hut in the garden, where she wrote in the summer months.
2. Of 52 Tavistock Square, which Duncan and Vanessa had decorated in 1924 when the Woolfs moved in.

lunch. It belongs to a village woman. Owing to a Labour meeting held in the drawing room, it discovered the hot cupboard, where it now lives.

I had something of the utmost importance to say; but cant remember what.

B.

Berg

2017: To Oscar Lewis   52 *Tavistock Square, W.C.*1

Typewritten
[9 April 1929]

Dear Mr Lewis,[1]
Many thanks for your letter. I have made a few slight alterations in the article and enclose it herewith.

I shall be much interested to see the book.[2] We are printers ourselves, and have printed some of my stories with our own hands.

With best wishes,
yours sincerely
Virginia Woolf

Columbia University   (Mrs Woolf)

2018: To Vanessa Bell   52 *Tavistock Sqre.* [*W.C.*1]

12th April 1929

Dearest Dolphin
This is not a letter because I don't think I shall have any time to finish it. Mere greed for cigars makes me fill my pen, which is one of the chief horrors of a writer's life (you know I have a cheap steel pen, bought years ago, and when I can get no more nibs—they are sold in Farringdon Market,—I have to stop writing) But Julian will be gone already.[3] The Keynes'es are back, have been heard, but not seen. People still seem to be away, and it is bitter; indeed it snowed yesterday; and I was just thinking that I was coming home to tea about Christmas time this afternoon, it was so black and so many lamps were lit when I picked up a primrose on the pavement outside Eddie Marshes'[4] flat in Grays Inn. This is my desolate state, to range about London with Pinker instead of having tea with you.

1. Oscar Lewis was the Manager of Westgate Press, San Francisco.
2. A limited edition of *Street Haunting*, which had originally appeared in the *Yale Review*, October 1927.
3. Julian was returning from Cassis. Virginia hoped that he would bring her a new supply of her French cigars.
4. Edward Marsh (1872-1953) edited several volumes of *Georgian Poetry*. In 1917-22, and again in 1924-9, he was Private Secretary to Winston Churchill.

I believe I've found Angus [Davidson] a job—to be secretary to Hugh Walpole. Its only 4 months of the year; but its only 2 hours in the morning, and £4 a week. Anyhow, Hugh was to see him but I've not heard from Angus, and no doubt that old Bus horse (Angus) will be too cautious. Hugh requires someone not thin in the face, not supercilious. He must be over a certain age so as to avoid scandal, and discreet, because Hugh confides everything. If suitable, Hugh said, much more might come of it.

I had 3 hours talk alone with him, largely about the state of his soul, which is very dicky—because he can't help liking to be a success; but then nobody, like Vanessa, ever reads him; so what's the good of it? Yet perhaps, as he is only 45 and 3 months, he may yet reform. His father died over the tea pot the other night and was so heavy they had to coffin him in his arm chair. His daughter went out to answer the front door bell to a young curate and came back to find the Bishop holding a piece of bread and butter, dead.[1] The worst of it is, the Bishop hasn't left a penny, so Hugh has his family to support; in fact he now has 12 people, mostly singers, I gathered, to support; none of them related. There is something of the Curate in him.

But I daresay I must think of something else to tell you. Raymond was here to tea yesterday, and a young lady from France[2] who leads the men all a dance and translates Norman Douglas, who wears a buglass;—the better to pee and to prance—I dont know why I've made up this rhyme; it is a tribute to the romantic power of Dolph and Dog[3] across the sea. Raymond and Mlle.-so chattered we were halfdead.

By the way Mrs Mansfield[4] is groaning; I hear, under the burden of Morgan [E. M. Forster], Raymond (who's staying with him) and another gent coming tonight. I daresay Mrs M. will die in the basement.

I've not heard anything from Mr Drown,[5] nor yet from Mr Peck. What Raymond said about Clive I daren't repeat for fear of eavesdroppers.

Cabin this instantly.

But you will have left the key in the glass which holds, or once held your small hogshair brushes on the verandah.

Have you settled anything about Grace's[6] future? I ask with a reason which I must at present conceal.

1. George Walpole, Bishop of Edinburgh since 1910, died suddenly on 4 March.
2. Raymond Mortimer cannot now (1977) recall this lady, but the most recent translator of Norman Douglas's novels was a Frenchwoman, Ashley Andra.
3. Vanessa and Duncan Grant, who were at their house La Bergère in Cassis.
4. Caretaker of 37 Gordon Square.
5. William Drown, picture-restorers. Their premises were then at 8 Fitzroy Street, where Vanessa had her studio. Mr Peck was not a member of their firm. but a frequent customer.
6. Grace Germany, the maid at 37 Gordon Square.

I am asked to meet Mary at Sibyls, but have refused. If you want an amusing book of memoirs, rather randy and rollicky, I advise The retrospections of Dorothea Herbert[1]—She lived in Ireland at the end of the 18th Century, and talks as you might of the Chamber pot and how the gentlemen laughed when they saw the stream trickle through the door.

No news of Roger, but I saw his door open this afternoon when I came back with Pinker, having seen the primrose on the pavement.

I cant tell you how bitter and autumnal it is; not a leaf out; many indeed have gone in. And the snow falls in my heart too, slow soft flakes, salt tasting with tears. Why? Ah hah! Dolphin being a beast covered with brine who never shed a tear don't know the meaning of this pleasure. And Duncan, whom I adore, is cased in oil silk from the assault of all elements. The two of you swim seal like through the waves. However I adore you both, and must now go up to my dinner; poor poor Singe.[2] Does Angelica ever ask after me? I'm sending her a little present if I can get it across the water.

Please write fully and freely and frequently.

Yr
B.

Berg

2019: To V. Sackville-West   [52 *Tavistock Square, W.C.*1]

Friday 18th [19] April [1929]

Dearest Creature,

I do hope that Ben[3] is all right. Would you send me a line to say?

I found a letter from Harold here, uneasy about his future [in diplomacy], I'm glad to say, but cautious.

Lord, I did enjoy myself! You make me feel like a baby having drunk sweet milk. My room is full of flowers, and the pump[4] is a mere hum all owing to you. Now I must prepare for the ardours of the evening.

Do you love Potto?

Yr
V.

Berg

1. Published in two volumes in 1929-30.
2. One of the names ('ape') by which the Stephen family knew Virginia as a child.
3. Benedict Nicolson, Vita's elder son, had a minor illness. Virginia had stayed at Long Barn the preceding night.
4. See p. 3.

April 24th 1929

Dearest Dolphin,

I am overwhelmed, indeed touched to the point of tears by your generosity.[1] Vilest of vile animals to have such a scheme to spring on me! All the blue sorts of Dolphins are devils. But, on consideration, through my tears, I consulted Leonard; and what he says is that if you gave me the things, then we could never ask you to do us furniture again. And he is going to ask you to make him two tables—and there are other things I want. This being so, he says it would be best for everybody if I paid you what he thinks a very low price, and I think much too low: that is £25 for your share. As you would certainly charge a proper client like Dotty much more, I shall still think the chairs etc. almost a gift. I may tell you I get pleasure of at least three sorts every day: comfort; aesthetic; snob. Everyone who comes throws up their hands—says where do you get these lovely things? And I feel my gorges swell—for of course I don't deny that in aesthetics, about chairs and covers, I am so wholly snobbish I am ashamed.

There is a great deal to tell you; and the light is fading. It is a very cold day—not a single hot day yet—and here we are marooned. We came down without a hitch last night—this morning, going into Lewes, the car stuck on a hill. By dint of shoving, we reached Martins [garage], where they found that our clutch was burnt out, owing to mal-adjustment, and it will take two or three days to mend. So we must go up tomorrow by train—a profound sorrow to Leonard. He thinks of buying a second car to keep in case of emergency. Now I daresay your Citroen is a perfect angel. Julian came in, very late,—we had expected him to dine—but Fred[2] caught him and they got talking. He has got thinner, I thought; there was a lot to be said about cars, also about Apostles. He is growing like a crab—I mean he is only half covered with shell: he is very queer; one finds him noticing, and feeling, and taking up what last year was imperceptible to him. We argued about poetry as usual, and he said he has written a long essay on poetry, which he is sending us. The Bell sociability is so odd, mixed with the Stephen integrity. I daresay he'll give you a lot of trouble before he's done—he is too charming and violent and gifted altogether: and in love with you, into the bargain. It is very exciting—the extreme potency of your Brats; they might have been nincompoops—instead of bubbling and boiling and frizzling like so many pans of sausages on the fire. (I am just about to cook

1. In reply to Letter 2016, Vanessa refused to accept any payment for her decorative painting, arguing that she had received so much pleasure from Virginia's novels and had not had to pay anything for them.
2. Fred Harris, a local mechanic who had tried to teach Virginia to drive.

an omelette) I am so lost without any young life that I meditate plunging into Ann[1]—only what would happen?

Then theres the superb story of Angus [Davidson]. Would you believe it—he havered and hesitated to such an extent that Hugh thought he didn't want it, and has engaged a Captain? Now of course Angus is in an awful fuss; came round to see Leonard; says that both his other jobs have fallen through, and he never meant to hesitate—all he said was that of course Hugh's job wouldn't do for a permanency, and he might wish to get something else.

I did my best to impress upon him that it would lead to anything—for so it would—but his caution is such that he mumbles like a slobbering mastiff, and so will lose every chance that ever offers. Anyhow I shall never stir a finger for him again. This was worth at least £800 a year for life. On top of this, Miss [Alice] Ritchie came to Leonard to beg him to tell Angus she can't dedicate her life to writing plays with him—so Leonard had a confidential walk in the Square; and Angus hummed and hawed, and says he's now heard of something at Agnew's.[2] He is incredible—the truth is he enjoys a life at large, and thinks his old mother ought to support him, solely for the shape of his nose. Also he thinks that he can write; he thinks that he can correct what Alice Ritchie puts wrong—which he does, she says, very neatly in purple ink; and drives her mad.

Then, Lord Alfred Douglas threatens Leonard and The Nation with a libel action, because of an article Leonard wrote.[3] So we may be in court again. Leonard is going to defend himself. As Lord A. is mad, nobody knows if he means it or not; Maynard didn't want his letter published,— Lord A's letter—but it is now going to be published, so that he cant have any excuse to say that The Nation is afraid.

There is so much to say that I am dribbling along, in the dark. Whats the use of ever leaving London? It pelts—it whistles. All London is coming to life. Tomorrow I lunch with Sibyl to meet the Nicolsons; which I do to get out of dining. About 37 [Gordon Square]—we think you should certainly stick to the Premium, as it is part of the rent. I will hand on the other facts. The truth is, Harold doesn't know his own mind; but is very uneasy, I

1. Ann Stephen, aged 13, daughter of Virginia's brother Adrian.
2. The Bond Street art dealer. Angus Davidson did not obtain a job with them, but soon afterwards became the Secretary of the London Artists' Association.
3. Leonard had reviewed *The Autobiography of Lord Alfred Douglas* (*Nation*, 6 April 1929), condemning the book in all respects. Its author was particularly annoyed by Leonard's apparent defence of Robert Ross's study of Oscar Wilde, which Lord Alfred considered libellous (letters to the Editor, *Nation*, 27 April 1929), but he never brought actions against Leonard or the *Nation*. Several years later, when Lord Alfred could scarcely pay his rent, the Woolfs helped him to obtain a pension from the Literary Fund.

gather, about diplomacy altogether; still, as he hasnt a penny and now has to support his mother, the plunge is rather stiff.

Christabel asked us to the Opera—she is coming to life. On the other hand, Mrs Clifford[1] is dead, and I've just written a wreath like letter to Ethel [her daughter, Lady Dilke]. She is buried today, and I can't go.

We had Braithewaite[2] to dinner—and Miss Lyn Lloyd Irvine[3]—a pretty young intellectual, undebauched, to whom we talked of every subject—sodomy, and copulation; and at any moment, though he roared like a bull, I thought Richard was going to burst into tears. The modern way of being widowed is alarming—He took his old mother to Venice and to cheer him up, she came out with the most astonishing indecencies, carnous or uncarnous. "There ought to be rubber women" she said, when women are cold. Also she told him how much blood shed there was in marriage—this after complete reticence for 35 years. He mixed her water with wine, she being a teetotaller. What I find alarming is the sudden way of saying "Oh my future won't bear thinking on—" then roaring with laughter.

And we had William Plomer[4] who is going to be a great novelist to dine—fresh from Japan.—a very spruce and yet imaginative young man, born of parents in Pinner. I think I shall have to ask him here and bring him to Charleston to meet you. But what a mix up we are!—I pretending to be an Aunt and then a contemporary—I never know which. He says that they dont talk with much freedom in Pinner.

My great excitement is—I neednt say—building. Philcox will build two rooms for £320—whereas [George] Kennedy said it would be £450 for one. And he will do them by August—which is doubtful—So I'm ferreting my brains to think of doors and windows—handles and cupboards. They're to be built on next the Kitchen where the pears are—of brick, I think, painted white. Please make suggestions.

Here is dinner. I am devastated by the dull torpor of this letter. I let it go too long, and so I had too much to say, and could not put in any amusing or interesting things. So you must answer at once, in order that I may write at once; for letters are ruined by facts.

Lord! another must be added. I dont know about coming. I shall try to

1. Lucy Clifford, the novelist and playwright, whose husband had been a friend of Leslie Stephen, died on 21 April.
2. Richard Braithwaite, then aged 29. He later became Professor of Moral Philosophy at Cambridge. His wife had died the previous year.
3. She was beginning her career as a writer. Later she married the mathematician Max Newman.
4. At the age of 26 Plomer had already published one novel and two volumes of short stories. In October of this year the Hogarth Press published his book of poems, *The Family Tree.* Plomer went to Japan in September 1926. He was offered the Chair of English Literature at a provincial University in Japan, but refused it and returned to England in April 1929.

come, say the first fortnight in June; but L. rather inclines to motor out towards Perpignan—and not come to Cassis. But I dont think I can go without Dolphinery till August; even if I have my husband. Tell Jean[1] I hope to come anyhow myself about then. Write quick.

B.

Berg

2021: To Roger Fry   *Monks House, Rodmell*
                                                    [Sussex]

April 24th [1929]

My dear Roger,

I am so distressed to hear from Nessa that you're ill again.[2] This is only a line of enquiry. Perhaps the woman [Helen] Anrep might write and say how you are. Lord!—what an awful time you have of it! And I had hoped you were shaking off some of these diseases.

I wonder if you will be back soon. I pass your door and look in—it often seems to be open, but doubtless only to admit the whores of Bloomsbury, whom I'm sure congregate in that congenial atmosphere. I wish I were whoring—that is to say dining with you. It makes my blood run cold to think how seldom we meet in a world which may go smash the day after tomorrow. Yet I see Sibyl and Angus and the hinder parts of Bob Trevelyan[3] almost daily. London is, as you will gather, very busy, and as usual I get hooked in when I want to be left out. We have escaped down here, where the solitude is divine, but the cold so rasping that I have no skin left on my nose. We are seeing about building a room,—I wish I could tap your intelligence. You will have to come and stay with us, and then perhaps we shall get a little said of the myriads of things that must be settled one of these days. I should like incessant conversation for the next ten years, only getting up to relieve nature and sometimes look at a book. I should be reading one now on the war, a German diary, so horrible that I cant read it,[4] and then I think I must, since such things happened. It is a trick my Puritan blood plays me—otherwise I read a book by Vlaminck[5] which Clive recommends—only Clive's poor old wits seemed to me so devastated, last time we met, by his Poppets all a fluttering round and about that I can't believe him any longer. I daresay Nessa is pulling him through in the Sanatorium at Cassis.—wonderful woman! What we all owe to her!

1. Jean Campbell, a member of the English colony at Cassis. She lived with Colonel Teed at Fontcreuse, where Virginia had taken rooms on a previous visit.
2. Roger Fry was in Paris, suffering from a bad leg.
3. R. C. Trevelyan (1872-1951), the poet and an old friend of the Woolfs.
4. Perhaps *Roumanian Diary* (1929), by Dr Hans Carossa, who served with the German army medical corps on the Roumanian front.
5. *Tournant dangereux: Souvenirs de ma Vie*, by Maurice de Vlaminck (1929).

The Election is beginning to reverberate, or whatever the word is for the expulsion of wind. Lies, lies, lies, whatever paper you open; and the local lady has just stuffed a handful of pamphlets in at the window. Also Leonard is in for a libel action. Lord Alfred Douglas threatens one because of his article in the Nation.[1] I daresay it wont come to anything. But do come home and pull us all out of these imbroglios; and do please recover. Love from us both—

Yr
Virginia

Sussex

2022: To Ethel Sands

Monks House, Rodmell,
Lewes [Sussex]

April 24th 1929

Dearest Ethel,

It was delightful to get your letter—ages, ages, ages ago.[2] You were stuck on a mud-bank, and it was very hot and rather ugly—nevertheless you loved everybody as usual, and had made friends with a donkey boy. You were very exquisitely dressed, and you thought with charity of all your friends, not having even a laugh for Sibyl [Colefax], who stuck on a very much larger mud bank, I may tell you—but then she went in a private yacht, and saw many things that no European of her sex, which is female, has ever seen before. There! You see how malicious you make me—who am as sweet as honey by nature. It all comes of being Ethel; its the natural reaction: Nan and I discussed all this: "But Ethel never thinks a bad thought of anyone—she never has," Nan says—which explains Virginia.

I'm sorry to write such nonsense; I'm dozing over a wood fire, very sleepy after a walk by the river, in a raging wind, with Leonard and Pinker (the spaniel). We came down last night to see after our property and build a room, and there I saw your desk, and it is responsible for this. I daresay you would like news—but that again leads me to Sibyl. Aren't I lunching with her tomorrow to meet—of course—the Nicolsons; and we shall have to dress up, Vita and I, and behave like ladies, in the Kings Road, instead of toasting buns over my gas-fire. Thats one of Sibyl's lapses—to ask friends to cross London to meet. But enough of Colefaxiana.

I have been leading rather a recluse life—perfectly well, but determined never to spend a day in bed again. Heaven knows what happened in Berlin—it was a very odd affair; Count Kessler, pictures, operas, vast distances, icy

1. See p. 42, note 3.
2. Ethel Sands had written to Virginia in February from Egypt, where her tourist boat grounded on a Nile sandbank between Luxor and Cairo.

cold, Vita in snowboots at one end, Eddy,[1] Nessa and Duncan and I all far away at the other. It was hideous, and highly respectable in the midst of all its vice—we went to the Opera most nights, and even Leonard pined for the diamonds of Lady Londonderry[2] (is that right?)—so hairy and hearty and beery and cheery and like Bessie [Mrs R. C.] Trevelyan eating muffins in black kid gloves were they. Naturally I was ill.

Now I cannot begin another page, (but I see I shall,) as I have nothing to say—and I ought to be reading somebody's manuscript which I have lugged down here and never looked at.

By the way, I had ten pages from [Jacques-Emile] Blanche the other day, (I thanked him for an amusing spiteful article he wrote on me) and I gather he is ready to be more than a friend; and will paint my picture; and would like to give me the last half dozen books he has written. But I cant answer; indeed I cant even get through his letter, so by this time our relations (always of the purest) are no doubt again strained.

Perhaps you will write to me—I hope so. But I can't conceive where you are at this moment[3]—What wouldn't I give to see you, and to surprise you in some astonishing revelation! You may be just taking down your hair in a tent under a eucalyptus tree, the moon being obscured temporarily by a huge moth. Ah! You are a moth, I remember: red eyed, with a brown hood.

Goodbye
Yr V.

Wendy Baron

2023: To Vanessa Bell   52 *Tavistock Sqre.* [*W.C.*1]

Sunday 28th April 1929

Dearest

Here at last are the cheques;[4] I hope correct, and I have added the £2 you wrote about on the postcard.

I have left no time to write, as we have Mauron[5] and Morgan [Forster]

1. Edward Sackville West, Vita's first cousin, the musician, critic, and novelist.
2. Wife of the 7th Marquis of Londonderry. She founded the Women's Legion in 1917, and with her husband entertained lavishly at Londonderry House, particularly for the Conservative Party, although Ramsay MacDonald was one of her greatest friends.
3. Ethel Sands was now staying at the British Embassy in Constantinople.
4. Virginia sent two cheques. One was £31.11.9 for Vanessa's work as a decorator; the other, for £33.6.8, was the latest instalment of the funds made over to Virginia and Vanessa by their brother-in-law Jack Hills on the death of their half-sister, his wife Stella Duckworth, in 1897.
5. Charles Mauron (1899-1966), French critic and the translator of *Orlando* and *Flush*. Roger Fry had invited his friend to lecture in England.

upon us. Roger has more than surpassed himself, according to Morgan. He has gone down to Helen in the country leaving everything in complete chaos. Mauron is entirely unprovided for—Morgan and Mary are getting up a lecture at 37 [Gordon Square] on Wednesday; no preparations have been made at Oxford; Margery Fry [Roger's sister] has disappeared—the poor man is thinking of returning to France in despair. So we have had to ask him in, and instead of writing that long letter full of gossip I must fly.

I know I had a million things to say. I lunched with Sibyl—I sat between Sir P. Sassoon[1]—an underbred Whitechapel Jew, and Harold [Nicolson]. About 37—they want to leave it till the beginning of June, as Harold thinks his fate will be decided by the election, but naturally doubt that you can agree. Also; do you mean that you want the premium paid in one lump sum, or yearly? This last would suit them better if they took it. I doubt that these lunch parties are worthwhile. I had to dash into a shop and buy a bright red coat in a hurry, and gloves, and shoes; and then one only has ten minutes rational talk with Max Beerbohm, who is infinitely weary and discreet, and needs softly purring to get anything out of before we're interrupted. For the rest it was dull; and I could see Vita more happily over my own gas with a bun on a toasting fork.

I dashed into [Augustus] John's pictures afterwards, and there was so shocked that I came out again. You can't conceive—if I'm to be trusted— the vulgarity, banality, coarseness and commonplaceness of those works, all costing over £400 and sold in the first hour. Angelica with a gallipot would do better already. There I met old Dora[2] shuffling along like a half heeled sheep; has she adenoids? or why does she click at the back of her nose? She said that Daphne[3] is no more unhappy in Vienna than in London. We are dining with the Keynes'es; and I am taking Judy[4] to Baa Baa Black Sheep, since I can't go on entirely neglecting them, and I gather noone ever does them a good turn: but this may be servants gossip. Lottie has again violently quarrelled with Nelly over the grocer's boy, left her in the lurch, and gone pillion riding into the country. And Alice, looking out of the top floor window saw a one horse van draw up, out got a man with a key and unlocked a car that was standing there and was about to steal a bag when Alice screeched stop thief so loud that the milkman joined in the chase, the man dropped his key and bolted in the one horse van—infinitely to the excitement of everyone.

This is all the servants gossip. I am seeing Christabel [McLaren], and

1. Sir Philip Sassoon (1888-1939) was then under-secretary of State for Air. At his house, Port Lympne, he entertained the most eminent of his contemporaries.
2. Dora Sanger, wife of Charles Sanger, the barrister.
3. The Sangers' daughter, aged 23.
4. Judith, Virginia's niece, aged 11, the second daughter of Adrian and Karin Stephen.

Mary, and I believe we are taking the bull by the udders as you would say and having Faith[1] to dinner. But whats the point of all this when I want to be talking to you instead? I daresay we shall be ruined in the libel action, if [Lord Alfred] Douglas goes on with it, in which case I shall retire to my wood at Cassis. Here it is bitter cold, ink black, and no different from January save for six daffodils and two leaves.

But I doubt if what I write makes sense. What can Roger be about? He was talking of Mauron in January, and now not a notice has been sent out, or a thing done. I've not heard from him, but was supposed, according to Morgan, to be organising a lecture. I will write again in a day or two. but so may Dolphin—

B.

Berg

2024: To William Plomer   52 *Tavistock Square, W.C.*1

[April ?1929]

Dear Mr Plomer,

I must thank you for the lovely dish which Leonard says you brought back from Japan for us. It is extremely pretty, and I wonder what it is—I think it must be an old piece, from the lovely quality of the colour. You could not have given me anything more to my liking as I have a deep, though uneducated passion for china.

Thank you so much.

Yours sincerely
Virginia Woolf

Texas

2025: To Clive Bell   52 *Tavistock Square, W.C.*1

2nd May 1929

Shall I finish this letter? I doubt it, but I will begin it anyhow, with a new lizard-green fountain pen, a slippery sort of pen, golden, laxative, loose-tongued. But shall I end it? Did I not sit down in this very chair, yesterday at 6.30, when I should have been at 37 listening to M. Mauron on Mallarmé; and what happened then? The telephone rang; an acrid angular voice; agony and despair: Can I come round after dinner? No, Dottie, you can't, I said, because we are dining with the Keynes'. To cut the matter short—too short, for I never set pen to paper, round she came there and

1. The wife of Hubert Henderson, Editor of the *Nation*. As Faith Bagenal she was one of Virginia's younger friends in the earlier Bloomsbury period.

hen; and Heaven forgive me if I dont think Vita's choice of friends—of old friends to whom one must be loyal—a little crude. What d'you think? Check skirt, leather belt; loosely knotted tie. And then her Gerry[1] had been down for the week end. "Too awful, too awful, Virginia. And he gave me back the brooch I'd left on my dressing table the day I went. What a day! What life is! How one suffers! And Vita is I suppose the most popular poet in England!" This is Dottie, in agony: and then I got a trifle bored, and yawned three times, and she saw it, and said she must go and didn't. And then Leonard came from the lecture, where he had met Roger (just back from a new doctor, who says his thickened artery in the thigh is the cause of all his trouble—not a doubt of it; but nothing can be done); and Aldous [Huxley], very charming; and Logan;[2] and Molly [MacCarthy], mute on a sofa; and Mary [Hutchinson]; and I forget who else, as the servants say. But Bea [Howe] has a cold owing to staying in a Devonshire house which was a mortuary; and Christa [McLaren] had some other good reason; and Virginia had to take her niece Judy—a good nice child, full of brains, but not, alas, one of our sirens; she won't sing any songs, but her competence will no doubt serve instead—to the Coliseum, which, you know, begins soon after two, and does not end till 5.30: so Virginia did not go.

But all the same we've done our duty by Mauron, had him here for three hours—for as you so justly surmised, the whole weight of that rather obese and almost blind Frenchman was dumped without the least affectation even of interest on the backs of Bloomsbury by the dear old rapscalliony Roger, who had harassed us these three months, as you may remember, to do for Mauron whatever a human being can do for another. He went down to his Helen, merely posting to Mauron a letter beginning Darling Helen, I shall arrive at 2.30, and sending darling Helen a letter, so he says, a letter of full instructions about behaviour in England addressed to Mauron.

This perhaps gives you the hang of our situation. For the rest I am engaged in various enterprises which I would like to describe in detail if you were in the chair opposite, instead of Pinka, who has a newspaper under her, as she is violently on heat, yet must be exercised, and if you consider that there are ten fox terriers in the Square, all belonging to old, and mostly maiden, ladies, you can forgive the gusto with which, when I've written this, I must take her out.

But as you're not there, how can I begin? Life, as we all know, is made up of trifles. What amuses me, when I hear it in Tom's [Eliot] voice on the telephone, mayn't amuse you. Indeed it should not; it is tragic and sordid in the extreme. "Vivien's [his wife's] legs"—"*Legs*, did you say?" Yes, both

1. Lord Gerald Wellesley, later 7th Duke of Wellington, the architect, had been separated from his wife Dorothy for several years.
2. Logan Pearsall Smith (1865-1946), the American-born author of *Trivia* (1918) and other essays.

legs, but especially the left. "But what's the matter with it?" "She cant get a slipper on this week. Last week she was just able to come downstairs. So of course we have had to give up the Strachey's flat." "My God, Tom, have you seen a doctor?" "We have already had ten doctors." "And what do they say?" (here we settled in for an hour or two, I on the edge of a broken chair too)—Well the long and short of it all is that Vivien is now recumbent for ever; swollen, horizontal—for one can't get any footrest that fits her; 15 cousins from America call daily; what in short is the pleasure to be had from life if you've married Vivien and have only father Darcy[1] to fall back on? Ask of the frogs, ask of the nightingales which are even now singing to the lilies in the tank. How you play upon my vices! How violently you make me envy you! Don't you know I like my friends to be unhappy?—at least to be wet and cold if I'm wet and cold, and there you go and talk of sitting in the shade when we are cooped up under a perpetual umbrella—God's cotton umbrella which is nasty and slate-coloured and cheap and indescribably dowdy. Three leaves are out in the Square, where I must now take Pinka to make water; I am wearing a waterproof apron and a tweed skirt; and then you go and talk of the asparagus and the lizards. How can you have so entirely forgotten one of my most marked, though less pleasant, features! Envy; hatred.

Yes, I saw Harold, and Vita; and Harold squirms a little, like a gold fish hooked by a bent pin. He cant get off, and he cant get on. Ramsay [MacDonald] he thinks may re-call him. Meanwhile I can abuse him for a time-serving flunkey—This was at Sibyls, and as I write, here is another card, asking me to two more luncheons, though she is at the moment marooned at some ducal house in Dorsetshire. And we dined with the Keynes; because, as you may have heard, my husband is now party to a libel action. He wont apologise, and so Lord Alfred is instructing his solicitor to issue a writ. He is also suing the Nation, and Maynard is a little inclined to think that Leonard needn't have been so outspoken. However, no tears are shed, and though the one decanter was not entirely full, we had a fine dish of asparagus, and chicken, and an ice, much damaged by some cheap cherry brandy, however,[2] and clouded by the presence of Harland [manservant]. "Harland's been in bed with the Broncks", said Lydia,[3] "and Mrs Harland"; here she tapped her head with Harland proffering the lettuce. "She's odd *there*: and I have carbuncles on my bosom." They have all been vaccinated, owing to Maynard reading that 50 schoolchildren have a mild form of small pox in Ham. He is hand in glove with Lloyd George;

1. Father Martin D'Arcy, the Jesuit who was then teaching at Stonyhurst, and in 1932 became Master of Campion Hall, Oxford.
2. It was the common opinion of Bloomsbury that the Keyneses were remarkably economic in their hospitality.
3. Mrs Keynes was Lydia Lopokova, the Russian ballerina.

issuing a pamphlet, interviewing city magnates. Cecil Taylor[1] was there, whom I confuse with some other man always; and we discussed Peter and Topsy;[2] who will never come together again, Cecil says; Topsy is living in Pembroke Gardens; and Desmond [MacCarthy] is giving 8 lectures on Byron this week, in fact four are already given, so thats accomplished. And Julian [Bell], Maynard says, is undoubtedly the most important under-graduate at Kings, and may even get a Fellowship, and Maynard seems highly impressed by him altogether, and his poetry—Julian by the way says he tackled Maynard about Wittgenstein but was worsted; however, we shall hear the story tomorrow, when he's bringing Playfair[3] to lunch—why I don't know; but I shall try to get him in a corner and discuss the Apostles.

And then—as you perceive from the growing incoherence of this letter I am in some difficulty with the fountain pen. Yes I saw Christabel and gave her your message.[4] But, as she very justly says, if Clive had any affection for you and me, he wouldn't be gallivanting to Saigon. She had been entertaining 40 horticulturists at lunch, and was a good deal perplexed about a matter of conscience. That is to say, she was kissed last June on the top of a Welsh hill by Canon Bowlby. Canon Bowlby, as Nessa will tell you, has just been acquitted of improperly behaving to schoolgirls in a train.[5] Now what is my duty?, says Christa. Ought I to have given evidence of his behaviour to me? because not a soul in England will believe these wretched little girls. Well, that very night, Philip Heard (a bugger you may know) was dining here, and he said—this you will admit was a coincidence—that a very intimate friend of his had just consulted him about a Canon—Bowlby? I shrieked. Yes Bowlby, he said, who is certain to be convicted one of these days for tickling little girls in the streets of Chichester. So Christabel need not give her evidence: but I think Christabel would have liked to. But Christabel is very lovely, seductive and enchanting.

Tell Nessa that—no, its useless beginning another page. I must stop. I must face the dogs in the square. I must read Sachy's new book.[6] I must

1. A master at Clifton College until 1948.
2. Mr and Mrs F. L. Lucas. He was a critic and poet, and a Fellow of King's College, Cambridge.
3. Edward Playfair was Julian's greatest friend at King's. On going down from Cambridge, he joined the Treasury, had a distinguished career in the Civil Service, and became Chairman of the National Gallery Trustees in 1972.
4. The message was: Would Christabel write Clive a letter.
5. The Reverend Henry Bowlby, Canon of Chichester Cathedral, and formerly Headmaster of Lancing College, denied the charge. He maintained that he had done nothing to the children which he would not have done in the presence of their parents. At his trial on 5 April he said, "I did put my hand on them and asked if they were cold."
6. *The Gothick North* (1929), by Sacheverell Sitwell.

write to Tom. I must listen in to Vita.[1] What I want to do is to make you dissatisfied with Cassis. But I shant. So write me a long letter.

V.

Quentin Bell

2026: To Vanessa Bell   *Monks House, Rodmell*
                                          [Sussex]

Sunday 5th May 1929

Dearest Dolphin.

Now attend to the following plans: We have just had out the map of France and the calendar. Would it be possible for me to come on the 3rd or 4th of June for a week or ten days? As at present arranged, Leonard will motor, probably with Julian, on the 11th. to Perigueux, where it is proposed that I should join him on the 13th or 14th. What is suggested is that you and Duncan should consider making a short tour with us; going on for a day or two with us into desirable places, and then bringing Julian back with you. Please consider the plan, which can be modified of course to suit you. But I think I shall certainly come to Fontcreuse then, so could you speak to Jean,[2] paying her all my compliments. I shall bring some writing I expect, and thus be off your hands in the early morning; but I can do this perfectly in my bedroom, so she mustn't bother about the tower. or any other sitting room. I rather hope, I confess, that I shall be alone—I mean, that you wont have other visitors. But Leonard says that Roger, whom he saw at the Mauron lecture, means to go to Cassis very soon. I must admit I am rather excited at the thought of seeing you.

Here we are for the weekend—what a divine relief after London! Next year, with my new room, I shall certainly come here much oftener—if you were at Charleston, I should spend the summer months—what are called so. It pours and blows and not a flower scarcely is out; but still it is infinitely to be preferred to the telephone and the pump and Dottie dropping in, and Colefax ringing up. Even Christabel I could spare; the truth is with age one becomes crusty and solitary, save for a few crones who humour one's crotchets. However, you being away I do my best to frisk. How could I go to Lucy's [Clifford] funeral, seeing that I was here? All that remains of her in my mind is a cows black blubbering cunt: why that image persists I know not. Nor have I heard from Ethel.[3] My letter was not from the heart; it rang, as they say, hollow.

Julian came to lunch, without Playfair, I'm glad to say and we had a

1. Vita was broadcasting a weekly review of new books for the B.B.C.
2. Jean Campbell, See p. 44, note 1.
3. Ethel, Lucy Clifford's daughter, married Sir Fisher Wentworth Dilke, 4th Bt., in 1905.

52

long and animated discussion: about Clive and Quentin, whose state he finds very deplorable: because he says—but dont in God's name let this lie about —Clive is an elderly roué whose mind has gone grey and bald; but Quentin ought to know better—I gather the talk of love had rather bored him. He is very mature—one talks to him as to one's equal. He is in the thick of the Apostles of course, but what is so charming is that he mixes their bleak integrity with a general good will; and the most violent enthusiasms. We got into a long argument about poetry and then he drove me, at the risk of my life, to Berwick market to buy coffee and then to the London library— I thought we were smashed again and again, as the car is very stiff still, and he hasn't quite got the hang of it and doesn't know one street from another. He is coming up on Wednesday again, ostensibly to see Topsy [Lucas] who writes him moaning letters he says, very miserable and out of her element alone in London; but his real motive is to run off his 500 miles. I hope he will stay the night and come to a small literary party,—only Blunden[1] and I think Plomer and Eddy [Sackville West] and perhaps Roger [Fry].

But I haven't seen Roger. He went at once on landing to a new doctor, who knows exactly what is wrong—a thickening of one small artery— and says it is not serious and can be cured. This I had from Helen on the telephone, Roger having that instant left to take Mauron, I think, to Oxford. So he is at last shouldering his burden, or Morgan would have perished.

I dont myself see the phenomenal charm of Mauron—he's a heavy blind man, something like Kot, if you remember him, more Teutonic than French, very nice and slow and genuine, but not, to me, wildly exciting in the intellect or body. But then we only had three hours; in which I was the only conversationalist, my French coming in and out like the worms on the lawn last night. As we were going to bed, Leonard called me to see a marvel of nature, which it was, some ten million worms red and wet like rubber tubes writhing in all directions. It was precisely my idea of the floor of Hell— they made the grass heave and billow—you wouldn't believe it—wherever the torch lit, there were worms. I shall dream of them, I said to Leonard, and sure enough I dreamt all night of you and Hugh Walpole.

Which brings me—you see how the mind of a writer works—no nonsense about reason or order or logicality,—to Angus [Davidson]. I am sure your diagnosis is right—he is inwardly convinced of his greatness, and nothing will rouse him; .   .   .   .

.   .   .   .   *[three lines omitted]*   .   .   .   .

.   .   .   .

.   .   .   being I suppose, inwardly aware that his own mind is empty as a silk hat—which brings me—I dont see why—to Rothenstein,

1. Edmund Blunden, the poet, who won the Hawthornden Prize in 1922, and was from 1924-7 Professor of English at Tokyo University.

who in the most creepy crawly oblique and underhanded way has approached me, through a friend of Tom Eliots, and then through Tom, to sit.[1] Tom says he makes one look so noble, and loves it. I say, not for all the opals of Peru. Rothenstein is said to blame it on to the intolerable conceit of Bloomsbury. We are not popular—there can be no doubt.

There are two pieces of furniture I must buy, so do mark them down— one a poudreuse, not necessarily in good condition; the other a sideboard, or cupboard for the dining room here. I am immersed in questions of floors, windows and paint; and have a wild hope that work may start and the rooms be done by August. If only Kennedy and Durrant[2] between them hadn't wasted 3 months and £15! But it was all our fault, I suppose.

I will give Vita your messages.[3] All depends on the General Election. I think.—Harolds chance of coming to London I mean.

By the way, Julian was elected unanimously to the Cranium,[4] and poor [name omitted] heavily blackballed. Write. Write.

B.

Lord Alfred says he is going to bring a libel action against us; but so far nothing has happened. However, I am in trouble in America for saying that Henry James didn't write English.[5]

Berg

2027: To Molly MacCarthy   52 *Tavistock Square* [*W.C.*1]

Friday [10 May 1929]

Dearest Molly,

Are we never to meet again until we are old and wasted? I heard you were at Maurice's [Baring] lecture, when I couldn't go. But I am going to Argyll House [Colefax] on Monday, at 5, and could I come back to you afterwards for a short gossip?

1. Virginia never sat to William Rothenstein.
2. Whom the Woolfs had consulted on the extension to Monk's House.
3. About the Nicolsons' proposal to rent 37 Gordon Square.
4. The convivial society founded by David Garnett in 1925.
5. In her article *On Not Knowing French* (*New Republic*, 13 February 1929), Virginia had written: "A foreigner with what is called a perfect command of English may write grammatical English and musical English—he will indeed, like Henry James, often write a more elaborate English than the native, but never such unconscious English that we feel the past of the word in it, its associations, and attachments." A letter of protest, from Harriet T. Cooke, appeared in the *New Republic* on 24 April.

I hope that may be possible—and then I have to return to Argyll House to dine; but a respite in your company would be a great relief.

Anyhow, if this doesn't do, suggest something else please.

Your old attached but forgotten friend

Virginia

Mrs Michael MacCarthy

2028: To Quentin Bell   52 *Tavistock Square, W.C.*1

Typewritten
May 11th 1929

Dearest Quentin—oh, but youre Claudian. Well then Claudian

How you have seduced me by the charm of your language! I have thrown on to the floor the last page of my most hated book [*Phases of Fiction*]— it is dry as a captains biscuit—there is no food even for the weevil in it— and turned to this succulent sheet. For now thank God I need not say what I think of fiction and Proust and the future and the new orientation of the human soul, as Leonard and Dadie[1] insist—never were such taskmasters; now I can throw myself onto the back of life and grasping hard to the mane fly away and away. Where? How could I write when you were at Cassis and every page was left in the drawing room to be read by Clive Vanessa Angelica Duncan Sabine[2] Miss Campbell and Colonel Teed? You have a very elementary notion of the principles which should guide epistolary correspondence; though letter-writing on a typewriter is a mongrel, a mule; a sterile thing, compared with the handwritten letter. I say only what the typewriter likes to say. But I might have said things even so that I should not wish the whole population of Cassis to read. You admit your trousers have holes in them. Why at Lewes station you had to be covered with a potato sack in order to save the blushes of the young women who sell violets. But what was I going to say that is indiscreet? Only that I wish Clive would progress beyond love where he has been stationed these many years to the next point in the human pilgrimage. One cant kick ones heels there too long. One becomes an impediment. At your age a little talk and hubble-bubble of the kind does very well. One would not wish to cut you off from the society of your sex and mine. But take warning; dont outstay your welcome there.– I mean don't let people say Oh he thinks of nothing but love; oh he's off

1. George ('Dadie') Rylands, who had been assistant at the Hogarth Press from July-December 1924, and was now a Fellow of King's College, Cambridge. *Phases of Fiction* was originally intended by Leonard and Rylands to be part of the Hogarth Lectures on Literature, but it was finally published in the *Bookman* in three instalments (April, May and June, 1929).
2. The young French woman who looked after Angelica at Cassis.

on that old subject again. Why do I say this? Something Christabel MacClaren said about Clive and Miss—I dont know the name of the enchantress any more.[1] I saw Julian twice last week. He is a most marked and peculiar figure; so bulky, but so agile. We had an odd conglomeration—Roger and Helen and Mauron and Mr Plomer and Mr Blunden, the nature poet, and Miss Jenkins,[2] who teaches; and they all talked of every sort of thing; Julian vociferating at the top of his voice—Whats pure poetry? Whats assocation? Whats abstract? Whats concrete—half in French too; while little Miss Jenkins who is the size and shape of a mouse, piped up in the best Strachey voice —Lord how that persists!—its echoes will be heard when Pauls Cathedral is tumbling stone from stone; she piped up (forgive this typewritten incoherency) "But what am I to do if a young man asks me to go to France without saying if he includes copulation?" She said, what seemed odd, that it is now the convention that no young woman can demand a statement of intentions beforehand. She said that Bloomsbury has muddied the pure pool of convention and the young know not one hand from another, nor which is land nor which water.

Last night we had a terrific revivication; the resurrection day was nothing to it. Old Sydney Waterlow who dandled you as a babe, turned up from Abyssinia, which has nothing to do with dulcimers, he says; there he had a breakdown and is back again, ruminating, questing, like some gigantic hog which smells truffles miles and miles away. It is now Spengler.[3] But then, my dear, you were too young to know him; so what does it convey to you, this reference of mine to a tortured soul? He was impotent for years; and Clive heard his miracle, how he found a woman in Piccadilly and brought it off there and then—and Moore[4] converted him and Bertie [Russell] fathered him and I refused him and Leonard dished him; and still he quests like a hog for the Truth. So we all did once; save for myself; who was always distracted by some other flippancy.

Roger is growing a little older. One sometimes catches his nose in repose. Helen has flown to Paris, so I hear, to see her mother who is said to be dying; so you may be gallanting your Helen about Paris. Look here, I shall be coming through about the fifth of June or so; and might catch a glimpse of you, perhaps. But I'll let you know.

What other news is there? A great activity pervades London at the moment. Maynard has produced a pamphlet which is to turn the scale at the

1. Perhaps Joan Firminger (p. 23), or 'Susie' (p. 73).
2. Elizabeth Jenkins, whose first novel, *Virginia Water*, was published in 1929. She taught English at King Alfred's School, Hampstead.
3. Oswald Spengler (1880-1936), the German philosopher and author of *Decline of the West*, by which Waterlow was deeply influenced.
4. G. E. Moore, the Cambridge philosopher whose book *Principia Ethica* (1903) made a great impact on the young men who were the original nucleus of Bloomsbury.

elections.[1] He and Lydia are greying and weathering and so becoming more congenial. And Monks House is about to be rebuilt, so that you will have a room to sit in and will have to come and stay. An ecclesiastical ornament in stone has been found in my field which proves . . .

[*remainder handwritten*] here I was interrupted by lunch and am now away from my typewriter and so must stop. Leonard is probably going to drive Julian in the Sunshade [the new car] half way to Cassis.

Mauron and Roger last night confuted Leonard and Oliver[2] and proved beyond a doubt the non-existence of everything but an Idea. So there.

Write; at once
yr loving
Virginia

Quentin Bell

2029: To Hugh Walpole   52 *Tavistock Square, W.C.*1

14th May 1929

Dear Hugh,

I would willingly write in your copy of Orlando if it did not commit me to telling a lie. For the truth is that I did not give it you—and how should I ever have had the face to bind my books in red morocco? No, I am not the giver—I am the given. It is you that bought Orlando and bound Orlando. All that is left for me to do is to thank you, once more, for your generosity to my little paperbound book.

Yours ever
Virginia Woolf

The King's School, Canterbury

2030: To V. Sackville-West   [52 *Tavistock Square, W.C.*1]

Wednesday [15 May 1929?]

Oh curse, curse. Head has been slightly bothering and being a molly coddle I think I won't dine out tomorrow (I have to be out tonight) But I shall be here, in the basement, all the morning, or from 3.30 onwards, and have put off Lytton and Ottoline, so come any time. And then you'll go and dine with someone else, and I shall be furious: well, it can't be helped.

Come; I say, and let us sit by the gas and talk.

If you *cant* come, wd. you ring up. If you *can*, dont bother. I shall expect you.

Berg

1. *Can Lloyd George Do It?* by Maynard Keynes and Hubert Henderson, in which they argued that unemployment could be cured.
2. Oliver Strachey, Lytton's elder brother, the civil servant and cryptographer.

Monks House, Rodmell
[Sussex]

Saturday May 18 1929

Dearest,

I think Leonard has given up the idea of motoring, as it seems too difficult; and as at present arranged we shall both come for a week to Fontcreuse about June 4th—that is if the Teeds can have us. I'm not quite sure about dates but will let you know. It hardly seems worthwhile for Leonard to bring the car when he has such a short time. Julian was doubtful whether his springs would survive the French roads and therefore rather wanted a lift, but no doubt he will manage. He meant, he said, to leave the day after the Apostle dinner. I dont think he's exactly dangerous as a driver, but his springs and gears were very stiff, and he was not quite used to the new car the day he drove me. He came in last week after dinner, and was a great blessing—launching out into aesthetics in French with Mauron, discussing nature poetry with Blunden and sitting at the feet of Miss Jenkins, who is only the size of a fine grey mouse. He found her very attractive he said. I must say I think he does you great credit. If he had a little more cut and fashion to his face, he would be in every way desirable. As it is, he may get thin, and he has mentally and morally all the qualities anyone can want. He is very bitter about Clive, and had written a paragraph in a review for the Granta[1] saying something about "Mr Clive Bell who mixes aesthetics and love affairs" signed Julian Bell; but the Editor had wisely cut it out.

I have just had a long letter from Clive—rather distressing I think and deplorable, all about another mystery which is making life too exciting, but he cant tell me what—as if I didn't know all I ever want to know; but one doesn't want to know, no more than if Lotties in love with the Cowman or the green grocer. Even Christabel says she cant answer Clive's letters; and I think everyone is getting to feel that he's becoming dull and boring. Lord! what a week you must have had! To go to Cassis and to suffer that! Better almost remain in Gordon Sqre. There at anyrate you can't be talked to for a week entire. Roger and I feel some scruple about coming. However, its a scruple we seem to be getting over—at least I gather that Roger is starting almost at once. I think he may stay a night here on his way—in fact, he should be here now, for Whitsun, but rather basely we said we must have two days solitude after the racket of London (which I'll come to before long—all the gossip is coming, though I'm very cold, sitting in my lodge, looking at the rooks building—but that you dont want to hear about— Whats Rooks to me, or me to Rookeries you say, quoting Shakespeare, as your way is) Clive, as I say, is under a cloud in London. I think, as Leonard and I are perpetually saying, that something ought to be done about it, in self-protection. Think how he will make the downs resound this summer.

1. The Cambridge undergraduate periodical.

But I've done all I can do—which was to put a word of warning in a letter to Quentin against philandering, saying take Clive as an example, and see how he bores people; which I daresay will lie about in the hotel de Londres and bring my head to the block.

In duty to you I went off to Chelsea the other day, first to Mauron's lecture at Argyll House.[1] Then to sit with the MacCarthys, then back to dine at Argyll House, then home to bed with Waley.[2] What an afternoon— the lecture rather stiff to a mixed crowd of fashion and riff raff, poor Faith [Henderson] there without a chin, and then Mrs Maclagan[3] and other very highly furred women; and the French Embassy and little Read[4] and so on— As for Molly [MacCarthy]—do we all look like old women now, sitting by the open window, sadly reminiscing and sighing and getting up with difficulty? I was taken aback, to think she is 6 months younger than I am; and I feel as young as a flea. Her sorrows seem many. I washed my hands under a photograph of Philip Ritchie.[5] Desmond [MacCarthy] came in from lecturing at Cambridge, without any teeth, or only single ones here and there, and began undressing in the drawing room, as he was dining with Lady Lovelace[6] at 8—which it was then 10 to. But I find them congenial— and there were Rachel and Dermod[7]—she has been acting and he has just bought a skeleton—"Thats where our money goes to," Molly said; "one's children must have skeletons, and skeletons are dreadfully expensive." I find them more congenial than good kind simple worldly Sibyl; who had George Moore but there was Sir Arthur [Colefax] too, whose conversation, though full of substance, lacks atmosphere. George Moore sat on his chair like an old baby with a bib; however we had a little literary talk, and paid each other compliments. and now he has given me a book. But the thing you'll like to hear about is the resurrection of Sydney Waterlow. He came in the other night, having made it up with Leonard.—But I dont know that there's anything to say. He remains, like the pyramids, untouched. First he started abusing us all—at least lamenting the complete failure of our generation in every way; and said he was now cynical, sceptical, and independent. No one influences me any more, he said, blowing out his

1. Lady Colefax's house.
2. Arthur Waley, the orientalist and translator from the Chinese.
3. Elizabeth Maclagan, wife of Eric Maclagan, Director of the Victoria and Albert Museum, 1924-45.
4. Herbert Read (1893-1968), the poet and critic of literature and art. The Hogarth Press had published some of his early works.
5. He died in 1927 at the age of 28. Lytton Strachey had been much in love with him.
6. Edith, daughter of the Earl of Lichfield. In 1895 she married Lionel King, who became 3rd Earl of Lovelace in 1906, and died in October 1929.
7. Two of the three children of Desmond and Molly MacCarthy. Rachel married Lord David Cecil in 1932. Dermod was then a medical student.

cheeks, and then suddenly began booming and bellowing in the old way about Spenglers masterpieces (neither you or Duncan have ever read them) and how his life was completely changed by them, and he sees, or thinks he sees, the meaning of everything. He hopes to become Ambassador at Athens[1] (but this is a profound secret—don't go telling it to the Cruthers)[2] and we are dining with him at his Club next week. He would like to talk about his change of view.

And then I saw Hugh Walpole (all this is for you; and then neither you nor Duncan really care a battered fig for me—its a question of being magnets and being steel, if you understand, but I'm getting colder and colder) Hugh came to tea. His version of Angus [Davidson] was very funny.

Angus was so lackadaisical and so qualifying and so uncertain if he could get up on time and so certain that he was about to get another job that Hugh, who liked him, thought that he was clearly unwilling to take the place, and so gave it away to a Major in the army. He says it is clear that Angus has some reason for not wishing to take any place which works sub-consciously. I said he thinks he is the Racine of our time, to which Hugh agreed. I'm afraid Hugh wont altogether do—unless you can make him. He's own brother under the skin—it's a nice pink skin though—of Rose Macaulay[3] and the late Lucy Clifford. I mean he will talk about reviews and sales and dingy dirty literary shop, and drags me in, who am naturally so pure. Then (I'm now over the fire indoors) the telephone rang, and who should it be but Sir George Duckworth. It was lunchtime, but he kept me a good 20 minutes, first asking me to lunch to meet some literary bores, French people, who had heard of Leonard and of me; and then going on and on and on. "Wheres dear old Nessa? In France? But who's she living with? Clive d'you say? And her boy? Which boy? The painter? Is he a good painter? Well its too soon to tell, I suppose. How I should like to run over and stay with her! I've just had my last tooth out; and they've put in what they call a transformation—temporary of course—to last three months. Meanwhile my teeth fall out when I talk; when I eat; when I telephone. Margaret [his wife] and I want to come and see you. We're hoping to settle in Connaught Square—" At last, at last I dropped the telephone; he puffs and blows like a sea-horse, I daresay all his teeth were on the floor at the end.

We're here, as I've said; divinely lovely the country, and we've been picking blue bells in Laughton woods. Then we dropped in (Leonards incorrigible love of paying calls in the country) at Charleston and saw Raymond and Frankie, who say they are uproariously happy and content,[4]

1. After returning from Addis Ababa, Waterlow became Ambassador at Sofia in 1929 and Athens in 1933.
2. Permanent English residents of Cassis.
3. Virginia had first met the novelist and essayist Rose Macaulay in 1921.
4. Raymond Mortimer and Francis Birrell were living at Charleston during the absence of Vanessa and Duncan in France.

but seemed glad of an interruption; so we go to tea tomorrow. Such is life here—and no sooner had we turned into the village last night, than Widow Hawkesford[1] stopped us—but I like the widows of Vicars, carrying wreaths for their husbands tombs; and on the table here was a card from Nelly Cecil[2] who had called yesterday. and wants us to lunch. I'm not sure how long Sussex will be tolerable; but then I'm wriggling with rage. Philcox now says he cant get my rooms done by August—so I shant get them till Christmas—a whole (*this is the last page*) year wasted, owing to Kennedy and Durrant; and my chief pleasure in life knocked on the head. All the same I shall buy a table, a side board a cupboard, a chair, and a complete set of crockery at Aubagne.

I say—how you've spoilt me for the ordinary run of brats! Poor dumpy good clever Judith (Stephen). I thought I must have a little childish wit; missing Angelica as I do; but one might as well have old Ray[3] to tea. Lord, I wish I didn't miss you and your brood as much as I do: for never a thought do they give me.

Leonard now says, with his love, that we shall come on June 5th for a week and hope to find you alone.

The Singer is said now to be perfect.

There's lots more gossip but I haven't the face to write any more; besides you haven't read all this, and poor dear Duncan cant make head or tail of it.

B

No news from Drown about the drawing. Am I to do anything?

Berg

2032: To Lady Cecil

Monks House, Rodmell
[Sussex]

[18? May 1929]

My dear Nelly,

Why did you choose the day before we came? Our old woman gave me your card with great excitement, but I should have been better pleased to see you. Alas, we cant come over this time as we have people about. But couldn't we arrange a meeting for August?—or perhaps you'll be in London

1. The widow of the Rector of Rodmell.
2. Lady Cecil, whom Virginia had known since her youth. She was married to Viscount (Robert) Cecil and lived at Chelwood Gate, Sussex.
3. Rachel Costelloe, the sister of Karin Stephen, and therefore Judith Stephen's aunt, was married to Oliver Strachey.

and will come to tea? But not till the middle of June as I go to France now to stay with Vanessa.

August I think we must arrange.

And are you writing your life?

Yours affly
Virginia

Hatfield

2033: To V. Sackville-West   [*Monk's House,*] *Rodmell* [*Sussex*]

Tuesday [21 May 1929]

Lord what a donkey!

Lord what a donkey!

Lord, what a donkey!

I said, I can't ask you *for the night* as Roger will, or may, be here. But come to lunch and I'll get Raymond and Francis. All right, says Vita— and these were *her* last words, spoken as it were at the crack of doom, I'll come to lunch. Whereupon I order suet pudding for lunch. Rather hot, says Nelly; yes, I say, but its Mrs. Nicolson's favourite pudding. There is the suet turned out of its basin: where's Vita? We walk up the street. Has she been cut in two by a char-a-banc do you think? says Nelly. Anyhow the suet wont keep. Pinker is sick. They say when a dog is sick it means some one's in agony, says Nelly. I had an Aunt that dreamt of a dog being sick and her husband fell from a ladder next morning.

So we ate the suet. And then in I go to Lewes, all trembling with the char a bancs a cutting you in half, and you say as cool as cucumber—

But here are the young men, walked over to see Vita—

Look here: no nonsense: *lunch Thursday* 1 *o'clock sharp.*

Please dont go and be a donkey again. These calamities bring the white hairs to my head.

V.

Berg

2034: To Vanessa Bell   52 *Tavistock Square* [*W.C.*1]

Tuesday May 28th [1929]

Dearest,

I have not heard from you, so I don't know if you expect us on the 5th but we shall come, unless we hear to the contrary. They have taken off your train, and we reach Marseilles at about 7—am—an unearthly hour. So we shall take the train out or a car, and you may expect to see us in the course of the morning. Let me know if you want me to bring you anything.

By the way did Angelica get a pen?

I suppose one need only bring thin clothes. It is roasting hot here.

I will keep all news till we meet, as they say.

Leonards mother has again fallen down, and we have got to go off to Worthing to see her.

Lord—how nice to see a dolphin again!

B.

Dont on any account come and meet us.

Berg

2035: To Clive Bell   52 *Tavistock Square, W.C.1*

May 30th 1929

Dearest Clive,

I am sorry to have been a bad correspondent, but the summer is icumen in[1]—Every bee is abuzz. Also I hope to see you, and impart all my news by word of mouth. Alas, though, they have taken off the good train; and we shall arrive in Paris at 4 on Tuesday next, and leave again at about 7.30. Can you suggest any way of meeting—bearing in mind that we must cross Paris, convey luggage, and probably shall be late? Try to devise a plan and let me know. If Quentin could come, so much the better.

But these bees, you will say, that are abuzz. Oh Sibyl, Christabel, the Keynes, Sydney Waterlow, Desmond; and the election, which is today; and we are just off to Worthing to tend the aged, Leonards mother, who has broken her arm again; and the decay of the aged is so unspeakable that I cannot think of it. And then we are going to Rodmell for the night and hope to take Raymond and Frankie over to Eastbourne to hear Election results. (Maynard, by the way, bets that the Liberals will have 190 seats.)[2] We have seen a good deal of the Charleston playwrights;[3] Raymond has become the country gentleman, and will never, never touch a pavement again. All London goes there regularly. The place will have to be fumigated. They are in high spirits, and have almost finished a play, which clearly will

1. "Sumer is icumen in
   Lhude sing cucu."
                    (13th century lyric)
2. Baldwin's Conservative Government was defeated by Labour (Ramsay MacDonald), with the Liberals winning 59 seats and holding the balance between the majority parties.
3. Raymond Mortimer and Francis Birrell, who were living at Charleston, were writing a comedy about an emancipated couple who were under attack both from their parents and their children. The play was never produced or printed.

be the success of the age: and then they'll—they swear they will bury themselves in the country, even so.

I see a good deal of Vita; less than usual of Dotty, but then my voice on the telephone the other night was not, she said, cordial. Vita broadcasts; Vita lectures; Vita writes novels and poetry and reviews; her spaniel had 5 puppies (all well, you'll be relieved to hear) yesterday morning. Harold looks for great things from a Labour government; so does Sydney. Oh Lord, what a great gull Sydney is! as pompous, as insecure, as portly as ever; yet at a touch—and we give him many—he wobbles. Desmond looks rather like a man in a high wind whose hair is on end, tie flying, and teeth falling out. But he maintains his cheerful character, all the same. Lytton I have not seen—and here's Leonard come to hurry me off, to Worthing, to the aged, to the ugly. How I hate it—ugliness and age: but that doesn't apply to you, so please arrange a meeting and inform me in time.

yr V

Quentin Bell

Letters 2036-2078 (June–September 1929)

Virginia and Leonard left by train for Cassis on 4 June, and were away ten days. They stayed in a villa near Vanessa's, and negotiated the lease of a three-room 'peasant-hut' in the woods nearby, where they intended to spend part of the year. The hut was improved by inserting windows, and they sent furniture round by sea, but the negotiations were dropped before they occupied it. Most of the summer was spent at Rodmell. Virginia was at first busy with the proofs of A Room of One's Own, *then with journalism, and on 2 July she began the first draft of* The Waves, *but made slow progress. Her work was interrupted by frequent visitors, and by two minor illnesses, one of which was partly attributable to Vita's growing intimacy with Hilda Matheson. But the main cause was exhaustion after a social month in London, 'seeing' people, as she put it, 'and being seen'. 'It eats away all one's time and character', she wrote to Hugh Walpole, but in early October she returned to it.*

2036: TO MARGARET LLEWELYN DAVIES

Fontcreuse, Cassis,
Bouches du Rhône [France]

6th May [error for 6 June 1929]

Dearest Margaret,

I got your letters and the papers[1] just as we were starting—I didn't like to risk bringing them here, but I will read them as soon as we get back, in about ten days or so. I'm rather doubtful about doing a preface—I'm too much of a picturesque amateur—and I daresay none would be needed. But we can see about this later. Life is very pleasant here, in an old French villa in a vineyard. A retired Indian colonel [Teed] lives here with a mysterious but sensible lady [Jean Campbell]—not his wife (*she* remains in India;) and ekes out his pension by making wine. Nessa's villa [La Bergère] is five minutes off, and Leonard and I live up here, on a verandah, and go to her for meals—a delicious life, with a great deal of wine, cheap cigars, conversation,

---

1. Margaret Llewelyn Davies, who had been Secretary of the Women's Co-operative Guild, invited Virginia to contribute an introduction to a book which she was editing, *Life As We Have Known It*, a collection of autobiographical articles by working women. It was published by the Hogarth Press in 1931 with Virginia's Introduction.

and the society of curious derelict English people, who have no money and live like lizards in crannies, sometimes keeping a few fowls or breeding spaniels. Of course the mistral started blowing as we arrived, but it is baking hot, and I am hourly becoming more and more inclined to buy a small lodge, with two rooms, in a wood. I've just finished reading Rosalind Murrays novel;[1] and can't see why people want to have all the facts of life put out in sensible English. One goes on reading—in fact its very good, and well bred and interesting and creditable and real: but when I've done, I can't see what the point of facts about life in books is. But then I'm thwarted and perverse. It doesn't give me any of the things I go to literature for. Am I quite wrong? I dont want stories; and I dont want reality, and I dont want to think this is precisely what would happen to the son of a shopkeeper if he went to Oxford and married Gilbert Murray's daughter.

The night before the Election Maynard Keynes rang up and said the Liberals were sure of 190 seats. What a crow for you and Leonard! Even I, coldblooded as I am, feel some excitement. But do you think they'll do anything? Thats what I always want—instant and violent changes.

Of course Vita is half a peasant: her mother was the daughter of a Spanish station master and a dancer—illegitimate.[2] This is one of the things I like in her. But no room for more.

yr V

Sussex

2037: To Elizabeth Robins   52 *Tavistock Square, W.C.*1

[16 June 1929]

Dear Miss Robins,

Some time ago you were good enough to say that you would come and see us to discuss some plans—I hope for a book.[3] Anyhow this is to say that it would be a great pleasure to us to see you. Would you suggest any time; best a Monday or a Thursday, next week? I have left this a long time, but we have been moving about, and I still hope you may find it possible.

Yours sincerely
Virginia Woolf

Texas

---

1. *Hard Liberty* (1929). In 1913 she married Arnold Toynbee, the historian.
2. In fact, Vita's mother was the illegitimate daughter of the Spanish dancer, Pepita, and Lionel Sackville-West, later Lord Sackville.
3. The only book by Elizabeth Robins which the Hogarth Press published during Virginia's lifetime was *Ibsen and the Actress* (1928).

2038: TO HUGH WALPOLE   52 *Tavistock Square, W.C.*1

June 16th 1929

Private

My dear Hugh,

I hope you won't mind my writing to ask you to remember Angus Davidson should you have any opening or hear of one. I met him the other day and he seems convinced not only that he missed your job by his own idiocy but that it was the very one he would have liked and would still like should it be possible. No doubt the possibility is gone, but I said I would write, encroaching upon your notorious good nature. He seems depressed and willing and ready to understand that his methods of accepting offers are not the right ones. Of course this needs not a line of answer. I wouldn't write, if I didn't feel that there is a good deal to be said for him as a secretary after all.

We are just back from the South of France, where we lay in a blaze of heat, and I find it very difficult to attack London again. Shall you be coming through? Let us know if you are, any time before August.

Yours ever
Virginia Woolf

Texas

2039: TO HUGH WALPOLE   [52 *Tavistock Square, W.C.*1]

Postcard

[19 June 1929]

Do come to tea on Wednesday 26th 4.30.

No anger [about Angus Davidson] on our part only sorrow. Shall expect you unless we hear.

V.W.

Texas

2040: TO VANESSA BELL   52 *Tavistock Square, London W.C.*1

Tuesday 24th [25] June [1929]

Dearest Dolphin,

Many thanks for the covers.[1] I'm afraid we are reduced to having the printed one—I mean the one you re-arranged. The practical difficulties of the

---

1. In September 1929 the Hogarth Press began to issue the Uniform Edition of Virginia's books, of which the first titles were *The Voyage Out, Jacob's Room, Mrs Dalloway* and *The Common Reader*. All had the same pale peacock-blue dust-jacket, designed by Vanessa.

new are seen to be too great. One cant lock up type in that border, therefore each cover would have to be printed twice, or you would have to make a fresh design for each. So it seems simpler, though to my thinking duller, to use the re-arrangement. Anyhow that is infinitely better than it was. I'm annoyed; as this is my permanent edition; and if you were on the spot we could devise something. But there's the usual difficulty about time. I will send the size of the new cover as soon as it is settled—I mean the one called a Room of one's own[1] for the youth of Cambridge in October. I like the new cover very much.

This business has killed all desire in me to write a letter, and I am also hurrying off to lunch. I've seen a good many people, but in a crowded and confused way. I will write tomorrow to Jean [Campbell]—having just refused to go to Long Barn with Clive in his daimler. I dont think there's much chance that Harold will get a job in London. I've told Vita about the Penroses.[2] We caught our train—it began to pour in Paris. Here it is roasting hot.

B.

I almost wrote you, by the way, ten pages of adoration and deification of motherhood—but refrained, thinking you wd think it sentimental. Now if you sometime kissed me *voluntarily* perhaps I wd. not be afraid.

I'm seeing Hugh in order to discuss possible plan for Angus—arent I angelic!

Berg

2041: To Clive Bell   52 *Tavistock Square, W.C.*1

[late June 1929]

Dearest Clive,

Yes, we shall be in London and would like to sup with you on Sunday. 8. (I suppose). And I shall be happy to dine with you on Thursday July 11th —And I wish I could come tomorrow; but I have an assignation with Christabel, and a Labour party party.

I long to hear all the news.

yr V

Quentin Bell

1. Published in October 1929 with a pale-pink dust-jacket designed by Vanessa.
2. The possibility that Alec Penrose would take the lease of 37 Gordon Square.

Saturday June 30 [1929]

Dearest Dolph:

At any moment I shall have to stop and let in Saxon,[1] but if I dont begin to write, God knows when I shall. Such is London life. Take this afternoon for instance. I thought I would go and see the Sickerts.[2] Naturally they were shut. Turning to go to the National Gallery, I ran slap into Saxon, who therefore is coming at 5; I went to the National Gallery; saw Clives back going up the stairs; decided that all contemplation was impossible; and so made do with the bust of our grandfather[3]—a portentous object, and other cadavers in the National Portrait Gallery.

There is a mint of things to tell you. Before I am engulfed, let me first ask if you have got a receipt from the Pottery man at Aubagne. They wont deliver it unless we produce it; and he never sent us any—perhaps it came after we left; and no doubt you destroyed it. So help us all. Yes—there is Saxon.

But no—it was nobody. Never mind, he'll be here in a minute.

Life has been very interrupted. Theres Christabel—Clive—Vita—now Roger's back. You never write to me, so how do I know what you want to hear about? Politics? Theres William Jowitt [see p. 70, note 3] then. Indeed—another door bell. Yes, Saxon.

It is now 6.30 and Saxon has gone to meet Barbara[4] who is going with him to Paris tomorrow to meet the children. There's only one person in the world I want to see and that is Angelica, so I am glad to hear that she will soon be in this island (for of course England is an island). William Jowitt is what I was going to talk about. London rings with his infamy. We went to a Labour Party party the other night, held in cold weather in the vast Friends house in Euston Road. Well it was a deplorable enough night, as far as nights go—so much sweat, so much energy, so much deformity, so little of the illusive and transitory beauty which I love. I mean, there they stand up and crow—young women in short red flannel knicker bockers—young men in sweaters. However, suddenly a voluminous green woman bore down and said Vanessa? I said no. So she said Virginia? We used to know each other—I was Molly Bell.[5] And now you're in the Cabinet I said, referring to

1. Saxon Sydney-Turner, a Cambridge friend of Leonard and Virginia's brother Thoby Stephen, and an early member of the Bloomsbury Group. He made his career in the Treasury and remained a bachelor all his life.
2. The Retrospective Exhibition of Walter Sickert at the Leicester Galleries.
3. Sir James Stephen (1789-1859). The bust was by Carlo Marochetti.
4. Barbara Bagenal (*née* Hiles) had been a Slade student when Virginia met her in 1916. Sydney-Turner fell in love with her, but she married Nicholas Bagenal in 1918.
5. Mary Bell, the daughter of Sir Hugh Bell and wife of Sir Charles Trevelyan, who in 1929 became for the second time President of the Board of Education in a Labour Government.

Charles who is there, wearing a vast carnation: And isn't it splendid to feel that the future is with us! she said. And then I made off, crossing a windy court yard, with fish swimming in a shallow fountain. One was caught by a young man. And I ran into Dora Sanger and into Alice Russell,[1] and into an obliterated female called Low;[2] and suddenly a stout fashionable couple closed upon me, and after a painful hesitation, grasped my hand. These were the Jowitts, universally cut, abused, fallen among strangers, and embracing the Wolves as friends and comforters.[3] Leslie [Jowitt] told me an astonishing story: Even in well appointed houses there are black beetles she said. And I had German measles. One night the telephone rang. I answered it. I saw the beetles coming. You know how they come—First they hesitate; then they begin running. "The Prime Minister has offered me the Attorney Generalship" said William on the telephone. "Shall I accept?" Now what could one do with beetles coming nearer and nearer? So I shrieked yes—I assure you, they were round my ankles. So that you see is the true story. And her face was wrapped in a towel because she had German measles.

And now I must wash and go off to dine with Roger. I daresay you know more about Roger than I do. Leonard says he is going to do a cure now; but he has only been 3 days in London,—one he spent going to Bristol, another he spends going to Aberdeen, and then he's off.

No doubt you will find me in precious hot water when you come back—Clive, yes, I've wrought upon Christa's feelings and Clive is going to be spoken to. In fact, Christa entirely agrees. She dined alone with him; and he had a letter from Paris, and did nothing but finger it and say Have you ever been jealous? Have you ever been in Love? This is from a girl of twenty. I assure you I have never been so happy in my life, until Christa felt like an old gramophone record. Everybody feels the same, she said. It may be, she said that he takes drugs. He leaves the room very often. But I said That's all nonsense. What he wants is that some lovely and witty, young married woman should say to him nobody is impressed by these loves of yours. In fact, we are all bored. Cant you take a pull on yourself and write a history of French literature—or something?

This is what Christa is going to do. She buried her face in her hand, and I think, murmured a few broken prayers.

But I must finish this.

1. Alys (*née* Pearsall Smith) married Bertrand Russell in 1894 and was divorced from him in 1921. She was an aunt of Karin Stephen.
2. Probably Eveline Mary Lowe (1869-1956), who in 1929 became Deputy Chairman (Labour) of the London County Council and in 1939 its first woman chairman.
3. Although Jowitt had just been re-elected as Liberal M.P. for Preston, he was invited by Ramsay MacDonald to join the Labour Party and become Attorney-General. Jowitt immediately accepted (to the great indignation of his constituents and legal colleagues), but resigned his seat and was re-elected as the Labour Member for Preston in July 1929.

I will bless you for ever if you will see about my windows. I have caused great consternation by alluding to my villa in France[1]—not that people mind my going, but it shakes their belief in London.

Oh there's Angus. I think that man passes belief. I saw Hugh, who promises to see him in the autumn. I tell this to Angus, and he begins sighing and heaving and says he thinks Hugh is absolutely incomprehensible. He has been offered a tutoring job at Le Touquet; but boggles at it, because it may mean buying new clothes.   .   [*19 words omitted*]   .   .
.   .   .   . How can you explain him?—no malice, but a mere trickle of invertebrate vapidity—a positive danger on the road.

Well, dolphin, do write; and come soon. Meanwhile I hope for Angelica —adorable sprite—I dont think you like her half as much as—no, its Judith[2] I really adore. Poor hobgob.

Yr
B.

Remind me to tell you an amusing story of the Keynes, and Charleston.

Berg

2043: To Donald Brace   52 *Tavistock Square, W.C.*1

Typewritten
30 June 1929

Dear Mr Brace,

Many thanks for your letter and what you say about A ROOM OF ONE'S OWN. I return the agreement signed. I have only made one alteration, cutting out the words "and Canada". The Press now has an agent in Canada and as we have asked others of our authors to reserve their Canadian rights, I rather feel that I ought to do the same myself.

I have had an enquiry from the BOOKMAN about the serial rights for America and I have referred them to you, as you were good enough to say that you would deal with them. I should, of course, be glad if you could dispose of the serial rights before you publish.

With kind regards
yours sincerely
Virginia Woolf

Harcourt Brace Jovanovich

1. While Virginia was in Cassis she began negotiations for leasing a cottage called 'La Boudarde'.
2. Judith Bagenal, aged 10, daughter of Nicholas and Barbara Bagenal, had been staying with Angelica in Cassis.

Sunday [early July 1929]

Dear Lady Jones,[1]

(I had hoped we had cut off our titles, but submit)

There is nothing I should like better than your grand footmen's party—but I don't see any chance of being in London on the 25th. We're trying to avoid London this summer, and stick to Rodmell. If you saw what a turmoil we live in here, how all our lives are frittered on politics, authors, lawsuits, etc you'd agree it is the only thing to do. So dont tempt me. But later I hope you will, and then I (I dont speak for Leonard who is away) will willingly succumb. Many thanks anyhow.

Yrs ever
Virginia Woolf

Enid Bagnold

2045: To: Lady Ottoline Morrell

[52 Tavistock Square, W.C.1]

Postcard
[2 July 1929]

I should like to come, rather late, about 5, on Friday 12th. It is a long time since I saw you—

yr   Virginia

Texas

2046: To Vanessa Bell

Monks House [Rodmell,
Sussex]

July 6th Saturday [1929]

Dearest,

It seems as if I were reverting to the habits of our ancestors in writing long daily letters. I daresay Aunt Mary,[2] whom you much resemble, spent £100 a year on penny stamps, which would have paid for the keep of a butler. I am really writing to finish off the story of Clive, so far as it goes. I had a long, long quiet reasonable talk with him. Not a word was said about Christabel, but I think the poor woman has undoubtedly done some good. At anyrate, he was rather apologetic; and talked much more reasonably, and seemed cheerful, and quiet. He laid his case before me—he says the time has come, or will in October, when he must take action. Either he must

1. Enid Bagnold (who married Sir Roderick Jones in 1920) had already published two novels. Her best-known was *National Velvet* (1935).
2. Their maternal aunt, Mary Fisher, who died in 1916.

marry Susie, and live with her in France; or he must give up the attempt to find anyone, and continue detached in London. We debated the merits of both states very reasonably. Of course there is a good deal to be said, one realises, for a fling at happiness with Susie. He says she suits him very well, is in love with him, though he is not with her. He thinks they could make out a very happy life, for some years; and this is his last chance, and in no other way can he settle down and work. On the other hand, she might desert him, or he might get bored. Also she is penniless, and after five years he might find he had lost his old friends, and was stranded with an uneducated and poverty stricken and aging model in Dordogne. Again, if he decides to stay in London, he would be safer, financially; he would keep in touch with Bloomsbury; he might run against some paragon. All this he seemed to realise very clearly,—the dangers and the merits. All will be laid before you, or has been already. I could only advise him to wait, and point out the obvious risks, considering Susies youth, and lack of book learning. What is the truth about her? That is what I dont gather. He makes her out a sensible peasant girl, who has good wits, great charm, and general competence. If so, well, perhaps it is best—only in the back of my mind I feel that she is a figment and will pass like the rest of them. Anyhow, for the time, Clive seemed clearsighted, and under no illusion, and anxious to consider every-body and weigh all reasons.

At this point I went over to Charleston, and who did I see sitting with Dadie and old [Augustine] Birrell on the terrace? Mary [Hutchinson]! in grey and rose. Mercifully we hadn't asked Clive down, as we had half meant. We had no private talk. The clatter of tongues was prodigious; but I cant go into the full story of the Keynes' yet—Perhaps I will tomorrow. Here's your letter. I am very glad about the windows [of La Boudarde]. A thousand thanks. We have a vague hope of dashing over in October to furnish. Please get Elise to clean. I feel that one will soon need a refuge out of England. Sussex is becoming a talking house. Lord Gage[1] had been to Charleston and they showed him into the bathroom, thinking he was the plumber. But he showed no surprise and asked them all to lunch and threatened to call on us, but happily thinks he has not been asked. I found an enchanting letter from Angelica—really exquisite—how Saxon did not grunt, and talked, and she has been out with Judith [Bagenal] to look at a pony, and will I give Mrs Cart Wright[2] her love and tell her (not personly) not to mourn so much. I am going to get her for a day next week—without Judith.

Both Raymond and Francis thought Clive—to return to him, (and he has just sent in a note to say we must spend next Sunday with him as London

1. 6th Viscount Gage, owner of Firle Place, near Charleston, of which he was also the owner.
2. Mrs Cartwright had been employed by the Hogarth Press as Manager since July 1925.

Sundays are too oppressive)—they thought Clive much less personal and excited; so poor Christa is vindicated. I believe after he got over the first shock, it really gave him something to think about, and if he had a series of shocks he might come to his senses. I am dining there with Christa and Bea [Howe]—Lord Lord how I shall like seeing you! Would you like us to motor you and A[ngelica]. to The School?

B.

Berg

2047: To Clive Bell   *Monk's House [Rodmell,*
                                       Sussex]
[Sunday 7 July 1929]

Dearest Clive,
      About a variety of small matters.—
1) Vita is going to be in London next Thursday. I was bold enough to say that I thought you wouldn't mind if she looked in after dinner; but she is dining out, so would come late, if at all.
2) If I see Mary [Hutchinson] as is likely in the next week or so, do you wish me to say anything or nothing of your plans[1]—about which she may well ask?
3) Entranced by the fine, or moderately fine weekend we think of coming here again on Saturday. Couldn't you come too? I warn you that the house is in the builder's hands, but we could provide a bed and plain food and could go over and see the Charlestonians and crack some jokes. And you would be driven in the Singer both ways.
      So consider it and let me know when we meet. We are just off to see old Birrell.

yr   Virginia

(age has come upon me and I can no longer sign my name)

Quentin Bell

2048: To V. Sackville-West
                                52 Tavistock Square, London, W.C.1
[9 July 1929]

Darling, we are so unhappy about Pippin.[2] We both send our best love—Leonard is very sad.

V.

Nigel Nicolson (copy)

1. See the preceding letter.
2. Vita's spaniel, who died on 7 July.

2049: To Vanessa Bell   [52 *Tavistock Square, W.C.*1]

Thursday [11 July 1929]

Dearest

This is strictly on business, (to my great grief, for I have a million things
to say)

(1) We expect you Duncan and either or both boys to dine on Wednesday
(having put off a brilliant party on this account)
(2) We have a spare room, Nelly [Boxall] being away. Would you like it?
(3) Will Quentin dine with us on Monday? Clive says he will be in London.
(7.30 about)
(4) We will take you and Angelica to Chelmsford[1] on Thursday.
(5) I am furious that I was frustrated about Angelica. I had arranged that
she was to come for the day: then Louie[2] decided to go down to Norfolk;
and when I suggested another day, Barbara [Bagenal] objected that they
were busy with a bazaar and seemed to take it amiss that I should suggest
a day away from her. Never mind. I hope to see A. later

This is all. How I loathe facts!

Your devoted
Singe

Berg

2050: To V. Sackville-West   [52 *Tavistock Square, W.C.*1]

Friday [12 July 1929]

Yes, we would like very much to dine on Sunday if its all right for you—
Clive, Leonard and Virginia. We will aim at 7.30, but don't on any account
wait.

And only a cold mouthful,—and a kiss. And heavens be blasted, something has occurred which makes the night a blank—(I wont say what) I
mean a waste. So it would be better to fix August 7th say. Any day as soon
as you are back; any night.

V.

Berg

1. Angelica's school, Langford Grove, in Essex.
2. Louie Dunnett had been Angelica's nurse from 1922 until she went to school
   in 1928. Louie then married Fred Pape, but returned periodically to look after
   Angelica.

75

July 17th 1929

My dear Mr Birrell,

I am more than glad that I plucked up courage at Charleston and tried to tell you how much I admire and enjoy your essays.[1] Here they are in this splendid edition, and I have spent the evening foraging among them with a new delight now that they are mine and given me by you. I wish there were more I hadn't read. But I am going to re-read them, and then to put them where they belong—next my Hours in a Library.[2] It was very very good of you. Indeed I am almost precipitated by your goodness into the rashness of writing an essay upon Mr Birrell[3]—making an attempt to find how [*sic*] what is the particular thing you do so much better than anybody else. That will be a pleasant occupation,—And then there is one other demand I must make on you—to dock me of Woolf and leave Virginia only.

And may I call myself not only admiringly and gratefully but also your affectionate Virginia, as my father's daughter would like to?

George Rylands

2052: To: Donald Brace   52 *Tavistock Square, W.C.*1

Typewritten
4th August 1929

Dear Mr Brace,

I enclose a copy of the revised proofs of A room of Ones Own, up to page 64. I have made some alterations, and I think it would be best to print from these if you can.

With kind regards,
yours sincerely
Virginia Woolf

Harcourt Brace Jovanovich

1. Augustine Birrell (1850-1933), father of Francis. He had been President of the Board of Education and Chief Secretary for Ireland. He published three collections of essays, *Obiter Dicta* (1884, 1887) and *More Obiter Dicta.* (1924).
2. Literary essays by Virginia's father Leslie Stephen, published in three volumes (1874, 1876 and 1879). Virginia owned the three-volume 'new edition, with additions', 1892.
3. She did so for the *Yale Review* of June 1930.

2053: To WILLIAM PLOMER

Monks House, Rodmell,
Lewes, Sussex

8th Aug 1929

Dear Mr Plomer,

Could you come here for the week end of the 17th Aug.? We should like it so much if you could. This is only a cottage, so please bring no clothes, and we shall be alone.

Texas

Yours sincerely
Virginia Woolf

2054: To V. SACKVILLE-WEST

[*Monk's House, Rodmell,*
Sussex]

Monday [12 August 1929]

Dearest Creature,

I dont think I shall be able to come this week—I've had to retire to bed with the usual old pain, not very bad and the price of the value I set on your honesty. Lord! What a relief that was![1] But I doubt that I shall be very energetic this week; so I'll say the week after, and will let you know.

Meanwhile will you send at least a line to say what happened about Hilda—I particularly want to know the situation with respect to Janet, as I have anyhow to write to her. And please make Hilda see that it was all *your* donkeyism. I am lying in my garden room between open windows—, odd that 1 felt quite well when I saw you. And I wish I could see you now.

I feel very happy about Virginia and Potto and dear old Vita; yes, I do, and would say so more eloquently if I werent in bed.

V.

Berg

2055: To VANESSA BELL

[*Monk's House, Rodmell,*
Sussex]

Monday [12 August 1929]

Dearest

I have slight symptoms of headache, so do you think you and Roger would come to tea on Wednesday not Tuesday, and could we have the

1. Virginia's headache was caused, at least in part, by her distress about Vita's French holiday with Hilda Matheson. It appears (see Letter 2056) that Janet Vaughan, who was a friend of Hilda and the daughter of Virginia's youthful intimate Madge Vaughan, had inadvertently given away the secret of the trip, which Virginia insisted had been planned for several weeks or even months. On 10 August Vita, greatly upset by this accusation, attempted to reassure Virginia that it was a last-minute decision.

picnic on Friday instead of Wednesday. If we dont hear we shall understand
that this is all right and much look forward to seeing you. Of course I am
being more careful than is necessary

Yr
B.

Berg

2056: To V. Sackville-West   *Monks House* [*Rodmell,*
                                     Sussex]
Aug 15th [1929]

Dearest Creature

I am quite well again, and spent the morning writing. It wasn't you;
as you were only the tailend—I had been badgered by people in London,
and then this writing of four articles,[1] all pressed as tight as hay in a stack
(an image that comes you see from [Vita's] The Land)—that was what did
it—not that it was bad. These headaches leave one like sand which a wave
has uncovered—I believe they have a mystic purpose. Indeed, I'm not sure
that there isnt some religious cause at the back of them—I see my own
worthlessness and failure so clearly; and lie gazing into the depths of the
misery of human life; and then one gets up and everything begins again and
its all covered over.

And now I see Geoffrey Scott[2] is dead, at my age—no a year younger.
Do you mind? Does it bring back the hot afternoon when the Salvation
Army called, and the mews where he almost strangled you when you were
late, and the scene on the downs? I didn't like him; at least I didn't trust him
for some obscure reason. I met him at Mrs Ross's[3] over 20 years ago. Lord!
Mary Hutchinson was there. But I took up my pen to say that I hope, if you
see Hilda, you will make her understand, not merely superficially, that Janet
Vaughan was as blameless as anybody could be—mere joking and affectionate
at that,—I mean I shouldn't have minded to hear what she said of me; and

1. All were printed originally in the *Nation* and reprinted in the *New York Herald
   Tribune*. The subjects were Cowper, Beau Brummell, Mary Wollstonecraft
   and Dorothy Wordsworth. See B. J. Kirkpatrick's revised edition (1967) of
   the *Bibliography of Virginia Woolf*, nos. C 314-7.
2. Author of *The Architecture of Humanism* and *The Portrait of Zélide*. He had
   been deeply in love with Vita in 1923-4. At first she responded to him, and his
   wife divorced him because of her. When Vita's passion cooled, he went to America,
   where he edited Boswell's papers. He died in New York on 14 August, from
   pneumonia, aged 46.
3. Janet Ross (1842-1927), the author of several books about Italy, particularly the
   arts of Florence, where she had lived since 1867. Virginia met her there in
   May 1909.

to show how casual and lightly meant it was, she never even gave me a hint that Hilda could seriously entertain those passions. It was merely Oh how amusing it would be if Hilda could fall in love—and then nothing more, but what I took seriously—that the plan had been made many weeks or months.

When shall I come? I dont know. But what about next week—towards the end, say Friday, when I shall have written the last word of these excruciating little biographies. And what about a treat motoring to some place and spending a night in an Inn, first having dined?

I got out of all my engagements except Plomer, who comes for Sunday.

Leonard and Percy [gardener] are measuring the tank with a vast tape. I must go and see what its all about. Returning to Geoffrey, after all you gave him what was his phrase—rest and freedom? I remember he said something I was saying.

And then to be dead in New York—

Yr
V.

And what about your back?[1] Write and say.

Berg

2057: To V. Sackville-West   *Monks House [Rodmell, Sussex]*

Sunday 18th Aug. [1929]

I am very much distressed about your back. I wish you would answer, if only in pencil on a card, these questions. 1. Have you seen a doctor? 2. What does he say? 3. Are you better? Surely it has never been anything like as bad as this. Have you got rheumatism in it? Is it very painful?. Leonard says that the male principle [*sic*] of fern seed which paralyses the nerves of the stomach is miraculous—It cured Pinker's rheumatism in a moment, though meant to cure her worms. No, it would have been no good my coming, but when will it be any good, my coming? Leonard and Plomer are playing bowls on the terrace, and we are going to dine at Charleston and send rockets up into the sky—Quentins birthday party.[2] So you see I am recovered, and have, more or less, finished my articles.[3] The last was Dorothy Wordsworth, and if the written word could cure rheumatism, I think her's might—like a dock leaf laid to a sting; yet rather astringent too. Have you ever read her diaries, the early ones, with the nightingale singing at Alfoxden [Somerset], and Coleridge coming in swollen eyed—to eat a

1. Vita had stumbled while walking upstairs and hurt her back. She suffered from this injury all her life.
2. Quentin was 19 on 19 August.
3. See p. 78, note 1.

mutton chop? Wordsworth made his head ache, thinking of an epithet for cuckoo. I like them very much; but I cant say I enjoy writing about them, nine pages close pressed. How can one get it all in? Plomer is a nice young man, rather prim and tight outwardly, concealing a good deal I think; though I'm completely bored by speculating as to poets' merits. Nobody is better than anybody else—I like people—I dont bother my head about their works. All this measuring is a futile affair, and it doesn't matter who writes what. But this is my grey and grizzled wisdom—at his age I wanted to be myself. And then,—here is a great storm of rain. I am obsessed at nights with the idea of my own worthlessness, and if it were only to turn a light on to save my life I think I would not do it. These are the last footprints of a headache I suppose. Do you ever feel that?—like an old weed in a stream. What do you feel, lying in bed? I daresay you are visited by sublime thoughts —I saw Raymond yesterday who is off travelling for two months, and seemed vaguely aware of some change in Harold's life. And we hastily exchanged the last news of Vita in Lewes High Street, buying wines.

I shall be in London on Tuesday, and in the drawingroom at eleven o'clock; if you liked to ring me up. But I don't suppose you can ring me up, and so its no use my ringing you up either.

Here's a thing about Geoffrey Scott by Desmond.[1]—no I cant find it.

Anyhow, my dear Creature, let me know truthfully and exactly how you are. Potto kisses you and says he could rub your back and cure it by licking.

Virginia

Berg

52 *T.*[avistock] *S.*[quare, *W.C.*1]

[20? August 1929]

Dolphin;

Here is the bill that has just come for Boudard [La Boudarde, Cassis]. I expect it is all right, but perhaps you wouldn't mind just looking at it and sending it back. It doesn't include the ceiling and the other window which you wrote about, apparently. I cant remember what he said the cost would be. My sideboard apparently was put on a ship that is going by way of Algiers and Antwerp, but will arrive in time. Would you tell Quentin that I expect him to lunch on Friday at one; but, as I haven't heard from Miss [Lyn] Irvine I expect she's away, and so he mustn't put off Karin [Stephen] on her account. And finally would you tell Julian that thanks to his oil the car broke all records coming up this morning.

1. Desmond MacCarthy's obituary of Geoffrey Scott appeared in the *Manchester Guardian* of 15 August 1929.

I'm in London, and a damned place it is.
And when shall I see you?

B.

I forgot to say that I thought your cover most attractive—but what a stir you'll cause by the hands of the clock at that precise hour![1] People will say—but theres no room
I have just bought 4 goldfish and 2 carp.

Berg

2059: To Quentin Bell

Monks House [Rodmell, Sussex]

Wednesday [21 August 1929]

My dear Quentin,

We have to go to Dottie's[2] on Friday and intend taking you too. So be warned. I think we might pick some interesting observations out of it—anyhow, we have to go, and you might tell Nessa we hope she'll arrange to come too.

Lunch here at 1.

Virginia

We will leave you at Charleston coming back.

Quentin Bell

2060: To Oscar Lewis

52 *Tavistock Square, W.C.*1

Typewritten
Aug. 22nd 1929

Dear Mr Lewis,

I see from your letter of May 4th that you were sending me sheets for signing of my essay Street Haunting about June 1st. I have never received them, nor have I received the check for 125 dollars which you said you were sending on receipt of my corrected copy. As this was sent to you some time before the end of May I am afraid that something must have gone wrong.

1. Vanessa's dust-jacket for *A Room of One's Own* incorporated a drawing of a clock set at 11.05, forming a 'V'.
2. Dorothy Wellesley's country house, Penns-in-the-Rocks, Withyham, Sussex.

I should be much obliged if you would let me know whether you received the article safely, and whether you have also sent the sheets and check as arranged; as I ought to make enquiries if they have been misdirected. I see from your letter that you say you hoped to bring out the essay at an early date.[1]

Yours sincerely
Virginia Woolf
(Mrs Woolf)

Columbia University

2061: To V. Sackville-West

Monks House [Rodmell,
Sussex]

Saturday [24 August 1929]

Might I come on Wednesday for the night?—could you let me know?

I think there's a train from Lewes to Sevenoaks—for there's no question of your being able to meet me—but I've no time at the moment to look it out. The Vorn [Janet Vaughan], as you call her, is arriving. And I've no time to write a letter, much as your's deserved an answer.[2] And how are you? The best sleeping draught is audit ale at bedtime: any fellow of a college will get it, and if you don't like it, I will drink it.

A thousand different varieties of love are rained upon you, like the showers from a gigantic watering pot by Virginia and Bosman.

Berg

2062: To Frederick Bason

Monks House, Rodmell,
Lewes, Sussex

Typewritten
Aug. 25th [1929]

Dear Mr Bason,[3]

Many thanks for your interesting letter. I have told the Hogarth Press to send you a copy of their catalogue. "To the Lighthouse" *is* a novel, and I think you would find it at any library, such as Mudies.

I enclose an autograph, to save you the trouble of sending Orlando.

With best wishes,
Yours sincerely,
Virginia Woolf

J. Howard Woolmer

1. The Westgate Press published *Street Haunting* in May 1930.
2. Part of Vita's letter of 22 August is quoted in the Introduction, p. xiv.
3. An unknown London admirer.

Monks House, Rodmell,
                                      Lewes, Sussex

25th Aug. 29

My dear Hugh,

My conscience has been twinging me all August and part of July for not having answered your letter. But it was a tribute to you—I was so harassed and badgered that the idea of writing a letter, not a note, not a cheque, not a postcard, not a telegram, but a letter of sympathy and affection was abhorrent. Really you are right, and London is the devil—eats away all ones time and character, nibbles at one's friendships and leaves nothing but an old biscuit,—you know what one finds in a cupboard when the mice have been at it—of one's soul. Now I am settling into some sort of sanity. And I have bought a right to put windows in a farmhouse in a vineyard in Provence so solitude is assured and I am safeguarded: and I daresay I shall never go there.

When I was young I liked writing letters. Now I cannot remember how one does it. It is a fine hot day, and I am sitting in my garden room which has a fine view of the downs and marshes and an oblique view of Leonard's fish pond, in which it is our passion to observe the gold fish. There should be four, and one carp; but it is the rarest event to see them all together— and yet I can assure you that so to see them matters more to us both than all that is said at the Hague.[1] We are going off tomorrow to a pond at Slindon[2] where goldfish are so thick in the water that the village children ladle them out in their caps for passers by.

Why then am I reading La Fontaine with obdurate passion? I mean, why is human life made up of such incongruous things, and why are all one's events so perfectly irrational that a good biographer would be forced to ignore them entirely?

Here the church bells begin ringing and I am plunged as usual into anger and confusion—I hate to be disturbed; I hate the arrogance and monopoly of Christianity (and I'm writing to the son of a Bishop too!) but then I love the old women doddering along in their black bonnets, and the thought of all the years, and all the processions; and how buried there are their ancestors for centuries—I must explain that our garden abuts on the churchyard, and when we are looking at our beehives, they are often burying someone on the other side of the wall. Where shall you be buried, and shall you have a tombstone over you or none, and what do you feel about posterity, and have you any desire to be thought of in your grave—which questions bring me by a path which you will discern beneath the brambles—to your works: to your play; to the novel which I'm to be allowed to read. But you dont

1. In August 1929 a conference at The Hague endorsed the Young Plan, which removed allied control from Germany.
2. A village in Sussex between Arundel and Chichester.

say when its coming out. Is it this one that you are rushing up to Cumberland to write?[1] Please send me, what I'm sure there must be—a picture postcard of Hugh Walpoles house; or anyhow a view of the valley where he lives. I have a childish wish to consolidate my friends and embed them in their own tables and chairs, and imagine what kind of objects they see when they are alone. Of course it is quite true that I know nothing about human character, and to be frank, care less; but I have a cosmogony, nevertheless,—indeed all the more; and it is of the highest importance that I should be able to make you exist there, somehow, tangibly, visibly; recognisable to me, though not perhaps to yourself. Now *your* gift as a novelist—I was going to write an essay upon you, but I shan't, because you wont let me read your works.

Aren't you singularly vain, for a man of your reputation? I should have thought, selling ten million copies in a month, you would have long ago disregarded Virginia—perhaps you have—Perhaps it is only your sublime urbanity, and the quality which I most adore and that is man-of-the-worldliness, that lets her think that you care what she says.

Ought I to read Mr Priestley's book [*The Good Companions*]? by the way—From the reviews, chiefly by Jack Squire,[2] I am sure that I should hate it—but I suspect that I may be wrong, and if you say so I will send a card to the Times bookclub at once. What I am suspicious of is this manufactured breeze—what they call humanity—But you know my foibles in that respect —what I hate is having it done by electric fans and other machinery for making one sunburnt and rosy and jolly and cheery—but I may wrong him—he may be the real thing, not manufactured.

Leonard says he stayed in the very hotel you are in twenty years ago.[3] It was raining then; but he ate salmon and cream and strawberries, all off the same plate, and it is raining now.

What a letter!

Let us know when you are passing through again; I expect to be in London in October. Angus Davidson you'll be glad to hear, is provided for—has a quiet job looking after pictures which will suit him very well.

Your affte
Virginia

Texas

1. Walpole was in Sweden working on his play, *The Limping Man*. The novel which Virginia was 'to be allowed to read' was *Hans Frost* (published in September 1929; see Letter 2069), about which Walpole wrote in his diary: "I like this book. It's in a new vein for me, the vein of humour I ought to have tried long ago. Virginia Woolf has perhaps liberated me" (Rupert Hart-Davis, *Hugh Walpole*, 1952, p. 279). In the late summer of 1929 Walpole went home to Cumberland to begin *Judith Paris* (1931).
2. J. C. Squire, the poet and critic. He had founded the *London Mercury* in 1919 and was a regular reviewer for the *Observer*, 1920-31.
3. In the summer of 1911 Leonard and his brother Edgar stayed at Rattvik, Sweden, on Lake Siljan.

[27 August 1929]

Well then, I think I had better come next Tuesday, instead of tomorrow, for the simple reason that if I come tomorrow you will certainly drive the car and risk your back again. Admit that my psychology is correct. And then, as to see me is the light of your life, you will have to be extra careful all this week, because if you aren't well enough to drive me, then I dont come on Tuesday. All this is very well reasoned; but I admit I am rather disappointed—all the more that I have now no excuse for not correcting my articles—I shall do that tomorrow instead of coming to you.

I am sending a wire, as letters seem to take longer than an airship takes to go round the world travelling to Sevenoaks.

Janet Vorn [Vaughan] was here; and if I had to choose her or Hilda to love, it would be her. I explained the situation, which was all right; and she had seen Hilda, and nothing had been said or hinted. Also, Hilda never mentioned Vita, which she thought odd. So that, one way or another, your donkeyism has had good results.[1]

I am half asleep in my lodge, which seems to harbour the sun. I saw Dotty the other day, and she quoted passages from a letter I wrote to you— do you read her my letters? No, I dont suppose you do—only snatches, so dont be afraid that I am going to ring you up and make another explosion.

Thank God I'm not a rich woman and dont live at Penns—well, you cant read her that anyhow! I mean, it seems so cumbrous and unnecessary— 4 men mowing the lawn; things all settled round one like sticks in a stream.

Oh but heres Leonard and I must go to Lewes. Love from us both and write and be careful

V.

Berg

2065: To V. Sackville-West *Monks House [Rodmell, Sussex]*

Sunday Sept 1st 1929

My train arrives at Tunbridge Wells at 5.48. I wasn't serious in saying that I was afraid of Bosquet[2] driving me—so shall expect her—*not* you. If there is any difficulty, wire, and I will go to Sevenoaks and take a cab.

Damn Harold. And why should you attach any importance to the criticism of a diplomat?[3]

1. See p. 77, note 1.
2. Audrey le Bosquet, Vita's secretary.
3. Harold Nicolson had advised Vita not to publish *King's Daughter*, a collection of poems which contained some of a lesbian character. Later he changed his mind, and the book was published by the Hogarth Press in October 1929.

Have you got your proofs? I will read them—I had only one look at the type script here. No, I dont mind Dotties 4 gardeners; what I mind is the sense of stagnation, or rather ineffective agitation, among all that solidity. Now Vita could run 20 gardens and 10 houses with order and animation. But I cant now remember the impression that came over me, violent though it was, at Penns. Dotty seemed like a bit of wood that has floated into the midst of wrecked cupboards, kitchen tables, persian pots, great danes, priceless china, and they all knock and dash and wash about pompously. Put Vita there, and everything would at once take over and sail to the Antipodes under flying colours.

I am entertaining Miss L. Lloyd Irvine as I write, and throwing out sweeping views on chastity, fiction, and human life.

Are you really better? One asks these questions, and no answer comes.

I'm also, besides talking and writing, reading Mrs Meynell's[1] life. And getting together a picnic basket to lunch in the beech woods beyond Lewes.

We must wait to make plans until we see how your back is.

P [*squiggly design*]

She [Dotty] has just sent me her poems[2] for an honest opinion.

Berg

2066: To Dorothy Bussy   *Monks House, Rodmell,*
                                          Lewes [*Sussex*]

Sept 1st [1929]

My dear Dorothy,

I am not certain whose fault it was that we never met—except when you cut me in the street. But it was a lamentable fact, and must never happen again. However, I doubt that meeting in London is any good. It became more and more like a fried fish shop, and all my intercourse with my kind was merely barbarous. But what I want to suggest is that we might meet in France—where I suppose you to be. I'm having windows put in a small peasants hut in a wood near Cassis—I hope to be there off and on. Couldn't we postpone our tea till January?—and it would then be better than a tea; it would be wine and ices in blazing sun.

With the wisdom of a serpent, to which kind you belong, you have never attempted a regular life with your kind in London. Withdrawing as you do to some hole of your own, you avoid our miseries and irritations. And then you cut me—And I did try to make another attempt, and you

1. Viola Meynell (1886-1956), the poet's daughter, published *Alice Meynell: A Memoir* in 1929.
2. The Hogarth Press published Dorothy Wellesley's *Deserted House* in 1930.

never came—one night at Pippas.[1] That reminds me, I told a Lady Gerald Wellesley, a rich woman, about Pippa's flat—She wants something in Bloomsbury; and I hope it is still to be had.

I am writing under great difficulties—that is I am entertaining week end visitors. Do you ever let yourself in for that particular effort? One keeps looking to see if they are enjoying themselves. They aren't. Well then what can one do? Suggest a picnic. But the mutton is almost ready. Never mind—we will eat it at dinner. So that is what is happening this very instant in Sussex—we are going to boil some eggs and go off to a wood and sit on the roots of beech trees among pine needles and ants in a high wind and eat hardboiled eggs—dont you wish you were with us? Well, I rather do.

This letter, I must add, in case the fact has escaped you, is one of affection; pure and simple, and does not need an answer; but would like one. Love to Janie [Dorothy's daughter].

yr aff
Virginia

Texas

2067: To V. Sackville-West   [*Monk's House, Rodmell, Sussex*]

Sunday [15 September 1929]

A thousand congratulations from us both.
I daresay these are the happiest days of your life.[2]
No, alas, I go to London on Friday not Thursday.
Yes, very pleased about Kings Daughter.[3]
Thank Goodness, no more dealing with Lady S.[4]
Yes I've signed my name 600 times.[5]
Yes, I've read Hugh.[6]

1. Philippa Strachey, Dorothy Bussy's and Lytton's sister. She was Secretary of The National Society for Womens Service.
2. Harold Nicolson had decided to end his diplomatic career and accept an offer from Lord Beaverbrook to join the *Evening Standard*.
3. See p. 85, note 3.
4. One reason why Harold was pleased to leave diplomacy was that his mother-in law, Lady Sackville, had been making trouble about the marriage settlement which she owed her daughter. By earning a higher salary, he would be in a position to renounce their right to the money.
5. On the limited edition of *A Room of One's Own*.
6. Vita had written (13 September 1929, *Berg*) that Virginia appears in Hugh Walpole's *Hans Frost* as 'Jane Rose'. He prefaced the novel with the author's usual *démenti*, but of Jane Rose he wrote: "She had in her last novel spoken of the beam from a lighthouse 'stroking the floor of a lodging-house bedroom' —so her art illumined, gently and tenderly, the world that he knew. The debt that he owed her could never be paid" (p. 69).

Why need he say all his characters are dead, when its true?
How business like this letter is!
And looks like a sonnet.

Your red hat is here.

Berg

2068: To V. Sackville-West   [*Monks House, Rodmell,
Sussex*]
Tuesday [17 September 1929]

What a long and unexpected letter! a great treat. Also Pinka's comb.
Many fleas have already been analysed out. for it is searching and peculiar.
Many thanks; Leonard's and Pinka's.

What can I say about Hugh?—and I've got to write to him [about
Hans Frost]. The truth is its a day dream, unreal, all spangles, like a
Christmas tree, and to me rather exhilarating for that reason—all shivers
to violet powder. I expect all his books are gloried dreams of Hugh; Hugh
a great man, Hugh a sinner, Hugh a lover, Hugh prodigiously wicked and
so on—never a glimpse of any reality; and thats the trick—thats the glamour
and the illusion and the spangle: thats why he sells, and why nothing is left
but a little dent. I've only read 30 pages of Rebecca,[1] but I think really she is
another pair of shoes. I agree that the convention is tight and affected and
occasionally foppish beyond endurance, but then it is a convention and she
does it deliberately, and it helps her to manufacture some pretty little China
ornaments for the mantelpiece. One could read some of it again, but Hugh
never, never.

But what I want to know is as much as you think it discreet to say about
Beaverbrook and Harolds job[2]—what is it? What is the pay?—my word, I
think you are lucky to have brushed the bloom off diplomacy and then off
to another flower while the sun still shines—What a stallion, what a young
blood mare you are, to fling your head, kicking your heels.

And when shall we meet? I'm a little dismal. Another of these cursed
headaches. How I get them I can't imagine—Whether its writing, reading,
walking, or seeing people. Anyhow its not been bad at all—only it makes
Leonard gloomy, and tightens my ropes—I mustn't walk, or do anything
but sit and drink milk—you know the old story.

I am rather considering staying on here alone or possibly having a week
by some hot sea.

I wonder if I shall: I wonder if you'd be free: I wonder if perhaps we

1. Rebecca West, *Harriet Hume* (1929).
2. See preceding letter. The salary was £3,000 p.a.

might have 3 days or so together. It would be, if at all, about the 5th of October.

But I'm ever so much better today, and now must write to Hugh. Do let me know about Beaverbrook and all the rest.

Potto and Virginia

I have it in my mind to go to Lyme Regis.

Berg

2069: TO HUGH WALPOLE   *Monks House, Rodmell*
                                 [*Sussex*]

Sept 18th 1929

My dear Hugh,

This is awful—how long I take to answer you, and this time it isn't only a letter but a book, and a book I've enjoyed and read through so quick there was no holding me. We had visitors and I had an article to write and books to read, and then I sat reading on and on and on, pretending that I would only read one more chapter and then stop; and then arguing that as there were only 5 more chapters I might as well finish. Ask Leonard—he is a witness. How do you do it? What is your lure? Well, I'm not going to puzzle my head (though I see several very interesting questions rising). I had much rather some day soon meet and talk. I made all sorts of notes in my mind as I went along. There's a magnificent passage on friendship. There are odd peeps of all sorts of queer vistas. There's a general radiancy and Christmas tree lustre that I find adorable. Of course, I dont think its *my* world. I feel rather like the wife of a Pre-Raphaelite painter who has blundered in among Rubens and Matisse and Cocktails and Champagne and sits in a simple grey dress looking very odd and causing some alarm to her hostess.[1] Poor woman! She is a little out of place I agree, but enjoys herself hugely and trots off home to tell her husband, in their rather austere flat, all about it. Many many thanks; I did enjoy myself hugely she says.

I dont know when I shall see you to put my questions—I have an idea that I shall go off and bask in the sun by the sea somewhere before settling in for the winter. I have been talking too much, and I want to let the dust settle.

But let us know when you are up. Oh and many thanks too for the pictures which are pasted into Hans, for all the world as if Hans were Hugh: which he isn't of course. And do tell me—but these questions must wait; and the wives of Pre-Raphaelite painters, with their hair combed back dont go chattering on like this—

yr aff

Texas   Virginia

1. This is a paraphrase of a passage about Jane Rose in *Hans Frost*, p. 68.

Monks House, Rodmell,
                                                    Lewes [*Sussex*]

Typewritten
19th Sept 1929

My dear Desmond,

    I am a wretch not to have answered your letter before—but then you
write so beautifully on a typewriter with a secretary. I am going to write on
a typewriter too, but it always mis-spells, and often causes grave offence.
Ones style is apt to be abrupt. I have lost many friends this way. Irene[1]
among them.

    Thanks for the cheque. I will write you a better article one day.[2] I have
had to send the American articles[3] to the Nation as they all hang together—
four figures living at the same time—but I have others in my mind. Only I
want to write a story.[4]

    About your lady painter[5]—I have heard of her; she has been painting all
sorts of people. But as I have severely refused Will Rothenstein and a man
called Blumfield[6] on the ground that I have an antipathy to sitting still, a
morbid aversion, I dont see how I can agree to her. Rothenstein is rather
huffy as it is. Also I doubt that I shall be in London. Oh I see you say she
would come down here—but I dont think I could manage that—anyhow
by this time she will have gone and forgotten all about it. Yes I wish I came
sometimes into sight of you: it is odd to have a purely aural relationship—
to hear your voice addressing the British public [on B.B.C. radio]. I long to
get up and interrupt. I got so far as to hear that you were sitting on a seat at
Arundel, waiting for the Hutchinsons; and I sent my love to that precarious
point—But I daresay Mary never gave it. I have seen too many people—
Sussex is rather too available—I groan when I come in from my walk to
find Herbert Fisher[7] on the lawn. Peter [F. L.] Lucas is here at the moment—
I dont groan at all to find him. He is everything that is delightful, and I

1. Irene Noel, who married Philip (Noel) Baker in 1915. Before her marriage she
   had been engaged for a short time to Desmond MacCarthy.
2. Virginia's *Dr Burney's Evening Party* was published in *Life and Letters*
   (September 1929), which Desmond MacCarthy edited.
3. See p. 78, note 1.
4. *The Lady in the Looking Glass: A Reflection* (*Harpers Magazine*, December
   1929).
5. Unidentified. Possibly Ethel Walker, who painted Vanessa in 1933.
6. Possibly Harry Bloomfield, who exhibited in London from 1913 onwards; or
   Paul Bloomfield, a friend of Duncan Grant, who recommended him to Keynes
   as a possible artist-contributor to the *Nation*.
7. Virginia's cousin H. A. L. Fisher, Warden of New College, Oxford since
   1925, and formerly President of the Board of Education. She may have meant
   that he *might* have been found on the lawn, as an example of the sort of person
   she least wanted to find there.

am going to take him off to the river across my meadow now. And we shall talk about you. Last night we were singing the praises of Desmonds Sunday Times Articles. And I made a vow that I would print them in a book. Dont let them all vanish down the sink—they are much too good. Dont tinker at them. Let me print them as they stand. Please think this over, and resign yourself to my hands.

We are here till October when we all scatter like a covey of partridges—Clive to Spain, Angelica to school, Julian to Cambridge, Quentin to Paris, Vanessa to a studio in Fitzroy St—I have a wild desire to rush over to France and furnish my peasants hut—I told you I had three rooms in a wood didnt I, near Cassis?—and live on coffee and maccaroni and sit in the sun and drink quantities of Colonel Teed's cheap white wine; but I suppose I shant Do let us go there together one day—what fun it would be!

The despatch case, the swollen wallet which you said would suit you, is coming—inscribed D.M. 22 Wellington Square—is that right?

No I cant write letters on a typewriter.

Love.　Yours affectionately
Virginia

Mrs Michael MacCarthy

2071: To Molly MacCarthy　　　*Monks House, Rodmell,*
Lewes, Sussex

Typewritten
22nd Sept. [1929]

Dearest Molly,

Please forgive this machine—I have lost the use of my fingers. I will join you in throwing bats at Bob. He worries you; I can bear that; but he wanders off to the Press, suffocates them with boredom (Mrs Cartwright is at the time of life too) and lays not the tiniest egg in the long run. Never mind; we will kill Bob; that's one mercy settled; and drag the bloodstained pages from his coat tails. I will have them; alive or dead.[1]

I am dehumanised by the sun. It is like being in a Cathedral all day long. I wish it would stop and let me get back to my usual way of life. One feels so pure, so good, so high: and that is not really being happy. I should like to read, but then one feels, what a pity to read, in this weather. Finally we are going to Charleston to meet Lytton; who has torn himself from his bevy[2] for a moment. I envy you, talking to Giraffes. Do, if you want an occupation, write letters to me, supposing me to be in Australia. I assure you, this book would be fascinating; probably filmed; your fortune made.

1. The Hogarth Press published no further books by R. C. Trevelyan until *Three Plays* (May 1931).
2. Carrington, Ralph Partridge and Frances Marshall.

If you had ten thousand pounds, what would you do? I am glad Rachel is at the bookshop.[1] I shall order something very difficult at once. A six-and-sevenpence-halfpenny French novel, at $33\frac{1}{3}\%$ discount, allowing for fall of franc.

Please write again.

We shall be back soon—unless we decide to take the veil, as the weather indicates. Oh, Lord! As I was tapping this out, we caught our mongrel *in the act* with the neighbours' bull terrier.

Yes, I am revolving schemes. What is wanted is shabby, decent, pro-longed, varied, easy to come by talk; not dancing. I have an idea.

Yours very sincerely (this is the best one can do on a typewriter)

Virginia Woolf

Mrs Michael MacCarthy

2072: TO EDWARD SACKVILLE WEST   *Monks House [Rodmell, Lewes, Sussex]*

Sept. 23rd 1929

My dear Eddy

I am ashamed not to have answered your letter before—particularly as I liked getting it. Laziness; work, heat, visitors—those are my only excuses. No, I dont put the blame on us, for drifting apart as you call it. Its entirely life's fault—London seemed to me intolerable last summer—nothing but telephone bells and faces in endless succession—and everybody jerking wires and making me jump up like a jack-in-the-box, when I wanted to be ten miles deep under the sea. I've come to doubt whether London is possible —It seems to destroy all sensitiveness of perception—one person might as well be another. You as usual, manage better—but then, let alone your own red lineation (I mean gift for ruling a red line), you have Knole imposed on you, which is a considerable weight.[2]

Yes, I agree that we ought to have done *Brothers and Sisters*. It was annoying—mere slackness, I suppose. But I'd rather have done Eliot's poems and even Katherine Mansfield's Prelude[3]—There's something bleached about Miss Compton Burnett: like hair which has never had any colour in it.

Here I am, regretfully letting the last days slip through my fingers. I

1. The bookshop in Bloomsbury founded by Francis Birrell and David Garnett.
2. Edward Sackville West did not succeed to the Sackville title until the death of his father, the 4th Lord Sackville, in 1962, by which time the Sackville house, Knole in Kent, had become the property of the National Trust.
3. Although the Hogarth Press turned down *Brothers and Sisters* by Ivy Compton-Burnett, they did publish T. S. Eliot's *Poems* (1919) and *The Waste Land* (1923), and Katherine Mansfield's *Prelude* (1918).

suppose one must go back and begin again: "Hullo Sibyl is that you. No I'm afraid I cant come to lunch" etc etc.

I hope you are coming back triumphant and effective and will rule your red lines with the greatest decision over all of us.

I cant go into the history of Bloomsbury—I must go into dinner instead.

Yours ever
Virginia Woolf

Berg

2073: To V. Sackville-West   *Monks House* [*Rodmell, Sussex*]

Thursday [26 September 1929]

No, I didn't mean I was ill—only an ordinary headache, and I'm perfectly all right again.

We are going up to London; but alas, we get back too late to call in on you. And there doesn't seem to be any free time left here—. Theres Tilton[1] and Charleston this weekend, and then the Labour Party at Brighton to which we are going, and then Leonard must go back. So Harold must come and see us in London if he will. I had meant to stay on here and write and write, but the men are fuming to begin building, and so I dont expect I shall stay beyond the 7th or 8th, and then return very grudgingly to Tavistock and answer the telephone as usual. Lyme Regis, I'm told is completely spoilt—anyhow, I couldn't write in an Inn.

I'm reading an Oxford undergraduate ms novel, and his hero says "Do you know these lines from The Land, the finest poem, by far the finest of our living poets——" but for all that, we shan't publish him.

I have only one passion in life—cooking. I have just bought a superb oil stove. I can cook anything. I am free for ever of cooks. I cooked veal cutlets and cake today. I assure you it is better than writing these more than idiotic books.

I shall be alone, anyhow Friday and Saturday next week, if you'd come for the night, but I suppose you cant manage very well, with Harold. £1500 [after tax] is not a great sum, certainly; and damn your mother for making more bother. Well, God knows when we shall meet. You'll be off to Barcelona, and I shall be off to Cassis. (Mrs Bartholomew[2] here interrupted with an account of Colchester . . .) and now I must write [*five lines heavily crossed out by Vita*]

V.

Berg

1. The house near Charleston belonging to Maynard Keynes.
2. Rose Bartholomew, the daily-help at Monk's House.

Monks House, Rodmell,
                                        Lewes [Sussex]

26th Sept. [1929]

Dear Daphne,

What an amazing story![1] I wonder if the rather seedy looking man who came up from the basement and said you were all away one night last summer was one of the servants. He looked a little queer, we thought. I am very sorry about your father's gold watch and the silver—the books dont so much matter, and I am making bold to replace mine by sending you those which have just come out in a small edition.[2] They can be hidden away and take up much less room than the old ones.

It is so nice down here,—but you wouldn't think so—that I want to stay on and on, at least as long as the weather is fine and the water in the well lasts.

But when we come back I hope you will come and tell us all about the servants—I suspect that your mother was trying to reclaim a criminal, and therefore she has only got what she deserved and what one might have expected. Please give both of them (your father and mother not the criminals) my love.

yrs
V.W.

Daphne Sanger

[Monk's House, Rodmell,
                                         Sussex]

[30 September 1929]

No, no, no, I meant Dottie, not H. M. (about going to Barcelona) and the reference was to your late travels[3] and it was only a joke and Potto made it and said hah hah to show it was a joke and only Donkeys bray. Just off to sit for hours at Brighton,[4] Lord.

V.

Berg

1. One of the Sangers' servants had stolen the staff's wages and several articles of value while the Sangers were on holiday. Most of the articles were recovered, but not Virginia's books.
2. On this date the Hogarth Press began issuing the Uniform Edition of Virginia's works.
3. With Hilda Matheson to the Val d'Isère in July.
4. The Labour Party Conference.

2076: To Leonard Woolf   [*Monk's House, Rodmell,*
                                      Sussex]

Friday morning [4 October 1929]

Much relieved to get your card. I have had a very good night. Pinka gave no trouble but has been running round your study whining. Vita wired that she wants to come on Tuesday—so thats off. A letter from Mrs [Beatrice] Webb asking me to dinner. I opened a letter from Powell,[1] enclosed, thinking there might be some news. It looks very fine, so far.

Do you think you would like to change your mind, vast as it is, and come down on Saturday afternoon after all? I find that I can get all my things that I want into the small bag, so I shall go in by bus. I should be here till 12.45 anyhow. So if you think of coming, send me a wire.

If I *dont hear* I shall catch the 12.54 bus. Now that you have got up safely I dont feel so nervous. The petrol lid came this morning. I am sending it, in case you come.

A bag of bulbs has come, addressed to me, from Winchester: I'm giving it to Percy [Bartholomew].

I think thats all—Love from every animal. Come along marmots[2] and do your jublimmails.

Sussex

2077: To Leonard Woolf   Monks [*House, Rodmell,*
                                      Sussex]

Friday evening [4 October 1929]

This has just come by the second post. I've written to Maynard to say that you're in London, but that you will wire *if* you are coming down. I dont see any reason why you should, even if you do come, as it would be much nicer to be alone, and there is no reason to think Desmond is coming, I trust. This is the first I've heard of it.

I'm sending this on the chance it reaches you first post. We've had a very nice peaceful day—dull but fine. Pinka very good and sits with me.

A letter from Sibyl [Colefax]; a letter from Daphne Sanger; a letter from Saxon [Sydney-Turner]—10 pages of gibberish.

I am extremely well, the garden is heavenly, all we want is Mongoose [Leonard].

                                              Lovely Bird
                                              goodbye.

1. Humphrey Powell, agent to Lord Gage's Firle estates.
2. A name Virginia used for herself when writing to Leonard.

I had an awful shock—happily after getting your card. An unknown motorist was burnt to death yesterday afternoon between Chailey and Haywards Heath—you must have passed about the time. This makes me nervous—but I suppose unreasonably.

Sussex

2078: To Gerald Brenan   *Monks House, Rodmell*
                                          [Sussex]

Oct 4th 1929

My dear Gerald,
    I have just taken out your letter and re-read it. Probably you have forgotten that you wrote to me on the 11th July; and it is now the 4th of October. And I am not in a good mood for writing, being dirty—you know how physical states affect one—and lazy—so that I cant get up and wash; and lonely, Leonard is in London. But it is for this last reason that I write, because it is the last night for some months, perhaps, that I shall be lonely. Tomorrow I shall go back to London, and there already awaits me a string of inevitable experiences—what is called "seeing people". You don't know what that means—it means one can't get out of it. It means that Miss Winter has asked us to ask Mr Robinson Jeffers[1] to tea because he is only in London for a week and will then return to a cave in California and write immortal poetry for ever. Mr Jeffers is a genius so one must see him. Then Hugh Walpole is passing through London; Hugh is not a genius, and its precisely because of that sad deficiency, which so many of us share by the way, that he must be 'seen'. It torments him, his lack of genius, when, if only (so he says) the Bishop his father had had an ounce more spunk in him he, Hugh might have been something Titanic. Feel my biceps, he is always saying; and there's something so curious in his state, that again one must say I shall be in on Thursday at 4.
    And then there's that automaton Colefax your friend. Do you remember a curious autumnal tea party, with Logan and Clive and God knows who else, and how she forgot your name, and kept saying 'Mr — I can't remember who you are!' Happily time makes all these past scenes unspeakably beautiful—if one remembered the truth, life would no doubt be unbearable. And theres the Sidney Webbs[2]—they have to be seen. I wont go on. I only

1. John Robinson Jeffers (1887-1962), the American poet, who lived austerely near Carmel, California. The Hogarth Press published his *Roan Stallion, Tamar, and Other Poems* (1928), *Cawdor* (1929) and *Dear Judas and Other Poems* (1930). His friend Ella Winter married the American journalist Lincoln Steffens.
2. Sidney and Beatrice Webb, co-founders of the Fabian Society. In this year Sidney Webb was created Lord Passfield.

want you to realise how little control I have over my life; yours you say (July 11th) is all that it should be.[1] To counteract it I have bought a hut at Cassis, in a vineyard. There I shall imagine that I see Africa and hear nightingales and so attain to something of a prophetic strain, now lacking.

For, Lord, Lord, how much one lacks—how fumbling and inexpert one is—never yet to have learnt the hang of life—to have peeled that particular orange. As I said I am out of the mood for writing, and write because I shall never do it once I am "seeing": this being so, I shake these brief notes onto the page, like—what can I think of—only lice—instead of distilling the few simple and sweet and deep and limpid remarks which one would like to send to Spain in a letter. Suppose one could really communicate, how exciting it would be! Here I have covered one entire blue page and said nothing. One can at most hope to suggest something. Suppose you are in the mood, when this letter comes, and read it in precisely the right light, by your Brazier in your big room, then by some accident there may be roused in you some understanding of what I, sitting over my log fire in Monks House, am, or feel, or think. It all seems infinitely chancy and infinitely humbugging—so many asseverations which are empty, and tricks of speech; and yet this is the art to which we devote our lives. Perhaps that is only true of writers—then one tries to imagine oneself in contact, in sympathy; one tries vainly to put off this interminable—what is the word I want?— something between maze and catacomb—of the flesh. And all one achieves is a grimace. And so one is driven to write books—you see I'm shaking down unripe olives (if you like that better than lice.)

You say you can't finish your book because you have no method, but see points, here and there, with no connecting line.[2] And that is precisely my state at the moment, beginning another book [*The Waves*]; What do all the books I have written avail me? Nothing. Is it the curse of our age or what? The will o' the wisp moves on, and I see the lights (when I lie in bed at night, or sit over the fire) as bright as stars, and cant reach them. I daresay its the continuity of daily life, something believable and habitual that we lack. I give it up. Not writing books I mean; only understanding my own psychology as a writer. I thought I had anyhow learnt to write quickly: now its a hundred words in a morning, and scratchy and in [hand-]writing, like a child of ten. And one never knows after all these years how to end, how to go on: one never sees more than a page ahead; why then does one

1. Brenan was still living in Yegen, deep in the Sierra Nevada mountains, near Granada in southern Spain.
2. Brenan had written to Virginia (11 July 1929, *Sussex*): "Every few days something collects inside me and I write a page or two of my novel. It is nearly finished but there remain some difficult passages which I owe to my incapacity for thinking out a suitable plot." His novel, *A Holiday by the Sea*, was not published until 1961.

make any pretensions to be a writer? Why not pin together one's scattered sheets—I daresay one would be wise to.

I heard from Saxon yesterday from Madrid, where, as far as I can see, all Bloomsbury is now conglomerated,—Barbara [Bagenal], Ralph [Partridge], Frances [Marshall] and Mrs Sickert.[1] And Saxon goes on looking out trains and finding some hotels better than others, and this is the only fetching thing—being shown over the W.C's of a large hotel in building at Ciudad Rodrigo. I think it was late at night too, when the electric light was flashing in the W.C. basin, and an old man, on the scaffolding kept laughing. Saxon could not think what at.

I have just sent a postcard to the Times Book Club asking for God by Middleton Murry.[2] I would here launch into a dissertation upon literature, but I dare not begin another page when I am not only without the illusion that I am speaking the truth, but my pen has run out of ink.

However, you are not missing much. And if it should occur to you one night to attempt this curious effort at communicating what Gerald Brenan thinks on his mountain top, then I will first read it through very quickly, at breakfast, and come upon it a little later, and read it again and try to amplify your hieroglyphs—It is an interesting question—what one tries to do, in writing a letter—partly of course to give back a reflection of the other person. Writing to Lytton or Leonard I am quite different from writing to you. And now my log, shaped like an elephants foot, has fallen over, and I must pick up the tongs—goodnight.

V.W.

George Lazarus

1. Thérèse Lessore, the painter, Walter Sickert's third wife, whom he had married in 1926.
2. John Middleton Murry had written several books on religion, the latest of which was *God* (1929).

Letters 2079-2119 (October–December 1929)

The autumn was spent in London, with occasional weekend visits to Monk's House, where the new rooms were finished by the end of the year. The main excitement was the publication on 24 October of A Room of One's Own, *which was almost universally acclaimed and sold excellently. Virginia was now writing* The Waves, *slowly. "After a morning of grunting and groaning", she wrote to David Garnett, "I have 200 words to show; and those as crazy as broken china." She was distracted by social obligations, the demands of the Hogarth Press, and the noise of a dance-band in a neighbouring hotel, against which the Woolfs took legal action.*

2079: To HELEN McAFEE   52 *Tavistock Square, W.C.*1

Typewritten
4th Oct. 1929

Dear Miss McAfee,

Thank you so much for your cable. I had meant to write to you before, but I have been very busy. I am hoping not to write any articles for a little time, but to write fiction instead. But I shall probably write some more critical or biographical studies after Christmas,—I have not yet thought of them in any detail. Of course it would make a great difference if as you suggest The Yale Review were able to increase the fee to 200 dollars, but, if I may be frank, I find that I can dispose of my longer articles for a good deal more than that; and as I write journalism in order to earn a living, I have to accept the best offer. Would the fee you mention be paid for an article of say 3,000 words? There is also the difficulty that the Yale Review is a quarterly,— it means that the English editors are held up for so long. If at your leisure you would let me know what are the dates on which you have to have manuscript, it would be easier for me to make arrangements. I should like to write for you if I can possibly manage it. Please accept my best thanks for suggesting it so kindly.

Yours sincerely
Virginia Woolf

Yale University

Typewritten
8th Oct. 1929

Dear Mr Lewis,

I have to acknowledge with thanks the receipt of your cheque for £25. 13.4 as first payment on the 250 dollars due for the right to reprint my essay Street Haunting.[1]

I note that you are sending the sheets for my signature in due course, and I will sign and return as quickly as possible.

With best wishes
Yours sincerely
V. Woolf
(Mrs Woolf)

Columbia University

Friday [11 October 1929]

If Miss Bosqui [Bosquet] liked to answer these letters, just come, I would give her my copy of the London Mercury Book—gladly. and a million thanks.

If she wrote very kindly and said (to the Lady) that Knole was intended [in *Orlando*]—and the climate changes in sympathy with the age—and gave her my kind regards—And then to the boy of 16, perhaps she could say that 'Elizabethan' is probably inaccurate; but intentional; and that the grammar is colloquial: and give him my kind regards—Oh Lord! I cannot write any more letters about Orlando or anything else—so if she could—but dont let her bother—I daresay she has enough to do—

You will come on Thursday afternoon wont you? and then after dinner.[2]

Nelly [Boxall], being told it was Mr and Mrs Nicolson, insisted upon giving up her day and her love and her play and all. Such is the radiance and glamour.

Is this a dry letter?

V.

Berg

1. See Letter 2060.
2. On 17 October Harold Nicolson and F. L. Lucas dined with Virginia, and Vita came in afterwards.

Typewritten
21st Oct 1929

Dear Mr Brace,

Many thanks for your letter. I shall be very much interested to see your edition of my little book [*A Room of One's Own*]. I hope it will go well—I am sure it will not be your fault if it doesn't.

It is very good of you to have troubled about the serialisation. But I am sure that it was not possible, given the difficulty of separating the chapters, and the short time before publication.

I am sending a photograph [by Lenare] that was taken a few months ago. It is considerably later than the one you have, and we are using it over here.

> With kind regards,
> yours sincerely,
> Virginia Woolf

Harcourt Brace Jovanovich

2083: To V. Sackville-West
> [*The Hogarth Press, Bloomsbury, W.C.1*]

[22 October 1929]

There! if you want coronets, you can have them. [see Fig. 2b]

Yes I would very much like to see you on Wednesday, but I cant manage a matinée—for one thing I always snore; then we're very brisk at the Press, and my services are in demand—how I like it! doing up parcels, please remember open ends, Mrs Woolf, with bagmen coming in and out and saying Well good bye all when they leave; and we all say good bye. And then I'm given a cup of pale lemon tea, and asked to choose what biscuit I like; and we all sit on the edge of stools and crack jokes.

But couldn't you come to tea? Please do. or anytime. I shall be in.

Yes, I'm delighted you read my little book [*A Room of One's Own*], as you call it, dear Mrs Nick: but although you dont perceive it, there is much reflection and some erudition in it: the butterfly begins by being a loathsome legless grub. Or dont you find it convincing?

King's D[aughter]. is selling well; as I know, doing them up by sixes and 12's for the youth of Oxford and Cambridge.

Peter Lucas writes that he 'fell to Vita'—and what did you do?

Such a rush, but shall see you tomorrow

> V.

Berg

2084: To V. Sackville-West   [52 *Tavistock Square, W.C.*1]

Sunday [27 October 1929]

Please attend—

Leonard says he's going to dine out on Thursday. Could we dine somewhere after your [broad]casting, and either sit and drink or go to a play?

Let me know, would you, like an angel, and dont read into these brief words any adders tails or viper's gall. They are plain sense. I've been walking in Epping Forest. I think evening is more translucent and vibrating, or whatever the word is than afternoon—But dont hesitate to choose what you want.

V.

Berg

2085: To Ethel Sands   52 *Tavistock Sqre* [*W.C.*1]

Monday [28 October 1929]

Dearest Ethel,

What a pleasure to hear your voice! Nessa and Duncan assured me last night that you were in the highlands, Nan [Hudson] in the South of France, and I felt as if the nightingale had broken its promise. Yes, you must come to tea—Friday week, 8th. 4.30. Would that do? I'll try to get Nessa—She has just settled into a vast studio—the same door as the old one—I forget if its 6 or 8 Fitzroy Street. Next door, in the house which is vast, to Duncan, all very comfortable.

But my 'book' isn't a book [*A Room of One's Own*]—its only talks to girls, lectures I gave last autumn, and not for the adult and exquisite like Ethel—Excuse my illiteracy—I cant form words.

Yrs
Virginia

Wendy Baron

2086: To V. Sackville-West   [52 *Tavistock Square, W.C.*1]

Monday [28 October 1929]

Friday suits perfectly (only say what time—3.30 in Studio, unless I hear to the contrary). Providentially I had just put off Sibyl.

Lord! what a curmudgeon you must think me!—You write as if you were a dog that had been hunting. But you're not a bad dog. You're a good dog; you needn't go under the table. How could you not be with Harold?[1]

1. Harold Nicolson had been on leave since 6 September, and returned to Berlin for the last time on 31 October.

I shall be alone here, I think, on Thursday night, but I suppose you have to go back after seeing Harold off.

I hope you get your rooms.[1] I want to be given lobster and crumpets there, as Clive used to give them, 20 years ago.

V.

in hurry, but love somebody all the same.

Nigel Nicolson (copy)

2087: TO EDWARD MARSH   52 *Tavistock Square, W.C.*1

Typewritten
28th Oct 1929

Dear Mr Marsh,

Of course I shall be delighted to help your young Frenchman if I can. (Oddly enough, another, whether delightful or not I dont know, has just written to ask me the same question.)[2] T. S. Eliot wrote something in the Nouvelle Revue Francaise under the heading of Le Roman Anglais Contemporain, about three years ago, but I'm not sure of the exact date [May 1927]. E. M. Forster wrote an article in the Criterion, either at the end of 1925 or beginning if 1926 I think [April 1926]; Clive Bell wrote an article in the Dial I suppose five years ago [December 1924]; and M. Maurois wrote an introduction to the French Translation of Mrs Dalloway which came out last spring. There is also an article by Edwin Muir published in Transition, (Hogarth Press).[3] This I think writes at some length of Mrs Dalloway. I hope some of these may be helpful; but as far as I remember they are not in agreement.

I'm so glad you liked my papers in the Nation.[4] One of these days we want to approach you about a book for the Hogarth Press—would there be any chance of one? on any subject?[5]

Yours very sincerely
Virginia Woolf

Berg

1. Vita was negotiating for the lease of 4 King's Bench Walk, Inner Temple, as a flat for Harold when he returned permanently to London.
2. One of the two was probably Floris Delattre, who published *Le Roman Psychologique de Virginia Woolf* in 1932.
3. *Transition: Essays on Contemporary Literature* was published by the Hogarth Press in 1926.
4. See p. 78, note 1.
5. Edward Marsh never published a book with the Hogarth Press.

2088: To V. Sackville-West   [52 *Tavistock Square, W.C.1*]

Tuesday [29 October 1929]

Here are some remarks upon Orlando and Viola[1] that may amuse you—but will you bring them back, as I must answer the donkeys—nice good donkeys.

I have got into a muddle; (only having to buy a dress) and shan't be in till 4 on Friday: so, will you come and wait in the Studio if I'm out (I'll try to be earlier).

V.

Berg

2089: To Hugh Walpole   [52 *Tavistock Square, W.C.1*]

Thursday [31 October 1929]

My dear Hugh,

It is very nice that you are back. Could you come to tea on Friday 8th at 4.30? If you can, dont bother to write.

Yes, my book [*A Room . . .*], but I dont count it a 'book' is doing nicely—the expensive edition already sold out.

I'm furnishing my French [Cassis] house, but haven't yet been there. I'm told it is a paradise on Earth.

Yr aff
V.W.

Texas

2090: To V. Sackville-West   52 *T.[avistock] S.[quare, W.C.1]*

Sunday [3 November 1929]

Just come back from Rodmell.

Yes, I shall by good luck be alone for dinner on Thursday. Please let us dine somewhere and do something, or nothing. May I write later about the afternoon? I cant be sure if I can be here till late; but I'll try.

I thought your voice, saying Virginia Woolf, was a trumpet call, moving me to tears; but I daresay you were suppressing laughter.[2] Its an odd feeling, hearing oneself praised to 50 million old ladies in Surbiton by one with

1. Presumably a letter which Virginia had received, comparing Orlando with Viola in *Twelfth Night*.
2. On 31 October, in her bi-monthly BBC broadcast on new books, Vita talked about *A Room of One's Own* and Italo Svevo's *The Hoax*, also published by the Hogarth Press. Vita said about Virginia: "She enjoys the feminine qualities of, let us say, fantasy and irresponsibility, allied to all the masculine qualities that go with a strong, authoritative brain" (*The Listener*, 6 November 1929).

whom one has watched the dawn and heard the nightingale. I am at the moment groping to express these different levels of emotion—no, I'm too stupid after motoring even to get one word right. Isn't it surprising—your praise at once sells 100 of my book—not a copy of Svevo. Also, until this autumn, nothing the B.B.C. could say made an ounce of difference. So you will have me at your skirts for ever. Is your cold better? Are you fond of me?

Virginia [*squiggly design*]

Berg

2091: To Clive Bell   52 *Tavistock Square W.C.*[1]

Sunday 3rd Nov [1929]

Dearest Clive,

This is not a letter but merely a request that you should transact for me two, I fear, troublesome pieces of business.

(1) Could you place this cheque ($£5$) with your bookseller to my account and say that I shall write and order books from time to time?

(2) Could you subscribe to Les Nouvelles Litteraires for me (cheque also enclosed). Quentin promised, but Quentin is faithless, and as I have been on the verge of writing a letter to them for 2 years I must seize the chance.

Nessa says you are coming back soon [from Paris]; and I may tell you, as perhaps the truest compliment that you have ever received, that I wrote, spontaneous, not for publication, in my diary the other night [11 October] "I miss Clive"—But there is no reason to think that Clive misses Virginia. Anyhow, I will keep whatever news there may be for a possible hour between tea and dinner.

And please accept my thanks.

Virginia

Quentin Bell

2092: To Harcourt, Brace   52 *Tavistock Square, W.C.*1

Typewritten
3rd Nov 1929

Dear Madam [Margaret Cuff],

I have to acknowledge with thanks the receipt of your cheque for 475 dollars in payment of advance upon A ROOM OF ONE'S OWN.

I should be obliged if you would tell Mr Brace how much I like the appearance of the book.

Yours very truly,
Virginia Woolf
(Mrs Woolf)

Harcourt Brace Jovanovich

Tuesday [5 November 1929]

Dearest Creature,

Look here: attend:

I've got to see my mother in law Thursday, but shall be back by 6.30. Will you come then, and then we'll dine somewhere under red lights with foaming glasses, unless you'd prefer dinner with Nessa: She wants us anyhow to go in afterwards. Some crones are coming. But just as you like.

6.30 anyhow here.

Love from Potto-V.

Berg

Typewritten
Nov. 6th [1929]

Dear Goldie,[1]

It was very good of you to write. I cant tell you how pleased I am that you like my little book [*A Room . . .*]—seeing that I nourish a deep if inarticulate respect and affection for you. I'm so glad you thought it good tempered—my blood is apt to boil on this one subject as yours does about natives, or war; and I didnt want it to. I wanted to encourage the young women—they seem to get fearfully depressed—and also to induce discussion. There are numbers of things that might be said, and that arent said. The double soul[2] is one of them; and also education—I dont believe, though I'm a complete outsider, that its right for either sex as it is. But I'm certainly outstaying my welcome here. I was among your listeners the other night[3] and would have liked (this hardly ever happens to me—I mean with lectures in general) that you had gone on. And I laughed aloud.

Yours sincerely
Virginia Woolf

Sussex

1. Goldsworthy Lowes Dickinson, a Fellow of King's College, Cambridge, where he had lectured on Political Science.
2. One of the main themes in *A Room of One's Own* is that there are male and female parts of the mind and that they must unite before an artist can become fully creative.
3. On 4 November Dickinson broadcast a talk called *Points of View—A Summing Up.*

2095: To Theodora Bosanquet   52 *Tavistock Square, W.C.*1

Nov 7th [1929]

Dear Miss Bosanquet,[1]

One would need to be a very queer author not to be delighted by so kind a letter as yours. I am particularly glad that my little book [*A Room . . .*] should interest intelligent readers; I wanted to be readable and good tempered for the sake of the young women, and was afraid that my serious intention had suffered in the process. So it is very encouraging to find that you were interested.

Many thanks for your letter.

Yours sincerely
Virginia Woolf

Houghton Library, Harvard University

2096: To V. Sackville-West   [52 *Tavistock Square, W.C.*1]

Friday [8 November 1929]

I forgot to say that Faith Henderson, wife of the Editor of The Nation rang up to ask if I thought she might ring you up to ask some question about a school. I said I thought you wouldn't mind—so if she does, don't curse her but

V.

Berg

2097: To V. Sackville-West   [52 *Tavistock Square, W.C.*1]

Wednesday [13 November 1929]

Dearest Creature,

I am really awfully bothered about you, though George[2] was reassuring on the telephone that evening. Thank Goodness, you've got into a room with a fire—I dont mind if its a room with a double bed and someone else in it, as long as you are warm. Mercy! to think of you with a cold, a temperature of 102 in your primeval barn. But may I observe that even if it isn't pneumonia and isn't influenza, and isn't rhematic [*sic*] fever, appendicitis and jaundice, still it is *absolutely* necessary to spend the next week in a room with a fire; without roystering along passages, or into gardens. The telephone

1. Theodora Bosanquet was Henry James's secretary in his last years. She published an account of him in *Henry James at Work* (Hogarth Press, 1924).
2. George Thompsett, the butler at Long Barn.

can wait. All I ask is as many brief but veracious cards as possible: stating
temperature; whether in bed; when getting up. Now remember how lavish
I was of every detail, of my shiver and shake, for 3 weeks last winter; and
dont deny that you were on the whole, though bored, glad of it. Any small
fact will please me; and then I needn't bother George, whose telephone style
though warm is inexpressive. "Mrs Nicolsons love. She says no need for
worry with her love is sitting over fire". (I hope you were lying in bed.)

I was late ringing up, because Julian [Bell] was here. We discussed poetry.
And I said who in your opinion are the best living poets? He replied at once
Vita and [Edmund] Blunden. Well thats what I call a genuine rouser—what
I'd give my eyes for—the enthusiasm and generosity of youth; and Julian is
a most taking boy, and said to be the best of his time at Kings. And thats
what he says with a beautiful modest but glowing voice (having some
sentiment about you personally) of Vita—Also he much admires Kings
Daughter; and said when I told him Harolds view—What does Harold know
about poetry?[1]

Yesterday I was in mischief—in the arms of Osbert [Sitwell], and very
fat they are too; on the carpet of Mrs Courtauld,[2] and that is as thick and
resilient as Osberts arms. Lord! what a party? I flirted and I flirted—with
Christabel [McLaren], with Mary [Hutchinson], with Ottoline [Morrell];
but this last was a long and cadaverous embrace which almost drew me under.
Figure us, entwined beneath Cezannes which she had the audacity to praise
all the time we were indulging in those labyrinthine antics which is called
being intimate with Ottoline; I succumb: I lie; I flatter; I accept flattery;
I stretch and sleek, and all the time she is watchful and vengeful and
mendacious and unhappy and ready to break every rib in my body if it
were worth her while. In truth, she's a nice woman, eaten with amorosity
and vanity, an old volcanoe, all grey cinders and scarcely a green plant,
let alone a shank left. And this is human intercourse, this is human friendship
so I kept saying to myself while I flattered and fawned.

But I wouldn't have gone at all had I known you were ill. Its painful
how entwined I am with your aches and pains: and as I am honestly and
truly incapable of standing strain—really I cant—so for Gods sake be
careful; dont catch cold; do completely cure this one; dont give me another
panic; I assure you I shall be ill if you do. And you wouldn't like *me* to be
ill.

I hope, oh I hope, you are now comfortable and quiet and warm and
loving your

Potto and V.

Berg

1. See p. 85, note 3.
2. Elizabeth, who had married the industrialist Samuel Courtauld. Her house at
20 Portman Square was a centre of cultural life in London.

Friday [15 November 1929]

Dearest,

I'm so glad you're better—very glad.

I had an odd episode with Dotty about it—but I've no time to tell you.

Yes I'm dining with Sibyl [Colefax] on Monday, but I dont think its worth coming for that, as it wd. only tantalise, and Tuesday is an awful rush. Later in the week wd. be better; and there's not much sense anyhow in rushing up in this weather. Lord how vile!

And I must rush out to dinner.

Three 'rushes' in 6 lines—so rushed am I—people arriving—missing my bus—reading the ms of that d—d lecture wh. I've got to finish tomorrow (Maurons)[1]

I rather doubt that we shall go to Rodmell—too grim.

V.

Berg

Tuesday [19 November 1929]

What a bore you cant come! I'm so sorry about the sinus—I dont know whether its the same thing as an antrum—I hope not—anyhow I know theyre damnably painful. But it would be madness to come—The weather is unspeakable—a pane on my roof has been blown out. Everyone seems to be ill. Going to the garage yesterday the man said to me, "I've been ill for a fortnight; my wife has been ill for a fortnight; our little boy died of double pneumonia last night; and *the dog has distemper*." This he repeated three times, always winding up solemnly and *the dog has distemper* as if it were the most important of the lot. But there was the child dead in the cottage.

No, I never saw your message about the book, so I'm sending you my grand edition[2]—but dont *give* it away; exact at least £5—it is sold out, and therefore daily growing in value. The novel of the 90ties[3] sounds fascinating beyond description—Leonard says he would like to discuss the size with you later. But God knows when we shall meet. Dottie has asked us to come to Penns on Sunday, but I don't much expect that we shall. By the way,

1. Virginia took the chair at Charles Mauron's lecture.
2. The limited edition of *A Room of One's Own*.
3. Vita's novel *The Edwardians*, which she had begun to write in June and which the Hogarth Press published in May 1930.

that woman, your friend Dottie, gave me the fright of my life about you and I've not got over it yet (but dont say anything to her). She sounds, from Sibyls account, in a highly agitated state. We discussed it last night—Lord Berners[1] suggested that she should be "lunged" like a horse round her socks; I said he must be the ostler; I would crack a whip. Sibyls parties are improving—I rather enjoyed it—and flirted outrageously with Mary and Mary's Barbara.[2]

Lord! I've got so many things to tell you—but the most interesting is secret. All I can say is that I expect my life to change completely about Jan 1st[3]—Events seem to succeed each other as they say in the papers with bewildering variety. I shall be glad when my broadcasting[4] and my speaking at Mauron's lecture are both over. And, your Hilda—my God what friends you have!—has not proved exactly helpful—but there—I daren't say more for fear Hilda should be persuading you to take your medicine. If I had Hilda, I should not want medicine; but then of course you will say I am jealous. No. Its only that our taste differs. She affects me as a strong purge, as a hair shirt, as a foggy day, as a cold in the head—which last indeed I believe I am now developing (but its sure to be nerves) so if you listen in, you'll probably hear sneeze, cough, choke. But as, what with Hilda and the B.B.C, my poor little article has been completely ruined (but dont whisper a word of this) I'm not altogether looking forward to 9.20 tomorrow night. Also I am billed at 9.15—Oh dear oh dear what a tumult of things one does one doesnt want to do! At the moment, though I'm triumphant; I have put off Eddy [Sackville West] I have put off Mr and Mrs Bagenal [Nick and Barbara]. I have put off Professor Hornell,[5] on the ground of a previous engagement and am slipping round to tea with Nessa.

I've just read your letter again and I see you say that you may be coming up at the end of the week. If so, I'm having a morning off on Friday, and we might lunch somewhere. But I think soberly, not in the manner of Dottie, it would be madness to come.

V.

Berg

1. Gerald Berners was an amateur musician and artist of great talent, and wrote several novels and books of autobiography.
2. Barbara Hutchinson was then 18 years old.
3. Virginia was intending to free more of her time for writing by replacing Nelly Boxall with Annie Thompsett, a daily, and staying longer at Monk's House, where her new rooms would soon be completed. The 'secret' was that Leonard was planning to resign the Literary Editorship of the *Nation*.
4. On 20 November Virginia broadcast a talk on Beau Brummell for Hilda Matheson, who was Talks Director at the BBC.
5. Possibly William Hornell, who had been Professor of English at Calcutta, and was Vice Chancellor of the University of Hong Kong from 1924 to 1937.

52 *T.S.* [*W.C.*1]

Sunday [24 November 1929]

My dear Tom,

I was in the devil of a temper, if that is what you mean (by my terrifying worse than Dr [John] Donne). At the last moment the BBC condemned Dorothy Wordsworth and made me castrate Brummell—never again. But perhaps you refer to my treatment of B.B. Was I very harsh? These horrid little articles cramp one so the features always become rigid—too this, or too that.

I suppose you won't come in—and Vivien [Mrs Eliot] if she would—next Friday night, any time after 9 p.m. My Cambridge nephew [Julian Bell] is coming; and you know his opinion of T.S.E. I keep his respect by asserting that I'm by way of seeing you. And the truth is I never do.

My love to Vivien.

yr aff

Mrs T. S. Eliot   V.W.

Monk's House [*Rodmell, Sussex*]

Sunday [24 November 1929]

My dear Dadie,

Just a line to say how much I enjoyed your poem in The Nation.[1] I thought it really came off—and was lovely.

No answer needed.

Your

George Rylands   Virginia

52 *Tavistock Sqre* [*W.C.*1]

[26? November 1929]

It strikes me it would be much nicer if you would lunch here on Thursday, at 1. And then we could sit a little, and then go to Harold's rooms[2] or whatever you want.

Here is a letter which concerns you. Who is Angela [*unidentified*]?

Yr

Berg   V

1. Rylands's untitled poem, in which he implores Spring to return to the city, was published in the *Nation* of 23 November 1929.
2. 4 King's Bench Walk, Inner Temple, London, which the Nicolsons had now leased. Vita was re-decorating and furnishing the flat.

2103: To C. P. Sanger   52 *Tavistock Sqre* [*W.C.1*]

Wednesday [27 November 1929]

My dear Charlie,

 We were so distressed to hear from Roger [Fry] of your illness[1] that I cant help writing to send you Leonards and my best love. We think of you with such affection—I know you never believe me when I say it—and it is horrible to think that you are ill. Perhaps when you are better you will let me come and see you: That will be a great pleasure to look forward to. But now you must do nothing but get better. All your friends are thinking of you and wishing they could do anything to show their affection for you— It would really rather please you I think to hear the sort of thing that we are all saying.

 But now I shall stop, and only send our love dear Charlie,

             Your affectionate

Daphne Sanger   Virginia

2104: To Daphne Sanger   52 *Tavistock Sqre, W.C.1*

[27 November 1929]

My dear Daphne,

 I am so distressed to hear of your father's illness. It was only last night that Roger Fry told me. I dont want to be a bother—but if you could send me a line on a card to say how he is I should be immensely grateful. And please if there were anything I could do, will you let me know? We both send our love to you and your mother.

             Your affate

Daphne Sanger   Virginia Woolf

2105: To David Garnett   52 *Tavistock Sqre.* [*W.C.1*]

[28 November 1929]

Dear Bunny,

 Do you remember that we said we were coming to lunch on Saturday? It now proves to be impossible; what with one thing and another; but would it suit you and Ray [Rachel Garnett] if we aimed at lunch on Saturday 14th December? It would be a great pleasure to see you all.

             Your affate

Berg   Virginia

---

1. Charles Sanger (b. 1871), the barrister and an authority on Wills, died on 9 February 1930.

[early December 1929]

My dear Hugh,

No alas, the 6th wont do because I'm going away. What about your coming to tea on Friday 13th? That seems the most feasible. Anyhow I will keep that, and will try to be alone. But why "for ever"? I'd rather jump off Waterloo Bridge than spend 50 years (which is your prospect of life I daresay) in the USA.[1]

Friday, 13th, 4.30

Virginia

Texas

2107: TO V. SACKVILLE-WEST   [52 *Tavistock Square, W.C.*1]

Tuesday [3 December 1929]

This is just to say, dearest Mrs Nick, we do hope you weren't fearfully bothered going up to Knole today.[2] Potto thought of you. So did I too—a great storm came on, at about the very moment, on Southampton Row, orange and vermilion, and I thought Knole must have looked very tremendous.

No news—only my affection; and shall see you Monday lunch.

Oh by the way, was I very beastly to you, both the last times, about your friends and so on—From something Nessa said about something you said at Penns I think I must have rammed it in too devilish hard—it is my way when roused; but I'm only so roused once in a blue moon, and only then by the dearly loved and iniquitous. But if I was brutal, then do forgive and excuse. Please Vita, do forgive.

Potto and Virginia

How is the Sinus?

Berg

1. Walpole sailed for the United States on Christmas Eve to give a series of lectures, and returned in March 1930.
2. On 3 December Diana Sackville-West, Vita's first cousin, married Lord Romilly in the chapel at Knole. Vita did not attend the wedding. Between her father's death in 1928 and 1961 Vita never visited Knole, her childhood home, because she felt so passionately the injustice that she, as a daughter, could not inherit it.

Postcard
[4 December 1929]

Will you dine here next Wednesday, 11th at 7.45—Lytton Strachey is
coming.

                                              Virginia Woolf

Texas

2109: To C. P. Sanger   52 *Tavistock Sqre, W.C.1*

Thursday 5th Dec. [1929]

My dear Charlie,
    Your letter is the best news we have had for a long time. Of course you
must do exactly as the doctors say, and see no-one, otherwise you would
have us all round you. We were at Rodmell until today, but remembering
your opinion of English country I wont describe it. But we have built on
two dry rooms, where we shall hope to see you.
    Nessa and Julian were made very happy by the good news of you last
night—We dined at Charleston, in a gale of wind. Julian is evidently
inheriting our attachment to Mr Sanger and is such a nice young man that
I envy you his esteem.
    It is very very nice to think of you at least out of bed sometimes and we
both send our best love.

                                              Your affate
                                              Virginia

Daphne Sanger

2110: To V. Sackville-West   [52 *Tavistock Square, W.C.1*]

Friday [6 December 1929]

    Lunch here, Monday one.
    An intolerable bore—we're engaged in a lawsuit with the hotel and waste
all our time with lawyers, but I don't think it comes on till Friday.[1]
    So hope for Monday afternoon free, for anything:

                                              V.

Berg

1. Dance music from a new hotel in Woburn Place so disturbed the Woolfs that
   they took legal action to stop it.

52 *Tavistock Square, W.C.1*

Saturday [7 December 1929]

My dear Hugh,

A catastrophe has happened. We are in for a lawsuit with the Imperial Hotel, which is driving us crazy with a Jazz band; and I'm suddenly told that the case will be tried on Friday next. That is the day you were coming to tea. Whats to be done? I dont imagine that I shall get away till late. Is any other time or day possible for you? Let me know, and I'll try to arrange. This is a perfect curse, and has wasted all my time—and I'm particularly angry that the devils, having made my evenings intolerable, should now destroy my last sight of you [before he went to America].

                                                            Your
                                                              Virginia

Texas

                                    [52 *Tavistock Square, W.C.1*]
[December 1929]

Dearest Ottoline,

I've no doubt (from his book) that Lord D'Abernon[1] is charming; but I'd rather be in a humbler state with you. Would Monday 16th 5.30 do? All my life is now upset by a lawsuit against a Jazz band in an hotel, and I may have to put you off and visit the eternal lawyers: but if not, and if I don't hear, will come then.

                                                    Yr   Virginia

Texas

[52 *Tavistock Square, W.C.1*]

[9? December 1929]

Please may I engage the big tray with the figure	£5.5
The red tray	£2.2
And the small round purple tray (which Leonard wants to buy)	£1.5

Whom do we pay?
When can we have?

---

1. He was British Ambassador in Berlin 1920-6, and led several government delegations to international conferences, of which the most important was Locarno (1925). The first volume of his autobiography, *An Ambassador of Peace*, was published in 1929.

Theres no need for you to come on Wednesday to Islington[1] unless you like—as you could see the chairs anytime—only I think I must go then. I'll wait till you ring up on Wed. morning perhaps

V.

Berg

2114: To V. Sackville-West   [52 *Tavistock Square, W.C.1*]

[10 December 1929]

I dont think it will be worth your while to come tomorrow, because I'm going to Islington buying furniture with Nessa, and shant be back I suppose till six anyhow.—if then: Thursday I've got to go down to Rodmell, but shall be back by 5 I think—only does that leave time? If so, I shall be here and happy if you could come. Friday is the Lawcourts all day. And my mother in laws hotel [in Worthing] was struck by lightning but she escaped. Such is life.

Well I may see you Thursday evening perhaps—in haste

V.

The Cooling Show[2] is open after all in Bond Street.

Berg

2115: To David Garnett   52 *Tavistock Sqre.* [*W.C.1*]

10th Dec. [1929]

My dear Bunny,

I dont see any chance of coming now till after Christmas. We are engaged in a lawsuit. It is against the Imperial Hotel and their infernal band—so may be a nuisance, and begins on Friday.

But (to return to your letter) d'you mean to say your silken phrases are dug for and sweated out? I thought you dipped your brush and drew your stroke. And as for me, I write everything except Orlando 4 times over, and should write it 6 times; and after a morning of grunting and groaning have 200 words to show: and those as crazy as broken china.

These are sober facts; and then we, who live in the same age, and sometimes meet in the flesh, have these mistaken ideas about each other: What then is the worth of criticism?

1. See next letter.
2. The London Artists Association exhibition of watercolours and Christmas decorations at the Cooling Galleries.

I didn't like Hemingway. I dont much care for Graves[1]—
But here I must stop, hoping we shall meet this new year.

Yours
Virginia

Berg

2116: To V. Sackville-West   52 *T.[avistock] S.[quare, W.C.1]*

Sunday [15 December 1929]

Sorry to have been so long answering—rather whirled about. Yes, we shall be delighted to dine on Thursday before Keynes,[2] if invitation is still open. But if for any reason its difficult, lets dine at some pot-house and celebrate your scallawag baptism[3] in audit ale and Cheshire cheese.

Very nice to see Mrs Nick again.

Love from Pot.
Yr
V.

What time dinner?

Perhaps I shall see you first.

Berg

2117: To Helen McAfee   52 *Tavistock Square, W.C.1*

Typewritten
16th Dec. 1929

Dear Miss McAfee,

I am so sorry to have delayed so long in answering your letter. I should like very much to send you something for your summer number; but I dont feel that I can at the moment deal with the subject that you suggest— How should one know a person? It is of course, very interesting; but I cant see it as an article at the moment. I will bear it in mind if I may.

I have been making various arrangements over here for articles, and perhaps one of them might suit you. I am vaguely thinking of some studies of Elizabethan characters and also of short stories. I dont like to bind myself,

1. In 1929 Ernest Hemingway published *A Farewell to Arms*, and Robert Graves *Goodbye to All That*.
2. A large evening party given by Maynard Keynes, at which his wife Lydia gave a dramatic performance.
3. Harold left Berlin (and diplomacy) on 19 December, and a new way of life began for the Nicolsons.

as I find it far best to write as the mood comes. Would it suit you if I promised to send something—either literary article, essay, or short story—for your summer number?[1] I shall of course quite understand if you cant allow me so much latitude. I will at any rate put aside something to send you, and I note that you would have to have it by May 10th.

Many thanks for sending the Yale Review. I was much interested by Miss Sackville Wests article.[2]

With kind regards

yours very sincerely

Yale University   Virginia Woolf

2118: To Vanessa Bell   *Monks House [Rodmell, Sussex]*

Monday 30th Dec 29

Dearest Dolphin;

What should we find at the gate, coming back to tea on Saturday in the rain, but a seedy grey Rolls-Royce; with the detestable Edgar [chauffeur], and the Keynes'. I dont see that ones friends have any right to mutilate one's life in this way. There I was forced to rake the cinders of Bloomsbury gossip with Lydia—it was an insult—a murderous act and one has no remedy. They had a bag of crumpets, which Maynard steeped in butter and made Lydia toast. Its this kind of tallow grease grossness in him that one dislikes. But of course I admit they were amiable in the extreme. But then, curse them, we have to lunch at Tilton tomorrow. Leonard and I argued for an hour this morning—he says we are snobs and exaggerate; he says (but this is confidential) Clive in his present state is worse: and so on. However I must stick to facts.

(1) Could we come to tea on Saturday? because we are going up on Sunday morning. If this is impossible, perhaps we could come in on Sunday early and go on—but there will be rush and confusion and chaos—Let me know.
(2) Dont bring the trays. I will keep them in London now till I come down again. Could you put them where I can get them?
(3) We shall be delighted for you to have a Pither.[3] No doubt Philcox [builder] could take it off and dispatch it.*
(4) Here, at last, is the cheque for the chair. Please go and buy it *at once*.

* Let me know, as he is coming here, and I could give instructions.

1. Review of *The Collected Essays and Addresses of Augustine Birrell* (*Yale Review* June 1930).
2. In the September 1929 issue of the *Yale Review* Vita published *Thirty Clocks Strike the Hour*, which is not an article, but a short story.
3. A cast iron stove, its chimney fixed in the fireplace.

As I said, Maples seems to me as adequate, for the secondhand, as my Islington shop at the moment.

(5) Yes: we will keep the 18th against every temptation—afternoon, I suppose.

(6) Do let me see the letters.[1] I think Julian would be the right person to say if they are interesting impersonally. Perhaps one might add others—to Leonard (he has some long ones) and to Lytton. I dont think I had better write anything, if we should print them, because they seemed to me, the other night purely and entirely Cambridge: Lytton and Clive would be much better. Anyhow the cost of printing wouldn't be much. But we must go into the matter.

There—I think thats all the business transacted, and there is really no more to say—except that, should you be seeing Roger, you might remark that we haven't any rooms ready [at Monk's House]—which is the fact. He asked if he could come; and I never wrote.

What I want to do is to go to Boudard for April and May: to Italy for June: then to come here. I feel more and more inhibited and irritated by London life: I feel its meshes closing in—Goldie, Ottoline, [Richard] Braithwaite, a beautiful and brilliant young woman of his;[2]—perhaps Peter [F. L. Lucas]—all have to be seen next week: and what's the point? Here one can sit on the fender and read. Even I can write an occasional sentence about a Moth. (oh curse you for having invented them.)[3] All the processes of life, even in pelting rain, are pleasurable. One has no Nelly—no Lottie— no Mrs Mansfield. Domestic life transacts itself with perfect simplicity. Directly I go back I am badgered and worried; a thousand sucking vampires attach themselves to my ribs, and if I snatch up Milton once in a blue moon, its about all the reading for pleasure, I ever do. And that reminds me, who is Mrs Grants [Duncan's mother] Constance Llewellyn? I have a mad letter from a so-called woman, in which she says that she has 4 children, no money, and has been 14 weeks in a nursing home. Will I therefore write and advise her how to bring up her eldest girl, Hermione, who *longs* to write but is not clever, because they know Mrs Grant whom they love, with whom they stay, whom I am said to know. Is she a lunatic? a paying guest, or what?

Well; if I stayed longer here I should flood you out with letters. The brooches slightly conveyed the chill and fervour of your eyes to me[4]—

1. From Thoby Stephen, Virginia's brother, who died in 1906. Vanessa proposed to print them in a private edition with an introduction by Virginia. The proposal did not mature.
2. Marjorie Matthews, who had been at Newnham College, Cambridge, 1922-5. In 1933 she married the architect Marshall Sisson, and died in 1972.
3. See Volume III of this Edition, p. 372, note 2.
4. "The most lovely smoky blue cat's eyes pair of brooches came from you" (Vanessa to Virginia, 27 December 1929, *Berg*). Goode's shop was Cameo Corner then in New Oxford Street.

I daresay they were ugly: but Queen Anne is said to have worn them (only by Mr. Goode)

I want to live at least 2 months in France and see the anemones open and hear some 24 nightingales and go gliding in and out of the bays—but even though we have shed The Nation (I had the divine pleasure of telling Maynard that it cant be worse under Harold than under Hubert[1]) the press remains; and L. has taken against Cassis; so I shall never see my house, except perhaps for one week. However I will lay all this at your feet, whenever, God knows, we meet. I sent Angelica some toffee. I rather suspect Quinney [sweet-shop] never sent it.

B.

I suppose you are seeing Italian pictures—how odd—suddenly reading a completely new Shakespeare, Milton and I dont know who. You will be dazed—think of Roger.

Berg

2119: To Ethel Sands   *Monks House, Rodmell*
                                          [Sussex]

31st Dec. 1929

Dearest Ethel,

It is the standard that you set—you and Nan—the dove grey gloves, the pâté de foie gras—that's what makes you as slippery as an avalanche or an eel or an iceberg when it comes to finding what represents your idiosyncracy on a wet day in Brighton. There was a shining shelly box which took my taste, but then my taste is bad, and it was altogether too Brightonesque and lodging house when I put it beside the gloves and considered you. What would do for Ethel and Nan? I demanded; Well Nan is having some youthful poems sent her, because she is an austere woman, rapt to the heart of nature; but Ethel? Something dark, glistening, exotic, mothy, luxurious, soft, rich, rare. The only thing that in any degree combines these qualities is, so far as I can see, the sperm of the sturgeon. So this is going to you, but if you loathe it, send it back, for there is a glutton in Gordon Square [Clive Bell or Keynes] who lives on it. What I should like would be to think of Ethel sitting all alone in her glass green room, spooning caviare with the

---

1. In January 1930 Hubert Henderson resigned the Editorship of the *Nation*, and became Secretary of the Economic Advisory Council. He was succeeded by his Assistant Editor, Harold Wright.

bowl of a silver spoon onto brown bread and butter. But she shant, if she doesn't want to.

Love from us both to you and Nan for 1930.

Yrs
Virginia

The gloves are divine—But what party will ever be their equal—I mean, that I'm asked to? The foie gras is waiting till I get home.

Wendy Baron

Letters 2120-2145 (January-February 1930)

Virginia continued to write The Waves *in London, and made better progress than during the autumn. Having won their case against the Imperial Hotel Company, the Woolfs were left relatively undisturbed but accepted invitations to a large number of parties, including an Alice-in-Wonderland party for Angelica Bell, to which Virginia went dressed as the March Hare, and another (not recorded in her letters) at which she met Ramsay MacDonald, the Prime Minister. She was much upset by the death of her old friend Charles Sanger on 9 February, and soon afterwards she and Leonard both caught influenza. It was now that she began her correspondence with Ethel Smyth, who had written to her about* A Room of One's Own. *Their first meeting was delayed by Virginia's illness until 20 February, but they exchanged several letters in preparation for it.*

2120: To EDWARD SACKVILLE WEST   *Monks House, Rodmell*
                                 [Lewes, Sussex]

1st Jan 1930

My dear Eddy

I approach you as a supplicant—that is a bore. The cousin, of whom I spoke to you, Virginia Isham,[1] has written from Berlin to ask if I can give her any introductions or otherwise help her to get a job either in the theatre or films. She has gone out with a friend on the chance of getting some acting; failing that, she would teach, and is teaching a waiter, so as to earn enough to live on. I scarcely know her; but she seems nice; English; determined to break from her family with which I sympathise; penniless and adventurous. But she is not beautiful, and I know nothing of her gift as an actress. She appeared in the Seagull at Oxford and was said to be good, and has acted in repertory companies in the provinces. Her brother Gyles acted Shakespeare at Oxford.[2] She is also musical. Is this all too vague? Would an introduction to some of your friends be possible? Or could you give her any tips likely to

---

1. Virginia Isham was Virginia's first cousin once removed, and both were named after their common relative, Virginia, Countess Somers (1827-1910).
2. Sir Gyles Isham, Bt. (1903-76). As an undergraduate in 1925 he was President of the Oxford University Dramatic Society, and in later years acted leading Shakespearean roles at the Old Vic and Stratford-on-Avon.

be useful about approaching managers and film stars? It would be more than angelic if you could. I sympathise so much with her wish to break with the father and mother and their stodginess that I egged her on, and feel slightly responsible. Her address is

> Pension Rath
> Berlin W. 50
> Marburger Strasse 5

or write any comments or advice to me.

We come back next week. I feel neither sociable nor humane towards the race;—almost decided to vegetate here in solitude for ever. The Keynes' intervened, and there was the whole of yesterday gone bang. Lord how furious I was.—lunching respectably and discussing one's friends: yet they were both *very very very* nice.

Well anyhow I hope I shall see you, and get my new year ruled with red indelible ink—absolutely straight, without a blot—you know what I mean, [1] I apologise for being a bore.

> Ever yr
> Virginia

Berg

52 *Tavistock Square, W.C.*1

Typewritten
1st Jan. 1929 [1930]

Dear Miss Tyler,[2]

It is very good of you to write and tell me that you like my book A room of ones Own. It was the product of a highly unscientific mind, and I am therefore glad that you still find something true in it.

My knowledge of Greek history is small; but I suppose that writing poetry was, in one island and for a certain group of women, the habit at a certain period, and that Sappho was not a unique writer but supported by many other poetesses. That I think until the late eighteenth century was never the case in England. Why Sappho and the others were allowed to write, I do not of course presume to say. Historians perhaps might help. With thanks.

> Yours sincerely
> Virginia Woolf

Library of Congress

---

1. Eddy Sackville West, a man of neat habits, set out his diary with lines ruled in different coloured inks.
2. Of Detroit, Michigan.

Monks House, Rodmell,
Lewes [Sussex]

Thursday, 2nd Jan. [1930]

Dearest Ottoline

I meant to answer your letter in London—it was a very nice one; but O Lord you're mistaken if you think I enjoy what you call "being surrounded by admirers". What it means is that I am pinned down in my drawing room when I want to be wandering the streets to talk to some earnest American, or summoned to the bedside of Lady Cunard[1] where all I get out of it is the wonder of her golden silk stockings. Surely, in our time something better than this 'seeing' people might be contrived. But you will have forgotten the sentence that roused this cry of rage in me. Here in the country one loses a little the old match box feeling—the rubbed and scratched match box feeling. But I am nearly driven to set up my house in a pine wood in France.

This leads, inconsistently, to saying that if you, who are so much more modest than you should be, still think it nice to see and be seen, will you come in on Wednesday night (8th I think) after dinner—when you'll see Goldie Dickinson, a young man called Sprott,[2] another called something else, and the semblance—because I certainly shant be myself—of your irascible but faithful

Virginia

We only skip about in old clothes as you know. However I like to see you in your splendour.

Texas

Monks House, Rodmell
[Sussex]

2nd Jan 1930

My dear William,

As we left Tavistock Sqre before Christmas your presents arrived. Mine seemed to me inscrutable and fascinating. What is it? besides being an object of beauty? Leonard also wants me to thank you for the very good picture, which he is very glad to have. It will be an important picture in the Hogarth Press Gallery. Many thanks from us both.

---

1. Maud ('Emerald') Cunard, the American hostess who lived most of her life in London, and was an intimate friend of George Moore.
2. W. J. H. ('Sebastian') Sprott was a friend of Maynard Keynes and Lytton Strachey, and in 1926 was appointed Lecturer in Psychology at Nottingham University.

But this is to ask, as well as to thank—and say will you come in on Wednesday (8th) next after dinner, when we have one or two queer people,[1] and we want to put an idea for a book to you.

We go back on Sunday.

Yours ever
Virginia Woolf

I want you to tell me the name of the French man at your party.[2] I didnt catch it.

Texas

2124: To E. M. Forster

Monks House, Rodmell
[Sussex]

Jan 3rd 1930

My dear Morgan,

Many thanks for your letter. I think the only thing to do is to leave it entirely to Stock [French publishers]—they are very critical and have turned down several translators, and so far seem to give Mauron the preference over others. I never caught the Frenchman's name—somebody in the city, a friend of William Plomers. His point was, having been to a lecture of Maurons, that he talked bad French, had a bad accent, and was not on the strength of the lecture, intelligent. The other frogs were some of Clive's friends in Paris who remarked how well Mrs Dalloway was translated compared with the Passage,[3] which they professed to find very bad: but who they were I dont know. Raymond's [Mortimer] evidence was of the same kind. Why, I wonder, this hostility to Mauron in Paris? Is it disinterested criticism, or is there some motive behind? I shall tell Stock that I have no views, and will abide by them. From their letter to me, I didn't realise that they had already commissioned Mauron.

Talking of Professors, d'you know one who would like to follow Blunden in Japan?[4]

But there are many more interesting things to talk about than Professors. I must leave it to you, as a man of honour, to suggest a night when the Indians

1. The party consisted in Lady Ottoline Morrell, Goldsworthy Lowes Dickinson, Sebastian Sprott, Quentin Bell, Hilda Matheson and Plomer.
2. See next letter.
3. Forster's *A Passage to India* (1924) was translated into French by Charles Mauron, and the French translation of *Mrs Dalloway* was done by S. David. Mauron also translated *Orlando*.
4. Edmund Blunden had been Professor of English at the University of Tokyo, 1924-7.

are gone. We've got a nice room for you here now—it will be nice when the plaster has ceased to drip and the windows to sweat which they do by nature, the builder says, for 3 months now. You must come in February.

And—being my best critic, as I think,—how glad I am you liked A room! I was awfully afraid you wouldn't.

Love from us both
yr Virginia

and excuse the effusions of ink.

Sussex

2125: To Virginia Isham   52 *Tavistock Square, London, W.C.*1
                           [*Monk's House, Rodmell, Sussex*]

3rd Jan 1930

Dear Virginia,

I should be indignant if I had to call you Miss Isham. I wish we could have met before you left and discussed Berlin. I am very much interested—I wrote to Eddy Sackville West and asked him to send you any information or introductions so I hope he will. He lived in Berlin for about a year and knew a good many actors and film actors I think. But I daresay by this time you will have had some adventures and discovered everything yourself. It seemed to me the ugliest town in the world but thats all the more reason why they should have good theatres. We spent most of our time [in January 1929] at the opera, but it was in the middle of the great frost, and life was difficult.

Let me know if Eddy doesn't write. I think I could get hold of somebody from the Nicolsons.

I've not heard of Valerie Taylor[1] for ages. Best wishes,

Yours sincerely
Virginia Woolf

Northamptonshire Record Office

2126: To Ethel Sands   52 *T[avistock] S[quare, W.C.*1]

Sunday [12 January 1930?]

Dearest Ethel,

Lytton, of course, has not answered, but all the same I don't think I'll come: the thing is I am dining out—or having tea or some intolerable horror

---

1. The actress, whom Virginia had known in 1927-8 as a friend of Raymond Mortimer and Vita.

out of the past here so often next week that I am cross and distracted and should only be a blot on your table. And I like to be a radiance, as you know. So may I come another time, or you come to me here? How do you keep your suavity and adorability, seeing all the people you see I can't think.

My tongue dies, my heart crackles: but my love for you remains.

Yrs
Virginia

Wendy Baron

2127: To Clive Bell   52 *Tavistock Sqre.* [*W.C.*1]

Sunday Jan 18th [19]30

"I feel a qualm" said Lytton, as we came downstairs the other night. "I shall miss him" "So shall I" I replied. "And we never said good bye," "Shall we go back?" "No, we cant." "Perhaps he wont go after all [to Paris]" said Lytton. This is an authentic report of what was said by two old friends on your green carpet the other night. And of course, we didn't go back; and of course you did go. But as I cant very well leave off at this point at the top of the page I will make you eat your words about my never writing—disinterestedly too, in the service of truth, for God knows, I shant get an answer. I will just tell you the course of my life (dont complain of the writing—unless I dash it off before lunch, I never shall.)

Well, it was a fine spring day yesterday, and having failed to get the book I wanted at the London Library (where Mr Cox[1] has at last forgiven me my lack of baptism owing to Leonard's very generous subscription) we drove to Chelsea, to visit Charlie [Sanger], and take a walk in Battersea Park. But who can that seedy battered figure be, swinging along over the Bridge and talking aloud, under a vast black sombrero, with his bulging old ulster caught in by a strap? Can Francis [Birrell] really look like that from behind? He can. So we halted, and took him on board for he was going walking in Battersea Park too. It belonged to Lord Bolingbroke, he said, and there is a certain distinction I always think—some relics of the 18th Century. Pope lived here. Also there is a jackdaw. We have an aviary. I perceived that Battersea Park is one of the possessions which people in Chelsea secretly pride themselves upon: which was confirmed by the two ravens and the three owls (Look in the corner there—there's another owl in the corner) which Francis led us to look at, having modestly promised only one jackdaw. But to cut this short—Dora [Sanger], having appointed me to come to Oakley Street at 3.30, had of course left it to poor dumpy

---

1. Frederick Cox, who from 1882-1952 worked at the book-issue counter of the London Library. He had been shocked that Virginia and Vanessa had never been baptised. See Volume II of this Edition, p. 303.

desolate and crumpet complexioned Daphne [their daughter] to explain that Charlie lies some two miles north in Princes Gardens; so there we went. Footmen in maroon. Pile carpets in terra cotta. A lift. A bedroom like the back bedroom in a South Kensington second class hotel, and there was Charlie in bed—wizened, Arabian—I mean with starting blue eyes, tanned red cheeks, and intermittent teeth: he looked uncommonly ghoulish, and spider fingered and like some gnome which sits on a lamp and grins and then disappears in green flame. The decay of our friends is a miserable topic: he could only play with mathematics of blood pressure, in a fitful and exhausted way; unable to grasp some curious fact about the proportion to be observed between age, normality, and morbidity. Yet he has lost none of his tenacity—only some of his teeth. The future, I'm afraid, is rather hazardous. They say he must treat his profession [the law] as a hobby. I suggested that this was all to the good, considering the obscurer passages of Dante, the number of months that Virgil spent in Ancona, and other problems that remain to be investigated: but of course one must place in the scale—and she is not improved by misfortune, and stumps clumsily from room to room—poor Dora; and life at 58 Oakley Street.

Anyhow, off we went; and hearing a battering and booming in our basement, discovered Julian, who had been ejected by the painters, all crockery floor space and table space being needed for the preparations for the party. But he was in high feather, Miss Allanah Harper[1] having asked him for a poem. Time was when Miss Allanah could have sent a thrill through my spine by asking me for a poem—now I grumble for she mis-spells, mis-prints, and does not pay a penny. Also Julian had signed on at Lincolns Inn,[2] that moment, and altogether promises to do us all infinite credit, if he does bash in half a dozen cars or so meantime. But now, having prepared our dress, which consisted—and the point is not made vainly as you will perceive if you read on—in my case of a pair of hare's ears, and a pair of hare's paws (you remember the March hare) we went round to Fitzroy Street.[3] Roger [as the White Knight] had taken the place by storm. The children crowded round him like the piper. He was a masterpiece, having called out all the resource and ingenuity of Woolworths stores. Candles, mousetraps, tweezers, frying pans, scales—I know not what all—dangled from him by brass chains, infinite in number; his legs were bound in cricket pads; he wore chain armour on his breast; his cheeks flowered in green whiskers, and the surface of the body where visible was covered in

1. Founder and Editor of *Echanges*, the quarterly review of English and French literature, 1930-35.
2. Julian never became a barrister, and in the autumn of 1930 he returned to Cambridge to write a dissertation on Pope hoping that it might lead to a Fellowship at King's.
3. This party was given by Vanessa for her daughter Angelica who was just 11 years old. The guests were asked to dress as characters in *Alice in Wonderland*.

white yeager [Jaeger] tights. Encouraged by the extravaganza I turned lightly on my heels (a hare, you remember and mad at that) and tapped Dotty on the nose. Whether she was tipsy already or merely sour by nature, God knows; anyhow she flared up like a costermonger; damned my eyes; and this not in play; and swore I had wiped all the powder from her face. The worst of it was, that having recovered her temper she went by natural precipitation, into the opposite extreme of facetious and persistent amorosity, with the result that I spent the evening with her at my side—petulant, peevish, disconnected, incapable of a sensible, sober, let alone intelligent remark—all was high flown, rhapsodical and pert.

Enough, enough, I have vented my spleen where I dare hope it will be understood. In every other way the party was a complete success—hams disappearing—Angus [Davidson] assiduous and more than gentlemanly; Barbara [Bagenal] owing to her disguise negligible; and Angelica ravishing, flirtatious, commanding and seductive. Vanessa presided unperturbed—and going home Leonard, wearing a green baize apron and a pair of chisels as the Carpenter came in conflict with the police on behalf of a drunken prostitute, who, being insulted by three tipsy men, answered them back in their own coin. "Why dont you go for the men who began it? My name's Woolf, and I can take my oath the woman's not to blame. She called them bugger; but they called her whore"—and so on—holding his apron and chisel in one hand; upon which Lydia suddenly appeared out of the crowd; and by hook or by crook the affair subsided and we went home to bed.

Such is life. It is another fine spring day; and if it were not that I'm afflicted with Gumbo (you remember how we held her under, without success, off Swanage, 20 years ago?)[1] I should be tempted to go roaming. As it is, I must on the contrary fix my mind upon some definite but not to me romantic spot. Has she had Josh?—has she not had Josh?[2]—well, either way it dont matter that I can see: how sick she would have made you last night, in the housemaids flannel jacket and a false nose, like a turkeys wattle! Tomorrow I go to Puss in Boots with Angelica; on Tuesday dine with Ethel to meet Ruby that was Peto;[3] on Wednesday I hope Lytton comes to tea; on Thursday I introduce Quentin to Colefax: on Friday, praise Heaven, I go to Rodmell; and if the postman, on his motor cycle, were to stop in the dark, just as I'm lighting the lamp after tea, with a letter from Paris, how happy I should be. Its not likely though; nor that you will ever read through

1. Marjorie Strachey ('Gumbo') had been on holiday with Virginia, the Bells and others, at Studland, Dorset, in September 1910.
2. In 1927 Marjorie Strachey had written a novel, *The Counterfeits*, in which she thinly disguised her love for Josiah Wedgwood, the politician of the Staffordshire ceramics family.
3. Ruby Lindsay, a life-long friend of Ethel Sands, married Ralph Peto, from whom she was separated. In 1926 she re-adopted her maiden name.

this long ill considered and ill written letter, whose warmth of impulse must be its excuse. "I miss Clive"—that from Lytton and Virginia spontaneous and uncalled for, does seem to me, vain as I am, a bit of a tribute.

yr   Virginia

Quentin Bell

2128: To Desmond MacCarthy 52 *Tavistock Square* [*W.C.*1]

Monday [27 January 1930]

My dear Desmond,

It was a great delight to read your article.[1] I never thought you would like that book—and perhaps you didn't: but anyway you managed to write a most charming article, which gave me a great and unexpected pleasure. (Apart from that, you must let me collect your articles. This is no joke.)

By the way, did you refer to Lawrence? The novelist marked by an initial? He was not in my upper mind; but no doubt was in the lower.[2]

Ever so many thanks and I pray we may meet when Lord Buckmaster no longer asks me if I knew the late Lord Tennyson.[3]

Yrs affect.   Virginia

Love to Molly, I'm going to start an old-fashioned correspondence with her, if she is willing, on quarto sheets, all about the soul, the heart and the emotions.

Mrs Michael MacCarthy

2129: To Ethel Smyth 52 *Tavistock Square, W.C.*1

30 Jan. 1930

Dear Miss Smyth,

If you only knew how often I have wanted to write to you—and only didn't for fear of boring you—to thank you for your books and articles and to ask you about my great grandfather Pattle who shot up out of a barrel,

1. On *A Room of One's Own* in the *Sunday Times*, 26 January 1930.
2. In pp. 149-53 of the Hogarth Press (1929) edition of *A Room of One's Own*, Virginia discussed the androgynous mind, and cited a 'Mr A.' as an example of a novelist who 'protests against the equality of the other sex by asserting his own superiority'. In his review, Desmond MacCarthy referred to 'Mr A.' as 'an exceedingly gifted living novelist, clearly recognisable under an initial', but did not identify him.
3. For this incident, see p. 134.

as you say, in the Indian ocean[1]—then you wouldn't apologise. There is nothing I should like better than to see you—and you might like me. Who knows? Thursdays my husband, whom you would like, is here—but as you only come sometimes, please say which day suits you and we will keep it.

I am very glad you liked my little book [*A Room* . . .]. It was rather a wild venture, but if you think there is something in it, I am satisfied.

Yours sincerely and with as much admiration as you will accept,

Virginia Woolf

Berg

2130: TO WILLIAM PLOMER   52 *Tavistock Sqre.* [*W.C.*1]

Friday [31 January? 1930]

Dear William,

Its very good of the Oxford Society to ask me—but nothing will induce me to open my mouth in public so long as I live. I loathe lectures—to hear or to give—and how any rational person can think otherwise God knows. Can you put this politely, without mitigating the truth?

We have won our case [against the Imperial Hotel Company], did we tell you?—they want to settle it and pay expenses and screw all windows: a triumph—

Yrs Virginia Woolf

Texas

2131: TO SIBYL COLEFAX   52 *Tavistock Square, W.C.*1

[3? February 1930]

Dearest Sibyl,

The wretched Wolves cant think how to express their sorrow at your illness. At all times unmannerly, they are at their worst when they wish to show their affection. Are there any books that we could send? Leonard would like to give you a primula, grown from seed in his glasshouse. But these are nothing compared with the flu, which is only to be met by complete

1. James Pattle (1775-1845) was the grandfather of Julia Jackson, Virginia's mother. Quentin Bell, summarising the legends about him, wrote (*Virginia Woolf*, I, p. 14) that he was "the greatest liar in India; he drank himself to death; he was packed off home in a cask of spirits, which cask, exploding, ejected his unbottled corpse before his widow's eyes, drove her out of her wits, set the ship on fire and left it stranded in the Hooghly." Ethel Smyth had heard this story from her father, Major General J. H. Smyth, and retold it in her autobiography, *Impressions That Remain* (Volume 2, pp. 251-2), where Virginia read it.

quiescence—no luncheon, tea or dinner. Do not allow Jacques Blanche inside the house.

I saw Sir Arthur [Colefax] at Burlington House on Tuesday,[1] but was too conscious of the distinction of the lady in the chair [Edith Sitwell] to go up and ask after you. Lord! there were a lot of people, and many who had vowed never to meet again meeting there. How does one refuse the M. of Londonderry? Aren't I rising in the scale! It's true only so far as the party to which every plumber's wife in London is asked, but still—its rising. And I am plunged into the arms of Ethel Smyth. I feel them already hugging tight. It is a breathless rapture. And Vanessa has a show tomorrow; and all B———y is much excited. And we're asked to sell this house and must find another. Lady Frances Balfour should have asked her kitchenmaid's advice before she took to the pen.[2] However, she amuses me, with her ill-bred aristocratic manners. Do you know her? But of course you do, and could tell me the whole story if I had you here to tea: which I shall hope for next week. Please be careful.

Yrs V.

Michael Colefax

2132: To Ethel Smyth   52 *Tavistock Square, W.C.*1

Tuesday [4 February 1930]

Dear Dame Ethel Smyth (I'm afraid I miscalled you before)[3]

Alas, we are going down to the country early on Friday. But if you would name any day next week, I would keep it free. I'm sending you a book of pictures by a great Aunt of mine,[4] in which I quote your opinion of my great grandfather [Pattle]. But this is no return whatever for the immense pleasure I have had from your books (I dare not say music, because though willing, I am ignorant) in which my husband agrees with me.

Virginia Woolf

Berg

2133: To Clive Bell   52 *Tavistock Sqre.* [*W.C.*1]

6th Feb 1930

Dearest Clive,

I wrote you a very long letter [2127]—4 pages I think—so long a letter I've not written this 10 years—the week you went, to record a pleasing

1. A reception by Lady Londonderry at which Alfred Noyes read his poetry.
2. *Ne Obliviscaris: Dinna Forget* by Lady Frances Balfour (February 1930).
3. She was made a Dame of the British Empire in 1922.
4. *Victorian Photographs of Famous Men and Fair Women*, by Julia Margaret Cameron, with an Introduction by Virginia (Hogarth Press, 1926).

tribute paid to you after your party by Lytton and myself going downstairs: "We shall miss him" we said, and half turned back to tell you so. It contained also, besides affection and some gossip, various indiscretions about Dotty, with whom I happened to be in a temper. This I sent to the Hotel de Londres [Paris]; now Nessa says you never went there. There then it remains, mouldering in a wire cage, but unless Dotty passes and peeps, like Pippa, it dont much matter.

And now Eddy [Sackville West] will have whipped the cream off the gossip of Bloomsbury. Eddy will be arriving this moment, very trim, in spite of his night journey. As for your request about Brian Howard,[1] I'm quite ready to encourage, but dont see that I shall have the opportunity. As you know, Dotty refused to publish him,[2] for which I dont altogether blame her, seeing that his poems are steeped in Tom [Eliot]—a scent that sticks like the skunk or the musk and one can't smell any other. All the same, I thought they had merit.

Tom by the way writes today that he is just moving to a house, from a flat,—the 5th move in 6 months; which means I suppose that the worm in Vivien turns and turns, and not a nice worm at that.[3] Then of course we discuss the new paper—the Antidote it's to be.[4] Last week, I could have sworn it was accomplished—Roger had the £12,000 jingling in his pocket and was appointing Editors, calling board meetings, arranging for little men in the Boulevards to cry it by night. At dinner yesterday however, all this had sunk to a whisper. I doubt that he has more than a promise from some tipsy Lord. And also he is gravely disturbed by Raymond's suggestion to print on shiny paper. You know where shiny paper leads—to fashion, rank and Mayfair. So I doubt—but anyhow Leonard is quit of the Nation next week, and the amiable Blunden succeeds to the office stool and Mrs Jones's[5] somewhat ample favours.

The great world is not much with us. Sibyl has been raving, she says, with influenza, and the quick wits among us invent her sayings—indeed say they dont need much inventing. Christabel [McLaren] gave a party—did not ask me—on the other hand, Lady Londonderry gave a party and did ask me—at which my heart leapt up, as you can imagine, until I discovered that it was to meet 500 Colonial dentists and to hear Mr [Alfred] Noyes read his own poetry aloud. Not a distinguished gathering. Angelica has knocked two pieces off her front teeth. It doesn't show so much as might be,—and Julian goes booming about, like a gigantic dor-beetle. (When I was a child they

1. Brian Howard (1905-58), the extravagant aesthete whose *First Poems* were published in 1931 by Nancy Cunard at her Hours Press in Paris.
2. Dorothy Wellesley edited the *Hogarth Living Poets* series.
3. Vivien Eliot had been mentally and physically ill for years.
4. The *Antidote* never reached the point of publication.
5. Alice Jones, assistant to the Literary Editor of the *Nation*.

always hit the wire netting when we were playing cricket—but the sound means nothing to you.) I dined with Ethel [Sands], and was plucked by the hair from a tender and intimate—yes we were really growing intimate, after 30 years—tête à tête with Desmond to be asked "And did you ever know Lord Tennyson? Mrs Woolf?" by an aged enlightened Liberal peer, called Buckmaster;[1] who then recited, word for word, in tones of awful dignity (while I toyed with an ice, and you know how I love ices, and how good Ethel's are—but the poor woman's gone soft and sleepy like a pear in which even the wasps are sodden) No Coward Soul is mine [Emily Brontë]. The point of the story is that he has offered to give Julian every sort of introduction. And then we had snatches from the Ring and the Book [Robert Browning]. Ruby Peto Lindsay was there, and is said to be his mistress— Buckmaster's I mean: but time has blurred her fine features for fine they were, in the gaslight in Fitzroy Street when the century was no older than two or three.

Duncan gave a little lunch party to Lytton, Nessa and me, on the day of her private view[2] (I doubt if that is grammar) at the Gargoyle. Old Lytton sprinkled the Antidote with tepid sprays; and Duncan became inextricably involved telling a story about a—about a—oh I cant remember, if indeed I ever knew what Duncan's story was about, and so we went on, until the afternoon light was waning, and Duncan and I walked to Bond Street, and were so elated by every incident,—for one thing the discovery of Blake's house, for another an old man playing a violin said "Good bye to you," that we found ourselves inside one of the smartest shops in Bond Street asking the price of rings. Well they cost £120, and I had been ready to give £5. 10. So on, and with considerable dignity, to the Show; and there was that woman (and she's a good mother I grant you) Faith [Henderson]; but when she opens her mouth there should be a curtain before it, as before the doors of great cathedrals; things must pass in and out; but the vision of the altar with the red coral stripes, surely that should be concealed.

I am droning on, writing nonsense. Nessa sold 5 pictures I think the first day—needless to say not to Mrs Grenfell,[3] Lydia, or Dotty; who all stood in a group discussing how the man p—d in front of Vera Bowen's[4] house—its an old story and a dirty, but anything to save buying pictures. Lydia by the way has fallen and cut her lip skating.

1. Stanley Owen, who was created 1st Viscount Buckmaster in 1915, had been Lord Chancellor 1915-16.
2. In February and March Vanessa held an exhibition at the Cooling Galleries, 92 New Bond Street. The catalogue was introduced by Virginia.
3. Mrs Florence Grenfell (*née* Henderson), who in 1913 married E. C. Grenfell, a director of Morgan, Grenfell & Co., the bankers. He was created Lord St Just in 1935.
4. Mrs Harold Bowen, a friend of Lydia Lopokova, and composer of *The Masquerade* which Lopokova danced in 1922.

I'm afraid Charlie Sanger is very bad; but Heaven knows—the news comes through Roger, through Dora.

And now I'm going to dine with Nessa, while Leonard dines with the Cranium.[1]

Yes, I miss Clive.

Virginia

Quentin Bell

2134: To Lady Ottoline Morrell   *Monks House, Rodmell,*
                                    Lewes, Sussex

8 Feb. 1930

Dearest Ottoline

(Armada is a very good name too). We are down here, freezing and withered in the east wind. But its very beautiful too, all covered with snow, pink and violet. I shall be back in a day or two, but life has heaped up so many muddles next week that I am rather in difficulties. The week after? A Tuesday or Wednesday between 5 and 6? And alone or with your Lady, whom I met years ago, as you like. Send a card if you wish—I'm so unhappy about Charlie.[2] We got a desperate account as we came here, only from a maid—

Yr
VW

Texas

2135: To Dora Sanger   52 *Tavistock Sqre.* [*W.C.*1]

Sunday [9 February 1930]

My dear Dora,

I hope you won't mind my writing to you—it is only to gratify my own feelings. I have been thinking again and again at Rodmell of you and Charlie and wishing I could tell you how much your and his friendship has been to me. It began years ago, after my brother died, and all this time I have felt him there, with his extraordinary goodness and understanding. I don't suppose he ever knew how grateful one was. And yet—it is no exaggeration—one will need him and miss him all one's life. Your letter to Leonard makes me very angry with myself. How can I have been such a fool as to spoil those days with "merciless chaff"? It must have been some idiotic mood—probably nervousness—on my part. I do hope you will forgive me and believe in the sincerity of my affection.

1. See p. 54, note 4.
2. Charles Sanger died on 9 February.

We both send our love to you and Daphne. I hope she will think of us as friends (though so old) and come and see us sometimes.

Yours ever
Virginia Woolf

Of course, don't answer.

Daphne Sanger

2136: To ETHEL SMYTH   52 *Tavistock Square, W.C.*1

Tuesday [11 February 1930]

My dear dame Ethel Smyth.

If you knew how many lies I told all Sunday and yesterday about not having a temperature in order not to put you off, and then was caught out, and then said very likely you wouldn't catch it, and was then forced to ring up and explain, you wouldn't accuse me of telling lies—anyhow to you— I was never so truthful in my life. It did seem rather monstrous to let you come here and get the influenza at your first encounter: But what about Friday 4.30? I expect to be all right then; or Monday 4.30? I'll keep both till I hear.

And I have a request. I went to get Impressions that Remain[1] today, and found only vol 2. which I have read from end to end lying in front of the fire with my dog. But I cant leave you half in half—Could you LEND me vol 1? It would be an angelic charity—if you dont hate doing up parcels. What a fascinating book! How did you learn to write like that?

Yours very sincerely
Virginia Woolf

My husband is up again but says he is stupid as an owl.

Berg

2137: To V. SACKVILLE-WEST   52 *Tavistock Square, W.C.*1

Tuesday [11 February 1930]

Oh damn, I came back from Rodmell with the flu and am in bed so I'm afraid I cant dine on Thursday. I suppose you wouldn't come to tea tomorrow?—only if I'm normal though—(Leonard's had it too). But you shant run any risk. Perhaps you would ring up. It would be *very* nice to see you.

Yr
Virginia

Berg

1. One of Ethel's autobiographies, published in two volumes in 1919.

13th Feb 1930

My dear Dame Ethel Smyth,

But this generosity is absolutely unheard of and wrong. I said LEND and instantly two volumes [of *Impressions that Remain*] are shot at my feet. Well, if you will write my name in them, I can't ask more or resist. Of course I read them the year they came out, with rapture, and bought the red Edition later, which my sister Vanessa, who has only read 3 books in her life, stole, leaving me only the second volume. I think I could stand an examination in all your aunts, uncles, horses and dogs. I am now re-reading, with the additional delight of being the possessor, though I fear by unfair means. It is one of my favourite works, and I have even gone so far as to say so in print.[1] Yes, I think your mother adorable. So was mine.

What a relief to my mind that you are shabby! Then I needn't mend the hole in my solitary dress, as I had fully intended.

I am still in bed, and suppose should have had, in honesty, to put you off tomorrow, owing to a temperature; so Monday will be perfect.

Really I cant thank you enough for the books, to which I am now going to return

Yr grateful
Virginia Woolf

Berg

2139: To V. Sackville-West   52 *Tavistock Square, W.C.*1

Thursday [13 February 1930]

Look, Potto has written you this cheque. Its the only possible, and most painless way. Have you got it? (I mean influenza). I shall be alone to tea tomorrow, wh. is Friday, and, if you liked to come, wd. not ask anybody.

1. In a review of *Streaks of Life* (*New Statesman*, 23 April 1921) Virginia wrote: "Ethel Smyth is a lady of remarkable and original personality, and not merely a person to whom things chanced to happen . . . She is impressionable, but she is very discriminating . . . Can be strident, she is never sentimental . . . She possesses the combination of enthusiasm and shrewdness which fitted her for . . . the great pursuit of her life—the pursuit of friendship." In the same review Virginia wrote of Ethel's previous book *Impressions that Remain:* "Not that Miss Smyth possessed extraordinary literary power, or that she analysed her soul to the essence. Her method appeared to consist of extreme courage and extreme candour . . . Her astonishing vitality had led her into relationships and situations of such variety and intensity that the truthful account of them was of absorbing interest."

Perhaps you'd ring up. But for the Lord's sake dont bother about it.—I mean, I can get somebody else—not as nice though.

V.

Berg

14th Feb. [1930]

Dear Dame Ethel Smyth.

You will hate the sight of my handwriting. Honesty, which I loathe more and more, compels me to say that I am still in bed with a temperature, and the dr. says I am not to see anyone till I'm normal, and thinks there is no chance of this by Monday.

I'm so disheartened I dont know what to suggest. May I let you know when I'm well on the chance that you can come? There is nothing I should like more than to see you; it is infuriating to have got ill at this moment— All I can do is to read you and wish to goodness you had written 10 volumes not 2.

Well, I shall try for a later day next week. and please don't forget your promise in the meantime

Yrs sincerely
Virginia Woolf

Berg

[mid-February 1930]

Dearest Ottoline,

What a nice letter! I'm going to add Hispaniola to Armada. One of these days I shall write about you—what fun it would be—with the yellow silk sails all rent by shot, and the golden Eagles spread on the masts: but this is only a joke—I'm in bed with influenza and want to read your memoirs:[1] and like making up stories about you. The wilder and stranger the better.

But I am writing to ask could you give me the name and address of the man I met at your house in the summer who was connected with preserving downs? I am horrified to find that the Brighton Council propose to make a road through the loveliest part, behind us, and through our meadow, for no reason except to provide work and the sheer devilry of their hearts. This

1. In the early 1930's Ottoline began to write her memoirs based on her diaries, but they were not published until after her death, when they were edited by Robert Gathorne-Hardy in two volumes (1963 and 1974).

will mean villas, shops and ruin like Peacehaven.[1] If I write my fingers off, I want to stop it; but can only think of him, and how he said there was some Committee or Council—I cant remember what. His name on a postcard is all I want—unless in your bounty you can think of something else. It is still one of the loveliest places in the world, and then they want to have a coast road and omnibuses—oh the damnable stupidity of the English middle class!

Did you go to Charlie's [Sanger] funeral? I feel very unhappy about him —what you say is quite true—there was a great beauty about him, and I only wish one had made oneself see him more. Idiotic things prevent one— But I did go just before he died.

Yr
Texas   Virginia

2142: To Clive Bell   52 *Tavistock Square, W.C.*1

Feb 16th 1930

Dearest Clive,

What I should like would be a long long letter of affection and gossip. I have been in bed a week with influenza, and [Dr] Elly [Rendel] proposes to keep me on the sofa another week. You realise therefore my state of mind: and you sit naked in the sun!

I'm strongly tempted to fly to my pinewood at Cassis. If so, we may meet. London is too cold, too crowded, too full of funerals and influenzas.

I am reading Byron—well, there's a lot to be said about Byron—Maurois[2] does not understand him, but has the merit of making me think that I do.

Enough though: this is only a plea for a letter.

And hiss in Eddy's ears the words Virginia Isham.[3]

yr
Quentin Bell   Virginia

2143: To Ethel Smyth   52 *Tavistock Sqre.* [*W.C.*1]

Monday [17 February 1930]

My dear Dame Ethel

Once more. . . .

I suggest this very next Thursday[4] for the following reasons—

The temperature is now only a small one (I've often had them and they dont matter).

1. The new bungalow-town on the coast between Brighton and Newhaven.
2. André Maurois, *Byron* (1930).
3. See Letter 2120.
4. On Thursday, 20 February, Virginia and Ethel Smyth met for the first time.

I am *not* infectious.

You wont mind if I wear an old dressing gown.

You will excuse my stupidity and put it down to influenza.

If you dont come then, we may go away, and never meet for years.

Also, I can telephone on Thursday a.m. if anything terrible happens.

So I shall expect you on Thursday 4.30. Is this explicit?

Of course I want your book.[1] I think I missed that, though everything else, as I believe, of yours is known to me. You are, as I hope to explain a highly interesting portent to us old hacks—

Yours sincerely
Virginia Woolf

Berg

2144: To Julian Bell   52 *Tavistock Square, W.C.*1

Typewritten
17th Feb. 1930

My dear Julian,

    1. . . . Would you be so good as to take two tickets for the Marlowe (same as you get for Nessa) for Saturday night.[2]

    2. . . Would you be so good as to take two bedrooms at the Bull, same as Nessas, for Saturday and Sunday nights.

    3. . . Would you be so good as to take out a subscription for me to the Venture[3] and send me the first number. I will repay.

There! Even you, poor brat, cant pretend that this is illegible or obscure in intention. As for the spelling, it is so perfect that it may present some difficulty to those who . . . but enough.

I am sitting over the fire with influenza and would like to read your works. Lord! How precocious you are—flourishing in all the public prints at your age, when I, at the same, modestly cowered anonymous in the review columns of the Times!

Nessa's show is a great success. Leonard is fabricating the new paper [*Antidote*] tonight. Mr Empson[4] came to see us. A raucous youth, but I think rather impressive and as red as a turkey, which I like. I am reading Childe Harold. If Byron had lived to my age he would have been a great novelist. As it is, he is the worst poet.

1. *A Three-Legged Tour in Greece* (1927).
2. Virginia's illness prevented the Woolfs from going to Cambridge.
3. A Cambridge review in which Julian published his poems. It was founded in 1928.
4. William Empson, the poet and critic, who in 1930 at the age of 24 published *Seven Types of Ambiguity*.

Now Julian do go and see about the rooms and tickets and dont have us fobbed off with a dog kennel this time.

Your loving Aunt
Virginia

Quentin Bell

2145: To Quentin Bell   52 *Tavistock Sq.* [*W.C.*1]

Typewritten
17th Feb. 1930

My dear Quentin,

I have been having influenza, and being in bed, could not write to you, because I could not type, and so the most amazing letter in the world (which it would have been) remains unwritten. My brain was packed with close folded ideas like the backs of flamingoes when they fly south at sunset. They are now all gone—a few grey draggled geese remain, their wing feathers trailed and mud stained, and their poor old voices scrannel sharp and grating—that's the effect of typing; every sentence has its back broke, and its beak awry. Nevertheless, as I want nothing so much as another letter from you, I must eke it out.

I am sitting over the fire with masses of virgin—what d'you think I'm going to say?—typescript by my side; novels six foot thick to be read instantly or I shall be knived by cadaverous men at Bournemouth whose life depends on my verdict; and amorous typists. They write because they cant have their nights to their liking. This is hard on me. They write to revenge themselves upon the young man at the fish shop, or the young woman in red at the flower shop. So what news have I? Helen's [Anrep] been here; Roger's been here; and Nessa; and Vita; and just before I fell ill, your Miss Watson.[1] She is a nice girl—yes, I liked her. She stood fire from Roger very well. He was at his most sweeping and searching, raking her with terrific questions and denunciations. There was Julian's Mr Empson too—a black and red sort of rook, very truculent, and refreshing. None of your etiolated, sophisticated, damp, spotted, you know what I mean—Tonight theres a grand meeting, which I cant attend, of the new paper promoters, at Rogers. How young and ardent we all are at our age, flinging guineas on the waves and believing in the rule of reason and the might of art and the downfall of our enemies! But Raymond says the paper must be shiny; Roger says shine means shoddy; shine means Mayfair. Well, you can fancy how the argument goes and the tempers fly and the old friends are excoriated. I meant

1. Elizabeth Watson, then an art-student. She later became Mrs Sproule, and died in 1955.

to go to Heals to see your picture,[1] but was ill that moment; however if its there next week I shall try. Nessa has had a great success and members of the aristocracy rend their gloves asunder competing for her pictures. My foreword has roused Mr Rory Mahoney as his name suggests to fury.[2] He says I am indecent, and must be suppressed. Never mind, Sickert has asked me to foreword his show;[3] and I'm now asked to lecture on Art at the Royal Academy! only on Zoffany it is true, from the social aspect, still its the R.A., and I am very much set up to think how a writer can be of use in your sublime silent fish-world.[4] Still, I shan't. No; I can't. I can only write gibberish—oh you cant think what gibberish my next book will be. I fancy you tactfully apologising and tapping your forehead when you hear people say, Is that your Aunt?

I have a wild plan to go to Cassis next week to recover. If so, we might meet in the Gare de Lyons, and coming back recovered I should spend two or three days at the [Hotel de] Londres and then we would sit in the spring light quizzing and fizzing—what fun, oh what fun. And why does one never do, instantly, the things one thinks of?

I am now drifting to the region of questions. What did you have for breakfast? Where did you dine last night and so on? And are you in love? And are you happy? And do you sometimes write a poem? And have you had your hair cut? And have you met anybody of such beauty your eyes dance, as the waves danced, no it was the stars; when Shakespeare's woman— Lord lord I've forgotten all I ever knew—was born?[5]

Well here I will stop; It is five oclock on a fine evening, and if I were a painter I should take my colours to the window and do a brilliant little panel of the clouds over the hotel; how I should like bowling them round and filling them in with a fiery white and bluish grey.

Well dearest Quentin write me a nice long letter please.

Your poor dear old dotty Aunt V.

Quentin Bell

1. Quentin was exhibiting at a mixed show in the Mansard Gallery, which Eve Disher ran on the top floor of Heals, the furniture store in the Tottenham Court Road.
2. Unidentified. Perhaps Charles Mahoney (1903-68), the painter, who taught at the Royal College of Art. Virginia's foreword was to the catalogue of Vanessa's exhibition of her paintings at the Cooling Galleries.
3. Walter Sickert held an exhibition of his paintings at the Savile Gallery in March, but the catalogue had no Introduction by Virginia.
4. She did not accept this invitation.
5. "No, sure, my lord, my mother cried; but then there was a star danced, and under that was I born." Beatrice, *Much Ado About Nothing*, II, i, 313-4.

Letters 2146-2171 (February–April 1930)

The much-postponed meeting between Virginia and Ethel Smyth took place on 20 February, when Virginia had still not completely recovered from influenza. Although she described Ethel as descending on her like a wolf on the fold, she in fact welcomed her many visits and subsequent letters, and their friendship developed at breath-taking speed. Virginia resumed The Waves, *typing in the afternoon what she had written in the morning, and finished the first draft on 29 April. Leonard had now handed over to Edmund Blunden the literary editorship of the* Nation, *and was able to give most of his time to the Hogarth Press, which was about to publish Vita's best-selling novel* The Edwardians. *A threat that they might be evicted from Tavistock Square did not materialise, but Virginia was forced to spend much of her time searching Bloomsbury for alternative premises.*

2146:. To Ethel Smyth   52 *Tavistock Square* [*W.C.*1]
24 Feb. [1930]

I liked your extravagant telegram immensely and the book came and your letter. Shall I get another letter? Not unless I write one, perhaps. The truth is that I went out, inspirited by your visit, for a walk on Saturday and went into the question of church decoration at Hampstead garden suburb, and so, not unnaturally, had to retire to bed again, where I am. But this time it is what they call nerve exhaustion and not a temperature—if that conveys anything to you.

It is incredible stupidity and drowsiness. If I drop my book I don't pick it up—This explains why, except for 2 or 3 paragraphs, I have read none of the Prisoner.[1] But one of these paragraphs was so interesting that I thought I must have written it myself. This is the highest compliment I can pay any writer:

And that reminds me—you threatened to read my books—Please don't. I feel without doubt and without sorrow, but serenely and certainly that you won't like them; and that this is not one atom to your discredit or mine.

---

1. *The Prison: a Dialogue*, by Henry Brewster, with a memoir by Ethel Smyth was republished late in 1930. Its first publication was in 1891. Brewster (1850-1908) was a wealthy philosopher, half American, who lived most of his life in France and Italy, where Ethel Smyth met him when she was 25 and fell in love with him. He was the only man she ever loved. On his book, she based an oratorio, also called 'The Prison' (1930).

It is merely a matter of blue eyes or brown. Let us bury *my* pen, and never mention it. Yours is interesting, and so we can discuss it.

Very oddly and indeed as if sent by providence, George Duckworth my old half brother turned up the day after you came—which he has not done these 10 years—and told me that a cousin has left him a miniature of old Pattle surrounded by wife and daughters done in France. He is going to send me a photograph, which I will send you.

I do hope you dont think me a valetudinarian? All this bed sounds rather suspicious: You see how I cherish your good opinion.

I felt guilty letting you come up, as I found out by chance, merely to see me—But for me it was worth it—well.

Yr
Virginia

Berg

2147: To Janet Case   52 *T.S.* [*W.C.*1]

Monday [24 February 1930]

My dear Janet,[1]

The flowers came out and are only today shrivelled—all this time they have been wide open and exquisite—lovelier than all the flowers in shops.

I'm normal, but still in bed, because this horrid little temperature has given me the usual headache. But its going; and we hope to get to Rodmell on Friday. Leonard of course, spent 3 hours in bed,[2] and has worked hard ever since.

What a dull letter to send in return for the flowers. I much prefer having a temperature.

I've been having Ethel Smyth to see me—she sat for 4 hours, talking hard—great fun. But you must come and let us have a gossip. Ever so many thanks.

yr   Virginia

Sussex

2148: To Ethel Smyth   52 *T.*[*avistock*] *S.*[*quare, W.C.*1]

27th Feb. [1930]

Well if I did what I want, I should ring up whatever your number is and ask you to come tomorrow. But—oh damn these medical details!—this influenza has a special poison for what is called the nervous system; and mine

---

1. Janet Case taught Virginia Greek in her youth and was now living in the New Forest, writing nature notes for the *Manchester Guardian*.
2. Leonard had also had influenza.

being a second hand one, used by my father and his father to dictate dis-patches and write books with—how I wish they had hunted and fished instead!—I have to treat it like a pampered pug dog, and lie still directly my head aches. That is what I am doing; and on Saturday we shall go to Rodmell where I shall lie still out of doors, and then creep along the water meadows, and then perhaps read a novel, and not write a word, except this kind of word, and not see a soul except Leonard and Mrs Thompsett, who cooks the chicken, for a week perhaps: when suddenly I shall be cured and dash about the house inventing pleasures—of which the first will be to ring up Ethel Smyth and ask her to come instantly to tea. Will she come? I dont think the cure this time will take more than a week. I'm taking pro-digious care. You're at the bottom of all the spoonfulls of codliver oil and malt that I gulp down. But you see, I dont dare ask you tomorrow. Lord! what a bore! To think that my father's philosophy and the Dictionary of National Biography[1] cost me this! I never see those 68 black books without cursing them for all the jaunts they've lost me.

I too feel that the book—not that book—*our* book—is open, and at once snatched away. I want to talk and talk and talk—About music; about love; about Countess Russell.[2] Dont you think you might indulge me this once and tell me what she said thats so interesting? Yes. I think you are a kind woman, besides being such a . . . . etc etc. Those two happy dodges of yours come in useful on occasion, dot dot, dot—et cetera. I will write your character in that style one of these days. Years ago, 3 or 4 at least, when I first met Maurice Baring[3] he made my heart jump by saying "You must come and meet Ethel Smyth." but nothing came of it and I was, as you say, too 'delicate' to press. What a fool one is. Here is Leonard, come back from his committee—yes, yes, you showed your discrimination by what you say of him. But I cant write the history of my marriage on what remains of this paper, so good bye, and my address is

 Monks House
 Rodmell
 Lewes. Sussex
Should you give me the great pleasure of a letter
      Our love
       Yr Virginia

Berg

1. Leslie Stephen was the Editor of the *Dictionary of National Biography* from 1882, the year of Virginia's birth, until 1891, and he lived to see the work completed under his successor, Sidney Lee.
2. Elizabeth Mary, Countess Russell, who wrote several popular novels under the name of 'Elizabeth', and was a friend of Ethel Smyth, who had stayed with her at Cannes during the previous summer.
3. Former diplomatist, novelist, and man of letters, whom Ethel Smyth first met in 1893, when he was 19. In 1938 she wrote his biography.

52 *Tavistock Sqre.* [*W.C.*1]

27th Feb. [1930]

My dear Saxon,

This influenza has been rather a bore, and twice I have had to go back to bed. Indeed I still write from the sofa, and thus you must excuse the malformation of my hand. It's not mere senility as you might suppose.

I made a shot at the novels you want—because I am not sure which of the 3 are your old friends. If I did wrong, the Press will change.

We hope to go to Rodmell on Saturday for, roughly, a week; and I will leave your great grandfather in the Press, in case you want to call for him.[1] I rather regret that some chapters anyhow should remain unpublished. There is a good deal that interests me, and I still laugh over a story of a bull and an umbrella.

What is your opinion of Ethel Smyth?—her music, I mean? She has descended upon me like a wolf on the fold in purple and gold, terrifically strident and enthusiastic—I like her—she is as shabby as a washerwoman and shouts and sings—but the question of her music crops up—I don't mean that she cares what I think, being apparently indomitable in her own view, but one day you must tell me the truth about it. Anyhow, as a writer she is astonishingly efficient—takes every fence.

I'm sorry that Barbara [Bagenal] has been ill—The truth is that February ought to be torn from the calendar and thrown away—a vile, ill-conditioned, altogether unnecessary month. I daresay, if we only knew, it got there on false pretences—a mistake of the Pope's. I hope we shall meet some time, but I'm told you dine out every night covered with gold braid. That's the worst of middle age—one's friends become so distinguished.

Love
Virginia

Sussex

2150: To Donald Brace   52 *Tavistock Square, W.C.*1

28th Feb 1930

Dear Mr Brace,

Many thanks for your letter. I am glad that you are satisfied with the sales of A Room of One's Own. It has done a good deal better here than in America. We have sold between 10 and 11 thousand, and generally of course,

---

1. In 1926 the Hogarth Press had considered for publication the memoirs of Saxon's great-grandfather, the historian Sharon Turner, but decided against it.

our sales are much less than yours. But I am not surprised, as I think the subject is more interesting to us than to you.

Please excuse my hand—I am in bed with influenza at the moment.

Kind regards,
yours sincerely,
Virginia Woolf

Harcourt Brace Jovanovich

2151: To Ethel Smyth   [*52 Tavistock Square, W.C.1*]

Saturday [1 March 1930]

What a wonder you are—of instancy.
Here is the paper.
I'm dumbfoundered by Lady [?] R.[1] If ever hate and scorn were written on a woman's face I read them on her's. But then I'm not a novelist: and I'm awfully glad to be mistook; because she *is* a novelist and commands my deep respect.

We are just off.

Yr
Virginia

I am venturing to take the Prison[2] but will take care and return intact. I think (but I am not capable of much thought) that the words as you have done them ought to make a magnificent poem and I greatly envy you. . . . etc etc.

Berg

2152: To V. Sackville-West   *Monks House* [*Rodmell, Sussex*]

Tuesday [4 March 1930]

Leonard has just decided to stay till Saturday, so I dont think there's much use in asking you. I hope you didn't put anything off. He was to have gone on Thursday.—Well, I shall see you next week.

1. Probably Lady 'Elizabeth' Russell, the author of *Elizabeth and her German Garden*, etc.
2. See p. 143, note 1.

I think I shall come up with him on Saturday. I'm feeling—this is Keatsy? However, I'm feeling less like an old clothes bag.

But Lord! I wish Lawrence hadn't died—younger? than I am;[1] makes me feel in the way, though I never read him for pleasure. Still—and then the damnable hypocrisy of the papers.

Love

Let me know when you'll come, or every instant will be ravaged by the rapacity of Ethel Smyth

Virginia

I do hope you didn't upset any plans with a view to coming.

Berg

2153: To V. Sackville-West   *Monk's House* [*Rodmell, Sussex*]

Friday [7 March 1930]

A thousand congratulations from L and V on your finish.[2] I shall read it over the week end. Lord! What an excitement! And Lord! again I pray that the chicken horror may be stamped in the egg.[3] It is an outrage upon my view—which I saw when I sat among the currants or sank among the cushions.

I will ring up.

V.

Berg

2154: To Ethel Smyth   52 *Tavistock Sqre.* [*W.C.1*]

March 10th [1930]

I was annoyed to be down in my studio when you rang up; and I feel some guilt that you should have rung up. I ought to have written—a dozen

---

1. D. H. Lawrence died at Vence in France on 2 March 1930. He was three years younger than Virginia.
2. Vita had just finished the manuscript of *The Edwardians*, and sent it to Virginia on the next day.
3. A chicken farmer intended to buy up the fields in view from the terrace at Long Barn. This threat led the Nicolsons to search for a new house, and on 4 April Vita discovered Sissinghurst Castle, near Cranbrook in Kent.

times. But you said I neednt, and I like best writing letters in my head. One was about the Lighthouse. Lord! how glad I am you like it,—honestly I never thought you would: and then about your Broadcast. The gardener's wife stopped me in the road and gave me an account of it, and my sales jumped up. Then another was to be an autobiography, beginning "I was 48 last January, and have never suffered from indigestion in my life;" and another was about my mother and Lady Lewis[1] (I can't write a word, because I am talking to Leonard). That pleased me, your reference to Helen and the old man;—how intelligent you are, to quote the very quotation I had in mind about her![2] I met Lady Lewis once, and after taking a good look at me, she said "H-m, you're all very well my dear, but you're not a patch on your mother." I seldom meet any one who knew her without having this tribute paid me.—But as I began by saying, I never wrote these letters; They flamed up, looking at the logs at Rodmell.

I am, soberly and truly, again in robust health, but will leave health to settle this week and despatch a few dreary jobs, such as finding a new house.[3] And then next week—Will you suggest a time? Will you really come and begin again?—for I feel that we were torn asunder, just as we were opening our mouths to say something of the greatest importance.

A line, anytime; and I will keep the day—

Yr
Virginia

Berg

1. Elizabeth Eberstadt of Mannheim married in 1867 George Lewis, the eminent lawyer, who was engaged in almost every legal *cause-célèbre* during the late 19th century and became an intimate friend of King Edward VII. Virginia had met Lady Lewis in 1922 at a musical party.
2. Ethel Smyth's letter does not survive, but Ethel may have quoted from Edgar Allan Poe's poem *To Helen* which contains these lines suggestive of the beauty of Julia Stephen:

> "Helen, thy beauty is to me
> Like those Nicean barks of yore
> That gently, o'er a perfumed sea,
> The weary, way-born wanderer bore
> To his own native shore . . .
> Thy hyacinth hair, thy classic face."

3. The Imperial Hotel Company, which had lost the lawsuit which the Woolfs brought against them, now attempted to outbid them for the lease of 52 Tavistock Square.

2155: To Virginia Isham   52 *Tavistock Sqre., W.C.*1

10 March [1930]

Dear Virginia,

   I have just received this from Eddy Sackville West. I am afraid it is too late to be any use but send it on the chance.

   I hope you have had a good time.

                                          Yours
                                          Virginia Woolf

I believe that Herr Mendelssohn[1] is a person of great influence in the theatres and films.

Northamptonshire Record Office

2156: To Lady Ottoline Morrell
                                   52 *Tavistock Square, W.C.*1

Friday [14 March 1930]

Dearest Ottoline,

   I am a wretch not to have answered you, we have been away, and come back recovered. But I am in rather a rush next week house hunting (we may be turned out of this). Could I come the week after—any day I think, except Monday, between tea and dinner, if you'd let me know.

   I spend my time peering into cupboards and basements.

                                          Yr
                                          Virginia

Texas

2157: To Ethel Smyth   52 *Tavistock Square, W.C.*1

15th March
Sunday March 17th [16, 1930]

   As you say, and apparently mean, that you don't want me to write a letter, I, of course, begin to wish to—a wish I seldom feel now. But I have this reason—I want to know if it would conceivably suit you to come to tea next Tuesday, or next Thursday. These are the drawbacks—on Tuesday there will be a young man—very clever, kind, nice and all that—who would be thrilled to the marrow by meeting you. On Thursday if you came at

---

1. Francesco von Mendelssohn and his sister Eleonora were leaders of Berlin intellectual society. When Hitler came to power, they emigrated to the United States.

4.30 or 5, you would, I think, escape everything but some relics of the scent of Lady Colefax, who is running in and out: after which we should be alone. A line to say which if either (and these are the only chances next week) is all I ask. The week after—but thats too far ahead.

Where can I begin all the things that might be said. My mother? Your Niece?[1] The hermaphrodite?[2] Being vain, I will broach the subject of beauty —just for a moment—and burst out in ecstasy at your defence of me as a very ugly writer—which is what I am—but an honest one, driven like a gasping whale to the surface in a snort—such is the effort and anguish to me of finding a phrase (that is saying what I mean)—and then they say I write beautifully! How could I write beautifully when I am always trying to say something that has not been said, and should be said for the first time, exactly. So I relinquish beauty, and leave it as a legacy to the next generation. My part has been to increase their stock in trade, perhaps. But to leave this fascinating subject—Yes I would like to know all about your niece. Why briefly? Haven't you got a ream of paper which you might just as well fill, sitting over your fire (what sort of fire?) in your room (what sort of room?) alone? For what other purpose than to write letters to me brim full of amusement and excitement were you gifted with a pen like a streak of hounds in full scent? And the more odds and ends you stuff in the better I like it, for I have a habit of making you up in bed at night. Lets imagine Ethel Smyth, I say to myself. We will begin with the servant bringing in the breakfast etc etc. Marriage—yes?—What about marriage? I married Leonard Woolf in 1912, I think, and almost immediately was ill for 3 years.[3] Nevertheless we have nothing to complain of. Youth—I will give you scenes from my youth one day. But I cant take another blue slip now, so must trust that you will continue shooting letters into pillar boxes with a fling of your wrist— better still, that you may come and see me—

I am hoping not to have to leave this house after all.

Yr
Virginia

Berg

1. Elizabeth Williamson, who was in fact Ethel's great-niece, the grand-daughter of Ethel's sister Mary Hunter. Thus Ethel described her for Virginia: "She is 27. . . . Went mad on astronomy, and at the age of 21, set to work, urged by me, to study Greek and mathematics, and now lectures at University College to a class of greybeards on Ptolemaic astronomy. . . . Bursting with fun. No judge of character. I was better at that when I was only sixteen" (quoted in Christopher St John, *Ethel Smyth*, 1959, p. 221).
2. During her 1914 journey through the Nubian desert, described by Ethel in *Beecham and Pharaoh* (1935), she had met and photographed a hermaphrodite, the cast-off 'wife' of a Sheik.
3. Virginia married Leonard on 10 August 1912. She was intermittently insane from September 1913 until June 1915.

Sunday [30 March 1930]

What I have to offer this week (but for God's sake—no I am *not* religious—dont come up on purpose) are Wednesday 4. alone: Thursday 4.30 not alone, but with Leonard and a very good gifted enthusiastic Cambridge don [F. L. Lucas] who would rejoice to see you.

I'm ashamed to let my week run to tatters like this. I'm feeling like a trout in midstream. I'm trying to dispatch a chapter, or a passage, in a book: my head is bedded in it; meanwhile the telephone rings and my friends stream past. But dont take this illegible and inarticulate phrasing to mean that you are a weed or a waterfly or whatever signifies the bother of people who fritter and nudge and must come and wont be put off. No—however, since you have, so you say, and I incline to believe you, a profound and penetrating insight into character, I shan't bother with explanations.

And what is the apple on the bough?

Yr
Virginia

Berg

30th March [1930]

My dear Hugh,

No, not two letters from America—one; and that was clearly impossible to answer, as you were never spending a night anywhere in particular. I hope anyhow the gold is running out of your boots. Well, we had our lawsuit, and we won it, and then the hotel wanted to buy this house, and so I ran about Bloomsbury prying into basements, and always discovering a clergyman with a young lady having a meal; also a poor old solitary, drying her underclothes and they all apologised for being so untidy at the moment. Then the hotel didn't buy; then I got influenza; then I turned over like a slug and slept the month of February out. Meanwhile Leonard left the Nation; and we are now supporting ourselves entirely by the Hogarth Press, which when I remember how we bought £5 worth of type and knelt on the drawing room floor ten years ago setting up little stories and running out of quads.[1]—(the broad space with which one fills up lines) makes my breast burst with pride. Leonard is succeeded by Blunden, and has no more office hours to keep or authors to pacify, thank God.

---

1. The first publication of the Hogarth Press was *Two Stories*, one by Virginia, the other by Leonard, which they published in 1917.

I dont think we shall go to France just yet; but perhaps drive down to Cornwall, selling books—Vita's among them. (I'm very glad you are in favour of it, and hope your view will prevail. We still wait Miss—Somebodies decision).[1] And then I think we shall dash to Italy for ten days or so, but this again depends upon bookselling. But we shan't be away anywhere for long, so please try to hit us off when you are whizzing through again. I will write to the New Forest for a slab of honey upon which to feed your romance. Even if you dont give me your book, I shall read it. But not until I have written my own. My mind hardens itself and regrets all others. I cant write and read at the same time. Hence my deplorable ignorance of modern fiction—I've read scarcely any Lawrence; no Mr Ford Madox Ford,[2] and so on. But I shall read Rogue Herries[3] once my horrible little penance is over—for I must say writing books becomes more and more like entering a nunnery. I cant dine out; I cant go to the play. But all the same I shall read Rogue Herries I repeat. Of course I can read any amount of the dead and biographies and poems. But if I read Rogue Herries I shall write Rogue Herries; and I shall then puzzle Mr Arnold Bennett. But here I am at the end of the 2nd page: you cant complain I've not written a letter.

yr aff
V.W.

All the reviewers seem universally enthusiastic. Are you pleased?

Texas

2160: To Ethel Smyth   52 T[avistock] S.[quare, W.C.1]
Postcard
[1 April 1930]

Delighted you will come Thursday—No, I think I must take a walk—and let my ideas settle on Wednesday—too much talk. But my appetite for letters is measureless to man.

V.W.

Berg

1. Hugh Walpole, who was on the Selection Committee of the Book Society, had read the manuscript of Vita's *The Edwardians*, sent to him by the Hogarth Press, and recommended it. So did the novelist Clemence Dane ('Miss Somebody'), and *The Edwardians* appeared as the Book Society's Choice for June.
2. The literary reputation of Ford Madox Ford (1873-1939) was established by *The Good Soldier* (1915).
3. Walpole's most famous novel, published on 18 March 1930.

Monks House, Rodmell
                                                    [Sussex]

April 5th 1930

My dear Hugh,

That was awfully good of you to send me the book [*Rogue Herries*].
I shall put it aside until I have any wits to spend upon the works of others.
I hope this won't be long.

, Then there are two questions, of a plaguey kind, that I wanted to ask
you—trading upon the beaming and benevolent face which meets me, even
in sculpture, in the Bookman.[1] But dont answer if, as is likely, you have
nothing to say.

(1) We have a large drawing of Thackeray (inherited by my father) done
by Samuel Lawrence at the order of George Smith, as a present to
Thackeray's daughters when he was going lecturing in America.[2] This
we want to sell. Now is there any millionaire of your acquaintance who
would like to buy it? We used to dispose of Thackeray relics to Pierpoint
[*sic*] Morgan, who is now dead, and it strikes me there may be someone who
specialises in Thackeray since. If so, a word from you would greatly help.

(2) I have just had a cable from my American publishers saying that someone wants to make a play of Orlando; and he offers me half profits (also
£100 down on the option.) Is this the usual offer?—or ought one to
hold out for more? Any advice would be welcome.

Well, now I have bothered you enough.

I rather think we shall be here most of April. It is showery and damp, but
heavens how nice to see things growing and be out of the reach of the
telephone! No news of Vita's novel and the Book Society yet.[3] They take
their time, I must say, and until we hear, we cant settle our plans finally.
Thanks again—apologies again.

                                        yr
Texas   Virginia Woolf

52 *T[avistock] S[quare, W.C.1]*

Sunday [6 April 1930]

Good God, Ethel, I daresay you're perfectly right. I daresay I'm a
d——d intellectual. I know nothing about myself. And you coming in with

1. The bust of Walpole, which was illustrated in the *Bookman* of March 1930,
   was by David Evans.
2. Samuel Laurence did two chalk drawings of Thackeray in 1852, one of which
   is in the National Portrait Gallery. Virginia and Vanessa had tried to sell the
   other in 1921, but could not find a purchaser. Their father's first wife was a
   daughter of Thackeray.
3. See p. 153, note 1.

your rapidity and insight probably see whats what in a flash. The party wasn't my choice—I warned you.

But I think I see what you mean.—The [F. L.] Lucases. I've struggled and rebelled against them all my life, but their integrity always makes me their slave. Much though I hate Cambridge, and bitterly though I've suffered from it, I still respect it. I suppose that even without education, as I am, I am naturally of that narrow, ascetic, puritanical breed—oh what a bore; and its too late now. It cant be helped.

You'd be amused to see how I fret and worry when I am suddenly made aware of my own character. For months I forget all about it, and then some-one says But you're the most appalling liar I've ever met, and I rush to the glass (this sheet is a glass) as if I'd been told my dress was upside down, or my nose bleeding. As I told you, I am not a good psychologist.

The sort of thing I like is when you twist up a note out of a cover in the train—Thats life, I say. And I am only a spectator. I happened the other day to read an old article of my own, and I said "Good God, what a prig that woman must be!" I think I must go to some more parties—perhaps they would help. Only I hate dressing and coming into rooms.

Well good night—I'm just back in a flurry from Rodmell and found your note.

Virginia

Berg

2163: To Vanessa Bell   [52 *Tavistock Square, W.C.*1]

[April 1930]

Typewritten

I am taking up the question of the Thackeray drawing; but how am I to get into your studio? Could you send me the key of your room as soon as possible, so that I may get the photographer to come. I am going to offer it first to the Pierpoint [*sic*] library asking £500 unless you think we could ask more. Cartwright starts on May 6th so I want to hear from the Pierpoints first, and thus must hurry.[1] Mary, Barbara and Jeremy[2] had all been over to Rodmell on Saturday. Lord, lord.

Berg

1. Mrs Cartwright had been Manager of the Hogarth Press from July 1925 to March 1930. Presumably she had been asked to take the drawing with her when she went to New York.
2. Barbara and Jeremy were the children of Mary and St John Hutchinson.

Friday [11 April 1930]

Would you be so angelic as to post this? It is to say that I live entirely in the country. I dont think we shall be down till Tuesday or Wednesday, owing to the vicissitudes of the Press. Ethel [Sands] and Nan [Hudson] invited themselves to Rodmell on Easter Sunday; so I suppose that is the fatal date. Duncan has most obligingly undertaken the photograph [of the Thackeray drawing]. Raymond is coming to dinner, so I must I suppose wash. He is foaming with enthusiasm over your Dotty decorations,[1] and says she is as mild as milk now.

I should be with Ottoline at the moment.

We spent yesterday going over greenhouses at Waddesdon.[2]

This is all my news.

B.

There is no doubt but that Ethel Smyth is mad; and determined to know you also. I sat with her for 2 hours at the B.B.C. the other night—hearing her life history in a loud voice.

Berg

2165: To Hugh Walpole   *Monks House, Rodmell,*
Lewes [Sussex]
(*we go there tomorrow*)

Typewritten
April 15th [1930]

My dear Hugh,

Many thanks for your great kindness. (I use a typewriter because I am trying to be businesslike, and shall have to write figures clearly).

I have sent particulars of our [Thackeray] picture to Miss Green, mentioning you. Old [Pierpont] Morgan bought the Vanity Fair MS.[3] so this seems appropriate. We are asking £500, and I have a photograph

1. Dorothy Wellesley had commissioned Vanessa and Duncan to decorate her dining-room at Penns-in-the-Rocks, Withyham, Sussex. Each painted three large wall panels, and jointly designed the furniture. The room was not completely finished until 1931.
2. Waddesdon Manor, near Aylesbury in Buckinghamshire, was built in the 1880s for Ferdinand de Rothschild. Philip, Leonard's brother, was the Rothschilds' farm-manager, and the Woolfs had visited him there.
3. Virginia and Vanessa sold one page of the *Vanity Fair* manuscript to Pierpont Morgan in 1917.

which I could send if you wished it. But I will wait to hear from Miss Green
—it is only that if she fails to buy, then some friend of yours might be
willing. Anyhow a thousand thanks. We have had this drawing knocking
about for years, and at last wish to be rid of it. I am being sent a contract
by my American playwright [of *Orlando*. See Letter 2161] and will then if
you dont mind ask your advice on details.

Now thats all the cursed business.

I think we shall be away a fortnight now and then back anyhow for the
first part of May.

The Book Society has juggled about its dates so that we have had to
alter our plans according. Now the book [*The Edwardians*] comes out on
May 29th I think.

So we shall hope to see you in May which has a poetic and romantic
ring about it, as should be dear to your heart.

The typewriter is not an expressive instrument is it?

Yours affectionately
V.W.

Texas

2166: To Helen McAfee   52 *Tavistock Square, London, W.C.*1

Typewritten
15th April 1930

Dear Miss McAfee,

I have cabled to you today to apply to the Bookman for an article of
mine on Augustine Birrell,[1] as I gather from your cable that you are counting
on some thing from me for your summer number. I sent them this article
some time ago and as I have not heard from them, I should much prefer you
to have it. I believe they meant to print it, but they have kept it so long that
I do not think they can object to your having it.

I was just going to write to you on my own account. I have been held
up by an attack of influenza, and all my time is still used on a novel that I
am trying to finish this summer. Thus I have not written any story or article
since the autumn, and cannot yet say when I shall be free. The Birrell article
is thus the only piece I have at present in a state ready for publication.

Would you let me know as soon as you can when you intend to publish
it? It is to appear here in Life and Letters [July 1930] and I must arrange with
Mr McCarthy.

I am sorry not to have done the Lady Clifford;[2] but I am sure you will
understand how difficult it is to stop one piece of work and turn aside to

1. Review of *The Collected Essays and Addresses of Augustine Birrell* (*Yale
   Review*, June 1930).
2. Lady Anne Clifford. See p. 352, note 1.

another. In future, I shall avoid making any promises, for novels always take more time than one expects!

With kind regards,

yours sincerely

Yale University

Virginia Woolf

2167: To William Wyamar Vaughan

52 Tavistock Square, London W.C.1

April 18th 1930

My dear Will,[1]

I am afraid that I am interrupting a holiday, and that I have no right to address you personally. But I am asked by my brother-in-law, Philip Woolf,[2] if I could help him about putting his little boy's name down for Rugby. The child is 3, and his father particularly wants him to go to Rugby if possible, and naturally to the best house. Would you be so very kind to give me any advice about this that I could hand on? I should be extremely grateful to you, and so would they. The little boy is the only son.

I heard from Janet from America the other day.[3] It is a great pleasure to get to know her again, after knowing her as a child at Giggleswick—a time I always remember with great affection.

Your affate

John Vaughan

Virginia Woolf

2168: To Ethel Smyth

Monks House, Rodmell
[Sussex]

22nd April [1930]

Many congratulations. This refers to your publisher.

Oddly enough—I did precisely the same thing—that is wrote you a long letter and tore it up, owing I think to its egotism. Lord, how furious it makes me to think of the reams you destroyed! Please fish the ashes up and re-write them. You can't bore me; if thats what you were thinking.

1. William Vaughan, Virginia's cousin, had successively been Headmaster of Giggleswick, Wellington and Rugby. His wife Madge was an early intimate of Virginia and the original of Sally Seton in *Mrs Dalloway*.
2. Philip was Leonard's youngest brother, and his son Cecil was the only male grandchild of Leonard's parents. Virginia was in error about the boy's age. In 1930 he was eight years old. When he was four, in 1926, she had tried to obtain for him a place at Eton College. See Volume III of this Edition, Letter 1646.
3. Janet Vaughan, Will's daughter, was studying clinical pathology under a Rockefeller Fellowship.

I have just re-lit the fire, in order to be able to write this. And I may tell you that I cooked lunch today and made a loaf of really expert bread. We have our young widow [Mrs Thompsett] half the day—and she goes and leaves us; This is very nearly the ideal life I think; but we have our crosses; I mean people drop in. They are divine people, with whom everything is possible (and how can you suppose that you and your nakedness could shock?—if you heard us—no I'm ashamed even to sketch our bi-sexual conversations. You must revise your estimate of our society radically) Everything is possible I was saying; but I want silence. Today for the first time, I have seen nobody, and my book, a very flickering flame at the moment, begins to draw.[1] I dont know if music needs a shelter round it. Writing is so damnably susceptible to atmosphere. If I could sit here for three months alone, saying the same things, doing the same things, day by day—then perhaps a few pages would be solidly written in the end. As it is, I shall go back to London, and shiver it all to bits. What one wants for writing is habit; I am like one of Leonards fish (we have a pond) which is off at the shadow of a leaf—but I'm egotistical again, and no doubt shall have to burn this. No I cant be bothered to burn it.

I will try to keep May 24th if that is the day—I have left your letter in the house, and it is too cold to go and get it. (This house, you understand, contains two outer rooms, in which I live; it contains a large room where we sit and eat, play the gramophone, prop our feet up on the side of the fire, and read endless books). But then I may have to go travelling our new books in the West. We have no traveller this year, and are going to try it ourselves, in the car. It may be that week; it may be the one before. Bath, Exeter, Penzance, Lands End.

Well, what are you doing? I suppose Rottingdean is over; and you are back at Woking, carrying on the mysterious existence which I make up sometimes, in spite of the truth of your saying that I know less about human nature than anyone you ever met. (In the egotistical letter by the way I told you not to read The Common Reader—mostly school girls articles, done obediently to celebrate the great dead, for the Times; and so very submissive and long winded. They had to cover 4 columns.)

Are you writing? How does one write music? And whom do you see, and what do you say when you see them? Perhaps at Rottingdean you saw Lady Jones [Enid Bagnold]. I like to think so.

You see, our society is one of the freest I have ever met—to return to that. Even with little Don Lucas (whom I love and respect, but his asceticism as you know is icy and glittering) I would discuss, and have discussed, the most intimate details of sexual life. He and his wife [Topsy] are separated.

I had my lovely niece [Angelica] here yesterday, and my sister, who is

1. Virginia finished the first draft of *The Waves* on 29 April, and she began on 13 June to rewrite it.

erratically, after the way of middleaged women, even lovelier: also Clive Bell; and Duncan Grant; and we talked for 3 hours without a break.

Well, I cant get warm enough to hold the pen in such a way that one word is written differently from another—I shall go and get Leonard—no, he is planting hollyhocks: I shall get my dog then and go for a brisk walk on the marshes, returning at 7.30 sharp when my enchanting widow will dish up two grilled herrings. Our dinner will cost us 7d.

Yes you ought to be here now and see the bust of Venus against the pear tree (I have verified the tree by looking out of the window)

I dont want to come back to London in the least. Oh and I have 15 letters to write, and at least 3 foot of Ms. to read and two worrying, tiresome, authors, whose fate, they say, depends on me, to knock on the head.

Naturally therefore I warble on, unnecessarily to Dame Ethel Smyth; who won't read all this, being in a hurricane today, putting in trumpets, cello's and a trombone or two in the bass. She thumps it out on her piano; and is only roused to life by her dog; does she ever eat her dinner, or is it always cold?

VW.

Berg

2169: To V. Sackville-West   [*Monk's House, Rodmell, Sussex*]

Friday [25 April 1930]

"I dont think I can stand, even the Nicolsons, on happiness for three quarters of an hour" I said at 8.15.[1]

"Well, we can always shut them off" said Leonard. At 9 I leapt to my feet and cried out,

"By God, I call that first rate!" having listened to every word.

This is (for a wonder) literally true. How on earth have you mastered the art of being subtle, profound, humorous, arch, coy, satirical, affectionate, intimate, profane, colloquial, solemn, sensible, poetical and a dear old shaggy sheep dog—on the wireless? We thought it a triumph: Harold's too.

And shall you be in London on Monday? I think I shall—and free for tea or dinner. We might go somewhere. But let me know to 52 T.S. and I'll wire if, as is possible, I stay here, walking the downs and biting my nails.

Oh Lord if I could finish this book!

V.

Just off to Tunbridge Wells to travel books; and might look in on Long Barn; but shan't I suppose.

Berg

1. On 24 April Vita and Harold broadcast a discussion on happiness for the BBC.

Monday [28 April 1930]

I have just got back and found your letters. I am sure you are perfectly right to be angry with what I said in my letter. I dont remember exactly what it was, but I expect it was the sort of banter which (as Vita or any of my friends would tell you) I always scribble in letters. (I wasn't thinking of Dodo,[1]—it was something you said on the telephone to your maid; and I dont understand why my wishing you to see my pear tree annoys you— you wish me to see your daffodils)[2] But I dont excuse myself.

I am oddly (since I am the victim) glad that you should be disillusioned —I hate illusions. So no more.

Berg

Typewritten
29th April 1930

Dear Miss McAfee,

I just send a line to say that I have received your cable offering 250 dollars for the article on Mr Birrell[3] on condition that it does not appear here before July 1st.

I will accept the offer and see that the article does not appear until the time stated.

With thanks,

yours sincerely
Virginia Woolf

Yale University

1. In E. F. Benson's novel *Dodo* (1893), the heroine's aggressive, candid friend, Edith Staines, is modelled on Ethel.
2. Virginia's wish that Ethel could see the tree was expressed in passing (see p. 160), but Ethel was melodramatically offended. She again wrote to Virginia about the subject on 2 May: "But the difference between the pear tree and the daffodils was this: that if I didn't know that peace is chiefly what you want, I'd have implored you, *if* you ever take jaunts in the car, to look at my daffodils . . . whereas what you did was to wait . . . till I had left the neighbourhood, and then say to me (as Betty does to local givers of garden parties 'O that would have been nice') 'I wish you could see the Venus against the pear tree'. This seemed to me mockery . . . for I do care a lot about people's framework" (*Berg*).
3. See p. 157, note 1.

Letters 2172–2213 (May–July 1930)

For a week Virginia and Leonard toured the West Country, travelling by car as far as Penzance. Their main purpose was to canvass the current Hogarth Press list to booksellers, and they had little success, but Vita's novel The Edwardians *was an immediate best-seller on publication (29 May), and was chosen as the Book of the Month both in England and in America. Between bursts of journalism, Virginia was writing and typing her second draft of* The Waves, *finding it desperately hard work. She described her struggles only in her diary and in letters to Ethel Smyth (for example, Letter 2203), and although she told Vanessa that Ethel seemed to be off her head, she had begun to confide in her in other ways, particularly about her past. As a relaxation she continued to set type for the Hogarth Press. Whitsun and some other week-ends were spent at Monk's House, and the Woolfs went there on 29 July for their usual summer holiday.*

2172: To V. Sackville-West   *52 Tavistock Square, W.C.*1

Thursday [1 May 1930]

The Wolves are much ashamed of themselves, but it is a question of the pregnant dog [Pinker]. We dont think she will be welcome in hotels. Could she therefore spend the week with you?—but only if no one is upset. And if so, we could send her by any train convenient or by Ethel (Sands) on Saturday. And fetch her on Saturday or Sunday following. My head spins: ears ache: Ethel (Smyth) just gone.

                                                 Virginia

Potto *did that*

Berg

2173: To V. Sackville-West   *Castle Hotel, Taunton*
                                                        [Somerset]

May 5th [1930]

Yes, you are to *dine* with us, *not* tea, 8, or as early as you can, on Monday. Clive, I think and Lyn [Lloyd Irvine].

So far, a very good journey. Lord how lovely the Marlborough downs are! Why put up with Kent and Sussex? Then Bath: quite magnificent. Every street like Pope or Dryden: and everywhere Burke stayed or Sir

Walter Scott, Wordsworth and Fanny Burney. I can't see why it isnt more famous than Cambridge and Oxford together. We went on to Bristol, and saw your Mr Cleverdon; who bought 10 of the limited edition [of *The Edwardians*] and wd. have liked more. We have made about £10 today, though the booksellers are for the most part rude, ignorant, and out for lunch or tea or something. Then we went to Wells, saw Glastonbury in the rain; and it is still raining hard at Taunton.

Also I adore the life of hotels.—Endless grey haired single ladies with friends, all with wedding rings, and I daresay dead husbands; and they begin at breakfast "O dear, Minny says the footman and the housemaid started scarlet fever the very day dear Micky was going back to school"—so that I feel England is incredibly prosperous; eats enormous plates of porridge and bacon; and how they talk. The age of England becomes almost too much. Not a new house; and bits of a ruin even in the lounge, here—Tomorrow we go to Exeter or Truro. So no more. I'm so sleepy.

Yr.
Virginia

Ethel has made me a decration [*sic*] of violent but platonic love.[1]

Berg

2174: To Ethel Smyth   *Truro* [*Cornwall*]

Tuesday, perhaps 6th May [1930]

Well we have reached here safely, and found your letter, but we did not bring the dog, from cowardice. Excuse irrelevance, illspelling, psychological flaws. I'm so sleepy. We have been driving all day from Taunton over Dartmoor in a storm, and selling books where we saw a shop, but its disheartening business. No one reads, no one wants books, the booksellers say, and they keep us hanging about. But Lord what a lovely country this is —England, I mean; and ever so much older than I thought. I want to live on Marlborough Down, most. Here we are under your Bensons Cathedral, and my Hugh Walpoles Cathedral.[2] But how I yawn! The evenings are the

1. Ethel had written to Virginia: "Odd as it may seem to you I did love you before I saw you, wholly solely because of 'a room of one's own'. There is that in it— most of it far far away in the background, the inmost core of the book, that (as I since found out) is your essence" (2 May 1930, *Berg*).
2. E. W. Benson, later Archbishop of Canterbury, was Bishop of Truro, 1877-83. He was the father of the three men of letters—A. C., E. F. and R. H. Benson. Hugh's father, George Henry Somerset Walpole, held office in the Cathedral at Truro during the same years, and Hugh based his novel *The Cathedral* (1922) on it.

worst—nowhere to sit; or a room full of old, suspicious widow ladies, whispering to each other. Not an Inn from London here is without its six or seven. And once they were married, and once they had children. And my head spins wondering what they're doing in Truro tonight: but then they get up and go. Yes, I'm too sleepy to go into psychology. But you see; I make up stories; thats my downfall; imagine situations, and forget that the person concerned is flesh and blood, like myself, with feelings. I am therefore very treacherous. But enough of myself.

By the way, I heard the Wreckers[1] years ago, from the pit, in some theatre. Tomorrow we go to Penzance; visit my old home, St Ives[2]; and then back, by way of Salisbury and Rodmell. What a spin! Its a kind of dream—one glides from town to town, up hills, by rivers; always the same old ladies at night.

Virginia

Berg

2175: TO VANESSA BELL   *St. Ives* [*Cornwall*]

Wednesday [7 May 1930]

We are lunching at Hamlyns off cream and splits, which you may remember. It is a perfect day—Everything has gone well, so far, except that we cant induce the shops to buy much. We came over Sedgemoor and Dartmoor and saw the prisoners working with warders [at Princetown Prison]: today we went into the Arnold-Forsters garden [Zennor], they being away, and were glad to find it very inferior.

Bath is a magnificent city—far better than Oxford and Cambridge. The consistency of the architecture is amazing; which is true even of the people playing the viola in the pump room—all pure 18th Century. We went to a concert. Of course no letter from you, but several pages from E[thel] S[myth]: of mitigated madness—I have written kindly and calmly, and hope for the best. Should you be able to do me any service, so much the better; but I see you despise me for my predicament and will only keep out of one yourself.

The old ladies of England are a perpetual joy. They swarm in every hotel, knitting, writing letters, widows mostly. But, warned by E. S., I have made no friends. Now we are off to Bodmin. I'm sending you some cream,

1. Ethel's opera, composed in 1903-4, with a libretto by Henry Brewster. Virginia had heard its first English performance on 22 June 1909.
2. Talland House, where Virginia spent her childhood holidays.

for old sakes sake. The harbour is still incredibly beautiful. Lanhams there and Curnow.[1] You must bring Angelica soon.

B.

Berg

2176: TO V. SACKVILLE-WEST   *Kings Arms Hotel, Launceston*
                              [Cornwall]

Thursday 8? May [1930]

Look—isnt this nice.[2] As I was saying the antiquity of England is inconceivable. What is to be done about it? It must go on—(I'm waiting for the clergyman to leave the w.c. vacant.) Have you ever conceived the antiquity of England in a thousand years?—Every Inn we stay at has been an inn since the time of Arthur or Alfred. Here we have come down in the world—bells dont ring; hot water cold; but still a great air of the 18th Century in the coffee room, where we sit before a huge fire, with the clergy and the travellers in biscuits. Our sales have diminished steadily. The booksellers are often very rude and L. almost loses his temper. They are all violently against the Book Society and say it is ruining them. Then they won't listen when we say The Edwardians is next months book. They say it is all a wash out and favouritism. Whats odd is that in Cornwall they live entirely by selling Cornish novels; one small shop yesterday had sold 2,000 by an unknown (to me) man called Garstin.[3] We had a superb drive from Penzance over the moor to Zennor, all the gorse blazing against a pure blue sea, to St Ives; where I saw my Lighthouse,[4] and the gate of my home, through tears—thinking how my mother died at my age; or next year to it—Also we drove over Bodmin moor, solitary completely, with an occasional ancient cross. And now (if only the wc. were vacant) we are off to Sherborne, Yeovil, Salisbury.

V.

1. 'Lanhams' was James Lanham's, a general store at St Ives and printers of the local newspaper. The shop also dealt in painting materials for the growing colony of Cornish artists, who exhibited in Lanham's upstairs premises. 'Curnow' was a large café in St Ives, popular with local society, and also the town's bakery.
2. The hotel's letterhead device, crowned by the royal arms.
3. Crosbie Garstin lived at Lamorna Cove, near Penzance, and wrote novels, poetry, and books of Oriental travel. His novels, which were sagas of Cornish life, included *The Owl's House* (1923), *The West Wind* (1926), and *The Dragon and the Lotus* (1928).
4. Godrevy Lighthouse, St Ives Bay, the model for the one in *To the Lighthouse*.

We shall meet at dinner on Monday. My cheeks are the colour of old golf shoes; red brown with touches of pure crimson on the nose.

We have to come back on Sunday to see [Count Harry] Kessler[1]—damn him.

Berg

2177: To William Wyamar Vaughan

Monks House, Lewes,
Sussex

10th May 1930

My dear Will,

This is just to thank you for your letter. It was very good of you, and I have told my brother-in-law what you say.[2]

We are just back from a tour in a car through the West. We called in at Clifton[3] and I wondered where it was that you lived.

With love from us both.

your affte
Virginia Woolf

John Vaughan

2178: To Dorothy Brett

Monk's House, Rodmell,
Lewes [Sussex]

May 10th 1930

My dear Brett,

I am sorry to be such a bad correspondent. The older I grow, the more I hate writing letters, or rather, I still like writing letters, but hate writing notes, and have to write 20 dozen (so it seems) every day. But I like getting letters, so it was very nice of you to write.

It is monstrous that Lawrence should have died.[4] I never spoke to him, and only saw him twice—once, swinging a spirit lamp in a shop at St Ives, and once, two or three years ago when our train stopped outside Rome in the early morning and there was Lawrence talking to Norman Douglas on the other platform.[5]

1. See p. 11, note 4.
2. See Letter 2167.
3. Will Vaughan had been an assistant master at Clifton College (Bristol) from 1890 to 1904.
4. Dorothy Brett was one of D. H. Lawrence's disciples and joined him in Taos, New Mexico, in 1924, where he hoped to establish an ideal community. When he left Taos, Brett remained there for fifty years.
5. See Volume III of this Edition, p. 361.

The papers have been hypocritical beyond belief: I almost blazed into print in a rage; first abusing her [Frieda Lawrence] and then slobbering over him. I dont suppose it matters—And I couldn't write because I have never read any of his books, or more than half of two of them.[1] I hate preaching— and I can't read contemporaries; and I dont want to read novels, whoever writes them.

We have just driven from London to Penzance, selling our books as we went; and got here last night, very cold, but—though you wont believe it, much astonished by the beauty of England: for instance, Bodmin Moor. Will your eye be quite out for English beauty? Are your scales so much huger? What I envy is your warmth, and being able to sit in the sun and talk. Here it pours, and half one's faculties are for ever furled up useless.

I have been seeing Ottoline, who talks a great deal and very affectionately of Lawrence. They made it up I think when she was ill last year, and he began writing to her again.[2] Aldous Huxley is over here, buzzing about his letters;[3] and I hear that [J. M.] Murry has gone to be with Freda—you can imagine the sort of buzz and hum all this sets up. And Kot [S. S. Koteliansky] has come out of his hole and goes to tea with Ottoline which must be good for what remains of her soul.

I am very glad you liked A Room. It was rather popularised for the young and should have had more in it. But I wanted them to swallow certain ideas with a view to setting their brains to work. I get letters from every quarter revealing the horrors still of family life. I wonder how much was spent on your Education, compared with your brothers'—twopence half-penny I daresay. However you seem to have triumphed; you have your Indians, and they finance Life and Letters.[4]

Sydney Waterlow was here this summer; uneasily protesting his perfect happiness. Every sentence began "And are you *still*" doing so and so, from which we gathered that we are hopeless stick in the muds and failures, and that leads me to suppose that poor old Sydney is not quite so secure as he makes himself out. But he was amiable in the extreme.

yr
Virginia Woolf

Robert H. Taylor

1. She had read at least the following Lawrence novels: *Trespassers*, *The Lost Girl* (which she reviewed in *TLS*, 2 December 1920), and *Women in Love*. Later she wrote *Notes on D. H. Lawrence* (*see The Moment and Other Essays*, 1947).
2. Lawrence and Ottoline Morrell had quarrelled in 1921 when he drew an unpleasant portrait of her as Hermione Roddice in *Women in Love*.
3. Aldous Huxley, who had been with Lawrence when he died, edited his *Letters* in 1932.
4. The journal founded by Desmond MacCarthy in 1928.

Wednesday May 13th [14th 1930]

Lord how difficult it is to write a letter! You painters and musicians dont know the horror of pens that dry up and no blotting paper.

Also, what with you and Vanessa, I feel rather like a mouse pinned out on a board for dissection. I'm so odd, and I'm so limited, and I'm so different from the ordinary human being—so you say. I have a strong suspicion that I'm the simplest of you all, and that its my extreme transparency that baffles you too otherwise gifted women. I dont think I ever feel anything but the most ordinary emotions; but there—I wont begin cutting about the poor mouse, who is distracted enough without that. Shall I or shall I not go to the Opera—Parsifal—with Hugh Walpole? Shall I or shall I not go to a cocktail party at Raymond Mortimers? Shall I or shall I not read the three long MSS. on my table—or go on reading Hazlitt for an article that has to be begun tomorrow,[1] or take Pinka for a walk—but then she will have puppies on the pavement—or do nothing—nothing at all? Those are my predicaments. Yet we only came back on Sunday; and it is only Wednesday; and already I am spun over with doubts and impaled with thorns. Would you and Vanessa know how to burst through, free and unscathed? I suppose so. Well, I wont begin on you and Vanessa, or I should draw some of those fancy pictures for which I am so famous—(a joke—if I had any red ink, I would write my jokes in it, so that even certain musicians—ahem!)

I dont see why Miss E. Williamson[2] shouldn't come and dine with us. Why not? I dont see why she should be shy. I dont see how you can play your music because I haven't got a piano. I feel at the moment a helpless babe on the shore of life, turning over pebbles. You and Vanessa must really see to the whole affair. I forgot to say—there is no sequence in these remarks—that my life is further complicated by six letters daily from people telling me which is my best book; and it is always different. Then I puzzle over that. And you, E.S., say the opposite. And I have to write so many very polite lies—being myself I think the truthfullest of people. Did I once say I lied? Well, that was a joke. I cant pass a lie, no more than—Camel a needle. Leonard's printing. Pinka's snoring. Shall I go to the opera, shall I go to the cocktail party? So the ocean tosses its pebbles, and I turn them over, naked, a child, and no one helps me. There's Ethel at Woking among her pear—no daffodil trees; with her bacon mouldering on the piano. Dear me! I've gone and done it again! By the way, why do you take so much interest

1. Review of *The Complete Works of William Hazlitt* (*New York Herald Tribune*, 7 September 1930).
2. See p. 151, note 1.

in your own character? Or dont you? Why are you so fiercely and savagely aware of what is to me a transient and fitful flame?

V.

Berg

2180: To Julian Bell   52 *Tavistock Square, W.C.*1

Typewritten
13th May [1930]

My dear Julian,

Have you got Toms poems and Adamastor?[1] If not, I will send them; but I have forgotten so long, and been so much distracted by driving to Cornwall and back, that I daresay you have already bought them. Tell me in that case another book you want—for as you may remember, I owe you a birthday present; and it is now mid May, whereas, in the language of the poets, you were a February fair child.

Are you coming to dine one night? Bring Miss Sutar [Helen Soutar] if you will. Bring anyone. There are many things to be said—about Adamastor, I rather doubt that he's much better than a Byronic rhetorician; but people so much want a poet with guts that they cling to him like men in a storm. Poor old Desmond for instance. Toms hard boiled egg is hard boiled I admit; all this damnable Mary and Mother and God. Still he can write, oh yes, you may sniff. But he can. I'm told Peters poems are out;[2] shall I get them? Thank Heaven, I feel no more responsibilities as a critic. Nobody knows one from t'other. I've not read your poems in the Cambridge book yet [*Cambridge Poetry* 1929]; but that is because I so much reverence poetry that, though I cant judge it, I never read it till I can read and read, and let it sink and sink, till it reaches the bottom, and then rises again, like the dead, after seven days, and then I shall tell you, when I've let it sink for seven days, and it has risen like the dead, what I think.

The Singer went gallantly, because she was as dirty as a coal hole, Martins said; plugs were foul; engine a mere mass of carbon; yet she went to Penzance and back without a hitch.

Your loving Aunt
Virginia

Quentin Bell

1. T. S. Eliot's *Ash Wednesday* and Roy Campbell's *Adamastor*, both published in 1930.
2. F. L. Lucas, *Marionettes* (1930).

Typewritten
14th May 1930

Dearest Quentin,

What a delight to get your letter—and what, into the bargain, a miracle. For I had been dreaming of you, that very night, and you had been so brilliant, so charming in my dream that I woke saying Naturally he will never write to me: whereupon I looked at my letters, and there was yours. This happens, oddly enough to be true. Whether it is also true that you are charming and brilliant, is as Nessa would say, another pair of shoes. But let us be quit of that sinister woman, with her unparalleled truth speaking and say you are—very very charming—very very brilliant. You will have your father with you I suppose, and have sucked the egg of all its yolk. If he cant tell you the London news, who can? Its true I went to a cocktail party yesterday at Raymonds, and I could describe that. But it was given to pay off debts, and the debtors came flocking, nodding, ogling, mostly old women with purple noses; Ottoline was almost the freshest and fairest. No. There were also Barbara Hutchinson, with a head like the stopper of a Chinese scent bottle; one blob of crimson. And Mary had another head one blob of emerald green. This must be the latest fashion, because Barbara told me she was dressed up to the eyes, and couldn't face society undressed. Honestly I doubt that I think the career of a dressed girl sitting on a stool and waiting offers altogether satisfactory. It used to be the usual lot; now it seems somehow antique. And there were crowds of young men of a certain cast; and a German [Hamann] who does lifemasks, putting one straw up your nose and another down your throat. I shant be done; because to be exactly recorded has no longer any virtue in my eyes. But I am to be done on the floor of the National Gallery as Clio to Clive's Bacchus by Anrep.[1]

We have just been lunching with Peter Lucas and heard some news of Julian. Peter rather fears that Miss Helen [Soutar] has taken his mind off the poets and he wont cut such a good figure in the exam. as he should. They are inseparable and are asked out together, and interlock on every occasion. I thought her so like some warm blooded thick coated brown eyed sharp clawed marsupial in the Zoo that I cant attach any precise human value. Thats the worst of writing—images, often of the most grotesque, oust the sober truth. There are masses of things to say, but I dont think you would read them if I said them. Why were you on the downs when I came to

1. Boris Anrep was commissioned to design a mosaic pavement for the entrance hall of the National Gallery, in which Bloomsbury and other people were represented as classical gods and muses. In addition to Clive and Virginia, Mary Hutchinson appeared as the Muse of Erotic Poetry, Osbert Sitwell as the God of Music, Greta Garbo as the Muse of Tragedy, and Lydia Keynes as the Muse of Song and Dance.

tea at Charleston? Because we never meet now, and so I cant know exactly anymore what the shape of your mind is; no; perhaps you are elongated, tortuous and cloven, where I think of you still voluminous as a coal sack.

An old woman of seventy one [Ethel Smyth] has fallen in love with me. It is at once hideous and horrid and melancholy-sad. It is like being caught by a giant crab. She has just wired to ask me to meet her. Please let me have your advice. Now I am going off to tea with Nessa. Please write again dearest Quentin; to your old doddering devoted Aunt.

Quentin Bell

2182: To V. Sackville-West   52 *Tavistock Square, W.C.*1

[20 May 1930]

About 2,000 sold, not counting Book Club, very good. I think the other questions are answered.

L. says he told you he cdn't put on the sash,[1] for what reason I forget.
Well, we shall meet on Friday.[2]
Endless rings, notes, expresses, and other communications from E.S.
She says you say you have sold 170,000 of Edwardians already.

Berg

2183: To Ethel Smyth   52 *Tavistock Sqre. WC*1

Monday [26 May 1930]

Look—I have taken a new nib.

If only I weren't a writer, perhaps I could thank you and praise you and admire you perfectly simply and expressively and say in one word what I felt about the Concert yesterday. As it is, an image forms in my mind; a quickset briar hedge, innumerably intricate and spiky and thorned; in the centre burns a rose. Miraculously, the rose is you; flushed pink, wearing pearls. The thorn hedge is the music; and I have to break my way through violins, flutes, cymbals, voices to this red burning centre. Now I admit that this has nothing to do with musical criticism. It is only what I feel as I sat on my silver winged (was it winged?) chair on the slippery floor yesterday. I am enthralled that you, the dominant and superb, should have this tremor and vibration of fire round you—violins flickering, flutes purring; (the image is of a winter hedge)—that you should be able to create this world

1. A paper band folded around the dust jacket of *The Edwardians*.
2. On 23 May Virginia went for the first time to Sissinghurst Castle.

from your centre. Perhaps I was not thinking of the music but of all the loves and ages you have been through. Lord—what a complexity the soul is! But I wont scratch all the skin off my fingers trying to expound. But my dear Ethel it was frightfully good of you to let me come—dear me yes— what a generous woman you are—and how I adore your generosity and the vehemence with which you scatter the floor with hairpins and fumble in your placket for a spectacle case and embrace the Governor of Cyprus and enfold us all in the spontaneity and ruthlessness of your career.

Thats what I call living; thats the quality I would give my eyes to possess. Of course, in my furtive and sidelong way (being like a flat fish with eyes not in the usual place) I had read a good deal of this years ago in your books, and now I begin to read it and other oddities and revelations too in your music. It will take a long time not merely because I am musically so feeble, but because all my faculties are so industriously bringing in news of so many Ethels at the same moment. There I sit a mere target for impressions and try to catch each one as it flies and find its gold or its white or its blue ring for it. I only offer this explanation of my dumbness and fatuity yesterday. I couldn't say 'I like that best' or 'that' because I was sorting out, in a rapid elementary way, a myriad arrows: But perhaps you saw, with your hawk's glance, to the bottom of my silence.

Now Ethel, please do something for me really generous; and let me contribute my share to the entertainment: Please do. I had a ticket (which I lost) and tea, a very good tea, and I want to write a cheque to give to the gentleman like an enraged frog playing cymbals in the background. He wants a new tie—it is all gone shiny on the left hand side. Please convey this to him with my blessing.

Well: my cook [Nelly] has been stricken in the kidneys: I'm waiting for the doctor; I may have to take her to the hospital—A dismal sort of morning. But I recur to the rose among the briars, like an old gypsy woman in a damp ditch warming her hands at the fire. And then we have to give 3 Scandinavians lunch at a restaurant.[1]

Theres the doctor. No: a false alarm.

Nevertheless, I must bring this to an end and grapple with the problems of normal and natural human life.

By the way, Pinka has had 6 puppies, all black, in my arm chair at Rodmell.

I wrote to ask M[aurice]. Baring to dine, with Eliz [Williamson]: no answer: I sent it to the Chelsea address. What am I to do? O Ethel please tell me, what am I to do?

Virginia

Berg

---

1. Leonard's cousin Charlotte Mannheimer, her friend Mary, and Leonard's mother.

Thursday [29 May 1930]

Merely a post card:

Dont keep Wednesday—because I can't be sure at all—everything is very vague. We're going to Rodmell tomorrow, back Saturday, and away again for Whitsun.

I am, to tell the truth, rather harassed by all this business of cooks and hospitals and cant command my time: or sense; or pen. But I will write later.

Virginia

Tell Elizabeth not to expect much dinner on Monday; she must have an egg with her tea. But all the same she must come.

Berg

Typewritten
Monday [2 June 1930]

Darling Angelica,

What a treat to get your letter! Mummy gave it me, as we were having tea together. Mummy was making a beautiful white silk petticoat. How I wish I could sew like you and Mummy—but its too late I suppose for you to teach me now. When you come and stay at Rodmell will you give me lessons? Pinka sat on one of the puppies so there are only five—four daughters and one son—all coal black, except for three white paws, one white tail, and four white cheeks. We are going to call one Sheba. The son will be called Othello.

I went to Hamlet the other night. I will take you there when you are in London; or any other play you choose. Hamlet is very exciting. I met Ottoline there, and her hair has gone the colour of Pinka's coat, bright red. But this is a secret between us.

Oh dear how I wish you would run in now and then we could have some pranks with the sugar. Old Miss Pritchard[1] is doddering about on the roof—what can she be doing up there? Nelly is in hospital. I have a new cook [Mrs Taupin]. And she is making me a new pudding for lunch so I must go and eat it.

Love from Pinka, Sheba, Othello, Leonardo

Jinny

AND PLEASE WRITE AGAIN.

Angelica Garnett

1. The sister of the partner in the firm of Dollman & Pritchard, solicitors, who shared 52 Tavistock Square with the Woolfs.

*52 Tavistock Square, W.C.*1

Typewritten
3rd June 1930

Dear Mr Lewis,
    I have today sent off the signed sheets in three parcels. I hope they will reach you safely. I much look forward to seeing the finished book.[1]

Yours sincerely
Virginia Woolf
(Mrs Woolf)

Columbia University

2187: To Clive Bell   [*52 Tavistock Square, W.C.*1]

Postcard
[5 June 1930]

    This is just to remind you of the Empire.[2] I'm so scarified with domestic horrors—operations—kidneys—cooks—Nelly in hospital—dinners without any food—that I cant write: but with love to Francis [Birrell].

Quentin Bell

2188: To Vanessa Bell   *Monks House* [*Rodmell, Sussex*]

Saturday 7th June [1930]

Dearest Dolphin
    That old woman [Mrs Taupin] must be doddering, I think—She came and told me she had lost the key and Mansfield[3] and I poked about and found it—so if its lost, I think it must be in the street. Never mind.
    We've settled that the best plan is to pay her a week's wages and start another system, which I think will work better. (but I'm so bored with it all, I wont go into details) So I've written to her to say that we shant want her again, as the dr. says Nelly cant come before September and I've had to engage somebody else.

1. *Street Haunting* (1930), published in a limited and signed edition by The Westgate Press, San Francisco.
2. On the reverse side was a photograph of the Royal Horse Guards in Whitehall. Clive was in Paris.
3. Mrs Mansfield was the caretaker of 37 Gordon Square.

I've told her that Duncan will give her 15/- and the cheque is made out to him. Poor old creature—I think she's really on her last legs and would certainly drop dead if we kept her at it. I still maintain however that she has flashes of cookery worthy of genius. I expect gentle housework is all she is fit for now. If you could persuade her not to come and see me, I should be grateful. I'll look for the keys and send them if she hasn't been able to get in: supposing—as is necessary—that theyre there. Lord—thats over, thank God.

We wish to goodness you had sent us Maynards letter. After I left you the other evening I ran into Lydia. She was coming along Francis Street, and I waved with my usual cordiality. She bore on like a figure of stone, and I thought I must be mistaken, or she meant to cut me—However she stopped and addressed me like a mute—without a smile—about Wollaston's death and the awful shock to Maynard, and the disgraceful habits of the young.[1] Somehow I felt that most of it referred to you and Duncan; but no doubt we shall be told the full story by them both, over and over and over. What a lively summer is brewing! What a lark! How I do love quarrels and disagreements—talking of which Leonard and I both agreed with you about the Frys. The acerbity is very marked. Thats a comfort. I'm afraid you and Duncan are very happy though, and Eddys party was a great success. But I doubt that Helen's [Anrep] house can be as nice as this. To see nobody for 4 days is the pinnacle of human happiness. Even though I have to write about working women all the morning[2]—which is as if you had to sew canopies round chamber pots for Faith Henderson—I manage to get a good deal of pleasure one way and another. And there are no servants in the house Thank God; and nobody coming over to call (but this doesnt refer to you and Duncan)

I hope we may meet in London. But now you're such a success one has to catch you, of course, on the hop.

B.

Would you assure Taupin that I'm very sorry to part with her,—and its only because I must have some one who can stay 3 months.

Berg

1. Alexander Wollaston, the naturalist, ethnologist, and explorer of tropical mountain regions. He was elected a Fellow of King's College in 1920, and on 3 June 1930 was shot dead in his College rooms by a demented undergraduate named Potts, who killed himself immediately afterwards. Keynes wrote of him in the *Nation* (14 June 1930): "He could unlock hearts with a word and a look, and break down everyone's reserves, except his own."
2. *Memories of a Working Women's Guild* (*Yale Review*, September 1930).

Monks House, Rodmell
[Sussex]

Typewritten
June 8th [1930]

My dear Quentin,

I was just sitting down to strike the keys when fate plunged me into utter disorder. The kidneys. The cook. Yes, Nelly had an operation. I drove through London in an ambulance, half the glass is black so that you see life passing like a sepulchral procession. Then I saw doctors and sisters of mercy; and brothers and Aunts. Enough. I can't write when I must be planning dinner. How any woman with a family ever put pen to paper I cannot fathom. Always the bell rings and the baker calls. Then Nessa produced an old French lady [Taupin], reputed to be a cook. So she was in the year '70. But she had bad toes; no memory; had lost her husband in 1870 and so— I dont follow the argument—lost all the keys of the flat. And now I must go home and get another.

The incoherency of this is nothing to what it would have been a week ago. We are now at Rodmell for Whitsun, and the Austrians are gliding over our heads like gulls. Yes, this is a fact. They have tents on the downs and prove that one can fly up and down Asheham Hill without an engine. As I never doubted it myself, I take little stock of it. Tomorrow there is a village festival—our cook dances on the lawn—they act Midsummer Nights Dream and I am to guess the weight of a cake. All the receipts go to the church spire. And Pinka has five black pups—the sixth she sat on, conveniently, for to tell the truth five black bitches in my room are enough. Julian is coming to Charleston with a troupe next week. And they shot the senior tutor of Kings last week—Mr Potts did, as Lydia says must happen, when young men have no morals and wear coloured socks. There is a great row brewing between the Keynes' and the painters—Nessa will have told you. It is about their hanging themselves and not the young next the old masters in their show. Roger has resigned; and Maynard has disgraced himself once and for all. How I adore my friends to do that—and then they come over and confide in us; what fun it will be; Nessa thinks they will not dare draw water from the well. She thinks their friendship is what she calls a cruche cassée. Vita's book is such a best seller that Leonard and I are hauling in money like pilchards from a net. We sell about 800 every day. The Edwardians it is called. But you wont have read it, or heard of it.

Are you at Cassis? Basking, I suppose, and sipping vermouth at M. Somebodies, while the waves dont break, and the sardine boats come in at midnight. Has Col. Teed's nose put out a branch? I always think with a fine spring that might happen. But enough. I am cooking dinner.

Please write dearest Quentin and describe your life from the inside. Yes descend to the cellar, turn on the electric light and rejoice me with the sight of your veins and membranes all displayed. Dear me—to think that I must type all this and so never say a thing I want to say. The snap-snap of the typewriter frightens me as the snap of a turtle frightens fish. So good bye.

Your loving aunt Virginia

Quentin Bell

2190: TO MOLLY MACCARTHY   *Monk's House* [*Rodmell, Sussex*]

Sunday [8 June 1930]

Dearest Molly,

Yes, of course, I entirely agree with you about the collected works.[1] There should be a contract: Leonard should put it in business form, with dates for delivery of MS: fines upon failure; everything as solemn and awful as it can be. Then we ought to issue circulars, with photographs; to get the B.B.C to send addresses; to attend carefully to print, type, binding; which should be gay and alluring yet dignified. But of course the prime consideration is the MS: to get them I shall act the part of a gadfly, always disagreeable whenever seen; and you must be the domestic leech, sticking to his brow at breakfast, lunch and tea. Then when he is exhausted and pallid, you must snatch the sheets and post straight to me. I shall have printers in readiness, and the deed will be done, in one night. Six volumes on the table in six weeks. After this, nothing remains but to bask in fame and gold. The Americans are only converted by bound books. It will feather your nest in your old age. Guineas will go on dropping from the blue without a word more written. Of course, Desmond will loathe us both—You must expect to wear widow's weeds for a year; and I shall have my fingers dropped like a toad. But I don't care a jot. It must be done, in the grand style. I'm really feeling triumphant to get that book—which will be marblely masterly and stacked with delights—for the Press, and though I say it boastfully, I think after the Edwardians, (2 thousand in a month) we can manage a best seller as well as Heinemann, and with far greater distinction. I suppose I wouldn't help by taking a volume or two of the files down here in August?

But we can cabal about all this on Wednesday. Do you realise that Sydney Waterlow is back [from Addis Ababa], and says it is his *right* to come to Memoir Club meetings;[2] and then there's Mary [Hutchinson], at

1. Of Desmond MacCarthy. Virginia had been pressing him to publish his literary criticism since 1923 (see Volume III, p. 6, of this Edition). Ten collections of essays were eventually published (three posthumously), but none of them by the Hogarth Press.

2. The Memoir Club, organised by Molly MacCarthy, met for the first time in March 1920 and continued to meet until 1956. The original membership included most of Old Bloomsbury and Sydney Waterlow.

sight of whom Clive will bolt like a peppered Spaniel—altogether middle age is a trying time for these reunions, what with the ambassador [Waterlow], and the wrecks of your old lovers [Clive]. I leave it all to your tact—I'm worse than hopeless. I still wake in the night and bite the blanket through in spasms at the thought of the horrid things I've done. Do you? Awful things—worse than murder and rape.

I write surrounded by barking spaniels—Leonard and the old lady next door are forever lifting them up to judge their sex and points. Why is decency in complete abeyance with dogs?

Love
V.

Mrs Michael MacCarthy

2191: To V. Sackville-West   [52 *Tavistock Square, W.C.1*]

Thursday [12 June 1930]

If you are coming up let me know, before every instant is snatched by Ethel. We might do something nice—not buy food, this time.

Sales today 'close on 300'.

Let me know (as I was saying—but I'm dazed with reading mss. They flood us, all owing to Edians.) One poor woman thinks she completes your picture: about 6 foot remain to be read.—Poor dear Potto too with the mange on his nose—so let me know, as I was saying.

V.

Berg

2192: To Ernest Rhys   52 *Tavistock Square, W.C.1*

Typewritten
June 12th 1930

Dear Mr Rhys,[1]

It is very good of you to write to me so kindly about Orlando. If you knew how many letters I get pointing out the mistakes in that book, you would understand that your appreciation is very valuable.

I am also grateful that you should ask me to write an introduction to Middlemarch. But I have already written at length about George Eliot, and much though I admire her, I do not feel that I can begin again on that subject.

Please accept my thanks, and believe me,

Yours sincerely
Virginia Woolf

British Library

1. Ernest Rhys (1859-1946), the poet and the editor of Everyman's Library.

Monks House [*Rodmell,*
Sussex]

Sunday, June 21st [22 1930]

My dear Ka,

Yes, I agree, it is tragic about time and space. I no longer try to make them go my way. We came back from Cornwall and there was our cook ill in bed. Well, after 10 days or so, she had her kidneys out in a hospital. And first we had one char, and then another, and then by a series of coincidences so miraculous I cant describe them a born lady arrived in a car, with a son at Kings, and became our cook general[1]—God knows why—and does every mortal thing, so that at last I can ask somebody to dinner again—and now you are in Cornwall.

Every boy in England seems to have measles. I hope Mark is all right again. We liked your house[2] in your absence. The old lady, though alarmed, was very friendly, and offered pots of tea and bread and butter at once. We had a wonderful drive over the moor which I still think the loveliest in the world. But Bodmin Moor is sublime too—and Sedgemoor.

Well goodbye, and let us meet sometime.

yr V.W.

Mark Arnold-Forster

2194: To Ethel Smyth   [52 *Tavistock Square, W.C.*1]

Sunday, 22nd June [1930]

O Lord, I have been such a wretch—never to write even a card to thank you for the white flowers. You must have stripped your garden; and then found two huge boxes; and then borne them through Woking on a bicycle; and then up here in a taxi—and I receive all this with only a nod—dear, dear. And it is only on Friday that they were withered. But I buried my nose (why do you like that long proboscis?) 10 times daily in their deliciousness. And thus I was upborne through heaven knows what boredoms. Yes, so I am now saying thank you.

I send back Elizabeths [Williamson] very remarkable letter. What a terse and muscular mind she has! What a force she presses into her matter of fact statements; and it is this muscular mind that believes in God. I shall try to see her, alone if I can; and try to rake her mind with my erratic harrow; for she must be sown thick with all sorts of seeds—I cant finish this image; I see her mind; and I see my mind; but I'm so hot, so sleepy. I must leave

1. Mrs Walters, an American, formerly a journalist, with a passion for literature.
2. Eagle's Nest, Zennor, Cornwall. Mark was Ka's son, born in 1920.

it there. I began this at Rodmell, where we had a Scottish Ministers daughter in distress [Lyn Irvine]: should she take this job, or that? The angelic Leonard wrote a dispatch to her father in Aberdeen, while I sat mooning over my book,[1] furious to be interrupted; and the 5 black puppies bit my toes. But it is an impossible book—my book. No I don't much like Enid; maybe for knowing the sequel, that she married Jones and has a villa.[2] And I did not mean, though I must have said, that Leonard served 7 years for his wife.[3] He saw me it is true; and thought me an odd fish; and went off next day to Ceylon, with a vague romance about us both [Virginia and Vanessa]! And I heard stories of him; how his hand trembled and he had bit his thumb through in a rage; and Lytton said he was like Swift and would murder his wife; and someone else said Woolf had married a black woman. That was my romance—Woolf in a jungle. And then I set up house alone with a brother [Adrian], and Nessa married, and I was rather adventurous, for those days; that is we were sexually very free—Elizabeth owes her emancipation and mathematics partly to us—but I was always sexually cowardly, and never walked over Mountains with Counts as you did, nor plucked all the flowers of life in a bunch as you did. My terror of real life has always kept me in a nunnery. And much of this talking and adventuring in London alone, and sitting up to all hours with young men, and saying whatever came first, was rather petty, as you were not petty: at least narrow; circumscribed; and leading to endless ramifications of intrigue. We had violent rows—oh yes, I used to rush through London in such rages, and stormed Hampstead heights at night in white or purple fury. And then I married, and then my brains went up in a shower of fireworks. As an experience, madness is terrific I can assure you, and not to be sniffed at; and in its lava I still find most of the things I write about. It shoots out of one everything shaped, final, not in mere driblets, as sanity does. And the six months—not three—that I lay in bed taught me a good deal about what is called oneself. Indeed I was almost crippled when I came back to the world, unable to move a foot in terror, after that discipline. Think—not one moment's freedom from doctor discipline—perfectly strange—conventional men; 'you shant read this' and 'you shant write a word' and 'you shall lie still and drink milk'—for six months.

But enough. I must do whatever it is. This is really a letter to thank you for the vast cardboard boxes. How they must have banged about in your third class railway carriage.

Virginia

Berg

1. Virginia was writing the second version of *The Waves*.
2. Enid Bagnold married Sir Roderick Jones, Chairman of Reuter's, in 1920. They had a house at Rottingdean, Sussex.
3. Cf. the story of Jacob, Leah and Rachel (*Genesis*, Chapter 29).

[*52 Tavistock Square, W.C.*1]

Typewritten
Wednesday [25 June 1930]

Dearest Margaret,

Here is the photograph. I suppose we could get it back if we wanted it. Leonard has not yet read the papers,[1] but will. We are rushed at present by the huge success of Edwardians—it sells and sells. I think there is some truth in what you say—it was not intended seriously I imagine.

I heard no more of the widow lady; but have had another strange adventure to tell you when we meet. A cook [Mrs Walters] who is a lady; a coop; has a flat; a car; and insists upon acting as our daily general. Why?

Yours hastily
Virginia

Sussex

2196: To Ethel Smyth   [*52 Tavistock Square, W.C.*1]

Thursday [26 June 1930]

Oh this is such a bore—I've got rather knocked up—been out too much at night Leonard says—and have the usual headache—a pain that is in the back of my neck. So I've had to take to dressing gown and sofa and can't work. I shall be all right in a day or two: in fact I am better today; but it is a stealthy disease and pounces out if I give it a chance. So I shan't attempt your concert: and I shant attempt answering your letters. But do please write— I do like reading your letters; and will one of these days accumulate an answer. And tell me what the young man said about my life that was so interesting to Eliz: And dont for goodness sake think that when I call my mind a harrow, it is in a good sense: no: I'm not her match at all, in mind. About religion; isn't it sixth sense? I dont assert; I only lack. But here I must stop.

Lord—how I hate not being able to write! All the point of life gone. But enough.

V.

I am sorry about the Concert
Tell me about it.

Berg

1. Margaret Llewelyn Davies was editing some memoirs by working women which were published, with photographs and Virginia's Introduction, by the Hogarth Press as *Life As We Have Known It* (1931).

June 27th [1930]

My dear Helen,

It was a great pleasure to get your letter and to think of you and Roger [Fry] thoroughly wretched. As a rule, you are too happy; I like the balance to be redressed; and so I like to think of you sitting in a damp crypt with British spinsters to every meal. As for Roger, his spirit being what it is, I cant seriously suppose him unhappy, with his ten fingers and two legs. I'm glad they are healed. Then he must devote his life to friendship; now that his legs are healed.

London is awfully hot. At the same time, it is rather exciting and intricate, and like an aquarium, with that great crab, Ethel, pertinaciously gripping our toes, and Mary Hutchinson scuttling around, and poor dear Angus vagulating like some pale anemone in a cranny. I went to their show, and liked, spontaneously, without looking for a name, Rogers pictures. Can it be that artists go on ripening? I really think it looks like it. Angus was full of languor and bitterness. These quarrels he says upset him dreadfully; he was smoking cigarettes and reading French novels; but is a perfect gentleman all the same. I do not wish to say a word against him—only to say that I liked Rogers pictures. Maynard is back; Lydia fairly cuts me in the street, but deposits intolerable Russians upon me; so we are all agog for a summer of vituperation and discord—how jolly!

Your old Taupin is admirable and angelic for 3 days; on the 4th she arrives speechless and gaping; huddles in a chair; cant remember if she's bought a fish; has lost all the keys; feels her toes, and has to be bundled off in a taxi. So I leave her for you and Duncan. But then a real adventure dropped from the skies—I cant go into details—but we have an American lady whose sole ambition is to be cook general to the Wolves. Her car waits outside. Her son, at Kings, fetches my groceries. She tosses off every sort of luxury and mends my stockings—all for love, it is said; and a passion for Leonards books on Co-operation. You must come and dine.

I'm swamped with manuscripts. The success of the Edwardians has encouraged every old typewriter in Surbiton—they are all dishing up society fiction. Lord! why does one run one's head into such a panjandrum—which isn't the word, but I'm too hot to think what is. Love to my dear Roger; and tell him how much I liked his pictures and want to see him.

yr   V.W.

Sussex

2198: To Clive Bell   [52 *Tavistock Square, W.C.*1]

Postcard
June 30th [1930]

No, on the whole I think London is more entrancing [than Paris]. Very hot. Very gay: very—everything desirable; but for the lack of one person whom I cant touch with any stick.

Quentin Bell

2199: To Ethel Smyth   52 *T*[avistock] *S.*[quare, *W.C.*1]

Tuesday July 1st [1930]

Leonard will give you a ruthless and truthful answer—that I'm quite well and we'll come—thats what I expect since its true. But this is only to say that I must have misled you about this particular headache. There are 3 stages: pain; numb; visionary; and this stopped at pain, and only a little pain at that. And its gone; and I've been working, for me very hard. To continue medical details, though I think them rather sordid, it is 10 years since I was seeing faces, and 5 since I was lying like a stone statue,[1] dumb to the rose—(no it should be blind, but I write in a hurry)[2] In fact, I am now very much stronger than ever since I was a small child, in proof of which, I had a perpetual temperature, after influenza, for some years: this has gone; and a heart that was always leaping 5-barred gates; this is now steady as a cab-horse; and I dont get influenza nearly so regularly every winter. I am (by the way) greatly intrigued by your oblique and I suppose delicate reference to "the tiresome epoch in women's lives" for I had not yet begun to think about it, seeing what the month, to put it delicately, brings; nor has Nessa, who is 20 years older and so should precede me through these mystic rites. Are you right in your dates? And what does it feel like? Or are all your medical observations, as I suspect, founded upon the case of Pan [Ethel's sheepdog]—who is not really a case in point. "There now" as you say "I won't refer to the subject again"—unless you, being so terrifically psychologically minded like the analysis (oh I cant spell) of sensations.

1. In her diary for 8 August 1921, Virginia wrote of "all the horrors of the dark cupboard of illness once more displayed for my diversion. . . . The dark underworld has its fascinations as well as its terrors" (quoted by Quentin Bell, *Virginia Woolf*, II, 83-4). From mid-August to November 1925 she was intermittently in bed after collapsing at Charleston.

2.   A chamber deaf to noise and blind to light,
             A rose garland and a weary head.
                   Philip Sidney, *Astrophel and Stella*, Sonnet XXXIX

I am very glad about Beecham[1] (Lady Cunard has asked us to dine) and hope you prodded him between the joints: and wish I had heard the 4tet. Here is Leonard with my Will. Who is to witness it? Do you want a legacy? And now I must write to 70 almost congenital idiots who ask me among other things to write novels with them about plots which seem to them (and they are Oxford dons too I gather) so suitable. The flowers still flower: What a good heart, it suddenly occurs to me, speaking humanly as far I am able—you have—to care about my headaches.

Yr V.

Berg

2200: To V. Sackville-West [52 *Tavistock Square, W.C.*1]

[4 July 1930]

Yes—lunch, one, on Monday.
We have passed the 20,000—
I mean The Edwardians.
Just off to Rodmell after a champagne supper last night at Woking.[2]

Berg

2201: To Ethel Smyth *Monks House, Rodmell*
[Sussex]

Sunday, perhaps 6th July [1930]

I say Ethel—what a party![3] What a triumph! I can only assure you that when I saw all those hands stretched over the gate I felt I was being shut out from Paradise. I daresay it went on for hours after we left in the garden, under the roses. It was a superb affair, rolling and warbling from melody to melody like some divine quartet—no, octet. First the meeting; then the golf; then the returning; then the supper, and all interwoven with so many extraneous melodies, to me so fascinating; Lady Balfour,[4] Mrs Lyttleton[5] and then the champagne and then—oh millions of other things which I noticed at the time, but had hardly leisure to taste, and now single out and

1. Sir Thomas Beecham, the founder-conductor of the London Philharmonic Orchestra (1932-40). His operatic career began in 1909 when he produced Ethel's opera, *The Wreckers*.
2. See next letter.
3. At Ethel's house in Woking on 3 July.
4. Elizabeth, daughter of the 1st Earl of Lytton, who married the 2nd Earl of Balfour in 1887.
5. Edith Balfour, Alfred Lyttelton's second wife, known to her family and friends as 'D.D.'

brood over lights upon your life and character; sudden glimpses of buried truths which I had suspected dimly before. Lord! how I liked you! How I rejoiced in your existence! We are still talking it over, and saying "Do you remember the other night at Ethels—or Did you notice how . . ." and so on. By the way, Leonard was more overcome than I've known him by any party these 10 years. He was so warmhearted in his praise of you that nothing on earth (so slow and sure and everlasting is he) will now change his affection. Also he said he had seldom met anybody he liked better at first go off than Joyce Wethered[1]—he said he could have gone on talking to her for hours. He said he thought she had one of the nicest characters anybody could have—and so we go on. Now I must do a little very dreary work— boiling 2 articles in to one and spreading one in to 3:[2] that makes my years income; but I can assure you it is hardly earned. I have to wrench my head to the left when it's looking to the right.

52 Tavistock Sqre.

Home again, and found your letter. I say, who were the people who fell in love with Leonard? I rather like people doing that—yes; why shouldn't I come and be bored? I would like to—(now I dont suppose I say that I mean it once in a blue moon). But of course, what nobody, except you I daresay sees, is the difficulty of keeping one's atmosphere unbroken. If I could only live in my protected shell another 2 months, surrounded by the usual, I could finish this exquisitely irritating book [*The Waves*]. If I stay away, even between Sackvilles adulterous sheets, I break the membrane, and the fluid escapes—a disgusting image, drawn I think from the memory of Vanessa's miscarriage.[3] All the same, I shall come, for a night, and let the membrane break if it will. What a lark! I was tremendously interested (here we are off on the party again, which is already classical, like the Jane Austen Box Hill party [*Emma*]) by meeting Mrs Lyttelton. How she figured in my youth! though I dont think I ever saw her—she was one of Kitty Maxses stock instances of charm and interest, and as Kitty Maxse, my mothers greatest friend's daughter,[4] served us as foster mother in the ways of the world when we were left orphans in a sea of halfbrothers, her words were held by us more than inspired. She was always talking of D.D [Edith

1. Joyce Wethered won the Ladies Open Golf Championship three times in four years, the last time in 1929.
2. Virginia was currently writing two articles for the *New York Herald Tribune*, one on Hazlitt (7 September 1930), the other on Fanny Burney's half-sister (14 and 21 September).
3. At Broussa, Turkey, in April 1911.
4. Two of Mrs Vernon Lushington's daughters, Kitty and Susan, were among Vanessa's greatest friends in her youth. Kitty married Leo Maxse, the Editor of the *National Review*, and was the original of Clarissa Dalloway.

Lyttelton]. And then, what an extraordinary charmer I thought Lady Balfour—only I was tipsy. And heres Maurice sending me his book[1] and asking us to lunch—And here's a smart young man, called Beaton, notorious as a gate crasher at smart parties, asking me to be photographed:[2] Shall I? He does Edith Sitwell in her tomb.

But I am rambling and running in this heat, and must go and disinter the remains of our gammon. But why (to return to the party) this rancour against the soup? I thought it was a high bred, blue blooded soup—thick with the ichor of turtles, I thought. Was Elizabeth's [Williamson] golf so bad? Her figure was so exquisite—like the Greek Goddess at the Louvre that I forgot about sending the ball into a hole—I am no professional golfer you understand.

VW

Berg

2202: To V. Sackville-West   52 *Tavistock Square, W.C.*1

[8 July 1930]

Lord! What a go! £5,000 at least I imagine.[3]

And I'm sitting here so dolefully, trying to read Jimmy Sheehan,[4] when I want to be at the movie.

Look—wd. this do for Lady C?[5] It so wd. you post it—but please dont if there is any doubt—and ask Harold if you are hesitating.

Berg

2203: To Ethel Smyth   52 *Tavistock Sqre.* [*W.C.*1]

Friday [11 July 1930]

But that—ringing up on the spur of the moment—is precisely the method that does suit me, moody as I am. Also to arrange for Leonard and the car,

1. In 1930 Maurice Baring published *Robert Peckham*.
2. Cecil Beaton, the photographer and designer, had previously asked Virginia to sit for him in 1927; she refused on both occasions.
3. *The Edwardians* had been chosen by the American Literary Guild as Book of the Month for September.
4. James Vincent Sheean was an American foreign correspondent who achieved great popularity in English society.
5. Virginia's letter to Lady Cunard was never posted by Vita. It read: "I saw Vita Nicolson today and she encourages me to tell you that if you should (by a lucky chance) still wish me to dine with you on the 21st, I am now free that night and should of course like to come. But of course I dont expect that this is still possible. And I hope you wont mind my writing" (*Berg*).

is, in our much too organised life (interviews are always taking place with paper merchants, and a quavering old lady has just doddered in with a huge portfolio of what I know to be sketches of seaside resorts)—that is far harder than ringing up on the spur. What I will do, I hope next week, is to say there is a train that gets to Woking about 4: I will have tea and dinner with you; we will talk—how heavenly—then I will catch say the 9.40 to Wloo and be home for eleven o'clock bed. You will say, But I have to lunch with Beecham—then I will say what about Friday—I cant at the moment lose a morning, ridiculous as it seems—I am trying to get back, after a horrid burst of journalism, to fiction, and things are going so badly, that if I stop, I fall off my rock again—The truth is I dont know how to write this book—I might, given another 10 years of trying. No it is an impossible book—something that flashed upon me at Rodmell 3 years ago, as I was finishing The Lighthouse. And it will end in failure, the worst failure of them all. Why then make the attempt? For I could reel off books now that would do all right, and yet must beat my head against something that can't possibly do at all. But thats enough—only to explain the train home—

No, my gloves, if I may say it now they are dead, were among the world's beauties, a present from a lady [Ethel Sands] who buys at the best shop in Paris—the only shop—which she always knows. All the winter they have eked out the shabbiness of my stockings.—Cant be helped—I must have dropped them on the golf course—but that party deserves a ring dropped into the sea. No I won't lunch with M.B[aring]: nor dine with Lady Cunard; and I refused the Hutchinsons last night, and a picnic today— Each of these conquests over my gadding spirit is a tribute to you. But you're not, as I so futilely call myself, a novelist: things don't happen for you at parties; where I might pick up a crumb perhaps; suppose you were to hear some rare instrument; and then could not go, because of a horrible headache? Here is MBs letter[1] and the false gloves.

I will ring up about the day—perhaps Tuesday next? What about that?

VW

Berg

2204: To Ethel Smyth   52 *T.*[avistock] *S.*[quare, *W.C.*1]

Wednesday [16 July 1930]

O Lord—do all my letters to you begin O Lord?—O Lord again, that was a nice day Ethel. How I enjoyed it and the diversity of my sensations, as we went from solitude to society; and then back; and the wine, and the

---

1. Ethel had sent Virginia Maurice Baring's letter of thanks in which he said he "enjoyed seeing Mrs Woolf so much" (*Berg*).

duck, and the fire—oh and everything; always excepting some twinges of compunction (they came on worse after I had left you) at my own egotistic loquacity. I can assure you I dont romanticise quite so freely about myself as a rule—It was only that you pressed some nerve, and then up started in profusion the usual chaos of pictures of myself—some true, others imaginary; more were true than false, I think, but I ought not to have been so profuse. Next time it shall be the other story—yours. But in your benignity and perspicacity—its odd how the image of the soaring aeroplane seeing to the bottom persists—you can penetrate my stumbling and fitful ways: my childish chatter. Yes—for that reason, that you see through, yet kindly, for you are, I believe, one of the kindest of women, one of the best balanced, with that maternal quality which of all others I need and adore—what was I saying?—for that reason I chatter faster and freer to you than to other people. But I wont next time. And you won't think the worse of me, will you? You see, I am, I dont deny it, very excitable. And going home, as the wine went out and a cold sheen appeared on the roofs of Surbiton, I thought, My God what an egoist I am; and that was the only twangling wire in the whole composition. I was home by eleven; and slept; and still feel very, extraordinarily well. And I wont therefore accuse Leonard of always castrating my joys.

I dont like [J. C.] Squire, but am doubtless jaundiced by my sense of his pervading mediocrity and thick thumbedness. It seems to me a hot, sentimental, blundering poem; thick handed, as usual. But I have no trust any more in my critical judgments, for every year I live I become more dyed in my own juice; and I cant help it; but I cant any longer present a virginal mind to other peoples work, as you, who dont stew in ink, can do.

Well, this should be re-written, to comb out the tangles, but I'm writing in a hurry. We have to dine out (undressed) and I have to write to Hugh Walpole and so on; and yet I like writing to you, who are so good to me, and let me sit chattering, and keep so immensely wise and good all the time. Now do you think those epithets are right?

I'll send back the coat tomorrow.

Yr V.

Berg

2205: To Hugh Walpole   52 *T.S.* [*W.C.*1]

Wednesday 16th July [1930]

My dear Hugh,

Oh yes—the Press is flourishing, more than ever, what with Vita going into Edition after Edition. She has now made £5,000 too out of the American book Clubs.

I envy you, on the strength of your flying picture of German life:

Einstein etc.[1] But I always hope other people's lives aren't so wildly exciting as they seem. Another touch, and I should jump from my orbit in a vain endeavour to be you. I've been only Mrs Woolf of 52 T.S. all the summer, seeing Ethel Smyth, Vita, Christabel, Lytton and so on. I wish I could think of anything to make you envious. I like printing in my basement best, almost: no, I like drinking champagne and getting wildly excited. I like driving off to Rodmell on a hot Friday evening and having cold ham, and sitting on my terrace and smoking a cigar with an owl or two.

But you only want a post card: so here I stop. Dear dear, I cant write sense.

Yr Virginia

Texas

2206: To V. Sackville-West   [52 *Tavistock Square, W.C.*1]

Friday [18 July 1930]

Are you by any chance coming to tea with me on Monday? I'll keep it free on the chance. (But let me know)

Leonard wants me to say that he can possibly let you have 50 1st Edn. Edwardians if you still want them. About 21,600 now sold: still going strong.

How I dreamt of your mother last night. And it struck me, the other night, that Harold is one of the best hearted of people—Why did this so overcome me in a flash like a lizard creeping out of a chink? I dont know.

V.

Berg

2207: To Lady Ottoline Morrell

52 *Tavistock Square.* [*W.C.*1]

Friday [18 July 1930]

Dearest Ottoline,

It was very good of you to suggest taking me to Comus. It shows the optimism which your parties breed that I thought I would go—when I had people here to tea and have to spend tomorrow at Cambridge—Everything seemed possible, as I sat in your drawing room, but alas, outside it, not. I did enjoy myself, and thought Lady Hartington[2] charming.

Thank you so much

Your

Texas   Virginia

1. Hugh Walpole had recently returned from a lecture tour in Germany. The 'etc' included Carl Jung, Thomas Mann and the pianist Artur Schnabel.
2. Alice Cecil, daughter of the 4th Marquess of Salisbury, who in 1917 married the eldest son of the Duke of Devonshire.

2208: To V. Sackville-West   [52 *Tavistock Square, W.C.*1]

Thursday [24 July 1930]

It suddenly occurs to me—would you like me to come down tomorrow, Friday, for the night? But—

(1) Are you alone?

(2) Would it be in anyway inconvenient?

I should have to go early on Saturday.

Could you ring up?

A party has been put off, and it seems a good chance if it suited you.

Berg

2209: To Ethel Smyth   52 *T[avistock] S[quare, W.C.*1]

Thursday [24 July 1930]

Well, your cardboard boxes delivered by architects fairly make me gasp —the flowers, the scissors, the string, the telephone, and finally my room like a bower in a garden, all shades of pink, yellow lilac nodding together in great pale bunches. How is it done? I have garden, flowers, boxes, string— but the combination—No I cant envisage it. So I go on, sniffing and looking, and wondering—its like the edge of some sunset over a flat beach—my room at this moment. And they haven't dropped a petal. But I must confess that last night I woke in a stew, I forget about what—on the brink of per-dition, and dosed myself with chloral, and in consequence have a head like wood. I cant frame sentences at all. Tomorrow the dose will have worn off and I'll write a better letter. (It was only half a dose, now I come to think of it and I make this confession out of deference to you.) I'll tell you about that article next time

V.

Berg

2210: To Margaret Llewelyn Davies

52 *Tavistock Sq.* [*W.C.*1]

Typewritten

25th July 1930

Dearest Margaret,

I have been a long time answering your letter, but I have had an awful rush of work, trying to finish some articles which have to be sent to America and as usual finding them a much tougher job than I expected.

This explains why I have not yet gone through your suggestions about my Guild paper.[1] I am taking them to Rodmell, where we go on Tuesday, and hope in the quiet there to see what can be done to alter the paper as you and Lilian[2] think desirable. I am much relieved that you like it in the main. Of course I was aware of great difficulties. And in spite of your kindness, I admit that I feel grave doubts whether the thing ought to be published as an introduction. I think it might be better for the book to stand on its own feet, or to have only a formal note of explanation. But I have not read my paper since I wrote it, and I will go through it again with Leonard. I have a strong feeling against introductions—and this one is full of difficulties. But I will see.

Meanwhile an American editor, to whom I had promised an article, has read it; and wants to publish it in September as an article—or rather as fiction. What I want to know is whether you would object to my doing this, if I suppressed all real names, did not mention you or Lilian, and made it my personal view of congresses in general? I should put a note to say that it was based on some impressions received at a meeting of the Womens Guild and was intended as an introduction to a book by working women. The Americans, the editor said, are completely in the dark about co-operation and Guilds and it would be read as literature simply. It has to be sent off on Tuesday, and thus I have no time to make the alterations in detail which you suggest. Can you trust me to make the thing blameless? I dont suppose any Guildswoman is likely to read the Yale Review. Leonard says that this would make no difference to our publishing it in England. Would you send me a card to say if you have any objection?

Anyhow, I am awfully glad that you liked it—I felt it very imperfect. I dont think, by the way, that your swans, as you say, only provoked "a literary reaction" in me—or perhaps I include a good deal more in literature than you would. My difficulty always was the political attitude to human beings—that some were always right, others always wrong. I did hate that. And do still. But as you say one gets more sensible. Love from us both. Yes of course I will send the final form of the letter for you to see, if we decide to keep it.

[*in Virginia's handwriting:*]
Excuse the typing; but I think it is on the whole more legible than my handwriting.

yr Virginia

Sussex

1. Virginia's Introduction to *Life As We Have Known It.* The essay was published first as *Memories of a Working Women's Guild* in the *Yale Review* (September 1930).
2. Lilian Harris, Assistant Secretary to the Women's Co-operative Guild when Margaret Llewelyn Davies was Secretary.

2211: To Ethel Smyth

Long Barn, Weald,
Sevenoaks [Kent]

Saturday [26 July 1930]

Well here I am lying in Vita's adulterous sheets. I know I left a sentence unfinished in my drugged letter [Letter 2209], but cant remember what. It was a letter of thanks, wasn't it, for cardboard boxes; and then, with a graceful transition I hastened on to my own works. But aint it time that Ethel talked of her works? Yes, it is. Vita and I were talking about you last night. I sketched a fancy picture of a third class smoker from Woking to Waterloo. Theres Ethel between 2 city gents. (Vita is putting bath salts in my bath and talking agreeably—hence my intermittent pulse in narrative) Well, Ethel who has been all that a woman should be, reading the Daily Telegraph, is suddenly brought to bed of a phrase—a passage for flutes in the middle bass: what do the old city gents say? And does she write it, there and then? on an old envelope? Anyhow, what Vita and I said is, Thats true happiness, writing phrases in smokers—Life holds nothing better. Ethel, we said, is the most enviable of women: Now, my train

V.

Berg

2212: To Margaret Llewelyn Davies

[52 *Tavistock Square, W.C.*1]

Typewritten
Sunday [27 July 1930]

Dearest Margaret,

Leonard has given on another page his oath that it will be quite all right about America—we are always printing there first and it makes no difference. I feel it was my fault—I had promised to write an article and I never did and when the editor [of the *Yale Review*] came down on me for it I excused myself by saying that I had been writing an introduction which would *not* do for them. This put their backs up and they demanded to see it, and now of course out of perversity say it is the very thing. I have scrapped all names and otherwise abolished traces of the book and have sent it off. But I always write things twice over, and let the Americans, who are in a hurry, have the first version. No doubt when I get to Rodmell I shall want to rewrite a good deal of this, so that it wont be the same thing. I have only glanced hastily at your notes, and it may be quite easy—if they dont involve a change of view entirely—to put them in. I've always meant to ask what the writers of the letters feel about a book? Did they write with a view to publication? Do they want their things to appear in print? Are they all alive? What was their motive in writing?[1] It was stupid of me not to find out before I began.

We are off on Tuesday—oh dear how nice it will be to get away from London, but we shall be up weekly or fortnightly, and perhaps could meet you one day.

I agree about Vitas natural powers; the trouble is she writes with incredible ease and fills up any odd space of time by dashing off a book. This [*The Edwardians*] was done I think to wile away a few months leisure, and she has made about six thousand pounds!

Yr Virginia

Sussex

2213: To Helen McAfee   52 *Tavistock Square, W.C.*1

Typewritten
27th July 1930

Dear Miss McAfee,

I enclose the corrected copy of the paper. I think your suggestion of a title is very good and have adopted it.[2] I have also put a note as you see, and have made various alterations which will I hope make it quite plain to your readers. But if any further alterations occur to you, would you very kindly note them in pencil on the proofs and I will add them when I make final corrections. As you see, I have altered the last words.

I cannot find my copy of the article on Reading which you want to reprint. My memory of it is that I thought there were a good many alterations needed—if they should be too many I might of course be unable to let you have it, as my time is very full. But I will let you know as soon as I get the copy which you say you are sending.[3]

On reading your letter again, I am not sure if you are going to send me proofs of the Womens Guild paper. If not, I will send you any alterations that may occur for you to add yourself.

We were so glad to see you the other day.

Yours sincerely
Virginia Woolf

Yale University

1. *Life As we Have Known It* consists in autobiographical sketches by five working women, followed by extracts from the letters of another five. The whole was introduced by Virginia in the form of a letter to Margaret Llewelyn Davies. Virginia's questions about the letter-writers were not directly answered in the book.
2. *Memories of a Working Women's Guild.*
3. *How Should One Read a Book* was originally published in the *Yale Review* of October 1926, and revised, not for Miss McAfee, but for *The Common Reader: Second Series* (1932).

Letters 2214-2246 (August–September 1930)

Virginia was obliged to spend some time at Rodmell rewriting her Introduction to Life As We Have Known It, *a collection of essays by working women, but returned to* The Waves *as soon as she could, working in the 'tool-shed' or 'lodge', as she called her garden-hut. On 29 August she suddenly fainted, perhaps from heat-stroke, and was alarmed enough to refer to the incident in her diary as 'a brush with death'. It was three weeks before she had fully recovered. Ethel Smyth dashed down to Sussex to see her, and Virginia's letters of gratitude are evidence of how greatly she had come to depend upon her. Although she was well enough to drive with Vita to Sissinghurst on 10 September, it was not until the 19th that she felt able to resume serious work on her novel. Then she was continually interrupted by visitors—Morgan Forster, Ka Arnold-Forster, the Hutchinsons, George Duckworth, Leonard's mother—who little realised that an hour's visit could 'ruin 10 pages of my book'. The Woolfs returned to London on 4 October.*

2214: To V. Sackville-West

Monks House, Rodmell,
Lewes, Sussex

[30 July 1930]

This is merely to say that L. will be at the harbour at 10 on Saturday, unless we hear to the contrary; and will bring you back here.[1]

Also I left a sponge [at Long Barn]. (I think—a small one)
Also could I have Ediths [Sitwell] poems.
Thats all for the moment.

V.

Berg

2215: To Ethel Smyth

Monks House, Rodmell
[Sussex]

Saturday Aug. 2nd [1930]

Well it is extremely difficult to write letters here. One goes off, I find, into a kind of swoon; becomes languid as an alligator with only its nostrils

1. The Nicolsons were going on holiday to Italy, and Leonard saw them off at Newhaven. There was no time for them to visit Rodmell before the ship sailed.

above water. London keeps one braced; take away the tension and ones mind opens like a flower, or an old glove, in water. Also I have been to Worthing to see my mother in law. Also I have been tidying the house. One thing I did thanks to you—I re-read my Burney article,[1] which is a thing I never do (I have never read any of my books a second time, except when they were re-printed, I shudder past them on the shelf as if they might bite me) anyhow, I read this article again, thanks to you, and rather liked it. The truth is though, these articles, all architecture, a kind of cabinet work, fitting parts together, making one paragraph balance another; are such hard labour in the doing that one cant read them without remembering the drudgery. One starts full tilt; one sees a scene in a flash; but the working out is almost (with me) unbelievably laborious. However, when I read it, I got more pleasure and less sense of backbreaking effort than usual—thanks to you again. Some of it needs emphasising though—some of it is too condensed. And I have just written another.

But this letter written drowsily with a man hammering in the village and a dog barking next door is to ask you to remember when you write to tell me fully and explicitly what that rather sordid and absurd trait (these mayn't be the epithets) is which you say has come to light in you lately and must be extirpated.[2] I am really curious about this. You see, being an inexpert psychologist any help I can be given is very important to the health and stability of our friendship. Now, if I had alluded to a trait in me, you would have divined it at once, infallibly; and I cant and that worries me. So be full and garrulous and tremendously documented and illustrated, remembering my groping moles eyes.

Except for the dogs next door and the man hammering we are very quiet and content. I suppose my mind will cease to expand in a day or two, and contract; and take up the staff of life and trudge on. I went very sleepily to Worthing and sat in a little match box bedroom with my mother in law, aged 80, and as spry as an old tramp. It is the most exhausting expedition I know: all facts, all personalities, all compliments, all personal relations and family news. And I forget which Woolf is which—And we are given cakes out of tins from her cupboard. She had been visited by Colonel Carrington Smyth, very musical, and supposed therefore to be related to you. How I hated marrying a Jew—how I hated their nasal voices, and their oriental jewellery, and their noses and their wattles—what a snob I was: for they have

1. Ethel had read *Dr Burney's Evening Party* in *Life and Letters* (September 1929). Virginia's other Burney article was *Fanny Burney's Half-Sister* (*TLS*, 28 August 1930).
2. On 11 August 1930 Ethel wrote to Virginia accusing herself of jealousy of Vita and Long Barn: "I found myself thinking 'why have *I* not a lovely house, run on castors, with damask sheets, servants to do this and that—wherewith to entice Virginia?' " But Ethel also said that she understood and accepted the 'personal mothering' Virginia got from 'big un-small Vita' (*Berg*).

immense vitality, and I think I like that quality best of all. They cant die—
they exist on a handful of rice and a thimble of water—their flesh dries on
their bones but still they pullulate, copulate, and amass (a Mrs Pinto,
fabulously wealthy came in) millions of money.

Vita and Harold and the boys were to have breakfasted here today, going
to Newhaven, on a tour to Italy; but the boat went before its time, and I did
not see them, or I should perhaps have heard about your letter. I'm sure
nothing you could say would annoy, or embitter her—she is the most
entirely magnanimous minded of women—without a vanity in her; for which
I admire her immensely; and it is not that she is insensitive—merely that she
is made that way. And she was telling me, in her perfectly sincere fashion,
that she doesn't care a scrap for The Edwardians—prefers not to think of it,
though she likes the money to flaunt in that greedy old peasant woman's
face, Lady Sackville [Vita's mother], I mean. I was rather relieved they had
to catch the boat. My mind, this floating glove, or lily or whatever I called it,
wants to drift off into some obscure pool, and be shaded by weeds. I dont
want to talk or laugh or make engagements even with Vita. But I do want to
hear about the Prison,[1] and how you go on: it must be blazing up like a
furnace now; and I daresay you see everything a little fiery (thats the way its
spelt) and distorted. Even Pan, even Virginia. What a triumph when it is
done! How you will taste bread and tea again and look at the grass for the
first time this summer! But do remember, if you can put your mind to it,
about that sordid and absurd trait.

Virginia

(1) I have just been asked to write an introduction to a book partly by you;
and refused. How could I introduce you and the Bishop of London?[2]
(2) What is your cure for sleeplessness? Mine is walking on the downs—
but then you and Elizabeth [Williamson] dont know what walking is,
without a small white [golf] ball.

Berg

2216: To William Plomer   *Monks House, Rodmell*
                                           [Sussex]

Aug 6th 1930

Dear William,
I meant to answer your letter before—but London is an intolerable place
for that. The worst of it is, that I like getting letters more and more, and

1. Ethel's Oratorio, based on Henry Brewster's philosophical dialogues, was first
produced in 1931 by Donald Tovey in Edinburgh.
2. The Rt Rev. Arthur Foley Winnington-Ingram.

hate writing them. Yes, I have been in Greece [in 1906]; I have been in an hotel in Athens and seen the Acropolis as you describe. There were bugs everywhere. Once I sat up all night, reading the Christian Monitor in a drawing room to escape them, and was given a 4th Century pot by the hotel keeper (which holds spills)

Love from us both,

and remember us to Mr Butts.[1]

Your Virginia Woolf

Texas

2217: To V. Sackville-West   *Monks House [Rodmell, Sussex]*

9th August 1930

Yes, it must be dull, travelling without Virginia—nobody to say Brusque?[2]—oh no Harold would know the word for rough, and so would the boys; but then I daresay at Porto Fino, what with the vineyards and the olive trees, the mediterranean and the old crumbling cliff—(where Elsie Carnarvon,[3] the friend of my youth lived) you've forgotten me, and Potto, and how we crossed the Channel, and how I wept as the white cliffs disappeared.

You should be arriving about now, I daresay, I hope so. Yes, I still hope not to open the paper and read "Titled victims of motor smash"— and then to find you crashed down a precipice—in which case it would be incumbent on me to commit suicide like Colonel Green of the Cottesmore hunt.[4]

Life is so adorably pleasing at the moment, I dont know where to begin. I've just come in from a walk with Pinka across the fields, with 5 mushrooms in my hat. True it drizzles; and there is a cloud over Asheham, but I dont care; I feel so happy with poor dear Nelly away, and no rows, and no tears, and all my time free; and now Mrs. Walters[5] hints that she wants to come permanently. Lord, what am I to do? Please, as an English lady, tell me.

Yesterday, as I was dishing up my dinner, 2 chops, broiled in gravy with

1. Anthony Butts had travelled with Plomer throughout Europe, and later they shared a house in London. Under the name of William D'Arfey he wrote *Curious Relations* (1945), which Plomer edited.
2. In September 1928, when Virginia and Vita travelled to France, Vita overheard Virginia asking a French seaman on the cross-channel steamer, "Est-ce-que la mer est brusque?"
3. The Countess of Carnarvon, step-mother of Lady Margaret Herbert who married Virginia's half-brother, George Duckworth.
4. Colonel Sidney Green shot himself on 2 August 1930, leaving behind him a suicide note for his father, his sisters and his kennelman.
5. See p. 179, note 1.

green peas, there was a tap at the door; Leonard said, 'Curse these pedlars selling notepaper' and there was Lord Gage, with a plan of the downs under his arm. He had come to tell us about preserving the Newhaven down; and we gave him some wine, and he talked about you, and made us cry with laughing. When he lunched with Lord Curzon[1] the footman dropped methylated spirits on his hair and it blazed up. Lord Curzon had to put it out with a napkin. He was very shy—indeed, fascinate him though we do, in our sordid confusion, eating chops at 7, with a puppy howling, he is very frightened of us. Then I was in London—saw Raymond at the London Library. Why does he fill my throat with dust, and make me arch and clever and uneasy, and why is he so natty, modish, outwardly—why does no moss no verdure no shadow no sympathy no romance grow under his footsteps (for me) when he's everything good, kind, clever and tenderhearted? Is it all the effect of his nose—and why should noses have such a devastating effect? Ethel says mine makes her weep at night. Ethel however is over head and ears in work at this moment and only sends me frantic and flying sparks from her anvil. She promises a full blast next week. D'you think it can be all nonsense?—The Prison? If so, isn't nature odd, keeping an old woman in a state of positive frenzy for weeks, if its all nonsense, what she writes. I daresay I am just the same, with my Moths and waves. I wander over the downs, declaiming and making up and altogether working myself into a frenzy too: and whats the good of it?

The Edwardians is still selling very well. That being so, with the dead season in full career, I dont see any reason why we shouldnt sell 25,000; and what the sales will be in America—heaven help us—the imagination boggles, as they say.

Now I am going over to tea at Charleston. How fuliginous Nessa was the other day over Raymond and Francis! She had them for Bank holiday: they yapped like fox terriers, all about nothing, she said. And Clive was so cross with her; so she came over here, as monumental as a Sphinx and sat down and ruminated.

Dotty has sent her poem[2]—Leonard is, for him, rather impressed—says its good of its kind—I think (I've not read it) she deserves some credit for keeping her head up, and writing about cats and rocks this time instead of the birth of man.

Shall you be glad to see me—Breakfast Aug. 25th[3]

Yr

Berg   V [squiggly design]

1. At 1 Carlton House Terrace, where Lord Curzon lived following his retirement as Viceroy of India in 1905. He became Foreign Secretary in 1919 and died in 1925.
2. *Deserted House*, by Dorothy Wellesley, was published by the Hogarth Press in November 1930.
3. Vita actually returned on 29 August.

15th Aug. 1930

As it is a pouring wet afternoon, I will write a few disjected observations, like offerings to a magpie. (These birds make their nests of straw, hair-combings, and other things that have been thrown away.) Ethels great grandmother on the paternal side was a Magpie.

(1) Why dont you come down for the night? This is a sensible observation. Why not be our first dine and sleep guest [of the summer]? There is a train which gets you here about 4.30; met by Leonard: another takes you back about 9.30 or 2.30 next day. So that you wd. be home for tea again. I'm a little vague about dates; but I suggest, tentatively, Thursday 21st, or Friday 22nd. Please answer, and put this on a firm footing. We could talk the whole morning.

(2) As a psychologist I am myopic rather than obtuse.[1] I see the circumference and the outline not the detail. You and Nessa say I am so frightfully stupid because I dont see that fly on the floor: but I see the walls, the pictures and the Venus against the pear tree, so that the position and surroundings of the fly are accurately known to me. Say that you are a fly: what you actually do and say I may misinterpret; but your standing in the world being known to me, I never get you out of perspective as a whole. Therefore act and speak as frantically as you like; having (while I lay on the sofa that first afternoon) sketched your ambit —your wall, statue and pear tree, no minor agitation in the foreground will upset me. You see I like your circumference.

(3) Hence if I were ill I should be quite as ready to come to you as to Vita, though for entirely different reasons. When I was ill, 4 years ago, and had to spend 3 months in bed, she took me to Long Barn: there I lay in Swansdown and recovered. The sense of peace dwells thus, about her—those are some of my associations. But loving lights, pillows, and all luxury as I do, aesthetically largely, and often merely spectacularly, for I never acquire possessions myself, you, if I were ill, would be as soothing; no, not that; perhaps supporting would be the better word. Sanity is what I want. A robust sense of fact. Well, wouldn't you give me that? Haven't you—anyhow to my sense, warred with the world sufficiently to have made intervals of peace?

The object of this remark is I think to prove that I am diverse enough to want Vita and Ethel and Leonard and Vanessa and oh some other people too. But jealousy is not a very bad fault is it? I am often jealous of other

---

1. Ethel had written to Virginia: "You are supposed to be inexpert as a psychologist, not very 'human' and so on. And it is so. And yet I have a feeling of security with you in the matter of being understood" (11 August 1930, *Berg*).

people's gifts. Only to think I want the swansdown only is not an accurate picture of my mind.

(4) Then Perversion.

Yes, I am afraid I do agree with you in thinking it silly. But I suspect we are wrong. I suspect the ramrod and gunpowder of our East Indian grandfathers here influences us. I think we are being provincial and petty. When I go to what we call a *Buggery Poke party, I feel as if I had strayed into the male urinal; a wet, smelly, trivial kind of place. I fought with Eddy Sackville over this; I often fight with my friends. How silly, how pretty you sodomites are I said; whereat he flared up and accused me of having a red-nosed grandfather. For myself, why did I tell you that I had only once felt physical feeling for a man[1] when he felt nothing for me? I suppose in some opium trance of inaccuracy. No—had I felt physical feeling for him, then, no doubt, we should have married, or had a shot at something. But my feelings were all of the spiritual, intellectual, emotional kind. And when 2 or 3 times in all, I felt physically for a man, then he was so obtuse, gallant, foxhunting and dull that I—diverse as I am—could only wheel round and gallop the other way.[2] Perhaps this shows why Clive, who had his reasons, always called me a fish. Vita also calls me fish. And I reply (I think often while holding their hands, and getting exquisite pleasure from contact with either male or female body) 'But what I want of you is illusion—to make the world dance.' More than that, I cannot get my sense of unity and coherency and all that makes me wish to write the Lighthouse etc. unless I am perpetually stimulated. Its no good sitting in a garden with a book; or collecting facts. There must be this fanning and drumming— of course I get it tremendously from Leonard—but differently— Lord Lord how many things I want—how many different flowers I visit—and often I plunge into London, between tea and dinner, and walk and walk, reviving my fires, in the city, in some wretched slum, where I peep in at the doors of public houses. Where people mistake, as I think, is in perpetually narrowing and naming these immensely composite and wide flung passions—driving stakes through them, herding them between screens. But how do you define "Perversity."? What is the line between friendship and perversion?

Well, enough—especially as I read in your last letter that you dont want

* There is a Farm here called Muggery Poke.

1. Possibly Lytton Strachey, who proposed to Virginia in 1909, and was accepted by her. But by mutual agreement they broke off the engagement almost immediately.
2. Before she married, Virginia had flirtations with Hilton Young, Walter Lamb, Walter Headlam and Clive Bell. See the index under their names in Volume I of this Edition.

remarks about character. And I've no doubt these are all wrong; but I'm treating you as a woman whose paternal Grandmother was a magpie.

V.

See how incredibly stupid I am: I do not in the least know the answer to your question "Am I a dog with a poor appetite?." Please tell me what it means.[1] And what did Vanessa say one day to my face? Oh dear, oh dear. And who is Leo Piddington [*unidentified*]? Thrice oh dear! And now for tea.

Berg

2219: To Helen McAfee   *Monk's House, Rodmell,*
                                         Lewes, Sussex

Typewritten
17th Aug. 1930

Dear Miss McAfee,

I return the pages [of *Memories of a Working Women's Guild*] you sent for my corrections herewith. I quite agree to your alterations, and I see the point about [the] letter quoted on page 22. Yes, I think there is something rather fine in the very stiff words the woman uses. I have altered the comment in order to bring this out, as I agree that the meaning might not be taken without a little emphasis. I hope it is enough—one does not want to nudge the reader too much.

I am afraid this paper has given you a lot of trouble, but I hope that with these alterations the readers of the Yale Review will be able to read without difficulty.

Many thanks.

Yours very sincerely
Virginia Woolf

Yale University

2220: To Helen McAfee   *Monk's House, Rodmell,*
                                         Lewes, Sussex

Typewritten
17th August 1930

Dear Miss MacAfee,

I hope you will not mind my writing to you about the cable which I have had from the Yale Press, as they say they have heard from you about

---

1. Ethel had written: "It [perversity] is a bad trait if you have it. In the dog book you are told never to make a dog eat by pretending to take away his food. '*Let him go hungry.*' What about your angle to life? Is it like that of a dog with a poor appetite?" (Ethel to Virginia, 13 August 1930, *Berg*).

my "forthcoming book on Womens Cooperative Guild" and want to see advance proofs. I should be very grateful if you could tell them that the book consists of working womens letters with an introduction by me. It is not, of course, a book on the Womens Guild. Would you say that I should be glad to let them see the advance proofs, but that Harcourt Brace, who do all my books, might wish to do this, and I should have to give them the first offer.[1]

I hope this is not asking too much of you. I hope I am not wrong in supposing that you have some connection with the Yale Press which makes it easy for you to communicate with them.

Yours sincerely
Virginia Woolf

Yale University

2221: To V. Sackville-West   *Monks House* [*Rodmell, Sussex*]

Aug. 19th [1930]

I dont suppose this will reach you. Its only to say Yes of course, do come: shall expect you and the boys and the novel and the tragedy:[2] and if Harold would look in when he passes so much the better

I'm off to Charleston on a breezy evening to eat grouse and send fireworks up by the pond.[3] Isn't that English? Take care, crossing the Alps: dont fall over—Love from us.

Let me have a line by the way: and order your breakfast for the 30th.

Berg

2222: To Ethel Smyth   *Monks House* [*Rodmell, Sussex*]

Tuesday [19 August 1930]

(1) "I dont suppose I am really very fond of anyone"
I woke up in the night and said "But I am the most passionate of women. Take away my affections and I should be like sea weed out of water;

1. There was no American book-edition of *Life As We Have Known It.*
2. Harold Nicolson wrote his only play in Portofino. It was called *The Archduke,* and was a comedy (not a tragedy) about diplomatic life. The play was never performed and never published. The 'novel' was *All Passion Spent,* on which Vita had worked hard in Italy. With Ben and Nigel, she landed at Newhaven early on the 29th (not the 30th) and drove to Rodmell for breakfast.
3. It was Quentin's twentieth birthday party.

Virginia Woolf in January 1929, photographed by Lenare

Vita Sackville-West in 1929

Letter from Virginia Woolf
to Vita Sackville-West,
22 October 1929

Julian Bell

Hugh Walpole

Hilda Matheson

Molly MacCarthy, Harold Nicolson and Stephen Spender, 1929

Ethel Smyth with her dog Pan

Ethel Smyth

Virginia Woolf and Ethel Smyth at Monk's House

Virginia Woolf in about 1930

George Rylands and
Lydia Keynes in a
production of *Comus*,
December 1930

Virginia Woolf and
Angelica Bell, *c.* 1932

The bust of Virginia Woolf by Stephen Tomlin, 1931

like the shell of a crab, like a husk. All my entrails, light, marrow, juice, pulp would be gone. I should be blown into the first puddle and drown. Take away my love for my friends and my burning and pressing sense of the importance and lovability and curiosity of human life and I should be nothing but a membrane, a fibre, uncoloured, lifeless to be thrown away like any other excreta. Then what did I mean when I said to Ethel "I dont suppose I am really very fond of anyone"?"

(2) It is true that I only want to show off to women. Women alone stir my imagination—there I agree with you:

(3) how I enjoy your account of your talk![1] My word, how well you report! And what nice friends you have—what a credit to the race a talk like that is! And your sister's letter—now, you'd be surprised to know all I divine from a letter like that—what a light it throws from another angle. Perhaps my angle is (owing to my trade) an odd one. Certainly, I often get glimpses, as it were through the laurels in the kitchen shrubbery, which I dont get marching up to the front door.

So—I now come to the point—might I one day read some of your letters? Your diary? Remember what a lot has to be packed in. And remember—not I confess that you seem in any danger of forgetting this elemental fact—what a crazy piece of work I am—like a cracked looking glass in a fair. Only, as I write this, it strikes me that as usual I am romancing, led on irresistibly by the lure of some phrase; and that in fact Virginia is so simple, so simple, so simple: just give her things to play with, like a child. But enough. I am now going to look out your trains. (Should this need correction, Leonard will supply it).

Victoria 3.15   arr. Lewes. 4.32.

I suggest (unless you dislike mornings in other people's houses) that you should catch the 5.32 p.m. arr. Victoria 6.52 on Saturday.

But this can be arranged. I deserve a whole days holiday—I shall have finished a chapter (so-called) in my novel (again so-called for trade purposes)

But—look here: you say you are rather a wreck: you feel jagged, worn, fagged, have pains in your neck. May I point out that to add a railway journey, a visit, talk (for we must find time to say a word or two —it cant be all reading the newspaper and patting the dog) will be a strain. And seriously, I should be very very much annoyed if I made you spend even half a day in bed, or on a sofa. Next week would suit us —Dont let yourself be rushed. Of course, Friday would be very nice otherwise.

Yr V

Berg

1. In her letter to Virginia of 18 August (*Berg*) Ethel described her conversation with 'Betty', Lady Balfour (see p. 184, note 4).

Monk's House, Rodmell,
Lewes, Sussex

[27th August 1930]

My dear Dadie,

Any chance that you would come down for a night before October? I dont know where you are, but hope Kings may find you. We shall be here, anyhow till 25th of Sept. or so. We are having short visits from our most desirable friends, as we are happily provided only with a daily. O dear this should be re-written, to convey the real meaning: our happiness is being without a cook; not in having short visits. But its so hot I pour with sweat—the ink is pale with it. And it is the loveliest time here. So come soon.

This hot afternoon I have begun Rosamund Lehmann:[1] and read it with pleasure so far, which is so rare, novels being so abominable, that I think it must be good.

Have you written poetry? Please do. My old jaws can mumble nothing else.

yr V.W.

George Rylands

2224: To Ethel Smyth   [*Monk's House, Rodmell,*
Sussex]

Thursday, 28th Aug. [1930]

Now talk of affection—what can be a greater proof than that I sit up (I was slumbering) and write in answer to your questions

1. No I cant tackle Christopher St. John[2]—I never read a word of hers.
2. No. Elizabeths [Williamson] defamatory letter is not included—I wish it were.
3. What question in particular was it about the Waves that delicacy forbade? I think—but what's the use of thinking when I must correct Hazlitt and cant call an idea my own—they flaunt and fly like the shadows over the downs, yet the downs are like couchant lions today, yellow, unstained— I think then that my difficulty is that I am writing to a rhythm and not to a plot. Does this convey anything? And thus though the rhythmical is more natural to me than the narrative, it is completely opposed to the tradition of fiction and I am casting about all the time for some rope to throw to the reader. This is rough and ready; but not wilfully inaccurate.

Oh yes, I did enjoy your visit immensely. I was—if I'm allowed to say so— revived and fertilised. I'm floated over this dismal week of journalism and snipping and sitting; Proofs and signatures. But dont exaggerate my gifts

1. *A Note in Music* (1930).
2. Christopher St John is best known for her editions of Ellen Terry's memoirs and correspondence with Bernard Shaw. She published *Ethel Smyth: A Biography* in 1959.

or merits. I'm naturally vain but almost equally naturally fastidious: I mean, I adore being liked; but when I see how generous free and fierce you are, I feel (I think this is true) but I'm not worth it. But this theme will be developed later. I'm going to crawl to the post. Why wasn't it hot like this the day you came?

Do write please; do send me the love story.[1] If I'm inarticulate at the moment it is that the tide of the brain in me is so capricious I cant make it flow at all some days; not when I have to go to London, to arrange a dinner party, and to see about circumventing those intolerable hedgings that the Cooperative movement dictate.[2] Sand and shingles though I am, they crackle and blaze with genuine affection—oh yes they do—for you. Only I must one day explain how oddly my visual sense kept tricking me that night. Ethels 18: Ethels 30: Ethels someone, noble and austere, I've never known—all this as you sat in the light of the single candle and logs fire. And thus pulped, my emotions became like so many strange guests: as if chapter after chapter of your life, panel after panel of your psychology were opening and shutting in the twilight. But why try to explain?

I will write when I am rather more peaceful, and the silk knickerbockers dont stick to the sides of my legs.

Oh yes—no—I've no time to go into that, or the other. So goodbye.

Berg

2225: To Vanessa Bell   [*Monk's House, Rodmell, Sussex*]

Friday [29 August 1930]

I cant conceive what the bill is for—sheer robbery I expect. I had two bills and paid them last December, and thought it was long ago settled. Unless you or Duncan can throw some light, I dont know what to do—It seems hopeless to check it. What a folly!

Here's a letter from George [Duckworth]—still unanswered. We should like to come to tea on Sunday very much—Its too hot for anything but the garden, and the bees and flies swarm and the Keynes'es are just arriving for tea and we had Vita and the boys for breakfast and Worthing [Mrs Woolf] looms. So I should like a sight of Dolphin and some of my creatures to restore my balance.

B.

Berg

1. Apparently an account which Ethel once wrote of her romance with Henry Brewster: "My really outrageously fantastic love story" (Ethel to Virginia, 20 August 1930, *Berg*).
2. See pp. 192-3.

[*Monk's House, Rodmell, Sussex*]

Monday [1 September 1930]

Your telegram just come. Yes, I am much better. I am lying in the downstairs room today. I was showing some people [the Keyneses] round the garden on Friday and suddenly fainted. (It was awfully hot) Leonard carried me in here and then I fainted again—How odd being unconscious and coming to is! But it went off by degrees, and now there is nothing wrong but my old bother of a jumping heart—stops and jump, like a mulish pony. Its nothing wrong—with the heart I mean—only nerves. And that is better too. Dear me, what an angel L. has been. He almost makes me cry. I am lying in my room looking at the apple tree. I say, how I like your letter! How I shd. like to see you! What a pleasure if you walked in! Next best please send the lovers story and any other paper, and write.

I expect I shall be kept lying down most of this week; I had a plan to come up on Thursday and dine with you. I suppose thats impossible. I shall listen in.[1] Do you think I'm jealous and ungenerous about other writers, or people? You see I read your letters very carefully.[2] I can't do much yet in the way of long stretches. I say (this is repetition) what a pleasure to think of you—yes, I shd. like you when I'm ill. By the way, I never thanked you for the book. I will read it.

V.

Berg

[*Monk's House, Rodmell, Sussex*]

Monday [1 September 1930]

Your poor Virginia is in bed—I fainted in the garden the day you came, and was rather a long time getting right—Leonard carried me into the sitting room. How odd lying on the floor unconscious is.

However it went off, and I'm now in my dressing gown. Its only my jumping heart that remains—only nerves; and the heat.

But look here—I was going to London with L. on Thursday. I doubt if I shall be able to. Would there be a chance that you could come here for lunch and stay the night? I dont suppose so. But it wd. be nice if you could; and would palliate my anxiety about his driving. I daresay I shall be all right then. Anyhow I want to see you—

1. Ethel conducted the Promenade Concert on 4 September. She had written on 11 August that she would be 'a superb sight' (Ethel to Virginia, *Berg*).
2. Ethel had attributed many virtues to Virginia, but Virginia picked out the faults: "lack of generosity—jealousy—treachery—instability" (Ethel to Virginia, 31 August 1930, *Berg*).

I did think you so nice t'other morning. What a delicious pleasure you are to me.

I shall listen in to you this evening[1]—

V.

Berg

2228: To V. Sackville-West   *Monks House [Rodmell, Sussex]*

Wednesday [3 September 1930]

I have just with great reluctance wired to postpone your coming. Oh damn—It seems to have been some mild form of heatstroke and though I'm ever so much better, the usual headache is threatening and Leonard. . . . I think it would be silly to drag you here when perhaps I couldn't talk much. If I'm quiet now it'll go off.

What we suggest is that you would come on Tuesday (as early as you can) and spend the night and take us to Sissinghurst next day. I shall be in robust health by then. Please do this, or suggest another time—I do want to see you. And write me a full account of Gods own row with that Vampire.[2] I fully expected it; and hope it is final. Yes; my heart is hard for her. But not for you.

No—it was nothing to do with you—my tumble into the rose bush—It was sitting talking politics with the Keynes' and then showing them the hot house.

I say, I hope I haven't upset any of your plans.

V. and P.

Berg

2229: To Ethel Smyth   *Monk's House, Rodmell [Sussex]*

Wednesday [3 September 1930]

Your telegram just come. I will cut all singing of praises and thanks (though they've never been more genuine)—for you will in future take that for said (I mean how tremendously I enjoy seeing you, and how I thank you and shall to my dying day now once more remote for that terrific and superb effort yesterday). But to business. Now this is said; or not said. You did me nothing but good; that is honest truth; but, I've been a little bothered today with the rat gnawing pain—which almost invariably comes after

1. Vita was continuing her BBC broadcasts on current novels.
2. In her diary for 1 September, Vita wrote that she had had 'an appalling row' about money with her mother, Lady Sackville, and left her house in great distress.

my heart has settled—Its very slight; but I have put off Vita who was coming tomorrow; and dont feel that I can at the moment persuade L. to make promises about Friday—You know what I'd like—but I dont feel, after my demands on L., that I can—you will finish the sentence. Only again the pain is slight, and may well be gone tomorrow. One cant tell.

Shall we leave it then that if I am perfectly recovered I will wire tomorrow afternoon to Coign.[1] If I dont wire understand that I'm lying low. But dont understand that its anything but extreme precaution. And I'll trust you to fill in all that I wish—how invigorating, oh and more, it is to me to see you. I cant tell you Ethel, how I adored you for that dash here—for 2 hours only —how it kindled and enraptured me to have you by me. Irreligious as I am (to your eyes) I have a devout belief in the human soul—when I meet what can be called such emphatically; and your power of soul completely daunts me. Thats an odd phrase—but I cant stop—post going—to make a better, and will write anyhow tomorrow. No, no, no, the pain is always hanging about after any spill; you kept it off. I say, I shall listen in; and hear the shouts and the music.

V.

Berg

2230: TO ETHEL SMYTH

Monks House [Rodmell, Sussex]

Thursday [4 September 1930]

This is what I should like:
to see you come in to the room at 3 on Sunday afternoon, and to talk and drowse perhaps in the garden, till 7—(but the last hour to be left vague)

This is what I should *like*, I say; brutally stated, without considering your plans (L. is out and I cant get hold of your letter) or convenience. So state equally brutally. Of course its only Thursday and I dont know what fate intends. No plans therefore. Only tastes and wishes. The pain has gone; but the next stage is complete drowsiness. I cant think how I ever walked to the fishpond—seems like an expedition to the Pole; yet I did this yesterday. I read one line and go into a trance like smoke. Slept the whole afternoon. I'm like an alligator, nostrils only visible, and a kind keeper gives me bananas. Ethels one of my kind keepers. I was awake in the night; suddenly terrified and laid hold of you, like a log. One day I'll write the history of my spine: I think I can feel every knob: and my whole body feels like a web spread on the knobs, and twitchy and sagging and then sinking into delicious rest. But I wont go on at the moment. Here's L. 'Please stop writing'

At 8 we open our wireless. I lie here facing the door. L. in the big chair. Pinka asleep. I shall clap.

1. Ethel's house in Woking.

Blessings on you Ethel for all your goodness. No, Vita cant come anyhow before Tuesday, I've read—with vast looming intervals—50 pages of Ly. Russell ['Elizabeth']—enchanting—I laugh aloud

V.

I do want the lover's story.

Berg

2231: To Ethel Smyth   [*Monk's House, Rodmell,*
                                        Sussex]

Friday [5 September 1930]

Of *course* you must go to Mount M . . .[1] for the weekend—no possible doubt about it. I am touched, too, by her letter. Well, we listened in. 'How like she is to her music' L. said: a great compliment: for he sees you vividly and warmly. I thought the Anacreontic Ode[2] very exciting—even buzzed as it was across England. And the other, the songs, very satisfying (like a complete demonstration of something). Lord, how they knocked out Berners![3] How robust, and at the same time piercing. But no more words. I'm really better—less numbness in the back; and no pain; and here I shall lie all day (I've moved the other way round so that I can have the door open and see the hot pokers) I'm not even seeing Nessa today. I shall lie and dip into Elizabeth R[ussell]: who makes me shout with laughter. Some of her sayings are absolutely tophole: as good as Dickens. About the gent. not having shaved for instance. I shall sleep most of the afternoon, wh. I should not do if Ethel were in the garden. And I think I shall be up on Monday: I mean dress and go to the tool house. But with this cat and mouse illness, pouncing and dropping, one can't tell. I felt quite recovered the afternoon you came.

But go to Mt M: promise: the woman (I forget her name) has too much real feeling to be treated with any levity—I mean it is a serious thing, her affection

V.

Berg

2232: To S. M. Ellis   *Monks House, Rodmell,*
                                        Lewes, Sussex

6th Sept 1930

Dear Mr Ellis,

Please excuse the delay in answering—I have been ill. We shall like very

1. The rest of the name is illegible.
2. Which Ethel composed in 1908.
3. Gerald (Lord) Berners, the gifted amateur composer.

209

much, of course, to consider your book on Henry Kingsley.[1] If it is ready, will you send it straight here? I am afraid I shall not be in London before the beginning of October.

Yours sincerely
Virginia Woolf

Texas

2233: To V. Sackville-West

Monks House [*Rodmell, Sussex*]

Sunday [7 September 1930]

Yes, dearest creature, that will be great fun, if you will come on Tuesday, and dont let it be very late after lunch.[2] This disease has taken rather a lot of shaking off—dear old Ethel Smy: descended in the middle—but I've been for a little walk today and done what passes for writing—I mean correcting a damnable article on Hazlitt.[3] (We never went to Maidstone, after all)—so I shall be practically recovered on Tuesday and it will be a tremendous jolt and jostle and excitement, but of the same salutary kind, to have you to talk to. What a bore—a fortnight's hole knocked in the summer.

I dont pity that old termagant—ought one to?—your mother I mean. Now if the sun stroke descended on her head and left you £5,000 a year the richer I should think all the better of God. Why choose me and Potto, who have nothing to leave? It often strikes me that Heaven is a blundering affair—clumsy past belief.

I am lying in my downstairs room, looking out at the apples. Leonard—what an angel he has been, carrying me in here, fetching chamber pots, running about with trays and medicine—Leonard is grafting or pruning—which is it?—perhaps neither—and then goes to dine with the Keynes,[4] where Maynard will read a memoir of his dead life, and Molly will I'm sure get huffed and ruffed about something. She should have stayed with us.

What about your novel [*All Passion Spent*] and your poems? I ask in no idle curiosity; I look upon you now as the Woolf breadwinner, since it's more and more certain that my novel wont win us even a penny bun.

Yr.
V.

Berg

1. Stewart Marsh Ellis's book on Henry Kingsley was published in 1931, but not by the Hogarth Press.
2. Vita spent the night of 9 September at Monk's House, and on the next day drove Virginia and Leonard to Sissinghurst.
3. Review of *The Complete Works of William Hazlitt*, ed. P. P. Howe (*New York Herald Tribune*, 7 September 1930).
4. For a meeting of The Memoir Club at Tilton.

Monks House [Rodmell, Sussex]

Thursday [11 September 1930]

But Ethel why should I not have letters if I'm not well,—if I'm 300 miles away?[1] Its just then I do want them—every day, all day. Never see a pillar box without dropping a letter in. I miss them when they dont come— letters about everything—think when you're out, or at the dr's, that'll do for Virginia; or if you see a sunset or a butcher's boy or a shop full of cabbages, write and tell me. Writing letters comes as easy to you as rolling down a board does to a marble. But I'm impedimented, owing to—Oh but I'm not going to analyse my disabilities as a writer.

I am better, but, to be truthful, a little feeble still and apt to lie down and sleep. It takes some time to get back one's bodily vigour. My mind seems recovered—no headache, no heart leaping. But it's as if one had been in bed for a month with influenza—no, not really as bad as that—I exaggerate. But I dont yet look at a hill with any desire to climb. Leonard gently led me to the river his afternoon; and I go for drives; and I come in and lie down. And this morning I sat in the tool house and held my pen, but only sketched two shadowy sentences, and then came in and slept. However, I must re-construct my world before I can write about it—writing is a only a final and momentary flash—and I did begin that mysterious process so that I find myself fabricating a scene or two as I lie somnolent. And no doubt tomorrow I shall write 3 sentences; the next day it may be six. So one slips back into the process; and I feel certain now I shant have another tumble. Anyhow, the last one was nothing to do with you. I got (it happens every time) a spurt of ideas, and tried sitting up and working. Unless the sight of you causes ideas (and it well may) I dont see that you're to blame; but Lord, how I cursed fate that Friday, lying alone, a chair by my side, apples winking in the garden, and no Ethel.

This is—you will perceive—no letter; but only the swing of the pump handle to turn you on. Please Ethel, dont think you ought, for reasons of the highest morality, never to see me or write to me again. I should miss you. Oh yes I should. Now what should I miss? Well, I'm going to lie down when I've handed this to the postman, and I'll think of what I should miss. Tell me all you do—in spite of my inaccuracy, every fact is valuable to me: time of getting up, bath, breakfast: scraps of talk, stray ideas, what you wear, read, eat; if you dream; what the aurist [ear-doctor] looks like; does he wear a bow tie; do you walk; where?; have you a sitting room; how furnished; wine for dinner?; Mrs Woodhouse; and think about—what?—and feel— what? and what does your future look like?; also, your past. In short please

1. Ethel was staying with Violet Gordon-Woodhouse, the harpsichordist, who lived at Nether Lyppiat, Gloucestershire. She was consulting a doctor at Bath about her deafness.

Ethel, think, I shant be working or walking for another week seriously; and gape like a baby cuckoo for Ethels words. What a generous woman she is!

V.

Berg

2235: To Mrs Wilson　　　　　　　　*Monk's House, Rodmell, Lewes, Sussex*

12th Sept. 1930

Dear Mrs Wilson,[1]

I must ask you to forgive me my delay in answering your letter, and thanking you for it—it gave me great pleasure—and also in thanking for the white heather. The white heather must have been picked in adverse circumstances—no sooner did I put it in a vase then I fell down in a faint and have been in bed until yesterday. But I have now recovered, and might I suppose have died, so that I will consider it lucky all the same.

I am delighted that you have a new room and that I am the cause of so much discomfort. It is most encouraging to hear that there is one woman who is not going to write—since I published my little book I have been afraid that the writers would far outnumber the readers. But I shall now think with great pleasure that you are using your room to read in, and so shall hope to be counted once more among your far away benefactors.

　　　　　　　　　　　　　　　　　Yours sincerely,
Sussex　　　　　　　　　　　　　　Virginia Woolf

2236: To Margaret Llewelyn Davies
　　　　　　　　　　　　　Monk's House, Rodmell, Lewes, Sussex

Typewritten
14th Sept. 1930

Dearest Margaret,

(forgive typing)—I have at last gone through the Letter[2] and your suggestions, and enclose it for your inspection. I have made some alterations, but I'm afraid by no means all. We both feel, for Leonard agrees, that if I made all the alterations you suggest, the point of view would be so much altered that it would no longer give my own meaning. And as the only merit of the letter is that it gives a particular persons impression we feel that it would be foolish to publish a modified version. One would simply fall between two stools.

On the other hand we both think that you are very likely in the right,

1. An admirer of *A Room of One's Own*. See Letter 2299.
2. Virginia's Introduction to *Life As We Have Known It*.

and that to publish my version would give pain and be misunderstood—and that of course is the last thing we want. Of this we think you and Lilian are the only judges, and therefore we suggest that you should look through the paper again and decide whether you think it can be printed with the alterations I have made. Honestly, I shall not mind in the very least (in fact in some ways I shall be rather relieved) if you say no. I have had my doubts from the first. Then, if you feel that it wont do, we suggest that we should send the papers to Barbara Stephen,[1] unless you can think of anyone better, and ask her to write an introduction. We feel that there must be some introduction, other than a plain statement of facts, if the book is to make any appeal to the general public. I have always liked what Barbara Stephen has written, and I think that she would approach the subject from a much easier angle than mine.—I mean because she knows the thing from the inside and her account would therefore not be so dependent upon personal impressions. The difficulty with impressions is that if you once start altering from the best of motives everything gets blurred and out of proportion.

Its vile weather here, but we have our new sitting room and a roaring log fire and so are very snug. Leonards garden has really been a miracle— vast white lilies, and such a blaze of dahlias that even today one feels lit up. But other peoples gardens are an awful bore I know. Lydia wont buy the necklace—Keynes, Lopokova, I mean. I asked her, and she said she buys all her jewels at Woolworths for half a crown. Maynard has become a Protectionist,[2] which horrified me so that I promptly fainted. Now I am going to take Leonard and Pinka for a short walk in the wet. Excuse spelling. Much love

[*in Virginia's handwriting:*]
No, it was true. Vita has made between 5 and 6 thousand by the Eds.— mostly in America, and has bought a Castle.

V.W.

Sussex

2237: To Ethel Smyth   *Monks House* [*Rodmell,*
                                        Sussex]

Sept., perhaps 16th or 17th
anyhow Monday [15] 1930

Yes, Ethel dear, I did read your diary;
,,   ,,   ,,   ,, ,,   ,,   Burning of Boats.[3]

1. Barbara Stephen was prominent in the Women's Movement and wrote the history of Girton College, Cambridge. In 1904 she had married H. L. Stephen, Virginia's cousin, who succeeded his brother as 3rd baronet in 1932.
2. Keynes, formerly a Free Trader, now believed that home industries must be protected by high tariffs.
3. *A Final Burning of Boats* (1928), one of Ethel's autobiographical volumes.

(You see my economical use of words) I should have to write a dozen blue pages, 24 in all, if I expressed anything like my ideas on both; and as I have only 20 minutes, (my dinner is cooking) I hold off, for the moment. I can tell you though, that I'm building up one of the oddest, most air hung pageants of you and your life; indeed this friendship (if I do not annoy you by my exaggeration [*sic*] phrasing) is one of the strangest aesthetic experiences I have ever had; many people wd. say Lord how I hate your bookishness!— but you, who are so comprehensive (I feel great freedom, even after your angry letter, with you) will understand my use of aesthetic: then 'air-hung': you see, I evolve you and your life and your friends and your whole tremendous intricacy backwards, from letters and diaries; since we were so ill advised as to live many years without contact. Dear me, how badly this is written. Do you know, I shall never compass the plain narrative style that is your glory? And that brings me to:—

(1): We want to know if you will let us publish the speech to the girls about Lambert,[1] music etc? We have a series, day to day pamphlets. Please Ethel let it be about 10,000 words long; and do do it: let it be like a race; all your swiftness, fertility and long lean stride crossing any country you like. Years ago I suggested this to L: and he said "But she wont even write a review for the Nation!" So we gave it up. So we did not meet. So 5 or 6 years passed. What were the 2 important things? Please communicate fully. Oh yes I've enjoyed your letters: I lay in bed this morning fabricating the figure of your brother and sister. I am furnishing your house. Now I want a few theories, emotions, analysis of my character, of your character: there's the wardrobe; I want now to hear your voice.

I am better (you dont ask, but I daresay you wont think me a valetudinarian for alluding to health): but rather knocked up—I dont know why— and in fact I'm all right. Only if it comes to walking or writing for more than half an hour, I feel Lord, where's the place where I can lie back and put my feet up. You wd. be amused if you knew how crafty I am in dandling my body through these convalescences—how I alternate one thing and another. Yet sometimes I feel—no, no, I will not go into that. Tomorrow I'm going to London with L. and shall sit upstairs while he dictates to the clerks: and so back here, and sleep downstairs, for we've changed your bedroom into a sitting room, and I sleep and dress in full view of the garden; and having to change certain monthly articles t'other day, found the benign face of the gardener on me. Write, Ethel dear.

Yr V.

Berg

1. Constant Lambert (1905-51), the conductor, composer and writer on music. Ethel never published her lecture.

Monks House [*Rodmell,*
                                                        Sussex]

Sept. 19th 1930

I am rather like a bottle turned upside down when no water comes out. That is, I've so much to say, and seem never to get the time and the place all together. I answer your letters in my head, and the answers spread over miles of paper; then when I see this small sheet, I cant begin. To economise, and avoid transitions, I will ring round separate statements, one, two three. (But its tantalising to think what letters I could write, if, as I say I could merely print off my mind upon a sheet of blue paper about the size of the terrace, where Leonard is now instructing Percy on, perhaps, cabbages) But I want to catch the post.

(1) Hour: I say certainly, it can be legitimately two syllables; Leonard says, No: that is only done by the illiterate in writing, but can be done in music without offence.

(2) Coming back late from London the other night I was told by a very battered charwoman about to have a baby ("what will be will be, ma'am, and as its seven years since the last I cant complain) that a Miss Hodge had called, which translated means Dodge,[1] I suppose; and as I cant hit on her address, would you either send it, or somehow convey to her my gratitude and regret—that she should have come, that I should have been out—for really it was most cordial and kind of her to journey over that wet day, and I feel respectful and curious and interested and then grateful without knowing more than that Hodge is Dodge—O and she gave you a Kimono, and your house. So would you say what you can see that I mean?

(3) The Essay [on Lambert]: did I casually let fly 10,000 words? What a fountain of inaccuracy I am—perhaps its you, though, that are the hammer of fact. What I meant was that, if you were speaking, as is most usual, for an hour, and were doomed to it, then that—however many words—would be precisely what we should make a pamphlet of; and as I cant conceive that you are ever vapid, tedious, or anything but swift as lightning and ripe as a nut, I must print it—that was what I meant; but did not mean Ethel dear, that you were to go and make yourself take on a job you dislike, or write a single word not from the pressure of your own necessity. No, no. Let it be, and if one of these days something shoots into your head that you would like to publish, remember that the Press is a paying, a respectable, an eager, and devoted servant, who would immensely enjoy having your name to flaunt

1. Mary Dodge, a wealthy American who had settled in England. She was a great admirer of Ethel's music and often put her London house, Warwick House, at Ethel's disposal for private concerts. Coign was built on a plot of ground given to Ethel by Miss Dodge.

abroad. Ethel Smyth—published by L and V Woolf at the Hogarth Press. It is only a seed; the sort of thing one lets fall. No, I should hate to drive you into a lecture room, and innumerable legs.

(4) Of course, of course, of course, I should like to have you sitting by me if I were ill. Short of red ink or gold letters, how am I to make you understand that? That Friday when I was alone in bed, I could hardly keep myself from cursing Leonard for being so positive, against you, or any visitor. It seemed to me as I lay looking at the apples through the open door that you would heighten and establish and make everything right and cheerful and sound for me. If Ethel were here, then, instead of dangling my hand in all these books and papers, I said, I should hold her white cuff (of which I have a vivid memory) and she, who knows exactly how to settle the race and excitability of my mind, would tell me—oh what sort of wardrobe she has in her bedroom; And how did you get your Cook? I should say. Then at a certain moment Ethel would open her eyes, which are (here I was visited by an extremely vivid picture of your almost childish smile) so blue and laugh: and I should feel so set up, that I should lose whatever the pain happened to be—I think in my spine—no perhaps in my head—and toss life like a pancake; and then I should say, now Ethel, I am not going to talk, but you are going to tell me exactly what happened last August twelvemonth, so that I can build up that particular gap in my knowledge etc etc. I can't conceive that you would ever tire me; no; or agitate me; or harass me; but only make me feel like a good child, nestling its head into a perfectly fresh pillow.

But today is a great day, because I cant help thinking that with any luck I can say that this illness is now done with. Anyhow, I got up this morning, actually wished to put on my clothes, actually walked in the rain with energy to the tool house, and wrote, not in gusts, and jets, and bursts, like a runner just touching the goal, but with decision and composure for over an hour. Now if this lasts, and I feel some indescribable solidity as if I had rammed enough strength into my body to withstand all ordinary demands (Lord, how conscious I am, over conscious, of the exact poise of my health) if this lasts a few months, then I can reel off a good deal of the Waves: indeed I might, conceivably finish it. So I am going to say no more about my health; I consider, from today, that this illness is done with.

But I feel, at the same time, that you are vaguely unhappy; I talk of myself, of my being languid, and prostrate, and you meanwhile have pipes poked down your ears; are clogged with fibrous mushrooms; have indigestion; and are (perhaps) more than this, a little exhausted, unhappy, and have recourse to your death philosophy,[1] which I respect and to some

1. Ethel, in her letters to Virginia, often reflected on death and was fascinated by it, but had no wish to die.

extent understand; but I do dislike the thought that you in Bath and alone have to spend any minute of the day in melancholy. The trouble is, I'm so at sea with other people's feelings that I very often appear egotistical and unsympathetic because I'm afraid to discharge my sympathy when it is out of place and therefore offensive. That is I think a true note upon my own psychology. And I have many other notes, but look, I have written so much and at such a pace that the words scarcely cover the ideas—these are horrid splits,—and the writing is only an attempt to encircle a few signs. Do you ever show my letters? Do you ever quote them? Do what you like, but I rather hope not, because I am never able to write at leisure; (I'm trying to finish a good many things) and then I cannot be expressive (these interruptions are because of a double rainbow on the terrace—L. has dashed in from the rain to show me) As a professional hack, I detest making shots at sentences, and to you—anyhow for some time—I never do anything else—So send them in a proof that I repose on your understanding as Nelson on Trafalgar Sqre. But now that I am quite well, you shall write in any mood—about the wardrobe or the character; about the cruising widows (what a gift you have as a writer—how I enjoy your letters) or the finer parts of the soul.

So for the moment I pause.

V.

Berg

2239: To Ethel Smyth   *Monks House [Rodmell, Sussex]*

Monday 21st [22] Sept. [1930]

Well Ethel, I am vastly in your debt for your letters, which I carry out, like a dog its bone, to read in the Tool house. But my answers are never written—Oh I see too many people. All our diners and sleepers are flocking upon us like swallows on the wires. And my mind being unstable, one pebble is enough to send it rocking in waves to the shore. And stability is what I need. But I have said this; and can now only deliver a few paragraphs:

(1) Mrs Woodhouse. Would you convey to her, if she did ask us, and it was not only your frantic and rapturous anticipation that she would ask us, our grateful thanks: because it was very kind in her; and would you say how much I hope to meet her, and perhaps one day to come—one day soon I hope—to Nether [Lyppiat] whats its name—I love other people to have those houses, mats, tables chairs, pictures, china and tapestry over the 4 post bed, with lavender in the chamber pots and biscuits in a box shd. one wake hungry in the night: other people I like to have them, not myself.

(2) Would you like to read an Essay on Virginia Woolf[1] just come? or shall I send it back next mail? I ask, because, bat-blind as I am, I dont know if you like this sort of thing—None of my other friends would. And it may be vanity that prompts, or intuition. I dont know.

(3) We are throwing our hats up—no great exaggeration—about your essay. Morgan Forster (E. M. Forster the novelist, whose books once influenced mine, and are very good, I think, though impeded, shrivelled and immature) said "Lord! I should think you would like an essay by Ethel Smyth! She should write pamphlets—my word (he said) how good her thing in the train was[2]—how I laughed—what a born writer" and then, by a natural transition, passed to Lady Russell, and said (he's the quietest, but most inflexible of men) "No; I dont like her. I think she is unkind and selfish. But she has a wonderful way of making one wish to be nice to her"—and nothing I could say would change his inflexible opinion "I dont like her"—but then he was very young when he knew her[3]; and she was rude to the old mother whose sister, son, daughter and husband he is. They share a Surrey house; and live like mice in a nest.

This is a tiny sheet, because I have I daresay six very serious letters to write, one to a dying man—oh dear—a boy of 26, with wealth and an old house, and all to come[4]—and others to Cooks and publishers. Tomorrow I'm going to London in order to—but the story is so long and complex that I must leave it: but if Miss Rivett-Carnac[5] offered to be your general, and do entire work of flat, what would you say? Thats the question—what am I to say?

And its raining, Ethel, sweeping in filaments of mist across my marshes; but Ethel, all the same I walked to the top of the down this afternoon, and surveyed Sussex, and then tore my skirt my knickers and some tender parts not mentioned even between ladies on a barbed wire fence. Do you know, if I could sit still all the morning I could write straight ahead now— if I were you, and could drive one hour into another, I could finish the Waves in one blast—as it is I wake filled with a tremulous yet steady rapture, carry my pitcher full of lucid and deep water across the garden, and am forced to spill it all by—some one coming—Never mind. And write to me.

V.

Berg

1. Possibly one of the two essays published in April 1930: Jean-Jacques Mayou, *Le roman de l'espace et du temps—Virginia Woolf* (*Revue Anglo-Americaine*) and Paul Dottin, *Les Sortilèges de Virginia Woolf* (*Revue de France*).
2. *An Adventure in a Train* from *Streaks of Life* (1921).
3. As tutor to her children in 1905, when she was Countess von Arnim.
4. This young man has not been identified.
5. See next letter.

Monks House [*Rodmell, Sussex*]

Monday [22 September 1930]

Doran[1] is a vulgar brute to be sure, and about as inaccurate as he can be. But it was ravished from me by Morgan Forster, whose friend, the blind Frenchman [Charles Mauron], is translating Orlando, and wants a paragraph for the French papers about you.

So many people, one way and another. I can hardly settle to anything, and think on the whole Tavistock Sqre is a hermitage compared with Rodmell. Morgan F. says "Will you ask me to meet Vita?" I say yes.— so be ready.

I go up for the day tomorrow, to interview cooks. Only they're not cooks, but ladies of semi-royal birth (I mean Rivett-Carnac;[2] but you know nothing of the aristocracy of India): and she wants £1 a week; also the Miss Ibbotsons. But how does one know the points of cooks from their faces?

And when shall I see you?

etc. etc. etc.

Please write and say you still, in spite of Ethel, feel for me a respectful regard.

V.

Oh and thanks for the Shelley pictures:[3] I'm sentimental about them.

Berg

Monks House, Rodmell, Lewes [*Sussex*]

Tuesday [23 September 1930]
Dear Dorothy,

This valiant attempt must be crowned with success at all costs. What about Thursday, the day after tomorrow? Friday, Saturday and Sunday are all, I think hopeless (owing to hordes of relations) but Thursday would suit perfectly—at 4. So do contrive it with Elly.[4] I'll get Leonard to write full

---

1. Doubleday, Doran, who published the American edition of *The Edwardians*.
2. The Rivett-Carnacs were an old Derbyshire family, of which the most distinguished member was the 1st baronet who was Governor of Bombay, 1838-41. Mary Rivett-Carnac was about 35, impoverished, and a social worker. She stayed with the Woolfs only a few months.
3. Photographs taken by Vita of Casa Magni, Lerici, on the Gulf of Spezia, where Shelley lived for the last few months of his life.
4. Elinor Rendel, Virginia's doctor and Dorothy Bussy's niece.

directions tomorrow. We're up for the day and in a rush—pen wont mark—
but you must come.

V.W.

Texas

2242: TO VIOLET DICKINSON

Monks House, Rodmell,
Lewes [Sussex]

27th Sept. [1930]

My Violet,[1]

Yes certainly we will send you, straight from The Press On Being Ill,
and The Art of Dying[2] (a cheerful pair) The working women's book is
held up and wont I think be out till the Spring—which seems at the moment
very far off.

We are shivering over a log fire; but on Wednesday, you'll be amused to
hear, Nessa is giving a luncheon party to Sir George Duckworth and his
son [Henry]. He says he is about to die.[3]

What did I ever give you? I cant remember, and your hand is so
impressionistic that I cant read.

Leonards love—

Sp:

Berg

2243: TO HUGH WALPOLE

Monks House, Rodmell,
Lewes [Sussex]

27th Sept 1930

My dear Hugh,

I see you are making speeches and unveiling tablets all over England, so
I suppose you have returned [from France and Spain]. And though I hate
writing letters more and more—finish the sentence to your own credit.
My fingers are too cold. But we are sitting in a room with probably the

1. Violet Dickinson was Virginia's most intimate friend from 1902 until about
   1907, although Violet was 17 years older. The first volume in this series contains
   more letters to her than to any other person, but their friendship languished,
   and this is the only letter to Violet in Volume IV. Virginia always signed herself
   'Sparroy' ('Sp') when writing to Violet. See the Introduction to Volume I,
   pp. xviii-xix.
2. Virginia's essay *On Being Ill* was originally published in 1926, and was republished by the Hogarth Press in November 1930; *The Art of Dying*, an anthology
   of 'last words' edited by Francis Birrell and F. L. Lucas, was also published in
   November.
3. George Duckworth, Virginia's half-brother, died in 1934.

finest view in Sussex: marsh, down, church and pear tree. Last Sunday Morgan Forster was here and we skulked behind the churchyard wall and watched the Bishop arrive to bless the spire (to which I contributed £5. 10: and also bought, in its behalf a bottle of bathsalts, and six cakes of variegated soap at a Bazaar). Morgan was moth like and evanescent, abjuring fiction,[1] but—what is the opposite word?—cant remember—anyhow writing criticism for Cambridge—a chilly fate. We come back on Saturday, and settle in to pack up parcels of new books. All are worthy—all will fail. I see our nice heap of gold from the Edwardians melting in the sun. We have discovered a good novelist,[2] homosexual, a waiter, I think, in Cardiff; but he wont help—his rags will further diminish our hoard. I think we shall travel then again along the East Coast this time—I want to see the Wash, and the Humber, and King's Lynn, and the moors where the wild duck come.

Then we shall be in London again, and then—but this is far far off—I've heard of a yacht that one can charter, and visit all the Isles of Greece.

By the way, my American publisher writes that Mr Hugh Walpole says that Mrs Woolf's novel is finished. This is so wildly fantastic a statement that I consider it equivalent to an offer to finish it yourself. The last words, written this morning with fearful labour were—"Listen," she said, "Look".[3] Now go on. What a good game that would be. In 12 months I have written 29,000 words.

I hear also that you met Dadie [George Rylands] somewhere—So romantic is my view of friends in absence that I at once leap to the conclusion that it was down a back street in a wine shop in Seville. But I've no room to sketch my vision of what happened there.

Leonard sends his kind respects.

yr V.W.

Texas

2244: To Ethel Smyth   *Monks House, Rodmell*
                                                        [Sussex]
Sept. 28th [1930]

But, Ethel dear, I have left your letter in the tool house, and it is too cold to go and fetch it, as you'll agree, so I can't be exactly precise about dates.

---

1. E. M. Forster's last novel published in his lifetime was *A Passage to India* (1924).
2. John Hampson, whose novel *Saturday Night at the Greyhound* was published by the Hogarth Press in February 1931.
3. What Virginia had written that morning was: " 'Look, listen' said Rhoda" (*Virginia Woolf: The Waves: The Two Holograph Drafts*, ed. J. W. Graham, 1976, p. 540). The final version read " 'Look,' said Rhoda; 'listen' " (Hogarth Edition, 1931, p. 146).

All I know for certain is that we go back next Saturday 4th; then I shall have a week entirely devoted to seeing servants, who will all come at the most inconvenient hours. You say you are passing through about the 10th?; I say will you fix whatever hour suits you then; either to come to 52, or— no I think it had better be 52. I expect to be in full command of my life by then. What other subject had I in mind to write about? Lesbianism? Thats your theme; I await illumination anxiously. Being alone in Bath and turning yellow and having your teeth scraped and writing in a hotel lounge with old widows cruising has my intense sympathy: why is it that such forced maroonings are so violently detestable? I remember once being stuck for 10 days in Brighton[1] and almost dashing my head out against the pillar boxes; and have hated Hove ever since, even going with you.

Your strictures on my weakness in wasting these last days that will never never come again, talking, when my entire year, almost, wastes in talk, are apparently justified, but actually, if you were in my shoes, what could you do? I'm lounging after tea—the fertile hour, the hour for hatching and planning and imaginatively surmounting all obstacles in The Waves— when there's a tap at the window, and there's Jack Hutchinson and Barbara; there's Mary Hutchinson; theres Lord Gage—the local nobleman who drops in to see how eccentric intellectuals can be, and is not disappointed; or worse, I get a letter, imploring me, because she's going away for a year to see Madame Bussy, who was Strachey, and is about to return to France; or from Ka Arnold-Forster who's motoring to Cornwall, and wants lunch— what can I do thus trapped and implored, but say O all right, come in; you've ruined 10 pages of my book; I shall never catch that mood again; but by all means sit down while I boil the kettle, make toast, and show you the goldfish. Worst, superlatively worst, my mother in law has settled at Worthing. Occupation she has none. Her youth passed in childbirth. Now nothing can make the innumerable days tolerable but frequent teaparties and conglomerations of children and long tables covered with little cakes, which she adores, and presents on birthdays, and remembering anniversaries; so that if she says can she come over on Friday, as Harold, Bella and Tom[2] are staying with her and want to see Monks House, what can I do, but race off to Lewes, buy pink, red, and yellow cakes, cakes striped with sugar bars and dotted with chocolate spots, return just in time to collect chairs, light fire; and then—here they are, dressed, like all Jews, as if for high tea in a hotel lounge, never mixing with the country, talking nasally, talking incessantly, but requiring at intervals the assurance that I think it really jolly to have them. "I am so terribly sensitive Virginia" my mother in law says pensively, refusing honey, but sending me into the kitchen to

1. The Stephens often stayed in Brighton during Virginia's childhood.
2. Harold, Leonard's younger brother, Bella, Leonard's oldest sister, and Thomas Southorn, her husband.

find strawberry jam; and then, like a perfectly aimless airball, off she drifts into long long anecdotes about Mrs Luard; girls who looks [*sic*] 14, and Mrs Watson's cook having a a baby which died—oh no it was Mrs Watson's cook who died—all this goes on till 7: when she says her head aches: I say, I will go off then, and show Bella, Tom and Harold the church. And leave me all alone? she says. Tears well up. Down I sit. Off we go again about Herberts[1] temper and her own tremendous sorrows, virtues, courage and endurance in raising 9 Jews, all of whom, with the single exception of Leonard, might well have been drowned without the world wagging one ounce the worse.

There! Thats a long sentence: and an ill natured. But when you say why do I see people? I say Ethel as a believer in the Christian religion has brought about this state of affairs, and believes that crucifixion is good for the soul.

Ah, but now they are gone, and I wrote this morning; and then took one of Leonards large white pocket handkerchiefs and climbed Asheham hill and lost a green glove and found 10 mushrooms, which I shall eat in bed tomorrow, with bacon, toast and hot coffee. I shall get a letter from Ethel. I shall moon slowly dressing; shall loiter talking, shall hear about the funeral of our [Rodmell] epileptic, Tom Fears, who dropped dead after dinner on Thursday; shall smell a red rose; shall gently surge across the lawn (I move as if I carried a basket of eggs on my head) light a cigarette, take my writing board on my knee; and let myself down, like a diver, very cautiously into the last sentence I wrote yesterday. Then perhaps after 20 minutes, or it may be more, I shall see a light in the depths of the sea, and stealthily approach— for one's sentences are only an approximation, a net one flings over some sea pearl which may vanish; and if one brings it up it wont be anything like what it was when I saw it, under the sea. Now these are the great excitements of life. Once I would have written all this twice over; but now I can't; it has to go, with its blood on its head. I have 3 whole days of solitude still— Monday, Thursday and Friday. The others are packed with this damnable disease of seeing people. Please tell me what psychological necessity makes people wish to "go and see" so-and so? I never do. Do they resent obscurely, the effort that L. and I make to be alone? that I make to write? And Lesbianism, to return to that?

V.

I warn you, this is an egotistical letter, which says nothing about my really complete sympathy for you, and your rheumatism, diarrhoea, and ears.

Berg

1. Leonard's older brother.

Monks House [*Rodmell, Sussex*]

Typewritten
Wednesday [1 October 1930]

We think it would be fun to go and see the Barretts of Wimpole Street[1] on Monday. Would you come and dine with us first, and come to tea before that. And would Boski be such an angel as to telephone for tickets? Perhaps there are none—anyhow she is in command of wits and telephone—more than I am. Off to lunch with Sir George [Duckworth] and shall refer delicately to our past.

V.

Berg

2246: To Ethel Smyth [*Monk's House, Rodmell, Sussex*]

Typewritten
Friday Oct. 3rd [1930]

This is merely a formal acknowledgement of your MS just come.[2] We will be remorseless and plain spoken.

Here is Ursula Greville[3] to put you in a rage, in case you have escaped her. Very good for the liver—to be put in a rage.

Just lost my watch in the meadows, but found (to put me up in your esteem) a white knife with four blades.

My God—if leaving your letter about will make servants go, I shall have it broadcast. My whole endeavour now is to be rid of the most faithful and enraging of her kind.[4] (Yes, no servant will ever leave me. In 48 years I have had three.)

Lunched with Lady Margaret my half sister in law and Sir George and have been given Pattles picture[5] as reward. You shall have it. I will write about plans when I can get my head above these vast whirlpools of departure.

V.

[*in Virginia's handwriting:*]
No, I dont think you are convincing on the subject of Lesbianism

Berg

1. The play by Rudolf Besier, first performed in this year.
2. See p. 214, note 1.
3. The soprano and writer on musical subjects.
4. Nelly Boxall had been ill since May and had undergone a serious operation. Virginia's attempts to dissuade Nelly from returning to her service did not succeed.
5. See p. 144.

Letters 2247-2299 (October–December 1930)

The autumn in London was varied by occasional weekends at Rodmell. Virginia was trying to write 'the very difficult passage' in The Waves, *Bernard's soliloquy, but was as usual interrupted by social engagements and work for the Press, reading many unsolicited manuscripts from unknown authors. Not for the first time Leonard considered abandoning the Press, which was now almost monopolising his time. They intended a book-selling tour of East Anglia, but cancelled it when the pressure of work proved too heavy. The threat of eviction from Tavistock Square was renewed and there were servant troubles, but on the whole it was a happy and productive autumn. Virginia's friendship with Ethel Smyth continued to prosper, and she also saw much of Vita. But Vanessa was in Cassis and Clive had serious eye-trouble. The Woolfs returned to Rodmell for Christmas, when Virginia caught influenza again. The year ended with* The Waves *still unfinished.*

2247: TO ETHEL SMYTH   52 *Tavistock Sqre.* [*W.C.*1]

Sunday [5 October 1930]

Yes Ethel dear dinner next Sunday will be delightful (I'm not talking of the food, which may be harum scarum, odds and ends, cooked by me)— at 7.30—But come when you like—only tell me what time suits.

We shall probably go on an East County tour soon afterwards. but thats not fixed.

Am I to vote for the Opera merger?[1] a post card, with a stamp, has been sent me; as if Sir Thomas [Beecham] means business: I'll put on 1½ if by so doing I can ensure a perfect performance of the Wreckers [Ethel's opera].

Lord what a shindy and a gloom London is! I'm dismal all through and have taken L. to walk in Regents Park and look at the pinched Cockneys and the dying flowers instead of roaming the downs and putting up a hare.

So no more.

                                                                                V.

P.S. Monday [6 October 1930]

I forgot to post this scrawl; so add, in answer to yours of this morning, I was speaking personally, no doubt frivolously (what a pity there aren't

1. It was Beecham's plan to amalgamate the Imperial League of Opera with the Covent Garden Opera in order to form a National Opera.

accents to convey tone of voice $\phi \, \mathcal{C} \, \curlyvee$ and so on, to mean I'm laughing, I'm ironical, I'm glum as the grave—) about your being unconvincing on the subject of Lesbianism. I was referring to what you said, (but I've locked your letters at Rodmell) about the shape of my nose not going, to your taste, with that particular vice. Well but then, to another, my shaped nose may be a perfect monstrosity without that addition. But I was laughing, and no doubt misquote. Anyhow I hardly ever think half a thought about these matters—if Eddy [Sackville West] chooses to plunge his poker in an ant heap or a woman or the next young man he meets in Bond St. its all the same to me. No room to develop this subject seriously.

Now to write seriously about the essay [on Constant Lambert] which seems to me so perfect for its end that I'm not sure how far it would suit another. I mean, the girls, the school, the cropped heads. The legs are so completely visualised and assimilated as in all first rate lectures—that to switch off to another audience seems impossible without injury. But L. has not read, and I must read again.

Lord its good!

V.

Berg

2248: To Viscountess Rhondda
52 Tavistock Square, London, W.C.1
Typewritten
7th Oct. 1930

Dear Lady Rhondda,[1]

Many thanks for your letter. I am afraid that luncheon is a very difficult time for me, but would it be possible for you to come to tea with us either Monday October 20th or Thursday 30th, at 4.30?

We should so much like to see you, and should be much interested to hear the other side of Ethel Smyth's story.

Yours sincerely
Virginia Woolf

Texas

2249: To Ethel Smyth   52 *T.[avistock] S.[quare, W.C.*1]

Wednesday [8 October 1930]

I'm awfully pleased—thats a great relief about Elizabeth [Williamson]. They can be, I know, an awful bore,—glands. In spite of the Pattle blood, some of my cousins have them. But Lor! (as you would say) what punish-

1. Editor of *Time and Tide*.

ment can be inflicted on Harley Street for these entirely false verdicts—and all the agony they give. Once [in February 1922] (having a temperature) I was told that my right lung was diseased; then that my heart was inflamed, and L. and I walked away prepared (so the man said) for death in a fortnight. Give E. my love, and congratulations in spite of the soot, and hope to meet.

Lor! (as you would say) the egotism of the male! Two completely solid hours of Eddy [Sackville West] this afternoon, and every second a complaint about his stomach. Every other aspect of the world barred. My time wasted and all I could do was to suppose the ant heap was on him.

But about Sunday. Isn't there a train that wd. allow you comfortably to get here say 5.30? then we could stretch our legs a little before the cold pale ham and the argument with L.

Anyhow I shall be in, should this suit.

In a hurry, or I would write at length about Rivett Carnac, my new general and the domestic comedy, which is at present exercising all my diplomacy and temper. Lor (as you would say) what a go domestics are! And nothing I can do will prevent their loving me! hah hah—a tribute that, which in spite of haste and disgusting handwriting I can't deny myself.

But to what quality in me do you attribute it?

Yr V.

Berg

2250: To V. Sackville-West   [52 *Tavistock Square, W.C.*1]

[8 October 1930]

Dearest,

would you be a great angel and send me, on loan the Ladies of Llangollen[1] —if that is their name? I cant find anything to do for Mrs Van Doren,[2] and this might suit, and stingily I dont want to buy and dont want to use my Times subscription and much prefer to worry you. That is my principle in life.

Such a visit from Eddy—all peeve and grieve and now I'm sick and trembling because Nelly is about to descend upon me in the flesh. Good lord, why are these things so much worse than operations for cancer? And shall we meet some day?

Your
V.

Berg

1. *The Hamwood Papers of the Ladies of Llangollen*, edited by John Travers, (1930).
2. Irita Van Doren, Editor of the *Weekly Book Supplement* of the *New York Herald Tribune*.

Thursday [9 October 1930]

Look here—dont be later than 5.30 because I may have to go out at 9 to say goodbye to Vanessa etc who have suddenly decided with no tact to fly to France. So no more, till we meet.

Love to Eliz—I'm much relieved about the glands.

So no more.

Berg

2252: To Margaret Llewelyn Davies

52 *Tavistock Sq.* [*W.C.1*]

Typewritten
Oct. 10th 1930

Dearest Margaret,

I am a wretch not to have written before but—there have been endless interruptions, and now of course our head clerk [Miss Belcher] is ill, in the height of getting books out, and Leonard has to take on her work as well as his own. So I havent faced him with your questions about publication— partly indeed because I know he thinks the Press will be very glad indeed to do the book quite apart from my introduction (which is only a flourish.) But he will tell you about facts—date of publication and so on. I am very pleased that Mrs Barton on the whole approves—at the same time I'm amused at the importance attached to the size of the Guilders.[1] Vanity seems to be the same in all classes. But I swear that Mrs Barton shall say exactly what she thinks of the appearance of me and my friends and I wont think *her* unsympathetic. Indeed I wish she would—what fun to hand her a packet of our letters and let her introduce it! What rather appals me (I'm writing in a hurry, and cant spell, and dont please take my words altogether literally) is the terrific conventionality of the workers. Thats why—if you want explanations—I dont think they will be poets or novelists for another hundred years or so. If they cant face the fact that Lilian [Harris] smokes a pipe and reads detective novels, and cant be told that they weigh on an average 12 stone—which is largely because they scrub so hard and have so many children—and are shocked by the word "impure" how can you say that they face "reality"?, (I never know what 'reality' means: but Lilian smoking a pipe to me is real, and Lilian merely coffee coloured and discreet

1. Margaret Llewelyn Davies added a Note to Virginia's Introduction to *Life As We Have Known It*, saying that the Women's Co-operative Guild had nearly 1,400 branches and 67,000 members. Mrs Eleanor Barton was the current General Secretary of the Guild.

is not nearly so real). What depresses me is that the workers seem to have taken on all the middle class respectabilities which we—at any rate if we are any good at writing or painting—have faced and thrown out. Or am I quite wrong? And how do you explain away these eccentricities on the part of your swans? It interests me very much. For you see, it is that to my thinking that now makes the chief barrier between us. One has to be "sympathetic" and polite and therefore one is uneasy and insincere. And why, with such a chance to get rid of conventionalities, do they cling to them? However, I must stop. And we must meet and go into the question by word of mouth—if you want me to make them sylphs I will.

Yours Virginia

By the way, I have had a cable from the Yale Press who want to see the book for America.

Sussex

2253: To V. Sackville-West   [52 *Tavistock Square, W.C.*1]

Wednesday [15 October 1930]

Yes, do come to dinner on Monday. I'll see if I can get tickets [for *Private Lives* by Noel Coward] tomorrow. Rivett Carnac will cook.

I want to take 2 days complete holiday on Tuesday and Wednesday and packed with pleasure, in the open air, anywhere. Could you come? And where could we go? Lord, how happy you must be cutting Nettles.

Yes, I heard about Lily[1]—it would have served Eddy right had you been killed. But I dont want him served right, peevish though he is. I can imagine his complaints, Vita dead—and now I cant have my roast apples as I like them.

Osbert [Sitwell] has sent a book for you (I think) I'll keep it till Monday. At Rodmell on Friday, thank God. Come as early as you can; and let me know about Tuesday and Wednesday—

Vita's first letter at Sisshurst[2]

Berg

1. Lily Jimenez had been Vita's cook at Long Barn for some years, and then cooked for Edward Sackville West at Knole. On 9 October she went off her head, seized a revolver, descended on Long Barn, and was only prevented from shooting Vita by the intervention of the other servants. Next day Eddy and Vita had her committed to Maidstone asylum.
2. On 16 October Vita spent the first night of her life at Sissinghurst, which had hitherto been uninhabitable.

Thursday, 16th Oct [1930]

Well, Ethel dear, I daresay its all right about 'masterpieces'—I accept your definition a thing done as well as it is possible to do it—only I think somehow one ought to discriminate between 'things'. [King] Lear for example and Trilby[?].¹ Its not a question of roast beef v. omelette. One must find some other metaphor, or is this a simile, or even an analogy—(I'm infinitely stupid this morning and cant write fiction miserable to relate). One must I mean indicate that one 'thing' is colossal and the other tiny. That being understood I bow my head and pass on—No, not instantly. I think these discriminations rather more important than you do; I think if one ignores them by habit one becomes woolly headed; one chokes people off. And enthusiasm (as Nurse Cavell said)² is not enough. No, nor discrimination either. It is the rare and blessed combination that I find truly imaginative— and I grant that having been born within the Polar region of Cambridge I tend by education not instinct to frigidify. Enough. enough.

Rivett: an admirable cook. Light handed, adept, adventurous; but this is on the strength of six meals. Whether being a lady born, she can scrub and sweep without collapse I rather doubt. Today is the first day of trial, because so far the country widow [Annie] has been helping. Anyhow, there are no dark pockets of discontent; everything is above board and plain sailing. The question of Rivett or Carnac is still hedged; but I've hardly been alone with her, and so say 'Miss' and then stop. Now Nelly looms; and how to deal with the devoted servant, whose mind is riddled with jealousy, suspicion, and poverty—thats my horror. One cant be ruthless; they are so weakly and devoid of all support, and one sees their poor fluttering lives as one talks,—its the dependence and defencelessness that queers the pitch, and take the sting from their violently infuriating unreason—yet leave one hopeless, helpless—have I ever felt such wild misery as when talking to servants?—partly caused by rage at our general ineptitude—we the governors —at having laden ourselves with such a burden, at having let grow on our shoulders such a cancer, such a growth, such a disease as the poor are. Again, enough.

Monday or (or is it 'and'?—see, how seldom I look at my own works) *Tuesday.*³ If one put comparatives for all your superlatives, you're a very

1. The manuscript is unclear. But the probable reading *Trilby* (the romantic novel by George du Maurier, 1894) suits the sense well.
2. Edith Cavell, the English nurse, who was executed by the Germans in 1916 for assisting Allied prisoners to escape. Her last words were: "I realise that patriotism is not enough. I must have no hatred or bitterness towards anyone."
3. Virginia's collection of stories, *Monday or Tuesday*, was published by the Hogarth Press in 1921. The contents were *A Haunted House, A Society, Monday or Tuesday, An Unwritten Novel, The String Quartet, Blue and Green, Kew Gardens*,

good critic—that is, have singled out the phrase I liked (the pigeon)[1] and the stories I liked; and lighted with your aeroplane eye upon the generally acclaimed successes—that is Mark on the Wall and Kew. You are perfectly right about Green and blue and the heron one [*Monday or Tuesday*]: thats mainly why I won't reprint. They are mere tangles of words; balls of string that the kitten or Pan [Ethel's dog] has played with. One of these days I will write out some phases of my writer's life; and expound what I now merely say in short—After being ill and suffering every form and variety of nightmare and extravagant intensity of perception—for I used to make up poems, stories, profound and to me inspired phrases all day long as I lay in bed, and thus sketched, I think, all that I now, by the light of reason, try to put into prose (I thought of the Lighthouse then, and Kew and others, not in substance, but in idea)—after all this, when I came to, I was so trem-blingly afraid of my own insanity that I wrote Night and Day [1919] mainly to prove to my own satisfaction that I could keep entirely off that dangerous ground. I wrote it, lying in bed, allowed to write only for one half hour a day. And I made myself copy from plaster casts, partly to tranquillise, partly to learn anatomy. Bad as the book is, it composed my mind, and I think taught me certain elements of composition which I should not have had the patience to learn had I been in full flush of health always. These little pieces in Monday or (and) Tuesday were written by way of diversion; they were the treats I allowed myself when I had done my exercise in the conventional style. I shall never forget the day I wrote The Mark on the Wall—all in a flash, as if flying, after being kept stone breaking for months. The Unwritten Novel was the great discovery, however. That—again in one second—showed me how I could embody all my deposit of experience in a shape that fitted it —not that I have ever reached that end; but anyhow I saw, branching out of the tunnel I made, when I discovered that method of approach, Jacobs Room [1922], Mrs Dalloway [1925] etc—How I trembled with excitement; and then Leonard came in, and I drank my milk, and concealed my excitement, and wrote I suppose another page of that interminable Night and Day (which some say is my best book). All this I will tell you one day—here I suppress my natural inclination to say, if dear Ethel you have the least wish to hear anymore on a subject that cant be of the least interest to you. And, I add, Green and Blue and the heron were the wild outbursts of freedom, inarticulate, ridiculous, unprintable mere outcries.

My word—what a bore—here's Leonard to say that some agent has made an offer for this house, and he, Leonard, thinks we ought to consider

---

and *The Mark on the Wall*. All these stories, with the exception of *A Society* and *Blue and Green* were among those reprinted after Virginia's death in *A Haunted House* (1943).

1. "The shadow of a thrush crossed the carpet; from the deepest wells of silence the wood pigeon drew its bubble of sound" (*A Haunted House*).

231

it seriously, for we've only the fag end of a lease to run—which means that I must rout up and look at houses again, I suppose.

In the immediate future however we go to Rodmell, Friday to Sunday; then to the East Coast, travelling our books, on Thursday. And as the devil will have it, I have somehow injured the usual nerve in my spine and am rather done up for the moment—cant even open the Waves; dare not think of the next sentence. But I did grind a bit, last week, and can't therefore do more than grumble to you if I have now to knock about like an aimless fish, for a week. But the light in the sky certainly depends upon my own little taper—the green goes out of the leaf—I am rather below the level of the woman one meets in omnibuses. I shall lounge about for a day or two, and slowly—oh its nothing to grumble about.

Please write a nice long letter. And hows the d i a r r h oe a? Thats the way its spelt. I'm told its the very devil of discomfort. Ah hah! How much you suffer that I dont! Isn't that a comforting reflection? But I dont actually wish you to suffer.

Yr V.

Your rose has come out and is a perfect marvel, like a red globe in the window.

Berg

2255: To V. Sackville-West   [*52 Tavistock Square, W.C.1*]
[17 October 1930]

Look here I'm not getting tickets for Noel Coward [*Private Lives*] because
  (1) I forgot
  (2) I've been rather headachy and want to be dull.
  (3) I dont think we shd. have got any.
  (4) We suggest going next week, if you will.
  (5) We expect you to dinner after Broadcasting.

Berg

2256: To David Garnett   *52 Tavistock Sqre., W.C.1*
[18 October 1930]

Dear Bunny,
    Could you in your very great kindness tell me which is the right Inn to stay at at Kings Lynn [Norfolk]? I'm told that there are two—one good,

the other bad. We are going there travelling our books up the East Coast, and any information will be gratefully accepted.

> Your aff.
> Virginia

Berg

2257: TO KATHERINE ARNOLD-FORSTER
Monks House, Rodmell
[Sussex]

Saturday 18th Oct [1930]

Dear Ka,

In spite of your prohibition, the flowers were really too lovely not to be thanked for. They were burning blue yesterday when we left—Leonard is envious, the emotion you gardeners most like to rouse. It was odd to open the paper and read that Mrs Brooke was dead,[1] after your letter. I remember her sitting on the step at Talland House with Rupert or, perhaps Dick; her face covered with wrinkles—thats what struck me as a child—Lord, what years ago. We are here for one merciful week end and then go travelling our books up the East Coast. Miss Rivett-Carnac is now my cook—but how far born ladies can abide scrubbing remains to be seen. Its rather an odd situation. The end of the paper, so goodbye and thanks.

> V.

Mark Arnold-Forster

2258: TO ETHEL SMYTH   52 *Tavistock Square* [*W.C.*1]

Friday [24 October 1930]

Yes I am better—that is I have done two mornings work—one hour each, and rather indifferent work; but its a beginning.

Being a creature of moods, and not now in the mood for Belgrave Sqre and music, may I ring you up on Tuesday and settle the matter—according to the Tuesday mood?

How are you? Anyhow a clear still day, and I rather envy you, seeing many men and cities.

> V.

And I never thanked you for the rose, but that goes without saying.

Berg

1. Virginia had met Mrs M. R. Brooke when with her three sons, Rupert, Alfred and Richard, she spent a holiday at St Ives in 1893.

Sunday [26 October 1930]

Yes, Ethel dear, disgracefully gushing as your letter was, I enjoyed it all the same. You almost tempt me to gush, but then I shouldn't do it with the speed and abandonment and lavishness and generosity with which you (having been up all night too, and locked in a WC. and rescued by a young man stark naked—Lord what fun) achieve these incomprehensible pinnacles. I daresay I shall catch the hang of it one of these days—but you must allow for the fact that many kinds of writing are forbidden the professional writer —a sad fact, but a fact.

No, no. I didn't quite mean that about the 'astounding' concert going— I didnt mean that you implied that there was nothing wrong. Or rather I meant two things at the same moment. I thought, Now she's saying she coddles herself; or she's saying, what a fool she is, what an ungrateful wife, to run these risks for the sake of an evenings pleasure. For years people, like Ottoline for instance, who have mysterious and chronic diseases, used to say to me, and do still, if I plead a 'headache', Oh if I could only take as much care as you do; and then the other set say, "God's teeth Virginia you deserve to be ill when you've been told a thousand times not to do this and then do it." Both flashed to my mind simultaneously—this is only for your instruction should the same thing happen again. Its a sore point—I've been too often beaten there—about being too careful, about not being careful enough.

(1) Rivett has many merits and I like her; but she's too refined for hard housework. I think it will only be a temporary liaison; but it has worked well, personally; and is much more to my liking, though rather a strain, as she will buy dogs biscuits full of weevils and then I have to remonstrate, and the hares blood makes her squeamish—then the regular domestic: Nelly's pistol will be at my head next week, I fear.

(2) Nothing further has been heard from the agent who wants to buy us out. I hope he thinks better of it. We shall never be so congenially lodged again, and I would stay, even if the Duke fleeces us: but I'm afraid we shall be ejected in 1934, to make room for hotels.[1]

(3) I cant make plans: I cant settle whether to accept or reject invitations. Its a failing of mine. To be asked is a form of mild torture. But I'll let you know on Tuesday

VW

(4) Health. Really I think its over this time, and with luck I shall be in what for me is full swing next week. The trouble is, its a difficult book.

Berg

1. The Bedford Estate wished to pull down 52 Tavistock Square and redevelop the area. But the Woolfs did not leave until 1939, and the house was badly damaged by bombs in 1940.

2260: To Lady Ottoline Morrell

52 *Tavistock Sq.* [*W.C.*1]

Sunday [26 October 1930?]

Dearest Ottoline,

Yes we are back. I'm not sure about being able to come tomorrow—in fact (though you wont accuse me of modesty) it is much much nicer not to meet admirers: much much nicer to see you alone. But if I can I will.

Your Virginia

Texas

2261: To V. Sackville-West

52 *Tavistock Square, W.C.*1

Monday [27 October 1930]

Hilda is dining here next Monday—will you come on with her, and dine, and perhaps crack a joke with me, while they discuss BBC.

Then we might arrange Cowards play.

And are you still——— (Can you finish that sentence?)[1]

V.

This letter has just come.

Berg

2262: To Vanessa Bell

52 *Tavistock Sqre.* [*W.C.*1]

[27? October 1930]

Dearest Dolphin,

Yes I quite agree that it was time you wrote to me—its your duty, being so idiotic as to go to your Mediterranean blue [Cassis]. Thats what makes letter writing a necessity, and I cant write, never again probably, my career's at an end, I leave it all to Julian, because my steel nibs cant be had any more, they've given up making them, and there's only this slippery slidy detestable gold nib, which I cant think with. Probably this is the last letter I shall ever write. I feel a little like Clive, trying to give you a brisk and breezy account of the Beau Monde. Well, everyone is buzzing about— we dined with Raymond; and there was [Arthur] Waley—waly waly up the Bank and waly waly down the Brae.[2] And we had cold pineapple chunks, prepared by a char—all rather pared down and abstemious, which I prefer to high cock a dandy, but there's too much talk of money and America,

1. . . . in love with Hilda Matheson.
2.
O waly, waly, up the bank
And waly, waly, doun the brae,
And waly, waly yon burn-side,
Where I and my Love wont to gae!

Traditional ballad

and shares going down. When Dolphin [Vanessa] loses £100 she merely casts a damn and its over: Raymond forever nibbles and scratches and is full of pimples, poor man. Also Hyslop[1] was there, and went into a back room and fetched out a document—literally 60 pages of foolscap, typed: so many baskets of loam; so many tons of bricks; so many gallons of nails—all made out to a T for the Nicolsons house, with provisions for treasure trove, ancient tiles, and rights of way, underlined in red, so naturally the total was £1600 instead of £800, and there's what they call a hitch; in fact some embarrassment. He was a month making out this document, and is worn and pernickety and takes it amiss, seeing that the Nicolsons make about £800 weekly that they wont run this up instantly. So Vita, who merely wanted to be rid of the boys in the Christmas holidays now has them on her till Easter. And Eddy's mad cook—did you hear—went down to Long Barn one evening, and if it hadn't been for the bootboy thinking her queer and sending for the secretary who sent for the doctor who came by a miracle and tapped her on her thigh and found there a revolver loaded in 6 chambers Vita would have been shot at her writing table—whereas now Eddys cook is lodged in Maidstone Asylum and Eddy is lodged at Long Barn, because, he says, its all Vita's fault that he has had to part with his cook—also she was to have shot Eddy later that night, it turns out, so that Eddy is said (but dont spread this abroad) to be more intolerably peevish than ever. Further, I had Lady Rhondda to tea, and she has made old Ethel eat her words, from the root up, about St John Ervine[2] and Christopher St John— but I dont think I ever told you all that story, about Ethel and the girls school at Bath and how she libelled Lady Rhondda, who wrote to me, who came to tea and is a great hacked hewn woman like Ray and once swam for ten minutes, it is said, under water, when The Lusitania sank, and then she saved herself and her father who subsequently died from shock, leaving his Alice [Margaret] £20,000 a year, which she spends on Time and Tide, which is a newspaper; and thats about all.[3]

Then I had Dotty here; who will only say "I adore Vanessa—I love Vanessa—I want Vanessa"—this sort of thing I find so boring; and yet with your fame mounting and your beauty still alas not sunk behind the hill—

1. Paul Hyslop, the architect and Raymond Mortimer's intimate friend. At this moment he was designing an extension to the children's cottage at Long Barn, but it was never built.
2. The playwright and drama critic, whom Christopher St John would have known through her friendship with Ellen Terry and her daughter Edith Craig.
3. The real story was that when the *Lusitania* was torpedoed in mid-Atlantic in 1915 Margaret and her father, Viscount Rhondda, floated in a lifeboat for three hours before being picked up unconscious. Lord Rhondda died in 1918, and his daughter inherited his title and fortune, most of which she spent on sustaining *Time and Tide*, the journal, initially left-wing and feminist, which she founded in 1920.

whats to be done? Suffer, and clasp the serpent to my breast I suppose. And I am growing my hair; but its a secret; and theres a way of avoiding hair pins; which is also a secret; and it's all due to Angelica who says I'm so ugly; and I'm so ugly—and so old that noone knows if I have hair or haven't hair. To return—I've only ten minutes to dinner.

Well, Rivett is an odd fish: I think rather a nice woman; rather like Sylvia Milman,[1] only more subdued; somebody I think failed her; she is saddened; refined; can cook very well, but cant scrub; so though I daresay she would last a lifetime, its too much strain on the whole; also she has heard of a job in a hostel; on the whole I think she'd better stay her month and then go—and then—well, now Annie wants to come permanently; and next week Nelly is on me. Lord knows what to do; but I say I shall be firm and explicit, and temporise till Xmas, and then install Anny forever. You cant think how nice it is—The house empty at 9—simplicity, reason, taste and logic in the ascendant, after all those broils. Rivett has some humour too; and we save about £1-10 a week—(oh these d—d pens—wont mark—) on groceries alone. What with one thing and another, I was so distracted last week I almost came to France—not to you but to Beaune. I thought there one might be silent. But now you have Slavs and Teeds and Tryons[2] and Frys—so where is solitude—where is silence? Nowhere. About the furniture I am pleased that Boudard [Virginia's cottage at Cassis] is unsold, as I am less foolish than was thought; and also I might get it—say at Christmas. I think thus it wd. be best to keep anything that Roger dont want—Keep any chairs that cd. be useful to you, and the beds. in case we could use them later. Is the settee any use to you? Of course, if they're in the way, give them to any of your mouldy quayside aquaintance—the man who crawled, for instance—or Teed. I doubt that they would be worth the carriage.

Now having had dinner I will wind up. Owing to the incessant drudgery at the Press (this must be ended—its becoming too much, even if one makes £2,000—Leonard is at it all day and I have endless novels to read) owing to Dotty's anthology[3] etc. we couldnt go to the East coast, so did not see Angelica; no news of Julian. Everyone is in a stir about Wyndham Lewis and his Bloomsbury Black Book in which every sod and every Saph is to be pilloried;[4] the publisher won't print, so we have offered, as a gesture, which is thought by some flippant. And on Wednesday the Jews assemble

1. An old friend of the Stephen family. She married John Mills Whitham, the novelist.
2. Wyndham Tryon, the painter.
3. *A Broadcast Anthology of Modern Poetry*, edited by Dorothy Wellesley.
4. In 1924 Wyndham Lewis, the author and painter, had satirised Lytton Strachey and others in an article which he entitled *Apes of God*. In 1930 he expanded it into a novel, and published it under the same title in a limited edition. He described Bloomsbury as substituting "money for talent as a qualification for membership. . . . The tone of 'society' (of a spurious donnish social elegance) prevails among them."

and pour 80 chocolates in the form of sovereigns into the lap of the Mother Woolf who is 80; and there will be a cheque among them for that sum; and Sibyl Colefax comes to dinner. And when shall you be back?

B.

Berg

2263: To Quentin Bell   52 *Tavistock Sq.* [*W.C.1*]

Typewritten
28th Oct. [1930]

Dearest Quentin,

You see how obediently I answer your letter at once. For all your illiteracy and difficulty with the pen—your letter might be written by a large wild cat that had fallen with all its paws into a well—you yet contrive to make me see you and your miraculous companions. Now if Wyndham Lewis instead of writing a Bloomsbury Black Book in which every sinner of either school is to be pilloried were to write what is the truth—that we are merely wild, odd, innocent, artless, eccentric and industrious beyond words, there would be some sting to it. But to represent us as he does one seething mass of correlated villainy is so beside the point (I cant remember any of the right words—but I have been writing for two hours and they have flown) that it glances from the back. No, not from Eddy and Harold, and Raymond. They are all providing escapes for themselves, it is said; they propose to live abroad. That is what we are talking of at the moment. Today I am going to a party at the Austrian Embassy to hear a Viennese string quartet with Ethel Smyth. She will be in an old rabbit fur coat and thick boots; I feebler but dowdier. There will be princes and dukes. Tea and cakes. Women and violins. Ethel will almost certainly commit some rape. That is why I go, to tell the truth, for God knows I cant listen to quratets at Austiran embassies. (There you see how this typewriter seplls.)

It has been the finest October on record. The gravel pits at Warlingham [Surrey] where we went on Sunday are precisely like Cézanne pictures— why go to the South of France where the wind blows and the mosquitoes bite, then? What I most envy is Rome. Oh to be Quentin and going to Rome! But my dear child, do you know that in half a century there will be methods of circumventing these divisions of Aunt and Nephew? By attaching a small valve something like a leech to the back of your neck I shall tap all your sensations; the present system is a mere anachronism; that I should be here and you there and nothing between us but a blue sheet (of paper I mean).

I have not heard of Julian but I see his book[1] is advertised and no doubt

1. *Winter Movement*, Julian Bell's first book of poems, was published in this month by Chatto and Windus when he was 22.

he will be celebrated by the time you are back. But then you are not jealous. John Strachey[1] has just sent me an invitation to a show of his pictures— but I thought he was a novelist. Shall I go? Is he a good painter? I thought again that he was like me—subject to visions. You know what I mean. I thought he spent many months incarcerated.

Oh I wish Nessa hadnt told me that silly story about the moths![2] I spend day after day writing and scratching out. Then Mr Kahan[3] who is like a moth without any wings, a poor little deformity of a Jew, comes at six and stays till eight, saying, among other things, that he is a virgin; and so are all the young men now he says. But are all young men without legs I say. In Hampstead yes, he says.

Does this bring about you the old savour of Bloomsbury? Please dearest Quentin write me a full account of Rome. I shall be there in the spring. We will sit in the Boboli gardens together and eat dinner on the Pincio. I may have got it wrong; but the fact remains that you will burn all your boats when you see Rome; dont let them take you to Florence. Logan [Pearsall Smith] lives at Florence; also Bob Trevelyan; by the way Luce[4] is in London, but so furtive and queer, he wont come out, save to lunch with Bob; think of coming from Burma and then lunching with Bob. Ottoline is on the ramp; but I cant go—not to meet Italian novelists, because when she says they admire me, it means they are cretinous, verminous and lecherous. If you were here we would go together.

This is a long letter; written in three minutes to catch the post; because I must now do up parcels; with Miss Belsher. All our books are coming out and my mother in law is eighty tomorrow. We are going to an Earls Court hotel with a bag of eighty chocolates; these will pour into her lap; she will then find they are gold. She will weep. I shall make a speech. There will be twenty five Jews all in tail coats.

Love to all the oddities.

Virginia

Quentin Bell

1. John Strachey was the son of Ralph, Lytton's elder brother. Although he had a nervous breakdown in the 1920s, he recovered, and became a talented, if not very successful, painter. His brother Richard was the novelist.
2. The origin of *The Waves* was a letter which Vanessa wrote to Virginia from Cassis in 1927 (See Volume III, p. 372).
3. Richard (later Lord) Kahn was 25 in 1930, the year in which he became a Fellow of King's College, Cambridge. Later he became Professor of Economics at Cambridge.
4. Gordon Hannington Luce, the poet and acquaintance of Julian Bell, had for several years taught English at the University of Rangoon. The Hogarth Press had published his poems in 1924.

30th Oct. [1930]

Yes, but why dont you write to me and say so—this refers to the last sentence in your letter. If you never say so, of course a black crust forms; try another intimate letter, like the one from The Pyrenees, theres a good Towser.

Highly alarming reports have reached me of what you said in The Schoolmistress[1]—why you wanted to lash out like that and take away my character as woman and as writer I cant conceive. Now your only escape is to send me the very words, but I suspect worse. O you old serpent; how you coil in your basket of fig leaves! (I have made so many enemies lately by writing letters in a hurry that I make a point of saying that I am *not altogether serious:* still, I should like The Schoolmistress: please bring her.)

But how am I ever to see you, apart from Hilda? Is an afternoon alone never possible? Not since Rodmell and then only for two minutes have we been alone in a room together—let alone the other place. I do hate these little slabs of meeting jammed in tight between other engagements. Potto positively loathes them—but I suppose nothing else is possible till you live in London, and as long as the sun is warm and the autumn leaves fluttering to the ground you wont come. Lord, to think how I spent the afternoon: buying ham in Fortnum and Masons, because Sibyl dines with us tonight. And you were in the field, I daresay.

Yes Ethel has pretty well done the trick—a triumph you must admit, for a woman of 73 She took me to a party at the Austrian Embassy, she in sweater and mouldy fur coat; I almost smart by comparison. And in the slow movement she said "This is like the movement of ones bowels"—at which the attache's sitting by us, jumped.

I wish that Dotty weren't convinced that the sign of a great poet is the inability to do anything practical. Leonards life has been made a burden to him, and I was in a rage (but kept it under) hearing Dotty dramatise her own incompetence And waste God knows how much of his time: He had to shoot her out and do the rest himself. And its said to be a bad book[2] into the bargain.

Now let us arrange a private meeting, dearest Creature: I have a mint of things to say: and dear me, how depressed I am about my book; and then you go and say in The Schoolmistress that V.W. is in your opinion an overrated writer! How true.

V.

Berg

1. In an interview published in *The Schoolmistress* of 23 October, Vita had only this to say about Virginia: "I suppose we may regard Virginia Woolf as one of the greatest prose writers of the day. She is more of a poetess by temperament than an actual prose writer."
2. *A Broadcast Anthology of Modern Poetry.*

30th Oct 1930

Well, I'm glad you caught your train. The guard said to me "She'll drop dead if she tries"—and I'm pleased that you did run, did not drop dead, and did catch the train. It seems to me marvellously gallant and efficient and sensible, as befits the daughter of an officer,[1] and a good omen for the Prison. Its odd how little scenes like that suddenly illumine wherever one may be— Waterloo station. I could swear a ring of light surrounded you me and the guard for one tenth of a second.

Well it was rather a glum, deliberate, middleaged assembly last night [Mrs Woolf's birthday party]—all, oh my word, so much like cuts off one long yard of cake—slice after slice; no beauty, no eccentricity. We stood about in the private room, with bunches of chrysanthemums tied up in orange sashes, and lots of carnations, incredibly unreal, in silver vases. And there were telegrams, cables from Sweden[2]—this was a great prize— and then parcels kept on coming in. And there we all stood about in very inferior evening dress, as was specially requested (not the inferiority—the dress) touching our hair with our hands. At 10 I was discussing with Mrs Harold, who is the black sheep, a divorcée and grown very stout, and the best bridge player in Maidenhead, floods at Staines; at 10.15 I was comparing Harrods and the Army and Navy stores with Mrs Edgar—who has always lived in Putney, and had a bad miscarriage several years ago, since when she has run the Stock Exchange Sweep stakes, and has an alsatian hound which she has painted in oils, "but he has not really that fierce look in his eyes" she says; and then at 10.30 the green baize tables were opened and we played a game called Pink Nines and I, being third won a prize of a plum pudding; and Leonard being Booby won a spotted tie; and at 11 we all went into supper (does this bore you) and I sat at the table of honour with my mother in law—there were four tables, some less honourable than the others—and cups of soup were handed, anchovy sandwiches and cold sausage rolls. And then Herbert, the eldest son, rose and drank to "Our mother, the most marvellous mother, mother in law and friend" and my mother in law thanked us, "The most perfect, loving and (she could not remember a third epithet) h.m.m of children" and what I liked was that though she was all tremors and quivers she ended, like a child, "And now lets finish our sausage rolls"—this spontaneous bubbling childishness—witness her passion for chocolate creams and sugar cakes—being her charm for me. Indeed, in spite of the glumness, grimness, and oh the intolerable middle class timidity

1. Ethel's father, John Smyth, was a Major-General.
2. From Leonard's Mannheimer cousins. For the Woolf brothers (Harold, Edgar and Herbert) see the Woolf family-tree in Volume III of this Edition, p. 522.

respectability and lack of accent distinction adventure dash, daring colour—
I cant describe to you the low level of all these childless people, with their
uniformity of cars, dogs, country houses and gardens,—in spite of my
damned snobbishness about them, I always feel slightly warmed and overcome by the entire absence of pretence, and the goodness, and the rightness
—if it is right so to people the world—of the vast family to which as Herbert
said, I have the honour to belong.

By the way, what are the arguments against suicide? You know what a
flibberti-gibbet I am: well there suddenly comes in a thunder clap a sense
of the complete uselessness of my life. Its like suddenly running one's head
against a wall at the end of a blind alley. Now what are the arguments
against that sense—'Oh it would be better to end it"? I need not say that I
have no sort of intention of taking any steps: I simply want to know—as
you are so masterly and triumphant—catching your train and not running
too fast—what are the arguments against it?

V.

Berg

2266: TO MOLLY MACCARTHY   52 *Tavistock Square* [*W.C.*1]

Sunday [October? 1930]

Dearest Molly,

I have spent a perfectly happy evening reading your book,[1] and now
alas, it's done and I must dash off one line to thank you. How I enjoyed it!
It's all so new and fresh and incredible. I galloped through Fitzgerald to the
end: the bear, the fight, the fiend [?], the rope breaking. You are an amazing
woman to dig out these characters, with all the facts and all the fun—so
solid and so amusing at the same time. Please write some more and so
enchant more Sunday evenings.

Yours in haste and admiration
Virginia

Mrs Michael MacCarthy

2267: TO VANESSA BELL   *Monks House, Rodmell*
[*Sussex*]

Sunday Nov 2nd [1930]

You are probably glutted by this time with letters from me, and your
aspersions on my habits are thrust down your throat.

I'm sitting here in a howling wilderness—rain, wind, not a glimpse of

1. *Fighting Fitzgerald* (1930) comprised four sketches of 18th century men, including
   Lord Edward Fitzgerald (1763-98), the Irish patriot.

sky, fog over the water meadows—any moment I expect the elms to be blown down, and in an hour we take the road and drive to London which is said to be in a thick fog. So what with falling trees, collisions and so on, this may well be the last time I hold the pen. I hope you are sitting in the sun; though I doubt it. As for Roger, tarpaulins and stakes will be needed to hold him down. I'm glad I didn't plunge off to Beaune, and sit in a public Inn; one can only just exist with all the comforts of civilisation. The unruliness of nature now passes belief. Honestly, I think the car will be blown back. It is a hurricane. If only Miss Younghusband who is now going to church could be lifted bodily to the top of the church spire and there stick, an example to church goers!

But you want gossip. Oh it is an incessant conversation—not so bad as it will be, for the bad weather always intensifies the life of Bloomsbury: we went to a party at James's [Strachey] to celebrate Saxon's 50th birthday, and [Albert] Einstein spoke in German through a hole in the wall. Tommy[1] was there, grown round as a snowball, in the last lap of destitution, and Carrington and Lytton. Next day I had a long tête à tête with Carrington, who is slightly shrivelled and to my mind disappointed, but then my mind is utterly untrustworthy. I judge these things by the way people blow their noses. Anyhow she was affectionate in the extreme, and we are to invite ourselves to Ham Spray. She said that Lytton often regrets that he does not see more of his old friends, and prefers us to his new friends, but how difficult it is to meet, and then we are all so busy, but the people he cares most for are Vanessa and Virginia. You would know to an ounce how much to believe, how much to be touched, inspired, sympathetic and moved by compassion (for I think Geralds desertion[2] is rather bitter, and Lytton is going to be in London, and [Ralph] Partridge never leaves the British Museum) by all this. Anyhow, she was very shabby; small; in her usual stupid petticoat and jacket, and said she spends most of her time with Mrs [Dorelia] John.

Then Lytton came to dinner to meet Lady Colefax. I spent 17/6 on a jar of pâté de foie gras; and Rivett really cooked admirably (she is erratic and has failures but on the whole I like her erraticity better than complete humdrum) and Sibyl has transformed herself into a harried, downright woman of business,[3] sticking her fork in the pot; and has lost almost all her glitter and suavity. Even her voice has changed. She is now of the family of Champcommunal[4] and other money makers. She is at her office from 9.30

1. Stephen Tomlin, who in July 1931 sculpted a bust of Virginia.
2. Gerald Brenan, Carrington's former lover, had recently fallen in love with Gamel Woolsey, an American poet, whom he married in 1931.
3. Sibyl Colefax started an interior decoration business in 1928. John Fowler later joined it as her partner.
4. Elspeth Champcommunal, a friend of Roger Fry, and the widow of a French painter who was killed in the First War. She was Editor of *Vogue*, 1916-22.

to 7: has had to give up entertaining, and on the whole is improved, though rather tragic. After all, she is 55, I daresay, and has practised society for 35 years; and now to become a hardhearted shopkeeper,—she is very successful too, decorating houses from top to bottom and standing on ladders and fixing sinks—must be a grind. She too has shrunk and faded. Lytton was smooth as silk and sweet as honey. You were praised. I think probably you do now represent the only island that keeps afloat. Everyone else seems at the moment money grubbing and precarious. And then there is old Ethel, who took me to one of the very smartest of parties in Belgrave Square, and unpeeled herself of sweater, jersey and mothy moleskin before all the flunkeys, knocking her pasteboard hat to right and left and finally producing from a cardboard box fastened at the edge by paper fasteners a pair of black leather shoes, which she put on, because she said "The truth is I'm a damned snob, and like to be smart." She also said, "Isn't this slow movement sublime—natural and heavy and irresistible like the movement of one's own bowels." All the dapper little diplomats blushed. She is half crazed about a memoir of HB. which she writes all day and all night, and has just sent me to criticise.[1] Such is my life; and we go back—the storm is if anything worse, and the mist is now sulphur coloured—to Hilda Matheson and Vita to discuss the future of the BBC. on Monday; dine with Hope[2] Tuesday; Wednesday I fear Nelly will come; Thursday Tom Eliot; Friday tea with Ott:—and no Dolphin, no Fitzroy, no buns and toast, no Angelica, no rational converse. Even dear old Duncan seems to me sometimes to speak a more inspired tongue than these articulates.

My household plans are now vague again, as Annie thinks she cant come for a year, because of her child; and Rivett goes in a fortnight—but there doesnt seem to be much difficulty; and the living out system I'm sure emerges triumphantly. Or does one grow hermitatious? To be alone in the house is now my greatest pleasure. Even a mouse annoys me—And I can cook a simple dish very well. But Dolphin would not annoy me—oh dear no.

B.

I've only had one picture postcard from Clive—

Berg

1. *The Prison: a Dialogue*, by Henry Brewster, with a Memoir of Brewster by Ethel Smyth, was published later this year. For Virginia's opinion of it, see the next letter.
2. Hope Mirrlees, the writer. The Hogarth Press had published her *Paris: A Poem* in 1920. She had lived for some years in Paris with the classical scholar, Jane Harrison, who died in 1928.

Monks House [*Rodmell, Sussex*]

Sunday 2nd Nov. [1930]

Yes. I think even allowing for Woolf coldness, that it is a perfect little memoir—humorous, tender intimate at the same time reserved, presenting HB [Henry Brewster]. not as a black silhouette pinned to a sheet but as a coloured and rounded being moving of his own free will in the open air. Its extraordinary how you have got such space and movement into so small a compass.

Being a Woolf, of course I make one or two reservations—that there is perhaps a little too much of justification, as if you felt called upon to defend HB. (but then I suppose his obscurity necessitated this); and a little too much Maurice Baring, or rather, for MB. is admirable, too little Ethel. (Its just conceivable, but this I advance with great hesitation that the juxtaposition of H.B. on M.B. and M.B. on HB. is a little too close—has a little the effect of a duologue of admiration—but I dont feel certain and only make this remark sketchily) And certainly I should have liked more of HB's own letters, because however delicate and discriminating the testimony of friends nothing describes character like a letter. (But then, there is to be a long one, left out in my copy.)

But these reservations advanced, and I am the first to understand your wish to be compressed and unegotistical, I dont see that it could be better, or more vivid, or more complete. How I enjoyed your hit at Gosse[1]—perfect; and the freedom and sweep of all your gestures, combined with their directness and precision—never a word wasted, no diffusity, and yet all so easy as if you had reams of paper to write on and chose only to use ten pages. This is an effect I can never attain, and the proof of mastery.

Only I do wish, all the more, for a whole book; for Ethel in all her force entire to her prey attached.[2]

A violent gale here, the smoke blowing down the chimneys, and if we escape death by falling trees on the road up this afternoon, so much the better. My reflections on suicide I leave to a later date.

V.

Of course Heinemann will take it—even Evans[3] isnt such a thick skull as to refuse that.

1. In her memoir Ethel recalled buying a second-hand copy of Brewster's *The Prison* which had once belonged to Edmund Gosse ('no student of metaphysics'), and noting that only the first six pages had been cut.
2. *C'est Vénus toute entière à sa proie attachée* (Racine, *Phèdre*, I, iii).
3. Charles Evans, Director of William Heinemann Ltd. since 1921, and Managing Director 1932-44. He accepted Ethel's book.

Back at 52 and find your letter. By all means come tomorrow 5.30. I shall be in, though probably not alone—

Berg

2269: To T. S. Eliot   52 *T.[avistock] S.[quare, W.C.*1]

Typewritten
Nov. 2nd. [1930]

Yes, my dear Tom, come to tea on Thursday next, at four thirty, and you will find your ancient and attached Wolves very glad to see you. No, I'm not generally held to be ambiguous by the clients of the Hogarth Press— I give much pain and receive much abuse. But then Mr Eliot is not a candidate for publication—far from it; and I cant (no false modesty intended) suspect him of any very great concern about Mrs Woolf's opinion; and Mrs Woolf would have to dig among the roots of what it pleases her to call her mind were she to give it; and she is lazy; and catch Mr Eliot committing himself about Mrs Woolf in the same circumstances. But my smoke screen isnt made of doubts of you, but doubts of myself rather, and of the whole business of criticising prose or poetry. Perhaps in talk—but then we never meet. Not for a whole year I think—except visions in streets which though inspiring arent substantial. Such is life. But one of these days we may some-how contrive to say something in spite of the smoke—who knows? And anyhow I have the honour to sign myself with sincerity your devoted and humble admirer

Virginia

Ella Strong Denison Library, Scripps College, Claremont, California

2270: To Vanessa Bell   52 *T.[avistock] S.[quare, W.C.*1]

Tuesday Nov. 4th [1930]

Clive has asked me to write you a short account of his misfortunes—not to be taken too seriously he says, however annoying. About a fortnight ago he woke up to find he could hardly see out of one eye. However he didn't think much of it and went on travelling, until, as it did not get better, he decided he had better come home and see an oculist. This he did yesterday, and the oculist says that it is due to some inflammation behind the eye, caused by some germ. He is going to see Freeman[1] who will test his blood and try to discover what the germ is. Possibly it is the same germ that caused his eczema and if so they will be able to cure it quickly. but it may take

1. Dr John Freeman, Director of the Department of Allergic Diseases, St Mary's Hospital, London.

some weeks to discover. Meanwhile he is forbidden to read or write and has to wear black spectacles. He dined here last night and seemed otherwise very well and in high spirits. He has engaged a reader who comes for two hours in the afternoon and he says everybody is being very nice and coming to see him. They dont think there is any danger for his eyes—it is only a question of getting at the germ—it is apparently the same thing Alix[1] had. He takes it with great composure and said you were on no account to worry or change your plans. I think Joan [Firminger] is in London. Grace [Germany] is doing for him. I expect we shall see a good deal of him and I will let you know what Freeman says.

This is merely a bulletin

Yr
B

Berg

2271: To ETHEL SMYTH   [52 *Tavistock Square, W.C.*1]
Wednesday [5 November 1930]

Well, didn't I say so?

A thousand congratulations;[2] but no more. because I'm expecting company, distracted. and so I was t'other day, distracted, not bored—Vita, Hilda Matheson and Clive dining.

Keep in the warm; be careful, and a thousand congratulations mixed with some regrets[3]

V.

Berg

2272: To V. SACKVILLE-WEST 52 *T.*[avistock] *S.*[quare, *W.C.*1]
Thursday [6 November 1930]

Dearest Creature,

I was so much touched by your staying up to dine with me last night— Potto and I were so happy. And Lord!—how can *you* be jealous! Looking at one picture and then at the other—no I wont go into that business. And of course I'm rather glad that you can be jealous, even of that old sea-monster encrusted with barnacles [Ethel Smyth]; I had felt slightly in the shade—like a toad under a plantain; owing to your husband and so on.

1. Alix Strachey. In June 1920 she and her husband James Strachey had been to Vienna to study under Freud.
2. On the acceptance by Heinemann of Brewster's *The Prison*, with the Memoir by Ethel.
3. That the Hogarth Press did not publish the book themselves.

and'all your lustre and activity, general splendour; however, now there's an end, with a soft wet warm kiss from Poor Potto.

Here's Clive rung up to say that his mistress [Joan Firminger] has been flung against a lampost in a car smash, delivered at his flat at 2.am. all cuts and blood, and is now in bed, at her flat, for 3 weeks. So he's more at a loss than ever, and we have to dine with him. But I count on Tuesday or Wednesday next week.

V.

And Tom Eliot is bringing his wife [Vivien]—raving mad, seeing insults if I say China or India or do you like more water?

Curse oh curse.

I am sending you as a tribute of affection, a wretched little book,[1] another old essay, meant for America only; so hide it. and say nothing; but it is a tribute of love.

Berg

2273: To Lady Ottoline Morrell
52 Tavistock Square, W.C.1

[6 November 1930]

Dearest Ottoline,

If I came in tomorrow, Friday, at about 5.30, would there be a chance of seeing you?[2] I should so much like to. I've been away so much this summer that I've seen nobody, and now I suppose you are going: But dont bother, if you are busy. I shall hope to see you in the autumn.
Your affat
Virginia Woolf

Texas

2274: To Vanessa Bell
52 Tavistock Square [W.C.1]

Nov. 8th [1930]

Dearest Dolphin,

About this business of the furniture [at La Boudarde, Cassis]: I'm surprised to hear how much there is; I expect I could use it all at Rodmell,

1. *Beau Brummell*, published in a limited edition by Rimington and Hooper (New York) in this month, and originally in the *Nation*, 28 September 1929.
2. Virginia met W. B. Yeats and Walter de la Mare at tea with Ottoline on Friday, 7 November.

as I have two rooms now to furnish; so would you get an estimate for sending the whole lot by sea.

At the same time, I wish you would take anything you want, as a gift; I dont want to sell it, and as I feel I have put upon the Teeds, wouldn't Jean [Campbell] let me give her the sheets, if she wants them? I give you full authority to close with the removers, as its clear that nothing will be done if its left till after you go. I've not heard from you about Oreste; I'm hoping you made him climb down. If he insists that the 2nd item on the bill was also Convenu [agreed], I think you had better give way, if by so doing we are quit of him. But otherwise its obviously an imposture. (I think it was 300 francs)

As for Clive's affairs, I suppose you have heard that the very day after his return Joan was in a motor accident, and they rang him up at 2 am to say she was all cut about, and he got the Stephens' [Adrian and Karin] and doctor, and she was brought to 50 [Gordon Square] and sewn up, and taken off next morning to her own flat, where she will be in bed more or less for 3 weeks, but not they think permanently disfigured. This was coming back from a Bonfire night [5 November] party at Dick Wyndhams, and it is thought that the young man who drove into a lamp post was drunk.

It is very unfortunate, as Clive is therefore left more to his own devices—and Lord! to tell the truth a dinner at Clives with Cory[1] and Raymond [Mortimer] is not the height of joy to me. But one feels rather a brute not to go. He's in great fettle, as a matter of fact, with every sort of lady and gent. swarming to his help—Christabel [McLaren], etc. and I hope in a short time his engagements will be so many that we have no conscience about him—Its odd how difficult he makes easy and natural talk very often: its all pirouetting and boasting, and I boast and pirouette, and then I fall into despair, where Leonard is to begin with. His eyes seems a long business though; they're taking X rays, but so far without result. I should be terrified; he seems amazingly cheerful. You were a bold woman to marry into the Bells: the mixture is pretty thick, so I thought listening to Clive and Cory. And the new lighting system reduces one to a coma—light pours from white spittoons everywhere—no escape—I feel like a Rabbit looking at a Cobra.

Your Christmas sounds appalling[2]—its their rough gritty good sense I think—; the only consolation I can offer is that on the whole I'd rather compound for one week a year than suffer as I do about 35 afternoon teas, and visits to Worthing [Leonard's mother] and birthday parties. Last week we had a terrific one—the 80th birthday; 18 Jews in an Earls Court Hotel, 80 sovereigns presented, bad champagne, card games, speeches, sausage rolls; but the horror was such that it reached a point of magnificence and

1. Colonel Cory Bell, Clive's brother.
2. Vanessa was intending to spend the Christmas holiday with Clive's family at Cleeve House, Seend, Wiltshire.

was over by 12.30. Only now there are Bella [Leonard's sister] and Tom [Southorn] to be invited—

Why didn't we marry into interesting families? Why did we choose—well, what did we choose? I mean, not husbands, but families?

As you say, I've got no news. Yet I've seen so many people I could fill 8 pages: but its only chatter. My most horrid experience was a visit from Tom Eliot. This had been arranged for weeks. At the last moment he rang up to say that Vivien wanted to come too, and would we pretend that we had asked her. This sounded ominous, but was nothing to the reality. She is insane. She suspects every word one says. "Do you keep bees?" I asked, handing her the honey. "Hornets" she replied. "Where?" I asked. "Under the bed." Thats the style, and one has to go on talking, and Tom tries, I suppose, to cover it up with longwinded and facetious stories. And she smells; and she throws cheap powder over the bread; and she opens his letters, suspects me of being his mistress, so far as we could gather; and finally said that I had made a signal which meant that they were to go. So they did go, in about half an hour, and now he writes that he wants to come and see me alone, to explain I suppose; but I expect Vivien will appear too. I went to Ottolines yesterday, and must unsay my abuse, as there I found Yeats, whom I think (naturally, wrongly) our only living poet—perhaps a great poet: anyhow a good poet: and there was also [Walter] de la Mare, who is very odd, very charming, rather daft, but at the same time surprisingly on the spot. Being now almost incapable of discretion I said all the wrong things about poetry and we had a long discourse—very amusing to me: as I can't think why they dont write poetry about interesting things any longer. Yeats admitted it—but then, as he believes in the unconscious soul, in fairies, in magic, and has a complete system of philosophy and psychology —it was not easy altogether to understand: at the same time, I agreed with many of his views; and he also is surprisingly sensible. He has grown tremendously thick, and is rather magnificent looking; in fact seeing how seldom one meets interesting people (with Dolphin away) this was a great success. It is old Ottolines function, undoubtedly. She has the atmosphere for that, though she now has a black trumpet hung to her side for she is rapidly growing deaf. All the time we talked in the drawing room I heard Pipsy [Philip Morrell] talking to a lady in the dining room—Could it be Mrs Jones?[1]

Also we had a terrific visitation from Hugh Walpole. If you want a book from the Times, get Cakes and Ale by Somerset Maugham. All London is ringing with it. For there poor Hugh is most cruelly and maliciously at the same time unmistakably and amusingly caricatured [as Alroy Kear]. He was sitting on his bed with only one sock on when he opened it. There he sat with only one sock on till 11 next morning reading it.

1. Assistant to the Literary Editor of the *Nation*. See Vol. III of this edition, p. 380.

Also, we gathered in tears. He almost wept in front of Hilda Matheson, Vita and Clive, in telling us. And he couldnt stop. Whenever we changed the conversation he went back. "There are things in it that nobody knows but Willie and myself" he said. "There are little things that make me shudder. And that man has been my dearest friend for 20 years. And now I'm the laughing stock of London. And he writes to say he didn't mean it for me." "Oh but he undoubtedly did that" said Vita cheerfully. "And he might have been jugged" said Hugh. "You dont know the kind of life that Willie has led. I do. I could put him in a book. But then I call it a dastardly thing to do." And so on, round and round, round and round, like a dog with a tin on its tail, till it was half past 12. Then he said it was all in the strictest confidence, and he had told no one else. But of course, Clive met Christabel next night, and Christabel had met Hugh that afternoon—and had been ever so much more tactful than Vita.

I've written to Nelly; and had one line from her, merely acknowledging the cheque. but then she went off to her doctor [Alan McGlashan], and now he has written to say that there must have been a misunderstanding and that she is perfectly well able to come back to our place. So we have now written to him. We have given him a hint—I think it might have been stronger— and hope that he may mitigate Nelly somewhat, but I see we're in for a visit and a tempest of rage next week—cant be helped. Meanwhile Rivett has improved—anyhow the present system is so much better I cant think how we ever stood the other.

Heavens what a letter! And none from you.

B.

Of course if you were likely to spend 4 or 5 months annually at Cassis, it might be worth while to keep some of the things, as in that case for love of you, I should probably go to Boudard; but I dont suppose you can tell, and even if you could, L. so much dislikes Cassis, or prefers other parts, that I daresay I shouldn't manage it.

Berg

2275: To Vanessa Bell   52 T.[avistock] S.[quare, W.C.1]

Monday [9 November 1930]

I wrote to you last night at Cassis, so you won't get it. But there was not much of importance.

Clive is still being Xrayed and no result has been reached. Unluckily, the second night after his return Joan was rather badly cut about the face in a motor accident and will be more or less in bed for 3 weeks at her flat.

So I'm sure your company will come in very useful. Of course, everyone is swarming round him at the moment, but I daresay he has a good many dull times. He is now coming round here to dinner with Fanny Marshall,[1] so I've time for no more and all my news, such as it was, went to Cassis.

I told you by the way to give Jean [Campbell] the sheets, whose existence I'd forgotten, if she wants them. But we can talk. I cant make any sense of Oreste's claims. I remember perfectly your letters and the two separate lots of work, and you said the whole wd. come to £30 which was about what it did. I think he's simply swindling, on the chance one doesn't keep cheques; and he sends no receipts. But this too will keep.

Lord, how nice it will be to see you again. I'll arrange with Clive about Thursday evening. I've told Grace. I heard from Quentin today on board ship and in high spirits. No news of Julian or Angelica.

Yr

Berg

B.

2276: To Ethel Smyth   [52 *Tavistock Square, W.C.*1]

Friday [14 November 1930]

I'm awfully sorry to hear from Mary[2] that you're in bed—I dont like your being ill. No, thats the truth. But perhaps by Sunday you'll be recovered. She said you were to avoid draughts. So please, when a draught comes round the door, think of Virginia. This is only a brief spider line—we're just off to Rodmell. There I shall read the letters[3]—sitting out I daresay, in the fish garden, if its like this. I'm better—I put this in, only from duty, feeling myself a robust woman compared with you: a day's idleness will cure me; and then splash into the Waves again.

Well, anyhow, you must feel you've earned your illness, which is sometimes a gratification; and got your way with life triumphantly, so that the colour of the sky, as seen from your bed (what do you see? leaves, branches, creepers?) must wear a certain glory, like—oh I have only the tail of an image in my head—cant catch it—must let it go—must throw my nightgown into my bag, avoiding 24 sanitary towels, which from charity to a bankrupt woman, I had to buy; "And my brother" she said "has £100,000; and here am I hawking these towels round to ladies who are kinder to me than my own mothers son" Here she produced the two swollen blue packets, in the middle of the Press, and the clerks who were blushing and giggling

1. Frances Marshall, who married Ralph Partridge after Carrington's death in 1932.
2. Probably Mary Hunter, Ethel's sister.
3. See Letter 2278.

finally subsided and had to help me to find 5/- Well Ethel dear this is all great nonsense, and I wish dear Ethel I could see you—

VW.

Berg

2277: TO ETHEL SMYTH

Monks House [*Rodmell, Sussex*]

Friday [14 November 1930]

Not a letter; a scribble over the fire, waiting for dinner, which my dear Ethel will consist of roast chicken and some masterpiece of Annys, all fluff and cream; something you know with jelly sunk to the centre in it.

I will now tell you about my parties (you say its a case of eating 6 meringues and being sick). Now thats unjust; thats the rasp of whooping cough; thats whats worse to me, *untrue*. Think of this: my 1st party was by command to Ottolines; and it was a shabby between the lights party, which is a compromise, for one can slip in without even putting on those black shoes which you carry about to propitiate the British aristocracy in a cardboard box mended with safety pins—no paper fasteners. In this twilight all the Italian furniture and pomegranates are faded to rose and amber, and now and then she flings a handful of cedar shavings upon the fire; dips her hand in a basket and brings up skeins like the entrails of flying fish, coloured wools, all tangled: these she drops again. And on one side of the fire sat the poet Yeats on the other the poet de la Mare—and what were they doing when I came in? Tossing between them higher and higher a dream of Napoleon with ruby eyes. And over my head it went—for what do I know of the inner meaning of dreams, I whose life is almost entirely founded on dreams (yes, I will come to the suicide dream one of these days) I mean I know nothing of the spiritual significance of ruby eyes, or a book with concentric rings of black, purple and orange. But Yeats said, as it might be a man identifying a rather rare grass, that is the third state of the soul in contemplation (or words to that effect—it will not surprise you if I got them wrong). And then? Did I like Milton? Yes. And then—De la Mare does not like Milton. And then—dreams and dreams. and then stories of Irish life in brogue; and then the soul's attitude to art; and then (here I was touched, you I daresay not—) then, as the talk got more and more rapt, refined and erratic, I saw Ottoline stoop her hand to what seemed a coal scuttle and apply it to her ear: An ordinary black ear trumpet it was, ungilt unfunelled, and the apparition of this bare and ghastly object had somehow a sepulchral effect—and I cried out, in the midst of all the poetry. Heavens Ottoline, are you deaf? And she replied with a sort of noble negligence which struck me very much "Yes, yes, quite deaf—" and then lifted the trumpet and listened. Does that touch you? Well it did me, and I saw in a flash all I admire her for; and think what people overlook, in the briarwood bramble of her obvious tortuousness and hypocrisy.

Well thats the meringue; then the next. Did you know old Parry,[1] who wrote a March, which in some circles supplanted Mendelssohn? Of course you did; and he had two daughters; and one was Gwen and the other was Dolly. The sound of their violins used to float across Kensington Square, and sometimes as a child I worshipped their bright eyes, feline ways, laughter and so on; and there she was, Gwen, at dinner, the wife, I suspected indeed widow, of Plunket Greene. All her colour had faded; her face was pouched; and still she had something arch and flamboyant; but in addition an action of the neck such as I have only seen in a rather absurd fantastic bird—reaching, pecking, sidling, retreating advancing and making sidelong dashes, as at an imaginary seed. What is she after? I asked myself, and then saw her, still dangling and darting, slip an odious shiny manual into our hostesses hand. And out it came: they were both perverts—I mean converts—I mean lately born into the Roman Catholic church—And that was what I had felt in her—even while she ate her pheasant.

Now I have eaten my chicken—in the most straightforward way in the world. I am smoking my cigar and L. is clipping gramophone needles. I wish Ethel—she shall finish the sentence to her own advantage. Yes, I think HB[Henry Brewster]. had a mind with a very fine close texture. This comes into my head from dipping into extracts: a fine pattern, full sprigs and thorns, like the background in an Italian picture. But I hold off reading him till my brain clears tomorrow. In love of you, I did *not* take chloral at 4.30 this morning—but lay wide eyed; and rather doubt if chloral isn't the less drugging of the two.

One more meringue, or little maccaroon rather, prevising that you're in bed, and have time for all this chatter.

You know Colefax? Now often you have said to me, Fool that you are to darken their doors and drink their vermouth—And I have always answered, with my inimitable niavity [*sic*], Peace Peace—Well (thats one of your tricks of style—a convenient stepping stone). Well, a year ago Colefax lost all her money; gave it to a son to invest, and he chose America, and every penny vanished—all her provision for age and retirement; simultaneously, Sir Arthur lost his hearing, his practice, his £20,000 pa: and there they were with a beggarly thousand in whats to provide all London with vermouth. She said, I will not be beaten; and promptly turned house-decorator; ran up a sign in Ebury Street, sold her Rolls Royce, and is now, literally, at work, in sinks, behind desks, running her finger along wainscots and whipping out yard measures from 9.30 to 7. So I said, Come and dine, and

1. Sir Charles Hubert Hastings Parry (1848-1918) the composer and writer on music, whose most popular work was the anthem *Jerusalem*. His second daughter Gwendolen married in 1899 Harry Plunket Greene, the singer, who died in 1936.

she came; and there was an ordinary paté; and there was I jumping up to fetch the chicken and L.; running round with cheap French wine: and there and then, she took her fork and plunged it into the truffle; and all to match. All ease, hunger, shabbiness, tiredness even; no red on her nails, and merely lying in an armchair gossiping and telling stories of this sale and that millionaire, from the professional working class standard, as might be any woman behind a counter.

Enough.

V.

Berg

2278: TO ETHEL SMYTH   *Monks House, Rodmell*
                                        [Sussex]
Typewritten
Sunday [16 November 1930]

Well, I have read them[1]—very good indeed—very subtle, very various, very finely shaded. Here is my tabulation:

31st May 97:* I agree (this means to the part scored by you)

30th July 1900.* I agree. I also like the last paragraph. "Now I am going to bed etc" to the end. It gives a touch of daily life, and theres very little daily life for the most part.

8th March 1901. This is the letter I should print whole if you have room. In fact, I should shorten others to print it whole. It gives a general map of his psychology which to me at least, explains much otherwise evasive. Nor should I edit and omit personalities. After all, the story is told in *Imps;*[2] which disposes of the intimacy bogey, and a whole letter seems to me to have far more persuasive effect than one dotted, even if the dots leave out nothing of importance. One feels one has all the facts at ones disposal.

22nd May 1907.* I agree (I suppose Ottoline must be suppressed?)

7th Jan. 1902. I agree. I like the Annamites[3] very much.

6th Oct. 1902.* For some reason, possibly wrong, I dont much like this. It seems a little out of tune, and nobody remembers John Oliver Hobbes,[4] and it reads fadedly, rather—out of date.

1. Letters written to Ethel by Henry Brewster, part of which she published in her new edition of *The Prison.*
2. *Impressions That Remained* (1919), the first two volumes of Ethel's auto-biography.
3. Annam was a district of French Indo-China, whose tonal language Brewster compared to Swinburne's.
4. The pseudonym of Pearl Craigie (1867-1906), the American novelist.

3rd [5] *April* 04. I agree. I think the description of bad thought and good thought very true—very good.

7th Sept. 1904.* I agree. Again I suppose Vernon[1] cant be printed.

22nd March 05.* Yes, quite good, but his [Brewster's] literary criticism is not so interesting here as some other remarks, for which I would omit this, if its a case of wanting room.

1st March 08. I agree.

About the snippets[2]—yes, thats very good—that gives many facets in a bunch. My word, though I should like to have all the letters at length. There is so much fineness; and continuity of thought and individuality— I mean to cut out bits is only to show one bud, one thorn, one leaf. of a very complex pattern. And he is a quiet and evasive writer who does things by shades so that the interest is diffused, and not in spots and splashes that can be cut out. But I dont see that it could be better done than you suggest. (This letter, I admit, could be better done, a great deal, but I must type for clearness, and the voice of the typewriter snips my mind to bits. And its not a clear mind owing to distractions; but I'd better write now before I begin London again where the distractions will be worse.)

Let me know if I can explain anything more clearly or fully. And say how you are. I will keep the letters till you instruct me. I'm all agog to read the finished version of the memoir.

Berg

2279: To V. Sackville-West   *Monks House* [*Rodmell, Sussex*]

Sunday 16th or 15? [16] Nov. [1930]

Well, that is a nice good poem.[3] Yes, I like it. I like its suavity and ease; and its calm; and its timelessness and shade; and its air of rings widening widening till they imperceptibly touch the bank. Thats what I like best in your work. And the sense that you have shed all the meretricious horrors of life and have taken to the waters; fishlike, absolved. Oh so much better than bothering about human relations, and dining out, and buying white

---

* These letters were not printed in *The Prison*. Ed.

1. Vernon Lee, the pseudonym of Violet Paget (1856-1935), the novelist, critic and cultural historian.
2. In addition to the four letters mentioned above, which were printed at length, Ethel included short extracts from others.
3. *Sissinghurst*, a short poem which Vita had written in the form of a letter to Virginia. It was published by the Hogarth Press in July 1931.

satin shoes to dine with Lady Rhondda. Lord yes—you infected me last night with nostalgia for the lake and the farm cart; "tilted stupidly";[1] and the returning horses; and the old men.

I think it is a very harmonious and complete poem; and very stately and urbane. And after all this I come to the point—

Sunday Nov. 24th [23]

(I find this beginning, crumpled up; unlike you, I send it. But then how I tower above you in the intimacies of life—) the point was, I suppose that you should let us print it. Will you? Here, faithfully, is a cheque for £1-6.1.

Ethel met me with a quarto sheet, on which were written things to ask Virginia: 1. 2. 3—and so on to 20. Without stopping she went on till 5: and her veins were swollen on her forehead.

To give you a sample: 1. Suicide. 2. About Nelly. 3. What is Vita writing. 4. Relations with Ottoline. 5. 6. 7 8—all Brewster and the memoir. But she is a game old Bird and I respect her to the point of idolatry.

Alas and alas—Friday is no good. Leonard has promised to address a village meeting at Rodmell. I forgot. Any chance the week after? All days I think free.

And when shall I meet you.

O you were a nice good Vita—

Berg

2280: To V. Sackville-West   [52 *Tavistock Square, W.C.*1]

[19 November 1930]

This is pure business.

Would Friday night be possible, for you, I mean could I come, if I could come? I'm not altogether sure—but want, oh yes, do want, to see you.

I wrote a letter, or began it, about the poem [*Sissinghurst*]—to me a very good one—was interrupted—Oh curse theres the bell—there's Plomer —so will write another—Oh yes I liked it—the poem.

Sorry for the scrawl.

Are you lunching with H. on Friday?[2]

Yr V.

Berg

1. In the published version Vita changed the line to read: "The waggon stupid stands with upright shaft."
2. Virginia and Vita attended a lunch party at the Garrick Club on 21 November to celebrate Harold Nicolson's 44th birthday. Afterwards Virginia went to Long Barn for the night.

[November 1930]

Dearest Ethel,

Yes, do come and gossip—what about next Wednesday, 4.30, when I shall be alone?

Might I be asked to dine another night later—if this is not asking too much—That week has become a rubbish heap of horrors.

Of course I am going to see your pictures [at the Warren Gallery], but I'm so perpetually snubbed by painters that I creep into galleries and never venture a word.

Yours
Virginia

I'm so furious at being in Beaton's Book[1]—I was never asked—never sat—never saw the horrid worm—and there I am seized for ever.

Wendy Baron

2282: To Ethel Smyth   52 *Tavistock Sqre.* [*W.C.*1]

Saturday 29th Nov. 1930

Ethel dear, I have been a wretch not to write, but I have been out of the mood (not at all for reading letters though) trying to spread my mind in calm to get this bothersome chapter [of *The Waves*] right, and for ever called off to fit in quite impossible engagements. In this mood, I cant sit down and answer—but there's no need to go into these explanations I daresay if I didn't write for 6 months, all you'd say would be well—

One cant keep a clear head in London. There's my poor brother in law suddenly struck blind of one eye while travelling with a mistress in Italy. The oculist says it may be a serious matter—anyhow he cant read, upon which his rational life depends. Whereupon his old mistress Mary Hutchinson, says "Cant I read to you?" and comes and pitches her tent in his room; and has now summoned me, as I suppose to go into the whole question of their relationship this afternoon. You cant think what an odd tangle of emotions this sets tingling. She used to be so jealous of me; I am now her confidante; Clive used to be so passionate, and now says he wants nothing but peace; then Vanessa, strangest of women, who never could tolerate Mary cordially, now, whether in cynicism or earnest I dont know,

1. Virginia had refused Cecil Beaton's request to photograph her, but in *The Book of Beauty* he included two drawings of her by himself. Beaton claimed that only Virginia and Queen Mary had declined to sit for him (*The Wandering Years*, 1961, p. 175).

suggests that I should suggest that Mary should take Clive out to Zurich where the greatest oculist in Europe lives, and so launch upon another decade of passion, or rather embroilment. For by this time of course, Mary has developed a love affair, it is said with a Royal Prince or a negro chauffeur —(somebody either way entirely beyond our sphere) which puts all her feelings for Clive into the shade. Yet, she says, if going to bed with him once a fortnight would be any use, I could safely offer that. And I, who am bat-blind and mole-deaf to all these questions, have to decide what effect once a fortnight if combined with the Royal duke would be likely to have on Clive's stability. Happily, all people want is to talk about themselves; advice giving is a mere farce.

Yes I think you're entirely ruthless—if it comes to that. I have noticed more small things, ways of eating and sitting (I get things through odd channels, thats all) which have built up by this time a very decisive portrait, than you imagine. I daresay I know as much about you as you about me. Anyhow I dont think you exaggerate lopsidedly; I mean, one day you may be as rapid and enthusiastic as—(oh a hawk must do) and the next deadly shrewd, caustic, rational, severe—the daughter of the General in short. She sometimes shocks me—the daughter of the metaphysician.

No, I dont think that L. or I 'snarl'—we analyse each other's idio-syncrasies—(you will like that phrase) in the light of psycho-analysis walking round the square. My reports, however, are apt to twist up into balls what is really amicable, serious, disinterested, and almost wholly affectionate. It's true that Leonard sees my faults.

A man wrote to the Observer last week to ask for some method of keeping letters written to the edge. No doubt there will be 20 dozen replies—which I'll send you.

My letter, I now hear, has created consternation in the Times office— a principle is involved—half the Times in favour of printing, half not. So far the half not have prevailed. But they are still fighting—my letter about Beatons book I mean[1]

These remarks about Clive are I need not say highly confidential.

Berg

2283: To V. Sackville-West   [52 *Tavistock Square, W.C.*1]
Wednesday [3 December 1930]

Is there no chance that we could have a happy day one day next week,

---

1. The *Times* declined to publish her letter of protest, but it and one other appeared in the *Nation* of 29 November and 20 December 1930.

and go to the Mint or the Tower or The Zoo or eat muffins in a shop?
Answer.

Or do you want to drop me? Answer.

Do you bequeath me to Ethel? Answer.

Have you no power of the pen left? Are you merely the mouthpiece of English poetry speaking at ancestral dinner parties, along with Milton, Shakespeare and Sir Walter Scott? Write a letter instantly. I could have dined with Lady Astor last night if it comes to that.[1] I dined with Ethel Sands—oh dear, so many things to say and no chance to say them in. The truth of it is I suppose, that you live largely in the Tower at Sissing-hurst and sometimes descend to talk to the Old Bulls. A man fell from his Tower last week—was killed. Dont lean on the bastions. I wrote to Dotty, in trembling, and got no answer, so tremble all the more. And can you tell me anything about a Hart Davies[2] who is with Heinemann?

V.

Berg

2284: To Anon   52 *Tavistock Square, W.C.*1

Typewritten
10th Dec. 1930

Dear Madam,

As one of the guilty parties I bow down to your strictures upon the printing of On Being Ill.[3] I agree that the colour is uneven, the letters not always clear, the spacing inaccurate, and the word 'campion' should read 'companion'.

All I have to urge in excuse is that printing is a hobby carried on in the basement of a London house; that as amateurs all instruction in the art was denied us; that we have picked up what we know for ourselves; and that we practise printing in the intervals of lives that are otherwise engaged. In spite of all this, I believe that you can already sell your copy for more than the guinea you gave, as the edition is largely over subscribed, so that though we have not satisfied your taste, we hope that we have not robbed your purse.

Yours, with apologies,
Virginia Woolf

Washington State University, Humanities Library

1. Vita and Harold had spent the previous weekend with the Astors at Cliveden.
2. Rupert Hart-Davis, the author, editor and publisher. After leaving Oxford, he was an actor for three years, and then joined the staff of William Heinemann the publisher.
3. Virginia's essay, *On Being Ill*, was limited to 250 signed copies, printed and published by the Hogarth Press in November 1930.

2285: To Lady Ottoline Morrell

52 *Tavistock Square, W.C.*1

Friday [12 December 1930]

Dearest Ottoline

How extraordinarily nice of you to write! It is a surprise to find these little articles[1] liked—especially by you. I was impressed by Christina—but what nonsense these lives of her are!

Life has become such a cascade that I dont see how to come round at the moment—its this abominable Christmas and going away—but I will ring up if I may, and anyhow shall be back in the New Year and shall hope for a quiet evening gossiping over the fire then. Once more we are looking at houses, in the expectation of being turned out.

Your

Texas

Virginia

2286: To Ethel Sands

52 *Tavistock Square, W.C.*1

Sunday [14 December 1930?]

Dearest Ethel,

How can you divine my tastes so exactly—what's more, add to them your own exquisity? And, moreover, if you knew how I hate shopping, and for weeks have been saying I must buy a tie, and making shift with an old Julian handkerchief from sheer cowardice!—So I'm immensely grateful, could I daresay face a Chelsea lunch without blushing. Life is such a rush—but I hope in spite of that you'll include us in it—I don't know why—but I spend all my time seeing people, and never anyone I want.

Yours

Wendy Baron

V.W.

2287: To Alan McGlashan

52 *Tavistock Square, W.C.*1

Typewritten

15 Dec 1930

Dear Dr McGlashan,

I must apologise for the delay in sending you this little book [*On Being Ill*]. The edition was a small one and was sold out, so that I am now sending an out of series copy which has, I fear, no value from a book collectors point of view, but I hope you will accept it with my thanks all the same.[2]

1. Review of *The Life of Christina Rossetti* by Mary F. Sandars, and *Christina Rossetti and her Poetry*, by Edith Birkhead (*Nation*, 6 December 1930).
2. Dr McGlashan had been looking after Nelly Boxall during her illness, and Virginia had agreed to take her back for three months from the first of January.

There is no reason why the same title should not be used again for your poems,[1] which I shall hope to read when they come out.

Yours sincerely
Virginia Woolf

Please dont bother to acknowledge this.

Alan McGlashan

2288: To Ethel Sands   52 *Tavistock Square, W.C.*1

Sunday [21? December 1930]

Dearest Ethel,
    The little book [*On Being Ill*] is coming to you as an inadequate Christmas present, with my love. At the moment I can't lay hands on a copy, but shall have one in a day or two. You must excuse the printing—and the waiting too.
    Let me know when you're back. And then we'll have our cold bone and a long talk in which, I swear Virginia shan't be mentioned, and Ethel shall.
    I looked down on your head the other night at the play—rather a stiff play too.

Yrs Virginia

Wendy Baron

2289: To Edmund Blunden   *Monk's House, Rodmell,*
                                       Lewes [Sussex]

[December 1930]

Dear Mr Blunden,
    Many thanks for sending me the little book on Christina Rossetti,[2] which I shall like to read. I felt some hesitation in writing of a poet, with you as editor, but am very glad if you liked the article.[3]
    We are trying to enjoy the country, in spite of fog, and the horror of new houses, with which they are spoiling these downs, to my great rage.

Yours sincerely

Texas   Virginia Woolf

1. Dr McGlashan's poems, to which he had provisionally given the same title *On Being Ill*, were published as *St George and the Dragon* (1931).
2. Probably *Christina Rossetti* (1930), by D. M. Stuart, which was part of the English Men of Letters series.
3. Her article on Rossetti had appeared in the *Nation* for 6 December 1930.

Monk's House, Rodmell
[Sussex]

Wednesday [24 December 1930]

Dotty wires that you're not going to Penns for Friday but next week, and wants us to come then. So will you say which day. Such a bore—have had to take to my bed with bad throat and temperature. So anyhow Friday I suppose couldn't have done. And no books. If you have any memoir or other book fit for one completely imbecile it would be a charity to send it. Any chance of seeing you here? That would be nice. Long letter would be nice too.

V.

Nigel Nicolson (copy)

2291: To Vanessa Bell *Monks House [Rodmell, Sussex]*

Xmas day [1930]

Dearest Dolphin

I rang you up on Tuesday, but you were out. It was only to say that we sent you a black coat; and that if you hate, it, or it doesn't fit, you can change it. I thought it might come in useful in the evening; anyhow keep you warm in the country.

I have had to retire to bed which is rather annoying. I got a bad throat and made it worse I suppose coming down and so had a temperature and spent yesterday in bed. However it is only a little over 99 today so I expect I shall be up and about tomorrow. I have just had my lunch off a fish (but we shall have turkey tomorrow) L. is lunching with the Keynes, to taste Mrs Harland, Lydia says, for the last time. I gather that there is a good deal of business about the future of The Nation to be discussed—of course in strict confidence—as if anybody cared what happened to that dead dog except that it should be buried. I had a queer adventure by the way, the day I got your coat at Marshall and Snelgroves. I was given £6 to buy Xmas presents; I put my bag under my moleskin, and turned, for one moment, to try on your coat. Then I thought I ought not to leave the bag, so turned to get it—and behold—in that second a thief had snatched it! There was then a great hue and cry, and a detective appeared, and they said a woman in brown fur had been seen; but of course they could not catch her; so there I was, penniless, without key, spectacles, cigarette case or handkerchief. Marshall's refused to lend me a penny as they said I was not on their books; but the detective gave me 10/- of his own. Later that night the bag was found, thrown in a drain; and marvellously, though the £6 were gone, the thief had left my spectacles, keys, and one old earring. I had just bought two for a present. So didn't do as badly as I might.

I was sad to part with Rivett [Carnac], who is really very nice, and might be very good with training. She aked me to get her another job if I could among my friends; as she enjoys so much being with people like us. I rather dread Nelly—but this I have said before. It is very fine and spring like here, but I haven't yet had my nose out of doors. I am in bed in my top room with a fine log fire, and new bookcases—all very snug. Duncan's table is arriving on Saturday, and will be only just in time as the accumulation of parcels and papers is terrific. Two telegrams have already come from Dotty—but as I shant be able to go tomorrow, we have got out of our lunch till next week. Perhaps you will come with us.

Roger [Fry] dined with us, and Lord! how bitter he is! Now I laugh at my friends, but not with a black tongue. First he abused Vita; then Ethel Smyth; then Maynard; then of course complained of his poverty and the neglect of his art—but not as of old with tolerant grumps: bitterly, savagely, with morosity. We think his mésalliance is souring him and Helen [Anrep] to wit. Have you noticed it? I found myself in the unusual position of standing up for Edith Sitwell, Maynard, Vita, Ethel and so on—and how do you psychologically speaking, account for his morbid desire to be thought poor? He told me I could quite well afford to lose £6—which is true; but that he was so bankrupt that to spend £30 on a new gramophone was impossible—and his mothers death had been a complete fiasco.

This is all my news and very doddery and dull I fear; but perhaps Christmas at Seend is even dodderier. When are you coming?

I want to discuss with you the propriety of my now making a small annual allowance to Angelica. I think she ought to have a little money to throw away on clothes etc. Dont you think I might? We were always too poor. Please consider this.

J. Lehmann[1] is coming to see us. Do ask Julian what he thinks of him from a practical point of view.

B.

Berg

2292: To Ethel Smyth

Monks House [Rodmell, Sussex]

Christmas day 1930

It was very nice getting your letter this morning Ethel dear.

But this is only a scrawl, because I'm in bed. That cold I had when you came has been burrowing about, and coming here made it worse—Hence

1. John Lehmann was 23 years old. He had recently come down from Cambridge, where he had been a friend of Julian Bell, and the Hogarth Press had accepted his poems for publication. In the new year Leonard invited him to become Manager of the Press, and he eventually became a partner.

a temperature; hence bed in my top room; where I lie, before a great log fire. And the temp. only rather over 99 this afternoon; and my alarum clock cough (like yours I imagine) whirrs only now and then. And my throat is less red and raw. Still I'm blasted if I ever take special care of myself for 10 days with a view to finishing a book if this is what happens. There's the poor old Waves on the shelf; and I cant do a thing. And I'd just got the swing, I thought, of the end. Never mind; I'm quite happy in many ways; and hope for turkey and wine tomorrow. Any letters instead of sole and milk pudding will be gratefully received. But they take such an age coming, I shall be well by the time you get this. Yes, I wish I'd got your book;[1] it would be the very thing. I dip into Q Victoria's letters;[2] but mostly lie and look at the fire. L is as usual a perfect angel; he carried my bed up, wraps his own silk dressing gown round me, and cooks dinner and prunes his trees, and does every single thing just when I thought he wd. have a fortnights holiday: what a curse I am to him, to be sure!

Its turned balmy and fine, and I can see the rooks in the Churchyard trees, and the downs all pink and yellow if I look over my head.

So no more at the moment. I am not in the least bad—only its annoying —at the moment—worse though to be you correcting your drunken copyist.

Love V.

I will write properly again.

Berg

2293: To V. Sackville-West   *Monks House [Rodmell, Sussex]*

Saturday [27 December 1930]

It seems to be my usual influenza—cough practically gone, but this idiotic little temperature goes on. So I'm staying in bed.

Yes, do for Heavens sake drop in any time, and take your luck if there's any food—How nice to see you. I expect I shall be all right by Monday. (Possibly the Keynes's come on Monday—otherwise we're alone and shall be here till Tuesday week.)

I'm raging at not finishing The Waves here as I hoped—otherwise bed is not a bad place.

Sorry about your mother, at least about you, and going to Brighton, and Christmas and mud and decorations.

1. *Streaks of Life* (1921), one of Ethel's autobiographies.
2. The first of G. E. Buckle's three-volume edition of Queen Victoria's *Letters*, 1886-1901, which was published in 1930.

Let me know when you'll come—I dont suppose we shall get to Dotty
Love from Pot,
Who's rather
Hot.

V.

Berg

2294: To Ethel Smyth   *Monks House* [*Rodmell,*
                                         Sussex]

Saturday 27th [December 1930]

Book [*Streaks of Life*] come this morning, perfectly correct, and very
welcome. How clever you are to get it here!

Still in bed; throat cured, cough much better, but temp. still goes on its
silly way—never over 100, never under 99. I suppose it is the same influenza
I had last Feb:—that celebrated occasion when you came to see me; and I
must make up my mind, what with being careful about headaches and so on,
to give up the time here to nothing but mooning and lazing. I expect the
temp. will be normal in a day or two—its only the, what are called after
effects that have to be swept up. I try to philosophise and suppose that my
mind will store itself and that I shall pour out the last chapter [of *The Waves*]
all the fuller for this break.

As you see from this egotism, one's mind gets choked and not a fish rises.
It pours and blows. The char's baby is ill. I keep very snug in bed in the
top room. L. prunes in a leather coat. I have lots of Christmas cards and
bits of paper on top of me. Of course I snatched the [marked] red ink
passages in Streaks at once, with delight. I wish I hadnt read it already, but
shall try again. I read about the Stars, and try to imagine what is meant by
space bending back.[1] Eliz [Williamson]: must take me to her telescope.
Thats about all my news.

I was sad to part with Rivett—she got nicer and nicer and the relief of
being on a footing, socially, I find immense. No huffs, no feelings. And she
liked us and wanted to stay and so I feel indisposed for poor old Nelly and
her kidneys. Whats your next job? You say you've done this for the time. I
imagine something blowing through your hair off the shingles at Cromer—
never been there but imagine shingles and cobbles, wind bitten evergreens.
And I'm allowed no wine till I'm normal! So write. Love to Eliz; and please
excuse this awful drivvle and the egotistic soliloquy. Heres L: Who sends
his love

V.

1. Virginia had been reading one of Sir James Jeans' books on astronomy, perhaps
The Mysterious Universe (1930).

I will send you (if you like) On Being Ill—another copy turned up. This is my erratic Xmas present.

Berg

2295: To Vanessa Bell   *Monks House* [*Rodmell, Sussex*]

Monday [29 December 1930]

Dearest Dolphin

The necklace is exquisite—like the inside of white grapes—and as my consumption of necklaces is huge, will come in most useful as well as ornamental. Leonard is so enamoured of his caddy that he is making it into a tobacco tin for London. Also, I am finding Angelica's blotter of immediate use—for one thing, I never have any blotting paper, and as I am writing in bed it is essential to have a hard block. In fact all the presents were entirely on the spot and much in contrast to the hideosities my poor old mother in law sent—for instance a vast sham brass fish slice.

I am hoping to get up today and receive the Keynes's. I have gone on having a slight temp: not over 100, but over 99, so I suppose it has been the same influenza I had last year. But I'm almost normal today and am going now to dress.

Nothing much therefore has happened—in fact nothing. The Keynes's go back tomorrow, so you will miss them. There is a lot of Nation gossip and Harland [Keynes's servants] gossip—they're leaving to better themselves with a rich prostitute in Mayfair. I shall hear it all again this afternoon.

Duncan's table has come and is so lovely in the drawing room I can't have it up here, and thus shall have to buy another. Jean [Campbell] writes about the furniture, which should come by sea [from Cassis], she says; and wont take the sheets without paying.

It pours and pours.

I must say the necklace is lovely—so much that I have it on the table to look at. I shall wear it this afternoon

Any visits wd. be much appreciated; I expect we shall come anyhow on New Years day, but shall be here in solitude till 6th. so hope to see you soon

V.

I'm so furious—I had meant to finish your intolerable Moths [*Waves*] here, and of course havent been able to write a line—all your fault.

Berg

2296: To Ethel Smyth *Monks House [Rodmell, Sussex]*

Monday 29th Dec [1930]

Your wire has just come. Look here—dont spend all your fortune in wiring—L. wd. at once tell you if I were worse. But I'm better—much. In fact I'm going to put on stockings and dress when I've had lunch. The temp. is almost normal this morning—it has been between 99 and 100 until today, but now I think this is the end. I feel much better; dont sleep all the time; have no headache; cough almost gone; eat everything, and hope for a drop of wine tonight. I shant try to write—Waves I mean—for a few days, as these things hang about; but I dont feel as done up as I did last time, and can keep so quiet here that I shall have no temptation to exceed. Its a bore of course, but I'm beginning to plan a walk; and to plan what my next sentence will be, and to think with rapture of roast mutton.

You see the higher faculties aren't playing up—One gets muffled in one room. All the same, last night I read practically all Streaks again with the highest relish. Its the very book I want—as good as watching Joyce Wethered[1] play golf—I found I cd. read it almost as if new—a great tribute to your English and vigour, which hoards enough heat to warm one a second time. Lord what fun it is!—Any letters, any documents will be welcome. So if you've nothing to do—wh. is unlikely—do that. I'm ashamed of this invertebrate jerkiness. The muscles in one hand are highly susceptible—cant form a word after 6 days in bed; but it comes back. Now the sun is actually in the left hand corner of the room and making the Church tower a silvery yellow, and the pear trees bright green. And my lunch is coming—how nice! Are you buffeting against the gale? What are you doing? And what wild spate is rushing through the giant chambers (reference to your size in hats) of your brain?

V.

Berg

2297: To Saxon Sydney-Turner *Monks House, Rodmell [Sussex]*

30th Dec. 1930

My dear Saxon,

It is a long long time since I saw you—your birthday party was the last occasion. Here I am marooned in bed with what appears to be influenza. A country cottage is a chill place to come to late on a December night with a bad cold. So I took to my bed and have lain by the fire for 5 days, but I'm practically normal today, so shall put on a dressing gown and become a rational being again.

1. See p. 185, note 1.

I suppose in these 5 days you would have read Plato through. What a pity it is that we cant pool our reading!—I mean, if I could attach a little sucker to the back of your neck and drink through it without any effort, all your knowledge, I should be able to die content. I dont suppose, as things are, I shall ever read Plato through, or Theocritus, or Thucydides: and then I suspect you of having spent Christmas reading some entirely obscure, rather late and imperfect, but absorbingly interesting and very indecent, satire by an Alexandrian—why not? But I shall never know.

I heard of you making the Baboons howl at the Zoo with Roger. How much does it cost to become what you are—I dont mean in spirit—I mean a Fellow of the Society, so that one can go on Sundays? I want to make Leonard a member. Now that we're all so old, I daresay one can afford it, and what a refuge for extreme old age, to sit with the baboons!

Maynard and Lydia came over in their Rolls Royce yesterday; Nessa and the children—but Julian is likely to become a fellow of King's they say[1] —came to Charleston yesterday. I am reading Defoe's Tour of England[2] —the sort of book one can read all day, turning the pages as a sheep eats grass. I go on and on. In his day, a new house was a most creditable and welcome sight—that is what strikes me—whereas, whenever I go out here I find some horrid little red bug on the downs, and feel more rage than about almost anything.

As you can see, I've no news. Gerald Brenan seemed at one moment to be hovering over us with his wife [Gamel Woolsey], but we did not manage to meet. Have you met? Why do you think one comes to the country at Christmas? The gale is battering at the windows. Why do you think one makes up these romantic stories about owls and clear sunny days, when the owls are dead and the sun sunk? Please write a long long fascinating letter full of reflections upon life.

Leonard's love—
yr V.W.

Sussex

2298: To Ethel Smyth   *Monks House [Rodmell,*
                                        Sussex]
Last day of old year [31 December 1930]

This can only be a line as the postman may be here any minute. Therefore the usual egotism; up; been for a walk as far as the Post office; a little wobbly; temp. stays about 99, but thats of no account.

I've read the paper (Prison) with the usual admiration at your dexterities

1. Julian Bell never became a Fellow of King's.
2. *Tour Through the Whole Island of Great Britain*, published in three volumes, 1724-7.

and audacities. I think there's one fault of grammar somewhere I forget: anyhow I've no big envelope so will keep it a day or two. I'm going to stay almost entirely speechless till we go back—no more exertion than ordering dinner—and as I cdn't swear to be speechless if you were in the room I'm going to forego that extravagant offer.

So you must write instead

V.

Happy New Year 1931

Berg

2299: To William Plomer   *Monks House, Rodmell*
                                  [Sussex]
31st Dec. 1930

Dear William,

We were very sorry to miss you, but we came here two days before Christmas, and, developing influenza, I had to take to my bed instantly but am now up.

We are very much interested to hear of your visit to Simpson[1]—how astonishing that he should be mixed up with Mrs Wilson[2] whom I remember vaguely through a wild letter she wrote me, enclosing a bag of lavender and a bunch of heather. She also gave me some particulars of her life—I cant remember what, except that nothing would induce her to write, for which I commended her. But how the Wilsons and the Simpsons have come together, with all other details, we must wait till we see you to hear. We're very glad you liked the Greyhound. I still think his first purely sodomitic novel[3] was the best.

We go back about the 6th and shall be in London all January, except for occasional weekends, so let us know when you can come and dine.

I doubt that the country is possible at this time of year—one cant walk far, it rains incessantly; night sets in about 3 pm. But then London is a racket of people, so perhaps the only salvation is a Greek island.

Our best wishes for a happy year.

Yours
Virginia Woolf

Texas

1. John Hampson Simpson, who under the name of John Hampson wrote *Saturday Night at the Greyhound*, which the Hogarth Press published in February 1931.
2. See Letter 2235.
3. John Hampson Simpson published no novel before 1931, but in 1934 appeared his *Strip Jack Naked*, of which Virginia may have seen a typescript.

Letters 2300-2353 (January–April 1931)

On 7 February Virginia finished the second draft of The Waves, and wrote in her diary the famous sentences:

"I wrote the words O Death fifteen minutes ago, having reeled across the last ten pages with some moments of such intensity and intoxication that I seemed only to stumble after my own voice, or almost, after some sort of speaker (as when I was mad) I was almost afraid, remembering the voices that used to fly ahead. Anyhow, it is done." (A Writer's Diary, p. 169). It was not quite done. She still had to retype it, and revise again. But she took a holiday from the book, writing journalism, including five articles on London for Good Housekeeping, and exposed herself once again to London parties. After one of them at Lady Rosebery's, she wrote to Ethel Smyth (2335) a letter of bitter protest against 'this chatter and clatter', and in another (2341) contemplated, apparently quite seriously, taking her own life. Other events of this period were the advent of John Lehmann to the Hogarth Press, a day's visit to the Webbs, and another to Cambridge. Virginia's moods varied. At one moment she felt that life was 'a childish, happy affair'; at the next, 'My days are nibbled from me by rats'. She much looked forward to her holiday with Leonard in France. They left England on 16 April.

2300: To V. Sackville-West   Monks House, Rodmell
              [Sussex]

1st Jan 1931

Here, in the first place, is a letter from a lady whose aunt translated Mrs Barclay,[1] for which reason the niece wants—what a nice compliment!—to translate you. L. says you deal with these bugs yourself.

The Books have been a godsend—for some reason, the London Library took to sending me third volumes only, and I was in despair. Anderson[2] seems to me extremely good—puts a line round herself completely, as Katherine Mansfield used to wish to do, when she bought a tailor made coat.

1. Florence Barclay (1862-1921), whose novel The Rosary (1909) sold over a million copies.
2. Stella Benson, whose best-known novel was Tobit Transplanted (1931). She married J. C. Anderson of the Chinese Customs Service in 1921. Vita had probably sent Virginia The Man Who Missed the Bus, a collection of Benson's short stories.

Are you staying at Penns [Dorothy Wellesley's house]? I dont know what to say about coming—I'm much better, but go on with the usual little temperature, and thus have to keep warm and so on. It may vanish—one never knows. I fume a good deal—There's is my wretched last chapter—should have been poured out in a rush and done with. I've written 2 sentences, and dont see when I shall manage more. For this reason the whole burden of the Spring season rests on you. Make a note of this. A charming young man, John Lehmann, brother of Rosamund, wants to become our manager, and perhaps buy a share later. If he turns out possible—I rather suspect charming young men who write poetry—this may solve our difficulties. He is coming to see us in a day or two. Anyhow our spring season must be worked. Easdale,[1] the 17 year old poetess, wants us to bring Dotty to see her act a play in a shed in the garden. Ethel, marooned at Cromer, has just sent me all her love letters—I mean Brewster's letters, and keeps up a daily fire which I sometimes dont read all at once. It is very difficult to be intimate with such a blazing egotist—the flames shrivel one up. You'll be glad to hear. And at the moment I want coolness and calm; and old oxen, and merely to sit with Vita and be told that Milton did not come to the dinner. I suppose you cant come over from Penns? Anyhow I'll write again—my word, I could have spared this influenza—any other time but this. You dont know anyone who wants Rivett-Carnac I suppose? I parted from her with sorrow, and she has no job; and I return to Nelly without enthusiasm; but must go through 3 months I suppose. Write me a nice letter.

Your
VW.

Sissinghurst Thursday,[2] is announced.

Love to D.

V.

Berg

2301: To V. Sackville-West [*Monks House, Rodmell, Sussex*]

Friday [2 January 1931]

A brilliant idea—wont you and Dotty come over tomorrow? (I think L. has written this) We go back on Wednesday, but shall be so cumbered with things that L. says we must go home straight. I seem stuck at 99, which is nothing: so am taking up the burden of life—chiefly Ethel. An idol

---

1. The Hogarth Press published two books of poetry by Joan Easdale, one in 1931, the other in 1932.
2. Vita's letter-poem was headed 'Sissinghurst, Thursday'.

is not necessarily what one wishes in the home. Have you finished correcting Sissinghurst Thursday?

VW.

Just off for a walk on the downs Oh how heavenly!

Berg

2302: To Ethel Smyth   [*Monk's House, Rodmell, Sussex*]

Friday Jan 2nd [1931]

O a thousand congratulations. Well, you've got the greater part of your wishes this year already I imagine. I'm very grateful for HB.[1] in whom I'm dipping with great curiosity, and have many questions to ask. But not now. I'm off for my first walk—my ½ hour round, in this blazing sun. I remain 99 but don't suppose it matters. And if I get out I have a much better head-piece

Love and thanks and congratulations
V.

Berg

2303: To Julian Bell   *Monks House* [*Rodmell, Sussex*]

Typewritten
Friday [2 January 1931]

My dear Julian,

I meant to get you a book for a Christmas present but as I dont know what you want I send you a cheque instead, which can be spent on anything —dogs, drink, what you like.

Your father cut me off so short yesterday that I dont know what arrangements were arrived at—possibly Dotty and Vita are coming tomorrow, but I doubt it. Anyhow we must meet and go into the question at length— I mean about the nature and character of poetry etc etc.

Virginia

Quentin Bell

1. Henry Brewster's love letters to Ethel.

Monks House [Rodmell, Sussex]

Saturday [3 January 1931]

Dearest Clive,

Have you by any chance got Madame du Deffand[1] Letters to H. Walpole, (Mrs Toynbee) vol I? The London Library of course have only sent 3rd vol, and I should be greatly obliged by the loan. I'm in bed with some feverish distemper and read all day—Hoping to see you.

yr V.

Don't send—bring with you, or we could fetch.

Quentin Bell

2305: To Lyn Lloyd Irvine   *Monks House, Rodmell [Sussex]*

4th Jan [1931]

Dear Lyn,[2]

As you see, we're down here. We came for Christmas, and come back on Wednesday. I spent Christmas in bed with influenza,—am still stupid and sleepy beyond words. May we take our chance of coming on Saturday for tea? I've not faced my engagements yet, and dont know what we mayn't find waiting us. But we shd. like to come if we can—provided I'm capable of intelligent conversation, which seems doubtful.

Our best wishes, as they say, for 1931. I'm dipping into Madame du Deffand (your edition) and shall be interested to hear what you make of her. My theory of letterwriting is now complete: but no room to explain it.

Yrs V.W.

Sussex

2306: To Ethel Smyth   *Monks House, Rodmell [Sussex]*

5th Jan 1931

I swear I will go through the article [*On Being Ill*] and find the bad grammar this evening; I daresay all my own inaccuracy. Well (as you would say) my letter writing faculty has dried up. This bloody temperature stays a little over 99, and I daresay when we come to London I shall see a doctor—

1. The 18th-century French intellectual. Her letters to Horace Walpole were edited in three volumes by Mrs Paget Toynbee in 1912.
2. In 1932 the Hogarth Press published her edition of *Ten Letter-Writers*. In 1934 she married Maxwell Newman, Lecturer in Mathematics at Cambridge, 1927-45.

no thats no use—I shall get a febrifuge. We come up on Wednesday, I expect the germ can't be ousted here, as, though I can keep one room hot, the others are like cold baths, whatever one does. No doubt a dry house and a large gas fire will do the trick. No: spittoon never needed. Meanwhile I feel vaguely ashiver, and vaguely dull, and vaguely hot, and then want to sleep, and try to write a sentence to keep the Waves on the simmer, but cant get up the right pressure. However its an Italian day—there should be cypresses against the sky and lizards in the crannies, and Leonard is going to take me for a drive. So there's no great damage to cry over—except my fortnight wasted.

Whats the use of beginning to ask or answer questions? None. A bottle turned upside down represents my state of mind. Theres the Brewster letters —theres the Wreckers[1]—theres the question of repeating compliments. As for this last, I've come to the conclusion, in my 99's, that no: theyre not good for me. I dont like them. I mean I do; but dont want them—they tingle and quiver and leave me displeased. So I'm going to be austere, and you shall never again repeat what people say (with certain exceptions) You, now, flourish on praise; its part of your strange psychology—I believe you need it: why it upsets me. I cant at this moment decide—Mrs Woodhouse[2] on my nose for instance. And was HB. a man of wealth? Did he ever do any-thing, by way of profession? What did his father and mother do? Why did he live in Rome? I feel him, though so near in some ways, in a vacuum in these respects. I've finished the letters—awfully (to use my childish slang) intriguing, I must wait, for I'm going to catch the sun. It is so warm, so blue, one could fancy it was early on a June morning, the downs on the other side of the marsh have that soft burning, yet dim look of a very early summer morning.

Love
V.

Berg

2307: To Quentin Bell   *Monks House, Rodmell,*
                                         Lewes [Sussex]

Typewritten
5th Jan. 1931

Dearest Quentin,

I am tired of waiting for a letter, though I can take my oath that it is your turn, not mine. However since it is the Christian season, and charity prevails, I write, and enclose this small douceur, as no doubt you can spend it to better advantage in Italy than I here.

1. Ethel's opera, first performed in England in June 1909 under Sir Thomas Beecham, and revived in 1931 at Covent Garden.
2. See p. 211, note 1.

Now for news, as your father would say—well, very little. On Christmas eve I took to my bed with influenza and thus was spared a visit to Dotty, a visit to Tilton, a visit to Miss Easedale, the poetess of the Goat who lives at Sevenoaks. (To explain, I may say that she is 16, and imagines herself spiritually in touch with Miss Chutneygrove—a virgin, who keeps, not for their milk, he goats) But in solitude news dies out. Only profound thoughts survive, and those you quite rightly interdict. However, getting better, I saw the Keynes's, Lydia slightly depressed by her comparative failure to tempt the British public with slabs of Paradise Lost recited by half naked young men in American cloth.[1] It was a depressing exhibition, unless you are of the persuasion. Which? Well, in a fascist country I darent say. And that I'm not.

Last night we dined at Charleston off a fine brace of pheasants shot by the Colonel [Cory Bell]. Everybody was there—Clive, Julian, Duncan, Angelica, Vanessa. And we had a bottle of audit, and got very merry. We sang old catches—three blind mice, white sand and grey sand, Angelica conducting with a rod of iron, so that I was suppressed most of the time, oh and Clinker had the mange, and lay by my side, while Leonard sang Lay by my side a bunch of purple heather. Duncan is as mellifluous as ever, but how he can spend three months alone with his Russian who by all accounts is sheep headed, bird witted, and not nice into the bargain, we in Bloomsbury cant imagine.[2] Or do you think each of us in proportion to our virtue requires some such outlet? Then Duncan's virtue must be very great. But hush—this is not to be said above a whisper. Poor old Clive is to be found reading in black spectacles. He goes to Zurich next week, alone, to a nursing home, I gather, for two months; and is very solid and sensible about it—more than I should be, to whom the thought of eyes failing would bring misery unending. This is where the Bell blood shows itself— so I doubt not did Cory stand with his feet in the water for five years in a trench. Julian is spurting and whizzing ideas. I look over his shoulder and see rows of books—territories conquered. He is going to write poetry, history, criticism; he is going to read. He is going to immure himself at Cambridge with all the books of all the ages. Before one can be a poet, he says, one must stand on a pinnacle made by the convergence of philosophy, history and art and survey the world. But in the interval of erecting this gigantic pile—and I believe he means it and will do it and will bring lasting credit on your name—meanwhile he scribbles an ode or two, and takes

1. Lydia Lopokova had taken part in a performance of Milton's *Comus* at the Arts Theatre Club, London in December 1930. George Rylands was Comus, and also the producer; Frederick Ashton was the choreographer; and Constant Lambert the musical director. (See Plate 7a.)
2. This was the painter George Bergen, who had exhibited his work in London. He was partly Russian and partly Dutch. Subsequently he emigrated to America, where he married.

Helen [Soutar] for drives in the fog. But Nessa says Helen is not to be Mrs Bell—only as it were the prelude to the footsteps of that dove-toed woman.

There—I have scratched together lots of little bits of news. Now tell me about your pictures and about the Roman world. Have you been outside along the Roman roads? have you seen Nemi? Have you seen the galleon? And have you dined on the hill? Oh dear—if I were there! It was spring when we came [April 1927], and I used to sit in the gardens at the top of the steps and merely palpitate, like a frog, sucking in and out my flanks with sheer joy. Isn't it infinitely beyond any other town—Munich, Berlin, London, Paris?

I shall come in May. You will find me a nice room. We will drink a glass together. And you will beckon to some shabby slouching figure and say Heres my Aunt.

Old Ethel Smyth has sent me all her love letters written from Rome in the 90ties when it was thought daring in the highest for a woman of 40 to share occasionally a flat with a widower of 45. She is a game old cock—we go home tomorrow, and there write me a letter.

But of course if I must type write I can hardly make sense—all cogency, fluency, and intimacy is lost. Goodbye.

[*in Virginia's handwriting:*]
In my own hand, what a tender, brilliant, subtle and penetrating letter I could write!

Virginia

Quentin Bell

2308: To Harcourt, Brace   52 *Tavistock Square, W.C.*1

Typewritten
7th Jan 1931

Dear Miss Cuff,
    Many thanks for the cheque for 784 dollars in accordance with your statement of October 25th.

Yours very truly
Virginia Woolf
(Mrs Woolf)

Harcourt Brace Jovanovich

2309: To V. Sackville-West   [52 *Tavistock Square, W.C.*1]

Thursday [8 January 1931]

We only got back yesterday.—what about Monday or Tuesday? Let me know which and when. Rather bothered with headache after this d—d little temp: but shall be in full health then. L. says you [*Sissinghurst*] are advertised in The Times tomorrow. O Lord London is a horror! back 24 hours and 24 visitors telephones and general scrimmage.

But how nice to see you in peace

Let me know in time so as to ward off people.

V.

Berg

2310: To V. Sackville-West   52 *Tavistock Square, W.C.*1

Sunday [11 January 1931]

I rang up to ask when you cd. come, but was told Mrs N. was in London. Alas—Tuesday is now full, (Dotty etc.) and I shd. like to see you without a crowd. What about Monday, tomorrow? tea? or earlier.

Perhaps you'd ring up.

Wednesday is no good. But there are other days: let it be soon.

V.

Berg

2311: To Edmund Blunden   52 *Tavistock Sqre.* [*W.C.*1]

Jan. 14th [1931]

Dear Mr Blunden,

No, I had not seen the translation;[1] and am delighted with the improved version, which I think I shall let stand. Many thanks for sending it. And, if, by the way, it was you who reviewed Julian Bell [*Winter Movement*] in the Times [*TLS*, 8 January] (he is my nephew) this is to say that he was very grateful.

Yours sincerely

Virginia Woolf

Texas

2312: To V. Sackville-West   52 *Tavistock Square, W.C.*1

[January 1931]

Here's a card for our [Hogarth Press] display, but I don't advise you to come.

Will you come to tea on Monday? But dont let Eddy know, or Ethel.

1. Possibly part of Charles Mauron's French translation of *Orlando.*

278

On the other hand, let me know—and come, because I want a little quiet pleasure.

V.

And Bring Poem [*Sissinghurst*]. Lehmann engaged.[1]

Berg

2313: To Clive Bell   52 *Tavistock Square, W.C.*1

Jan. 19th 1931

Dearest Clive,

Well, I'm full of sympathy for your state [of his eyes]–how entirely damnable. The only consolation I can offer is that you're not at any rate what I have been at various stages of my career—both shut up and mad. But perhaps a few illusions would be welcome. Therefore I will hastily tell you about life in Tavistock Square—how we have almost settled to take John Lehmann, if his guardian can be persuaded that the Press is worth a thousand pounds—how Leonard has been summonsed for a fifth time in 3 years to sit on a jury—how old Miss Pritchard [solicitor's sister] says this proves the Under Sheriff has a down on him—how Lydia has just been in to tea and says that the master of Mrs Harland's mistress is a cousin of Florry Grenfell's[2]—As you can imagine this seems to Lydia a fact of some importance—and the husband of Mrs Harland's mistress who is Florry Grenfell's cousin has a flat at Hove—so that the Harlands will be over at Tilton in their new car. But the most illusory part of Lydia's visit was that she proposes to set a scene in Orlando to music and to dance to it behind a microphone at Savoy Hill [B.B.C.]—Will I therefore rearrange the words to suit music to be written by Constant Lambert? Also Maynard's secretary is dying of large white bubbles in the blood. This Maynard highly resents as they are at the moment without a cook.

So we go on. I am scarcely brought nearer to sanity by a long most amusing letter from Quentin, telling how he killed a dog with a hammer on the Apulian road in order to gratify a humanitarian American lady, a friend of Shaws, who tried to buy chloroform at a chemist but was refused. Roger and Helen were pretty crusty together the other night, as Helen heard a wheeze in their gramophone, which Roger could not hear. Tomorrow is

1. John Lehmann started work at the Hogarth Press on 21 January. The original arrangement was that he would serve an eight-month apprenticeship, and if found satisfactory, would enter into a partnership with the Woolfs. Before this plan was realised, he left them in August 1932, but in March 1938 he returned, buying out Virginia's share of the Press.
2. The Harlands had recently left the service of the Keyneses. For Mrs Grenfell see p. 134, note 3.

Angelica's party, where I hope to pick up a little gossip. Lyn is finding life hard—and poor Miss Belsher, our manager, has broken her engagement, and so cant get the accounts right. Such is life. I will depend on Nessa for news of you.

V.

Quentin Bell

2314: TO ETHEL SMYTH   *Monks House [Rodmell, Sussex]*

Saturday 24th [January 1931]

No, I cant answer riddles by letter—besides I'm naturally obtuse, as you guess. Put the question to me in a plain manner on Wednesday and you shall have, after due deliberation, a plain answer. About the speech—I dont think I shall print mine, as it stands, because as you doubtless perceived, with your supernatural apprehensiveness, it was clotted up, clogged, partly owing to the rush I was in—no time to comb out—partly because, the very last morning in my bath I had a sudden influx of ideas, which I want to develop later, perhaps in a small book, about the size of a Room[1]—But this must wait—Lord—if only I could finish the Waves!

Your speech, meanwhile was divine and entirely expressive—Leonard says about the best of its kind he ever heard, and done he says with supreme skill, wh. I interpret to mean that you liquidated your whole personality in speaking and threw in something never yet written by being yourself there in the flesh—Anyhow, we must print your speech, by itself entire. But this I leave for discussion. I'm a little dashed—no not that—its too fine a day for that—but disappointed to find that the infernal though enjoyable racket of Wednesday has—after buoying me up for 24 hours so that I felt like a stallion in a field, capable of any enjoyment or effort (excuse the image) let me down again on Thursday night into the usual headache. I've not written, oh dear, for 3 days, but hope to start afresh on Monday. I suspect this little temperature (I've just taken it after a fortnight) 99 pt. 4 gives one a fillip, and then a drop—but its, as I say, a very fine day. We've been on the down and seen a magpie.

And now I'm back in London, and have, with incredible virtue refused an invitation to the play tonight—God what an effort, what virtue!

Well, anon, anon. (These are lifted from your style)

Virginia

Berg

1. On 21 January Virginia and Ethel spoke to a meeting of the London National Society for Women's Service on professions for women. Virginia's speech is printed in *The Pargiters* (ed. Mitchell A. Leaska, 1978), the novel-essay on feminism which she began in 1932 and ultimately developed into *The Years*.

Jan 25th 1931

Dearest Clive,

Well now, as you would say, whats the news? Whereupon your poor battered untidy sister-in-law, does what is called by the ready-writers, cudgelling her brains. There's Tom [Eliot] on the phone—by no means a trivial event, because as you are aware, the state of Vivienne's bowel is not a matter to be despatched in a moment—he wants us to meet a New Zealander who admires Leonard, was an intimate of the Empress Eugénie, and is hand in glove with the Pope. Is this Tom's wit? Goodness knows. Eddy has been taken short with the quinsy at his sisters house [Lady Romilly]—the malicious (I'm not one, nor you either) say that since he fell over a rock at Penns and failed to sprain his ankle he has been peeved with the world, and the quinsy, in Mount Street, was his means of redress. This comes through Vita who is incapable of malice, you'll agree. Dotty, on the other hand, at Angelica's party the other night, sizzled and sputtered like a herring on a fork, exposed to the torture of her books failure, her marriage's failure,[1] and various other failures which, do what she will, turn her £10,000 a year to grit and shingle between the teeth—or should it be in the hair? However I respect her for this: we were sitting talking of life and its miseries—how the Nation won't review one, and the Spectator calls one Lady Dorothy, thus insinuating one's an aristocrat and cant write poetry, when I noticed a vast hole on her forefinger. I mean her ring was without a stone. Good God Dotty, I said—you've lost your ring. Now this she took with perfect calm—it was a ruby too worth between 6 and 700 pounds. Lord, dont bother—dont make any fuss, she said; and only after the party, agreed to ask Nessa, who of course had picked it up, thinking it was out of a cracker and put it on the mantelpiece. Its a pity one must admire one's friends. Then I met a limping little creature called Geoffrey Whitworth,[2] who asked after you. Then I met Miss Scott[3] who's building the Shakespeare theatre. Then I met incredibly old Katie Lewis[4]—all of them at a party, given by the young women of England, to meet Ethel Smyth and Virginia Woolf. But you dont care about that kind of thing, instinct warns me. Your sons want muzzling—theres Quentin killed a dog

1. Dorothy Wellesley was Lady Gerald Wellesley, but she parted from her husband in the early 1920's.
2. The Honorary Secretary of the Shakespeare Memorial National Theatre Committee (1931), and previously art editor at Chatto & Windus.
3. Elizabeth Whitworth Scott won the competition for designing the new Shakespeare Theatre at Stratford.
4. Katherine, the youngest daughter of Sir George Lewis, the solicitor. His wife Elizabeth was a friend of Ethel Smyth and Virginia's mother.

with a hammer, and Julian killed a don[1] with a review. A poor old creature called Thornley wrote a book: Julian reviewed it with such tremendous severity and truth that the Editor has had to resign, and the don to retire. The spirit of Sir Leslie [Stephen] is undoubtedly abroad again—all this speaking the truth, I mean.

Well, I shall write again and hope for news from Nessa in a day or two.

V.

Quentin Bell

2316: To V. Sackville-West   [52 *Tavistock Square, W.C.*1]

Monday [26 January 1931]

Could you come to tea on Thursday next 4.30? Lehmann wants to discuss some suggestions about your poem, wh. he thinks "superb".

Could you come early and take us to Persian show[2] first?

Could you then lavish some kindness on me?

Let me know

V.

Berg

2317: To William Plomer   52 *Tavistock Sqre., W.C.*1

26 Jan 1931

Dear William,

I think I once told you how I dont write letters and now I have gone and proved that fact—also, the more you write to me the silenter and the happier I become. Your book was the very thing—I've been stewing over the fire with the relics of this damned influenza, and I read nothing but the Welsh Squires[3] all one day. I have certain connections among them—the Vaughans are my cousins, and was therefore much amused to trace their oddities to the source. What a picture it gives me of a little crazy society, flourishing all by itself! Thanks very much. Here is a cutting about Hampson or Simpson[4] that may interest you. I think there must be something queer—I mean of the illegitimate bar sinister kind—behind the swimming mistress, but perhaps you know.

Let us hear when you're in London again.

Yours ever,

Virginia Woolf

Texas

1. Thomas Thornley, Fellow of Trinity Hall, Cambridge, and author of *Cambridge Memories*. He died in 1949 at the age of 93.
2. At the Royal Academy, Burlington House.
3. *The Fivefold Screen*, by William Plomer, published by the Hogarth Press in 1932.
4. See p. 270, note 1.

Wednesday 28th Jan. [1931]

Dearest Clive,

Only time for a short gossip. I daresay you've heard all my news too—about the Nation amalgamating, as they call it, with the Statesman;[1] and its not very interesting anyhow. Thats what we're talking about, however, if you want to know. And I've been hoarding this precious secret for 5 weeks—Sharpe, you see, is dead drunk—went to America and broke out again; and the Nation is dead, not drunk, but sober; and so they thought poor little [Edmund] Blunden was to be made an Oxford fellow, which he aint; anyhow they thought they could pension off Mrs Jones, and make a fresh start. The telephone rings perpetually: Kingsley Martin—d'you remember meeting him here in the days of the Strike [1926]?—is to be Editor; and the new paper, perhaps re-christened, is to come out late in February. Frankie [Birrell] and Raymond [Mortimer] are again like gulls on a rock clamouring for work; and I think Frankie is to be retained as film critic, but Raymond, being disagreeable in his views to Mr Ellis Roberts, who is anglo-catholic and literary editor, is alarmed.[2] I cant doubt though that they'll all fall on their feet and things go on much the same as before. Its amazing that at our age, after all our disillusionments, we can still prick up our ears, neigh, and gallop wildly about the field believing that the time has come for a new paper, better than any that has ever been before.

Young Mr Lehmann is now installed in the back room behind the W.C. at a small table with a plant which Leonard has given him on the window sill. Far from tending the Press and slipping the burden from our shoulders, we are of course rushed into all sorts of fresh projects, and I shall think myself lucky if I see the shores of France once in ten years—what with all the cursed realistic novels I have to read, and Blanche Knopf coming to tea tomorrow, because she's the wife of a publisher [Alfred A. Knopf]. I met Aldous Huxley last night at a concert—more of a windmill and a scarecrow, more highbrow, purblind and pallid and spavined than ever; but all the same, sympathetic to me, so I asked him to dinner, with his wife, whom I mix up with Ottoline's governess, wrongly.[3] Tonight Lord Passfield [Sidney Webb]

1. On 28 February 1931 the *Nation* and the *New Statesman* were amalgamated under the editorship of Kingsley Martin, who remained Editor until 1960. Clifford Sharp had been the Editor of the *New Statesman* from its foundation.
2. Soon after the amalgamation, Ellis Roberts was succeeded as literary editor by David Garnett, who was in turn succeeded shortly afterwards by Raymond Mortimer.
3. Maria Nys was a Belgian refugee, who had lived with the Morrells at Garsington. In 1919 she married Aldous Huxley. In the same year his brother Julian married a Swiss girl, Julliette Baillot, who was the governess-companion to Ottoline's daughter.

dines with us to discuss Kenya, and Kingsley Martin comes in afterwards—
his table manners are deplorable—harking back to the days when meat was
dear and two vegs. a luxury—to discuss the New Statesman. It blows a
black and bitter wind, Pinka is said to be trembling on the verge of heat;
the tobacconists young woman is bringing her black cocker round at 7 to
see if he could be mated with a red—not bitch, but what she calls "lady dog"
—that's about all; and I wish my poor brother-in-law were round the corner
for a little rational conversation.

No more now: I'm afraid this is very disconnected, but I have to rush
upstairs and get tea for Ethel Smyth.

V.

Quentin Bell

2319: To Molly MacCarthy   52 *Tavistock Sqre.* [*W.C.*1]

30th Jan. [1931]

Dearest Molly,

I was so annoyed yesterday only to catch a disturbed glimpse of you,
among all those motor cars, when I wanted a little peaceful conversation.
And now Vita says you've gone to live in Wiltshire.[1] I hope this is an
exaggeration—why should you live in Wiltshire, unless Wilson has given
you her folly for life, on condition that you write some more stories of
Fitzgerald[2]—which is the only reason that will satisfy me. Do go on, and
write the whole history of Ireland; but surely for that you will need the
British Museum, and then might drop in for a cup of tea.

I've had a long and no doubt exquisitely written letter from Logan[3]
about the collected works, but to my demand, when will you let us have the
first volume, he returns no answer. We have just taken on this last week a
young poet, John Lehmann, brother of Dusty Answer,[4] to be eventually
our partner, and the Press therefore far from dying or resting on its oars,
is now in midstream and must be fed with Desmond's books. I held them
out to Lehmann as a bait. So let me know when you can, if anything can be
announced. Two volumes of Portraits to begin with would be admirable:
and they must be illustrated.

1. Periodically the MacCarthys let their Chelsea house and returned to their cottage
   at Oare in Wiltshire, where one of their neighbours was Mona Wilson, the
   writer, who lived there with G. M. Young, the historian.
2. In 1930 Molly MacCarthy published *Fighting Fitzgerald and Other Papers*.
3. It is probable, given the context which follows, that Virginia wrote 'Logan'
   (Pearsall Smith) in error for 'Desmond' (MacCarthy). Desmond published
   Portraits I in 1931, but not with the Hogarth Press, although Virginia had been
   soliciting his books for many years.
4. The novel (1927) by Rosamond Lehmann.

There were too many people at the [Persian] Exhibition for my taste—
I occasionally caught sight of a small blue spark between old women's bodies
which I took to be a manuscript—that's about all. That is more or less what
happens in London; so perhaps you are wise to retire to Wiltshire, but
Sussex is a mere swamp, and the devils are putting up electric posts in the
middle of our view. Clive writes dismal letters from Zurich, where he is
being treated for his eyes, and asks me to ask his friends to write to him:
so do if you can, the address is,

Schwesternhaus vom Roten Kreuz, Zurich 7

Now I must return to my daily task, which is to read manuscripts—
masses and masses of manuscripts, with their authors screaming like gulls
for an answer. If they were only worse, or only better—as it is, I have to
plough on, hoping always that something will turn up.

yrs
V.

Mrs Michael MacCarthy

2320: To Ethel Smyth   [52 *Tavistock Square, W.C.*1]

[1 February 1931]

A declaration

Just to clear myself from being called a valetudinarian by Dame Ethel
Smyth: (as she may incline to after a talk on the telephone)—this is to testify
that I only saw the dr. by accident, she having come to look at Ls. ears;
that I scouted her suggestion of tuberculous trouble with ribald laughter;
that I refused to see a specialist; that I only take my temp. under coercion:
that in short I attach no importance to the matter whatsoever and only (I
think this is true) mentioned health on the telephone because dame Ethel
started the subject herself—So help me God.

V.W.

If I dont come tomorrow it will simply be that I think it more sensible, on
aesthetic grounds, to listen to only one musical masterpiece on the same day
—Nevertheless, I may look in for a time,[1] if I dont interrupt.

V.

Berg

1. At Lady Lewis's house in Portland Place, where Ethel was rehearsing *The
Prison*. Later Virginia went to a concert at Mrs Samuel Courtauld's house.

Sunday [1 February 1931]

Dear Dadie,

We shall be delighted to come (D.V.) on Saturday February 14th.[1]

Would you add to your goodness by taking two bedrooms at the Bull [Cambridge] for that night? We shall return on Sunday—to read and read and read worthless MSS.

No, John[2] terrifies me far too much for laughter at present.

Your
V

George Rylands

2322: To Margaret Llewelyn Davies
52 *Tavistock Square, W.C.1*

Typewritten
Sunday. Feb 1st [1931]

Dearest Margaret,

I have been meaning to write and thank you for your letter, but have been rather somnolent owing to the usual curse of influenza. Of course, of course, the introduction[3] was a gift (though as a matter of fact I was handsomely paid by the Yale Review.) But about royalties—I'm afraid they wont amount to more than a pound or two, but whatever they do amount to, (my share I mean,) please let me hand that over to you to spend on any thing acceptable to the Guild. They must want money for something or other, and I should only feel I was paying my due for the immense interest their letters gave me. But that can wait. Leonard has explained to you the reason of this most irritating delay. Ones clerks ought to be made of bone and rubber—not the human heart. It is devastating in an office. Children are bad enough, but broken engagements, divorces and so on are the very devil, as we used to find when we had Mrs Joad.[4] I'm very anxious to see that the book looks attractive—has a good bright binding of some sort. I'm writing to tell my American publishers, Harcourt Brace, about it.

By the way, when I came to read the proofs, I rather came round to your view that I made too much of the literary side of my interest; its partly a

1. For a performance of Purcell's *Faery Queen*.
2. John Lehmann had been recommended to the Woolfs by Rylands, who had himself been an assistant at the Hogarth Press for six months in 1924.
3. To *Life As We Have Known It*, edited by Margaret Llewelyn Davies.
4. Mrs C. E. M. Joad (Marjorie Thomson), 'wife' of C. E. M. Joad, the popular Professor of Philosophy, worked at the Hogarth Press, 1923-5.

habit, through writing reviews for so many years. I tried to change the tone of some of the sentences, to suggest a more human outlook, and also, I brought in a few cigarettes in Lilians ash tray[1]—do they matter? A little blue cloud of smoke seemed to me aesthetically desirable at that point. But the corrections were as usual done in a rush, and when I get my final proofs I will look at it carefully again. Perhaps we may meet and have a final revision. But lord, the rush of London—I sometimes long for nothing but Rodmell, even in this damp. This is the result, of not seeing you, but seeing without stopping overdressed American publishers wives [Mrs Knopf] with their eyelids picked out, so that one pencil of hair remains in the middle of the forehead. Have you ever seen that effect? It is one of perpetual surprise, and to me unpleasing.

Love to Lilian.

Virginia

Sussex

2323: To Vanessa Bell   52 *Tavistock Square, W.C.*1

Tuesday [3 February? 1931]

Here is the cheque for the table. Dirt cheap, I consider.

Would you take a commission to make tiles for the upstairs room at Monks House?

I dont know if you expect me tomorrow or not—late, about 5.30—Shall have had tea.

Cant ring up because you'll be engaged with Ethels nephew—no not nephew [*unidentified*]. But perhaps you'll let me hear.

Berg

2324: To Gwen Raverat   52 *Tavistock Sqre., W.C.*1

3rd Feb. 1931

My dear Gwen,

What an age since we met!—I dont even know your address, so must send this to the Keynes's.[2] This is only a dull business letter, to ask if you think that anything could now be done—since Mrs Brooke is dead—about Rupert's letters. I came across a copy of some of those to you and Jacques,

1. ". . . the ash-tray in which many cigarettes had come amiably to an end."
2. Gwen (*née* Darwin) was the widow of Jacques Raverat, the French painter, who died in 1925. During the last 1½ years of his life, Jacques and Virginia exchanged frequent and intimate letters. Maynard Keynes's brother Geoffrey was married to Margaret Darwin, Gwen's sister.

that you sent me and I rather think you said at the time that they must wait till Mrs Brooke was dead. It seems more and more idiotic that Eddy Marsh should be allowed to parade his hairdresser's block.[1] Let me know if you think anything can be done. A vile and repulsive book about him by a man called, I think, Maurice Brown,[2] an American, was sent to us the other day. But we refused to touch it—not the beautiful Brown who wrote to me 2 or 3 years ago, but another, an actor, I think.

I suppose you're never in London, and I suppose you're always busy, so I send this instead of meeting.

Is your new house nice, and the children—and painting—and Cambridge—and life altogether?

Yours ever,
Sussex   Virginia

2325: To Ethel Smyth   52 *T*.[*avistock*] *S*.[*quare, W.C.*1]
Friday [6 February 1931]

No we dont go this week, unless Sunday is fine, and we go for the day. But I rather hope Sunday won't be fine—I want to do nothing but write.

I'm rather ashamed—but have no time to explain—of my egotistic soliloquy—God knows what set me off—on what was true and what fiction. But I entirely trust to your perceptiveness.

And if only I'd not fired off like this, I had meant to enquire into ever so many questions about your sensations, what d'you feel at going to Edinburgh;[3] and so on; all lost now in my flood of egotism: And I'm so sleepy, I cant write; 6 hours talk on end last night.

Are you very very very tired? Not ill? Not about to collapse I hope?

I will keep Tuesday night—either here or in Br Sqre.[4] So no more. (but you can write to me all the same.)

E[thel]. (at Courthauld Concert) O Virginia, how ill you're looking!
M[ary Hutchinson]. (yesterday) O Virginia I havent seen you look so well for years!

Berg

1. *The Collected Poems of Rupert Brooke*, with a Memoir by Edward Marsh (1918) was reviewed by Virginia, who wrote at the time to Ka Cox: "I think it was one of the most repulsive biographies I've ever read. . . . He contrived to make the letters as superficial and affected as his own account of Rupert" (Volume II, Letter 959).
2. Maurice Browne's *Recollections of Rupert Brooke* was published in Chicago in 1927.
3. For the first performance of *The Prison*, sponsored by Donald Tovey and conducted by Ethel herself.
4. 38 Berkeley Square, Lady Rosebery's house.

7th Feb. 1931

Dearest Clive,

It suddenly strikes me on writing the date, that this is the 24th Anniversary of your wedding day—so next year we shall all be giving you silver shaving pots. What is the anniversary of my wedding day, I cant remember. Anyhow, this is a topic—anniversaries—I tend to avoid, in favour of gossip. For instance—you've doubtless heard all and more—how awkward —one cant go on grammatically—that—than—is to be known about Peter [Lucas] and his lady. Nessa will have told you about the affray outside the bedroom door.[1] Besides it only comes through Helen [Anrep], a dirty— I mean no offence—filter. My week has been, let me see, Eddy scratching like a dog on a mat, at a concert, scratching, pimply, queasy, querulous to a degree, as they say, all because he inherits Knole and cant write a play. Then he swears his novel, Simpson,[2] is a masterpiece, and when I say, 'Isn't that enough?' he rounds on me and tells me I know nothing of life. The truth is I cant take Buggerage seriously—now if it were a wench, a girl even out of a haberdasher's shop in Shepherds Market, I should be the first to pull a long face; but when it's Jimmy who's gone off with Tommie, irreverence seizes me, and if it were not that by turning to hide my smile I run into Koteliansky[3] that fervid Jew (this was at a concert) I should have turned to hide my smile.

Then to dine with Raymond where the talk was all about the Nation; about Mr [*name omitted*] who's got himself photographed in a state of more than copulation, and left it on a table and been blackmailed; about Rouse, the blazing car murderer and how he should be let off;[4] about the Nation, and again the Nation and again the Nation, until I said to myself, Is it female perversity, or do these young men think too much about money? Ask Clive, I said to myself, for anyhow, no one can accuse him of buggery. Then Christabel [McLaren]; who had asked me to a play which begins at 6 and ends at 11.30—an American play, where the actors speak their private thoughts, and their private thoughts are nonsense; and this nonsense lasts 7 hours;[5] so I didn't go, knowing what the private thoughts of Americans

1. See letter 2328.
2. Edward Sackville West's *Simpson*, about a children's nurse, was published in 1931.
3. S. S. Koteliansky, the Russian émigré, who had collaborated with Virginia on translations from Tolstoy and other Russian writers.
4. Alfred Arthur Rouse was condemned to death on 31 January for the murder of an unknown man, whom he wished to be identified as himself. The man's remains were found in Rouse's burnt-out car, but the evidence against him was circumstantial. In the condemned cell, Rouse confessed to the murder.
5. Eugene O'Neill's *Strange Interlude*, a play in nine acts.

are by instinct. Christabel asked tenderly, repeatedly, lowering and raising her lovely eyes, after you. There's no such sure road to popularity, I may tell you, as to go to Zürich, and I'm thinking of coming myself. Elly [Rendel] tells me I have a bug in my body; but it wouldn't be for the sake of the bug that I should come to Zürich. What I want is that people should talk of me with affection. And tonight we meet Aldous and Maria [Huxley]; and I think thats all, save a waste, a pother, a litter of people you wouldn't touch with a short stick. Molly has gone to Wilson's Folly—a castle built by Mona Wilson in a farmyard at Oare—to write 6 talks about life for the benefit of the incurable in hospitals. The first is devoted to the lunacy of Mary Lamb[1]—such is our life, and Lord, I could relish an evening with my brother in law.

V.

Quentin Bell

2327: To Lady Ottoline Morrell

52 *Tavistock Square, W.C.*1

Sunday [15 February 1931]

Dearest Ottoline,

I'm so sorry not to have written before. Like everybody, I've been having influenza, and though I'm alright again, I have had endless bores to see, who have been heaping up. Would one day, not this week, but the week after, suit you—the usual time between tea and dinner? Any day I think, except Monday.

Just back from the Fairy Queen at Cambridge and 48 hours conversation.

Yr

Texas

Virginia

2328: To Ethel Smyth   52 *T.[avistock]* S.[*quare, W.C.*1]

[16 February 1931]

Its so difficult to write, because,—well, after finishing a book, the mind bobs like a cork on the sea—I hate the feeling; I had forgotten the horror. I am irritable and melancholy and I doubt not, if you were here, egotistic. All the same, I have sympathy enough to think of the wind whistling through Edinburgh and you standing at a desk 6 hours a day; and the Prison emerging I hope; here an arch, there a column.[2]

1. Molly MacCarthy published these talks in *Handicaps* (1936). Mary Lamb, in a fit of insanity, killed her mother and was removed to a mental hospital, but eventually she was allowed to return home, where she collaborated with her brother, the essayist Charles Lamb, on *Tales from Shakespeare* (1807).
2. See p. 288, note 3.

No; you can't want letters when you're waving your hands over that chaos.

I am glad to think of the wig [Ethel's] anyhow. My word, its so bitter, so broken, so desolate here, all fractured, all inanimate; The Huxleys (Aldous) are dining here, and I cant summon my spirit to wait on my guests. What a vast inane—I mean, I'm fluttering like a leaf in a gale in some corridor or antechamber, outside life, outside the room; all because I've finished a book. And one must wash now.

But how are you? And are you verging on triumph or despair? Years and years ago we dined together and drank champagne. Yesterday I was at Cambridge hearing the Fairy Queen, oh and talking 10 hours at a stretch, and hearing that Don Peter [F. L. Lucas] has fallen in love with a married woman and come to blows with her husband outside the bedroom door. (I must see if the soda water and whisky have come). I have been driven like a yellow cat by a pack of dogs. Thats my state—friends, business, people ringing up. MSS. to read. I should like to see somebody sane, wearing white cuffs, somebody frightfully intent on whats said. Thats a quality of yours—attentiveness: you respect facts, if I said its 6; you wd. confirm this by looking at your watch. I daresay you're too tired to read any more. So I'll stop, because I feel these disturbances acutely—how many worlds we live in, and the incongruity of things, and why should this little wail (but there's affection in it and desire to see you) ever reach you, storm bound as you are, standing at a desk 6 hours a day, bidding the broken columns and the blue flowers arise, all orderly. I say, you must remember all your feelings and tell me. I shall soak drowsily and one day wake with a start and say thats what Ethel felt in February? And how are you? Any cold? Very tired?

Love
V.

Berg

2329: To Clive Bell   52 *Tavistock Sqre., W.C.*1

16th Feb. 1931

Dearest Clive,

I return your Valentine, but what a farce! Cold and gloom and sleet; no lovemaking in prospect; every nose nipped—my oldest friend, Sibyl Roskill, burnt to death;[1] three corpses on the road going to Cambridge,

---

1. Sybil (*née* Dilke) was born in 1879 and married John Roskill K.C. in 1901. The Dilkes had lived next door to the Stephens in Hyde Park Gate, Kensington, when Virginia was a child. Sybil Roskill and her maid were burnt to death in her London house.

three more in a field coming back from Rodmell—all the same we remain brisk, and have just been at Cambridge for the weekend.

I enjoyed myself more than I expected. The opera was to my taste: Dadie [Rylands] very charming: Richard [Braithwaite] full of argument about the universe: Julian full of violence and spirit and has written 70,000 words about Pope merely by way of preface: also there was a young Mrs Roger Clark whom I took for Helen Soutar [Julian's friend] and addressed accordingly; and old Bogey Harris,[1] highly preserved, in a corner—God knows why; and Alex and James [Strachey], and Morgan [Forster] and two South African lady doctors—in short Cambridge in its February festal mood, with the snow falling and a bell tolling for I don't know whom. From the little private gossip I had with Dadie I gather that Peter's [Lucas] affair is cooling off on her side; at least she won't do anything extreme; and so he looks round for another, so Dadie says; but Dadie is always apt to take a sardonic view of Peter in every capacity, why I dont know. Old Lytton is on the sofa in slippers, and we had an old time gossip about Madame du Deffand[2] which I find consoling, though I suspect that Lytton would rather be romancing with Mr Peter Morris [the painter] than with me.

Eddy's book [*Simpson*] is out and, I gather, a great success. Arnold Bennett, who has been dying but is now recovered,[3] whispered over the telephone that it must be declared a masterpiece—for my part, its too much like an Arnold Bennett to inflame me—the first chapters that is—later I'm told—an albino appears, and mystic taps on moth-eaten tapestries—Nessa however thinks well of it. Our Cardiff waiter, Simpson,[4] is also booming; and Leonard (forgive the disconnection, but I'm too cold to write) has just been to the Nation for the last time, to sign a copy book bound in full morocco which is being presented to Harold Wright by the Staff on his demise. Maynard has influenza; so has Desmond. Tonight Raymond and the Huxleys dine with us. Aldous is bringing out a play[5] and supervising Freda Lawrence—that is, trying to persuade her not to make love to the waiter, and not to buy a Rolls Royce, and not to sell all Lawrence's MSS. twice over to every publisher in London. The pressure of Lawrence being removed, she has sprung up like a cactus hedge, and all is prickly and precarious.

This is a sad jumbled letter, but if I dont send it I doubt that I shall

1. Henry Harris, a Trustee of the National Gallery and a well-known figure in London society. The Omega Workshop decorated a room in his house in Bedford Square.
2. On whom Lytton Strachey had written an essay in 1912.
3. Arnold Bennett died on 27 March 1931.
4. *Saturday Night at the Greyhound*, by John Hampson Simpson, was published in this month by the Hogarth Press.
5. *The World of Light*, Huxley's first play, was produced at the Royalty Theatre in March.

think of anything more to the point. The truth is that February is justly called killjoy and fillgrave; moreover, we are having electric fires installed—hence the racket is continuous, and one steps across the drawing room on a plank.

V.

Quentin Bell

2330: TO CLIVE BELL

Monks House [Rodmell, Sussex]

21st Feb. 1931

Dearest Clive,

I hear rumours that you are soon to be out of your prison [the Zurich eye hospital], and also that you can see a great deal better—both I hope are true. But perhaps there is still time for a letter. We are down here to see some electricians about putting in electric light; but of course they haven't come. No: but they have defaced the country with bare black poles at intervals, so I suppose they have done their best. Probably we shall be burnt down—as my oldest friend was there the other night, Sibyl Dilke. She married a man called Roskill, and had long gone out of my life; but we took walks in Kensington Gardens together, 35 years ago; and now she is black as a cinder. Aldous and Maria dined with us, and Raymond and Lyn [Lloyd Irvine] and our John [Lehmann]. Our John is panning out well, in his doghole behind the W.C. Lytton says the Lehmann's are middle class—you can tell it by their eyes, and their ancles [*sic*]—I forget which, nor do I know if there should be a c or a k in ankles. He—John—touches on a very odd world: the Barry Pains, A. A. Milnes, Mrs Hammersleys (she, too, had the top of her house burnt off the other night, but escaped). I gather they knew all the minor lights of 1900; and Lisa Lehmann who wrote drawing room melodies was an Aunt.[1]

Aldous astounds me—his energy, his modernity. Is it that he can't see anything that he has to see so much? Not content with touring Europe with Sullivan[2] to ask all great men of all countries what they think of God, science, the soul, the future and so on, he spends his week in London visiting docks, where with Maria's help he can just distinguish a tusk from a frozen bullock: and now is off on a tour of the Black Country, to visit works, to go down

1. Barry Pain (1864-1928) wrote humorous sketches; A. A. Milne's (1882-1956) most popular works were the Winnie the Pooh books for children; Violet Hammersley was a patron of Wilson Steer, the painter, and a friend of Duncan Grant and Logan Pearsall Smith; Elizabeth ('Liza') Lehmann (1862-1918) had a career as a soprano as well as a composer of song cycles.
2. J. N. W. Sullivan, the writer on scientific subjects.

mines: and then to Moscow, and then America. I am very envious in my heart. I should like to die with a complete map of the world in my head. But shall I ever see a naked savage? I doubt it. Your son Julian, who dropped in yesterday, says the sight of Duncan is odder far than any savage. I think by the way from what I gathered at Cambridge that he has a very good chance of a fellowship—how odd that is too. I mean, how time passes, and how the young improve upon us, for none of us were ever made fellows, and remained charming and amorous and adventurous like Julian into the bargain.

Arnold Bennett lies, it is said, like the picture of a dying fox in Uncle Remus,[1] staring straight at the ceiling and beating the air with his front paws as he tries to say "I met him in 1906". After an hour's effort he comes out with this momentous fact; but will live they say to write another fifty novels.

I have finished my book [*The Waves*]—yes—but it is a failure. Too difficult: too jerky: too inchoate altogether. But what's the point of writing if one doesn't make a fool of oneself? Anyhow I am left high and dry and can turn my mind to other people's books. Will Rothenstein has brought out his memoirs,[2] in which Vanessa, Stella and Virginia Stephen figure, most inaccurately, all in black, like Watts paintings, having tea in the basement, very beautiful, but shy, and only responding with freedom to Phil Burne-Jones and Arthur Studd.[3] Also there is my grandmother,[4] a violent old lady rapping the floor with a stick and descending to scold Will for his iniquitous portrait of her beautiful daughter, the stepmother [mother] of Mrs Bell and Mrs Woolf, who are now so well known. Do you think that all memoirs are as mendacious as this—Every fact I mean, all on one side? Lytton's little book of biographies is coming out,[5] and he wants to call it Lives in Aspic, but Carrington and Pippa forbid. And I am turning to Don Juan [Byron] and Aurora Leigh [Elizabeth Barrett Browning], together with all those vile memoirs, for which as you know, I have such a gluttonous appetite. Coles journey to France was a bitter disappointment however. I had promised to do it for the first number of the New Statesman and Nation, but had to cry off and do an article, in the form of a letter to you instead.[6] Raymond and Francis have both got jobs on it and both seem once more in high feather.

1. The American folk tales by Joel Chandler Harris (1848-1908).
2. *Men and Memories* was published in two volumes in 1931-32.
3. Philip Burne-Jones (1861-1926), the son of Sir Edward Burne-Jones, and also a painter; Arthur Peter Studd (1863-1919), the artist and collector.
4. Maria Jackson (*née* Pattle), 1818-92.
5. *Portraits in Miniature* (1931).
6. Virginia wanted to review the new edition, by F. G. Stokes (1931), of William Cole's *A Journal of My Journey to Paris* (1765). What she did write was *All About Books* (*New Statesman & Nation*, 28 February 1931), which begins with a quotation from a letter to her from Clive Bell.

On Tuesday I go to a party at Lady Rosebery's.[1] You may well ask why: but it is to celebrate the first performance [in Edinburgh] of that old maniac Ethel Smyth's masterpiece [*The Prison*]. She has cajoled Lady R. into giving a supper, at which fashion and art are to join hands. And Lady R. says Clive Bell is on her list, and he must come. So we may meet in Berkeley Sqre on Tuesday night at a gilt table with champagne leaning out of buckets.

And now, having seen a man catch a fish in the Ouse and the hunt in red coats since I wrote the first page, I must stop; and congratulate Roger on his show.[2] My word—the picture of Nessa[3]—Your wife by the way stayed at Tommies [Stephen Tomlin] party till 7 am and was universally acknowledged the beauty of the evening. Not that you'd think so from Roger's picture.

V.

Quentin Bell

2331: TO ROGER FRY   *Monks House, Rodmell*
                                               [Sussex]

Saturday 21st Feb. [1931]

My dear Roger,

I was very late in getting to your show owing to various horrors, but none the less I am going to lay my tribute at your feet. How fascinating it is! I felt all the elements of an absorbing novel laid before me. I could trace so many adventures and discoveries in your pictures, apart from their beauty as pictures—and some seemed to me surprising in their beauty—but then as you know I'm a partial and imperfect judge of that. What intrigued me and moved me to deep admiration was the perpetual adventure of your mind from one end of the room to the other. How you have managed to carry on this warfare, always striding ahead, never giving up or lying down and becoming inert and torpid and commonplace like other people, I cant imagine. That is what one realises from seeing the show as a whole, and as I say I found it enthralling to follow after you and try to see how you get from point to point. My only complaint is that there aren't more portraits—

1. Eva Isabel Bruce, the second wife of the 6th Earl Rosebery.
2. A retrospective show at the Cooling Galleries.
3. The present owner of this portrait of Vanessa by Roger Fry is Mrs Pamela Diamand, Fry's daughter. It was painted in 1915. Vanessa wrote to Clive Bell in February: "When I last went to his [Roger's] house I was horror-struck to find an enormous portrait of myself looking like a handsome but shapeless cook in a red evening dress painted about fifteen years ago . . . The show will be very trying, I expect. All sorts of things one hoped never to see again are being fished out."

the Carpenter[1] I thought magnificent—what a character monger you are! And I wish you had asked me to write a preface, but then it would have run to 6 volumes of small print.

My word, what a character you are!

And finally—could you and Helen Anrep dine next Thursday? We never meet, but I intend to make a despairing effort.

Yrs ever
V.W.

Sussex

2332: To Lady Ottoline Morrell

52 Tavistock Square, W.C.1

[25 February 1931]

Dearest Ottoline,

I was so sorry to put you off this evening; but Ethel Smyth insisted upon dragging me to her concert and then to an extraordinary party at Lady Rosebery's, so I could not sleep. So I am as heavy as an owl, and should be a load upon you. It was an incredible evening. But if you would let me come another day, I would refuse all parties.

Yr
Virginia

I do hope I did not put you out. I thought my head might clear up: instead it grew more and more cloudy.

Texas

2333: To Vanessa Bell

52 T.[avistock] S.[quare, W.C.1]

1st March [1931]

As I find I can easily contribute £30 this year to Angelica's clothes or whatever you like I send £15, and shall send the other £15 on September 1st. which is by my reckoning 6 months ahead.

Berg

1. Fry's full-length portrait (1894) of Edward Carpenter (1844-1929), the champion of love between men.

Typewritten
Monday [9 March 1931]

Well Ethel wheres your chapter on Vanity? Surely I might have that—we are never to meet again, I agree. But you have a pen—you have a purpose. Mine is gone utterly. Didnt I say I wanted solitude? What have I got? Oh Lady Oxford, Ottoline, all Leonards family dining, two or three parties, interviews with agents, with authors, the man come about the electric light, about the bell that dont ring—heres Roger, heres Clive, heres Miss Pearn[1] with a project, and Mr Simpson again. But no discourse from Ethel on Vanity. I sit under a pall of snow and think I could write one myself—the vanity of wishing to be left alone. In six years perhaps I may actually have three days to think in. Never mind. Write me your sane and sensible reflections on vanity.

Virginia

Berg

11th March 1931

I feel, no doubt wrongly, simply from your voice and what you say mysteriously about 'discipline' that I have annoyed?—no, not annoyed, but perhaps hurt you? Well, I'm so blind and deaf psychologically, that I have to put these, to most people certainties, as questions, and now, because I'm blind and deaf. I'm going to lay before you the reason of the misunderstanding, if there is one. I expect you to ridicule me, but I dont mind being ridiculed, if you understand me, as there is always the chance that you will understand.

It was the party.[2] I dont know when I have suffered more; and yet why did I suffer? and what did I suffer? Humiliation: that I had been dragged to that awful Exhibition of insincerity and inanity against my will (I used to be dragged by my half-brothers against my will—hence perhaps some latent sense of outrage) Then, that you liked the party—you who are uncompromising, truthful, vehement. "Ethel likes this sort of thing" I said, disillusion filled me: all belief fell off me. "And she has planned this, and worse still, subjected me to it. Gulfs separate us." And I felt betrayed—I who have spoken to you so freely of all my weaknesses—I to whom this chatter and clatter on top of any art, music, pictures, which I dont understand,—is an abomination. Oh then, the elderly butlers, peers, champagne

1. Nancy Pearn, the literary agent, of Pearn, Pollinger and Higham.
2. The party for Ethel Smyth at Lady Rosebery's on 24 February.

and sugared cakes! It seemed to me that you wantonly inflicted this indignity upon me for no reason, and that I was pinioned there and betrayed and made to smile at our damnation—I who was reeling and shocked, as I see now, (to excuse myself,) by my own struggle with The Waves—who had vainly perhaps but honestly tried to understand you, H.B. the Prison: there I was mocking and mowing, and you forced me to it and you didn't mind it. I went home therefore more jangled and dazed and out of touch with reality than I have been for years. I could not sleep. I took chloral. I spent the next day in a state of horror and disillusion. When you rang me up you seemed to guess at none of all this, and I felt that I could never approach you so as to touch you again. (And without exaggeration you dont know how I have honoured and respected you—come, oddly, to depend upon your sanity) So then I put off [Sibyl] Colefax and Ottoline and resolved to be quit of the posturing and insincerity and being hauled about and made to exhibit myself for ever.

This no doubt seems to you wantonly exaggerated to excuse a fit of temper. But it is not. I see of course that it is morbid, that it is through this even to me inexplicable susceptibility to some impressions suddenly that I approach madness and that end of a drainpipe with a gibbering old man. But this is me; and you cant know me and merely brush this aside and disregard it as a fit of temper. I dont attempt to rationalise; but I can now, after 2 weeks, see how selfish, cold, and indeed brutal I may have seemed to you, when in fact I felt more strongly about you and therefore about your betrayal of me to wolves and vultures than ever before. Excuse this; and continue whatever your scheme may be. I dont suppose I shall understand your explanation, if you give one, or you mine. But I venture it, trusting in your sanity as I do: and because of what I call my respect for you.

V.

Berg

2336: To V. Sackville-West   52 *Tavistock Square, W.C.*1

Thursday [12 March 1931]

Curse Clive! What a tatler he is! I was sworn by Nessa to tell no one of her parties,[1] and he tells everyone. Oh I had meant to ask you to dine. And now Clive has. You see its a question of room—one cant tell people she's in every week. But you—Oh yes—*you* You're all right.

I am jealous of Elena Richmond.[2] Did she say she loved me? Years ago, pared down, with her head held high, she was divine. Since then, her poor dear wits have sunk in the oil and gone out. But still I love her.

1. Vanessa was reviving her Thursday evening parties in Bloomsbury.
2. The wife of Bruce Richmond, Editor of the *TLS*.

Oh and I've talked so much—so much too much—and I have to go to Lady Cunards: and then Lord David [Cecil] and then George Duckworth and then—and then.

Honey, tell me when you're coming I want to sink into your arms and feel the festival and the firelight. (This is a line from an old description of you I've just read [in *Orlando*].) Write.

V.

Love to Harold.

Berg

2337: To Lady Ottoline Morrell

52 *Tavistock Square, W.C.*1

Friday [13 March 1931?]

Dearest Ottoline

I can't come today, but could tomorrow, Saturday, about 5 if that suited you. I didn't come last week being in a rage with the world—Lady Cunard etc etc. and so shut myself up.

How do you manage not to hate everyone?

But I don't hate you—its this chatter-chatter.

Yrs Virginia

Texas

2338: To George Rylands   52 *Tavistock Square, W.C.*1

Friday 13th March [1931]

My dear Dadie,

Of course I would have written, instantly, to thank you for all the million delights—I enjoyed myself hugely [at Cambridge]—but I have been told that no one writes a Collins now—indeed they dont. I never have even a postcard written to me—So not wishing to be out of date, I curbed my natural impulse, and bit my tongue. Thats just as well, seeing that I can hardly form my letters anymore.

'Yes,' said Leonard, as we got into the car to drive home, 'thats the best weekend we've spent for ever so long.'

'And how fond I am of Dadie!' I said.

'You've always had a tenderness for Dadie' said Leonard. And then, as if to rebuke my effusion, the ballracing burst and we limped back at 20 miles an hour, in danger of losing a wheel.

V.

George Rylands

2339: To Ethel Smyth   *Monks House, Rodmell*
                                              [Sussex]

22nd March 1931

Vanessa says she has chosen Thursday next for the supper party.—
What time I dont know, nor what company. But I hand on the message
as I was bid.

I thought I should feel in the mood for letter writing between tea and
dinner, after a walk over the downs. But I have wasted the time reading a
manuscript—the slow sickliness of which, falling on me drop by drop, has
completely extinguished my love of words. And I have at least six more to
read. When you analyse my moods, make allowance for the pervasion of
bad fiction or do I mean perversion?

I dont think—though I've left your letter in London—you made out your
case against me as a critic. After all, you never liked my books till you liked
me: then if I'm too tolerant of Vita's fiction because I know her, why do
I rate her poetry (as you say) too low, since I know her? And again, I'm
only criticising the early letters of HB. which you yourself admit were the
product of isolated and petrified days. As for your letters in T and T and
New Statesman[1]—no: I think you would carry more conviction if you let
the Turners turn in silence. Any answer, any explanation, any refutation
weakens one's case—so I feel, and so I act; but I may be wrong. You say
you dont read criticism, and then you reply to it—on general grounds I
admit, but any acknowledgement of what you despise seems a tribute to the
despicable. There! there's my perversity for you again; and I daresay as you
always point out, whats well enough for a writer, doesn't apply to a musician.

I have been dipping, down here, into a life of Alice Meynell[2]—the lady
who wore Jaeger, didn't you say, in her bath, and one of her letters remarks
that she went to Ethel Smyth's new opera, which was a great success, and
then to a brilliant party at Mrs Hunter's.[3] I at once long to be there—with
magnificent inconsistency. O you asked about my party—I've no room, or
I wd. repeat a little talk which oddly proved the violence and incompre-
hensibility of my moods. I had given a young man a horrid shock, it seems—
and he, being rational, read into it all kinds of profound emotions on my

1. In the *New Statesman* of 7 March W. J. Turner, their music-critic, wrote:
   'Both Ethel Smyth and Henry Brewster have made brave attempts at mediocrity,
   but both have failed without attaining that bottomness which is completely
   diverting.' Ethel replied to this in two articles in *Time and Tide* (21 March and
   4 April), saying in the first, 'I never study English criticism of my work . . .
   having passed my life in hoeing a particularly lonely furrow', and in the second:
   'There are some things that should not be taken lying down . . . I want other
   women, and especially those who ply in my trade, the hardest of all for a woman
   in a man-run world, to realise they are not alone on the battlefield.'
2. *Alice Meynell: A Memoir* (1929), by her daughter Viola Meynell.
3. Mary Hunter, Ethel's sister.

part—all I had felt was a violent sweep of anger at being made to talk at luncheon when I wanted, with a passion no one can understand, to eat my mutton in silence. And then my party was spoilt rather, by various queer discomforts at what people said. I'm being bored to death by my London articles[1]—pure brilliant description—six of them—and not a thought for fear of clouding the brilliancy: and I have had to go all over the Thames, port of London, in a launch, with the Persian Ambassador[2]—but that I liked—I dont like facts, though.

V.

Berg

2340: To Helen McAfee   52 *Tavistock Square, W.C.*1

Typewritten
25th March 1931

Dear Miss McAfee,

Many thanks for your cable about my article on Mrs Browning.[3] I have now arranged that it shall appear here [in *TLS*] after July 1st. I will therefore send you the copy so as to reach you by May 10th which I think you told me was the date necessary for your summer number. I have not quite finished it, but think that it will run to about 4000 words. I hope this will be all right. It is really a study of Aurora Leigh, which I read by chance with great interest for the first time the other day.

We are starting next week for a little motor tour in France, but shall be back early in May. Is there any chance that you will be coming over this summer?

With kind regards from us both,

Yours very sincerely
Yale University   Virginia Woolf

2341: To Ethel Smyth   52 *Tavistock Sqre.* [*W.C.*1]

Sunday [29 March 1931]

Just back from the [Sidney] Webbs; and left rather in a fluster, though I enjoyed it—hence can't write a letter. I dont remember saying I wanted a

1. A series of five essays on 'The London Scene', published in *Good Housekeeping* from December 1931 to October 1932. The subjects were: The Docks, Oxford Street, 'Great Men's Houses', Abbeys and Cathedrals, and the House of Commons.
2. On 20 March Virginia went with Leonard, Vita and a party organised by the Port of London Authority, to visit the Docks. The launch went as far as Tilbury, and the party lunched with the P.L.A.
3. *Aurora Leigh* (*Yale Review*, June 1931).

301

violent letter—though its true I was feeling violent—any letter: you know my tastes. Why did I feel violent, after the [Rosebery] party? It would be amusing to see how far you can make out, with your insight, the various states of mind which led me, on coming home, to say to L:—"If you weren't here, I should kill myself—so much do I suffer." (I flatter myself you guessed nothing). I wonder how jealous I should be if you preferred Vanessa to me? Or what I should feel? I wonder what new light was thrown on my personality, and why it was disgusting? I wonder how the group, as a group, if it seemed to you a group, struck you?

I wonder—but whats the use of wondering? because I dont see how I'm to get an answer. I've got to get in House of Commons and Lords before Thursday,[1] and various people; so that I dont see at the moment any prospect of a quiet time for talk—only for talk perpetually cut up by people opening the door. But should the hubbub clear, I'll telephone on the chance.

Yr V.

Berg

2342: To Ethel Smyth   52 *Tavistock Sqre.* [*W.C.*1]

1st April (fools day) [1931]

Well Ethel you are a clever woman, a novelist wasted if ever there was one, and I could write pages in praise of your gifts if I could write at all. But that delightful art I shall not attempt till I sail out of this flotsam and jetsam of misery—ordering groceries I mean, tearing up bills, and trying to find lost manuscripts—into the green haven where I live, solitary, praise be to the Lord, in my sitting room, looking over the marsh. Among odds and ends stuck behind boxes I find these letters which I think you wanted sent. The woman Holtby[2] doesn't altogether attract me on paper, but I take your word for it she is not quite so indiscriminate as she seems.

Where's the bill for the Wig?[3] Write me long letters. In the country—they unfurl like flowers in water. The worst of my suffering is that its half the scratching of an eczematic dog. Little things people say; nods and hints: these stick in my pelt; and not the arrows always of destiny. No: what you give me is protection, so far as I am capable of it. I look at you and (being blind to most things except violent impressions) think if Ethel can be so downright and plainspoken and on the spot, I need not fear instant dismemberment by wild horses. Its the child crying for the nurses hand in the dark. You do it by being so uninhibited: so magnificently unself-conscious.

1. To obtain material for her article *This Is the House of Commons* (*Good House-keeping*, October 1932).
2. Winifred Holtby (1898-1935), the novelist, who published the first full-length study of Virginia (*Virginia Woolf*, 1932).
3. Perhaps Virginia's present for Ethel's birthday on 23 April. She would be 73.

This is what people pay £20 a sitting to get from Psycho-analysts—liberation from their own egotism. Never mind now—here's Vita coming like a ship in full sail. I think you're right—we all cry for nurses hand.

V.

Let me know what happens, or has happened, to Mrs Hunter [Ethel's sister] or Elizabeth [Williamson].

Berg

2343: To Ethel Smyth   *Monks House* [*Rodmell, Sussex*]

7th April [1931]

Your letter just come, with a great bundle, from London. We go back—didn't I explain our plans?—on Thursday. But Ethel dear, are you really ill? Why does the dr: prescribe bed for your ears? I am (in spite of the ossified and rigid heart to which you allude) anxious to know the truth; and more annoyed than you, the woman who takes me for a snake, would think likely. Why, didn't I lie awake last night calming myself out of some momentary fear by inventing your reasons for not being afraid?—And I wrote you a long letter by the way, which was all on the theme of the absurd and irrational happiness of our lives—yes, even poor Leonard, whose breast I pierce daily with hot steel, is divinely happy here; we giggle and joke, and go and poke at roots and plan beds of nasturtium; and altogether, life is a childish happy affair—no reason for happiness, dear me no: and therefore one never talks of it, I suppose: but only of the other state which can be made to sound reasonable. "I'm the happiest woman in England" I said to Leonard yesterday, for no reason, except that we had hot rolls for breakfast and the cat had eaten the chicken. But also the most egotistical—no I think, with all due respect, Ethel's that. Lord, Ethel, did you think I was ever so blind as to say that you, of all people, had conquered egotism? It is only that you ride it so magnificently that one doesn't care if its egotism or altruism—its your uncautiousness I envy; not your selflessness.

Forgive this drivvle. I've been a long walk, have had Nessa Clive and Angelica to tea, and the loudspeaker is pouring forth Wagner from Paris. His rhythm destroys my rhythm; yes, thats a true observation. All writing is nothing but putting words on the backs of rhythm. If they fall off the rhythm one's done—But write I must this evening, because all tomorrow I must be toiling to finish an article on Gosse,[1] whom I hope to hit off

1. Review of *The Life and Letters of Sir Edmund Gosse*, by Evan Charteris (*Fortnightly Review*, 1 June 1931).

303

smartly, without malice, but without much love either—for he was a crafty, worldly, prim, astute little beast—tomorrow. I've written and written—so many articles—8 to be exact. Five on London; one on Mrs Browning;[1] one on Lockhart;[2] one on Gosse; and all have to be sand papered, made to fit, smoothed, pressed, curled, and sent off before we go. We go on the 16th—and dear me, how glad I shall be to wake up in France and not write. Think of being free from 10 to one to sit and look out of the window!

But when shall I see you? You'll be surprised to hear that I'm in a mood when I should like to hear the particular accent you put on Vir-gin-ia! Shall I come down to Woking one day? Shall we go on with our disquisition? I like this feeling that we are in the middle of a tremendous argument—no, discussion: its not 'seeing' Ethel; its going on with what we were saying last week—About the Prison—about women's disabilities; about HB; about death; garters,—Oh and Lord I was forgetting The Wig. Here is a cheque: fill it up: I trust you not to increase the sum; not to pay for an extra fine Lombard wig instead of dog's hair British, which I expect yours to be. I know all about wigs: the best are plucked from the centre mesh of the hair of Italian peasants: the worst come from China—the cheap coarse wigs you see in the pit of provincial theatres, or in Whitechapel on Sundays. Yours, I should say, is a middle class wig; plucked very likely in Croydon from a butcher's daughter. So pay it, please; And that reminds me of your terrific family doings—what a set you are to be sure! I envy you your family temperament—so rich, so fruity, so high blooded, and fox hunting. Mrs H[unter]. rigid as she is—she always looks to me to move all in a piece as Sir Thomas Browne said the elephants did—is superbly sympathetic as a discredited and ruined woman. And whats happening to Elizabeth [Williamson]? What farm? Anything better than Connaught Sqre. I should imagine. I return all letters instantly—what a woman of business and character—what a soldiers daughter I'm becoming! Dr Gordon I dont understand, but credit her with good intentions. All right; I'll widen my mind and see if it cant embrace the urgent necessity and rightness of your proceedings re women in orchestras etc. I never said you were obsessed; all I ever said was that I hate all forms of principle. Whats the good of saying This is true, when nothing is true, except that some sounds are nicer than others and some shapes? No views are true. This is said, you'll see, to annoy a valiant woman turning to a lobster in bed. Do you grow whiskers to match?—those long jointed whiskers that the Cornish lobsters used to have, and I to break off, in the kitchen, as a child? I hope so—six on each side of your nose, bright red and very bristly like a cavalry officer's moustache.

Thank God, Wagner has stopped murmuring among the forest leaves,

1. See p. 301, note 1, and p. 301, note 3.
2. Review of *Lockhart's Criticism* (*TLS*, 23 April 1931).

and I'm my own mistress again; but dare not start another page, in this finicky little hand (I'm writing with the only pen, a gold one, slippery and false and fickle as Edmund Gosse—) so must stop; though I've millions of things to say—warmhearted, passionate things, things that bubble and squeak; and bleed red blood. By the way, why do you say and think I'm heartless? Why, Ethel, why? when I'm only anxious to know how you are, and to—there's no room to say what.

V.

No big envelopes, so the soldiers daughter (thats me) must wait, reluctantly and impatiently, till tomorrow; for this most important, indeed urgent letter, must catch the 11.10 sharp.

Berg

2344: To Beatrice Webb

Monks House, Rodmell,
Lewes [Sussex]

Typewritten
8th April 1931

Dear Mrs Webb,

I would have written before, but waited for Leonard to have read your chapter of autobiography, and have been vainly trying to go into Lewes and send it back by registered post.

We are both agreed that it is extremely interesting, and that it would be a great pity to cut any of the diary.[1] We feel that the reality that the diary gives is better than any more general account could be. I was extremely interested and amused throughout, and this is a good test, as few people can know less about Trade Unions than I do. We only wish you could write it straight off, as your next book, so much do we want to see how your story with its most interesting commentary develops.

We enjoyed our Sunday with you and Mr Webb so much. I wanted to tell you, but was too shy, how much I was pleased by your views upon the possible justification of suicide. Having made the attempt myself [in 1913], from the best of motives as I thought—not to be a burden on my husband—the conventional accusation of cowardice and sin has always rather rankled. So I was glad of what you said.

1. Beatrice Webb had probably sent Virginia and Leonard part of the first draft of her second volume of autobiography, *Our Partnership*, which includes many extracts from her daily diary, woven into a narrative framework. It was not published until 1948, after her death.

I hope to send the MS. and the Russian diary,[1] which is very interesting, tomorrow, when we go back to London.

Yours very sincerely,

The British Library of Political Science,   Virginia Woolf

University of London

2345: To V. Sackville-West   52 *Tavistock Square, W.C.*1

Thursday [9 April 1931]

Just a line, as my aunts used to say; we're back here till Thursday, and shall I see you, and if so when? Because the telephone rings and rings and my days are nibbled from me by rats—Eddy for one. Lord, how lovely today was; how hateful this blasted black town is! All I can do is to hop up and down on my perch like a parrot till Thursday; but to see you would be to me what—is it sugar or hemp or worms?—would be to a parrot.

Did I tell you that I heard from Bruce Richmond that Percy Lubbocks life is a burden to him because of his Sibyl's fandangoes—cant sit and write without a thump on the ceiling from Sibyl, who wants a hot water bottle or an air cushion. No more work in this world from Percy: and thats your doing.[2] I've written so many articles and so bad—Gosse the last, about whom I've been candid and caustic. Lord what a letter to Robbie Ross.[3] Did you read it? How cold cautious and clammy—like the writhing of a fat worm, red, shiny—disgusting: yet Harold likes him—Gosse, I mean.

Yr

Berg   V.

2346: To Ethel Smyth   52 *Tavistock Sqre.* [*W.C.*1]

April 9th 1931

Well Ethel dear, I suppose I must fulfil my duty as a general's daughter and go and find a big envelope for your letter (surely, though, E[lizabeth Williamson]'s: letter, in a thick envelope was returned?) What a bore it

1. The 'Russian diary' was almost certainly that of H. D. Harben, the wealthy Fabian who had financed Christabel Pankhurst and the early *Daily Herald*. He had been in Russia in 1930, and lent his diary to the Webbs in anticipation of their own visit there in May 1932.
2. Lady Sibyl married Percy Lubbock after she divorced her husband Geoffrey Scott in 1927 because of his love for Vita.
3. Robert Ross (1869-1918). Born a Canadian, he became a journalist, art dealer and writer. He was literary executor to Oscar Wilde, and when the scandal about his friend broke, he received a letter from Gosse which Virginia thought cowardly. See her review of *The Life and Letters of Sir Edmund Gosse* (*Fortnightly Review*, 1 June 1931, reprinted in *The Moment and Other Essays*, 1947).

must be, really being a general's daughter, and always getting envelopes, catching trains, answering letters and all the rest!

No particular news has accumulated since I wrote—on my knee, with a gold pen. It was a divine day yesterday—O how happy we were!—mildly sauntering down to the river, and protecting Pinka's chastity, now in bloom, from Botten's yellow cur. And then again, how happy I was to finish Gosse (provisionally) this morning—the last of the lot: but unhappy to pack and come home and find, among a welter of trash no letter from a lady that lies in bed at Bath. No she dont: she drives in a car to stay with friends. She drinks champagne with retired guards officers. She sees the Severn—what was your brilliant phrase—like a mad King's white hair?—No—thats mine. And I have never seen the Severn.

Do you really like Vanessa much better than you like me? We argue about it. She thinks its on the cards, because she thinks you and she have, what is called, 'much in common' And I have not that faculty. Please wire by return.

I'm glad you dislike Osbert's book:[1] so do I. All foliage and no filberts. I'm alone tonight—hence this erratic style. I'm rather used up in the brain—hence this style. Writing articles is like tying one's brain up in neat brown paper parcels. O to fly free in fiction once more!—and then I shall cry, O to tie parcels once more!—Such is life—a see-saw—a switch back. Once I get moralising I'm as good as you any day. Three people have rung up in 2 hours, and I have made 2 engagements. If I could linger out my days in the fields, sometimes driving through a country town and buying a pocket knife at the ironmongers, my moods would flatten out in one long roll of calm. Should you like me, all calm? On Thursday we go to France for 2 weeks, motoring. and then here for what remains of the summer—And shall I see you? What shall you be doing? Writing music? Have you lit on a theme? What response have your T and T [*Time and Tide*] articles had?[2] Is the bone now gnawed? Well Ethel dear this is only by way of good night —last Post, I suppose they call it in military circles, like yours. About your whiskers and your wig—do tell me. And—whats the ending you so much like—lots—no tons of love. Well then, tons of love. (I dont like your style in endings—but cant be helped)

V.

From a French article Le Style de V. Woolf dans Mrs Dalloway.

La ponctuation ne lui est pas, comme à la plupart des écrivains, un moyen d'éviter d'essoufler son lecteur, elle ne lui est jamais un moyen de faire passer un laideur, une gaucherie, elle lui est moins encore un artifice pour parer à une faiblesse de pensée ou d'impression, elle n'est jamais un signe

---

1. *Collected Satires and Poems* (1931), by Osbert Sitwell.
2. See p. 300, note 1.

négatif, elle est un signe positif, et les signes de ponctuation sont à la phrase de V. Woolf ce que les gestes sont à la parole, ils la presisent, l'enrichissent. So there.

Berg

2347: To Quentin Bell   52 *Tavistock Square, W.C.*1

Typewritten
11th April 1931

Dearest Quentin,

I wrote you a most brilliant letter—perhaps the most brilliant I have ever written—full of scandal, confidences, self reproach, remorse, revelation, together with character sketches of Lady Oxford, Ethel Smyth, President Wilson and others; but, being unable to find your address, never sent it, have now lost it, and must—since its the only way of drawing you, prince of letter writers as I think of you, write another. Also, my letter contained full instructions for meeting me in Italy. I was to arrive in May. Now, curse the Hogarth Press, curse literature, curse Lehmann, curse life—I shall get no further than France, where we go on Thursday. But only for one beggarly fortnight; so write here. And Nessa starts for Italy. Oh I could shoot her dead for having my holiday. Still, they say France is very lovely— La Rochelle, Brantome, I dont know where. We are taking the Singer; and by way of trial, drove to Kew today, got as far as the Euston Road, broke down, collected the police, had to send for an ambulance, and were towed to the garage, where a piece of hair, coiled into innumerable inter-lineations, was removed from the auto-vac. That was all. But no Kew.

Well, dearest Quentin, what about your life? I hear vaguely of Americans. I was ravished by the story of the dead dog; I long for more. But you will want our news. Julian, Helen [Soutar], Barbara [Hutchinson] and so on. I gave the young couple—Julian and Barbara—a little dinner. Dear old Julian looked like a man taken from digging out a badger—all earth and clouts; Barbara as clean and cut as a Shepherdess; but they got on very well, and if I have to choose a niece, I choose half of Barbara rather than twenty six dozen Helens. I met [Edward] Playfair the other day; and he implored me to use all my influence—but aunts have no influence with their nephews I said—to detach Helen; because they say she makes their lives one long labour and toil. There she is, cant be got rid of; worse still, when alone Julian says My God what a lovely siren Helen is, and gives a catalogue of her virtues, then of her beauties, then of her favours, which they say, lasts three hours; and is only psychologically interesting as a proof of what the heart can do. He has her this moment in Tommies [Stephen Tomlin] cottage. On this lovely spring evening, they are hearing lambs bleat together.

And one can only be young once; and love not so many times. Take warning.

I have had to work absolutely like a devil for two months. I have finished the worst novel in the language [*The Waves*]; I have written ten articles. The writing I like; its the winding up of the affair I detest—cutting out, putting in, commas and so on. Duncan is in the same state, finishing 28 pictures for his show,[1] after which he leaves the country. And Clive leaves the country. Peter Lucas was here yesterday, but timed his visit with Pernel Strachey[2] so that, as they sat each other out, I heard only hints of his sorrows; but Alan[3] is behaving like a young man in Byron a hundred years ago. Happily Peter has the muse for his wife; and is writing an epic about Ariadne [1932]. When we write so seldom there are too many facts to be got in. I hate facts. I do not know how to arrange them.

I am taking Leonard to a modern comedy, by Maugham.[4] Aldous has had a great success with his play.[5] He bids fair to be the great man in succession to Arnold Bennett. Bennett is dead, and I had the pleasure of being almost the last to talk to him before he drank a glass of water swarming with typhoid germs. 'Then' he said, as he got up to go, 'men will say one morning 'He's dead'. I, thinking this referred to his works, said 'Oh you mean your books?' 'No no no—myself'. So we parted, and though his books are dead as mutton, he had a relish for life—wore waistcoats of incredible beauty—so I'm sorry because I myself dont want to drink typhoid from a tumbler yet.

Are you writing? Now thats your gift. The brush is merely the tail end of you. Angelica is a whirlwind of beauty and destruction. She sweeps all before her—we are dead leaves and old tin cans when she comes our way. I rather think she'll marry the Prince of Wales. Lord David is not engaged to Rachel,[6] and I doubt that he's a man [to] have mistresses. No more room.

Virginia

Quentin Bell

2348: To Vanessa Bell   52 *Tavistock Sqre.* [*W.C.*1]

Sunday [12 April 1931]

Dear Dolphin;

Many thanks for the cheque—father's books do remarkably well, I think, considering it will be his centenary next year.

1. *Recent Paintings by Duncan Grant.* Cooling Galleries, June-July 1931.
2. Pernel was Lytton's elder sister. In 1923 she became Principal of Newnham College, Cambridge, where she remained until 1941.
3. Alan Clutton-Brock, for many years art-critic of *The Times.*
4. *The Circle* by Somerset Maugham, at the Vaudeville Theatre.
5. *A World of Light* closed after a short run.
6. David Cecil did marry Rachel MacCarthy, in October 1932.

Life has been full of telephones—Eddy the first moment we arrived; then Pernel [Strachey] and Peter [Lucas] in person, simultaneously, so that I couldn't gossip with Pernel, nor hear from Peter the secret of his love, which obviously pressed, as the Greeks say, like a great ox on his tongue. I shall be glad to get off on Thursday, though if we shall ever move beyond Dieppe seems doubtful. Both yesterday and today we tried to get to Kew, and yesterday broke down in Judd Street and had to be towed home, and today in Paddington. It's said to be a piece of dirt in the auto-vac:; and they hauled out a thing like a large burr, but apparently there is more to come. Pinka's hair it looks like.

I am enclosing a cheque for £20, as a contribution to Angelica's Cornish tour, which will be more costly than you think: also I find I am absurdly rich through American articles, and the Press accounts L. says are very satisfactory. Next year I hope to be penniless; when we pay John and can leave all to him.

If I get through my corrections of that awful dull bad book The Waves, or Moths, in May I think I may take a little flight in June; but I suppose you'll be no longer in Rome then—The heart of my desire; and if L. wont come, I dont suppose I shall.

We shall be back on the 2nd—Saturday. So if you are in London let us dine together.

If you'll let me have your addresses I will write.

We shall have tea at Monks House on Thursday, but I dont suppose you will want to come over. But do if you can. 4' o'clock. And as I say, I suspect we shall stop permanently outside Newhaven.

V.

Would you let me know when I can get your and Duncans new chair stuffs?

Berg

2349: TO JONATHAN CAPE   52 *Tavistock Square, W.C.*1

Typewritten
April 12th 1931

Dear Mr Cape,
    I am much interested to hear that you think of reprinting some of Miss Thackerays novels.[1] I have a great admiration for the early ones, and would like, if I could, to write an introduction to one of them. Could you tell me

1. Anne Isabella Thackeray, Lady Ritchie (1837-1919) was the elder daughter of W. M. Thackeray and herself a writer of novels, of which the best known are *The Village on the Cliff* (1867) and *Old Kensington* (1873). Thackeray's younger daughter, Harriet Marian, was Virginia's father's first wife.

when it would be necessary to have the manuscript?—I am very much engaged at present, and should have to fit it in. Also, might I assume that I am free to publish the introduction simultaneously in America?

Yours sincerely
Virginia Woolf

Jonathan Cape Ltd

2350: To Hugh Walpole   52 *Tavistock Square, W.C.*1

Typewritten
Sunday April 12th 1931

My dear Hugh,

—forgive this typing, but my hand staggers like a drunken washer-woman after writing innumerable articles, so that is in kindness to you— We are just back from Rodmell, and just off, motoring, to France. But I was very glad to get your letter. And I dont suppose we shall be away more than two or three weeks; so please come for your usual tea—why not dinner—in May. Lord, though, how hopeless seeing people in May is. If we had any sense we should all live in Cumberland.

The girl poet [Joan Easdale] is my discovery—she sent me piles of dirty copy books written in a scrawl without any spelling; but I was taken aback to find, as I thought some real merit. How far it will go, I dont feel sure. It may be a kind of infantile phosphorescence; and she is a country flapper, living in Kent, and might be from behind a counter. Very odd. I'm glad you're recommending them. The Waves is done; but a failure; however I enjoyed it; and have some others brewing, which is all I ask of life. Yes, Arnold's death was queer.[1] I never knew him, as you did, I suppose, but had two hours tête à tête at a party just before he drank the fatal tumbler; and we abused each other as usual, and as usual I liked him; and was bored; and yet found him impressive, as a presence. You must explain his character to me. I implore you, dont be buried by the Bishop of Wakefield. We went home and drew up instruction for silent dispersal in a field. Look how my type is running, so good bye.

Yrs ever
V.W.

Texas

2351: To Jonathan Cape   52 *Tavistock Square, W.C.*1

Typewritten
14th April 1931

Dear Mr Cape,

I am afraid that I could not possibly write the introduction within six

1. Arnold Bennett died of typhoid contracted during a holiday in France.

weeks. I am just going abroad for a holiday, and when I come back I expect to be very busy for some time. I thought from what you said that the books were not to be published for some months. As it is, I am sure that it would be better for you to get somebody else to write the introduction; as it would be a great pity that the publication should be delayed.

I shall hope to write about the books when they are published, and I much look forward to seeing them. Many thanks for the suggestion.

Yours sincerely
Virginia Woolf

Jonathan Cape Ltd

2352: To Ethel Smyth   52 *T[avistock] S.[quare, W.C.1]*

Wednesday April 15th 1931

Well Ethel dear, no greater proof could there be of my devotion than that I should atttempt at the present moment to write a letter and copy out, with complete accuracy, a list of addresses. However it will be one of my joys to go to the Post and find a packet from you. I shall study your character with a care and space that I have never yet given it, over my bottle of wine after the days adventures, Anything may result. You will be under the scrutiny of an idle traveller, removed from life—oh thank God, removed from life. I am putting in a frigidaire, having walls distempered, sending mattresses to be re-made, cleaning covers, directing electricians—I—who am a soldiers daughter only with the effort of an elephant blowing soap bubbles. The articles swarm round me. My head is a hive of words that wont settle. I scratch and correct. Enraged, and idiotic editors go on demanding Gosse at once, Browning instantly. Of course, as you know, I put money far above friendship; and shall despatch this all by tomorrow. Then I have to buy shoes, and my shop suddenly declares the human foot has broadened, and no longer make my fitting. Why is it broadened? An open air life they say. I have also been listening to two love lorn young men[1]: they caterwaul— with an egotism that, if I were a feminist, would throw great light on the history of the sexes—such complete self absorption: such entire belief that a woman has nothing to do but listen. Then Murry—the one vile man I have ever known—has written a book about D. H. Lawrence, making out that he is Judas and Lawrence, Christ.[2] What do you think? You who know the characters in question? These I say are some of the little pellets that sting my hide at the moment and make me think of a table before an Inn at La Rochelle where all the boats have green and purple sails as a heaven scarcely

1. F. L. Lucas, and possibly Alan Clutton-Brock.
2. *Son of Woman* (1931), by John Middleton Murry.

to be reached. Its cold though: and our car broke down twice going to Kew. O but think of new hills, and French towns, and rolls, and views, and the sea, and buying old looking glasses, and wandering out with L. to see a church, or buy a glass of wine—and then we're going to visit Montaigne's house, for which I have a veneration. I will try to collect myself and write a vinous amorous line from some Inn.

Meanwhile, please dont let yourself succumb to the incubus of Bath vapour and cruising widders. What can Mary Hunter mean? Those bobbing spirits who defy life and always float in triumph are the wonder of my days. I had a great aunt once—but enough. There's Gosse got to catch the post: and I've written the last sentence I daresay 10 times and cant get the hang of it. One more shot, and so goodbye Ethel dear, and do write fully frankly freely; for I shall be so pleased to see the thick white envelope among the W's in the wire cage.

Yr V.

No, I cant 'do' the Ladies [of Llangollen]. They've done themselves too perfectly for anything to be written. That does happen: besides, never so long as I live do I write another little article.

You never said you were going to Lyppiatt:[1] how could I know?

Just off to France.

Berg

2353: To V. Sackville-West   [52 *Tavistock Square, W.C.*1]

Typewritten
Wednesday [15 April 1931]

Dearest Creature, I am in the devil of a hurry, so only enclose—lord how lovely my typing is—our list of addresses; and mind and send long letters to meet me in foreign parts. I cant lay too much stress on the delight of finding them. It will make me cautious about hens and old women, typhoid, over eating, lorries, revolutions. And do you be fearfully cautious about your bronchial tubes—they easily turn to a chronic wheeze; to general decay; to rheums and pleurisies, I assure you, Dont cast if you still have a pain. O Ive been so worried, imagining cancer and other trifles these two

---

1. Nether Lyppiat, near Stroud, Gloucestershire, the house of Ethel's friend Violet Woodhouse-Gordon.

days. You know, I must have a heart—its the only explanation. So good bye, and make the nightingales sing for me in May—about the 10th.

How happy to see you again we shall be.

V. & P[otto]

Eddy [Sackville West] was almost suicidal yesterday. What is to be done?

Joanne Trautmann

Letters 2354-2367 (April 1931)

From 16 to 30 April Virginia and Leonard went to western France for a week's holiday, driving slowly to the Dordogne. Virginia loved it, in spite of rain, hail, cold and punctures, and she wrote more letters and postcards than on any other of her foreign travels, selecting from all her correspondents, Ethel, Vita, Vanessa and Quentin. Montaigne's tower and Joan of Arc's castle were the two places which made the greatest impact on her, but the whole of France once again so captivated her that she half-wanted to live there permanently.

2354: To Ethel Smyth

Hotel de France et d'Angleterre, La Rochelle [France]

Monday 20th April 1931

Well Ethel dear, I will sit down at once and attempt to write, though Heaven knows its hard enough; before going out to see the town. O for a little warmth and colour! Bitter cold and rain; with a few hours of dazzling sun: then a grey cover over the sky again. This is our only plaint—and that I didn't bring a fur coat. Otherwise all has been very successful: 2 punctures; one mended in hailstorm; and I helped by scraping a hole in the road. Here we are, arrived last night, late. It looks like Bologna,—arches I mean: roofs made of red flower pots; a lilac in full flower; roman remains in the garden below the window. A very nice hotel, the floor shining; a toothless old servant in black; a hint of imagination in the sauces: the south beginning to warm and tumble: I mean one can imagine heat—everything's made for heat; but still all grey as a goose's back. I love tripping even in the rain down road after road; all with their avenues; and old women sitting under umbrellas minding two sheep. And we saw the Plantagenet tombs at Fontevrault yesterday, lying red and blue in a superb scraped abbey—the tombs like the Sitwells.

But enough guide book. I'm reading Lawrence, Sons and Lovers, for the first time; and so ponder your question about contemporaries. [J. M.] Murry, that bald necked blood dripping vulture, kept me off Lawrence with his obscene objurgations. Now I realise with regret that a man of genius wrote in my time and I never read him. Yes, but genius obscured and distorted I think: the fact about contemporaries (I write hand to mouth) is that they're doing the same thing on another railway line: one resents their distracting one, flashing past, the wrong way—something like that: from timidity, partly, one keeps ones eyes on one's own road. Stella Benson I

315

dont read because what I did read seemed to me all quivering—saccharine with sentimentality; brittle with the kind of wit that means sentiment freezing: But I'll try again: I'll think about jealousy. Its true that death makes judgment easier. My Gosse[1] wont be out for some weeks—has to appear in America. I think it comes out in the Fortnightly. Browning In July.[2] Your letters just been brought in by L. I've looked hastily—not yet read. No, I never got the letter about Lyppiatt. O the sun at last! I shall read the 3 letters carefully at lunch—gulped them down—you're all right I hope—O the sun! the red flower pots shining—the lilac—So we go out, and I shall post this: Aren't I a soldiers daughter:

Please write fully to Brantome

V

This is the paper on which I take notes for my critical works. In the margin I note p. 241. Here I note that I'm on the whole attracted to E.S.

Lord what an illegible hand! The Gosse gold pen which I detest.

Berg

2355: To Ethel Smyth   *Marennes [France]*
Postcard
[21 April 1931]

Leonard has been eating oysters here just off the sea. Sun at last. Cold. Go to Brantome day after tomorrow. A lovely marsh land. No accidents. Lunch off paté and cheese in the marsh. Old walls, cows, women, all lovely and solitary.

V.

Berg

2356: To V. Sackville-West   *Marennes [France]*
Postcard
Tuesday [21 April 1931]

Here we are, safe, hot at last: L. has just eaten a dozen oysters fresh from the sea in your honour. What a good book Sons and Lovers is! All well. How are you?

Love   V.W.

Lyn Dunbar

1. See p. 303, note 1.
2. See p. 301, note 3.

2357: To Ethel Smyth   *Chastillon [Castillon, France]*

Postcards
[22 April 1931]

1.

Just dined off eels, artichokes and wine—slightly tipsy. Tomorrow we go to see Montaignes Tower; Lord how nice: how far from Woking. Will write from Brantome.

V.

2.

And a lovely river; and poplars; and vineyards, and the most divine country I've ever seen This is a rural Inn, on the banks of Dordogne: commercial travellers; picking oranges. Not seen an Englishman yet—

V.

Berg

2358: To Ethel Smyth   *Bergerac [France]*

Postcard
23rd April [1931]

Oh so tipsy after drinking a bottle of Montizillac—delicious—and eating paté de foie gras—and visiting Montaignes tower[1]—a bare, ragged room, with 3 windows, on top, and his old saddle, a chair and table, and steps, room and chapel below and chair. dear me how I shd. like this life to go on for ever

Berg

2359: To V. Sackville-West   *Bergerac [France]*

Postcard
23rd April [1931]

At the end, where I have, with trembling fingers after a whole bottle of Monbazillac, drawn an arrow, Montaigne wrote his essays. There we went this morning: a divine country all round—vineyards, oxen, spring. We must come again together. O so drunk; and have eaten a whole paté de foie gras.

V.

Jane Lancellotti

1. Michel de Montaigne (1533-92). The family took its name from the Château de Montaigne, which they inherited, and where the essayist was born and died.

317

2360: To V. Sackville-West   *Hotel Moderne, Brantôme*
[France]

24th April [1931]

Well I got your letter last night—your rather melancholy letter. And it was so lovely here—a fine evening, a stone bridge, a river going in circles like the lash of a whip; a boy fishing, a man cutting down a poplar tree: And a whole colony of gipsies nested in a rock. But this is the most coherent sentence I shall write, as I'm occupying a table in the dining room, and next me is a fat Frenchman, rather like Bogy Harris,[1] munching great hunks of roll. It has recovered, the weather, which for 3 days was appalling; and everybody is sitting in the street, and swarming. No; its clouding over again. Anyhow we have had no accidents, save punctures. France is entirely empty and we drive a whole morning under avenues and meet perhaps two oxen and an old woman sitting on a bank with sheep attached to her umbrella by a piece of string. Yesterday was the best of all. We went to Montaigne—a hill in the middle of vineyards, where the Tower still stands; and the very door, room, stairs, and windows where, in which—grammar gone—Montaigne wrote his essays: also his saddle and a view precisely the same he saw. Does this excite you? (in spite of grammar: but the French don't eat breakfast without noise).

I see why one is so happy here: no visitors. No being in at 5 to see Sibyl; to see Eddy; to dine out. Thats the horror of our lives. I intend to stop it; I cant get back into that squirrel cage again. Here, in spite of packing, motoring, sight-seeing, I've actually read two or three books in peace; from start to finish—a thing incredible in London. Now for the summer, I intend a weekly expedition with Vita; and no 'seeing' at all. Can it be done? I am sure the root of your melancholy lies in the disordered odds and ends—one thing starts—its broken—this exhausts and exacerbates more than anything. Now I've no room to discuss Sons and Lovers—what a good book, my word: I must read him all: Murry so disgusted me, I never faced him. We shall be back at Dieppe today week—

V.

Berg

2361: To Vanessa Bell   *Brantôme [France]*

April 24 [1931]

Dearest,

I have just got your letter from Okehampton [Devon], and write, at once though I dont feel sure that you will ever get it. We have had no

1. See p. 292, note 1.

serious adventures, though two punctures in hail storms; and several nuts and bolts flown off, and pebbles got into the works. Still the car has been very considerate. But God—what weather to start with! Icy cold, storms of rain, clouds so black we could not see beyond our noses. Suddenly it got brilliantly fine; and then again storms; then again fine; but not really hot till yesterday. La Rochelle in fine weather would be lovely; though Ethel's green sails turned out to be fishing nets. Marenne is I think more lovely; and Chastillon [Castillon] most lovely of all. Here we adventured off the road to a small village on the Dordogne, where we had the best food for about 3/- and drove off to Montaigne's house, which excited me immensely. His tower is still standing, in the loveliest vineyards, high up, and we wandered all over the gardens with some very humorous dogs at our leisure. Then we went to Bergerac for lunch and gorged upon pâté; and wine and sauces and eggs and in consequence I nearly bought 6 old chairs, and several looking glasses, but as they weren't as good as might be and very expensive just reframed. We got here last night. It is lovely—as you remember; and we have the Inn to ourselves. The people say they remember you and two Mr Gores[1]—but I doubt it. It is cold again, but fine. They say this weather is unknown, and it was hot as summer 2 weeks ago. Why we dont live in France I cant conceive—in fact we have a plot to uproot you from Cassis, leave it to Clive, and settle hereabouts. It is a perfect country, and no tourists. In fact, we've not seen an Englishman or woman since we left.

It is market day and all the old peasant women are tramping in with kids in their arms and chickens in baskets. I hope St Ives will still move your rather stony heart. But the Times, just in, says it still rains in England. Lord— I dont in the least want to go back, and be again tormented by Sibyl, Hugh Walpole etc. Here one feels perfectly free and casual and can sit and read or consider the world by the hour. Once in London all is hurry. scurry. I am thinking out a plan for the amendment of my life. One could easily settle down—write books here. How I envy you Rome! This is duller than ditchwater—this letter—but I've no gossip—only letters from Ethel Smyth, and [McKnight] Kauffer and Koteliansky, who all accuse me of being unwilling to see them. Why is the male so happy?—counting Ethel a male? Please write again. And then I will. Love to the Brats. I wonder what Angelica will think of St Ives. I dreamt last night that you'd had a child by Hilton Young.[2]

V.

Berg

1. One was possibly Spencer Gore (1878-1914), the painter and friend of Sickert, who was the first president of the Camden Town Group (1911).
2. In 1909 Hilton Young had proposed to Virginia. He entered politics and became Minister of Health (1931-5), and was created Lord Kennet in 1935.

2362: To Quentin Bell

Hotel Moderne, Brantôme
[France]

24th April 1931

It's all very well, dearest Claudian,[1] telling me to write instantly, but I have only my natural hand available, which you can't read. Also, it thunders and lightens, and the old half wit grandmother of the proprietor turns to me for confidence. Rassurez-vous, Madame, I say from time to time, those whom the Gods love die young. She thinks this a great joke. Yes, we are on tour—naturally: naturally there hasn't been such a spring since the Dordogne overflowed its banks in 1846. Nevertheless, in spite of hail, lightning, punctures, steering wheel on the point of breaking, we are enjoying life and eat patés absolutely mellow and yellow with liver. It's a disgusting taste which I expect we share with the dogs, but for once I like to feel wholly and rabidly canine. But I mustn't use long words or you won't be able to read. My hand is stiff with cold. I write at a café table. We have an hour to dinner. Tomorrow we go to Angouleme, and so home—oh dear— to Bloomsbury rampant—opera and ballet and disappointed lovers, and lovers that feed on vapours. I've had lots of confidences lately—a tribute to my grey hair; and Clive has become a misogynist, a tribute to Mary [Hutchinson]. Barbara says she will stay at Monks House this summer—I must scrape poor Julian free from his Great Barnacle. Why don't we live here —far lovelier, lovelier far, than Cassis—plains, heights, poplars, vineyards, of a subtlety and distinction like a moth's wing compared with the shell of a lobster. Write to me.

V.

Quentin Bell

2363: To Ethel Smyth

Brantôme [France]

April 24th, perhaps. 1931, certainly

What an angel I am! Every day, whatever the pressure of hunger and thirst, in lightning and rain, I've stopped at some mean shop and bought a card for a musician. And now, I may tell you, I'm stiff with a violent scramble along the banks of the Dronne (I think) which are blue, yellow, and suddenly purple; with bluebells, cowslips and gentians; when the lightning flashed, the thunder rolled, and we took shelter in a ruined arch; waited; started; waited; started; at last fled, under a sky like a blue banner bellying down, among white poplar trees. When we reached the cemetery L. who has only one thick suit, ran; I, puffing like a grampus, got involved with some cadaverous mourners, carrying tin wreaths—what a livid and sinister and sulphurous scene!—and then, crossing the old Bridge, again

1. See p. 24, note 1.

the lightning flashed, and I thought, Really now, Ethel believes in God, does she? How very very queer! And here I sit in my socks and slippers, at the café table, waiting dinner. I cant describe: I hate the gradualness which is necessary to carry conviction or I would fill this entire sheet with the amazing loveliness of France: vineyards: poplars; rivers; then of Montaigne's tower. My word Ethel, the very door he opened is there: the steps, worn into deep waves, up to the tower: the 3 windows: writing table, chair, view, vine, dogs, everything precisely as it was—when?—I cant remember. Also 4 ancient saddles.

There—thats all the guide book you shall have. As I spin along the roads I remodel my life. What is wrong, what is detestable, what shall be altered, this very moment—is 'seeing' and being seen. Now I ask you, why should I go back to 52 T.S: and there be jerked daily by the telephone; never have a space in wh. to read; gulp my books; curtail my walks, fritter away there, perhaps the last summer evenings, at the beck and call of Colefax Kauffer,[1] Koteliansky, Mioux,[2] and a thousand others, who buzz even now: and blacken my sugar? No. A vast vista of intense and peaceful work stretches before me—a whole book on English lit; some stories: biographies: this is as I spin. I got your letters here: love the violent breath of the Bath hotel; but shall get no more till Monday. What are you writing for the Statesman?—a hard, heartless sheet? What music is beginning to trumpet and whistle—or how does your work begin—mine in phrases—yours in bars, tunes? I apologise for the extreme disjectedness—oh this pen—of the blue sheet; but the white wont be any better. We start early for Angouleme, though, so unless I post earlier still, you will say, looking out at your dripping creeper, Adieu spanish ladies—meaning that you cant abear the thought of one who, stuffed with yellow mellow pâté, cant spare a word for a soldiers daughter in Woking. I daresay Lady Balfour is dropping in before dinner to tell you something very warm, like a bird on its nest. I should find her talk infinitely delightful; but cant write it all out for you in this thunderstorm. So you will settle my life for me, wont you: its all a question of buying a waterproof and thick shoes and being downright and upspoken.

Leonard and I have been discussing God and Ethel; with the not unexpected result that Ethel survives and God—no—God we say, God is merely a—a what?—our English is going—is miazma a word? Lord how you'd laugh at my voluble sanguine French—half Madame de Sevigne; half schoolgirl English: but I cant resist branching out, and then, too late, realise my predicament cut off, alone.

V.

1. Edward McKnight Kauffer (1890-1954), the American painter, whose best-known works were posters for the London Underground.
2. Possibly Lady Meux, widow of Sir Hedworth Meux, Admiral of the Fleet, who in 1930 married Lord Charles Montagu, son of the 7th Duke of Manchester.

Dinner thank God, so I can stop writing; and they think of putting a little green wood on the stove.

Berg

2364: To Vanessa Bell   *Chateau du Loir [France]*
Postcard
27th April 1931

I hope you're having better weather than we are. It is violent April weather. However, we are enjoying ourselves, eating I think most delicious food: and often tipsy. No adventures. Car as good as the Baby.[1] Let me have your address. This is a small inn on a river.

Berg

2365: To V. Sackville-West   [*Chinon, France*]
Postcard
April 27th [1931]

Very glad to get your letter here. O dear what a bore about B.M.[2] etc: I will write tomorrow. We stood on this pinnacle and heard Joan's clock strike.[3] Almost enough castles here for you. Divine food. Weather violent— rain, hail, sun gale, in turns. Back Friday.

V.

Jane Carr

2366: To Ethel Smyth   [*Chinon, France*]
Postcard
[28 April 1931]

Have found your letter, very welcome but too short; and lunched

---

1. Vanessa's car.
2. 'Bonne Mama', Vita's name for her mother, Lady Sackville. See Letter 2367.
3. Joan of Arc first met the Dauphin at the Château de Chinon in 1429. Vita wrote her life in 1936.

322

magnificently and heard the same clock Joan heard. Very wet and cold with bursts of splendour.

V.W.

Berg

2367: To V. Sackville-West   *Hotel du Paradis, Dreux*
                                [France]

28th April 1931

Yes, I like that way of beginning your letters—Please keep to it in future. E.S. has no such beginning—and last night I dreamt she was dead; but have just had 6 pages from her.

Here we are, safe, ever so cold, shivering and shaking with cold. Can it be like this in England? Even when the sun is out, it is still bitter. We have violent storms of hail, thunder and lightning. I cant remember a more blasted fortnight—though its lovely too: amazing green, blue, purple, poplars like young birds feathers—Still the hotels at night are getting rather a trial. No central heating: or the machine failed. We sit under the one light, wrapped in a rug, as now: try to read; get into bed about 9: and then theres a movie next door—tonight a wedding. They've been dancing since 5—skinny young women in silks, readymade, skimpy: pale young men in grey trousers: vast stout mothers: and little boys and girls in black velvet suits and patent leather shoes. I peeked in and was fascinated; but L. wdn't let me stay, though I saw the whole of French provincial life exposed before me. A young man suddenly stood up alone and sang. Lord—but the noise they make!

I'm sorry about your mother,[1] and feel vaguely guilty, but anything would have fired her off in her morbid and thwarted state; I dont think its me particularly. I'm glad you stood out. And anyhow you needn't go there weekly—but I see the discomfort, what with her being your mother (odd though it seems) and so on.

Lord—Lord—again—this time about Harold and Parliament.[2] I admire the way he takes his fences—thats what I should have done had I been Harold—been rash, foolish, perverse, incalculable—like a large bouncing cod in a pail of water. I think he'll get in: but a member's wife isnt nearly so much of a wedding cake as an Ambassadors, I imagine. Now if I'd married Hilton Young—

1. Vita's two sons had just visited their grandmother in Brighton, and Lady Sackville reiterated her abuse of Virginia, whom she had hated since the publication of *Orlando*.
2. Harold Nicolson intended to stand for Parliament at the Chiswick by-election as a candidate for Sir Oswald Mosley's New Party.

We go to Caudebec tomorrow: cross by night boat on Thursday: London Saturday evening.

And when shall I see you?

This 4t night (is that the way to spell it?) seems at least 4 4t nights: I've thought over all the books I shall live to write, spinning down endless roads: and you're going to be a farmer are you?

This pen is vile.

V.

Berg

Letters 2368-2406 (May–July 1931)

The Waves *was moving towards publication. Twice Virginia had written it, and three times typed it. The third typing was completed on 22 June, and then it was typed a fourth time by a professional, whose typescript required further revision and in one passage extensive rewriting. At last, on 17 July, it was finished, and Virginia gave it into Leonard's hands, who pronounced it a masterpiece. These final months of painful creation were disturbed by Ethel Smyth's growing egotism, and her friendship with Virginia was nearly ended by her wearisome complaints that her work was ignored, particularly her new oratorio,* The Prison, *which had met with lukewarm success. Virginia was further distracted by smart parties and frequent sittings to Stephen Tomlin for the bust he made of her. That she never grudged time to those she loved is shown by her happy references to evenings spent alone with Leonard or Vita, and a charming letter (2380) describing her visit to Angelica's school.*

2368: To Ethel Smyth   *Monks House, Rodmell*
                                          [Sussex]

Typewritten
Friday May 1st [1931]

Here we are—we crossed yesterday afternoon, having, as you foretold, run into our first fine day. It is entirely divine here. But naturally after sitting in a cold bedroom at Brantome, and having forgotten my fur coat, I contracted a sore throat, which is now running from my nose and eyes in a streaming cold, so I am stupid as a bat. Also my good English steel pen is lost, and the gold one intolerable. So I pick out these few words with infinite pain. Odd how ones fingers lose the tip of writing.

Hence, my many observations upon your profound and interesting remarks re society, re health, must wait. All I will whisper, or rather croak now is, that thanks to L. I have devised steps by which I think society will be considerably modified this summer. Not that that cuts off certain military musicians. But again, I must wait, since all my letters remain unanswered. As to seeing a doctor who will cure my headaches, no, Ethel No. And whats more you will seriously upset L, if you suggest it. We spent I daresay a hundred pounds when it meant selling my few rings and necklaces to pay them,★ without any more result than that if I get a pain, go to bed, and eat meat it goes. No other cure has ever been found—and the disease—well, all the nerves meet in the spine: its simple enough. No complicated mysteries

325

about my headaches. Not like your fybroid ears, which Im delighted to think now hear the nightingales. I say, it will be nice seeing nobody, except one or two people. Crossing yesterday, we ran into the wife[1] of my old lover Sidney Waterlow. She told us how she had claimed precedence from Lady Clifford on the passes of Himalaya—that would have been my fate. So good bye. I'll write when I am less sore in the throat boiled in the eyes and red of the nose.

V.

[in Virginia's handwriting:]
★ Sir G. Savage. Sir M. Craig. Sir M. Wright. T. Hyslop. etc. etc.[2]

Berg

2369: To Jonathan Cape   *Monk's House, Rodmell,*
                                          Lewes, Sussex
Typewritten
May 1st 1931

Dear Mr Cape,

I am sorry to have delayed so long answering your letter, but we only got back from abroad late last night.

On the whole, even though you **are** so kind as to suggest delaying publication, I dont think that I can undertake to write an introduction to one of Miss Thackeray's books.[3] For one thing, I dont like making engagements so far ahead, but the real reason is that I should much prefer to write a longer and more general article upon her books. I find these short introductions very difficult to do, and unsatisfactory from the writer's point of view. But I much appreciate your kindness in asking me to do it, and hope that my delay has not inconvenienced you.

Yours sincerely
V. Woolf

Jonathan Cape Ltd

1. Margery Eckhard. Sydney Waterlow proposed to Virginia in 1911 before he was divorced from his first wife.
2. Sir George Savage (1842-1921), a specialist in mental illness, and President of the Neurological Society; Sir Maurice Craig (1866-1935), Consulting Physician in Psychological Medicine, Guy's Hospital; Dr Maurice Wright, member of the British Psychological Society, and author of *Physical Aspects of Neurasthenia* and *The Psychology of Freud and its relation to Psycho Neurosis;* Dr Theo Hyslop (d. 1933), Lecturer on Psychological Medicine, St Mary's Hospital and London School of Medicine for Women.
3. See Letters 2349 and 2351.

[9 May 1931]

Oh dear, I had meant to buy that book, had the address lying on my table—and now of course I am ashamed—Please send me the bill. I know its something like 3/7¾; it was the getting the order that was insuperable. A vast amount of business has accumulated—

1) L. says—for some good reason I dont know what—that we cant go to Bradfield[1] that day. So here is the paper returned.

2) Here is the handkerchief found in the W.C. and therefore attributed to you.

3) About being "misunderstood" (but I thought that was the title of a novel)[2]

'God' I said to Leonard, after you had gone "Whats clear to me is that Ethel, with all her shrewdness, will never, never understand me."

"But I'm the only person who does" said L: "You and Shakespeare" I said—on top of which comes your letter, saying the very same thing only t'other way round, of V-W., Montaigne, and H B [Henry Brewster]. I think its perfectly true too, though whether its to be accounted for as you suggest by my being a don's daughter from Cambridge, and you a General's daughter from Aldershot, I dont know. Whats odd is that we are both understood (I will agree that this is an unfortunate term) by poets. Which suggests, but I've no time to follow this up,—that all inwoven, complex, hidden, and curious people—which we both are—are abraded by human contacts—feel shut up, enclosed, petrified by meeting (in Tavistock Sqre say) but take down Montaigne, take down Shakespeare, and at once flow, flower, expand and are at rest—Only you, being so damned practical, for ever seek for understanding; and I, in whom Cambridge has bred a large measure of unalloyed melancholy, never look for it now: sit and look at Ethel, raging, with resignation; and never say half whats in my mind.

Yes—your article was a good deal better than Turners;[3] that I agree; but now, read Laura Riding's protest on the next page, and see whether

1. Bradfield School, Berkshire, which annually produced a Greek play in the original language.
2. *Misunderstood* was a popular children's novel by Florence Montgomery (1869).
3. The battle between Ethel and W. J. Turner (see Letter 2339) had continued throughout April, Ethel accusing the music-critics of ganging up against new composers, especially if they were women, and Turner retorting (*New Statesman*, 18 April) that much modern music was 'imitative work, cleverly fashioned, but essentially commonplace." Ethel replied (*New Statesman*, 9 May): "He who damns contemporary creative music shoulders a grave responsibility . . . It is monstrous that a work may be sneered, *pro tem*, out of existence by unfortunates on whom harsh criticism has imposed a career. . . . *The Prison* is the coping stone of a long life devoted to art."

you dont get the feeling that here's a shallow egotistical cock crowing creature, to bother what people say of her.[1] And The Cause suffers: I mean, I feel, what will people say of the vanity of women? But then I dont believe in causes. And she's a writer, not a musician: all the same, read Laura Riding (in Time and Tide)

No: handkerchief has been sent to the wash.

Berg

2371: TO JONATHAN CAPE   52 *Tavistock Square, W.C.*1

Typewritten
9 May, 1931

Dear Mr Cape,
    I am afraid that you misunderstood my letter. What I meant was that I definitely could not write an introduction. If I write at all, it must be a general and critical article such as I would not wish to appear as an introduction to one of Miss Thackeray's books.[2]

Yours sincerely
Virginia Woolf

Jonathan Cape Ltd

2372: TO ETHEL SMYTH   52 *T.*[*avistock*] *S.*[*quare, W.C.*1]

Typewritten
12th May [1931]

    No Ethel, dear, no; I didnt make my meaning plain. I wasnt alluding to any particular instance, of misunderstanding, so much as to the general impossibility, which over comes me sometimes, of *any* understanding between two people. This instance—your behaviour about critics and your music—doesnt seem to me of importance. That is, if I give my mind seriously to it for five minutes—a thing I seldom do—I can imagine, by imagining you as a whole,—with all your outriders and trembling thickets of personality, exactly why you do it; and sympathise; and admire; and feel the oddest

---

1. Laura Riding's letter was not in the *New Statesman* but in *Time and Tide* (9 May). She complained that a reviewer had damned four of her books. "He became so exhausted by his own point of view that by the time he reaches the fourth and most recent, he is capable of discerning only 'a very poor performance'. I thank him for leaving it at that."
2. See Letter 2369.

mixture of admiration and pity and championship such as I used to feel for a white tailless cat of ours which we forgot to have castrated. This superb brute used to spend his nights fighting; and at last got so many wounds that they wouldnt heal; and he had to be put out of life by a vet. And I respected him; and I respect you. Only I think you dont altogether realise how, to the casual onlooker you seem exaggerated—how it strikes an outsider. I think sometimes you let the poison ferment. Never mind. I can't altogether lay hands on my meaning. The other thing anyhow interests me much more— the impossibility of one person understanding another. Oh, and when I write to you, I put it off till the end of the day when my careful typed letters to publishers and so on are done with and I write with a flick of the pen, leaving things to be understood. Hence my unintelligible remark about 'not believing in causes.' This, as I see, now, reverts to Murrys life of Lawrence [*Son of Woman*]; the whole doctrine of preaching, of causes; of converting; teaching etc which has been working vaguely in my mind and penetrating into my Waves; so that I let it fly, casually, in my letter, without a word to explain it. I think what I mean is that all teaching at the present moment seems to me a blasphemy; this hooked itself on to your cause; and so obliquely, to Laura Riding, whom I despise for writing perpetually to explain her own cause when reviewers say what is true—that she is a damned bad poet. There! Not very well put I admit; but hurried.

What is the misery that weighs you down so that you can't write? Talking of miseries, I went in with L. to see the furniture and found Mrs H.[1] sitting at her desk (about to be sold) as pink and cool as a rose; very kindly. Would we go everywhere? I felt much disconcerted. I felt how awful for her to be selling at her age—and me to be lounging round. But she carried herself like a general on a battlefield; there was a fat critical, censorious daughter in an arm chair; Mrs H. was superb; as if it were a nuisance, shutting up ones houses, selling every stitch, but not a thing to cry over. If one must squander twenty million this is the way to do it. We may look in this afternoon, partly from curiosity, and buy a looking glass.

About Friday—lord, thats our black hole [social] day. Begins at three; goes on till seven. And I choke with a tickle in my throat and cant talk. I dont see any use in your coming on top of Mrs Hueffer,[2] Mr Plomer, Hugh Walpole, et cetera. Wednesday I'm in; also perhaps Thursday; Saturday we go for a walk (not away) I dont know what to suggest, therefore; but leave you to make your own terms; and shall be happy to stroke the head of the

1. Mary Hunter, Ethel's sister. "So extravagantly had Mrs Hunter lived beyond her means that in her old age she was penniless, and Ethel had to join other members of her family and her friends in raising a sum to support her" (Christopher St John, *Ethel Smyth: a Biography*, 1959, p. 241). Her furniture was sold by auction.
2. Violet Hunt (1866-1942), the novelist, and daughter of A. W. Hunt, the painter. She lived with the novelist Ford Madox Hueffer (Ford).

indomitable and uncastrated cat. By the way excuse typing; I'm so sick of my utterly disgraceful pen—

[*in Virginia's handwriting:*]
Look—it wont make a single letter right. When I've time, I'm going to the city to look through a wholesale pen seller—surely there must be one pen, somewhere—one heart for me to share (it sounds like an old song)

V.

Berg

2373: To Vanessa Bell   52 *Tavistock Sqre.* [*W.C.*1]

14th May [1931]

Dearest Dolphin
    I would have written before, but I somehow thought that you said that you were going to camp outside Rome, and would send me your address. Here are some letters from Angelica, who seems to be in the highest spirits. I've sent her a bathing dress, but I gather her summer coat has gone wrong. Shall I do anything about it? We shall go and see her as soon as she lets us know that it is allowed.
    London is at the moment rather enchanting, chiefly because most people think we are still away. Also, though thundery, it is really warm— Lord, the cold of France!—I wore all my winter things—they said it was La Lune Russe—whatever that may be. I'm sorry it has moved on to Rome, which doesn't sound so dazzlingly romantic in your account as I thought it— but then we had a perfect May week. And I rather think the days of cheap travel are for ever over—the prices in France seemed considerably higher than the English: no old furniture that I could find at possible sums. And in one's age one begins to dislike hotels.
    Yes; Mrs Hunt[1] is dead, knocked down by a motor van in High St. Kensington; had her arm cut off; is now buried in St Pauls. But I kept to myself and did not go. Among the living I have seen Desmond, whose collected works it is said we are to print; slightly worried about Michael [Desmond's son], who has bought 400 goats, and finds them more sympathetic than sheep, but at the same time more active, so that he spends his time chasing them, and recovering them from Leopards; and so wants to sell them and start life afresh. Also Rachel [Desmond's daughter] is not much of a hand at managing life—which may refer to Lord David [Cecil]. He calls her very childish. Then I saw Cory [Bell], and came to the conclusion that you were a bold woman to marry into the Bells: they materialise everything, and with such good sense there seems no escape. He told me that the

1. Marion (Mrs Holman) Hunt, the widow of the pre-Raphaelite painter, died on 1 May. She was 84.

young need discipline and his son and daughter dont seem to get it. And O what an encounter I had on the Channel boat; a squat sallow lynx eyed woman—Dawks [Mrs Sydney] Waterlow, returning with 3 of the ugliest children ever misbegotten from Sofia. And so we've got to go and stay with them at Oare. Then, domestically speaking, Adrian has dismissed his cook—at a moments notice; and Mrs Goldsmith has written to tell me that old Uppington[1] has had all her savings stolen and can't get any work. Can I help? I say you (V.B.) will. The truth is, I think, that Alice and her Tony have gone off with £50; as he is in difficulties, but I dont see how I'm to intervene. They say now in the underworld that it was Tony and Alice that lost Lotty [Hope] her place with the Harrisons—God knows.

Thats not very interesting I fear, but you know what life is—one thing and then another: Hugh Walpole tomorrow, and Mrs Violet Hunt-Hueffer. There is another great literary scandal on foot, about a book that caricatures Somerset Maugham this time;[2] and Hugh, like the Galahad he is, has intervened to stop it. Desmond says he is a perfect ass; but I shall hear his story tomorrow. Old Ethel adores you beyond any chance of quarrel: she says your life is too full for her. Its one of her points that she takes facts to heart; and I have snipped her back considerably by saying that I've got too much work at the moment to see anyone. But she came yesterday, and was melancholy beyond words; old, battered, depressed; because (though she wont explain) I rather think the Opera has refused The Wreckers, owing to the failure of The Prison. Anyhow she says she has seldom found life harder, and wakes at 3 am., when she has to wet, in such despair that she cries aloud Courage, courage! and prays to God, who has deserted her. I've promised her a champagne dinner at Boulestin's, but even that is not of much avail.

I cant conceive why [Winifred] Holtby[3] wrote to you. I tremble to think what a character you would have given me: she then applied to L: so I saw her myself, and find her a Yorkshire farmer's daughter, rather uncouth, and shapeless, and Heaven knows what sort of lies I didn't tell her—Chiefly about you, for whose work she has a great admiration.

Who is David Bomberg?[4] He has asked me to sit, but only if I admire modern painting. So I said I loathed sitting and thus hope to escape.

London, as I began by saying, is rather amusing at the moment (though its deplorable to have no dolphinry) and I go to the gallery at the Opera, and to Aldous's play [The World of Light], and to the movies—there's a

1. Who occasionally helped with the housework at Rodmell.
2. Gin and Bitters, by Elinor Mordaunt, published anonymously in America. Hugh Walpole, who had himself been caricatured by Somerset Maugham in Cakes and Ale (1930), wrote to Maugham offering to help him obtain an injunction against the book's publication in England.
3. See p. 302, note 2.
4. Bomberg (1890-1957) was a founder member of the London Group (1913), which Vanessa joined later.

very good French one[1]—and sometimes merely saunter and meander through the streets, looking about me. Its English country that's such a pin cushion after France: all these little fields and houses. I think one ought to live 6 months in London and 6 at Brantôme or Castillon. John Lehmann shows signs of melancholia—otherwise all is well As his father went mad,[2] I'm rather apprehensive. Please write, and then you'll get further sheets.

B

I will hand on to L. your remarks about the wine. And all shall be attended to.

Berg

2374: To Ethel Smyth   52 *Tavistock Sqre.* [*W.C.*1]
18th May 1931

It occurs to me, at L's suggestion, that I probably misled you about the writing table, on the telephone. I did buy a writing table; but *not* the one your sister was writing at. That, which I coveted, went for £37—to whom I dont know, too much for me: and the £6.10 one was the high immense rosewood desk-cabinet in the drawing room, a far less distinguished object, but exactly right to impose order on the obliquities and diversities of my studio. It stands over me at the moment like a policeman. Behold your envelope, just come. The soldiers daughter must have been in a bad way when she wrote *Woking*.[3] But I somehow infer, atmospherically, that your sulphur and rotten eggs are lightening. I think Wednesday, 4, will be all right. I dont see why not, at this moment. if its true you are in London anyhow.

Isnt it odd—I saw my new pen, (which is not all I could wish,) and said, now of course I can write a full and expressive letter; that is my perpetual illusion. I never can. I am always interrupted: My page is never filled; just serves to throw odds and ends into. But the illusion persists that this time I am going to write a long, entirely satisfactory letter. Perhaps letter writing is a thing one does in youth. Yes: I was rather flown with wine last time you came. I had a brief season of thinking, well anyhow these pages, (of the Waves) are brimfull. I've only to seal them up: send them to Mrs Jarrett (a village girl who had a baby through falling downstairs with a typewriter, she said) the things done. But yesterday was vile beyond words. Couldn't stagger along over the burning pebbles at all. In fact, I cant help thinking that

1. *Le Million*, written and directed by René Clair.
2. Rudolph Lehmann (1856-1929) had a distinguished career as a barrister, Editor of the *Daily News*, Liberal M.P., and the writer of many books. His son John wrote: "My father died, after ten years of illness bravely borne, but tragic for his family and friends to watch" (*The Whispering Gallery*, 1955, p. 157).
3. Ethel had been at Bath.

this book contains the dreariest of all my patches. And pity me for this: the tickling throat has taken away all pleasure in smoking. Not a single cigarette have I enjoyed these seven days.

The Black hole was as well as can be expected. That is to say, L. and I looked at each other, about 6.30 (it had begun at 3 sharp) and signalled, thank the Lord only another hour of it left! Whether this is the right mood in which to see the human face divine I dont know. Now, about Causes. Of course, and of course, I'm not such a pacifist as to deny that practical evils must be put to the sword: I admit fighting to the death for votes, wages, peace, and so on: what I can't abide is the man who wishes to convert other men's minds; that tampering with beliefs seems to me impertinent, insolent, corrupt beyond measure. I never pass through Hyde Park without cursing separately every God inventor there. This is partly because; unbaptised as we were, our religious friends, some cousins in particular,[1] the daughters of Fitzjames, rasped and agonised us as children by perpetual attempts at conversion. As they were ugly women, who sweated, I conceived a greater hatred for them than ever for anyone. And even now, when no one tries, I still draw in and shiver at the suspicion—he's got a finger in my mind. I will try to read Tobit[2] one of these days but the repulsion of the early book, whatever it was, still poisons my mind. And I cant read when I'm writing; everything flies off at such an odd angle (This is another pen: no: no: I must revolutionise my life—a new pen: no smoking)

Now this is not in the least the letter I meant to write: but the illusion of the perfect letter still hovers. A Mrs Stack to see you "Who is Mrs Stack?" "A lady who wishes to talk about your book" "To hell with Mrs Stack." L. comes in. "I've an estimate to show you". This is life: and I adore it

V.

Berg

2375: To Vanessa Bell   *Monks House* [*Rodmell, Sussex*]

23rd May [1931]

Dearest Dolphin,

I have only just got your letter, and here I am answering it at once. First, business: will you get yourself a birthday, I was going to say wedding present, with the enclosed cheque—something entirely useless, I recommend, not combinations or umbrella; (2) if you should see an old looking glass or frame in my taste, which is bad—say a shell between 2 mermaids—gilt,

1. Katherine (1856-1924) and Dorothea (1871-1965) Stephen. See Volume II of this Edition, pp. 488-9 and 492.
2. *Tobit Transplanted* (1931), by Stella Benson. Virginia had earlier read *The Man Who Missed the Bus* (1928).

would you get it? I've no glasses here; but then I expect the prices are ruinous—I'd go up to £5—And also the bringing back impossible, and also I daresay there are as good to be had in London. I enclose a review of your show,[1] to which I cant go, partly because I'm here for Whitsun, partly because all your shows are rendered impossible to me by Angus who drops round, gently disparaging, and I feel myself sucked under like a lily by a dead fish—a thing that often happens, specially in Scotland.

I've had to retire to bed for 2 days with a headache, but am now practically recovered. This was not due to my Jolly, but to Ethel Smyth, whom I think, seriously, to be deranged in the head. We'd spent the morning trapesing round the Chelsea flower show, a very remarkable sight, banks and banks of flowers, all colours, under a livid awning, for it was perishing cold, and all the county families parading with their noses red against the lilies,—a fascinating but rather exhausting performance, and then Ethel appeared, stamping like a dragoon with a wallet full of documents. For 3 hours she nailed me to my chair while she rehearsed the story of her iniquitous treatment by Adrian Boult.[2] I cant (you'll be glad to hear) go into it all, but she seems to have gone into the green room, after he'd been conducting a Bach Mass for 6 hours, and insisted that he should do the Prison at the BBC; whereafter, according to her, he grossly insulted her, in the presence of the finest artists in Europe, and finally after a screaming and scratching which rung through The Queen's Hall, ordered her out of the room. She then went through, with the minuteness and ingenuity of a maniac, the whole history of her persecution for the past 50 years; brought out old letters and documents and read them aloud, beat on my chair with her fists; made me listen, and answer, and agree at every moment; and finally I had to shout that I had such a headache that unless she stopped talking I should burst into flames and be combusted. One is perfectly powerless. She raves and rants; yet has a demoniac shrewdness, so that there's no escape. "You've got to listen to me—You've got to listen" she kept saying and indeed the whole of 52 rang with her vociferations. And its all fabricated, contorted, twisted with red hot egotism; and she's now launched on a campaign which means bullying every conductor and worrying every publisher, and rich man or woman, as well as unfortunate friends, until she gets that hopeless farrago of birds and last posts played and all HB's rubbish printed again. I dont feel I can even face her unless 2 keepers are present with red hot pokers—at the same time, considering her age, I suppose she's a marvel—I see her merits as a writer—but undoubtedly sex and egotism have brewed some bitter insanity.

Meanwhile, Mrs [Mary] Hunter has gone smash, owes about £10,000,

1. Some of Vanessa's paintings were included in the exhibition of Contemporary British Art.
2. Musical Director of the BBC (1930-42) and founder conductor of the BBC Symphony Orchestra (1930-49).

has pledged her pictures to Duveen,[1] and then sold them to pay an overdraft
—in short, she has had to sell all her possessions. You remember the house
stuffed with furniture? Well, I went to the sale, for a joke, and before I had
been there ten minutes had bought a vast writing desk for £6.10, and bid
for several chairs, cupboards and carpets, in a state of complete irresponsibility. Mercifully I for the most part failed to get my lots, but Hugh Walpole
was landed with 2 dessert services and all the bed linen for £40. It was a
sordid scene—old Jews clutching hold of pen trays and shaking pots in case
they might be cracked. I found myself wedged against a semi-familiar looking
lady who said she did not wish to bid against me. After a time I seemed to
suspect that she was Lady Rothenstein, as indeed she was, but highly
respectable, even sanctimonious, all black, at which I wondered, but saw that
she was presented at Court the following night, and behold this cutting about
the Queen and the Veteran. What a humbug Will [Rothenstein] is with his
lecture about the evils of aristocracy—and then dressing Alice like a plumber's
widow and sending her to Buckingham Palace.

Then we had Violet Hunt-Hueffer (it appears she's a married woman in
certain streets in Berlin, where she signed a document; but not otherwise)
and had a lewd and lascivious talk about her statements as to Ruskins private
parts and so on. It is all based upon things she heard gentlemen saying to
her mother as she was going up to bed at the age of 8. These she has since
reflected upon and drawn her own conclusions—erratic, slightly; and I
ought to be going through the revised version at this moment, instead of
scribbling to you. Its hot, ink black: now its pouring; now blue as a rooks
egg: very odd weather; The only advantage over November is that its hot.
Lytton and Raymond (to go on gossiping) dined with us—Lytton, as one
always says, very charming: Raymond with every virtue except charm.
Lytton's book [*Portraits in Miniature*] is out—I think its far better than
Elizabeth [*and Essex*], indeed rather masterly in technique, and the essays
read much better together than separate. Also, I think he's combed out his
rhetoric somewhat in respect for us. He had seen Julian and Helen he said,
and deplores the Cambridge infection, as I do—but whats to be done? He's
bound to get a Fellowship, and there Helen will sit forever, talking, Lytton
said, minute provincialities about exams; and Cambridge parties.

Percy [Bartholomew] has got appendicitis, so we have a day gardener
from Glynde and it is said our flowers wont be as good as usual. Nevertheless, our garage and our new rooms are very remarkable: the frigidaire is
installed, but not working which matters the less as nature is seeing to it;
and we have electric light everywhere. I dont see what further improvements
can be made—Our way of life here—cooking messes, cutting fresh asparagus
from the earth seems to me almost divine (quite if there were a Dolphin in the

1. Joseph Duveen (later Lord Duveen), the art dealer and Trustee of the National
Gallery.

pond with the fish) and I dont (you'll be sorry to hear) really envy you Rome, as I want to write, which needs a table, and then—Lord—how violently our taste in friends opposes itself! Thus you can go to Rome and there meet Jimmy Sheehan [Vincent Sheean]—to me the dullest of good Americans—and Peter Morris, who is explained by your brilliant analysis, as the cousin of a duke without a skin—I cannot imagine. Far rather would I stay in Surbiton and consort with Ida Milman and Emma Vaughan.[1] Those are my sentiments—not, I suppose yours. I suppose Jimmy, Peter and Angus have some mystic charm as I see that Vita has none in your eyes. I suppose its something to do with the illusion of sex: the male sex illudes you; the female me: Thus I see the male in its reality; you the female. Or how do you account for it? About books and pictures our taste is respectable; about people, so crazy I wouldn't trust a dead leaf to cross a pond in it. But I daresay it is a matter of no importance, as long as you needn't sit in the Pincio with Vita, nor I with Peter. I'm amused by the way to find that Vita has been told the story of Eddy and Jimmy by a friend under strictest secrecy, and she much deplores it, not so much for Eddy as for Knole, for Eddy swears he will never marry owing to J[immy]; thus the house will go to a cousin who will sell it in building lots, all because of a wretched American who talks through his nose! Had it been an actress, or a duke, I gather they wouldn't so much have minded; but I daresay its all for the best—that Knole should be cut up into villas, I mean.

Now I must really stop. (Its due, my garrulity, to my taking a holiday). Lytton said Maynard had asked him to write an introduction to Duncan's show, which very naturally he refused, thinking Duncan in no need of Introductions. Angelica, who writes like the Ladies Complete letter writer in imitation, I suppose, of some other girl, with sudden flashes of pure folly in her own manner, wants us to go down next Sunday. I shall try to, if it doesn't interfere with your seeing her. But I dont suppose you'll be back much before August.

[Walter] Sickert has some (to me) very witty pictures on show; and Varda[2] is said to be also very good, by Raymond. We go back on Thursday, and shall be in the thick of publishing Vita's book.[3] So please write and write and write good Dolphin.

B.

Berg

1. Ida Milman was one of four sisters (with Sylvia, Enid and Maud), grand-daughters of the Dean of St Paul's, Henry Hart Milman, and family friends of the Stephens since their childhood. Emma Vaughan was Virginia's first cousin and one of her earliest correspondents.
2. Yanko Varda, the Greek painter.
3. *All Passion Spent* was published on 27 May.

Sunday [24 May 1931]

Dearest Creature,

We've decided not to come on Tuesday, as I've been in bed with a headache for two days, and though much better today, the Expedition [to Penns-in-the-Rocks] and talk with Easedales[1] would probably bring it back. What a curse. I suppose you wouldn't come here on Tuesday—lunch? instead. We have a room if you'd stay the night.

I had such an awful doing with Ethel on Wednesday. That woman's egotism is scarcely credible, and she is now in full flood with a new grievance gainst Boult and the BBC. I'm sure its all her heated invention, but it took 2½ hours to hammer into me on Wednesday, at the end of which I felt like a stoat nailed to a barn door.

Not without foreboding did I say that I preferred Vita to Ethel when I'm ill. And this is the second time she's come between us, and I feel powerless in her hands. If she stays with you, keep off the Prison and Boult and the BBC like fire—if its possible—or you'll be burnt to cinders too. And I've wasted 4 days when I wanted to write. And I've spent them partly reading Princess Daisy of Pless,[2] speculating upon her real character and life and longing for a full account from you—who appear in a footnote as a distinguished author. What a chance the British aristocracy had and lost—I mean if they'd only grafted brains on to those splendid bodies and wholesome minds—for I cant help liking her, in her wild idiocy, and her frankness "7 days late—can it be a child—" seems to me the highest human quality, if it werent combined with a housemaids sensibility and the sentimentality of a Surbiton cook. Could Bloomsbury be grafted on to Mayfair: but no: we're too ugly and they're too stupid. And so the world goes to rack and ruin. I see Harold is standing[3]

                                                              V.

Berg

Sunday [24 May 1931]

This is to say—what I've written also to Long Barn—that we must put

1. The family of Joan Easdale, the young poet whom the Hogarth Press published.
2. *From My Private Diary* (1931), by Princess Daisy of Pless (*née* Mary Theresa Olivia Cornwallis-West). She was the daughter of Colonel W. ('Poppets') Cornwallis-West, and distantly related to Vita through the De la Warrs.
3. For the Chiswick by-election, which did not, after all, take place.

off coming on Tuesday, as I've been in bed with a headache and afraid to risk another by an expedition. What a bore. If you could come here on Tuesday—lunch one—or stay the night—what a pleasure.

I'm practically all right—only keeping quiet.

V.

Berg

2378: To V. Sackville-West   *Monks House [Rodmell, Sussex]*

Wednesday 27th May [1931]

Yes, dearest Creature, come to dinner on Monday do—8, I suppose, after [broad]casting. I pity you today, roasting in the hot fire of Ethel's egotism—though I cant lay all the blame of my headache on her entirely, poor old woman. Its partly this silly little temperature, no doubt, and partly that we spent that morning brushing in a crowd round Chelsea flower show —where, by the way we bought a little minute cedar tree, 50 years old; and I want now to find a very small breed of nightingale to sing on its branches. Find me some at Sissinghurst.

I'm quite recovered and have been sauntering over the downs alone— Lord—why go back to London? They look so lovely this evening, from my garden room, with the low barns that always make me think of Greek Temples. And we've been to a village wedding and seen the bridal party perched on kitchen chairs driven off in a great blue wagon, drawn by colossal farm horses with ribbons in their tails, and little pyramids of bells on their foreheads. What an odd mixture English country life is of squalor and magnificence! I should like to read The Land [Vita's poem,1926] tonight, but haven't got a copy here.

So instead, if my frigidaire is working, I shall eat frozen gooseberries and cold asparagus fresh cut, and perhaps a bottle of Spanish wine white with frost—but of course, though they hammer all day, it wont be working. Leonard says we have sold over 4,000 copies of A.P.S. [*All Passion Spent*] before publication. Its a great day today for the press—I dont envy you the usual rotten eggs and sticky sweets of reviewers, all the same.

Monday 8. (or before): now note: I dont mean breakfast—

V.

Perhaps Ethel is sleeping with you tonight?[1]

Berg

1. Ethel Smyth was staying the night at Sissinghurst.

2379: To V. Sackville-West   52 *Tavistock Square*, *W.C.*1.

[28 May 1931]

I didn't make it clear just now on the telephone (I think) that we had been engaged to go to the Opera[1] for three weeks or so—it was my idiocy that I forgot: only I don't wish you to think that we put you off, for a superior engagement. No. No. Thats all. Monday, then.

V.

Berg

2380: To Vanessa Bell   52 *Tavistock Square* [*W.C.*1]

Typewritten
June 1st [1931]

What an angel I am to write, seeing youve never written in answer to my long last—but good hearted as I am, I write to say we spent yesterday with Angelica [at Langford Grove School]; who was in high spirits; in blue; in a new coat; we went off to a field to picnic; but owing to my sense of duty we took Judith [Bagenal] too. They were very amusing—both brought gloves. Angelica a pair of furred ones. Judith brought only one, because as she pointed out, one only brings gloves to show that one has gloves, so that one is enough; and then if one loses it one can bring the other. Angelica saw the sense of this, but of course left both of hers in the car. Then she refused to touch tongue, but devoured tomatoes raw; and lettuce and liqueur chocolates and a whole box of pineapple chunks. Then we went down to the sea, and she caught a furry bear caterpillar and put it in her hat. Then we stole up behind an old gentleman who was sketching. We also found a lamb being led by a boy on a string, and she stroked its ears. We then went to tea at the Blue Lion where you stay, because she said there is a dear old lady who knows all about her and gives one hot buttered toast. It was a broiling hot day. We had a good deal of conversation at tea. They were both extremely pathetic (to me) about their being so bad at arithmetic that they would never be able to to go to Cambridge as Mrs [Elizabeth] Curtis [Headmistress] would say they could not pass the entrance. Angelica said that she had been able to do decimals, but they had put her so low in the class she was not now allowed to learn any sums. They spoke with great sadness about this. She said Quentin had never written to her, and she is so devoted to him that she cannot bear his being so long away. I said he had gone to Cassis. She said Thank goodness, then he will come back at last; but he may have grown very thin, or very fat. She said you were coming

1. *The Magic Flute.*

back in a week to Paris. We are all to come to what they call Parrots day. She sang us some drinking songs in a rollicking voice. Also some Mozart. She blacked all her face by accident and I had to wipe her, then she went to the looking glass and said how dreadful she looked. Of course she looked like a fantastic blue butterfly beside a tidy cob. Not but what Judith is not a sensible child with a very sad view of life and her responsibilities. She always knew the right road and Angelica never did. This rather depressed Angelica. Then we went back to school and A. asked me not to come and see Beetle,[1] as it would make her shy. Beetle has fallen off a desk and torn her ligaments, so that she has to lie on a chair in the garden. A. tied up the few remaining cherries with gold string from the sweets and took them to Beetle. Then she implored me to come and see Mrs Curtis, which I did not want to do, but A. was so pressing that I yielded, and we went off to the drawing room but Mrs C. was at a service. So I went over the school with A. and saw all the bedrooms and photographs of army officers and a new dress which A. admired very much. As you see I have fallen in love with her, but think her mother very heartless, gallivanting in Rome and never casting a thought my way. Then we left them, they were going to be read aloud to and do hymn practise. It was on the whole very fine and a great success but how pathetic children are to be sure; full of the wildest feelings I could see, and adumbrations of the future and jealousies and torments, though I think very happy there. Judith said the worst of school is one is never alone, but A. seemed to like this. So no more. Though had you written I would have told you some very interesting pieces of news and one that bodes no good to us all this summer. So there.

B.

Berg

2381: To Margaret Llewelyn Davies

52 *Tavistock Square* [*W.C.*1]

Typewritten
June 1st [1931]

Dearest Margaret,

We were so sorry about last Sunday, especially for the reason. I wish you werent always called upon to take part in these catastrophes, though I daresay its natural enough that they should call upon you. No, we cant manage this Sunday anyhow; and I'm afraid not next, but we must try again. We get tempted into going to Rodmell when we can, and Sunday is the only day L. can leave the press, which has now published what we hope to be

1. Elizabeth Carr, a fellow-pupil of Angelica at Langford Grove.

another best seller [*All Passion Spent*] by Vita Nicolson. I like it a great deal better than the Edwardians.

I have just read through the letters,[1] and feel greatly relieved. I somehow thought many of the women would dislike my butting in, and ask what business I had. They seem very generous on the contrary, and I am delighted they are so appreciative. But as a matter of fact I agree with your sister in law. I doubt that I was the right person to make people interested in the womens stories, because if one is a writer by profession, one cant help being one. It would be far worse to pretend not to be. And I think, as your sister in law says, that gets between and makes a distraction from what is the point of the book. However it cant be helped—old age makes one feel one cant change ones spots; much though I should like to. I've had a letter from the American Yale Press who asked to see the proofs, but they say they cant publish it. "Since there is no organization in the U.S. like the Working Womens Guild, the letters prove to deal with matters rather far from the experience and interests of possible readers here". I thought the Coop. movement flourished in America—perhaps theres no Guild. I have had some very enthusiastic comments on the book from very unlikely people—young intellectuals, who had never heard of working women or guilds or coopera- tion. They thought the letters amazing. I wish we could have had more.

We stayed at a good Inn [Talbot Inn] in Dorset at a place called Iwerne Minster—lovely country, near Shaftesbury, and a model village run by Mr Ismay.[2] I could find the address if you want it. This was about 4 years ago —cooking good, and all clean and quiet, as far as I remember.

[*in Virginia's handwriting:*]
L. wants to read the letters and so I am keeping them, but will send them in a day or two.

                                                                        V.

Sussex

2382: To Vanessa Bell   *Monks House* [*Rodmell,*
                                          Sussex]

Saturday 6th June [1931]

I wrote to you in Rome, about our visit to Angelica, but I dont suppose you will get it—and it was only to say she was in fine feather, and we at any rate enjoyed ourselves greatly. Its odd, considering her parentage, how very little she resembles the Bells:[3] or Bagenals for the matter of that. To me this is most sympathetic.

1. Written in response to the publication of *Life As We Have Known It.*
2. James Ismay (1867-1930), one of the Ismay family who managed the White Star shipping line.
3. Duncan Grant was Angelica Bell's father.

It is a fine day, and in a short time Jack and Mary [Hutchinson] will be upon us. Judge my horror! Mary rang up and said they were taking Southease [a house near Rodmell] for the summer, and were coming down to see it, and might she spend the night. Mercifully, she rang up a second time to say Southease had fallen through, but they were set upon getting a house near Lewes and were coming to see agents. I doubt that they will find anything. I couldn't bear to meet Mary in full finery and fashion on the downs. Other news, is chiefly to the discredit of English surgeons. Perhaps you've heard how Rosamond Lehmann, who is going to have a baby was seized with pains. A specialist was sent for and said that the conception had taken place in a wrong part; and she would certainly die if not operated upon instantly. So they operated, and found everything perfectly normal, but it is thought that the shock will certainly bring on a miscarriage. The same day Alix [Strachey] was seized with pains. Elly [Rendel] said she thought it was not appendicitis, but the specialist said it was, and must be operated upon instantly. So they cut Alix open and found that there was nothing whatever the matter with her. John L[ehmann]. is in a nursing home having 4 wisdom teeth extracted—I make no doubt they'll pull out the wrong ones. I've seen various oddments—Peter Lucas one day and Alan and Sheilah [Clutton-Brock] the day after. Peter seems as merry as a grig; and Alan and Shelah did nothing but squabble about a parrot—I'd rather marry Peter than Alan who looks wild weak mad and vindictive. I tried to calm them by suggesting that they should own a dog in common. Yes, I think you're right about Ethel. The sad thing is that she had some gift, but now it's utterly distorted. She is now raving against my having headaches and says theyre all liver, and could be cured by Calomel. Also she's spending all her savings on having The Prison done at her expense. Heavens how nice to see you and Duncan—if Duncan—again. But why in God's name does Ott: open his show?[1] Maynard's doing I imagine. It will need some courage to go, as the whole of art and fashion will be there. I thought you'd catch me a clout on the snout for my present[2]; but next year I shall be coming to you for half crowns I warn you. Its only our bumper crop. L. says he has paid a bill from Cooks, for your wine, but could not take any other steps as he doesn't know the name of Teed's[3] agent.

Berg

---

1. See p. 309, note 1.
2. Vanessa's birthday had been on 30 May. She was 52.
3. Colonel Teed of Cassis.

2383: To CLIVE BELL   [52 *Tavistock Square, W.C.1*]

Postcard
9th June [1931]

Yes I've no doubt France is very nice, but then you don't see Ottoline leading a pug dog down Oxford Street.

V.

And Waller[1] is engaged to marry a girl of 22.

Quentin Bell

2384: To V. SACKVILLE-WEST 52 *T.[avistock] S.[quare, W.C.1]*

Thursday [11 June 1931]

(1) Would you like me to come down on Tuesday for night, to Sissingt, (or Long Barn) I shall be alone.
(2) We have sold 6500 of Passion. Sales *very* good. We are today considering printing a new edition. Lord! What fun! Orders come in like pilchards in a net.
Ethel yesterday much subdued. Had you said anything I wonder? Let me know about Tuesday.

V.

Berg

2385: To ETHEL SMYTH   [52 *Tavistock Square, W.C.1*]

Friday [12 June 1931]

No, I haven't got a moment, or a thought, because I've been working for me, very hard at this bloody book—3 hours this morning, and 2 from 5 to 7. this evening (the publisher [Leonard] yesterday says he must have it, God save his soul, by the end of the month) All I therefore can attempt to say is that yes, certainly, in one word, ALL cards flat on table and faces up. Thats my disposition; nothing else is any use at all. But of course you may not feel so disposed, which alters the case.
I'm trying to make no engagements, except one to go to Vita, next week; because I find myself hopelessly behind hand, and dont see how I'm to be

1. John Waller Hills had married Virginia's half-sister Stella Duckworth in 1897. She died in the same year. In 1931 he married Mary Grace Ashton. Hills was a Member of Parliament and had been Financial Secretary to the Treasury (1922-3). He was now 64, and died in 1938.

ready with my MS. in just over a fortnight. (And Lord how bad it is)—unless I work between 5 and 7 every day if I can: but I'll write later.

Cards on table please without waiting.

Saturday: forgot to post: flowers just come—exquisite—fresh—scented —amorous—glad about Prison.

Berg

2386: TO ETHEL SMYTH   52 *Tavistock Sq.* [*W.C.*1]

Typewritten
[15 June 1931]

No—its the Fortnightly, here. So I send it,[1] to save you 2/6 which it aint worth. Will D.D [Edith Lyttelton]. let me have it back some time, and will you, correctly, inform her of the rectification sent by Evan Charteris. as I feel is Gosses due, not that it alters my opinion one straw. No, it isnt 'work'—I wish it were. my five hours only the deadliest of drudgery, copying, cutting out, putting in, re-reading and so finally sending to the typist; who then leaves out and puts in on her own account, so that has to be altered too, twice, for America and here; a dismal business, but not worse than picking up stitches in knitting—which neither you nor I know nothing of. So by next week I shall be ready for all cards. One of my most vivid memories is of Toveys[2] boredom. We crossed a small bridge at Eton together—the Cloisters, the MacCarthys wedding;[3] and he was facetious about prodding the arch of the bridge with an umbrella; also foamed at the corner of the lips; also irresistibly reminded me, to look at, of cold fowl, such as comes up at Sunday supper covered with a thick white paste. His own music struck me stiff with horror; but I accept all you say about his playing of Bach, and shall go to hear him. There was also a Miss Weisse,[4] wasnt there? And he sets Bob Trevelyan's unreadable plays to unplayable music, an economical arrangement on the part of Providence. So no more.

V.

What about the Prison?

Berg

1. Her review of *The Life and Letters of Sir Edmund Gosse*, by Evan Charteris (*Fortnightly Review*, 1 June 1931).
2. Donald Tovey was Reid Professor of Music at the University of Edinburgh from 1914 until his death in 1940. He produced the first performance of *The Prison*.
3. Desmond and Molly MacCarthy married at Eton in 1906. Molly was the daughter of Francis Warre-Cornish, the Vice-Provost.
4. Sophie Weisse, headmistress of a girls' school at Englefield Green, Surrey, noticed Tovey's exceptional musical precocity, and he owed to her his entire education until he was 19.

2387: To WILLIAM PLOMER   52 *Tavistock Sqre.* [*W.C.1*]

Postcard
Wednesday [17 June 1931]

Could you come in tomorrow, Thursday night—about 9? Lady G.
Wellesley is coming and would like very much to meet you.

V.W.

Texas

2388: To ETHEL SMYTH   52 *T[avistock] S[quare, W.C.1*]

Typewritten
[19th June 1931]

Very well, I'll keep Nov 11th and be prepared for a party at Lady
Londonderrys—for which I shall buy a new dress, all spangles. So for Gods
sake dont let me down and go off to a pot house alone with a crony. I count
upon splendour in Park Lane.

This is however by way of thanking you for the sweet smell of my
drawing room, all white with Simkins[1]—is it? Probably not. I seldom hit
off a name. But any pink by any name would not smell sweeter than yours.
Now I must throw all my MSS into my bag and go off to Rodmell there to
continue this everlasting scratching and copying. And it seems to get
slower and slower and the 1st of July rushes nearer and nearer. Why does
this happen every time; and every time I say it shall not happen again. I
bought one of D[uncan]s pictures.

V.

Berg

2389: To V. SACKVILLE-WEST 52 *T.[avistock] S.[quare, W.C.1*]

Friday [19 June 1931]

After waiting 3 weeks, the books arrived today.[2] I suppose an instance of
thought transmission—your exquisite French must have crossed the Channel
and stirred them to activity without words. But I am keeping the French
letter for future use. O Lord how I enjoyed myself—what a fine brand of
calomel you keep.

Sales going on uninterrupted: at a nursing home yesterday I was told
how one patient recommended AP.S to another 'because its so exquisite,

1. Mrs Sinkins, a dianthus.
2. The French translation of *Orlando.*

345

and also the very book for you, since you're looking for a house"[1] The psychology of the reader is obscure.

Dotty dined here last night, in the oddest jumble of a party, hastily run up to induce her (but dont say this) to continue the series [Hogarth Living Poets]: I'm afraid it wasn't very effective.

Monday, 3.30

V.W.

Berg

2390: To Ethel Smyth   52 *T.[avistock] S.[quare, W.C.1]*

Monday [22 June 1931]

Well if you dont want to see the great grand daughter of the Barrel man,[2] why do you suggest flowers on Wednesday at 5? God knows—to copy your military language what you're at—with your champagne at 2.15 and knocking your cards off the table and damning Virginia because that bald and blameless man Maurice Baring does not write about her—The psychological current at Woking seems to me in my simplicity criss-cross to say the least of it.

However: I shall be in anyhow at 4.30 on Wednesday: tea; if you wish to come, on your way some where else: I'm having a holiday, thank God for a few days having outpaced my typist. for the moment. But you baffle and surprise me so that the formation of the simplest words becomes a problem.

V-W.

And the table will be there for the cards.

Berg

2391: To Lady Ottoline Morrell
                                52 *Tavistock Square, W.C.1*

Friday [26 June 1931]

Dearest Ottoline,

Yes it would be very nice to see you again. (By the way, did your ears blush, or whatever the phrase is, at lunch yesterday, when Goldie and I sang hymns in your praise?)

1. *All Passion Spent* is the story of an 88 year old woman, Lady Slade, who after her husband's death decided to set up house on her own, in defiance of her children's plans for her to live with them.
2. James Pattle. See p. 131, note 1.

Could you come in on Wednesday (July 1st) night, any time about 9?—
We shall be in, and one, possibly 2, others. That would be very nice; and I
hope to come if not on Thursday, another time if I may.

The Saturday night man is most curious—ravaged, exhausted, has been
a bootboy, a waiter, also in prison—but so shy its difficult to catch him.
Next time he's in London I will try to get him here with you, if you can.

But this we can talk of on Wednesday

Yr
V.W.

Texas

2392: To Jane Bussy   [52 *Tavistock Square, W.C.*1]

Friday [26 June 1931]

Dear Janie,

I cant alas come on Wednesday, as I have to go to a concert and hear a
poetess [Joan Easdale] sing; her own works, which makes it even more
formidable. But perhaps another time—?

Also, if I sent you, with my love, Orlando in English and French could
you tell me if Orlando by [Charles] Mauron has any relation to Orlando by
Woolf?—I've heard conflicting reports—not that it much matters. Only
2 passages need be compared and those short ones.

Yours
Virginia Woolf

Texas

2393: To Ethel Smyth   [52 *Tavistock Square, W.C.*1]

Typewritten
Saturday [27 June 1931]

Yes, I've read it twice[1] and think it a very felicitous and persuasive article
in your best style (one or two corrections I've made—my uncles name for
one) My only literary criticism is that it might be improved by greater
compression. Its a little diffuse I think. Your nail is a good nail and a shining
one—that there should be no musical criticism in daily papers but it might
be knocked in a little harder. Owing to the pleasing variety and circum-
vagulation of your mind one gets a little doubtful about the nature of the
nail and what your remedy is. But then on no account would I give up the
man's face like apples and a banana or other Smythian pleasantries (except
'critic and cricket' which savours to me too much of after dinner speaking)

1. Ethel's article *Composers and Critics* (*New Statesman*, 9 May 1931).

so your indirectness is justified and delightful and full of ripeness and richness. But considering the obtuseness of the public and the many hares they'll hunt might it not be a good thing to give the article some simple hammer stroke of a title—A plea for the Abolition of Musical criticism—something like that, but better and shorter. Of course you lay yourself open to one charge I think—that if youre criticised by the papers its your own fault for sending them press tickets; just as I should be told, if I didn' want to be reviewed, why then send out review copies? Marie Corelli[1] never did. And was never reviewed.

Otherwise I think its very true and convincing, your points, even to me purblind and distorted as I am. What I think you dont realise, perhaps, is that (no doubt owing to my own vanity which imputes vanity to others) you *seem* in *talk* to attach such enormous importance to praise to recognition, when on your own showing the best judges (Walter[2] etc) know your worth; when critics are vile; when youve enough to live on; when you spend months of ecstacy (see the Prison and your letters) in the act of composition. What I should like would be, in another article, a purely objective statement of the exact disabilities (not being allowed to play in orchestras etc which women suffer in music.) Also, though you make out a good case, the critics, damn them, cant be so destructive or why are the classics the classics; and why is this so, even in the case of Wagner, so often during their life time? Somehow the big apples come to the top of the basket, and generally before the composer is under the sod. But of course I realise that the musician's apple lies longest at the bottom and has the hardest struggle to rise—thats clear. And then I detest people dwelling on their own injuries—its so infinitely sterile. And then I think the creative thing to do would be to furbish up some orchestra and run the things on your own. This I did— oh yes, in a modest way, when the publishers told me to write what they liked. I said No. I'll publish myself and write what I like. Which I did, and for many years, owing to lack of organisation travellers etc. lost much money thereby. Yes there I am blowing my own trumpet. But its a harsh raw noise —ones own trumpet. If I were you I'd train typists and street singers rather than go on whipping these gentrys hard and horny behinds. You will say however that I know nothing, feel nothing and understand less than nothing. So be it. I realise why I am so essential to you—precisely my quality of scratching post, what the granite pillar in the Cornish field gives the rough-haired, burr-tangled Cornish pig—thats you. An uncastrated pig into the bargain; a wild boar, a savage sow, and my fate in life is to stand there, a

1. Marie Corelli (1855-1924) was one of the most popular novelists of her day.
2. Bruno Walter (1876-1962), the distinguished conductor, once wrote of Ethel's music: "I consider Ethel Smyth a composer of quite special significance who is certain of a permanent place in musical history" (quoted by Christopher St John, *Ethel Smyth*, 1959, p. 111).

granite pillar, and be scraped by Ethel's hoary hide. Yes, because not another soul in Woking but lies under you like sweet lavender; there you roll and trample and bellow. I'm the only friend you have who is thoroughly and disgustingly upright and blind and deaf and dumb. Now isnt that a psychological discovery of the first water? But I cant be here till 5 or so on Wednesday owing to my infernal fate—to listen to a poetess singing her own songs to music written by a brother at some blasted hall. I've seen Barretts;[1] rather feeble I thought; and have written (to come out next week) an 'essay' on Mrs Browning.[2] But perhaps we may meet, if youll arrange it—one scrape more, one more grind of your infuriated hide and rasping tusks. What you call euphemistically 'putting cards on the table;' when its more like rending a rib open with a knife.

—hah hah. V,

[in Virginia's handwriting:]
(written in a hurry, but I'm always now in a hurry so I send it as it is, with all its faults on its face)

Berg

2394: To Vanessa Bell   52 *Tavistock Square, W.C.*1

Sunday [28 June 1931]

   Would you convey to Angus that I will offer £40 for the chairs, which I think is about fair—I do this through you, (and will send you the cheque when my money is paid in*) as I find him so depressing he'll probably dissuade me.
   Perhaps I might come to tea on Tuesday?—God knows.

B.

* this maynt be for 3 weeks.

Berg

2395: To Jane Bussy   52 *T.[avistock] S.[quare, W.C.*1]

Sunday [28 June? 1931]

My dear Janie,
   I must say it is amazingly good of you to have ploughed through so much of the translation [of *Orlando*], and I accept your word as gospel truth. [Charles] Mauron is much blown upon in certain quarters and I was

1. *The Barretts of Wimpole Street* (1930), by Rudolph Besier.
2. 'Aurora Leigh' (*TLS*, 2 July 1931).

349

told that any competent French scholar would see through him. As you're more than competent, I'm greatly relieved by your report, and shall bruit it abroad. Is there any book or books of mine, or Shakespeare's Hardy's Scotts, that I can give you, in token of gratitude? Or a puppy, or a fantail pigeon, or a piebald mouse? Ask and it shall be yours.

God knows I wish I could come to your basement on Tuesday: all this week I must be chained to mine. I have positively to finish my latest, which is of indescribable horror, so that to try and get it right at the last moment is like washing a black baby white, or stitching a 4th leg to a lamb born with only 2 and ½. But the week after, please God, I shall be free and at yr service.

V.

Robert H. Taylor

2396: To Ethel Smyth   52 *Tavistock Square, W.C.*1

June 29th [1931]

I have read your letter twice and shall read it again. I am very glad that you have written with such frankness.[1] I dont think there is much for me to say but, as I suppose from your tone that you want to come here on Wednesday I just want, very briefly to say that I think you are completely justified in your conclusion that "such a person ought not to be thus loved." But I dont think that I've ever made out that I possessed qualities which entitled me to your love. I have from the first insisted on my faults—blindness, selfishness etc. So that if you have now discovered that I have not an ounce of perception etc. it is not that I tried to delude you. And I think I've always said that you exaggerated my merits as a writer.

But please believe that I am very glad of the frankness with which you have written.

Of course I could go on to justify and excuse myself, but I dont feel that there's any good in it.

V.

Berg

2397: To Sibyl Colefax   52 *Tavistock Square [W.C.*1]

Typewritten
[June? 1931]

My dear Lady Colefax

Wasn't I clever to avoid the seductions of your voice? I sat in my bath an hour but it was worth it. If you want to rend the domestic veil, here you are.

1. Virginia returned Ethel's letter with the most sentimental and hysterical passages underlined.

If I dine with you, I shan't sleep; if I don't sleep, I cant write. You say this dont matter a straw. I quite agree with you. But my next year's income depends on sending a book to America in August. It aint half done, owing to dining out. So theres no more to be said. Your mercenary soul (didn't you throw me over for half a crown the other night?) will understand.

Ever your obedient and now extremely clean

Virginia Woolf

Michael Colefax

2398: To Vanessa Bell   [52 *Tavistock Square, W.C.1*]

Wednesday [1 July? 1931]

Will you dine here with me tomorrow? I shall be alone, and perhaps you would like to bring your pencil and do a sketch. Anyhow you must come, as I've got your picture,[1] which is the apple of my eye. I dont know how to hang it. Ethel Sands was in great admiration of it.—but all gossip when we meet.

8 or earlier.

B

Berg

2399: To Helen McAfee   52 *Tavistock Square, W.C.1*

Typewritten
July 2nd 1931

Dear Miss McAfee,

Many thanks for the cheque for 250 dollars for my essay on Aurora Leigh. I must also thank you for the very useful list of errata—I am ashamed that so many got past me in the typescript. I had already found some of the worst myself, but too late to send them on to you. They have been corrected in the English version, and I am very grateful for the help.

The Barretts of Wimpole Street goes along here, apparently without any slackening. I myself was rather disappointed, though amused by the astonishing story—which is not an exaggeration. But they might have made it hit harder I thought. However the Barretts themselves are furious, threatening libel actions as it is.

Many thanks for enquiring about another essay. I fear that my mind, over which I have little control, is leading me away from contemporary

1. Perhaps the 'picture of Angelica' referred to in Virginia's diary for 30 June 1931 (Berg).

life in the direction of the Elizabethans. I want to explore there a little, and may at last go into the Lady Clifford Diaries[1] which have been on my shelves for more than a year. But if anything likely to interest the Yale Review occurs to me I shall of course be very glad to suggest it to you.

Believe me, yours sincerely

Virginia Woolf

Yale University

2400: To Ethel Smyth   *Monks House* [*Rodmell,*
                                         Sussex]

Typewritten
Saturday [4 July 1931]

Let me put it like this.

As I think I told you, I had promised to have the Waves done by July 1st—last Wednesday. I discovered however that I must make one very difficult and radical change before I could let it go. I calculated that by giving up Monday Tuesday and Wednesday to writing, and not merely to writing out to concentration of a very complete kind I might be able to do it (But I have not).

On Monday morning your letter arrived. At the same time I was told something in confidence about a friends life that moved and upset me very much;[2] at the same time I was asked to consider a plan that needs considerable thought and it may be action. I confess that your letter with its multitudinous embroidery of a personal grievance seemed (quite apart from its damaging references to my character and conduct) to make a huge and at the moment unwarrantable demand on my sympathy. I had the sense afterwards to reflect that such demands upon the sympathy and attention of your friends are inevitable. One must remember your temperament, your struggles, your difficulties, your loneliness, your unhappiness, and the peculiar strain which as a musician you have to undergo. It is quite natural, as I see, that a chance joke gets upon your nerves and rouses you to a sense of intolerable hardship. I dont blame you; I see it must be so; I see that it is the penalty that life exacts.

1. Lady Anne Clifford was the daughter of the Earl of Cumberland and heiress to his vast estates. She was twice married: her first husband was the Earl of Dorset, and she left a diary, published in 1924 (with an introduction by Vita), in which she described life at Knole in the early 17th century. Her second husband was the Earl of Pembroke. Apparently Virginia never wrote about her.
2. Virginia makes no further reference to this in either her letters or diaries. The 'plan' was Leonard's idea to go to America and then around the world.

352

But it does I think put great difficulties in the way of intercourse. And I dont think that they are the difficulties that you speak of. Scenes and rages and moments of misunderstanding are a bore and a pity and take up time and harass ones mind; but they pass and one forgets them. What does not pass, and is not forgotten is the feeling that one is prevented from intimacy. Your extreme susceptibility to criticism and your vast (if entirely natural) need of sympathy inevitably make one feel that one cannot be at ones ease, and free, and careless with you as with other people; that one cannot expect the same intuition and understanding from a woman who is naturally and rightly as absorbed as you are in your own past and present and future. One therefore feels that one is limiting oneself, being simpler, cruder and less communicative than is natural. The same thing has happened to me twice before—once with my father whom I adored. But then, he had had a very hard life with his deafness, my mother's death, and his sense of being, as a philosopher, a failure. Thus he demanded and needed perpetual sympathy and was apt to fly into violent rages and despairs in what we thought a most unreasonable way if anyone spoke a careless word about his work, or his life. Hence by degrees one felt that one had always to pick and choose what one said to him and never dared tell him the small events that interested us, for he might at any moment fly off with 'Oh but think what my life has been, what my sufferings are, what I have been going through since your mother died.' And I think this queered the pitch and made us much more formal and cautious with him than was right. And it happened again with a woman who was in love with me, and used to write me reams about not understanding her life and her misunderstood virtues (for she thought herself the greatest psychologist in England) [Ethel herself] and so we parted.

Now to brush all this aside—this quarrel—and say "O but I'm so devoted to you; lets kiss and be friends," seems to me childish. Yet as I say I dont see how you can help yourself. When the Wreckers is done you naturally need much more sympathy than I do when the Waves is published. And one is sure to laugh and be casual about it. (Also I dont think you realise how much you emphasise, from good motives I'm sure, the difficulties of the musician; your own struggle; the horror of the critics—I believe I could pass an examination in whats been said and written about you and by you since you were six years old—but here again, you reiterate partly because of your championship of the under dog—but its a nail that has gone through my head) Therefore there will be other quarrels. And what is worse I shall be feeling; well, surely she might see that one has other difficulties, other struggles, other interests—Of course I see that this is not so with your old friends, like Mrs [Violet] Woodhouse or Lady Betty [Balfour], but how can it help being so with you who were seventy, and I who was 48 when we first met? I'm sure this is crudely put, for I'm hurried; but perhaps you'll see how it puzzles me. I dont care for unreal friendships;

and if one thing emerges from these letters it is the extreme unreality of a relationship which leads to all these words.

P.S.
I forgot to say that I underlined in blue your remark about the Interim passage in the Waves by mistake. It didnt in the least annoy me. It interested me very much, and I meant to ask you what you meant. I should like to know.

No Leonard does not think you a 'tame tiger', but another animal, less dignified, but more sonorous.

[*in Virginia's handwriting:*]
Monday 4.30 would suit me better than Wednesday if its the same to you.[1]

V.

Berg

2401: To Ethel Smyth   52 *Tavistock Square, W.C.*1

Tuesday [7 July 1931]

Well Ethel dear, I'm very glad that the poor cat—oh no I mean the happy the hirsute, the erect, the brindling and bristling cat—in fact the hedgehog, has gone to bed happy—though I dont approve of a woman who has pawned her last hairpin to produce what she considers—hum-ha—one must be very careful in future—no jokes, no allusions to certain foibles—I'm sorry I was going to say before my evil devil led me astray, that you should express letters so that they cost 7d. instead of one. But then I like getting things at irregular hours, with the emphasis of the unexpected in them— lying stamped on hall tables when I come in, hot, dreary, from moving one pillar in the Waves half an inch to the right, having moved it yesterday three quarters of an inch to the left. Its not the writing of the Waves that takes the time, but the architecture: and its not right yet, and God knows if my eyes not out, and I'm only moving round in a circle. But this explains perhaps certain absences of mind, and cannon bolts down the telephone— Lord! how I like the thud of my abuse upon your hide. I think I shall make a practise of it "Ethel. d'you know you're a damned Harlot.—a hoary harpy—or an eldritch shriek of egotism—a hail storm of inconsecutive and inconsequent conceit—Thats all" And I shall ring off. I forgot what I started out to say. Never mind—this is just a pelt at your hide.

V.

1. During this visit Virginia and Ethel made up their quarrel.

A furious old gentleman in Manchester, coeval with the Brownings has attacked me[1] for what he's pleased to call iconoclasm. I'm replying, in my well-known style, something spicy about orgasm making a rhyme.

Berg

2402: TO ALLANAH HARPER, EDITOR OF ECHANGES
52 *Tavistock Square, W.C.*1

Typewritten
7th July 1931

Dear Madam,

I understand from the Hogarth Press that M. Mauron gave you authority to publish an extract from Orlando in Echanges. But, as a matter of fact, that authority can only be given by Stock, who publish the translation of Orlando, and to whom any money due should be paid. I am therefore returning the cheque for £5 which you sent me, as it is clear that I have no right to it.

Yours faithfully
Virginia Woolf

Texas

2403: TO V. SACKVILLE-WEST 52 *Tavistock Square, W.C.*1

Wednesday [8 July 1931]

I've told Ethel that you have long promised to take me for a treat—say to the Blackwall tunnel—on Monday next, thus gracefully avoiding a visit to Lady Lewis's to hear Tovey play Bach. So please confirm this or some part of it.

Then, years, no weeks ago I met Maurice Baring who wished me to exculpate Gosse from writing that letter to Ross,[2] with Harold. And here's a letter from Evan Charteris to prove it. All of which is out of date and forgotten now; but never mind.

And oh Lord these senile old women with their perverted passions—here's Lady Oxford on me—bringing Ebth Princess of Bibesco[3] to tea, demanding my picture and—O Lord again—that my next book shall be

1. Her essay on *Aurora Leigh*.
2. See p. 306, note 3.
3. Elizabeth Asquith, the daughter of Lady Oxford, who married Prince Antoine Bibesco. She wrote several novels.

dedicated to her. What Poppy or Mandragora[1]—no, its keep away[2] I'm
thinking of—the room still ringing with Ethel on the phone. So to bed.
And whats bed without—? And when—? And what—?

V.

Berg

2404: TO ETHEL SMYTH   [52 *Tavistock Square, W.C.1*]

Sunday [12 July 1931]

What G. Lowes Dickinson said was (not to me but to Leonard) that he
had been reading, first I think, The Prison: with great interest, and great
admiration: He had then gone on to Law and Anarchy which he found also
most sympathetic; he admired the writing, found the ideas akin to his own;
and so went on to read a third, in French;[3] and was increased in his admiration. Leonard said that HB was doing much what G.L.D. does, or attempts;
but G.L.D. said No, HB. was doing something of his own, and something
which interested him (G. L. D) very greatly. GLD. is a writer, as you may
know, of Platonic dialogues, about law society the soul, duty, love, work
etc: and a very charming man, and the fine flower of Cambridge culture—
How he got at HB. I dont know: anyhow he seems to have put up a good
fight against whatever objections L. made, and to have been discriminating,
detailed and impressed. There—I dont suppose I've given GLD. his words
verbatim; but you can gather the gist. And I think this a great compliment,
because, like the rest of his tribe, GLD is very fastidious, instructed and only
says what, on deep consideration with complete regard for the truth, he
thinks. How unlike us, Miss Beale and Miss Buss.[4]

I dont suppose I shall be able to come tomorrow, greatly though I
should like to hear the cold chicken [Donald Tovey] play Bach. Life is too

1.   Not poppy, nor Mandragora,
                    Nor all the drowsy syrups of the world,
                    Shall ever medicine thee to that sweet sleep
                    Which thou ow'dst yesterday.
                                        Othello, III, iii.

2. Keepaway was a substance designed to keep dogs away from bitches on heat.

3. Dickinson had read these books by Henry Brewster: *The Prison; The Theories
of Anarchy and of Law;* and *L'Ame Païenne.*

4.   Miss Buss and Miss Beale
                    Cupid's darts do not feel.
                    How different from us,
                    Miss Beale and Miss Buss.
                                    Anon., 19th century.

Miss Beale was Principal of the Ladies' College, Cheltenham; and Miss Buss,
Headmistress of the North London Collegiate School.

much with us, late and soon, getting and spending, we lay waste our powers. (another quotation)[1] Once this bloody book is done, I shall fling my hands in the air, and be quit for ever of writing sentences. Lord what a happy life—never to write again. At the moment the thought of not writing fills me with delirious joy, too far and fair to be true.

Whats the use, if a book is fundamentally unreadable, like the Waves, of correcting commas?

So you can judge the mood in which I scribble these hasty lines, hoping to find you in the Pink as they leave me—Some evenings I write all quotations.

Yr Virginia

Berg

2405: To Elizabeth Robins   52 *Tavistock Square, W.C.*1

16th July [1931]

Dear Miss Robins,

We shall be delighted to look at the verses, if you will send them here. I wish that they were by you! A vague dream remains in my mind that you once said you would write your memoirs and let me see them—but perhaps it was only a dream.

Yours sincerely
Virginia Woolf

Texas

2406: To Ethel Smyth   [*Monk's House, Rodmell, Sussex*]

Sunday [19 July 1931]

Well Ethel, Leonard has read it—The Waves—and likes it, and I'm so relieved I'm like a girl with an engagement ring.[2] Its true he thinks very few people will survive the first 100 pages. And I must now see if I cant simplify and clarify a little on his hints; but he doubts that I can. Anyhow thats over: and I'm, as I say, as light as a trout, with sheer irresponsible relief, and feel now I can spend a whole hour putting sweet peas in water and needn't hurry down to my commas and semi-colons in a state of torpor, distrust, and somnolent sordidity. Here's an eldritch screech of egotism if you like. But my word—think of getting that MS. out of the house on Tuesday perhaps, and no proofs for a fortnight. A very stormy week end:

1. Wordsworth. Sonnet XXXIII.
2. " 'It is a masterpiece,' said L., coming out to my lodge this morning. 'And the best of your books' " (*A Writer's Diary*, 19 July 1931, p. 173).

elm trees almost down, and flowers broken by rutting cats howling all night in the wind. They made their marriage bed in the sweet williams, and their progeny will be pied, I imagine. And I'm buying a boat and taking to the sea. Why should all physical delight rest with you—why shouldn't I stretch my muscles in a gale and haul down sheets and anchors and fly before the North East to the Pole?

Berg

Letters 2407-2450 (July–October 1931)

Virginia rapidly corrected the proofs of The Waves, *finishing them by 17 August. The book was published on 8 October. As she awaited the verdict, she felt her usual misgivings about the book's quality, and was distressed that one of her first readers, Hugh Walpole, was said to have found it disappointing. Her spirits were restored by the praise of John Lehmann, Harold Nicolson and, above all, Vanessa, and she felt confident enough to write in her diary, 'I'm the hare, a long way ahead of the hounds my critics'. But the waiting period, between proofs and publication, was a strain. She went to bed with a week's headache, and visitors forced themselves on her at Monk's House—Sibyl Colefax, Ethel Smyth, the Easdales, the Duckworths. For relaxation she had a few new pleasures, a camera, a frigidaire, a rubber boat in which she paddled down the Ouse, and a new book,* Flush, *the biography of Elizabeth Barrett Browning's dog.*

2407: To V. Sackville-West   52 *Tavistock Square, W.C.*1

Wednesday [22 July 1931]

Lord! was there ever a woman I knew called Vita? And was she ever fond of a woman called—Well my life's a running sore, and I write only to say are you dining with me on Monday? If not, when am I seeing you? And will you tell me, so that I mayn't be ravished to Woking. But my life's one pustulence and pestilence—I cant tell you—Only, are you dining with me on Monday? or what? And are you fond of me, or what? D'you know what I bought today[1] and what it bodes?—and what a change is impending? No:'cos you dont care, heartless daughter of the stationmaster at Barcelona.[2]

Berg

1. Virginia had bought an inflatable rubber dinghy.
2. It had been rumoured (inaccurately) that Vita's mother was the child of the stationmaster at Boulogne, where her mother Pepita, the Spanish dancer, was stranded overnight by bad weather.

Wednesday [22 July 1931]

My dear Dorothy,

This is ghastly—I mean the flight of time and no tea party. But the truth is that the man I hate most in the world, your nephew Tomlin,[1] has me by the hair: I waste afternoon after afternoon perched in his ratridden and draught-riddled studio: cant escape. If I do, all the bonds of friendship are (he says, and I wish it were true) torn asunder. I mean, I have to sit daily for his bust, and Nessa's portrait.[2] What I suggest is that you should come, tomorrow, 4.30. to tea *there*, 8 Percy Street, off the Tott. Court Road; where you'd find too I think, that immortal old harridan Ethel Smyth. Next week seems altogether hopeless, and we go away on Thursday.

So what's to be done?

Yours
Virginia

Forgive this scrawl. My fingers tremble with rage. Day after day thrown into the pit, and all for a woman's face, or whatever Swift, if it was Swift, said. You see how sitting disintegrates every faculty.

Texas

Thursday [23 July 1931]

I'm afraid I cant manage to come tomorrow because I've got into such a muddle that I must take a day off in order to deal with horrors.

But I want to lay this question before your wisdom. Do you really think it is worth while for me to go on sitting [to Tomlin]? I'm quite prepared, as I said, to sit until we go away, but I have a feeling that the bust won't conceivably be finished by then, and that the question of further sittings in the autumn will arise. Now that I've tried it for four days I see that it would be sheer idiocy on my part to pretend that I can do this. I dont believe sitting regularly is possible in London, leading the lives we lead, and simply involves both painters and sitters in endless difficulties and a general

1. Stephen Tomlin, the sculptor, married Julia Strachey, the daughter of Dorothy Bussy's brother Oliver.
2. Virginia was sitting for her portrait-bust by Tomlin, and Vanessa kept her company by simultaneously making a sketch of her. There were four castings of Tomlin's bust: which are now in the National Portrait Gallery, in the garden at Monk's House, at Sissinghurst Castle, and belonging to David Garnett. The original plaster-model is at Charleston.

rush and scramble and chaos and horror. This being so, it seems rather a waste of all our time to go on, even these next few days, which are very full for both you and me. However, as I say I'm ready to come on Monday (we go to the Waterlows on Saturday) if you think on sober consideration that it is worth it. Of course the bust may be on the brink of completion—I only write because I dont want to waste all our time if it should be a waste; I mean if further sittings in the autumn should be necessary.

Here are the measurements of the fireplace.Please understand that I've commissioned this and charge me not pauper's prices but those that befit mature and well grounded citizens. We bought a camera today, in the wildest fashion, and now they say my Kodak can be made perfect for 5/—Would you accept it—? I'm sure its incurable, so there's not much virtue in the offer.

B

Berg

2410: To Ethel Smyth   [52 *Tavistock Square, W.C.*1]

Thursday [23 July 1931]

Ethel, C.BE,[1]—I felt very compunctious and rumpaxtious and gromboolious into the bargain. When I saw you go off, dripping, into the furnace this afternoon—Also red roaring rackety tackety rampagious at the thought of that multi faced Austrian [*unidentified*] making off with your nest egg, your very small bantam egg, laid with such prodigious labour too, and by such a magnificent dawn fiery cock—I should say hen—How d'you like my new vocabulary? I'm so delighted to be relieved of the Mrs [Alice] Meynell claustrophobia—no word not cut on Miltons tombstone to be used ever again, and all that hard boiled aridity—when my veins run liquid language, and red hot rum. By the way, owing not to you, but to those thridoled and thrummed, danderhopscottery [*all these words sic*] painters, slap-dander them, we missed our appointment with the Loud speaker man— he has a tip for making every fiddle squeak divinely even at Rodmell—we rushed with violent impetuosity into a camera shop instead and bought a superb Zeiss camera, costing £20, and said to be unrivalled in the portrayal of the human—if mine can be said to be human—face. So I shall send you a whole series of Virginia, and you will say very properly curse the woman for a quick silver mine of vanity—Those will be your very words, and justified too: but also it shall record the noble features of the dripping cat, the uncastrated cat, the fighting indomitable cat, who began this letter by

---

1. Commander of the British Empire. Ethel was in fact a D.B.E., which Virginia well knew.

being a cock, then became a hen, and is all the time a Dame of the British Empire

Shame! Shame! on her!

V.

Berg

2411: To V. Sackville-West

52 *T.[avistock]* *S.[quare, W.C.*1]

[25 July 1931]

Yes, come at 5.30 to sign[1] and return at 7.30 to dine. (That is a poem— a lyric I think) But poetry is far from my thoughts. I have to break a sad piece of news to you.

Potto[2] is dead.

For about a month (you have not been for a month and I date his decline from your last visit) I have watched him failing. First his coat lost lustre; then he refused biscuits; finally gravy. When I asked him what ailed him he sighed, but made no answer. The other day coming unexpectedly into the room, I found him wiping away a tear. He still maintained unbroken silence. Last night it was clear that the end was coming. I sat with him holding his paw in mine and felt the pulse grow feebler. At 7.45 he breathed deeply. I leant over him. I just caught and was able to distinguish the following words—"Tell Mrs Nick that I love her. . . . She has forgotten me. But I forgive her and . . . . (here he cd. hardly speak) die . . . of . . .a . . . . broken . . . . heart!" He then expired.

And so shall I very soon. Just off to spend Sunday with the Waterlows [at Oare, Wiltshire] Oh my God—my Potto.

And Mrs Nick has deserted us.

V.

Oh no I dont suppose we shall dine alone; because L. must see you—must, must, must.

Berg

2412: To Ethel Smyth

52 *Tavistock Square, W.C.*1

Tuesday [28 July 1931]

A miracle happened.[3]

I turned over all my papers; was in despair; found only a rough first

1. The limited edition of Vita's poem *Sissinghurst*.
2. Virginia's name for herself when writing to Vita.
3. The typescript of *The Waves* had been lost and found.

draft; sat down to re-write; gave a sweep of my hand; looked up; there was the carbon copy before me. The mystery remains, about the original; but I sent off the carbons; so saved my sanity. But it's bad, alas—

Yr V.

Berg

2413: To Ethel Smyth   [52 *Tavistock Square, W.C.*1]

[30 July 1931]

No, no—I wasn't alone—I wasn't meaning to dine here, but at Boulestins. L. was here. It suddenly occurred to me that we might have our ceremonial dinner—but it was too late to arrange and as L. pointed out, it was an absurd idea, on my part, considering I had left a thousand things to do. I'm sorry I disturbed you with the suggestion, a mere phantasy born of the delicious relief of having done with sitting [to Tomlin] I spent the evening in virtuous preparation for flight today [to Monk's House].

Berg

2414: To V. Sackville-West

52 *T.[avistock] S.[quare, W.C.*1]

Thursday [30 July 1931]

Poor poor angelic creature—I'm desolated to think of you racked [with lumbago], not moving, in bed, full of crumbs, with perhaps a book or a glass or your pocket handkerchief out of reach, and Louise [Genoux] banging about next door. Potto's last wish by the way was that I should send you a jar of caviare to be eaten in his memory—so take it thus, eat. slowly. with tears.

Here's my half brother on pigs (the 3rd copy he's sent me).[1]

Life's a bad business—all hurry and riot and sitting for my bust against my will. I think of you as I sit aching with my eyes blazed out of me in a top light. Not as bad as the lumbago, I say to myself. But almost.

I hear A.P.S. [*All Passion Spent*] has beaten the Edwardians, and now if its a play, will run on and on. Oh and out of the profits—did I tell you?— I've bought a boat and a camera. Such are the blessings you shower. Yes— any day we shall have a spare room: so let me know. Or I will come over. Just off

V.

Berg

1. George Duckworth had published a short letter on pigs in *The Times.*

2415: To Ethel Smyth   [*Monk's House, Rodmell, Sussex*]

Sunday [2 August 1931]

But I dont see any possibility of meeting you on the pier. Some sort of meeting, at a station perhaps, could have been arranged for Tuesday had it not been fixed—and Lord Lord why do I hate these necessary formalities so violently?—that we should spend Tuesday at Worthing, in a hotel bedroom, with lots of sugar cakes and almond paste taken from a cupboard. My mother in law—poor old lady—yes, I know all that: she's been ill; is alone with a maid; hates all other old ladies; sends me large pots of cream by way of a bribe. I've been out in my boat though, and had one walk on the downs;—and so can't I suppose complain. And tonight we develop our first photographs. But I came in from my walk to find 5 people calling. All very very nice; but after those sittings, not to see, not to be seen, is all I ask.

Well goodbye.

If you should have time to write, of course you know an address where letters are welcome. Pen is hopeless.

Berg

2416: To Sibyl Colefax   [*Monk's House, Rodmell, Sussex*]

[4? August 1931]

Dearest Sibyl,

Yes let me know if you're anywhere near[1]—but what's the use of coming here? My view's entirely ruined—galvanised iron sheds, [Asheham] cement works, bungalows. God save us all. Better be in London.

Yrs. V.

Michael Colefax

2417: To V. Sackville-West   *Monks House [Rodmell, Sussex]*

Tuesday [4 August 1931]

Oh dear what a bore, and more, it is that you are still so bad. Are you taking any steps about it—seeing an osteopath, or a surgeon, or having treatment? These sort of questions are a nuisance, I know; but it seems such a wearisome long time, to lie in pain on ones back, occasionally shifting to

1. Sibyl Colefax visited Monk's House on 14 August.

one elbow. But I suppose Harold and Dotty are on the look out, and it remains for me merely to curse.

I have been slightly knocked up with headache (liver I suppose; a dose of calomel is what I want) and therefore cant suggest at the moment coming; but I'm much better today, and shall be cured by Thursday completely. Let me know if you'd like me to come. We would drive over.

London became the usual treadmill. I dont see much point in London in July without Vita, and Potto expiring. But you're right—he's not dead. I brought him here—put him on the terrace—he stirred yesterday—today he's nibbled on orris root which I happened to have by me.

And its roasting hot. This I hope may filter down your spine and dissolve the knot.

There's a million things to say, and I have little control of what passes for my pen. What about Mary [Hutchinson]? I had not heard. Nessa seems to think Clive's eyes rather bad, but so wrapt in mystery, because he wont say whats wrong if indeed he knows, that she cant tell how bad they are. I'm going on the river in my boat and out to sea—no lily ponds for me. We take photographs which develop in a slope of mist undulating from one end of the film to another. Sibyl has invited herself to stay: George and Margaret themselves to lunch: and Ethel whirls round me like a circulating thunderstorm, so far mercifully averted from this actual roof. Leonard somehow has conveyed to her that he does not like her.

Yes yes; I am still unfortunately attached to the woman I never see; the vision in the fishmongers shop.[1] I was thinking of that scene the other night, and wondering if there was a porpoise in a tank, or whether that was merely an emanation of you—When is your play being done?[2] Are you writing it? Is your fortune made? What about Harold and Mosley?[3] But dont write if it hurts. I will write. A spare room is always ready for you

V.

Berg

2418: TO V. SACKVILLE-WEST   [*Monk's House, Rodmell, Sussex*]

Saturday [8 August 1931]

Well, I'm hugely pleased to hear that you're up, even if you look like a corkscrew. But please dont do it again. Dont think the antiquity of Sissinghurst requires a mistress like an old fire tongs. Please get your muscle

1. Vita herself.
2. *All Passion Spent* was dramatized in 1933, and performed at Croydon, where Jean Cadell played Lady Slade.
3. Harold was soon to leave the *Evening Standard*, and edit *Action*, the journal of Sir Oswald Mosley's New Party.

replaced. Go to a doctor. Yes: I know how this annoys you on the lips of Dotty and Harold, but not on my lips, which you love. I cured myself with only one day in bed. And I thought I should be there 3. But I find, after 25 years, that to be still, flat, silent, dark, instantly, is a perfect cure, and might have saved me years, had I done it ages ago. And then I should have written more books. But I rather doubt that one wants more books (witness Hugh, whose new book[1] is being given me by the author in a day or two) But what I was saying was Yes, yes, for Gods sake come. Come on *Wednesday* not Tuesday, as early as you can, and stay the night—the chaste night— We have a mint of things to say to you—about Eddy for one thing, who says if we will pay his fare he will come to England [from Germany], stay here, and sign his books. Then theres a French duchess—I always talk to you about duchesses—who insults me on the telephone. Clermont-Tonnerre.[2] But I've warded her off for the time. As for Katherine [Mansfield], I think you've got it very nearly right. We did not ever coalesce; but I was fascinated, and she respectful, only I thought her cheap, and she thought me priggish; and yet we were both compelled to meet simply in order to talk about writing. This we did by the hour. Only then she came out with a swarm of little stories, and I was jealous, no doubt; because they were so praised; but gave up reading them not on that account, but because of their cheap sharp sentimentality, which was all the worse, I thought, because she had, as you say, the zest and the resonance—I mean she could permeate one with her quality; and if one felt this cheap scent in it, it reeked in ones nostrils. But I must read her some day. Also, she was for ever pursued by her dying; and had to press on through stages that should have taken years in ten minutes—so that our relationship became unreal also. And there was Murry squirming and oozing a sort of thick motor oil in the background—dinners with them were about the most unpleasnt exhibitions, humanly speaking, I've ever been to. But the fact remains—I mean, that she had a quality I adored, and needed; I think her sharpness and reality—her having knocked about with prostitutes and so on, whereas I had always been respectable— was the thing I wanted then. I dream of her often—now thats an odd reflection—how one's relation with a person seems to be continued after death in dreams, and with some odd reality too.

But why be ashamed of wanting a garden and poets? Whats there to be proud of in Fleet Street, and daily papers.

I assure you—only the post is going and I have no time to think what it is that I assure you of—that one walk here fills my poor old head with a sense of such natural happiness as I never get a whole summer in London. And you, being a poet—O how I wish I were!—you being a poet have no

1. *Judith Paris* was published on 28 August.
2. Marie Louise, daughter of the Duc de Brissac, who married the Comte de Clermont-Tonnerre. She was 74.

use for the odds and ends, the husks, the fragments, the general confusion and vibration which I can make myself believe I find in London. If I were you, I would lie on a bank all day and make one phrase—for Virginia.

Potto is distinctly better.

V.

Berg

2419: To Ethel Smyth   *Monks House, Rodmell*
                              [Sussex]

Monday 10th August [1931]

Oh yes, my dear Ethel, I did notice that there were no white envelopes on my plate with your rapid masterly hand—but I said to myself, with a sigh, she is otherwise engaged. Why should she think of me? This beautifully modest beginning to the day has been of great service to me spiritually. For the rest—let me see: headache; bed; (too much of my mother in laws cream affecting the liver is it?—the spleen?) up: boating; down tide at a rush; meeting 22 embattled swans; necks stretched hissing; towing boat home;—one or two walks; some callers; photography; developing at night in a cavern hung with red calico—hence many films spoilt; but some are tremendously ugly and very like;—I am jotting these facts down to soothe my own agitation; now that I have read, two minutes ago, my first batch of proofs: so dont be too hard on me. No, I swear its worse being a writer than an operatician; anyhow you can say its love, or the tenor has a cough; or the conductor, having copulated 10 times in one night with the soprano is not up, now, to the scratch. Whereas faced by cold print which can neither cough nor copulate, what excuse is there for the Waves? That is what I ask myself this cold rainy morning, sitting out here in the Lodge, with the lively prospect of people to tea. And from the lilies and lavender of Woking will come no answer. What a farce letter writing is to be sure! Why do we want letters? All I say is false. I mean, so much has to be left out that what remains is like the finger print in salt of some huge pachydermatous quadruped which no private house could contain. My brain is rather on the hop; I rip and skip: haven't settled, as I should, to read all Donne, all Sidney, all a writer you've never heard of called Lord Brooke.[1] When I've had my last proof I pray God that I may recover my balance; and settle in and wrap myself in philosophy against the winter and all its blows.

Well, you say we shan't meet? Why, if you're at Rottingdean dont you— but hush! I feel myself on the verge of one of those obtusenesses which my psychological blindness so often produces. I know so little what people feel,

1. Fulke Greville, 1st Baron Brooke (1554-1628), the poet and statesman who wrote the *Life of Sidney* (1652). Virginia published essays on John Donne and Sir Philip Sidney in *The Common Reader: Second Series* (1932).

want, are: For example, are you enjoying life? Are you happy? What is your opinion of the Wreckers?[1] And Virginia; and Leonard; and life as a whole? Also is the Duchesse de Clermont-Tonnerre a friend of yours? Because I dont wish her to be a friend of mine. So please Ethel write and explain everything.

V.

Berg

2420: To Ethel Smyth   *Monks House* [*Rodmell, Sussex*]

Sunday [16 August 1931]

That all seems to me perfectly straightforward and clear—the Synopsis I mean. I dont see that even I, who boggle at plots, could get this one wrong. Of course, as you say, its the bones of a mammoth merely—but I dont find any essential, say a rib or a spine missing. Only the brain; which will be there when the orchestra starts the first bar.

I see you ask for a definite answer about the 21st-24th. If thats so, I think it had better be alas, utterly impossible: for these reasons: on Friday I go to London for the day (you dont believe it, but I always go up when L goes, about every 10 days). On Saturday we may have our partner, Lehmann, whom we have to take to Charleston on Sunday. On Monday my mother in law comes to lunch and stays, I suppose, till 6 or 7. It is possible, but that I cant know yet, that Lehmann cant come: he's abroad. There remains London, Lunch on Friday. But I daresay thats no good to you: anyhow Lunch is a horrid meal—I offer it vaguely, desperately. You, who are so expert at organisation, can decide whats possible, what impossible—I give it up.

I sent on your letter to Lady Craik[2]—it seemed to me a brilliant portrait of Virginia Woolf, a lady I respect, but do not like; and have nothing much to do with. And then one says one 'knows' people! That austere priestess, who only wants one human being, is half of one,—a recluse—a fanatic— thats the woman you think it worth coming to see! Thats the woman you do see. But my dear Ethel, why not sit at Maurice Baring's window and look at the marine view, or the noble and immaculate downs?—why trouble to touch such a frigidified frump—Lord! I exclaim again (not for the first time) what a farce friendship is! But I'm delighted that this version should be current, because the more people think V.W. a statue, chill, cold, immaculate, inapproachable,—a hermit who only sees her own set—the more free I

1. Ethel's opera, composed in 1904, for which she was now rewriting the synopsis for a new production at Covent Garden.
2. Mary Frances, the daughter of Alfred Lyttelton, married Sir George Craik, Bt. (1874-1929), the barrister.

myself am to be myself. And then I need not see Lady Craik. I've not had my boat out all this week—But I've taken some photographs and am now coiled in a desperate grapple with the last pages of that wearysome book: I shall finish tomorrow; but must then go through all the corrections again, copy into a second proof, and finally get a revision of one chapter gone wrong. So excuse, pity, and lend the shade of your august umbrella to this unfortunate. I gather your life as an artist is now all triumph and jubilee. But then you feel sure of the Wreckers—a thing I've never felt with my work. And why does one do them, these works? That's a question I put myself as I reach page 327. or shall do when I reach it tomorrow morning.

And if friendship is futile, and letters futile, and art futile, what remains? Well for me at the moment a walk on the downs. So goodbye and let me know about plans.

V.

Berg

2421: To Ethel Smyth   *Monks House* [*Rodmell,*
                                        Sussex]
Tuesday [18 August 1931]

Another suggestion.
My mother in law is *not* coming on Monday. How would it be if you came here on Monday? instead of lunching in London—which would be a rush, and full of interruptions. L. says there is a bus which leaves Brighton at 2.35. passes Rottingdean somewhere about 5 to 3; and reaches Rodmell at 20 to 4. We could have a quiet tea and talk in the garden here, till you want to catch your train at Lewes. If this is not possible, we will stick to the lunch in London: in which case will you arrive at 52 at 1.

Let me know which: remembering that I leave here on Friday before the morning post.

You must verify the arrival of the Bus at Rotting[dean]: But it passes through Rodmell anyhow

Berg

2422: To V. Sackville-West   *Monks House* [*Rodmell,*
                                       Sussex]
Thursday [20 August 1931]

Gosh yes—very natty and sporty she looks to be sure[1]—just your style Mine is the very opposite—But to speak seriously, God knows you're right,

1. Possibly a photograph of Evelyn Irons, a journalist on the *Daily Mail*, with whom Vita had been intimate for about six months.

369

and I shant come, and you'll find another, and forget me, and make excuses when we meet, and I shall be driven to the rough Coast of the Wreckers [Ethel]: Anyhow, you must, as they say, make your plans without considering me.

I dont think there's the ghost of a chance of my coming. (I've reconnoitred, and so it seems but no doubt I exaggerate my own importance)

But—I want answers:

(1) have you seen the osteopath?
(2) What did he say?
(3) Are you smoking?
(4) How's your jumping heart?

Finally. please put up in a penny envelope and send Harold's pamphlet.[1] As I'm always being cross-examined, and put to the block.

And its a gale and a hurricane—the trees are being torn up by their roots—and we're off to Charleston to drink champagne. No doubt this is my last letter. Sibyl came, Ethels coming: Shall I see you? before you elope?[2]

Eddy's not coming Thank God.

Berg

2423: To V. Sackville-West   *Monks House* [*Rodmell, Sussex*]

Sunday [30 August 1931]

Well, you old wretch, what a skin flint you are with your letters. Here's poor Virginia in bed, and Potto too. The headaches wont let me out of their clutches (curse this intolerable gold pen—) so I am taking a week in bed. Then I shall be in robust health. But I've promised to keep in a state of lethargy the next week. What about the week after?—I should think the 5th September week? Couldn't we meet one day about the middle? We might come to Sht.—too many S's in that word [Sissinghurst]—and go to the Easdales. Let me know—and dont be so stingy with your words—take example by Hugh [Walpole]—I feel like a tea cup—I mean I feel very small, broken, lying under a tap—a tap that never stops—a lukewarm tap, a tap that one cant hold in, stop, take count of—And you sit under it too, I suppose; and what we poor tea cups are to say to Hugh, except that he'd better send for the plumber, I dont know.

What books are there, *not* by Hugh? I feel as if the whole of English

1. Harold Nicolson's Zaharoff Lecture (Oxford, 1930) on *Swinburne and Baudelaire*.
2. Vita was planning to go on a walking tour in Provence with Evelyn Irons, starting on 26 September.

literature were submerged by Hugh. All is wet, dripping; not a frog can find as much as a dry leaf to sit on.

Eddy's [Sackville West] coming—oh yes—if we'll pay half his fare [from Germany] and [Count Harry] Kessler the other. How like him! Mercifully, I've put off all other visitors for the time being; but had a stormy visit from Ethel, and she dragged me to the top of the downs in a hurricane, talking about God and the Wreckers. Which is which? I dont know. The truth is, desire, gone mouldy, is not a sweet smell; venerable though the vessel of lust may be. I respect her—yes—I've said that before: but dont like the smell of old lust. So you've found someone [Evelyn Irons] sweet and pure to sit with under live Oleanders by the Bay of Biscay is it? But you'll never find anyone you like as much as me; because I'm so clever, so good, so pure—so extremely interesting. There! I'm now going to shut my eyes and think about my being so interesting. L. says Kessler's misprint will increase the value of the books.[1] Did you see high praise of Sissingt (the poem) in the Manchester Guardian? Will Harold be Lord Sh? Is the New Party—no, I wont go on. Please write a long long letter, because I'm in bed; and if you have a copy of Harold's latest[2] LEND it me. I cant remember the name. Talks I mean. And the Pamphlet. Find—well, just say, in so many thousand words, why you love me.

V.

Berg

2424: TO ETHEL SMYTH   *Monks House [Rodmell, Sussex]*

Sunday [30 August 1931]

The photographs are now being printed. I'll put them in, if L. has done them. The negatives look good. I cant write, because I'm in bed: and shall be for a few days (headache) hence gold pen; hence general imbecility. The parcel came safe. Wonderful woman! I've got a lot to say about God, but won't attempt it at the moment And I expect you've no time to write. Otherwise letters would be acceptable.

Curse this pen.

V.

Berg

1. In October 1931 the Hogarth Press published Vita and Eddy Sackville West's translations of Rilke's *Elegies from the Castle of Duino*. Count Harry Kessler designed the format of the book and supervised its printing.
2. *People and Things*, a selection from Harold's BBC talks during the previous year.

Monks House [*Rodmell, Sussex*]

Wednesday [2 September 1931]

September cheque[1] enclosed.

Nelly Cecil has written to ask if we can go there before Sept. 17th—bringing Sonia—who is I suppose a form of Angelica. What am I to say? Or she suggests coming here, but I think it would be better to go there [Chelwood Gate]. Let me know.

B.

The stuff has come and the covers are being made.

Berg

2426: To Ethel Smyth *Monks House* [*Rodmell, Sussex*]

Wednesday 2nd Sept [1931]

Well, here are the prints. What d'you think of them? I think one of them magnificent, but wont say which, as you may hate them all. Why did you tear up the Wreckers letter? I've often told you, letters are a way of penetrating for those who are, like me, blind into the dark damp deeps of your soul. No, the headache isnt the period—how you love periods, w.c's, excrement of all sorts—it interests me—I'm going into that in my life of you—not the period but God. I was struck with a brilliant idea; wrote and wrote; he smashed his fist on my head. Lord, I said, I will write. Then he altogether took from me the power of adding word to word. So I went to bed. A head like wood, instead of one like fire—thats your God. What he likes is to take away, to destroy, to give pain for pleasure—L. says if I'll stay in bed till Monday God will let me alone for another 6 months. But no: bed, with Ivanhoe and Hugh Walpole [*Judith Paris*] for my companions, bed with God for my protector, is intolerable. I'm up, but dont dare go to the Lodge and write. That little inspiration therefore is doomed. I shall never catch it again. And it rains and what is life without writing?

I was highly amused, and maliciously pleased by your letter, saying how you had never seen me in such good condition—no social, sober, cheerful and healthy (I mean spiritually, not bodily). Lord Ethel—that day you came I was so bothered, so irritated in a rage about everything (unreasonably as it turned out) that I almost put you off; thought I could never sit an afternoon of talk out; had a mind, on top of the down to explain and excuse; almost write to ask pardon for having given you such a wretched time. And

1. For Angelica's clothing allowance. The cheque was for £50.

you saw nothing! Then you talk of your insight—then you wonder that I dont 'want' more than 2 people—Here we sit in dark tunnels, tapping on the wall—Thats friendship—thats communication. But do tell me why that visit was so momentous—I thought you must be bored, disillusioned, and caustic though restrained. But of course (forgive this leap) you have Style. Never a postcard without it. Its the flight and droop of the sentence; where the accent falls, the full stop. Ah, how beautifully you wing your way from phrase to phrase! When one feels something remote, separate, pure, thats style. And, I think, almost the only permanent quality, the one that survives, that satisfies. And now why was that visit momentous?

V.

Berg

2427: To Lyn Irvine   *Monks House, Rodmell*
                                       [Sussex]

Sept 2nd [1931]

Dear Lyn,

Its disgraceful of me not to have written before. My excuse is that I've been in bed—too many proofs to correct, too much talking, too many headaches. But I'm recovered.

The 26th will suit us very well. If you'll let me know your trains or buses later, I expect we could arrange something with the car. I dont for a moment think it will be fine. My boat lies swamped in the garden, and I've only used her twice. But she is great fun—one blows her up like an airball and she can be used also for a bed. But most days I stump across the fields in heavy boots—Lord what a summer! But like you we spend hours in violent political argument.[1]

Yours
Virginia Woolf

I hope this will reach you, but I daresay you've left Norfolk by now.

Sussex (copy)

1. This is the first mention in Virginia's letters of the political crisis which had racked Britain for the past month. Against the will of the great majority of his Cabinet colleagues, Ramsay MacDonald formed a coalition government on 24 August to deal with the economic crisis, and the Labour Party was split in two. Most of its members accused MacDonald of betraying the working people who had elected him.

2428: To Ethel Smyth   *Monks House* [*Rodmell,*
                                        Sussex]
Friday [4 September 1931]

Very glad you like one of the pictures. I think I know which—If you
want it reproduced, let us know, and we will get a special print done.

No no no—you cant ride off like that—thinking yourself such a fine
psychologist—Your words (here's your letter before me) are: "face so
smooth and hard-fleshed, so un-harried, such condition—dearest V. I was
glad to see this *and to feel your spirit is in similar condition*" when my spirit
was torn, rasped, distracted. A fig for your psychology, I say!

                                                            Yr V.

No: you're a completely befogged and besotted owl—One came into the
orchard yesterday and let L. catch him. He—a she—was brought to me,
and I said instantly "Thats Ethel" The creature looks wise I admit, and
doubtless thinks itself omniscient.

Berg

2429: To Ethel Smyth   *Monks House* [*Rodmell,*
                                        Sussex]
Sunday [6 September 1931]

Well, well, Ethel dear, have it your own way. Be a miracle of psychological acuteness if you will, only why, if you saw all that you say you saw,
you didn't catch the early train but stayed on to dinner I cant think—Unless
indeed, as I expect, the fascination of the new born babe detained you—
I think I know what the infant is, and shall wait its development with silent
expectation.[1] As for your brilliant medical diagnosis—that headache is
caused by inspiration—why then did I have two fairly complete attacks
earlier in the month when inspiration was miles away—if inspiration it was,
Or do headaches indicate the distant approach of that delightful state?—
Anyhow, inspiration has gone, and I doubt that it will ever occur again—
a mercy to be thankful for.

But here I come to a serious statement—I mean one I intend to abide by
—never again to mention the subject of my health to you. If I'm stricken
by cancer, typhoid or hydrophobia, you will no doubt be notified on a
postcard by Leonard. And this leads to a request, which I've meant to make

1. On 11 September 1931 Ethel explained to Virginia that the 'babe' was "one
begotten by you all unconsciously . . . what brought home to me that a new
thing was born in me was this—I had evidently been making silent demands on
you, which I'd always promised myself not to do. I'll always care for you, but
the 'tragedy element' is gone" (*Berg*).

this many a day,—please in future dont speak of my health to me, or say if I'm looking well, or ill, or tell me what other people say. In short, from today (Sunday 6th Sept) I want to ignore the whole subject of my health with you, for very good reasons which I needn't go into: and hope for your co-operation.

What an amiable donkey that woman Holtby is! Why doesn't she send the biography straight to me? I told her not to consult my friends; after all I'm the chief authority—you I'm sure, know nothing of the facts—who taught me Greek and so on—Please tell her—or shall I?—to let me have the chapter and I'll make all corrections.[1] Why she should impute such delicacy to me I cant imagine. Short of being pilloried by that bloody bounder Beaton[2] I dont mind what people write about my 'life'—indeed should be immensely amused and interested by their interpretation. And she is far too kind, gentle, and well meaning to hurt a hair on the hinder leg of a fly.

Well, its not very cheerful here. Floods and tempests: Downs gone out like wet paper. And my poor brother in law Clive Bell steadily getting blinder. All the oculists—even the Swiss—seem helpless, and one doesn't dare even to show sympathy, though to see him trying to see this and then that and giving it up as a bad job is enough to wring even my abnormally unsympathetic heart. And his love [Mary Hutchinson] (the old one) has had a bad operation, but is recovering; and shall one try, as she hints, to help a reconciliation? If he's to be blind—my God, Ethel, when his only (non-sensual) pleasures are looking at pictures and reading 6 hours a day—whats one to say of the divine providence that inflicts this on him with at least 20 years of life before him? Its for you Christians to solve these little problems.

Let me see Holtby: and what shall I do about the photograph?

Yr V.

Berg

2430: To V. Sackville-West   *Monks House* [*Rodmell, Sussex*]

Monday [7 September 1931]

Could we come to lunch at Long Barn on Tuesday 15th about one?—and go on to Easedales afterwards?[3]

(how you must hate this phrase—Could we come—)

1. In her author's note to *Virginia Woolf* (1932), Winifred Holtby stated that she met Virginia only once while she was writing the book. Virginia gave her some help with biographical details, but Holtby relied mainly on information supplied by Virginia's friends, particularly Ethel Smyth.
2. See p. 258, note 1.
3. The Hogarth poet Joan Easdale and her family lived in Sevenoaks.

We feel that we ought to advise Dotty and suggest that she should come too.

I've had a divine week of doing nothing and seeing no one, and am now deep in Lady [Anne] Clifford. Headaches cured I think. Dont let Ethel drag you to the top of the Tower; and be discreet—if as I think you are lunching with her.

No: Harold never sent his pamphlet. John [Lehmann] is here, very nice, pink, fresh, enthusiastic, and I must take him to the river.

I should very much like to see you, alone, before you go off—where, with whom?[1] O Lord, shall I ever see you again when you've been off?

And what about the winter?

Dont let Ethel break your back again, with telling you the story of the Wreckers, from the beginning, as you climb the Tower.

Let me know about Tuesday lunch.

It's actually hot today

V.

If you have the Ellen Terry Shaw letters[2] would you LEND them to me?

Berg

2431: To Ethel Smyth   *Monks House* [*Rodmell, Sussex*]

Tuesday [8 September 1931]

L. says much the best thing would be for you to send the negative to the printer who is making the reproduction. So here it is. Will you let us have it back when done with?

No, I didn't mean you were "never to tell me I think you look well"—but Lord! its hopeless to make you see what I did mean so I give it up, from this day forwards. But I too have a child growing in me, and this incident is the sort of thing it battens on—so all's for the best in the best of all possible worlds.

[Winifred] Holtby's written me a long list of enquiries—I'm sorry she bothered you. Haste for post

V.

Berg

1. See p. 370, note 2.
2. Edited by Christopher St John, Ethel Smyth's friend and biographer, in 1931.

376

Monks House [Rodmell, Sussex]

[10 September 1931]

Yes much against my will, L. insisted upon sending an advance copy [of *The Waves*] to the Book Society. But what did Hugh say? Damned it utterly I suppose from your silence on this head. Please tell me. You know how I mind even the workhouse cats view, vain as I am. But I'm not as vain as Ethel, by God.

We shall meet on Tuesday for a few flurried moments.

And did Hugh think it hopeless? (Potto asks this)

V.

Berg

2433: To Vanessa Bell   *[Monk's House, Rodmell, Sussex]*

Thursday [10 September 1931]

Yes I'm glad to find you have some relics of common sense still knocking about in your distracted head. I dont know what to say about the tiles—I'm getting attached to them, but think perhaps the proportions are wrong. What did Duncan think? He was found looking at them. We can settle when we meet. Will you bring the children to tea on Sunday, and will as many grown up come as like, and play bowls? We're off to London tomorrow. I've arranged with George.[1]

God!—what a crowd we live in! even I, who dont let friends sleep, if I can help it. I hope Goldie [Lowes Dickinson] and John [Lehmann] are gone. I'm seriously thinking of buying a house in Dorset or Cumberland—theyre going to build endless villas here. And then retire, and never speak, except to you and Angelica ever again.

But I shall expect you to Sunday tea. Haste

B.

Berg

2434: To John Lehmann   *52 Tavistock Square [W.C.1]*

Friday [11 September 1931]

Dear John,

Lord! To think you are reading The Waves! Now I shall be immensely interested to have your opinion—brutally and frankly—so please write it down for me. At present it seems to me a complete failure. And please don't

1. George Duckworth and his wife Margaret came to tea at Monk's House on 18 September.

tell anyone you've read it, because I'm already pestered with demands for copies, Hugh Walpole apparently having said that it's out.

By the way, are you nervous about your book?[1] What d'you feel about critics? I meant to ask you about all that; but was swept aside by the tide of life at Rodmell. We enjoyed having you enormously, though in such a tempest of kittens and photographs. Some of them (the photographs) are good; not your portrait though. I'll send them.

I'm waiting for L. to finish the eternal conversation with Miss B.[2] (whose language has been purity itself) and then, thank God, we're off.

Yours,

Texas   Virginia Woolf

2435: To V. Sackville-West   [*Monk's House, Rodmell, Sussex*]

Tuesday [15 September 1931]

Oh my God Vita, how fearfully depressed I was getting your wire. I think you'd have been touched. Was it sinus that gave you a throat [tonsillitis]? I rather suspect the damp there—the sweat of ages in those bricks. I say, cd. you possibly let me know instantly on a card how you are? And how are we ever to meet now?

I dont know when The Waves will come out. If there's a General Election L. says it must be put off till November—otherwise October I suppose.[3] But you know I honestly think it a complete failure—only a very interesting (to me) experiment. And why one should spend 18 months writing what wont interest any one, God knows. I'm astonished at the oddity of one's own psychology as a writer.

I'm greatly relieved that you think J[udith]. Paris damned. I found it so bad, so hatefully and completely bad, that I had persuaded myself that it was in fact a work of genius; I being now blind of both eyes to all the true merits of fiction. Now however that you, whose eyes are wide and bright, agree, I feel once more some return of confidence—I mean that it is absolutely bad. Not that that makes it any the easier to write to him [Hugh Walpole]—as I must, O Lord; for he knows I've read it.

Now, as you see I am scribbling, all trembling with hurry, because that accursed car is at the door, and we must be off to the Easedales—

But I've had tonsilitis—doesn't that make one immune? Not that you'd wish to see me today

1. In this month the Hogarth Press published Lehmann's *A Garden Revisited*, his first book of poems.
2. Miss Belsher (or Belcher) became an assistant at the Hogarth Press in March 1928.
3. *The Waves* was published on 8 October, although the General Election was held on 27 October.

Please say what your temp. is and how you are.
Please Vita do this. I'm a devil for imagining disaster

Yr
V.

Berg

2436: To V. Sackville-West   *Monks House* [*Rodmell, Sussex*]

Wednesday [16 September 1931]

This is just by way of a kind enquiry—not that I shall get an answer. Tonsilitis is a very painful disease, as I remember it, and one's throat is spotted with white spots—isn't that it? And to lie in bed today—what a crime—on the part of God, I mean, for what you've done to deserve it I dont know, poor creature. And it would have been such fun, lunching with you—I daresay we should have had mushrooms on toast—and then going to the Easdales. You cant imagine anything more what one expected—a lavish hospitable sloppy mother—a great spread for tea—a small old tumble-down house in an orchard. The son writes music in one room. Joan writes poetry in another. They have meals whereever it takes their fancy—sometimes in the kitchen, sometimes in the bedroom. As it turned out Mrs E. is the sister of a bad painter called Adeney[1]—thats where the art comes from, and was in some dubious relation to an old prophet called Hale White[2] who lived at Groombridge. She had a drawer of his letters which she wanted me to take off and read. She had endless odds and ends of old stuff and bead mats and early Victorian umbrellas—Joan is the mystery—She looks like a chocolate box flapper, talks like one, about how lovely the lilies are, and the sunset, and the dog, and the cat, and yet produces those strange poems. I daresay she's hypnotised by the man servant, a half wit, who does all the housework and was dressed in seedy black I think for your benefit. They were terribly disappointed that you didn't come, and had laid in five cakes and some biscuits, all for you, made by the seedy man. When they gave a birthday party he implored them not to bother about lamps, as he would fill the garden with glow worms. He went out with a huge basket into the woods and returned with two—which did their best, but what are two glow worms in a whole garden, Mrs Woolf, Mrs Easedale asked me,

—here I was called out to play bowls, and now continue next day over the fire, the rain pouring of course; and I dont so much pity you in bed. (But I hope you're up) There's nothing more to say about the Easedales, except that a young musician there confirmed me that Ethel has infinite

1. Bernard Adeney (1878-1966), who exhibited with the London Artists' Association, and had been President of the London Group.
2. William Hale White (1831-1913), the novelist, philosophical writer, literary critic and civil servant, who wrote under the name 'Mark Rutherford'.

competence and not a note of music in her. So think of me, who hate opera sitting under 5 hours of Wreckers [on 14 October] with her beside me, I suppose. Another row, I make no doubt.

What about your French tour [with Evelyn Irons]? Dotty said something, but I was immorally discreet, and said nothing—discreet without reason I expect. O I'm in such a rage—a serious rage that caught me by the throat and constricted my heart—They've sold the Down above the village, and its all to go in plots, and two bungalows are already being run up, and its all ruined for ever and ever. What are we to do? I would sell instantly: but dont tell L. this. I dont see any point in living here in a suburb of Brighton. I dont suppose there is any pleasure in my life like walking alone in the country: no, I'm not exaggerating. And then to see the downs spoilt—by an infernal labour candidate[1]—his blasted villa will be there for all time— My God, Vita, I wish one hadn't picked this age to live in: I hate my kind. And you've fallen to the blandishments of Benn.[2] I'm sorry, selfishly for the press; and his oiliness made me wish him none but the ignominious tribes of Walpoles and Storm Jamesons—not you—in his gizzard. Another line, please, to say how you are. Tomorrow George and Margaret [Duckworth] come over—God knows why, and she's so lame she cant get up stairs, and he so fat he lies where he falls, like a sheep, and will fall. Dotty was as nice as could be, showing her grounds surrounded by dappled spotted, brindled dogs. That reminds me—have you a photograph of Henry?[3] I ask for a special reason, connected with a little escapade [*Flush*] by means of wh. I hope to stem the ruin we shall suffer from the failure of The Waves.

This is the worst publishing season on record. No bookseller dares buy. So I'm glad Passion is spent.[4]

Berg

2437: To John Lehmann   *Monks House, Rodmell*
                                             [*Sussex*]

Sept 17th [1931]

Dear John,

I'm most grateful to you for your letter. It made me happy all yesterday. I had become firmly convinced that the Waves was a failure, in the sense that

1. F. Hancock, who stood for the Lewes constituency in 1931 and 1935 as a Labour pacifist. Leonard commented on his new house: "You have spoilt the view for everyone else, without even having gained a good view for yourself.'
2. Vita's two stories, *The Death of Noble Godavary* and *Gottfried Künstler*, were published together by Ernest Benn in June 1932.
3. Harold Nicolson's cocker spaniel.
4. Vita's novel, *All Passion Spent*, published by the Hogarth Press.

it wouldn't convey anything to anybody. And now you've been so perceptive, and gone so much further and deeper in understanding my drift than I thought possible that I'm immensely relieved.

Not that I expect many such readers. And I'm rather dismayed to hear we've printed 7,000: for I'm sure 3,000 will feed all appetites; and then the other 4 will sit round me like decaying corpses for ever in the Studio (I cleared up the table—for you, not the corpses). I agree that it's very difficult —bristling with horrors, though I've never worked so hard as I did here, to smooth them out. But it was, I think, a difficult attempt—I wanted to eliminate all detail; all fact; and analysis; and my self; and yet not be frigid and rhetorical; and not monotonous (which I am) and to keep the swiftness of prose and yet strike one or two sparks, and not write poetical, but purebred prose, and keep the elements of character; and yet that there should be many characters, and only one; and also an infinity, a background behind —well, I admit I was biting off too much.

But enough, as the poets say. If I live another 50 years I think I shall put this method to some use, but as in 50 years I shall be under the pond, with the gold fish swimming over me, I daresay these vast ambitions are a little foolish, and will ruin the press. That reminds me—I think your idea of a Letter most brilliant—To a Young Poet?[1] because I'm seething with immature and ill considered and wild and annoying ideas about prose and poetry. So lend me your name—(and let me sketch a character of you by way of frontispiece)—and then I'll pour forth all I can think of about you young, and we old, and novels—how damned they are—and poetry, how dead. But I must take a look into the subject, and you must reply, 'To an old novelist'—I must read Auden, whom I've not read, and Spender (his novel I swear I will tackle tonight).[2] The whole subject is crying out for letters—flocks, volleys, of them, from every side. Why not get Spender and Auden and Day Lewis to join in?[3] But you must go to Miss Belsher, and I must go to my luncheon.

This is only a scribble to say how grateful I am for your letter.

Yr

John Lehmann   Virginia Woolf

1. In his letter to Virginia about *The Waves* Lehmann had suggested 'that it was high time for her to define her views about modern poetry, which we had discussed so often together' (John Lehmann, *The Whispering Gallery*, 1955, p. 170). Virginia published *A Letter to a Young Poet* in July 1932, as one of The Hogarth Letters series.
2. Stephen Spender had submitted a novel to the Hogarth Press. See p. 383, note 3.
3. Stephen Spender (aged 22), W. H. Auden (24), and Cecil Day Lewis (27) were all friends of Lehmann. Day Lewis's *From Feathers to Iron* was published by the Hogarth Press this month, and all three poets appeared, together with Lehmann, Julian Bell and four others, in *New Signatures*, edited by Michael Roberts and published by the Hogarth Press in 1932.

Monks House [Rodmell, Sussex]

Friday [18th September 1931]

I admit I've been a wretch about writing, but O how I hate writing and the futility of all human intercourse has never seemed to me greater and these feeble little efforts to patch up whats called understanding—how idiotic. And, these being my views on the universe, letters from all sides accumulate, and as I look at them unanswered, I put off writing again and again. What is there to be said in writing? Except facts. That is, many thanks for the oculists proper name—Clive is in Venice, and I shant see him till mid-October, I suppose: and will then try tactfully to tell him of this man. Only he's as sensitive as can be about his eyes—poor man. I imagine you living in a storm and hurricane—rather exciting and overwhelming I imagine—and so unlike anything thats ever happened in my life. Here we go on eternally 'seeing' and being seen. At this moment I write at a gallop, expecting my seducing half brother and his wife [George and Margaret Duckworth]—why they drive 30 miles to see us I cant imagine. And the drawing room's all of a litter, and we sit down 7 to tea, and there's not enough tea spoons, and we shall talk about his prize pigs; and Margaret will wonder how George ever put up with such half sisters so long.

I shall slip into a back seat somewhere one of these nights—not the first night—at Covent Garden and absorb silently. The gallery's what I like where one needn't dress. No; Waves postponed; anyhow till 8th perhaps longer. Dont read it. Dont lets indulge in these high flown remarks about genius; lets settle down in silence to think ourselves very small beer indeed—which is what I am. And here's George.

V.

Berg

[Monk's House, Rodmell, Sussex]

Wednesday [30 September 1931]

Shall you be [broad]casting on Monday and will you come and see me?—or are you off with Dotty somewhere? I haven't the remotest idea.

We come back—Lord knows why we do these things—tomorrow, for L. to broadcast, and I must now tear up ten dozen letters (not from you) and all the rest of it. Lord, how I hate the thought of London, except that I like seeing some people—Who? not Eddy, by the way.

V.

Please give Dotty my love—I was sorry about her—her mother.[1] O yes—
I understand about yours [Lady Sackville].

Berg

2440: To John Lehmann   *Monks House* [*Rodmell,*
                                          Sussex]
Wednesday [30 September 1931]

Dear John,

I am a wretch not to have thanked you for your book [*A Garden
Revisited*], which will not only stand on my shelf as you suggest but lie
beneath the scrutiny of my aged eyes. I want to read it with some attention,
and also Auden [*Poems*, 1930], and Day Lewis [*From Feathers to Iron*]—
I dont suppose there's anything for me to say about modern poetry, but I
daresay I shall plunge, at your bidding. We must talk about it. I dont know
what your difficulties are. Why should poetry be dead? etc. etc. But I wont
run on, because then I shall spurt out my wild theories, and I've had not a
moment to read for days and days. Everybody in the whole world has been
here—the Easedales in cartloads etc. etc. And now I should be packing.
And then we go back. And then there'll be all the books fluttering about us;
alas: its going to be a bad season[2] I'm afraid.

But I want to go into the question of poetry all the same. I'm stuck in
Spender's novel, by the way.[3]

                                                       Yrs ever
John Lehmann   V.W.

2441: To Ethel Smyth   *52 T.*[*avistock S.*[*quare, W.C.*1]
Thursday [1 October 1931]

Well, here we are back again, but I confess in a vile temper, complete

1. Dorothy Wellesley was the daughter of Robert and Lucy Ashton. After Ashton's
   death, her mother married the 10th Earl of Scarborough. She died on 24
   September 1931.
2. The 'bad season' included *The Waves*; Leonard's *After the Deluge: A Study in
   Communal Psychology*, Volume I; and Lehmann's own book of poems.
3. Virginia, on behalf of the Press, rejected this novel. Spender wrote in his
   autobiography: "It interested her and she spent some part of an afternoon
   discussing it with me. As she made several favourable comments, I asked how I
   could re-write it. 'Scrap it!' she exclaimed with force. 'Scrap it and write something completely different.' When she said 'Scrap it!' I had a glimpse of the
   years during which she had destroyed her own failures" (*World Within World*,
   1951, p. 157).

confusion and rage at leaving Rodmell this fine day. O we had so many people last week end—unknown, undesired, unattractive—why I can't think. And now, as L. has to broadcast every Thursday night, here we are in this grime, in this chaos (I've not unpacked) in this sordidity and squalor, and I've only to put my nose out of doors to run into a friend—no, an acquaintance, who wants me to write an article—as if I wanted to write articles—for this cursed paper by Wednesday. Being so irretrievably humane I half said I would—And to put all this against my downs and marsh and slipping home, alone, and lighting a wood fire, and hearing an owl or two in the elm tree.

By the way; was the Wreckers good, on Thursday? I only caught the roar at the end [of the broadcast], as our local Colonel of course made electric light that evening, and all your singers and choruses sounded like bees in a swarm. Indeed I shut off in a fury. But I suppose they'll now do it in May with all the court there in their diamonds. I shall slip into a back seat if I possibly can on the 14th. But then I'm in such a rage. So I go on raging; but if you could see the litter in this room—all the letters I've not answered —the MSs. I've not read, and the grime, after Rodmell—I repeat, why does one waste the few fine October Evenings that remain in going off at 7.30 to Savoy Hill to listen to L broadcasting about democracy. Do I believe in the future of the human race? Do I care if it perishes or survives? And there's Colefax—I mean I see peeping out of the slag heap one of her invitations, unanswered. Please forgive these groans. Its time to be off to broadcast now. And I suppose you sit triumphant answering letters by the score, and receiving laurel wreaths, harps made of chrysanthemums, or whatever great and successful composers like Ethel

No room

V.

Berg

2442: To Ethel Smyth   52 *T.*[*avistock*] S.[*quare, W.C.*1]

Typewritten
Saturday [3 October 1931]

Ah my dear Ethel, how you would have laughed yesterday—its on these occasions I most vividly recall you, when theres something ridiculous in my situation, for as I said I'm making a new image of you, bearing a fresh child; and she—the new Ethel is a sardonic, brutal, truculent, savage, an irredeemable lover of reality in its least flattering guise—but shes not finished yet, my new Ethel—but how you would have laughed I thought. I was drawing in after a violent helter skelter day, assuming some control of my faculties, about six; then the door opens. Then push in, shuffling past

Nelly who did her best to bar their way, three small shabby dowdy, speechless figures; one, an old apelike man; two young women with shiny noses, cheap shoes, and unkempt hands. Holding out an envelope the man approached and there I found myself addressed by a poet I hardly know called Blunden and asked to receive Mademoiselle Rousel, who is writing about my books. They stood round shuffling in silence uneasy guilty as I read. Thus assaulted what could I do but say Sit down. What can I do? What do you want of me? Dead silence. More shuffling, The grey monkey old man then made a very much impeded speech to the effect that he is an elementary school teacher in Kent, but directly descended from the author of Ralph Roister Doister, the first English comedy, who as I doubtless knew was called Udall, as he was. Upon which I bowed. "And therefore with this blood in our veins, he said, we tend to try as a family not very successfully, far from it, to write. My daughter here, she writes, stories for children, as yet unpublished. Yes, Mr Udall, I said. And what can I do? And this young lady, Mademoiselle—she lets me call her Susanne, pointing to the other silent sweating damsel, who had not yet broken silence but wrung her red hands almost incessantly, she is a guest of ours, for my sister, who—for were all a bit eccentric—runs a boarding house in the old mansion where Sir Harry Vane was born she—Susanne she lets me call her—stays with my sister,—that is my sister, who's eccentric like the rest of us, desires to encourage what I may call reciprocity among the young of different nations. How it strikes you, Mrs Woolf, I dont know; but as an elementary school teacher, (Ive tried to write but failed, owing I may flatter myself to the fact that my ideas arent other peoples)—I say Mrs Woolf, we need reciprocity to understand the viewpoint of other races. So Susanne as she lets me call her is staying with us—that is with my sister. And so Mr Blunden, who was taught by my sister—she used to keep a school—he told us, very kindly being interested in Susanne, to call on you—since the young lady who's at the Sorbonne has been studying—which book?—oh Mrs Dalloway—and wants to ask you—now Susanne, what are the questions you want to ask Mrs Woolf?"

"Ive forgotten, Madame; said Susanne, wringing her red bald hands. "I dont rightly know now what I want to ask you—except—can you tell me perhaps, do you differ in your views from other people? And what—could you tell me quite simply—what is your—its a hard word to pronounce—pheel—o—so—phy—That is could I ask you to explain as Mr Blunden has so kindly introduced us what why that is you have written your books?" Here she broke down twisting her shabby shoes like an eel on the mat. "That is, said Mr Udall, she wants to ask you madam, if you had any reform to advocate in writing these books, which I understand attempt rather a different viewpoint from our English classics. Now I in my plays had an end in view: I am by nature a reformer Madam, though through circumstances I am an elementary school teacher in Kent. Now if you could very kindly put into a simple form what was your intention in writing let me see the Walk to the Light house—thats I think what this young lady would like to ask you."

"Our students said Susanne, do not know English well; but would gladly know madame, have you any meaning in what you write, could I tell them simply, I should be so very grateful, but alas, I am so upset at coming into your presence, that what I was asked to say, I cannot now remember, I do not speak well. I do not explain myself. It is a thesis I am writing upon English fiction; and Mr Blunden says you have written English fiction—with a philosophy—which reminds me, here broke in the small apelike man, to ask, could you help me with your advice about my daughter here, Amy (pointing to the other silent shiny girl who had so far made no remark whatsoever) She's turned twenty; and a hard worker, Mrs Woolf, I may say; if shy. But she too is set upon writing—for so we all are in our family, being the descendants of Nicholas Udall who wrote our first English comedy—which you might have seen acted three years ago by the students at Highgate college—And we cant, having a boy coming on, let her write, save she makes a living. Thats what we'd like to ask you to tell us—could Amy—thats my daughter—make a living and still have her mornings free for writing? And could she in your opinion do so in some circle that involved the society of educated literary people, since I hear society is now so important in a literary career. Thats what we want to ask you; and also, Susanne here would like to know so as to put it before the students at the Sorbonne, have you any special meaning when you write your books?

I assure you, so we went on from six to seven thirty.

[*in Virginia's handwriting:*]

Sunday.

I dont know why I've scribbled all this—however, let it be. About Wednesday, I think 4.30 would be safer than 4, as I have to go out. Lord! do you really read my letters to your friends—to Elizabeth [Williamson], whom I dont know? Well, in future they shall be of a primness, of an exemplary decorum suited to the company you keep. Every t crossed, every i dotted.

V.

Berg

2443: To WILLIAM PLOMER   52 *Tavistock Sqre.* [*W.C.*1]

Sunday [4 October 1931]

Dear William,

We are back, and should like it so much if you could dine with us on Thursday 15th, at the odd hour of 8.15, but Leonard is broadcasting. An admirer of Sado, Bonamy Dobrée[1] is coming—I don't know if you like meeting admirers. You seem to have many, judging from reviews.

Yours

Texas   Virginia Woolf

2444: To V. Sackville-West

52 *T.[avistock] S.[quare, W.C.1]*

Thursday [8 October 1931]

Why do I only get a letter from you today, Thursday, which was written on Monday? God knows. Yes, do come on Monday, afternoon, let me know what time—I've a mint of things to say, but I cant remember any of them at the moment. Just off to buy a large house in Bedford Square—I'm sending The Waves, but I dont much think you'll like it. Please congratulate Harold warmly upon the Book page in Action[2]—especially the novel reviews. First copy just come in. Let me know about Monday. Dont talk of Ravenna—it makes me ill to think of it.

V.

We go down to Rodmell, thank the Lord, tomorrow till Sunday night. O to escape from people! And the ceiling in my studio has fallen and I've nowhere to sit and all Freud's works[3] were ruined and—and—and—. . . .

Or, what about lunch on Monday, 1.

Berg

2445: To Vanessa Bell   [52 *Tavistock Square, W.C.1*]

8th Oct. [1931]

As I consider you entirely responsible for this unfortunate book, here is a copy.[4] But you needn't read it.

Berg

1. Plomer's novel *Sado* was published by the Hogarth Press in September 1931. Bonamy Dobree (b. 1891), the literary critic and historian, had published two books with the Hogarth Press.
2. The first number of *Action*, the New Party journal which Harold Nicolson edited for Sir Oswald Mosley, was published on 8 October. Harold reviewed *The Waves* in this issue, calling it 'difficult' yet 'superb'.
3. The Hogarth Press had for several years been publishing *The International Psycho-Analytical Library*.
4. Vanessa's letter about the moths at Cassis (see Volume III of this Edition, p. 372, note 2) was the origin of *The Waves*, which was published on this day.

Thursday [8 October 1931]

My word, what a kind woman you are to send a wire at that hour of the morning!¹ Well, well—I shall want your whole and considered opinion some time. This is only a scrawl, as I'm off to bed, but must thank you, having been much cheered by your impetuous and extravagant ways— (I hope this comes out of the saved bacon rashers)

V.

We go to Rodmell thank God, tomorrow till Sunday

Berg

2447: To Vanessa Bell   [52 *Tavistock Square, W.C.1*]

Friday [9 October 1931]

I wrote a post card to ask you and Duncan and Julian or anybody to dine at Monks House on Saturday at 7, but I rather think it was lost so I repeat this and hope it may manage to get sent. But we live in such chaos owing to the ceiling falling down, John putting his hand through a window etc etc that I doubt it. And now we're just off to Rodmell. Hopeing [*sic*] to see you

B

Berg

2448: To Ethel Smyth   [52 *Tavistock Square, W.C.1*]

Sunday [11 October 1931]

No, no my dear Ethel, it was only a jaded phrase of mine—'tell me what you think"² I almost crossed it out, but was too hurried and bothered. Dont for goodness sake add this to your other worries. We'll talk quietly one day perhaps—in six months or so: not now. I'm perfectly content. We had 2 days of complete happiness at Rodmell—O so lovely and so calm; and have just come back to letters innumerable and endless interruptions.

So no more—

V.

Berg

---

1. On 8 October Ethel wired Virginia: "Book astounding so far. Agitatingly increases value of life"; and on 10 October: "Final paragraph almost smashes the machine of life with its terrible duty" (*Sussex*).
2. The phrase Virginia wrote in the copy of *The Waves* which she sent to Ethel.

2449: To Ethel Smyth   [52 *Tavistock Square, W.C.1*]

[13 October 1931]

Oh but I didn't mean I didn't want your criticism (Of course I do.)
Only that I thought you were worrying yourself when you had a million
distractions to give it. Oh yes, any criticism—every criticism. I'm tremendously interested.

How odd this is—so far most of the low-brow reviewers (whose sense
I respect) find the Waves perfectly simple: and it is selling beyond all my
other books! Now why?

But I shall see you in the distance tomorrow.[1] This is only a scrawl—

V.

I dont for a moment suppose that I shall be able to say anything whatever
about the Wreckers—not for some time anyhow. I'm incredibly ignorant
and slow about music. Your wig I shall enjoy.

Berg

2450: To John Hayward   52 *Tavistock Sqre.* [*W.C.1*]

Oct 13th 1931

Dear Mr Hayward,[2]

I'm sure you dont know how glad I am that you should like The Waves.
Though I was immensely interested, I admit, in writing it I came to feel
that it would never mean anything to anybody. Also I found it a very
difficult book to write. So I am delighted that my halfpenny means something
to you, and thank you for saying so.

Yours sincerely
Virginia Woolf

Mrs Henry A. Dewenter

1. On 14 October Virginia and Vita attended a performance of *The Wreckers*
   and afterwards took Ethel to supper.
2. John Davy Hayward (1905-65), the literary critic, bibliographer and anthologist.
   Virginia had met him as an undergraduate at King's College, Cambridge in 1925.

Letters 2451-2500 (October–December 1931)

The Waves *attracted reverential reviews, and although some of Virginia's friends found it hard going, Vanessa's and Morgan Forster's opinions counted most with her, and they were ecstatic. The novel sold nearly 10,000 copies before the end of the year, and Virginia's reputation now stood as high as any living writer's. For a time, she made little progress with* Flush, *and was occupied mainly in revising or writing essays for her second* Common Reader, *and in late December, after a month's illness, began* A Letter to a Young Poet, *addressed to John Lehmann. He was still working in the Hogarth Press, and he brought to it Wystan Auden, Stephen Spender and Cecil Day Lewis, whose names have begun to appear in the letters for the first time. Leonard had published the first volume of his* After the Deluge, *on which he had been working for ten years, but the response to it was disappointing. Christmas at Monk's House was clouded by the news of Lytton Strachey's severe illness, and he survived the first crisis only to die on 21 January 1932.*

2451: To Vanessa Bell [52 *Tavistock Square, W.C.*1]

Thursday [15 October 1931]

Dearest dearest Dolphin,

O what a mercy that you should like that book! I cant tell you, (this is literal truth) what it meant to me getting your letter this morning.

Nobody except Leonard matters to me as you matter, and nothing would ever make up for it if you didn't like what I did. So its an amazing relief— I always feel I'm writing more for you than for anybody: only I cant express this, as I'm rushing off, and have been interrupted by Peter [F. L. Lucas] coming. Never mind—I couldn't say if I'd the whole day how happy you make me.

And Lord—what I owe to you!

But I cant write more now, and only send this as an inarticulate thanksgiving and shall write again tomorrow—

You didnt think it sentimental, did you, about Thoby?[1] I had him so

---

1. Vanessa wrote to Virginia about *The Waves:* "For its quite as real an experience as having a baby or anything else, being moved as you have succeeded in moving me—Of course there's the personal side—the feelings you describe on what I must take to be Thoby's [Perceval's] death. . . . Even then I know its

much in my mind,—I have a dumb rage still at his not being with us always.

Dearest Dolphin, how I adore you, whether you like what I write or not

B.

I'm frightfully interested about your picture.[1]

Berg

2452: To Vanessa Bell   [52 *Tavistock Square, W.C.*1]

Sunday [18 October 1931]

This is merely to ask whether there's any chance that Clive wants a cook? Lottie [Hope] is again out of a place, through no fault of hers she swears, and is quartered upon us. So I said I'd ask you.

London pullulates with people, and is incredibly horrible at the moment.

Thats all. One day perhaps we may meet, but not I daresay for many months.

B.

Berg

2453: To Margaret Llewelyn Davies
                    52 *Tavistock Square* [*W.C.*1]

Typewritten
Sunday 18th Oct. [1931]

Dearest Margaret,

How very nice to see your hand again—especially since you can write legibly, which is more than I can. Yes we are back; but so hurried and busied at the moment with the Press and L's broadcasting which leads to endless

---

only because of your art that I am so moved. I think you have made one's human feelings into something less personal—if you wouldn't think me foolish I should say you have found the 'lullaby capable of singing him to rest' [*Hamlet*] (October 1931, *Berg*).

1. "Will it seem to you absurd and conceited or will you understand at all what I mean if I tell you that I've been working hard lately at an absurd great picture I've been painting off and on the last 2 years—and if I could only do what I want to—but I can't—it seems to me it would have some sort of analogous meaning to what you've done. How can one explain, but to me painting a floor covered with toys and keeping them all in relation to each other and the figures and the space of the floor and the light on it means something of the same sort that you seem to me to mean" (Vanessa to Virginia, October 1931, *Berg*). Vanessa's picture does not survive. It may have been destroyed when 8 Fitzroy Street was bombed during the Second War.

letters that he says he doesnt yet see a chance of making a plan to come up to Well Walk [Hampstead]. But we shall take our chance and ring you up. We've had the usual catastrophes in the thick of business—a ceiling falling, our young man, Lehmann, cutting his hand badly, one clerk going, and so on. Now theres the election, and then we shall have to rouse up the book selling business again which is bound to flag, though doing well at the moment. Did you see a very good review of L's book by Laski in the Statesman?[1] I must say I feel rather triumphant that he has come through with that book in spite of all his other occupations: and now there are seven more volumes to be written. I cant conceive how you politicians can go on being political. All the summer we had nothing but political arguments with Maynard and others; and I finally felt it so completely silly, futile, petty, personal and unreal—all this about money—that I retired to my room and read poetry in a rage. Well, I know you dont agree; but if everyone read poetry then there'd be no politics; no crisis; none of this place hunting and party spite. All they do is to abuse each other. This shows you how little I grasp the true meaning of events. Lilian [Harris] must instruct me. I suppose you dont know of anyone who wants a cook—Lottie, our old servant, that wild but in some ways admirable character, is out of a place and Mrs Hunt [domestic agency] says she wont take servants, as there are no "places. So I am trying to enquire, incredible though this seems.

I must say my grammar has gone to blazes—so I must stop. I like Mrs Burman's letter [about *Life As We Have Known It*] which I enclose. Well we must meet and have a good argument. Love to Lilian. I do hope her illnesses are better and long for news of the Harris family—a constant source of joy to me, especially if I wake at night.

Yrs V

Sussex

2454: To George Duckworth   52 *Tavistock Square, W.C.*1

18th October [1931]

My dear George,

I am delighted you find the Waves plain sailing and common sense. I shall quote your opinion I daresay in an advertisement. Yes, the plague of half wits from America is already considerable, and one cant even be pleased with their compliments, since they are clearly incapable of adding 2 to 2.

---

1. A review of *After the Deluge* by Harold Laski, Professor of Political Science at the London School of Economics. There were to be two more volumes of Leonard's book. The next appeared in 1939, and the third, under the title *Principia Politica*, in 1953. They dealt with the ideas of liberty, equality and fraternity, and their effect upon communal political motivation.

I'm so sorry they sent off your copies before I had signed them. I would send another, as a tribute of respect and affection, but I dont think one house can possibly want 3 copies of a book.

Why are statues being erected to you in the Abbey and all the villages of England [*inexplicable*]? I'm not in the least surprised—I only want to know which of your many virtues have been at last discovered by the public? Well, I shall go to the Abbey and find out. We are back in London I am sorry to say, and in the chaos of publishing and general election.

Many thanks from

Your affectionate
GOAT

Henry Duckworth

2455: To Ethel Smyth   52 *T.[avistock] S.[quare, W.C.*1]

19th Oct [1931]

Oh yes; I have several times thought I was going to sit down and write a long long letter on a vast white sheet about the Wreckers; but then the bell rings, or something interrupts. Moreover, I dont suppose my views are anywhere close enough to sense about music to count. Isn't it odd though that all yesterday, running about London, in tubes and so on, I was singing the 2nd act—How you'd have laughed, at the mess I was making: but what a good tune; and I wanted it to flare into flower again: But, as the late Mrs Pankhurst was it, used to say, 'enough'. I'll describe the Wreckers to you someday by word of mouth. I've very little to offer by way of 'seeing' time this week, God help me: We go to Rodmell on Friday; and on Thursday I have an old friend, dejected, down trodden, and faithful, from Cheltenham —but she'll have spent her confidences by 5.15 or 5.30—so if you'd come then, anyhow we could carry on a general conversation. She—a Miss Snowden[1]—has one of those provincial illusions about you and the glamour of your life, so that to see you in the tailor made and tie would give her a whole chapter to talk about during the long winter nights when they sit—she and her 2 sisters—mournfully thinking what life to Ethel Smyth must be—O dear I hadn't meant to take another page, which I shant have time to finish, as we're going to the Courtauld concert, I dont know why.

No, I rather think the Waves are striking a rock, and wont roll many more guineas to shore. But I'm so thankful to be free of them, I dont mind if I never hear a word of them again. Yes, I should like to discuss them with you, however; for a flashing moment, having some dread of your insight. Nessa is enthusiastic, which pleases me immensely—and unexpectedly.

1. Margery Snowden, who had been at the Royal Academy Schools with Vanessa in their youth, but never succeeded as a painter.

And—as I say, I must wash, being all covered with curious ink stains: So—I shall expect you about 5.15, is it, on Thursday. And I must go at 7 to hear L. broadcast.

His book's out—the work of 10 years; and a masterpiece, so the learned say, and I think its probably true.

V.

Isnt L. a modest man, never to have told you about it? Yes, and I married him. Here he is.

Berg

2456: To Virginia Isham   52 *Tavistock Sqre., W.C.*1

Oct 22nd [1931]

Dear Virginia,

I would like to go to the play in St Bartholomews[1] and will try, but we are rather in a rush with publishing at the moment. I saw a long and enthusiastic review of it.

How are you getting on? I wonder what happened at Berlin.[2] I hope we may meet again some time.

Yours ever
Virginia

Northamptonshire Record Office

2457: To Ethel Smyth   52 *T.[avistock] S.[quare, W.C.*1]

Typewritten
Sunday night [25 October 1931]

Forgive this typing, but I'm in such a rush, coming back to find a mass of week end rubbish, that unless I write in type you couldnt read my scrawl. No, I dont see any chance of Wednesday or of any day this week, God help me. I'm awfully tempted by Maurice [Baring] and supper and rehearsal, but as I'm going out Tuesday night, and Thursday night (my mother in laws birthday feast) and we have people here Friday night, let alone I dont know how many odds and ends and one day at Cambridge electioneering— Leonard will say, damn you not Wednesday night too. And I'm out to tea, or have people here Wednesday. And though you were angelic to the

1. A play about the 12th-century cleric Rahere, who founded St Bartholomew's Hospital in London in 1123. It was acted mainly by amateurs, and produced by Ida Teather.
2. Where Virginia Isham had gone in 1930 in the hope of obtaining theatrical work.

Cheltenham lady [Margery Snowden], still its a waste, always shouting across three heads. So we must wait for calmer times, if they ever come.

About the Waves—your letter I mean, which Ive only read once, but will again. I think you have said exactly what I expected you to say, with your usual vigour.[1] Thats the effect I thought it would have on you, only I'm surprised that it makes so much impression. Different as we are—O lord how different—didn't I feel that at the Wreckers—I'm amazed that we can even see so far eye to eye as that this book should have any power to make you read it. (I write clutching at words) But of course you dont solve what for me remains a troublesome problem at the moment—since every one must write me their views or speak them—I mean, what The Waves is. Here, by this same post I get a letter from Lowes Dickinson—the man who liked the Prison so much; "Your book is a poem and I think a great poem (and then he goes on about how its the summing up of all my books.) And then he says "For there is throbbing under it the mystery which all the poets and philosophers have felt" and by this I understand he finds precisely what you dont: I mean a morality, a principle.★ Well, but then the next letter I open, from a very fine critic, says all sorts of nice things but . . . oh oh oh how he hates Percival and all I write about death—more than anything in any of my books—and then here's another, from a writer I also much respect who says "When I am wretched I shall always turn to Bernards soliloquy for comfort and encouragement." and theres another who says the very opposite—how its damnably depressing, those last words. And here I sit buffeted from one to the other; and cant think how to make them all fit—what the thing is itself, finally and absolutely. But enough, and indeed seeing the rubbish I write, too much. And in fact I feel that I am a thousand miles removed†

Rodmell was unspeakably lovely; but my fury about the building on the downs makes me wake at night in an agony. Think—a house one sees miles off breaking that sweep for ever and ever.

V.

[*in Virginia's handwriting:*]
★ "it deals with what is perpetual and universal" these are the words—

† from the thing itself.

1. Ethel wrote to Virginia on 23 October: "The book is profoundly disquieting, sadder than any book I ever read. And because it has no adorable human being in it (like [unlike?] the Lighthouse, sad as it is) there is no escape from its sadness. For the first time I felt that beauty alone . . . is not enough. I think what makes King Lear bearable is one's consciousness of a moral principle in it all. I don't believe you can banish it—when, Prometheus like, you are at work with the divine element or are forming men and women. I feel all these people lack something necessary to the human equipment and the best of them all is Neville because he was anyhow capable of love" (*Berg*).

Ive lots of letters from Hugh, but always signed Hugh only.[1] I enclose one in case it will do.

[*in Virginia's handwriting:*]
Just found another earlier Hugh.

Berg

2458: To George Duckworth   52 *Tavistock Square, W.C.*1
25th October [1931]

My dear George,
    I have torn up your cheque, as this third copy was meant as a gift.
    If Sophie[2] is with you please give her my love and thank her for a most charming letter.

Your affectionate
GOAT

Henry Duckworth

2459: To V. Sackville-West
52 *T.*[avistock] *S.*[quare, *W.C.*1]
[27 October 1931]

    Yes, do come on Monday. Lunch? I shall be alone. One. Leonard will be in for tea and dinner. So choose which suits and let me know. Yes, I was pleased with Ben's [see Letter 2465] tribute—how enchanting the young are—and sent him a copy—how different his feelings from his mothers. What she said was "Stunted. The woman who wrote that book was fed on gin." And then Dotty rang up, and Vita and Dotty both said "Stunted"[3]— How I love that story, better than any—though its true I'm said, by a Cambridge don [G. Lowes Dickinson], to be the greatest living *poet*; which I repeat not so much from vanity as from the noble desire to annoy another poet—one I could touch with a stick about as long as from here to Sevenoaks—but Lor' bless you, she don't mind—Thats the worst of Vita— she has no vanity. Mine is at the moment fed largely by the letters of

1. Ethel had requested one of Hugh Walpole's autographs, 'for an absurd female who wants it' (23 October 1931, *Sussex*).
2. Sophia Farrell had been the cook for the Stephens when Virginia was young, and now worked for George Duckworth's family.
3. In her diary for 17 October Virginia wrote that Vita and Dorothy Wellesley had found *The Waves* "boring in the extreme" (*Berg*).

lunaetics [*sic*]. And Lord—we're almost certainly taking a great house in Gordon Sqre. [No. 47] where we shall live for ever: and all my time will now go in tying up our books with string for the move. Still hoping to see you before that.

Yr.
Stunt

Probably you will never see me again but we're just off in the fog to Cambridge to take voters to the poll in the fens.[1]

Berg

2460: To G. L. Dickinson   52 *Tavistock Square, W.C.*1

Typewritten
Oct. 27th 1931

My dear Goldie,

How extraordinarily nice of you to write to me—I cant tell you what pleasure your letter gave me.[2] What you say you felt about the Waves is exactly what I wanted to convey. Many people say that it is hopelessly sad— but I didnt mean that. I did want somehow to make out if only for my own satisfaction a reason for things. That of course is putting it more definitely than I have a right to, for my reasons are only general conceptions, that strike me as I walk about London and then I try to fit my little figures in. But I did mean that in some vague way we are the same person, and not separate people. The six characters were supposed to be one. I'm getting old myself—I shall be fifty next year; and I come to feel more and more how difficult it is to collect oneself into one Virginia; even though the special Virginia in whose body I live for the moment is violently susceptible to all sorts of separate feelings. Therefore I wanted to give the sense of continuity, instead of which most people say, no you've given the sense of flowing and passing away and that nothing matters. Yet I feel things matter quite immensely. What the significance is, heaven knows I cant guess; but there is significance—that I feel overwhelmingly. Perhaps for me, with my limitations,—I mean lack of reasoning power and so on—all I can do is to make an artistic whole; and leave it at that. But then I'm annoyed to be told that I am nothing but a stringer together of words and words and words.

1. The General Election took place on this day. The result was a triumph for the Conservatives, who won 473 seats, and Labour 52.
2. The letter is quoted by E. M. Forster in his *Goldsworthy Lowes Dickinson* (1934), and reprinted in *Virginia Woolf, The Critical Heritage* (ed. Robin Majumdar and Allen McLaurin, 1975).

I begin to doubt beautiful words. How one longs sometimes to have done something in the world—So you see how it comforts me to think that anyhow you had me in mind on the river bank. Then the world I live in— for I dont see how to live in any other—seems at any rate to have that justification. So thank you again—very very sincerely—for writing.

We started off for Cambridge this morning meaning to take voters to the poll in the suburbs, but North London was black as pitch and we had to grope our way home. Now we are going round to James's [Strachey] to hear Election results read out, and I shall try to make myself believe in that reality; and then fail; and try again; and fail again. I dont thank people for their books unless I like them,—but I quiet my conscience by never giving them mine. That reminds me—I told old Ethel Smyth, on Leonard's authority, that you had liked Brewsters Prison. She now writes to ask if she may say that Mr Lowes Dickinson admired it in a preface she's writing to a concert she's giving of a setting she's made to The Prison. I dont suppose you'd mind; and as she dotes upon HB. and found your words of the highest comfort, perhaps you'll let me assure her so. But this needs no answer.

Yours always
Virginia Woolf

Sussex

2461: To Ethel Sands   52 *T.[avistock] S.[quare, W.C.*1]

Oct. 28th [1931]

Dearest Ethel,

Alas, its my mother in laws 81st birthday party tomorrow night, and I dont think I can manage tea first. I wish I could. But on Wednesday next I shall be here for tea, only Ethel Smyth may come,—but if you'll risk it, it will be charming. I can, as you know, stand any amount of praise without flinching. You cut me the other night at a concert by the way.

And would you be so angelic as to tell me in confidence who is Antonia White,[1] and must I see her? She says she is a friend of Logans—and I must answer her—[*nine words omitted*] I'm sure you must know of her.

Yours
Virginia

Wendy Baron

1. Antonia White (b. 1899), was Assistant Editor of *Life and Letters* (1928-9) and was now a freelance journalist. Later she wrote several books, and translated Colette.

2462: To Ethel Smyth   [52 *Tavistock Square, W.C.*1]

Postcard
[29? October 1931]

Is it possibly this?—

"This is the true joy in life, the being used for a purpose recognised by yourself as a mighty one; the being thoroughly worn out before you are thrown on the scrap heap; the being a force of Nature instead of a feverish selfish little clod of ailments and grievances complaining that the world will not devote itself to making you happy." G. B. Shaw. Preface to Man and Superman.

Berg

2463: To Harcourt, Brace   52 *Tavistock Square, W.C.*1

Typewritten
31 October 1931

Dear Sirs,

I have to acknowledge cheque for $950 being advance account of royalties on THE WAVES.

Harcourt Brace Jovanovich

Yours faithfully,
Virginia Woolf

2464: To Ethel Smyth   52 *T.*[avistock] *S.*[quare, *W.C.*1]

Typewritten
Sunday [1 November 1931]

Just the usual hasty typed line to say:

I had a letter from G. Lowes Dickinson about quoting him on the Prison. He had some qualifications to make. Now I've lost his letter. I think thus it might be as well if you wrote him a line, enclosing your statement—not that he'll object, I'm sure; but this would make it all safe. His address is, G. Lowes Dickinson Kings College Cambridge.

As I said on the telephone, I shall be in on Wednesday 4.30; but Ethel Sands, a Chelsea hostess, exquisite and amiable and elderly, has asked to come then; also Lord David Cecil, young and mild; both would be enchanted to see you; but I cant guarantee that theyll go early—Lrd. D. is rather a stayer. And Thursday a girl is coming to talk about her novel[1]—Ive

---

1. Rosamond Lehmann, whose novel *Dusty Answer* appeared in 1927, published *Invitation to the Waltz* in 1932.

promised to give her a solitary talk—she's gifted, wrote Dusty Answer; and is in some despair about her work. Monday I'm out to tea—no, I'm not, but Nessa comes first and then Vita and possibly an unknown youth who wants to write poetry—No; Ive been rather knocked up—(excuse this hasty mention of a forbidden subject) and put off our party on Friday so I didnt ask Elizabeth but will when I can. Time as you see is not my strong point at the moment. But this will blow over—is always the afterblast of a book out—people remember one and come and come and come.

I'm amused at your trap—catch me looking up quotations so innocently again [see Letter 2462]. Also amused at your insinuation that *thats* what youre after, and I'm not—losing the egotistic self I mean. That never struck me certainly as your prevailing characteristic—a complete lack of interest in your own doings. And I shouldnt like you if you were entirely altruistic and swept on the current of others lives—what rot it all is, to be sure, this perverted pagan Christianity that you try to palm off on me! Its no use trying to have it both ways; thats your downfall; egotism again; you want to be in Heaven and on earth, one foot in either, and so sure of salvation. I cant now remember what I said, I suppose in a fury of haste, about the Waves; I cant have said that *I* had any opinion about it. That's whats entirely washed out of one by the vociferations of readers, reviewers and friends. I have ceased indeed to believe that there is such a book—merely that somehow I have stirred up a dust dance which makes my friends bonnet ribbons and whiskers fly this way and that east north south and west, and prevents me from getting on with what I'm doing now. But the dust dance soon dies down. Oh and I'm taking a new house, and shall have all the glory of a move in January;[1] oh the type the tables, the books—pity me, though you despise.

V.

Berg

2465: To Benedict Nicolson   52 *Tavistock Sqre.* [*W.C.1*]

Nov. 1st [1931]

My dear Ben,[2]

What a charming letter you wrote me! Take care, or I shall send you all my books. I shall be very much interested to know, if you get to the end of The Waves, what you think. The end is always apt to come to grief, because one gets so sick of writing. Also, do you find it very gloomy?—Some

1. On 29 October the Woolfs made an offer to the Bedford Estate for the lease of 47 Gordon Square, but the Estate refused their offer, and the Woolfs remained in 52 Tavistock Square until 1939.
2. Benedict Nicolson, Vita's elder son, was aged 17.

people say it is very happy, others, so sad they cant have it in the room. And Vita says its so bad that only a small dog that had been fed on gin could have written it. This pleases me greatly.

I'm so glad you dont like being a soldier [in the Eton O.T.C.]. Are you able to do any painting and do you know a nephew of mine called Henry Duckworth—I'm told he's very stupid—the stupidest boy at Eton. My love to Nigel [Ben's brother]:

Yours ever
Virginia Woolf

Benedict Nicolson

2466: To Ethel Smyth　　　52 *T[avistock] S.[quare, W.C.*1]

Sunday [8 November 1931]

Very well, I'll come on Wednesday[1] to the seat wherever it is. And then on to the supper, if I may go early, for L. swears he wont sit up after 12 waiting me. Lord no—he wont come to supper for any body: and I ask, what can be the miraculous joy of eating quails and drinking champagne after hearing one's most solemn music played under the beautiful but oh so stupid eyes of Lady Diana [Cooper]: and Duffs little gentlemanly ones? "I ask what age are you? Answer 3." (not 73, at all) Still I've no doubt we shall all enjoy it enormously. Will you thank M. Baring for me—I dont remember his address—miles away in Chelsea—O Lord—and if I fail through sheer devilry, not of my own seeking dont blame me.

V.

Berg

2467: To Hugh Walpole　　　*Monks House [Rodmell, Sussex]*

Sunday [8 November 1931]

My dear Hugh,

And I'd been meaning to write to you, but unlike you I never, never do what I mean to. How do you get the time? Here am I wedged in between two piles of MS—each it seems to me six foot high—all novels—most commendable alas—That's my excuse. But we are here, Rodmell, for the moment, both well, and enjoying a fine spring day with the advantage of autumn thrown in—gold leaves, ploughed fields, the downs incredibly lovely.

1. To hear *The Prison*.

Well—I'm very much interested about unreality and the Waves—we must discuss it. I mean why do you think The Waves unreal, and why was that the very word I was using of Judith Paris [Walpole's novel]—"These people aren't *real* to me"—though I do think, and you wont believe it, it has all kinds of qualities I admire and envy. But unreality does take the colour out of a book of course; at the same time, I dont see that it's a final judgment on either of us. You're real to some—I to others. Who's to decide what reality is? Not dear old Harold, anyhow, whom I've not heard, but if as you say, he sweeps us all into separate schools one hostile to the other, then he's utterly and damnably wrong, and to teach the public that's the way to read us is a crime and a scandal, and accounts for the imbecility which makes all criticism worthless. Lord—how tired I am of being caged with Aldous, Joyce and Lawrence![1] Can't we exchange cages for a lark? How horrified all the professors would be! Yes, greatly to my surprise The Waves is selling better than any of my novels, which pleases me, and E. M. Forster says it moves him more than any of them, which pleases me still more.[2] Otherwise, opinions good and bad, seem to me increasingly futile and beside the mark.

I'm reading Middlemarch with even greater pleasure than I remembered: and Ford M. Ford's memoirs[3]—fascinating, and even endearing; but I long to know the truth about him—the truth which I'm sure you know, as you know the truth about all these great figures. I wish, to please me, you'd write your own memoirs—why not? The truth and nothing but the truth.

Anyhow come and see us; for we must discuss Reality and Ford M. Ford at length. Why is he no longer the same name as he was 20 years ago when I met him—and her—at the Protheros?[4]

Yours

V.W.

Texas

1. On 29 September, in the first of his ten BBC talks on 'The New Spirit in Modern Literature', Harold Nicolson labelled as 'modernist' writers Virginia, T. S. Eliot, D. H. Lawrence, James Joyce and Evelyn Waugh. He excluded John Galsworthy, James Barrie, J. B. Priestley and Hugh Walpole on the grounds that "from the scientific standpoint, they are all old-fashioned" (*The Listener*, 30 September 1931).
2. Virginia quoted from E. M. Forster's letter in her diary for 16 November: ". . . I've the sort of excitement over it which comes from believing that one's encountered a classic" (*A Writer's Diary*, 1953, p. 176).
3. The first of Ford Madox Ford's three autobiographical volumes, *Thus to Revisit* (1921).
4. George Walter Prothero, the historian and Fellow of King's College, Cambridge. Ford Madox Hueffer changed his Germanic surname to Ford in 1919.

12th Nov. 1931

Yes, dearest Dadie, it was my intention to extract a letter from you. I regret to say that I was not purely disinterested in sending you The Waves. I wanted, and still want, your opinion. For I was turning over the Adelphi, and read backwards a very subtle and erudite article, signed to my surprise (whats brought you there?) Rylands.[1] Can it be my Rylands I said, the one with whom (and here my mind spurted off to the old days with Miss Kipps[2] and the paste pot . . .) anyhow, to cut the matter short, I began at the beginning and found your brief mention of the Waves—hence the desire to get a letter out of you—criticism I mean.

So far I've had practically none, in public (dear Hugh finds it all most unreal and unsatisfactory) and you raise all sorts of interesting questions about poetry and prose: which I long to go into. What sort of emotion does it produce: are the characters still characters: how far has one lost by losing touch with reality—and so on.

But as you're teaching Keats, I mustn't run on,—and indeed a dozen MSS wait me—one about a woman, called Virginia too, who trained an Orang Outang from birth upwards, with the result that she raped him, he strangled her, and going into the garden, found one single cabbage which he planted on her dead breast. Now is this real, I ask you. Echo answers, I no longer know.

Perhaps though you'll come and see me one of these days and go into the matter of orang outangs, Shepherd[3] etc.

Volumes pour hourly, daily, into the Press: and there dear John, whom I love, sits like Prince Consort on the Albert Memorial, which seems to imply that I'm Queen Victoria. But I'm not, am I? Again, this perpetual note of interrogation.

Running out to water Pinka I dashed straight into Raymond, with his Lido tie on. But you know its better to be teaching Keats in the mud flats [Cambridge] than doing many of the things we in B—y [Bloomsbury] do: for example, last night, sweating with horror, I listened to the Prison, set to music—if cat calls, early birds and last posts can be called music—and Lord the defunct butlers and ladies maids who sang—by Ethel Smyth. When Maurice Baring emerged, bald as a coot, and leering for all the world like George 4th—and asked me to sup, I vomited there and then on the red

1. Rylands reviewed John Middleton Murry's *Countries of the Mind* in the *Adelphi* for November 1931.
2. A nickname for Miss B. Higgs, who worked at the Hogarth Press with George Rylands in 1924.
3. J. T. Sheppard, Reader in Classics at King's College, Cambridge, from 1931-47, and Provost of his college.

carpet. But I was going to say I much prefer your way of life with all its manifest disadvantages to Lido ties, last posts, and having the Princesse di Bassiano,[1] escorted by Tom Eliot, to tea.

Now dearest Dadie, you must write me a long letter about the future of the English novel.

Lord what a repulsive remark to end with!

Yr
V.W.

I have not said how immensely pleased I am that you do like The Waves.

George Rylands

2469: To Lady Ottoline Morrell

[*52 Tavistock Square, W.C.*1]

[mid-November 1931]

[*second page only survives*]

. . . Thanks for the second letter about the house [47 Gordon Square]. After keeping us on tenterhooks and making me visit every agent in Bloomsbury for 6 months, the Duke, Bedford, suddenly announces that he's not going to pull us down for 7 years: but will double our rent and make us paint the bricks. So here we stay.

Yes, I went to Bolsover once—in my remote past, when we were lent houses by old Lady Carnarvon. I remember that and Hardwick and Haddon Hall.[2]

Texas

2470: To Hugh Walpole   52 *T.[avistock] S.[quare, W.C.*1]

Sunday 15th Nov. '31

My dear Hugh,

Alas, I'm made to stay in bed at present and keep quiet. So what's the use of thinking I can discuss reality with you? But I shall be all right in a

---

1. The American wife of the Duke of Sermoneta, and the publisher of *Commerce*, the Parisian cultural journal.
2. This is the only record of Virginia's youthful visit to Lady Carnarvon's house, Bretby Park, near Burton-on-Trent. From it she could easily have visited Bolsover Castle, Hardwick Hall and Haddon Hall, which are all in Derbyshire.

week or 10 days. Only I can't make any engagements for certain, don't want you to bind yourself to tea when I might put you off. So may I write on the chance and ask you to come later?

How long are you in London? I hope some time.

My mind teems with arguments.

Yrs
Virginia

Middlemarch finished: now Dizzy:[1] then Trollope—but which?

Fitzpark Museum, Keswick, Cumbria

2471: To Ethel Smyth   [52 *Tavistock Square, W.C.*1]

Typewritten
[16 November 1931]

As far as I know at the moment I shall be in on Wednesday; but dont for gods sake make any engagement on that footing because anybody may insist upon coming then—I cant manage to keep my days apart at the moment—and how could we talk about the Prison in the presence of some American duchess—such as make my life a burden to me? My head is stupid with letter writing and therefore no more at the moment, but hope to write later. I'm much better, but you inspire me with such healthy dread of being caught malingering (is that the word? military I think, so youll know) that I skate off the subject as soon as I can. A very good thing. I hate that sort of talk myself. And all talk at the moment. Ten to talk tother night—whats the use of talk, I go on saying, and go on talking. A lovely and solitary—that is with L—walk today over Hampstead Heath; trees like chandeliers in holland bags with mist; dogs copulating. L. is buying a mixture called Keepaway to be smeared on the hinder parts of Pinka next week—thats what I'm trying for the American aristocracy. Think what a cost it is to telegraph Princesse di Bassiano, Madame de Clermont Tonnerre etc instead of plain Smyth.

So enough.   V.

[*in Virginia's handwriting:*]
I will let you know for certain later about Wednesday

Berg

1. Virginia was reading Benjamin Disraeli's *Coningsby* (1844).

Tuesday [17 November 1931]

By some miracle, all the duchesses have retired to Rome, so I shall be alone tomorrow, if you like to come up instead of sitting in the basement; and shall expect you at 4.30.

V.

Please hand the enclosed with my love to the very stout lady who sang [*The Prison*] on the top left hand corner the other night.

Quite recovered, so no need to mention health.

Berg

2473: To Ethel Smyth   *Monks House* [*Rodmell, Sussex*]

Saturday, Nov? [21 November 1931]

It came over me, directly I had delivered that appalling bunch of cuttings to the care of Miss Walton [*unidentified*] that I had forgotten the H[enry]. B[rewster]. letters. I daresay this was a nudge from the sub-conscious, which is said to nudge—I mean, I dont want to give them up till I've read them. Cant you give me till New Years Day? I'm promising myself—I'm always talking to Virginia the 6 year old and saying "If you'll be good and do—so and so, you shall have so and so—" and I've promised her a whole 4t night here at Xmas, without a single MS. to read or duchess to pacify, or anything but sitting over a log fire and reading what she likes. So do wait to drop dead of a stroke in the street till Jan. 2nd or 3rd.—when I'll give them to your executors, and buy a laurel wreath, and go to Woking in time for the disposal of the corpse. (The wireless is chanting Western European folk songs as I write—like a gale in the shrouds—Highland songs, the man says—sung by women while they shrink cloth. Lord how I'd like to write that kind of thing myself—but I wouldn't wail so—why do 'folk' wail, always? Never a tune, always up and down, like a cats tail gliding over the kitchen floor. Do you like folk songs? To my thinking they're the ruin of all modern music—just as [J. M.] Synge and Yeats ruined themselves with keening Celtic dirges. And then to set our dish in the oven: and then for a wholly blessed evening over the fire. By the way, I've asked E[th] [Williamson] to dine on Monday, and hope she can—very good funny poetical political nephew [Julian Bell], who's never met anyone but earnest girls in tweeds at Cambridge—to meet that stargazer. (Now they're singing the Earl of Moray; but still keening, though its a question of love, halters, dagger, in the snow, all bloody, as far as I can make out) One day I want to come down to Woking and Coign [Ethel's house] that is: lunch with Dame E: walk with her on just such a lovely thrush-egg milk-soft day as this to Triggs Lock[1] (my word how silken and sensitive like a race horse skin the sea at Brighton was this evening, with a dozen ripples, such as one draws across a silk sheet, and two black fishing boats, almost drawing tears from my eyes. Save for a strong smell of stinking fish which reserved my sanity)— I say, we will go to Triggs Lock on such an afternoon: home to tea; I to catch the dinner train home. Really that would suit better with my mood than any hour over the fire. I want air, movement, and to see things changing —now a horse, now a tree, perhaps an old man in a comforter taking an airing—not any longer to survey the inside of my own head, even when kindled into fiery electric bulbs by Ethel. (Now they're singing Jacobite ballads—rather better; more like a frothing horse and less like a cats tail).

But its a quarter to 7. at which hour I light my oven, and put in my chicken brew; and a divine blood red soup, made of beetroot, onions, carrots and I think a dash of some spirit: after which we end with two gigantic Bath buns, made by the widow of a man who was called Booth, and dying he left her nothing but the receipt for buns, on which she's made a fortune; and serves one herself, aged 102, with ringlets to her shoulders, like hollow barley sugar.[2] Now its Helen Fair—Beyond Compare O What lovely words —and now Mr Middleton[3] on pruning, whom we cut off, and so I must stop and to my oven.

Well Ethel this is a long letter—the longest far I've written this six weeks, and all in ten minutes too, so its thick as a bun with howlers, solecisms, and no true expression, I daresay, of my affection and admiration for the valiant uncastrated cat with the unhealed wound.

O I spent the morning so agreeably talking about spaniels to the lady next door—and Mrs Ebbs the clergyman's wife has given notice she means to ask me to tea; though I'm, she hears, so dreadfully shy, very likely I shan't have the courage to come. But I shall. Thats the society I long for— Mrs Ebbs and Miss Dixey who breeds lemon coloured cockers. She said to me, "Mrs Woolf, I've planted this bed with yellow and white roses, because my yellow and white bitch is buried there; and that one with red and orange roses, because thats the grave of the red bitch. Its a mistake to have so much sentiment, aint it? But I'm like that" etc. etc

V.

Berg

---

1. On the 18th-century River Wey Navigation Canal, near Woking.
2. Booth's was a confectioner in East Street, Brighton.
3. C. H. Middleton, who for many years broadcast gardening talks for the BBC.

Monks House, Rodmell
[Sussex]

Nov. 22nd [1931]

Dearest Dadie,

I should have thanked you for your letter before, but London is such a parrot house, with all the fowls pecking and screeching at the same moment that I waited for a quiet day here. By the way, if King's were to offer me a room in a quadrangle, with fellowship attached on condition I teach nothing I will accept—(the woman next door breeds cockers, who bark—thats whats determined me to become a Fellow of King's.)

Why I'm so grateful for your letter is not merely for the sake of the intelligence and discrimination of the praise (vain as I am) but because I'm full of ideas for further books, but they all develop from The Waves. Now if the Waves had seemed to you a barren and frigid experiment—merely Virginia hanging to a trapeze by her toe nails—then I should have felt, Why go on?, and as I can't go back, even so far as Mrs Dalloway and The Lighthouse, I should have come to an awkward pass, and have probably taken a vow of silence for ever. Thats why your encouragement is a draught of champagne in the desert and the caravan bells ring and the dogs bark and I mount—or shall in a few months—my next camel. Not that I mean to begin another of these appalling adventures yet awhile.[1]

When are you coming up? I never know, and so can never suggest a dinner or some way of meeting. I leave it to you to drop a postcard in the press and say. Did you like the look of your poems?[2] And are you writing more—and criticism? Now (though you'll suspect the origin of my praise to be author's vanity—which it is not) I think you have a real gift for what I call poetry and what I call criticism; and wish you would throw Keats at the wooden heads of your jackasses and sit in a garret and write, write, write.

But on this point you have little respect I know for the opinion of old women like me: though why Peter Q.[3] and Shephard [J. T. Sheppard] should seem to you in this respect venerable and virile guides, and me a flibberti-gibbet, God knows. And there's a hair in the pen: and a flea, alas, in L's right trouser, so no more.

V.

1. Virginia wrote in fact only one more 'adventurous' novel, *Between the Acts*, which was published in 1941, after her death. Her other remaining books were *The Common Reader: Second Series* (1932), *Flush* (1933), *The Years* (1937), *Three Guineas* (1938), and *Roger Fry: A Biography* (1940).
2. Rylands's *Poems* were printed by the Hogarth Press and published in December 1931.
3. Peter Quennell, the author and editor, then aged 26, had published *Poems* (1926) and *Baudelaire and the Symbolists* (1929). He was regularly contributing literary articles to *Life and Letters*.

That copy of The Waves I sent you was the last—this is a boast—of the first edition: I snatched it from John's maw: so if you keep it very carefully in brown paper ten years or so it may be worth 10/4½. This is advice to you as a book collector.

George Rylands

2475: To Ethel Smyth   [52 *Tavistock Square, W.C.*1]

Wednesday [2 December 1931]

I've been in bed for a week, but am up today and much better—Still I've promised not to see anyone, so cant call you up as I should wish. Yes, I entirely agree with you about L's book [*After the Deluge*]—and hope you'll infect your old Tories at Woking with the desire to read it. Here's a book you lent me ages ago. We're off to Rodmell I hope on Friday and please write me letters and I shall be all right (D.V.) when I come back

V.

Berg

2476: To Ethel Smyth   52 *T.*[avistock] S.[quare, W.C.1]

Sunday [6 December 1931]

Yes, Ethel dear, I am quite aware of the warm and generous cat who goes to Ringwood on the spur of the moment. Indeed its that Ethel I clasp to my breast at present. I admit that I've been rather depressed, considerably sunk between the sea, with these incessant headaches; and when I've been tempted to say what is the good of it all?—I've remembered with gratitude how often you've told me—how openly and generously—that I'm one of your—what shall I say?—objects—necessities? I mean, if I ceased to exist, Ethel would feel her glass of champagne less sparkling. There—you've done me a lot of good, though I seldom say so—I've had to agree with L. that I shall spend the weeks till Christmas in an invalid state—no writing, no going to parties or plays, but taking a walk and coming back and lying on the sofa. Every time I do more the pain comes back; but it certainly ceases when thus given in to, and so give in I must. But by Christmas I think I shall be in full fettle again. I'm going to read science—as the least like to my own ideas—which I beat down; and yet how they swarm! I've 3 books in my head at the moment.[1] I'm going to read Wells and Huxley, and

1. Virginia was writing some new articles and revising old ones for a second *Common Reader*, which appeared in 1932. She had begun to write *Flush* (1933) and a copy-book called *Diary* or *Calendar*, never completed. She was contemplating two further books, a novel, briefly mentioned in her diary as *The Tree*;

a man called Heard;[1] and perhaps you'll find me a nicer, quieter, less remote
and arrogant and moody character, when scientific. Elizabeth [Williamson]
we both liked immensely; and she was so intelligent—I doubt that L.
would throw her from her perch. Well—I'm not going to write long letters.
Yes, Ethel dear, I find the thought of you very comforting.

V.

Back from Rodmell. Very lovely in gusts.

Berg

2477: To V. Sackville-West   52 *Tavistock Sqre* [*W.C.*1]

Sunday [6 December 1931]

Oh that was very nice, getting your letter. I had a nightmare that you'd
discovered say Enid Jones or someone altogether nicer than I am. And now
you say you love me—what a relief. I'm better, but O dear, I spent all last
week in bed—curse these headaches, all due to Waves, the stunt book;[2]
and now have promised to remain invalidish till we go away at Christmas:
no writing, no going to parties, lying down, taking a short walk; it seems the
only way to stop the usual pain—not that its been bad only forever coming
back. And what I want is to see you—But when? I mean, when would it
suit you? Here I am all day. I'm dining alone next Wednesday (9th, I think)
and if you cd. come, we'd dine quietly (L. wd. allow you, tho' no one else)
Let me know soon if you can. But dont bother. I mean tell me a day you're
up. Roses come: are being planted under my lodge window. Are you really
fond of me?

V

Dont put yourself out to come, if as probable, youre in an awful rush

I'm afraid I must put off Pennshurst[3] till Christmas

Berg

---

and a feminist book on women's emotions, a sequel to *A Room of One's Own*,
called at this time *The Pargiters*, but eventually written as *The Years*.

1. Gerald Heard, the writer on science. From 1930-33 he gave fortnightly broadcasts under the title of *The Surprising World*. In 1931 he published *The Emergence
   of Man*. Virginia also intended to read *The Science of Life* (1931), by H. G.
   and G. P. Wells and Julian Huxley.
2. See Letter 2459.
3. Penshurst Place, near Tonbridge, Kent, the great medieval and Tudor house
   of the Sidneys (Lord De L'Isle). Sir Philip Sidney was born there in 1554, and
   Virginia had been writing about him for the second *Common Reader*. Virginia
   and Vita did not go to Penshurst until 1940.

52 *Tavistock Sqre.* [*W.C.*1]

Sunday [6 December 1931]

Dear William,

I should like nothing better than to come to your party, but I'm afraid its not likely. I go on getting bad headaches, and the only cure, as I've found from long experience, is to lead a hermits life without pleasure or excitement. I'm afraid I must follow this rule till Christmas. But I shall remind Leonard and Vita, and I'm very sorry for myself, remembering how greatly I enjoyed the other party in the bloodstained house.[1] Perhaps you'll let me come when the house is warmed.

Yours
Virginia

If its Canning Place, where you live, then I used to learn Greek at no. 6 from Clara Pater, sister of Walter;[2] no bloodstains there: all blue china, Persian cats, and Morris wallpapers: but thats ages ago.

Texas

2479: To Ethel Smyth   [52 *Tavistock Square, W.C.*1]

Tuesday [8 December 1931]

Well anyhow next Wednesday if not this. I think *probably* I should do better to ward you off till I'm recovered: but if I wake very rigorous tomorrow I'll ring up before 11 on the chance you're free. My blessings for letter— So sleepy I cant write

Berg

2480: To Hugh Walpole   52 *Tavistock Square, W.C.*1

Typewritten
[December 1931?]

Dear Hugh,
    I've had this by me for weeks.[3]
    Why should I know about Hugh Walpole's beds?

1. The landlady of Plomer's previous house in Bayswater, a young Jewess, was butchered by her husband in the presence of their child, while Plomer was away. He tells the story in his autobiography (1975) pp. 240-3, and wrote a novel, *The Case is Altered* (1932), based upon the crime.
2. Clara Pater taught the classics to Virginia from 1900, when she was 18, until 1901.
3. Virginia's enclosure, and Hugh Walpole's reply, do not survive.

I told you we were getting mixed in the public mind and so it is.[1]
Very nice to have seen you, excuse typing.

Virginia

(no answer needed unless at will.) And dont return the German.

Texas

2481: To Lytton Strachey   52 *Tavistock Sqre.* [*W.C.*1]
10 Dec [1931]

"I arise from dreams of thee"[2]—that's why I write. I have just woken from a dream in which I was at a play, in the pit and suddenly you, who were sitting across a gangway in a row in front, turned and looked at me, and we both went into fits of laughter. What the play was, what we laughed at, I've no notion, but we were both very young (no, for you had your beard) and at the age when we used to write to each other. Why are these dreams more vivid than real life?—Anyhow while it hangs about me, I can't help writing to the bearded serpent, especially as Clive tells me you are off to Malaya for months[3] and the chances are we shan't meet till Gordon Sqre. is full of tulips and [Arthur] Waley is playing tennis with Alix [Strachey] in white flannels.

I'm recumbent, lazy, content, reading book after book. And what are you doing? Reading Shakespeare I hope and occasionally making a note very neatly in a very beautiful book. By the way I read As you like it the other day and was almost sending you a wire to ask what is the truth about Jacques—What is it? His last speech reads so very odd.[4]

This is all my news, as I see no one, not Ottoline, not Charlie Chaplin[5]— no one but Clive who runs in to see me between a lunch party that ends at 5 and a dinner party that begins at 8.30 and goes on till the sparrows are rising in flocks from the Embankment. Lord—how I'd like to lead his life.

Well this is only a dream letter and needs no answer, unless you can tell me what we laughed at; but when you're in London with the tulips and Waley's white flannels, please come and see your old and attached friend

Virginia

Strachey Trust

1. See Letter 2467.
2. *The Indian Serenade*, Shelley.
3. In fact, although Virginia did not know it, Lytton was seriously ill.
4. "To see no pastime, I: what you would have
   I'll stay to know at your abandon'd cave."
5. Charlie Chaplin, who was then 42, was paying a prolonged visit to London, and was much lionized by Sibyl Colefax and Ottoline Morrell.

Saturday [12 December 1931]

I fell asleep like a sucking pig after dinner and so cant catch the post. This is only what they call a line to say that on the contrary, I wasn't at all tired but I think refreshed by your visit. Its a fact that to listen to conversation when the converser is as discreet well balanced and racy as Dame Ethel cheers and invigorates. I liked Ethel very much on Wednesday. I think she has a tender and understanding nature, in spite of appearances. I'm really better, only mustn't, as Leonard says, think of writing so for another 10 days: when I say now I'll begin to think of a book, he puts a shade over me just as I used to shut up my canary.

What a blessing to have a critical string to my mind. I dont feel I could write another novel under a year. But to collect my thoughts on Sir Walter Scott is to use a quiet sober string that wont twang me awake—Forgive these metaphors, this egotism, this breathless abruptness. Nelly is going to buy my dinner and post this, and I daren't be found writing by L when he comes up from the Press.

He's much excited about the Cole question[1] and is going to get his facts correct—rather wishing I think to force you to say to the widow, "D'you know, Nell, your husband was a murderer?" It would be a lark—as a conversational opening.

So no more

Yr
V.

What about the Village?[2]

Berg

12th Dec. [1931]

Dear Ralph,

Could you by any chance advise me as to how to get Niger goat skins?—I want two to make a writing case. My old merchant has disappeared.

---

1. Galbraith Cole, the son of the 4th Earl of Enniskillen, married Eleanor Balfour ('Nell'), the daughter of Ethel's friend Elizabeth, Countess of Balfour. Cole died on 6 October 1929, in Kenya.
2. Leonard's novel *The Village in the Jungle* (1913), which was reprinted by the Hogarth Press in 1931.

But dont bother if you're no longer in touch with the trade[1] and forgive me for being a nuisance.

I hope you and Frances [Marshall] will come and dine after Christmas— oh no, you'll be in Spain I suppose. I wish I were.

Yours ever
Virginia

Robert H. Taylor

2484: To Dora Carrington   52 *Tavistock Sqre.* [*W.C.*1]

Tuesday [15 December 1931]

Dearest Carrington,

We're so unhappy to hear that Lytton is ill. We didnt know it. If you or Ralph could ever let us have a card to say how he is we should be more than grateful.

Our best love. If there was anything I could do you would let me know wouldn't you—

Yours Virginia

I'm so sorry I bothered Ralph. Please thank him for his letter.

Robert H. Taylor

2485: To William Plomer   52 *Tavistock Sqre.* [*W.C.*1]

Dec 16th [1931]

Dear William,

It's not ingratitude that has prevented me from thanking you for the book—merely laziness. I can't write letters, as you know. But my love of reading books, specially books on Scandinavian literature, grows;—how queer and crabbed their names are: and I've never heard of them or read them.

Alas, your party was last night, and I'm sure it was a gigantic success, and I wasn't there. But I hope I shall see you after Christmas when I shall come back from a fortnight at Monks House quite recovered.

Yours
Virginia

Leonard had hoped and meant to come to the party, but was caught here, and was very much disappointed—which is seldom true of him and parties, but is this time.

Texas

1. Ralph Partridge had taken up book-binding when he left the Hogarth Press in 1923.

2486: To Ethel Smyth   [52 *Tavistock Square, W.C.1*]

[19 December 1931]

This is only again 'just a line' to catch the early post so that you may get it this evening. L. S. is about the same. The next days are the critical ones—fear of perforation.[1] But there's nothing to be done. Nessa comes back tomorrow, and I shall know on Monday if its any use our going for the night on Tuesday. I suspect Nessa has told them not to ask me, unless she sees they really are in need of an outsider. They—all the relations—sitting there waiting find it a relief to drive over to Hungerford—and anything one can do, as you will realise, is to me a relief. After all, I dont suppose I care for anyone more than for Lytton. (after my Jew) He's in all my past—my youth. But never mind. Its my form of tenderness, that—well, I wont go on. I feel your form, dearest E—oh yes—sitting by me so strong—so quiet. Yes. Its the being used up, after these attacks of headache—thats the nuisance now. Its always so—a general complete influenza drowse. But fresh air at Rodmell will cure that in no time

Will write tomorrow.

Yr
V.

Berg

2487: To Ethel Smyth   52 *T.[avistock] S.[quare, W.C.1]*

Sunday [20 December 1931]

Here is the questionnaire duly answered.[2] I must say it doesn't reflect well upon the Woking posts. But something like it happened here with some MSS—since arrived, and said to be due to Christmas.

No change in L.S—except that the drs. now incline to call it ulceration of the colon, and not typhoid. He is very ill, but they say not hopelessly. I rather expect we shall go after Christmas, but shant know till tomorrow. If not, we shall go to Rodmell on Tuesday. I'm better, and think if I can get fresh air and not too much talking I shall be well again and able to write next week perhaps. (Excuse egotism: you draw it on yourself)

O what a dull letter? Why did I ever think I could write? Ah, but *you* can write letters, and I hope the horror of Christmas will be starred for me by frequent white envelopes. And I will reply, anyhow egotistically.

I'm going to get up and dress tomorrow after breakfast.

So with that proud boast

Goodnight
V.

Berg

1. The doctors' latest diagnosis of Lytton Strachey's condition was an ulcerated colon.
2. Ethel frequently fired at Virginia a volley of numbered questions.

Monks House, Rodmell
                                                              [Sussex]

Typewritten
Monday [21? December 1931]

My dear Julian,
    I have vainly tried to write to you many times to ask if you'd like me to
give you the new Nonesuch [Press] edition of Dryden for Christmas. They
have done the two first volumes, and I would give you the lot as they come
out if you liked. Only I don't know if its a good edition, or if you already
have one. Sometimes the Nonesuch are execrable to all true scholars I'm told;
but let me know, and if you don't want that, think of something you do
want. I expect and hope that we shall meet shortly.
                                              Your loving Aunt Virginia
Quentin Bell

2489: To Ethel Smyth   *Lewes [Sussex]*

Postcard
Tuesday Evening [22 December 1931]

    Bad news of L. S. today, and I'm not sure what we shall do—will let
you know. Just arrived here, warm through owing to your wonderful
warmer.[1] I'll write tomorrow—

                                                              V.

Berg

2490: To Vanessa Bell   *Monks [House, Rodmell,*
                                              Sussex]
Wednesday [23 December 1931]

Dearest,
    I have just heard from Quentin. I will ring you up tomorrow at 9.30
on the chance of catching you. I should be glad of any news you could
send [about Lytton]—as I dont suppose the caretaker can tell me much.
I find I only gave Angelica 10/- when I thought it was £1—so will you
give her this

                                                              B.

490 Lewes will always find us—its next door and they will send round.

Berg

1. A car-heater.

[*Monk's House, Rodmell, Sussex*]

Wednesday [23 December 1931]

A new specialist [John Ryle, a surgeon] saw L. S. yesterday and thinks badly of him—I only had this on the telephone this morning. I think they are afraid that the poison is affecting his heart. We are staying here, but shall go to Hungerford if they want us. I suppose the next 2 or 3 days must decide.

Well, I dont know what to say: in fact I couldn't say anything. I seem to have lived about 20 years in the past week—so much we have shared—so many states of mind; such intimacy. I find myself now talking to him whatever I read or think. But no: I wont think of it: and he may still live.

Your heat box saved my life yesterday. It kept me hot all the drive, and it was a very long one, and we got here late. Wonderful woman to have such a thing! I've had (you asked for details) a little pain again—naturally; but am better today, and have 3 weeks good rest behind me.

A letter from Miss [Mary] Dodge[1] about the Waves—how odd!—and odd that you should have met Gwen Raverat[2]—a tragic figure—now L. is going to drive me into Lewes. Anyhow I have a husband—no, I will not open any vein of feeling. I still believe that if one can stir about briskly, even buying sausage and turkey, its the best course for Lytton. I'm sure you understand all this

V.

Berg

2492: To Ethel Smyth   [*Monk's House, Rodmell, Sussex*]

Thursday [24 December 1931]

L. S. seems unchanged. I suppose he is just holding his own, and there is still a chance. Especially as they can give him more food now that theyre certain its not typhoid. Very lovely here. I'm going to Brighton now with L. so no more—oh and I feel better and hope for a letter and will write a longer letter soon—I'm reading science—

V.

Berg

1. See p. 215, note 1.
2. Whose husband Jacques Raverat, the French painter, died painfully of multiple sclerosis in 1925.

[*Monk's House, Rodmell, Sussex*]

Christmas Day [25 December 1931]

Your Wednesday letter just come. I hope you've had a scrap from me before this. Last night they thought he [Lytton Strachey] was dying: but Nessa has rung up to say he is a shade better this morning. It may mean nothing, or it may be the turn. But he is conscious again, and has taken milk after 24 hours taking nothing. I cant be positive about plans,—I mean we should go at any moment if they wanted us—but I expect now we shall stay here till Monday anyhow, as Nessa is going over from her home at Seend:[1]—in fact I doubt that we should go, even next week, for more than a night; and I would wire if we did. So write here with certainty.

Its difficult to settle down, to read, write or think. But I'm better in spite of all. The air is so fresh, and I've been a walk with L. over the marsh, and we feel unreasonably cheerful again.

But one's mind seems to freeze and you get the effects in these spasmodic scraps. I've not tried yet to write, but dip into The Sciences of Life, (Wells) and Goethe and various poems—and then there's the old woman in the cottage aged 91, who cant see, or move; and we give her 10/- and she says we are her best friends but she wishes to die—and then there's the cesspool to be emptied, and there's the greenhouse full of carnations, and Maynard Keynes, and Lydia giving us Christmas dinner, and so on and so on.

Goodbye for the moment

V.

Berg

Monks House, Rodmell [*Sussex*]

Christmas day [1931]

Dearest Ethel,

How extraordinarily nice of you to have sent me this lovely book!— Its one I've always meant to read, and never have: and now it stands in my new bookcase. How odd that Lytton gave me the letters from Portugal, in much the same edition![2] Nessa has just rung up to say that he is a shade better—they thought he could not live through the night. This may mean nothing, or it may mean the turn. As you can imagine, we're not able to

---

1. The house of Vanessa's mother-in-law in Wiltshire, near Ham Spray, Lytton's house at Hungerford.
2. Virginia's two books may have been Shelley's *Letters from Italy* (1818-22), and Robert Southey's *Letters Written During a Short Residence in Spain and Portugal* (1797).

think of much else at the moment—but when we're back, do come and see me—(I've been so stupid in the head, I didn't ask you) and tell me if there is any book of my own or anybody elses I could give you.

What a lovely binding—how discreet, so distinguished and like you—the Italian letters have!

Yrs

Virginia

Wendy Baron

2495: To Ethel Smyth   [*Monk's House, Rodmell, Sussex*]

Sunday 27th [December 1931]

The latest news of L. S. is that he's rather better if anything, and though the dr. wont say that this is lasting, I cant help feeling that 48 hours of improvement must mean something solid. They now again think its typhoid, and are having fresh examinations—What seems clear is that Lytton himself is making a fight, and not sinking into unconsciousness, as they feared. All this keeps one oddly numb in the head—though I'm much less anxious One feels there's the telephone at 5—what's the news—Even at 12 in the morning. But for the first time today I feel a wish to write and have no pain, and so hope that with luck I may glide into words tomorrow. I've been a muddy walk to the river. Your letter and Eliz⁵ came this morning. Tomorrow the frost of posts will be over, and newspapers, etc. In some ways a pity—there's a certain luxury in being isolated. As you see I can't write. I'll let you know if we decide to go to Hungerford. But anyhow not till the end of the week, I should think. Nessa comes on Tuesday. All the Stracheys are consumed with family love: 7 of them are sitting in an Inn and there are, as you may suppose, complications with the different varieties of wives, and which are amusing at a distance but harrowing in the house itself. Glad of letters as long as possible.

Yr

V.

Berg

2496: To Ethel Smyth   [*Rodmell, Sussex*]

Telegram
[28 December 1931]

Please say how you are. Lytton rather better

Virginia

Berg

　　　　　Monks House [Rodmell, Sussex]

Dec. 29th [1931]

Well, dearest Mrs Nick; there was once a woman called Virginia, and she had a small hairy animal called Potto. Does this bring anything back to mind? The sound of your lovely balmy voice coming across the marshes last night advising me to read Lady somebodies Book[1]—as I shall—stirred the embers of desire. Oh we've had such a wretched Christmas—telephones, wires, ready to start for Hungerford at any moment. Though you dont care for Lytton, you'll understand my feeling. Why is one thus attached to people? On Christmas Eve we thought he was dying. He is still very ill,—but now, apparently, its going on, up and down,—a thing called ulcerated colon.

And naturally my head which is not screwed right, began its infernal aching. Lord—I'd sell it cheap at auction. Why shouldnt Hugh [Walpole] buy and bequeath me his diabetes? Thats only a matter of not eating sugar, whereas here I am, since Nov. 25th, abstaining altogether from love, frolic, excitement, Vita, ink. Not a word have I written; and I've 4 books all surging in my head, and shall be 50 next month, and how am I ever to write them? And does it matter if I dont? Why not give up writing and lavish my days in joy? I'm reading, reading; and have rambled down to the river; its this cursed being fond of my friends thats my downfall. Old Ethel is sick or fevered or somehow stricken—with Lady Balfour by her side, and a [hand] writing like 6 paralysed frogs hopping. But she's better. And how happy the sound of your voice made me, coming over the fields, and lighting up the fish mongers window as it did this time how many years ago? Potto cant count after 5—so whats the good asking.

As for seeing you, whats the chance? You did say something about coming to your mother with the boys. But by this time doubtless she's cut you out of her will again, and may have—who knows—ordered a pound of chocolate creams to be sent to me. I may go up to London on Saturday for the day—L. has to do some broadcasting nonsense—otherwise I shall be here till Sunday week I hope, unless the Stracheys want us at Hungerford. Poor people! Nessa says they all sit round an Inn, waiting for doctors, and all devoted, and all quarrelling, and no one knowing what to do next. And this has gone on since the first of Decr, or longer—so, should they wish it, we will go, and play chess, or take a walk or something. But I daresay not.

And what about Penshurst or Sissingt? I'm so behindhand—I was going to write about Sidney,[2] and cant get back into the mood. Dotty,

1. In her broadcast Vita mentioned *Book: Discreet Memoirs* by Lady Clodagh Anson.
2. See p. 410, note 3.

John says, is furious that we've not printed her poem for the New Year.[1] I'm sorry, but I couldn't finish the last page, and we didn't know she wanted it by then—but never mind—I sometimes think, privately, that Dotty would do well to endow the bedridden with her £200 and leave poetry alone.

But Vita, on the other hand, should write a long long poem for Virginia; and before she does that she should sit down and write ever so long and intimate a letter to Virginia. Now do try again, Vita; your first attempt in The Dolomites is among my most cherished possessions[2]

I wish I liked Desmond's book [*Portraits*, 1931] as much as I like him— too much in the style of [Edmund] Gosse: oh such flimsy criticism, not of people, but of books. But no more.

Yr
V.

Berg

2498: To Ethel Smyth   *Monks House* [*Rodmell,*
                                  Sussex]

Tuesday, 29th Dec [1931]

Well, Ethel dear, I was very glad to get your staggering whisky letter this morning, and to be in touch with you for a moment, even so. I dont gather what your illness is—a chill? influenza? rheumatism? fever?—Was it the after effect of that ghastly game of golf when the pain made you laugh? Any details will be gladly received, for I like to realise as you know, small facts. Whats your temperature, for instance—can you eat; can you read, have you pain, what pain, where?—but you mustn't articulate. I know the screw it means, extruding thought into actual words when one's ill. A great gulf lies between mind and words.

Lytton is if anything better. But its puzzling. On Sunday they say its typhoid; then get another specialist yesterday, who says positively thats out of the question, but it may be paratyphoid, is probably ulcerated colon, and if so, is an illness that must go on being serious, with ups and downs for weeks. The last man, however, said he had 'a good fighting chance', which is far more than they said last week, and all the doctors are amazed by his strength. Its the good Anglo-Indian blood; I always feel a toughness and sanity in Lytton, for all his look of weakness. Also he is determined to live. This being so, they think it better we should put off coming, as they are still all there—5 or 6 brothers and sisters sitting devoted playing cross word puzzles in the Inn. They will want friends later I imagine, and I'm selfishly

1. Dorothy Wellesley's *Jupiter and the Nun* was printed by the Woolfs and published in May 1932.
2. See Volume III of this Edition, Letters 1491 and 1502.

glad not to go this week, being rather liable to get pain if I make an effort. I woke up with rather a bout of it yesterday morning, so put off my writing. But it cleared off, and I'm very comfortable today, only shall take another few days of entire sloth by way of precaution. Also there is no great reason why I should write.

No, I dont think you're right about my caring for 'so few'. What would you have said had you seen me when I got no answer to my telegram to Woking? For some reason, none came till 7, though I wired at 3. By 6 o'clock I imagined you unconscious, so that the telegram hadn't been opened. By 6.30 I was in such a fidget I could not sit and read up here with L. I imagined telegraph boys knocks—went to the door—no one; imagined telephoning—but if she's unconscious whats the good? Mary would tell one nothing—And so on. At last to quiet myself, I went down to fidget with the dinner in the kitchen, and then unmistakably heard a feeble tap on the window, and there was the idiot boy, come to the wrong door, in a howling wind. I had him in and gave him all my spare coppers as thanksgiving. No, I think you grossly underrate the strength of my feelings—so strong they are—such caverns of gloom and horror open round me I daren't look in—and also their number. Do you know how I cared for Katherine Mansfield, for Charlie Sanger—to mention friends only? No, you dont. But then, for months on first knowing you, I said to myself here's one of these talkers. They dont know what feeling is, happily for them. Because everyone I most honour is silent—Nessa, Lytton, Leonard, Maynard: all silent; and so I have trained myself to silence; induced to it also by the terror I have of my own unlimited capacity for feeling—when Lytton seemed to be dying—well yes: I cant go into that, even now. But to my surprise, as time went on, I found that you are perhaps the only person I know who shows feeling and feels. Still I cant imagine talking about my love for people, as you do. Is it training? Is it the perpetual fear I have of the unknown force that lurks just under the floor? I never cease to feel that I must step very lightly on top of that volcano. No Ethel, there's a mint of things about me, I say egotistically, you've no notion of; the strength of my feelings is only one. So get well, and sit down to your A.B.C. again. It was angelic of Lady B[alfour]. to write. Now I believe she would see how fond of you I am, being simpler, more sensible than some wild cats, uncastrated and entire, that I know of.

Its bitter cold, all white snow over [Mount] Caburn one moment, iron black the next, and I'm sitting over the fire in my upstairs room, which you slept in; with lots of books, oh and unanswered letters. Everybodies taken to writing to me about The Waves. After 3 months they've just been able to get to the end, and write in triumph to say so.

About Gwen Raverat—(I trust you're in a state when gossip may amuse —leave the pages lying in your blankets and now and then lazily read a line—thats what I do in your state, and find it wiles away the time to lunch)

—well, Gwen is one of my oldest friends, George Darwins daughter, all Cambridge, all Darwin solidity, integrity, force and sense—What must she do, but take to art. This she did with a scientific thoroughness that used to make us jeer. But somehow she persevered, went to France, met—no this was at Cambridge—a French boy, Jacques R; fell violently in love; forced him, we used to think, to give up his lighter and more lascivious loves, to marry her. What a passion her love was! I came in for some flashes of jealousy—not of me—of another woman:[1] and was blinded—never saw such crude what they call elemental passion unscrupulous, tyrannic, pure— before or since. And then she married him: they both painted; she like a Darwin, by science, force, sense; and he rather gifted but lyrical, and exact and very French. And then he began to stumble; the doctors said his spine was affected: Through 10 years I suppose he slowly stiffened, till the paralysis reached his hands, which had to be tied to the paint brushes; and Gwen lifted him, rubbed him, drove him in a pony cart over the hills at Vence, to paint; and so he was finally tortured to death, watching it come, with rage, with obscenity—he wrote me page after page, and she at last wrote for him—of despair, of defiance—They were incredibly brave; and yet it was unspeakably sordid, for he couldn't die, and was jealous, and sexually tormented, and abused her, and loved her, and she suffered, as I imagine, more than seemed humanly possible, till at last she almost killed him, with one dose of morphia after another—the doctors saying she mustn't, and she defying them. After he died, 7 years ago, she came back to England, with the two children; and used to say to me, her unhappiness was such that she ought not to see me. She became set, frozen, like an old log dried out of all sensation, save for the children. And then she fell in love again:[2] and the man married somebody else. And somehow I got her a job on Time and Tide; and she stumps about, to me still frozen, formidable —I cant get over her past; but if you see her as a living and normal woman, probably its true. And I avoid seeing her, because I know of her past; and I feel that she wishes to avoid that, and so lunches with Lady Rhondda.

Good bye

V.

If you wish me not to have another headache, you will get well instantly.

Berg

1. Katherine Arnold-Forster (*née* Cox). See Virginia's letter to Vanessa of 19 April 1911 (Volume I, pp. 462-3).
2. With Jean Marchand (1883-1941), the French painter.

Monks House [*Rodmell,
                                                        Sussex*]

Wednesday [30 December 1931]

Could you—including Angelica, Julian Clive Quentin, anybody else,
come *here* to tea on Thursday? The bother is that the Keynes' who were
coming on Friday now want to come Thursday.

So you would meet them, but we hope you will for old sakes sake. Well
its marvellous about Lytton, considering last week and I cant help feeling
optimistic.

                                                                    B.

Berg

*Monks House, Rodmell,
                                                        Lewes* [*Sussex*]

30th Dec 1931

My dear Pernel,

I cant help hoping, from what Nessa says this morning, that Lytton
must be better; and that now we may all think of the future—which I
shouldn't like to do at all if Lytton weren't in it. What a Christmas you
had—and we too, for although the Stracheys and Stephen's may fight like
cat and dog I cant help thinking we are of one flesh when it comes to a pinch.

Are you staying on at the Bear [Inn, Hungerford]?

Well, I shall occupy the next ten minutes before lunch in gossiping, in
case you have a spare moment and feel as I do overcome with sloth, self-
indulgence, the desire never never to be anxious about anybody again. But
now I come to consider, there's precious little in the way of news. This
house, which you justly despised if you remember for having no bath, is
now luxurious to the point of electric fires in the bedrooms. Yes, you foresee
the day when you'll be asked to stay and won't be able to think of an excuse.
Shall I have Betty Jenkins to meet you? After all, your pain is little compared
with the lifelong joy it would be to her. She's written a second novel,[1] a
variation on the theme of Strachey—you're Kathy Winter this time—but a
theme so frail, so far, so impeccably well bred I can't recognise even the
way you have of putting the accent all wrong, say on the word 'donkey'.

Then I saw another of your admirers in London—Alice Ritchie[2]—
that formidable and to me slightly repulsive—no only acutely unhappy
like a beast that gets its paw in a trap—figure: she is now an orphan,

1. Elizabeth Jenkins's second novel was *The Winters* (1931). She had been at
   Newnham College, Cambridge, of which Pernel Strachey was Principal.
2. Alice Ritchie published two novels with the Hogarth Press, *The Peacemakers*
   (1928) and *Occupied Territory* (1930).

regretting her mother not her father; and when I said "But didn't he leave you say £50 a year?", she said, "Not a penny". "How then will you live?" I asked; whereupon she laughed, like a brown bear at the Zoo: all her means consist in the MS. of a novel which she alternately writes and burns; burns and writes. Now imagine yourself aged 30, in a small room, with a broken gas fire, sardines in a box, the sofa broken, facing life,—well would you call it life, my dear Pernel? Add to that a head which can fit no hat, feet which are impossible to cover, and a nature that suspects insults. But I have little skill in psychology; she may be a fairy (internally) aglow with rapture. But do you think it likely?

As for Ethel Smyth, whom you must meet, she has boiled over with a kind of effervescence of force—playing the trombone, golf, conducting, walking, riding, singing, loving, all at the same moment, so that she has, or had, a temperature of 104—and is nursed by a single maid with Lady Betty[1] at the bedside. I hear the vaguest strangest rumours of Mrs Sidgwick.[2] Amalgamation between her and Ethel seems to me difficult. Mrs Sidgwick sits with Gerald Balfour all day seeking evidence about ghosts. There's a hybrid called Piddinghoe[3], or some such name, who sits with them. Innumerable ghosts file before them, but always Gerald and Mrs Sidgwick say "There's no *evidence*" and Pid. pipes up, "None whatever". So the ghosts file out, and the three come up very late for lunch, and then mumble their food, Ethel says, so that its dark before they've masticated the celery: and then more ghosts. But there's a daughter, Kathleen, who's at Newnham, and says that Newnham is precisely and actually not an inch more nor an ell less, than Heaven. At that Mrs Sidgwick opens one eye, (the other being fixed on ghosts) and says "Ah"—as if she remembered Newnham; but Ethel doubts that she does. I say I'm like the Balfour, silent, submarine, profound, whereas the Smyths are foam and flurry on the surface. So we argue. So she takes the poker and flings it at me—and may it hit you when you come.

We are at your service at any moment of day or night, Leonard and I, so there is no need to say more.[4]

Here is my roast veal.

Yrs Virginia

Strachey Trust

1. Elizabeth, the wife of Gerald Balfour, who succeeded his brother, A. J. Balfour (the 1st Earl) in 1930. Their fifth daughter was called Kathleen.
2. Eleanor Sidgwick (1845-1936), the daughter of James Maitland Balfour, was Principal of Newnham College, Cambridge, from 1892-1910. In 1915 she published *Contributions to the Study of the Psychology of Mrs Piper's Trance*. She was a neighbour of Ethel at Woking.
3. Probably Leo Piddington, mentioned in the postscript to Letter 2218.
4. The Woolfs went to Ham Spray on 14 January, but Lytton Strachey was too ill to see them. He died a week later, 21 January 1932.

Index

The numbers are page-numbers, except in the 'Letters to' section at the end of individual entries, where the letter-numbers are given in italics.

Abbreviations: V. stands for Virginia Woolf; L. for Leonard Woolf; VB. for Vanessa Bell; and Vita for V. Sackville-West.

Beaverbrook, Lord, 87n, 88
Bedford Estate (Bloomsbury), 234 & n, 400n, 404
Beecham, Sir Thomas, xv, 184, 187, 225 & n
Beerbohm, Max, 17, 47
Belcher (Belsher), Miss (Hogarth Press), 228, 239, 280, 378n, 381
Bell, Angelica (Mrs David Garnett): 'in great spirits', 15 & n; 'adorable sprite', 71; school, 75 & n; at *Alice* party, 128-9; V. gives her allowance, 264, 296, 372; at Charleston party, 276; her beauty, 309; Cornish holiday, 310; as letter-writer, 73, 336; V. visits her at school, 325, 339-40, 341. *mentioned*, 22, 40, 61, 63, 69, 120, 133, 159, 237, 267, 330
    Letter to: No. *2185*
Bell, Clive: past love affair with Mary Hutchinson, 3, 4; in Paris with girl, 23, 34; his philandering ridiculed, 29, 44, 55-6, 58-9; in Cassis, 50; Julian Bell on, 53, 58; V. to Quentin on, 55; Mrs McLaren reproves him, 70, 74; contrite about 'Susie' etc and considers his future, 72-3, 74; to Spain, 91; article on V., 103; in Paris, 105; V. and Lytton Strachey miss him, 127, 183; Anrep's mosaic of, 170; accuses V. of coldness, 200; losing eyesight?, 246-7, 249, 258-9; accident to Joan Firminger, 248-9; renews relations with Mary Hutchinson, 258-9; to Zurich for eye-cure, 270, 279, 285, 293; eyes bad again, 365, 375; in Venice, 382; renewed social life, 412. *mentioned*, 2, 21, 118, 162, 178, 198
    Letters to: Nos. *1999, 2025, 2035, 2041, 2047, 2091, 2127, 2133, 2142, 2187, 2198, 2304, 2313, 2315, 2318, 2326, 2329-30, 2383*
Bell, Colonel Cory, 249, 276, 330-1
Bell, Julian: aged 21, 12 & n; elected to Apostles, 34 & n; at Cassis, 38n; character 41, 53, 58; may get King's Fellowship, 51, 269 & n, 294; criticises his father, 53, 58; elected to Cranium, 54; debates with Mauron, 58; admires Vita's poetry, 108; and Eliot's, 111; intends legal career, 128 & n, 134; like dor-beetle, 133; publishes poems, 140 & n; and Helen Soutar, 169, 170, 277, 292, 308, 320, 335; his poems 169; *Winter Movement*, 238 & n, 278; and John Lehmann, 264 & n; discusses poetry with V., 273, 276; reviews Thornley, 282; essay on Pope, 292; and Barbara Hutchinson, 308; in *New Signatures*, 381n; 'my poetical political nephew', 406. *mentioned*, 25, 29, 56, 119, 235
    Letters to: Nos. *1992, 2144, 2180, 2303, 2488*
Bell, Olivier (Mrs Quentin), xviii

Bell, Quentin: visits Berlin with V., 1; sometimes V. calls him Claudian, 24, 25, 55, 320; excellence of his letters, 37, 309; at Cassis, 55; in Paris, 63, 91; 19th birthday, 79; at Penns, 81; exhibits painting, 142 & n; in Paris again, 142; and Cassis, 176; 20th birthday, 202n; in Rome, 238-9, 277, 279; Angelica devoted to, 339. *mentioned*, 29, 53, 105, 252
    Letters to: Nos. *2003, 2012, 2028, 2059, 2145, 2181, 2189, 2263, 2307, 2347, 2362*
Bell, Vanessa: V.'s love for, 68, 390-1; opinion of Ethel Smyth, xvii, 307; and of Vita, 336; visits Berlin with V., 1; tours Austria etc, 20n; V. commissions furniture etc from, 33, 37; Fitzroy St. studio, 34, 39n, 91, 128, 391n; V. tells her about her affair with Vita, 36; refuses fee from V., 41 & n; V. visits at Cassis, 65-6; designs jackets for V.'s books, 67 & n, 68, 81; more furniture for V., 115-16; *Alice* party for Angelica, 128-9; exhibition of her paintings, 132, 134 & n, 142; decorates Penns-in-the-Rocks, 156 & n; 'dissects' V. with Ethel Smyth, 168; 'monumental', 198; to Cassis again, 228, 235; relations with Clive Bell, 258-9; portrait by Fry, 295 & n; Thursday evenings revived, 298 & n, 300; in Italy, 308, 330; in Cornwall, 319; exhibits pictures, 334 & n, her taste in friends differs from V.'s, 336; portrait of V., 360 & n; reaction to *The Waves*, 390-1 & n; attitude to painting, 391n; visits Lytton Strachey on death-bed, 418
    Letters to: *passim* (total of 49 in this volume)
Benn, Ernest, 380 & n
Bennett, Arnold: 153, 292 & n; dying, 294; dies, 309, 311
Benson, E. F., 161n, 163n
Benson, E. W., 163n
Benson, Stella (Mrs Anderson), 271 & n, 315-16, 333 & n
Bergen, George, 276n
Bergerac, France, 317, 319
Berlin: V. and L. prepare to visit, 1-2, 5; their activities in, 8 & n, 9, 45-6; ugliness of, 11, 15, 21, 126
Berners, Gerald (Lord), 110 & n, 209
Besier, Rudolf, 224n, 349n
Bessborough, Lady, 17, 23
Bibesco, Elizabeth, 355 & n
Birrell, Augustine, 73, 74, 76 & n, 118n, 157.
    Letter to: No. *2051*
Birrell, Francis ('Frankie'): 36 & n; at Charleston, 60, 62, 73; writes play with Mortimer, 63 & n; bookshop, 92n; V. meets in Battersea Park, 127; in Paris with Clive Bell, 174; yaps like a terrier, 198; *The Art*

Greville, Fulke (Lord Brooke), 366 & *n*
Greville, Ursula, 224 & *n*
Grizzle (dog), 4, 92

Haddon Hall, Derbyshire, 404 & *n*
Hague Conference, 83 & *n*
Hale White, Bernard (Mark Rutherford), 379 & *n*
Hamann, Herr (life-masks), 170
Hammersley, Violet, 293 & *n*
Hampson, John (Simpson), 221 & *n*, 270 & *n*, 282, 292, 347
Hancock, F., 380 & *n*
Harben, H. D., 306*n*
Hardwick Hall, Derbyshire, 404 & *n*
Hardy, Thomas, 4, 350
Harland (Keynes's servants), 11 & *n*, 50, 263, 267, 279
Harper, Allanah, 128 & *n*, 355. Letter to: No. *2402*
Harris, Fred (mechanic), 41 & *n*
Harris, Henry ('Bogey'), 292 & *n*, 318
Harris, Lilian, 191 & *n*, 213, 228, 287, 392
Hart-Davis, Rupert, 260 & *n*
Hartington, Lady (Alice Cecil), 189 & *n*
Harwich, 7, 8*n*, 16
Hawkesford, Mrs (Rodmell), 61
Hayward, J. D., 30 & *n*, 389 & *n*. Letters to: Nos. *2007*, *2450*
Hazlitt, William, 168 & *n*, 185*n*, 204, 210 & *n*
Heals (art-show), 142
Heard, Gerald, 410 & *n*
Heard, Philip, 51
Hemingway, Ernest, 117 & *n*
Henderson, Faith (Bagenal), 48 & *n*, 59, 107, 134, 175
Henderson, Hubert, 4*n*, 16*n*, 57*n*, 120 & *n*
Herbert, Dorothea, 40 & *n*
Hills, John Waller ('Jack'): financial aid to V. and VB., 46*n*; marries again, 343 & *n*
Hogarth House, Richmond, 31
Hogarth Press: V.'s original motive 'to write and publish what I like', 348; turns down Ivy Compton-Burnett, 92 & *n*; V. helps in, 101; L. almost full-time in, 143; V. proud of its success, 152; V. and L. travel books in West Country, 162-7; *The Edwardians* a best-seller, q.v.; too great a burden?, 237; 'amateur', 260; John Lehmann joins, 264 & *n*, 279 & *n*, 283; Works of Freud, 387. See also Woolf, Virginia, sub-head Hogarth Press
Holtby, Winifred (book about V.), 302 & *n*, 331, 375 & *n*, 376
Homosexuality, 200, 289
Honey, Dorothy, 24*n*
Hope, Lottie (maid), 11 & *n*, 15, 47, 331, 392
Hornell, Prof. William, 110 & *n*
House of Commons: V. visits, 302
Howard, Brian, 133 & *n*

Howard, Esme, 16 & *n*
Howe, Beatrice (Lubbock), 49, 74
Hudson, Nan, 22*n*, 45, 102, 120, 156. Letter to: No. *2001*
Hungerford, Berks, 424
Hunt, Mrs Holman, 330
Hunt, Violet, 329 & *n*, 331, 335
Hunter, Mary, xvi, 151*n*, 252, 300, 304; her bankruptcy, 329, 332, 334-5
Hutchinson, Barbara, 110 & *n*, 155, 170, 222, 308
Hutchinson, Jeremy, 155
Hutchinson, Mary: past love-affair with Clive Bell, 3, 4; might visit V. when ill, 9, 10; her character, 20; at Charleston, 73; in Anrep mosaic, 170*n*; at Monk's House, 222; renewed relations with Clive Bell, 258-9; may take house near Rodmell, 342; operation to, 375. *mentioned*, 49, 74, 78, 90, 108, 155, 170, 177, 365
Hutchinson, St John ('Jack'), 14, 15, 222, 342
Huxley, Aldous, 49, 167 & *n*, 283 & *n*, 290, 292 & *n*; character, 293-4; 309 & *n*, 402 & *n*
Huxley, Julian, 410*n*
Huxley, Maria (Mrs Aldous), 283 & *n*, 290
Hyslop, Paul, 236 & *n*
Hyslop, Dr Theo, 326 & *n*

Imperial Hotel Co., 115-16, 131, 149*n*
Irons, Evelyn, 369*n*, 370*n*, 371, 380
Irvine, Lyn Lloyd (Mrs Max Newman), 80, 86, 162, 180, 274 & *n*, 293, 373
Letters to: Nos. *2305*, *2427*
Isham, Sir Gyles, 122 & *n*
Isham, Virginia, 122 & *n*, 123, 126, 139, 150, 394. Letters to: Nos. *2125*, *2155*, *2456*
Islington, 116
Ismay, James, 341 & *n*
Italy: Vita in, 197; V. on Rome, 238-9, 277
Iwerne Minster, Dorset, 341

James, Henry, 32, 54 & *n*, 107*n*
James, Norah C., 29*n*
Jameson, Storm, 29 & *n*, 380
Jarrett, Miss (typist), 332
Jeans, Sir James, 266*n*
Jeffers, Robinson, 96 & *n*
Jenkins, Elizabeth, 56 & *n*, 58, 424 & *n*
Jews: V.'s attitude to, 195-6, 222, 241-2, 335
Jewsbury, Geraldine, 5 & *n*, 28, 30, 32
Jiminez, Lily (Vita's cook), 286 & *n*, 403*n*
Joad, Mrs C. E. M. (Marjorie Thomson), 286 & *n*, 403*n*
Joan of Arc, 322-3
John, Augustus, 47
John, Dorelia, 243
Jones, Alice, 133 & *n*, 250, 283
Jowitt, William and Lesley, 69, 70 & *n*
Joynson-Hicks, William, 14*n*
Jungman, Zita, 27 & *n*

Lushington, Mrs Vernon, 185*n*
Lyme Regis, Dorset, 89, 93
Lyttelton, Edith (Balfour, 'D. D.'), 184 & *n*, 185, 344

McAfee, Helen (Editor *Yale Review*): V.'s Burney article, 7; V. asks for higher fees, 99; Birrell article, 157, 161; Women's Guild article, 193, 201-2; meets V., 193
    Letters to: Nos. *1985, 2079, 2117, 2166, 2171, 2213, 2219-20, 2340, 2399*
Macaulay, Rose, 60 & *n*
MacCarthy, Dermod, 59 & *n*
MacCarthy, Desmond: lectures on Byron, 51; V. visits his whole family, 59, 64; broadcasts, 90; *Sunday Times* articles, 91; reviews *A Room of One's Own*, 130 & *n*; *Life and Letters* (ed.), 157, 167*n*; V. asks for his collected essays, 177 & *n*, 284; marriage, 344 & *n*; *Portraits*, 421. *mentioned*, 80, 95, 134
    Letters to: Nos. *2070, 2128*
MacCarthy, Michael, 330
MacCarthy, Molly (Mrs Desmond): 49, 59, 130, 177 & *n*, 210; *Fighting Fitzgerald*, 242, 284; *Handicaps*, 290 & *n*
    Letters to: Nos. *2027, 2071, 2190, 2266, 2319*
MacCarthy, Rachel (Lady David Cecil), 59 & *n*, 92, 309, 330
MacDonald, Ramsay, 50, 63*n*, 70*n*, 122, 373*n*
McGlashan, Dr Alan, 251, 261-2. Letter to: No. *2287*
McKnight Kauffer, Edward, 319, 321 & *n*
Maclagan, Eric and Elizabeth, 59 & *n*
McLaren, Christobel (Lady Aberconway, 'Christa'): 9 & *n*, 23, 26-7; 43, 47; and Canon Bowlby, 51; and Clive Bell, 58, 70, 72, 74, 249; V. 'flirts' with, 108; 289
Madrid, 98
Mahoney, Charles, 142*n*
Mahoney, Rory, 142
Mannheimer, Charlotte, 172*n*, 241*n*
Manning-Sanders, Ruth, 33 & *n*
Mansfield, Katherine: and Brett, 31 & *n*; *Prelude*, 92; 'put a line round herself', 271; V.'s considered view of, 366; affection for, 422
Mansfield, Mrs (caretaker), 39, 119, 174*n*
Marchand, Jean, 423*n*
Marennes, France, 316, 319
Marlborough Downs, 162, 163
Marsh, Edward ('Eddie'), 38 & *n*, 103, 288 & *n*. Letter to: No. *2087*
Marshall, Frances (Partridge), 15*n*, 91*n*, 98, 252, 414
Martin, Kingsley, 283 & *n*, 284
Mary, Queen, 258*n*
Matheson, Hilda: V. jealous of?, xiii, 5 & *n*; character, xiii; broadcast of *Orlando*,

27; walking-tour with Vita, 77 & *n*, 78-9, 85, 94; V. broadcasts for, 110 & *n*; V. on her character, 110; at V.'s party, 125*n*; dines with V., 235, 247
Maugham, Somerset ('Willy'): *Cakes and Ale*, 250-1; *The Circle*, 309 & *n*; caricatured in *Gin and Bitters*, 331 & *n*
Maurier, George du, 230*n*
Maurois, André, 103, 139
Mauron, Charles: lectures in London, 46 & *n*, 47, 48, 49; character, 53; 57, 58, 59; V. takes chair for, 109, 110; said to be poor translator, 125; translates *Orlando*, 219, 347, 349-50, 355
Maxse, Mrs Leo (Kitty), 185 & *n*
Mayou, Jean-Jacques, 218*n*
Memoir Club, 177 & *n*, 210 & *n*
Memories of a Working Women's Guild (V.'s article for U.S.), 175, 191*n*, 192-3, 201-2
Mendelssohn, Francesco and Eleonora, 150 & *n*
Meux, Lady, 321*n*
Meynell, Alice, 86 & *n*, 300, 361
Meynell, Viola, 86*n*, 300*n*
Middleton, C. H., 407 & *n*
Milman, Ida, 336 & *n*
Milman, Sylvia (Witham), 237 & *n*, 336*n*
Milne, A. A., 293 & *n*
Milton, John, 119, 276*n*
Mirrlees, Hope, 244 & *n*
Monk's House, Rodmell: two extra rooms planned, 30, 37 & *n*, 43, 54; VB. refurnishes, 33, 41, 54, 61, 115-16; Labour meetings at, 38; worms at, 53; new rooms delayed, 61; French pottery at, 69; goldfish, 81, 83; V.'s garden-hut, 83, 217, 302; new building starts, 93; well-water, 94; Pither stove, 118; new rooms finished, 126; use of rooms, 159; garden, 160, 213; V.'s bedroom, 214; new bookcases, 264; new Grant table, 267, 287; house damp, 275; VB. fireplace tiles, 287, 361, 377; garage, 335; view from upstairs room, 422; electricity installed, 293, 312, 335; frigidaire, 338; 'luxurious', 424
Monsell, Elinor, 27*n*
Montaigne, Michel de: V. visits his château, 317 & *n*, 318, 319, 321
Montgomery, Florence (*Misunderstood*), 327*n*
Moore, G. E., 56 & *n*
Moore, George, 32 & *n*, 59, 124*n*
Morgan, Pierpont, 154, 155, 156
Morrell, Lady Ottoline: memories of Garsington, 31 & *n*; V. visits again, 72; character, 108; her Memoirs, 138 & *n*; and D. H. Lawrence, 167 & *n*; at *Hamlet*, 173; her parties, 189; entertains V. with Yeats and de la Mare, 250, 253; opens Grant's show, 342; deafness, 253-4. *mentioned*, 170, 234, 346, 412
    Letters to: Nos. *2045, 2112, 2122, 2134,*

436

439